A Comparative Grammar of the Dravidian or South-Indian Family of Languages

Robert Caldwell

Alpha Editions

This edition published in 2019

ISBN : 9789353920241

Design and Setting By
Alpha Editions
email - alphaedis@gmail.com

A
COMPARATIVE GRAMMAR
OF THE
DRAVIDIAN
OR
SOUTH-INDIAN FAMILY OF LANGUAGES.

BY

THE REV. R. CALDWELL, B.A.,

MISSIONARY OF THE SOCIETY FOR THE PROPAGATION OF THE GOSPEL IN FOREIGN PARTS, AT EDEYENKOODY, TINNEVELLY, SOUTHERN INDIA.

LONDON:

HARRISON, 59, PALL MALL,

1856.

PRINTED BY HARRISON AND SONS,
ST. MARTIN'S LANE.

PREFACE.

It is many years since I felt convinced that much light might be thrown on the grammar of the Tamil language, by comparing it with that of the Telugu, the Canarese, and other sister idioms; and on proceeding to make this comparison, I found, not only that my supposition was verified by the result, but that the Tamil imparts still more light than it receives, and also, that none of the South-Indian languages can be thoroughly understood or appreciated without some study of the others.

Probably many other students of the South-Indian languages have been led to the same conclusion; but as the mission of the English in India is one which admits of little or no literary leisure,—as the old East, after the sleep of centuries, has begun to wake up and to clamour for the supply of its many material and moral wants, and as the majority of Anglo-Indians, whether they are engaged in the work of government, or in educational and Missionary labours, find that they have a world of work to do, and but little time or strength for doing it, this department of comparative philology, though peculiarly promising, has hitherto lain almost entirely uncultivated.

Much, it is true, has been done towards the elucidation of some of the South-Indian languages taken separately, especially the Tamil and the Telugu. Beschi's Grammar of the Shen-Tamil, and Mr. C. P. Brown's Telugu Grammar, rise far above the level of the ordinary Grammars of the Indian vernaculars. But the study of those languages, viewed as a whole—the inter-comparison of their grammars—is still in its infancy; and it is only when philology becomes comparative, that it becomes scientific and progressive.

The first to break ground in the field was Mr. Ellis, a Madras Civilian, who was profoundly versed in the Tamil language and literature, and whose interesting but very brief comparison, not of the grammatical forms, but only of some of the vocables of three Drâvidian dialects, is contained in his Introduction to *Campbell's Telugu Grammar.*

The next attempt that was made in this direction, was by the Rev. Dr. Stevenson, of Bombay, in some interesting papers on the languages of the Dekhan, which appeared in the *Journal of the Bombay Asiatic Society.* The main object which Dr. Stevenson appeared to have in view, was that of establishing the identity of the Un-Sanscrit element which is contained in the North-Indian vernaculars, with the grammar and vocabulary of the Southern idioms. He failed, as it appeared to me, to establish that point; but many of his remarks on the characteristic features of Drâvidian Grammar, and on the essential unity of the Drâvidian dialects were perfectly correct; and though his papers were of too sketchy a character to be of much permanent philological value, they were decidedly in advance of everything which had hitherto been published on this subject.

I was not aware of the existence of Ellis's or Stevenson's contributions to Drâvidian comparative philology, when my own attention was directed to this department of study; and when at length I made their acquaintance, I felt no less desirous than before of going forward, for though I had lost the satisfaction of supposing myself to be the discoverer of a new field, yet it now appeared to be certain that the greater part of the field still lay not only uncolonized, but unexplored.

I have not referred to Mr. Brian Hodgson's numerous and learned papers on the 'Tamulian' languages of India, though I have long been acquainted with them, because I regard them as a misnomer. Those valuable papers treat of the Sub-Himalayan dialects, which are styled 'Tamulian' by Mr. Hodgson, but which might as properly, or improperly, have been styled by any other foreign name; and though they throw much light on the languages, the physiology, and the inter-relationship of the aborigines of the north-eastern frontier of India, they leave the Drâvidian or Tamilian languages, properly so called, wholly untouched.

From the commencement of my Tamil studies I felt interested also in another question—that of the ulterior relationship of the Drâvidian family of languages; and before I was aware of the opinion which Professor Rask, of Copenhagen, was the first to express, and which has generally been adopted, I arrived by a somewhat similar process, at the same conclusion, viz., that the Drâvidian languages are to be affiliated, not with the Indo-European, but with the Scythian group of tongues, and that the Scythian family to which they appear to be most closely allied is the Finnish or Ugrian.

General statements of the Scythian relationship of the Drâvidian languages, with a few grammatical illustrations, occupy a place in Prichard's valuable 'Researches,' and have been repeated in more recent works on Comparative Philology; but as Prichard himself did not feel satisfied with general statements, impressions, and probabilites, and wished to see the problem solved, and as I was convinced that it never could be definitively solved without previously ascertaining, by a careful inter-comparison of dialects, what were the most ancient grammatical forms and the most essential characteristics of the Drâvidian languages, I found myself under the necessity of working out the entire subject for myself.

It was not till I had finished this work, and commenced to prepare to carry it through the press, that I became acquainted with Professor Max Müller's treatise, 'On the present state of our knowledge of the Turanian languages,' which is included in Bunsen's '*Outlines of the Philosophy of Universal History.*'

That treatise is the most comprehensive, lucid, and scholarly investigation of the general question which I have yet read; and I have been gratified to find not only that many of the conclusions at which the author of that treatise has arrived, but that many of his proofs and illustrations also, are identical with my own.

Notwithstanding our general agreement with respect to the Drâvidian grammatical system, and especially with respect to its Ugrian affinities, I have not found the following work forestalled by the Professor's. His work is generic, mine specific. His is an admirable survey of the entire field; but he does not profess to cultivate thoroughly any one portion of the field, or even to prepare it for cultivation. He does not occupy himself in clearing away the stones, breaking up the fallow ground, pulverising and analysing the soil, and turning up the sub-soil to the light. Occasionally, it is true, he enters into details; but though his conclusions are always correct, it is too evident that in dealing with details he furnishes an illustration of the principle for which, as he observes, Boehtlingk stands up, viz., that 'it is dangerous to write on languages of which we do not possess the most accurate knowledge.' Whilst the principal features of the Scythian relationship of the Drâvidian tongues are strongly marked, and whilst their grammatical principles and syntactic arrangement are of too peculiar a nature to be mistaken, there is much in the phonic system of these languages, in their dialectic interchanges and displacements, in their declensional and conjugational forms, and especially in the nature, uses, and changes of their formative particles, which cannot be understood without special study.

Drâvidian philology has recently attracted the attention of another writer, Dr. Logan, whose elaborate contributions to the ethnology of Eastern Asia, and of the eastern islands, form the most valuable papers in the *Journal of the Indian Archipelago.* That writer's ethnological learning and philological acuteness are very great, and some of his conjectures are remarkably happy; but he is too fond of speculation, and not a few of his generalisations and speculations respecting the forms and phonology of the Drâvidian languages, are far a-head of his facts.

Notwithstanding, therefore, the intrinsic general value of

the researches of Drs. Stevenson, Max Müller, and Logan, a work like the following still appears to be required. The Drâvidian languages still require to be compared and their relationship to other languages investigated by some one who has made them his special study for an adequate space of time.

Though I trust that the following work will help to supply this desideratum, yet it only professes to be a *contribution* towards the accomplishment of the object in view. I have laboured to be accurate throughout—and in a work of this kind accuracy cannot be attained without immense labour; but notwithstanding my endeavours to be accurate, I am conscious of the existence of many defects. I trust, however, it will be remembered that this is the only systematic treatise on this subject which has yet appeared; that in a first work on a new subject errors are almost unavoidable; and that, whatever be the defects of this work, it has at all events smoothed the way for those who may hereafter be disposed to investigate the subject more deeply.

During the period of my residence in India the work in which I was engaged as a Missionary was of too important a nature to allow me to spend much of my time in book-making. It was necessary for me to be content with jotting down occasionally a few notes and illustrations, and working out conclusions in my mind. Since my return to this country for a season, I have taken the opportunity of putting together the notes which I had collected, and moulding them into a systematic shape; and the result is now published, in the hope that this work will help to supply a want which I had long felt myself, and which must, I conceived, have been felt by many others. I trust it will be found to contribute to a more enlarged and scientific study of each of the Drâvidian languages, to a more accurate knowledge of their structure and vital spirit, and to a higher estimate of their phonic beauty, their philosophical organization, and their unequalled regularity.

During the period which has elapsed since the commencement of this work, a period of a year and ten months, it has been my lot to visit two hundred and fifty different parishes in various parts of England, and to deliver about three hundred and fifty lectures and addresses on India and Indian Missions. It may therefore be concluded that the composition and preparation for the press of a work of so laborious a nature, in addition to the duties of a 'deputation,' have not left much scope for the relaxation and rest which form the usual adjuncts of a 'furlough;' nevertheless, if the ulterior object which I have had in view should in any measure be accomplished—if in facilitating a more comprehensive study of the Drâvidian languages by those Missionaries and East India Company's Civilians who make use of them as instruments of thought or as vehicles of expression, the welfare of the Drâvidian people should in any manner, however indirectly, or in any degree, however small, be promoted—I shall have my reward.

I beg leave thankfully to acknowledge the facilities which have been afforded for the publication of this work by the kindness of the Honourable Court of Directors of the East India Company, in subscribiug for a hundred copies, and of the Madras, Ceylon, and Bombay Governments, in subscribing for a hundred and twelve.

R. CALDWELL.

Office of the Society for the Propagation of the Gospel,
79, *Pall Mall, London, June* 2*nd,* 1856.

DRAVIDIAN COMPARATIVE GRAMMAR.

INTRODUCTION.

It is the object of the following work to examine and compare the grammatical principles and forms of the various Drâviḍian languages, in the hope of contributing to a more thorough knowledge of their primitive structure and distinctive character. In pursuing this object, it will be the writer's endeavour to ascertain the relation which this family of languages bears to the principal families or groups into which the languages of Europe and Asia have been divided.

Whilst the grammatical structure of each Drâviḍian language and dialect will be investigated and illustrated in a greater or less degree, in proportion to its importance and to the writer's acquaintance with it, it will be his special and constant aim to throw light upon the structure of the Tamiḷ—a language which he has for seventeen years studied and used in the prosecution of his missionary labours, and which is undoubtedly the oldest, richest, and most highly organized, of the Drâviḍian languages,—in many respects the representative language of the family.

The idioms which are included in this work under the general term 'Drâviḍian,' constitute the vernacular speech of the great majority of the inhabitants of Southern India. With the exception of Orissa and those districts of Western India and the Dekhan in which the Gujarâthî and the Marâṭhî are spoken, the whole of the peninsular portion of India, from the Vindhya mountains and the river Nerbudda (Narmadâ) to Cape Comorin, is peopled, and from the earliest period appears to have been peopled, by different branches of one and the same race, speaking different dialects of one and the same language—the language to which the term 'Drâviḍian' is here applied; and scattered off-shoots from the same stem may be traced still farther north as far as the Rajmahal hills, and even as far as the mountain fastnesses of Beluchistan.

The Gujarâthî, the Marâṭhî (with its off-shoot the Konkanî), and the Uriya, or language of Orissa, idioms which are derived in the main from the decomposition of the Sanscrit, form the vernacular speech of the Hindu population within their respective limits: besides which, and besides the Drâviḍian languages, various idioms which cannot be termed indigenous or vernacular are spoken or occasionally used by particular classes resident in Peninsular India.

Sanscrit, though it never was the vernacular language of any district of country in the South, is in every district read and to some extent understood by the majority of the Brahmans,—the descendants of those Brahmanical colonists of early times to whom the Drâviḍians are indebted for the higher arts of life and the first elements of literary culture. Such of the Brahmans as not only retain the name, but also discharge the functions of the priesthood, and devote themselves to professional studies, are generally able to converse in Sanscrit, though the vernacular language of the district in which they reside is that which they use in their families and with which they are most familiar. They are styled, with reference to the language of their adopted district, Drâviḍa Brahmans, Kêrala Brahmans, Karnâṭaka Brahmans, &c.; and the Brahmans of the several language-districts have virtually become distinct castes; but they are all undoubtedly descended from one and the same stock; and Sanscrit, though now regarded only as an accomplishment or as a professional acquirement, is properly their ancestral tongue.

Hindûstânî is the distinctive, hereditary language of the Mahommedan portion of the population in the Dekhan and the southern peninsula,—the descendants of those warlike Mahommedans from northern India by whom the Peninsula was overrun some centuries ago. It may be regarded as the vernacular language in some parts of the Hyderabad country; but generally throughout Southern India, the middle and lower classes of the Mahommedans, who constitute the majority, make as much use of the language of the district in which they reside as of their ancestral tongue, and many of them are now unable to put a single sentence together in Hindûstânî.

Hebrew is used by the small but interesting colony of Jews resident in Cochin and the neighbourhood, in the same manner and for the same purposes as Sanscrit is used by the Brahmans. Gujarâthî and Marâṭhî are spoken by the Gujarâthî bankers and the Parsi shop-keepers who reside in the principal towns in the Peninsula: the mixed race of 'country-born' Portuguese are rapidly forgetting (except in the territory of Goa itself) the corrupt Portuguese which their fathers and mothers were accustomed to speak, and learning English instead; whilst French still retains its place as the language of the French employés and their descendants in the settlements of Pondicherry, Kârikâl, and Mahe, which still belong to France.

Throughout the territories of the East India Company, English is not only the language of the governing race and of its 'East-Indian' or 'Indo-British' off-shoot, but is also used to a considerable extent by the natives of the country in the administration of justice and in commerce; and in the presidency of Madras and the principal towns, it is daily winning its way to the position which was formerly occupied by Sanscrit, as the vehicle of all higher learning.

Neither the English, however, nor any other foreign tongue, has the slightest chance of becoming the vernacular speech of any portion of the inhabitants of Southern India. The indigenous Drâviḍian languages, which have maintained their ground for more than two thousand years against Sanscrit, the language of a numerous, powerful, and venerated sacerdotal race, may be expected successfully to resist the encroachments of every other tongue.*

* I admit with Sir Erskine Perry (see his valuable paper in the *Journal of the Royal Asiatic Society*), that English, the language of the governing race, should be employed as the language of public business in every part of British India; and I am certain that this end could be attained in a very short time by simply requiring every candidate for government employment, from the highest to the lowest, to pass an examination in English. The natives would everywhere adapt themselves to this arrangement, not only without reluctance, but with alacrity and pleasure; and English schools and other facilities for the acquisition of English would multiply apace, as soon as it was found that the new rule could not be evaded. I do not think, however, that English can ever become the vernacular language of any class of the Hindus, nor even that it is likely to be used to any considerable extent as a *lingua franca* beyond the circle of government employés. Before we can reasonably anticipate the employment of English as a conventional language, like Latin in the middle ages, or French in the more modern period, the number of the English resident in India should bear a much larger proportion to the mass of the inhabitants. That proportion is at present infinitesimally small: *e. g.* the population of the two Collectorates, or provinces, in Southern India with which I am best acquainted—Tinnevelly and Madura, amounts in round numbers to three millions: the number of Englishmen (and Americans) resident in those two provinces is considerably under a hundred and fifty! and that number includes the judges and magistrates who administer justice in those provinces, the officers of a single regiment of sepoys, the men belonging to a small detachment of foot artillery, a few cotton planters and merchants, and the missionaries belonging to three missionary societies! Including women and children, the number is about three hundred, with which handful of English people we have to contrast three millions of Hindus!

Enumeration of Drâvidian Languages.

The idioms which I designate as 'Drâviḍian,' are nine in number, exclusive of the Rajmahal, the Ûrâon, and the Brahuî. They are as follows:—

1. The Tamiḻ, by the earlier Europeans erroneously termed 'the Malabar.'* The proper spelling of the name is 'Tamiṛ;' but through the dialectic changes of ṛ into ḻ, it is commonly pronounced Tamiḻ, and is often erroneously written 'Tamul' by Europeans. This language being the earliest cultivated of all the Drâviḍian idioms, the most copious, and that which contains the largest portion and the richest variety of indubitably ancient forms, it is deservedly placed at the head of the list. It includes two dialects, the classical and the colloquial, or the ancient and the modern, called respectively the 'Shen-Tamiḻ' and the 'Koḍun-Tamiḻ,' which differ one from the other so widely that they might almost be regarded as different languages. The Tamiḻ language is spoken throughout the vast plain of the Carnatic, or country below the Ghauts, from Pulicat to Cape Comorin, and from the Ghauts, or central mountain range of Southern India, to the Bay of Bengal. It is also spoken in the southern part of the Travancore country on the western side of the Ghauts, from Cape Comorin to the neighbourhood of Trivandrum; and in the northern and north-western parts of Ceylon, where Tamiḻians commenced to form settlements prior even to the Christian era, and from whence they have gradually thrust out the Singhalese. All throughout Ceylon the *coolies* in the coffee plantations are Tamiḻians; the majority of the money-making classes even in Colombo are Tamiḻians; and ere long the Tamiḻians will have excluded the Singhalese from almost every office of profit and trust in their own island. The majority of the domestic servants of Europeans and of the camp-followers in every part of the presidency of Madras being Tamiḻ people, Tamiḻ is the prevailing language in all military cantonments in Southern India, whatever be the vernacular language of the district. Hence, at Cannanore in the Malayâla country, at Bangalore in the Canarese country, at Bellary in the Telugu country, and at Secunderabad, where Hindûstânî may be considered as the vernacular, the

* It is singular that so able and accurate a scholar as Dr. Max Müller should have supposed the Malabar to be a different language from the Tamiḻ: nor did he confound it, as would have been natural enough, with the Malayâlam, for he gives a distinct place (especially in his 'list of pronouns') to each of the Drâviḍian dialects which actually exist, including the Malayâlam, and thereto he adds the Malabar, on the authority, I presume, of some grammar of the last century, in which the Tamil was called by that name.

language which most frequently meets the ear in the bazaars is the Tamiḷ.

The majority of the Klings ('Kalingas'), or Hindus, who are found in Pegu, Penang, Singapore, and other places in the further east, are Tamiḷians: the coolies who have emigrated in such numbers to the Mauritius and to the West Indian colonies are mostly Tamiḷians: in short, wherever money is to be made, wherever a more apathetic or a more aristocratic people is waiting to be pushed aside, there swarm the Tamiḷians, the Greeks or Scotch of the east, the least scrupulous and superstitious, and the most enterprising and persevering race of Hindus.

Including Tamiḷians resident in military stations and distant colonies, and the Tamiḷian inhabitants of South Travancore, and Northern Ceylon, and excluding not only Mahommedans, &c., but also Brahmans and people of Telugu origin who are resident in the Tamiḷ country, and who form at least ten per cent. of the whole population, the people who speak the Tamiḷ language may be estimated at about ten millions.

2. The Telugu, in respect of antiquity of culture and glossarial copiousness, ranks next to the Tamiḷ in the list of Drâviḍian idioms; but in point of euphonic sweetness it claims to occupy the first place. The Telugu, called also the Telingu, or Telungu (nasalised from Telugu), is the 'Ândhra' of Sanscrit writers, a name mentioned by the Greek geographers as the name of a nation dwelling on or near the Ganges. This language was sometimes called by the Europeans of the last generation the 'Gentoo,' from the Portuguese word for heathens, or 'Gentiles.' The Telugu is spoken all along the eastern coast of the Peninsula, from the neighbourhood of Pulicat, where it supersedes the Tamiḷ, to Chicacole, where it begins to yield to the Uriya; and inland it prevails as far as the eastern boundary of the Maraṭha country and the Mysore; including within its range the 'Ceded districts' and Kurnool, the greater part of the territories of the Nizam, or the Hyderabad country, and a portion of the Nagpore country and Gondwana. Formerly Telugu appears to have been spoken as far north as the mouths of the Ganges. This appears both from the geographical limits which are assigned by the Greeks to the territory of the Ândhras, or northern Telugus, and from many of the names of places mentioned by Ptolemy as far as the mouths of the Ganges being found to be Telugu. The Telugu people, though not the most enterprising or migratory, are undoubtedly the most numerous branch of the Drâviḍian race. Including the Naiks or Naidoos ('Nâyakas'), Reddies, and other Telugu tribes settled in the Tamiḷ country, who are chiefly the

descendants of those soldiers of fortune by whom the Pâṇḍiya and Chôla kingdoms were subverted, and who number not much less than a million of souls; and including also the Telugu settlers in Mysore and the indigenous Telugu inhabitants of the Nizam's territory and other native states, the people who speak the Telugu language may be estimated as amounting to at least fourteen millions.

3. The next place is occupied by the Canarese, properly the Kannaḍi, or Karnâṭaka,* which is spoken throughout the plateau of Mysore and in some of the western districts of the Nizam's territory, as far north as Beder: it is spoken, also, (together with the Malayâḷam, the Tuḷuva, and the Konkani, but more extensively than any of them) in the district of Canara, on the Malabar coast, a district which originally constituted the Tuḷuva country, but which was subjected for centuries to the rule of Canarese princes, and hence acquired the name by which it is at present known. Under the denomination of Canarese many include the Coorg or Koḍaga, an idiom which is spoken by the inhabitants of the small principality of Coorg on the Western Ghauts, and which has generally been considered rather as an ancient and uncultivated dialect of the Canarese, modified by the Tuḷu, than as a distinct language. The Rev. Mr. Mögling, a German missionary, who has recently settled amongst the Coorgs, and who is our only reliable authority on the subject of their language, now states that Coorg is more closely allied to the Tamiḻ and Malayâḷa than to the Canarese. The speech of the Baḍagars ('people from the north'),

* 'Karnâṭaka' is not a Drâviḍian, but a Sanscrit word, and is properly a generic name for both Telugu and Canarese. It is defined to mean primarily 'a species of dramatic music,' or 'comedy:' it is used secondarily in Telugu as an adjective to signify 'native,' 'aboriginal,' *e.g.* 'Karnâṭaka mêlam,' Tel. 'native music:' it then became the common designation of the Telugu and Canarese, or 'native' languages: and, finally, was restricted still further, and became the distinctive appellation of the Canarese alone.

I should not have used the word 'finally,' for 'Karnâṭaka' has now got into the hands of foreigners, who have given it a new and more erroneous application.

When the Mahommedans arrived in southern India, they found that part of it with which they become first acquainted—the country above the Ghauts, including Mysore and part of Telingâna—called 'the Karnâṭaka country.' In course of time, by a misapplication of terms, they applied the same name, 'the Karnâṭak,' or 'Carnatic,' to designate the country below the Ghauts, as well as that which was above. The English have carried the misapplication a step further and restricted the name to the country below the Ghauts, which has no right to it whatever. Hence the Mysore country, which is properly the Carnatic, is no longer called by that name by the English, and what is now geographically termed 'the Carnatic' is exclusively the country below the Ghauts, on the Coromandel coast, including the whole of the Tamiḻ country and the district of Nellore in the Telugu country.

The word 'Karnâṭaka' was further corrupted by the Canarese people themselves into 'Kannaḍa' or 'Kannara;' from which the language is styled 'Kannaḍi,' and by the English, 'Canarese.' A province on the Malabar coast is called 'Canara,' properly 'Kannaḍiyam,' in consequence of having long been subjected to the government of Karnâṭaka princes.

commonly called Burghers, the most numerous class of people inhabiting the Nilgherry hills, is undoubtedly an ancient Canarese dialect. The Canarese, properly so called, includes, like the Tamiḷ, two cultivated dialects, the ancient and the modern; of which the former differs from the latter, not—as classical Telugu and Malayâḷam differ from the colloquial dialects of those languages—by containing a larger infusion of Sanscrit derivatives, but by the use of different inflexional terminations. The *dialect* called 'Ancient Canarese' is not to be confounded with the *character* which is denoted by that name, and which is found in many very ancient inscriptions in the Maraṭha country as well as in Mysore. The language of all really ancient inscriptions in the 'Haḷa Kannaḍa,' or Ancient Canarese character, is Sanscrit, not Canarese.

The people that speak the Canarese language, including the Coorgs, &c., may be estimated at five millions: but, in the case of both the Canarese and the Telugu, the absence of a trustworthy census of the inhabitants of *native* states, requires all such estimates to be considered as mere approximations. In the Nizam's territory four languages—the Canarese, the Marâṭhi, the Telugu, and the Hindustani—are spoken by different classes or in different districts; but it is impossible to ascertain the proportionate prevalence of each with any degree of certainty.

4. The Malayâḷam, or 'Malayâṛma,' ranks next in order. This language is spoken along the Malabar coast, on the western side of the Ghauts, or 'Malaya' range of mountains, from the vicinity of Mangalore, where it supersedes the Canarese and the Tuḷu, to Trivandrum, where it begins to be superseded by the Tamil. The people by whom this language is spoken in the native states of Travancore and Cochin, and in the East India Company's districts of Malabar and Canara, may be estimated at two and a half millions. All along the Malabar coast Tamiḷ is rapidly gaining upon the Malayâḷam. Though that coast was for many ages more frequented by foreigners than any other part of India; though Phœnicians, Greeks, Jews, Syrian christians, and Arabs, traded in succession to the various ports along the coast; and though permanent settlements were formed by the three last classes; yet the Malayâḷa people continue to be of all Drâviḍians the most exclusive and superstitious, and shrink most sensitively from contact with foreigners. Hence 'the lines and centres of communication' have been seized, and the greater part of the commerce and public business of the Malabar states has been monopolized, by the less scrupulous and more adroit Tamilians, whose language bids fair to supersede the Malayâḷam, or at least to confine it within the limits of the hill-country and the jungles.

5. Last in the list of cultivated Drâviḍian tongues is the Tuḷu, or Tuḷuva; an idiom holding a position midway between the Canarese and the Malayâlam, but more nearly resembling the Canarese. This language was once generally prevalent in the district of Canara, but is now spoken only in a small tract of country in the vicinity of Mangalore, by not more than a hundred or a hundred and fifty thousand souls. It has been broken in upon by many other languages, and is likely soon to disappear.

The four languages which follow differ from those that have been mentioned in that they are entirely uncultivated, destitute of written characters, and comparatively little known.

6. The Toda, properly the Tuda, or Tudava; the language of the Tudavars, a primitive and peculiarly interesting tribe inhabiting the Nilgherry hills, practising quasi-Druidical rites, and commonly believed to be the aboriginal inhabitants of those hills. Their number could not at any time have exceeded a few thousands; and at present, through opium-eating and polyandria, and through the prevalence amongst them at a former period of female infanticide, they do not, it is estimated, number more than from three to five hundred souls.

7. The Kôta; the language of the Kôtars, a small tribe of Helot craftsmen inhabiting the Nilgherry hills, and numbering about a thousand souls. The Tuda language may be considered as the indigenous speech of the Nilgherries; the Kôta as a very old and very rude dialect of the Canarese, which was carried thither by a persecuted low-caste tribe at some very remote period. Besides those two, two other languages are vernacular on the Nilgherry hills; viz., the dialect which is spoken by the Burghers or Baḍagars, an ancient but organized dialect of the Canarese, and the rude Tamiḻ which is spoken by the Iruḷars ('people of the darkness') and Curbs or Curubars (Tam. 'Kurumbar,' 'nomade shepherds'), who are occasionally stumbled upon by adventurous sportsmen in the denser, deeper jungles, and the smoke of whose fires may occasionally be seen rising from the lower gorges of the hills.

8. The Gônd or Goand; the language of the indigenous inhabitants of the northern and western parts of the extensive hill country of Gondwana, of the northern portion of Nagpore and of the greater part of the Saugor and Nerbudda territories.

9. The Khond, Kund, or more properly the Ku; the language of the people who are commonly called Khonds, but who call themselves Kus—a primitive race, who are supposed to be allied to the Gonds; who inhabit the eastern parts of Gondwana, Goomsur, and the hilly ranges of Orissa; and who have acquired a bad notoriety through their

horrid practice of stealing the children of their neighbours and offering them up in sacrifice.

I am unable to form a probable estimate of the numbers of the people by whom the Gond and the Ku are spoken, I think, however, that they cannot safely be estimated under half a million of souls.

The proportionate numbers of the several races by whom the languages and dialects mentioned above are spoken appear to be as follows:—

1. Tamil	10,000,000
2. Telugu	14,000,000
3. Canarese	5,000,000
4. Malayalam	2,500,000
5. Tulu	150,000
6. Tuda, 7. Kota, 8. Gond, 9. Ku }	500,000
	32,150,000

According to this estimate the Drâvidian race numbers upwards of thirty-two millions of souls. There cannot be any doubt of their numbers amounting to at least thirty millions; of whom about twenty millions are British subjects, and the remainder belong to the native states of Hyderabad, Nagpore,* Mysore, Travancore, and Cochin; the gross population of which, including all races, is estimated at twenty millions, but is probably much greater.

In this enumeration of the Drâvidian languages I have not included the idioms of the Ramûsies, the Korawars, the Lambâḍies, the Veḍars, the Male-arasars, and various other wandering, predatory or forest tribes. The Lâmbâḍies, the Gipsies of the Peninsula, speak a dialect of the Hindustani; the Ramûsies and the majority of the Korawars, a *patois* of the Telugu; the tribes inhabiting the hills and forests, corrupted dialects of the languages of the contiguous plains. None of these dialects is found to differ essentially from the speech of the more cultivated classes residing in the same neighbourhood. The Male-arasars, 'hill-kings' (in Malayâlam, Mala-araans), the hill tribe inhabiting the southern Ghauts, speak corrupt Malayâlam in the northern part of the range, where the Malayâlam is the prevailing language, and corrupt Tamil in the southern, in the vicinity of Tamil-speaking districts.

* Since the above was written Nagpore has been incorporated with the British territories.

In the above list of Drâvidian languages I have not included the idioms of certain rude tribes of Central India and the north-eastern frontier, which have sometimes of late been included under the general term 'Tamulian.' I refer to the languages of the Kôls and Sûras, the neighbours of the Gonds and Kunds towards the north, which might naturally be supposed to be allied to the Gond or the Ku, and consequently of Drâvidian origin; but which, though they contain a few Drâvidian words, belong to a totally different family of languages. Without the evidence of similarity in grammatical structure, the discovery of a few similar words proves only local proximity, or the existence of mutual intercourse at an earlier or later period,—not the original relationship either of races or of languages.

I leave also out of account the languages of the north-eastern frontier of India, which are spoken by the Bôdos, Dhimâls, and other tribes inhabiting the mountains and forests between Kumaon and Assam. These are styled 'Tamulian' by Mr. Hodgson, of Nepaul, on the supposition that all the aborigines of India, as distinguished from the Âryans, or Sanscrit-speaking race and its offshoots, belong to one and the same stock; and that of this aboriginal race, the Tamilians of Southern India are to be considered as the best representatives. But as the relationship of those north-eastern idioms to the languages of the Drâvidian family is a supposition which is unsupported by the evidence either of similarity in grammatical structure or of a similar vocabulary, and is founded only on such general grammatical analogies as are common to the whole range of the Scythian group of languages, it seems to me as improper to designate those dialects 'Tamulian,' or 'Drâvidian,' as it would be to designate them 'Turkish' or 'Tungusian.' Possibly they form a link of connection between the Indo-Chinese, or Tibetan family of tongues, and the Kôl; but even this is at present a hazardous assumption. Prof. Max Müller proposes to call all the Non-Âryan languages of India, including the Sub-Himalayan, the Kôl and the Tamilian families, 'Nishâda-languages,' the ancient aborigines being often termed 'Nishâdas' in the Vedaic writings. Philologically I think the use of this common term is to be deprecated, inasmuch as the Drâvidian languages are radically different from the others, as the Professor himself appears to have perceived. For the present I have no doubt that the safest common appellation is the negative one, 'Non-Aryan,' or 'Un-Sanscritic.'

The brief vocabulary of the tribe inhabiting the Rajmahal hills in Central India, contained in the *Asiatic Researches*, vol. v., and the fuller list of words belonging to the language of the same people, contained in Mr. Hodgson's collections, prove that the Rajmahal idiom is in the main Drâvidian. The proof of this fact will be exhibited in the sequel. This language is not to be confounded with its neighbour, the speech of the Sântâls, a branch of the extensive Kôl family inhabiting the Bhangalpore range of hills, whose language belongs to a totally different stock.

The Brahuî, the language of the mountaineers in the khanship of Kelat in Beluchistan, contains, not only some Drâvidian words, but a considerable infusion of unquestionably Drâvidian forms and idioms; in consequence of which this language has a much better claim to be regarded as Drâvidian or Tamulian than any of the languages of the Nipâl and Bhutân frontier, which had been styled 'Tamulian' by Mr. Hodgson. I have not included, however, the Brahuî, or the Rajmahal and Uraon, in the list of Drâvidian languages which are to be subjected to systematic comparison (though I shall give some account of them in the sequel, and shall refer to them occasionally for illustration), because the Drâvidian element contained in those languages bears but a small proportion to the rest of their component elements.

The Drâvidian Idioms not merely Provincial Dialects of the same Language.

Though I have described the nine vernacular idioms mentioned in the foregoing list as dialects of one and the same original Drâvidian language, it would be erroneous to consider them as 'dialects' in the popular sense of the term,—viz., as provincial peculiarities or varieties of speech. Of all those idioms no two are so nearly related to each other that persons who speak them can be mutually understood. The most nearly related are the Tamil and the Malayâlam; and yet it is only the simplest and most direct sentences in the one language that are intelligible to those who speak only the other. Involved sentences in either language, abounding in verbal and nominal inflections, or in conditions and reasons, will be found by those who speak only the other language to be unintelligible. The Tamil, the Malayâlam, the Telugu, and the Canarese, have each a distinct and independent literary culture; and each of the three former—the Tamil, the Malayâlam, and the Telugu—has a system of witten characters peculiar to itself. The Canarese *character* has been borrowed from that of the Telugu, and differs but slightly from it; but the Canarese *language* differs even more widely from the Telugu than it does from the Tamil; and the ancient Canarese character is totally unconnected with the character of the Telugu.

The Malayâlam being, as I conceive, an ancient offshoot of the Tamil, differing from it chiefly by the disuse of the personal terminations of the verbs,* it might, perhaps, be regarded rather as a very ancient dialect of the Tamil than as a distinct language. Its separation from Tamil evidently took place at a very early period, before the Tamil was cultivated and refined. Through the predominance of Brahmanical influence in the Malayâla country, the Malayâlam has not been cultivated *ab intra* to any considerable extent; and the infusion into it of a large proportion of Sanscrit words is almost the only refinement which it has received. The proportion of Sanscrit words which has been adopted by the Drâvidian languages is least in Tamil, most in Malayâlam; and the modern Malayâla character has been borrowed with but little alteration from the Grantham—the character in which Sanscrit is written in the Tamil country, and which corresponds to the Dêva-nâgari of Northern India. In consequence of these things, the difference between the Tamil and the Malayâlam, though originally slight, has progressively increased; and hence the claim of the Malayâlam to be considered, not merely as a dialect of the Tamil, but as a sister language, or at least as a very ancient and much altered offshoot, cannot now be called in question.

The Tulu has been represented by Mr. Ellis as a dialect of the Malayâlam; but although Malayâla characters are ordinarily employed in writing Tulu, in consequence of the prevalence of Malayâlam in the vicinity, and the literary inferiority of the Tulus, it appears to me capable of the clearest proof that the relation of the Tulu to the Canarese is nearer than its relation to the Malayâlam. It differs

* The derivation of the Malayâlam from the Tamil is well illustrated by the word which is used by it to signify 'East.' It is 'Kiṛakka,' meaning 'beneath,' or 'downwards,' which is properly a Tamil word, and corresponds to that which is used to denote 'West,'—viz., 'Mekku,' 'above' or 'upwards;' both of which words necessarily originated in the Tamil country, or the country on the eastern side of the Ghauts; where a lofty range of mountains rises everywhere to the westward, and where, consequently to go westward is to go 'upwards;' whilst to the eastward the country slopes 'downwards' to the sea. The configuration of the Malayâla country is directly and strikingly the reverse of this,—the mountain range being to the eastward, and the sea to the westward. Notwithstanding this, the Malayâla word for 'East' is 'Kiṛakka, "downwards,' identical with the Tamil word 'Kiṛakku,'—a clear proof that the Malayâlam is an offshoot from the Tamil, and that the people by whom it is spoken were originally a colony of Tamilians. It is evident that they entered the Malayâla country through the Paul ghaut Gap, and from thence spread themselves along the coast, northward to Mangalore, and southward to Trivandrum. Throughout the Malayâla grammar I have noticed only two forms which are not contained either in the colloquial or in the high dialect of the Tamil: those two forms are a dative in 'a,' which is used in some instances after 'n,' instead of the more usual sign of the dative, 'kka;' and a plural suffix of the second person of the imperative,—viz. 'in;' which is peculiar to this language,—except, indeed, it is derived from the high Tamil 'min.'

widely and essentially from the Tamil; and hence the tradition which is mentioned by Mr. Taylor, that the ancient 'Kurumbars,' or 'nomadic shepherds,' in the neighbourhood of Madras were expelled and their lands seized upon by Veḷḷâḷars from Tuluva, appears to be highly improbable. The colloquial Tamil of the neighbourhood of Madras is characterized by an infusion of the peculiarities, not of the Tulu, but of the Telugu.

Of the five cultivated Drâvidian dialects mentioned above—the Tamil, the Telugu, the Canarese, the Malayâla, the Tulu,—the farthest removed from each other are the Tamil and the Telugu. The great majority of the roots in both languages are, it is true, identical; but they are often so disguised in composition by peculiarities of inflexion and dialectic changes, that not one entire sentence in the one language is intelligible to those who are acquainted only with the other. The various Drâvidian idioms, though sprung from a common origin, are therefore, to be considered not as mere provincial dialects of the same speech, but as distinct though affiliated languages. They are as distinct one from the other as the Spanish from the Portuguese, the Irish from the Welsh, the Hebrew from the Aramaic, the Hindî from the Bengâlî. If the cultivated Drâvidian idioms differ so materially from each other, it will naturally be supposed that the uncultivated idioms—the Tuda, the Kota, the Gond, and the Ku—must differ still more widely both from one another and from the cultivated languages. This supposition is in accordance with facts. So many and great are the differences and peculiarities which are observable amongst these rude dialects, that it has seemed to me to be necessary to prove, not that they differ, but that they belong, notwithstanding their differences, to the same stock as the more cultivated tongues, and that they have an equal right to be termed 'Drâviḍian.'

Evidence that the Tuda, Kota, Gond, and Ku, are really Drâvidian Tongues.

It is unnecessary to state in this general introduction, the particulars in which the cultivated Drâvidian idioms agree with one another, and the evidences of their essential unity even in minor matters and of their common origin: but the Tuda, Kota, Gond, and Ku being rude uncultivated dialects, and little known, it appears to be desirable at the outset to furnish the reader with proofs of the assertion that those languages belong to the same Drâvidian stock as the Tamil and the Telugu. Their Drâvidian character and connections will appear from the following statement of particulars, which I have ascertained concerning each of them respectively.

(1.) TUDA.—It is a favourite opinion with many persons in India that the language of the Tudars is altogether *sui generis*, or at least that it is unconnected with any of the languages of the Drâvidian races of the neighbouring plains. In adopting the conclusion that the Tuda language belongs to the Drâvidian stock, and justly claims to be regarded as a Drâvidian dialect, the evidence on which I place most reliance is that of a list of words and short sentences which was kindly communicated to me by the Rev. Mr. Metz, German missionary at Kaity, on the Nilgherry hills. Mr. Metz's acquaintance with the language of the Tudars, is believed to be more accurate than that which has been acquired by any other European; and though his knowledge is confessedly defective in the department of verbal modifications and syntax, his list of vocables may be fully depended upon: and inasmuch as *his* knowledge of the Tuda has been acquired through the medium of the language of the Badagars, a language with which he is intimately acquainted, it cannot be supposed in his case (as was supposed by some persons with respect to the Rev. Dr. Schmid's inquiries), that he may have accepted Badaga words for Tuda, through ignorance of the dialectic peculiarities of the old Canarese idiom which is spoken by the Badagars.

The following words—'prerogative instances,' as they would be called by Abel Remusat—prove the Drâvidian character of the Tuda language.

	TUDA.	HIGH TAMIL, &c.
I	ân*	yân; ân, Ancient Can.
we	ôm	yâm, ôm
thou	nî	nî
you	nima	nîm, Ancient Can.
my	en	en
thy	nin	nin
he (proximate)	ivan	ivan
they (ditto)	ivar	ivar
he (remote)	avan	avan
they (ditto)	avar	avar
three	mûdu	mûdu, Tel.
four	nânku	nângu
six	âr	âru
ten	poth'	pattu
hundred	nûr	nûru
a person	âḷ	aḷ
father	appan	appan
mother	avva	avva, 'grand-mother' in Tel.
son	mach	mag-an
hand	kai	kei
foot	kâl	kâl
eye	kannu	kan, kannu
mouth	bai	vai
ear	kevi	kevi, Can.
moon	tiggalu	tingaḷ
sky	bân	vân-am
day	nâl	nâḷ.
night	ill	iruḷ, 'darkness' in Tamil
water	nîr	nîr
fire	nebbu	nippu, Tel.

* In the Tuda language â is pronounced broad like *aw* in "fawn."

The Tuda words given above scarcely at all differ from their Tamil, Canarese, and Telugu equivalents. In many cases, however, the word, though undoubtedly Drâvidian, can scarcely be recognised in its Tuda shape. The following are examples of this :—

	TAMIL, &c.	TUDA.
tooth	pal	parsh
tiger	puli, pili	pirsh
sun, or sunlight	veyil	birsh
finger	viral	bolh
belly	vayaru	bir
fruit	param	vom

In the above examples the regular change of *l* into *rsh* is especially deserving of notice.

In some cases the Tuda words correspond to the Telugu rather than the Tamil, *e. g.*

	TAMIL.	TELUGU	TUDA.
tree	maram	mânu	maëna
fire	neruppu	nippu	nebbu

Sometimes the Tuda corresponds with the Canarese, rather than with either the Telugu or the Tamil, *e. g.*

	TAMIL.	TELUGU.	CANARESE.	TUDA.
small	s'inna	chinna	kinna	kin
ear	s'evi	chevi	kevi	kevi

The Tuda generally agrees more exactly with the Tamil than with the Telugu, the Canarese, or any other Drâvidian idiom. In many particulars so close is this agreement that the Tuda might be considered as merely a corrupt *patois* of the Tamil, were it not that in a still larger number of instances it differs, not only from the Tamil, but also from every other Drâvidian dialect, pursuing a course of its own with a vocabulary of its own; in consequence of which it must be regarded as a distinct member of the family. On an examination of the Tuda words contained in the lists in my possession, exclusive of pronouns and numerals (which are throughout Drâvidian), forty per cent. are found to be allied to Drâvidian words belonging to the languages of the adjacent plains, whilst sixty per cent. appear to be either independent of those languages or to be so greatly corrupted and disguised that their relationship cannot now be ascertained.

The following comparison of the forms of the present and future tenses of the substantive verb in Tuda with those of the Tamil will illustrate the verbal inflexions of this language. The root of the substantive verb in Tamil and in Canarese is 'ir.' In Tuda the corresponding root is 'ers,' 'etars,' or 'esh.'

	TAMIL.	TUDA.
I am	yân irukkirên	ân eshken
thou art	ní irukkirâi	nî etersbi
he is	avan irukkirân	avan etarji
we are	yâm irukkirôm	âm etarsbimi
ye are	nîr irukkirîr	nima etarshi
they are	avar irukkirâr	avar etarshi

	TAMIL	TUDA.
I shall be	yân iruppên	ân ersbini
thou wilt be	nî iruppai	nî ersbi
he will be	avan iruppân	avan ersje
we shall be	yâm iruppôm	âm ersbimi
ye will be	nîr iruppîr	nima ersshi
they will be	avar iruppâr	avar ersshi

It is evident that the third person singular and plural of each of the Tuda tenses is destitute of personal terminations. This is in accordance in part with the usage of the Canarese, and still more with that of the Telugu.

The Tuda language contains exceedingly few words of Sanscrit origin, and those few have evidently been derived from the intercourse of the Tudars with their neighbours the Badagars, colonists from the Canarese country,—*e. g.*, 'der,' *God*, from the Canarese 'dêvar,' and the Sanscrit 'dêva;' and 'budi,' *wisdom*, from 'buddhi,' the Sanscrit word for *wisdom* adopted in the Canarese.

The substantial agreement of the Tuda with the other Drâvidian languages in its pronouns, its numerals, the first and second persons of its verbal inflections, and in forty per cent. of its stock of ordinary vocables, proves beyond all doubt the propriety of considering it as a Drâvidian dialect; and it seems scarcely less certain that of all the Drâvidian idioms the Tamil is that to which it is most nearly allied. Sixty per cent. of its words appear, indeed, to be unconnected with the vocabularies of the other dialects; but those words are chiefly such as are remote from the daily business of life, and which are therefore of all words the most apt to become corrupted by a barbarous, isolated tribe. It is also to be remembered that each of the cultivated Drâvidian languages contains a considerable number of roots of this secondary, fleeting class, which are not found in any other dialect of the family. Such words do not necessarily belong to an Extra-Drâvidian source; for no one language of any family whatever is in possession of all the roots which originally belonged to the parent stem. Each dialect of the Sanscrit, of the Classical, and of the Germanic families of tongues is found to have retained a certain number of roots which the other dialects have suffered to become obsolete.

(2.) KÔTA. Whilst the language and customs of the Tudars have always been regarded with peculiar interest, the Kôtars (a tribe of craftsmen, residing from an unknown antiquity on the Nilgherry hills), being exceedingly filthy in their habits, and addicted beyond all other low caste tribes to the eating of carrion, have generally been shunned by Europeans; and, in consequence, their language is less known than that of the Tudars. Notwithstanding this, the following paradigm of the Kôta pronouns and of the present tense of its verb, which was furnished me by the Rev. Mr. Bühler, of Kaity, will show that the language of this degraded tribe is essentially Drâvidian:—

	KOTA.	ANCIENT CANARESE.
I go	âne hôgabe	ân pôgdapên
thou goest	nî hôgabi	nîn pôgdapi
he goes	awans hôgako	avam pôgdapam
we go	nâme hôgabemme	âm pôgdapêvu
ye go	niye hôgabirri	nîm pôgdapir
they go	awane hôgako	avar pôgdapar

In this paradigm the first person plural, both of the pronoun and of the verb, and the second person plural of the verb, accord most with the Tamil; the other forms agree most with the Ancient Caranese, particularly the formative suffix of the present tense of the verb, which is 'dap' in Ancient Caranese, and 'ab' in the Kôta. In the use of 'h' instead of 'p' ('hôgu,' to go, instead of 'pôgu'), the Kôta accords with the modern Caranese. The third person of the Kôta verb, which is formed, both in the singular and the plural, by the suffix 'ko,' seems at first sight entirely unconnected with all other Drâvidian forms. If we consider it, however, not as a verb properly so called, but as an abstract verbal noun, which acquires the force of a verb from juxta-position with a pronoun, like the third person in the Persian verb, it may easily be brought within the range of Drâvidian analogies; for many such verbal nouns in the other dialects end in 'ke,' 'kei,' 'ka,' 'ge,' &c. The sign of the genitive case in Kôta is 'a,' of the dative, 'ke,' of the locative, 'olge,'—all which forms correspond with those which are found in the other dialects. The preterite is formed by changing 'ka' or 'ga' into 'ji' or 'di;'—*e.g.*, 'hôgako,' *he goes;* 'hôjiko,' *he went:* 'tinkabe,' *I eat;* 'tindibe,' *I ate.* In this also we see a family resemblance to the manner in which the other dialects, especially the Telugu, form their preterites. The Kôta forms its infinitive by the addition of 'alik' to the root,—*e. g.*, 'tin,' *eat;* 'tinalik,' *to eat.* The infinitives of the corresponding verb in Canarese are 'tinna,' 'tinnalu,' 'tinnalike.' On the whole, though certain analogies with the Tamil and also with the Tulu may be observed in the Kôta, I regard this language as more nearly allied to the Canarese than to any other Drâvidian idiom.

3. THE GÔND.—The very complete grammar and vocabulary of the Mahadeo dialect of the Gônd language, which was compiled by the Rev. Mr. Driberg, a late missionary of the Society for the Propagation of the Gospel in the Saugor and Nerbudda country, and which was published at Bishop's College, Calcutta, in 1849, together with Dr. Manger's interesting paper on the dialect of the Saonee (Seoni) Gônda, including 'The Song of Sandsumjee,' in the *Journal of the Bengal Asiatic Society,*—contain so many proofs of the close affinity of the Gônd language to the Tamil, the Telugu, and the Canarese, that it seems quite unnecessary to prove in detail that it is a member of the Drâvidian family. It is not so easy to determine to which of the cultivated Drâvidian dialects it is most nearly allied. In many respects it accords most with the Telugu, its neighbour to the South and East; but on the whole, it is more closely allied to the Tamil, though locally of all Drâvidian dialects the farthest removed from it—a proof that the claim of the Tamil to be considered as the best representative of the primitive condition of these languages is not destitute of foundation.

The chief particulars in which the Gônd agrees with the Telugu, rather than with the Tamil or with the Canarese, are as follows:—

(1.) The pronouns of the first and second persons, especially the second person plural, have most resemblance to the Telugu. Compare 'mîk,' Gônd, *to you,* Telugu, 'mîku,' with the Tamil 'umakku' and the Canarese 'nimage.'

(2.) Another point of resemblance to the Telugu consists in the absence of a feminine form of the pronoun of the third person singular and of the third person of the verb, and the use of the neuter singular for the feminine singular.

(3.) The Gônd preterite verbal participle is formed, like the Telugu, by the addition of 'si' or 'ji' to the root, instead of the 'du' which is so largely employed by the Tamil and Canarese.

(4.) A certain number of roots of secondary importance and a few Sanscrit derivatives seem to have been borrowed by the Gônd from the Telugu;—*e. g.*, 'nattur,' *blood,* from the Telugu, 'netturu,' a corrupt derivative from the Sanscrit, 'ractam.'

In some instances again the Gônd agrees remarkably with the Canarese; e. *g.*, the Gônd infinitive is in 'âlle,' or 'ille.' In Telugu and Tamil the infinitive is invariably in 'a:' the Tamil has a verbal noun ending in 'al,' of which the dative is used as a supine; and the High Tamil occasionally, but the Canarese ordinarily uses this very form 'al' as an infinitive. The Gônd also like the Canarese sometimes prefers 'k' where the Telugu has 'ch' and the Tamel 's;' *e. g., the ear,* is in Tamil, 'śevi;' Telugu, 'chevi;' Canarese, 'kevi;' in Gônd also, 'kaövi.' *To do,* is in Tamil, 'śey̆;' Telugu, 'chêy̆;' Canarese, 'gêy̆' (g hard); Gônd, 'ki.' Such agreements of the Gônd with the Canarese are rare; but the particulars in which the Gônd agrees with the Tamil, though the Telugu country lies between it and the country in which the Tamil is spoken, are very numerous and important. The following are specimens of this agreement.

(1.) The Telugu has but one form for the plural of nouns substantive, the suffix 'lu;' the Tamil has two, 'ar' and 'kal,' the former epicene, the latter neuter: the Gônd also has two, 'ar' and 'k.'

(2.) The instrumental case of the Telugu is formed by the addition of 'chêta:' the Gônd like the Tamil uses 'al.'

(3.) The Gônd differs from the Telugu, and accords with the Tamil in retaining unaltered the initial vowel of its pronouns in the oblique cases. Thus, from 'adi,' Telugu, *it,* comes 'dêni,' *of it;* Tamil, 'adin,' *of it;* Gônd, 'adena.'

(4.) The Telugu negative particles are 'lêdu,' *there is not,* and 'kâdu,' *it is not;* the corresponding particles in Tamil are 'illei' and 'alla;' in Gônd, 'hille' and 'halle.'

(5.) The Telugu systematically uses 'ḍ' instead of the Tamil vocalic 'ṛ:' the Gônd retains the 'r' of the Tamil; e. *g.*, 'êḍu' or 'aḍalu,' Telugu, *to weep;* Tamil 'aṛa." Gônd 'ara.' So also compare 'êḍu,' Telugu, *seven,* with Tamil 'êṛu' and Gônd 'êro.'

A considerable number of Gônd roots denoting objects of primary importance correspond with the Tamil rather than the Telugu; *e. g.*

	TELUGU.	TAMIL.	GÔND.
one	okaṭi	ondru	und
three	mûḍu	mûndru	mund
hand	chêy	kei	kai
tree	mânu	maram	marrâ
great	pedda	peru, paru	paror
to come	vachcha (vatssa)	vara	wara

In a large number of instances the Gônd, though retaining the same roots as the other Drâvidian dialects, modifies those roots after a fashion peculiar to itself. This will appear on comparing the following Tamil and Gônd words.

	TAMIL.	GÔND.
flower	pû	pungâr
belly	vayaru	pîr
boy	peiyal	perdgal
to fall	viṛa	ara
to fill	nira	niha
light	velicham	verchi
many	pala	walle

	TAMIL.	GÔND.
district	nâḍu	nâr (a village)
dew	pani	pîni (cold)
break	uḍei	urreha

Notwithstanding the affinities between the Gônd and the other Drâvidian dialects which have now been mentioned and illustrated, the Gônd possesses a large number of roots which are not found elsewhere, and exhibits peculiarities of grammatical structure of such a nature as amply to justify our regarding it as a distinct dialect. The difference existing between the Tamil and the Telugu sinks into insignificance when compared with the difference between the Gônd and every other dialect of the Drâvidian family. In the list of Gônd words given by Mr. Driberg, I have been able to identify only thirty-four per cent. as words contained in or allied to those that are found in the other dialects, which is a smaller proportion than that which is contained even in the Tuda.

The principal particulars in which the grammatical structure of the Gônd differs from that of the other dialects are as follows :—

(1.) Like the idioms of Northern India, the Gônd evinces a tendency to confound the dative with the accusative, though in possession of both forms.

(2.) It has a passive voice formed, as in some of those Northern idioms, by prefixing the past participle of the active voice to the substantive verb.

(3.) The remote and proximate demonstratives ('ille,' 'hic,') which in Tamil are 'avar,' 'ivar;' in Telugu 'vâru,' 'vîru;' are in Gond corrupted into 'wor' and 'yer.'

(4.) The base of the interrogative pronouns in all the other dialects is 'yâ;' in this it is 'bâ,' or 'bo.'

(5.) Instead of the regularly formed negative voice of the other dialects, the Gônd forms its negative verbs by simply prefixing the negative particles 'hille,' or 'halle,' to the verb. For example, *thou art not*, or *thou becomest not* (in Tamil 'âgây,' in Telugu, 'kâvu'), is in Gônd 'halle aivi.' A similar use of the negative particle is found in the Kota language. The only thing in the other dialects which at all corresponds to this, is the occasional formation in poetical Tamil of a negative verb by the insertion of the negative particle 'al' between the root of the verb and the pronominal suffix; *e. g.*, 'pês-al-ên,' *I speak not*, for 'pês-ên.'

(6.) The chief difference, however, in point of grammatical structure between the Gônd and the other Drâvidian dialects, consists in its peculiarly elaborate and complete conjugational system. The Tamil, the Malayâlam, the Canarese, and the Tulu possess only a present, an indefinite past, and a future tense,—the future more or less aoristic. The Telugu, in addition to these tenses, has a regularly formed aorist. The indicative and the imperative are the only moods which these dialects possess, and they are destitute of a passive voice properly so called. All modifications of mood and tense are formed by means either of auxiliary verbs or of suffixed particles. Whilst the more cultivated Drâvidian idioms are so simple in structure, the speech of the rude Mahadeo Gônds boasts in a system of verbal modifications and inflexions almost as elaborate as that of the Turkish. It has a passive voice: in addition to the indicative and the imperative moods, it possesses a potential: in the indicative mood, where the Tamil has only three tenses, it has a present, an imperfect definite, an indefinite past, a perfect, a conditional, and a future, each of which is regularly inflected: like the other idioms, it has a causal verb, but it stands alone in having also an inceptive. In these particulars the Gônd grammar has acquired a development peculiar to itself, perhaps in some degree through the influence of the highly inflected Sântâl, its Kôl neighbour to the northward.

(4.) THE KU.* The Kond, Khond, or Ku language, undoubtedly a Drâvidian idiom, has generally been considered as identical with the Gônd. It was stated long ago by Captain Blunt in the *Asiatic Researches*, vol. vii., on the authority of a native Jaghiredar, that the Gônds and Khunds are totally distinct races: notwithstanding this, I have not met with any account of their languages in which they have been regarded as different, though in truth their differences are numerous and essential. In many particulars the Ku accords more closely than the Gônd with the Tamil, the Telugu and the other Drâvidian tongues; in some things less so. For example:—

(1.) The Gônd forms its infinitive in 'alle,' or 'ille;' the Ku, like the Telugu, the Tamil, and the modern Canarese, forms its infinitive by suffixing 'a,' sometimes 'va,' or 'pa.' Thus, *to become*, is in Gônd 'aiâlle;' in Telugu, 'kâ;' in Canarese, 'âgal,' or 'âga;' in Tamil, 'âga;' in Ku, 'âva.'

(2.) The Ku retains the simplicity of the conjugational system of the other Drâvidian dialects, in contradistinction to the elaborateness of the Gônd.

(3.) The Gônd forms its negatives by prefixing to the indicative aorist the separate negative particles "hille," or "halle." In this point the Ku differs from the Gônd, and agrees with the other dialects. Thus, *I do not*, is in Gônd 'hille kion;' in Tamil 'seyyên;' in Telugu 'chêyanu;' in Canarese 'gêyenu,' in Ku 'giênu.'

In the following instances the Ku accords more closely with the Tamil and Canarese, though locally very remote, than with its nearer neighbour the Telugu.

(1.) The Telugu forms its plurals by the use of 'lu' alone, except in some of the oblique forms of the 'rational' demonstratives. The Ku, like the Tamil, makes a difference between the plurals of nouns which denote rational beings, and those of nouns of the inferior class. The Tamil suffix of the first class of plurals is 'ar,' of the second class 'kal:' the corresponding suffixes in Ku are 'âru' or 'ru,' and 'kâ.'

(2.) The Telugu forms its masculine singular by means of the suffix 'ḍu:' the Canarese and Tamil by 'anu' and 'an.' The Ku by means of the suffix 'âñju' or 'ânyu.' Thus, compare 'vâḍu,' Telugu, *he*, with the Tamil 'avan,' Canarese 'avanu,' Ku 'avâñju.'

(3.) The Ku pronouns bear a closer resemblance to the Tamil and Canarese than to the Telugu and Gônd, as will appear from the following comparative view:—

	TELUGU.	GÔND.	TAMIL.	CANARESE.	KU.
I	nênu	anâ	yân (ancient	ân (ancient)	ânu
we	mêmu	amât	yâm (do.)	âm (do.)	âmu
thou	nîvu	ima	nî	nînu	înu
ye	mîru	imat	nîr	nîvu	îru
he, remote	vâḍu	wor	avan	avanu	avâñju
he, proximate	vîḍu	yer	ivan	ivanu	ivâñju

* See a lucidly arranged grammar of this language prepared by Lingam Letchmajee, Deputy Translator to the Ganjam Agency, and published in Uriya characters in the *Calcutta Christian Observer* for May and June, 1853. I have not seen any notice in any scientific work or periodical of this valuable contribution to our knowledge of the Indian languages.

(*d.*) In the Drâvidian languages contingency is expressed by the addition of a particle to any verbal tense, person or number. This subjunctive suffix is in Telugu 'êni' or 'ê;' in Canarese 're,' 'rû,' or 'âgyu.' One of the suffixes employed in the Tamil is 'kkâl,' which in the speech of the vulgar becomes 'kkâ;' and this very particle 'kkâ,' added, as in Tamil, to the preterite, is the suffix by which the Ku also forms conditional or contingent verbs: *e.g.*, *If I do*, is in Telugu 'nênu chêyudunêni;' in Canarese 'nânu gêyidare;' in colloquial Tamil this is 'nân cheydâkkâ;' in Ku also, (from the root 'gi,' *to do*), it is 'ânu gitekkâ.'

On the other hand, in the following particulars the Gônd agrees more closely with the Telugu than with the Tamil or Canarese.

(1.) It uses the neuter singular to denote the feminine singular.

(2.) The oblique cases or "inflexions" of the pronouns of the first and second persons, singular and plural, are identical with those of the Telugu.

(3.) The case terminations of the Ku are nearly in accordance with those of the Telugu.

(4.) The pronominal signs suffixed to the Ku verbs accord on the whole better with the Telugu than with any other dialect: *e.g.*, in Tamil the second and third persons plural end differently, the one 'îr,' the other 'âr;' in Telugu they end alike—both generally in 'aru;' in Ku also both these persons end alike in 'eru.'

(5.) In Canarese all relative participles, including that of the negative verb, end in 'a;' in Tamil all relative participles, with the exception of that of the future, have the same ending: in Telugu the relative participle of the indefinite or aoristic tense ends in 'eḍi,' or 'eṭi;' and in the Ku also the relative past participle exhibits this ending. Thus, 'âna,' Tamil, *that became;* in Canarese, 'âda;' in Telugu (indefinite tense), 'ayyêti;' in Ku the same form is 'âti.'

The various particulars and illustrations which have now been mentioned prove the Ku to be totally distinct from the Gônd; and though it is allied to it, it is allied only in the same manner as to the other Drâvidian languages. In some points this language differs from all the other dialects of the family; for example, it forms its past verbal participles not by means of the suffixes 'du,' 'i,' or 'si,' the only suffixes known in the other dialects, but by suffixing to the root 'â,' sometimes 'sâ' or 'jâ,' after the manner of some of the languages of Northern India. In the other dialects of this family the negative verb possesses only one tense, an aorist; the Ku, in addition to this negative aorist, has also a negative preterite,—a decided advantage over the other dialects. The Ku suffixes of the present verbal participles are also different from those which are found in the other Drâvidian dialects. The formative suffix of the present verbal participle is in Telugu 'chu' or 'tu;' in the Canarese 'ta' or 'te;' in the Ku it is 'i' or 'pi.'

The four dialects referred to above—the Tuda, Kôta, Gônd and Ku—though rude and uncultivated, are undoubtedly to be regarded as distinctively and essentially Drâvidian dialects, equally with the Tamil and Telugu. In addition to these, there are two uncultivated idioms of Central India, the Ûrâon and the Râjmahal, which contain so many Drâvidian roots of primary importance that they may claim to be considered as originally members of the same family, though they contain also a large admixture of roots and forms belonging to the Kôl dialects. The Ûrâon is considered by Mr. Hodgson as a connecting link between the Kôl and the Râjmahal; and the Râjmahal as a connecting link between the Kôl and the Tamulian families. The Râjmahal is more distinctively Drâvidian than the Ûrâon, though the Males or aborigines of the Râjmahal or Male range by whom it is spoken, are locally more remote than the Ûrâons from the present seats of the Drâvidian race. The Kôls intervene between the Males and the Drâvidians; but whilst the Male is substantially a Drâvidian tongue, the Kôl belongs to a totally different family.

In the list of Râjmahal or Male words given by Mr. Hodgson, sixteen per cent. are purely Drâvidian; in the older list, given in the *Asiatic Researches*, the Drâvidian roots form only ten per cent. In the Urâon list the proportion of Drâvidian roots is fourteen per cent.

The principal and most essential analogies which I have noticed are as follows:—

	RAJMAHAL.	URAON.	TAMIL, &c.
eye	kânê	khân	kan
eye-lash	kan-meer	..	kan-mayir
hand	sêsû	kâhekhâh	chêyi (Tel.), kyê (Canar.)
ear	kkhêtway	..	kâdu, kêl, *to hear*
mouth	..	bâî	vây̆
tooth	pâll	pâll	pal
hair	tali	..	talei, *head*
father	âbâ	..	appa
mother	âyâ	ayyo	âyi
tree	man	man	mân-u (Tel.)
flower	pûp	phûp	pû; pûppu, *a flowering*
fish	mîn	..	mîn
dove	pûrah	..	purâ
scorpion	tîlah	..	têḷ
pain	nogi	..	nôgu, *to pain*
above	mêchê	mêyah	mêl, mêlê
below	..	kîyah	kîṛ, kîṛê
within	ûlê	ûla	uḷ, uḷḷê
I	en	enan	nân, ên
thou	nin	nîen	nîn (Can.)
he, she, it	âth	âsan	âta (Can.). *he*, adu, *it*; adum, (Tuda), *he, she, it*
we	nam, om	en	nâm, ôm
ye	nina (nim in nimki, *yours*)	..	nîm (Can.)
they	awâr, âsabar	..	avar
this	îh	..	î
that	âḥ	..	â
here	ino	..	inge
there	âno	..	ange
one	art, ort	ûutâh	or, ondru
two	(Sanscrit)	en-otan	renḍu (Tel.), ranu (Gond.)
three	(do.)	man-otan	mûnna (Malayal).
our	(do.)	nâkh-otan	nâlku, nânku

Unfortunately the inflexions of the Râjmahal and Urâon nouns and verbs are not given in any of the lists, so that, with the exception of a few incidental particulars, the grammatical construction of these languages remains unknown. In the particulars that follow they accord with the Drâvidian grammatical rules. The Râjmahal expresses the prepositions *to, in, on,* &c., by suffixes. Its dative suffix is 'ku:' 'm' is the sign of the plural number of the pronouns of the first and second persons, replacing 'n.' the corresponding sign of the singular; 'ar' is the sign of the plural of epicene pronouns of the third person. The sign of the possessive pronouns is 'ki,' or in the Urâon 'ghi,' corresponding apparently to the 'kâ,' 'kî,' of the Hindî, and more remotely to the 'yoka' of the Telugu.

The existence of a distinctively Drâvidian element in these aboriginal dialects of Central India being established, the Drâvidian race can now be traced as far North as the banks of the Ganges; and the supposition (which was deduced from other considerations) that this race was diffused at an early period throughout India is confirmed. The Brahui, the language of the Belûchi mountaineers in the khanship of Kelat enables us to trace the Drâvidian race beyond the Indus to the southern confines of Central Asia. The Brahui language, considered as a whole, is derived from the same source as the Panjâbi and Sindhi; but it unquestionably contains a Drâvidian element, an element which has probably been derived from a remnant of the ancient Drâvidian race incorporated with the Brahuis. The discovery of this Drâvidian element in a language spoken beyond the Indus proves that the Drâvidians, like the Aryans, the Graeco-Scythians and the Turco-Mongolians, entered India by the north-western route.

The following is an outline of the particulars in which the Brahui is found to be allied to the Drâvidian tongues.

(1.) In Brahui, as in the Drâvidian dialects, the cases of nouns are denoted by post-positions.

(2.) The gender of nouns is expressed not by their inflexions, but by prefixed separate words.

(3.) The number of nouns is ordinarily denoted by the use of separate particles of pluralisation, such as *many, several,* &c. When a noun stands alone without any such sign of plurality, its number is considered to be indefinite, and it is then regarded as singular or plural according to the context, or the number of the verb with which it agrees. This rule is remarkably in accordance with the Tamil.

(4.) Adjectives are destitute of comparatives and superlatives.

(5.) Pronouns form their genitives in 'na' or 'a;' *e.g.*, 'kana,' *of me;* 'nana,' *of us.* Compare Tamilian 'nama,' *of us,* and the Gônd genitive suffix 'na' or 'a.'

(6.) The Brahui dative-accusative is in 'e.' Compare the Malayâla accusative 'ê,' Tamil 'ei.'

(7.) The Brahui pronoun of the second person singular is 'nî,' *thou,* precisely the same as in all the Drâvidian tongues. The analogy of the plural of this pronoun, viz., 'num,' *you,* 'numa,' *of you,* is also wonderfully in accordance with classical Drâvidian forms. The Canarese is 'nîm,' *you;* the old Tamil possessive is 'num-a,' *your* (derived from an obsolete nominative in 'nûm' or 'num'), and the ordinary base of the oblique cases of this pronoun in colloquial Tamil is 'um' (the initial 'n' being lost), which is also the termination of the plural of the second person imperative.

(8.) Whilst 'nîm' or 'nûm' is to be considered as the most classical form of the plural of the Dravidian pronoun of the second person, 'nîr' is the form ordinarily used in a separate shape in Tamil, 'mîru' in Telugu; and in consequence of this plural termination in 'r,' in nearly all the Drâvidian idioms the second person plural of the verb in the indicative mood ends, not in 'im' or 'um,' but in 'îr,' 'eru,' 'âru,' 'iri,' &c. The same peculiarity reappears in the Brahui. Whilst the separate pronoun ends in 'm,' 'r' is the pronominal sign of the second person of the verb; *e.g.,* 'areri,' *ye are,* 'arer.' *they are;* with which compare the Canarese 'iru(tt)îri,' *ye are,* 'iru(tt)âre,' *they are.*

(9.) The root of the substantive verb in Brahui is 'ar,' in Canarese and Tamil 'ir.'

(10.) A remarkable analogy between the Brahui and the Drâvidian languages is apparent in the reflexive pronoun *self,* 'se.' In the Drâvidian languages this pronoun is universally 'tân' or 'tan:' in the Brahui 'ten.'

(11.) Bopp remarks that the three lowest numerals could never be introduced into any country by foreigners. The truth of this remark is illustrated by a circumstance of which Bopp could scarcely have been aware. From *four* upwards, the Brahui numerals are of Indo-European origin (*e.g.,* 'char,' *four,* 'panj,' *five,* 'shash,' *six*); and in the compound numerals *twenty-one* and *twenty-two,* the words for *one* and *two* are also Indo-European, but the separate numerals *one, two, three,* are totally unconnected with the Sanscrit family, and two of them are identical with Drâvidian numerals. In Brahui, *two* is 'irat;' compare Canarese, 'eraḍ-u,' *two;* Tamil, 'iraṭ-(ṭu),' *twofold* or *double.* In Brahui *three* is 'musit;' compare Canarese 'mûr-u;' Telugu, 'mûd-u.' The Drâvidian bases of these numerals are 'ir,' *two,* 'mû,' *three;* and if we notice the terminations of the Brahui numerals (1, 'asit;' 2, 'irat;' 3, 'musit;') it is obvious that the second syllable of each of these words, 'it,' or 'at' is merely a neuter formative, like that which we find in the Drâvidian languages (*e.g.,* compare 'ir,' the base and numeral adjective *two,* with 'iraḍu,' the abstract neuter noun *two*): consequently the agreement of the Brahui with the Drâvidian numerals, both in the base and in the formative, is complete. If we remember the interchangeable relation of 's' and 'r,' and if we regard the Canarese 'mûr,' *three,* and the Brahui 'mus,' as an instance of this interchange, as I think we may safely do, we may also venture to connect the Drâvidian numeral base, 'or,' *one,* with the Brahui 'as.' This connection, however, is doubtful, whereas there cannot be any doubt respecting *two* and *three.*

(12.) In the class of auxiliary words (prepositions, conjunctions, &c.) compare the Brahui, 'mont,' *opposite,* with the Tamil, 'munnê,' *before;* and also the copulative conjunction 'û,' *and,* with the corresponding Canarese 'û.'

In the limited vocabulary of the Brahui language, which is given in the *Journal of the Bengal Asiatic Society,* I notice a few Drâvidian roots. In the following list I include also a few Drâvidian words, which are found in the Laghmani, an Afghan dialect, containing an element allied to the Brahui.

	BRAHUI, &c.	TAMIL, &c.
water	dîr	nîr
eye	khan	kan
ear	khaff }	kâd-u
do., Laghmani and Cashgari	kâd }	
mother	lummâ	amma
do., Laghmani	âe	âyi
belly	pid	pir (Gond), bir (Tuda)
stone	khall	kal
bow	billa	billu (Can.)
mud or earth	men	man
bedstead	kat	kaṭ-(ṭil)
hare	muru	muyal
ass (female) Lagh.	karatik	kaṛudei, *ass*
cat, Laghmani	pusha	pûsei
to come	barak	bar-u (Can.)
to go, Laghmani	pak	pôg-u

It is true that the great majority of the words in the Brahui language are altogether unconnected with Drâvidian roots; but it must be evident from the analogies in structure, as well as in the vocabulary, which have now been exhibited, that this language contains many grammatical forms essentially and distinctly Drâvidian, together with a small proportion of important Drâvidian vocables. The Brahuis state that their forefathers came from Haleb (Aleppo); but even if this tradition were to be regarded as a credible one, it would apply to the secondary or conquering race of Indo-European origin, not to the aboriginal, indigenous Drâvidians. The previous existence of the latter race seems to have been forgotten, and the only evidence that they ever existed is that which is furnished by the Drâvidian element which has been discovered in the language of their conquerors.

The analogies between the Brahui and the Drâvidian languages which have now been pointed out, are incomparably closer than any analogy which subsists between the Drâvidian languages and the Bodo, the Dhimal, and the languages of the other tribes on the north-eastern frontier of India which have been termed "Tamulian" by Mr. Hodgson. Those analogies appear to me to be as remote as those of the Tibetan family; and are not only less numerous, but also of a less essential character and less distinctive than the analogies which are discoverable between the Finnish tongues and the Drâvidian.

Compare the following list of Drâvidian words of primary importance with analogous words in the Brahui, and with the words in the Bodo and Dhimal which correspond in signification:—

	DRÂVIDIAN.	BRAHUI.	BODO.	DHIMAL.
thou	nî	nî	nang	nâ
you	num	num	nangchûr	nyêl
we	nâm	nân	jong	kyel
self	tan	ten	goui	tâi

	Dravidian.	Brahui.	Bodo.	Dhimal.
one	or	as-it	chê	ê
two	irad-u	irat	gnê	gne
three	mûr-u	mus-it	thâm	sûm
eye	kan	khan	mogon	mî
ear	kâd-u	kâd	khomâ	nâhâthong
water	nîr	dîr	dôi	chî
stone	kal	khall	onthâi	ûnthûr

It seems unnecessary to give a larger number of instances; for whilst the Brahui does to a certain extent contain Drâvidian forms and words, the Bodo and Dhimal, and to them may be added the other dialects of the north-eastern forests, present no *special* analogies whatever; and contain only a few vague structural affinities, which they have in common not only with the Drâvidian, but with the Tibetan, and with every other language and family of languages of the Scythian group.

Use of the Common Term 'Drâvidian.'

I have designated all the languages now subjected to comparison by a common term, 'Drâviḍian,' because of the essential and distinctive grammatical characteristics which they all possess in common, and in virtue of which, joined to the possession in common of a large number of roots of primary importance, they justly claim to be considered as springing from a common origin, and as forming a distinct family of tongues.

This family which I style 'Drâviḍian' has been styled 'Tamulian' by some recent writers; but though the Tamil is the oldest and most highly cultivated member of the family, and that which contains the largest proportion of the family property of forms and roots, yet as it is but one dialect out of many, and does not claim to be the original speech from which the other dialects have been derived; as it is also desirable to reserve the terms 'Tamil' and 'Tamilian' (or as it is generally but erroneously written 'Tamulian') to denote the Tamil language itself and the people by whom it is spoken, I have preferred to designate this entire family by a term which is capable of a wider application. The word which I have chosen is 'Drâviḍian,' a word which has already been used as the generic appellation of this family of tongues by the Sanscrit geographers. Properly speaking, the term 'Drâviḍa' denotes the Tamil country alone (including Malayâlam), and Tamil Brahmans are usually styled 'Drâviḍa Brahmans.' 'Drâviḍa' means the 'country of the Drăviḍas;' and a Drăviḍa is defined in the Sanscrit lexicons to be "a man of an outcast tribe, descended from a degraded *Kshatriya*." This name was doubtless applied by the Brahmanical inhabitants of Northern India to the aborigines of the extreme South prior to the introduction amongst them of Brahmanical civilisation, and is an evidence of the low estimation in which they were originally held. In the Mahâ-Bhârata, in which the Drâvidas are distinguished from the Chôlas, or Tanjore Tamilians, the term is still further restricted to the Pâṇḍiyas of Madura, doubtless on account of the advanced civilisation and early celebrity of the Pâṇḍiya kingdom. The term 'Drâvidian' is thus in itself as restricted as that of 'Tamilian,' but it has the advantage of being remoter from ordinary usage, and somewhat more vague, and the further and more special advantage of being the term already adopted by Sanscrit writers to designate the southern family of languages. Consequently, by the adoption of this more generic term, the word "Tamilian" has been left to signify that which is distinctively Tamil.

The colloquial languages of India are divided by the Sanscrit Pandits into two classes, each containing five dialects. These are denominated respectively 'the five Gauras' and 'the five Drâviras.' By the Gauḍa or Gaura languages are meant the 'bhâshâs,' or popular dialects, of Northern India, at the head of which stands the Bengâli, the Gâura proper. Some of the 'bhâshâs' or Prâcrits anciently enumerated have ceased to be spoken. At present the Bengâlî, the Uriya, the Hindî with its daughter the Hindûstânî, the Panjâbî, the Sindhî, the Gujarâthi, and the Marâṭhi are the languages which may be regarded as forming the Gaura class; to which I would add the Cashmirian and the language of Nipâl, thus reckoning in this class nine idioms instead of five.

The five Drâvidas or Drâviras, according to the Pandits, are "the Telinga, the Karnâtaka, the Maratha, the Gûrjara, and the Drâvira," or Tamil proper. The Maratha and Gûrjara are erroneously included in this enumeration. It is true that the Marâthi contains a small admixture of Drâvidian roots and idioms, as might be expected from its local proximity to the Telugu and the Canarese; and both it and the Gûrjara, or Gujarâthi, possess certain features of resemblance to the languages of the South, which are possibly derived from the same or a similar source; but, notwithstanding the existence of a few analogies of this nature, those two languages differ from the Drâvidian family so widely and radically, and are so closely allied to the northern group, that there cannot be any hesitation in transferring them to that class. The three languages that remain in the classification of Drâvidian tongues which is contained in the Sanscrit geographical lists, viz., the Karnâṭaka, Kannaḍa or Canarese, the Telinga, Telungu or Telugu, and the Drâviḍa proper or Tamil, are certainly the principal members of the southern or Drâvidian family It will be observed that the Malayâlam and the Tulu are not contained in the Sanscrit enumeration. The first was considered to be a dialect of the Tamil, and was included in the denomination of the Drâvida proper; the second was probably considered as a dialect of the Canarese. The uncultivated dialects—the Tuda, Kôta, Gônd, and Ku—appear to have been unknown to the Pandits; and even had they been known, probably they would not have been deemed worthy of notice.

No term belonging to the Drâvidian languages themselves has ever been used to designate all the members of this family, nor are the native Tamil or Telugu grammarians, though deeply skilled in the grammar of their own tongues, sufficiently acquainted with *comparative* grammar to have arrived at the conclusion that all these idioms have a common origin and require to be designated by a common term. Some European scholars who have confined their attention to the study of some one Drâvidian idiom to the neglect of the others, have fallen into the same error of supposing these languages independent one of another. The Sanscrit Pandits had a clearer perception of grammatical affinities and differences than the Drâvidian grammarians; and, though their generalisation was not perfectly correct, it has furnished us with the only common terms which we possess for denoting the northern and southern families of languages respectively.

The Drâvidian Languages independent of the Sanscrit.

It was supposed by the Sanscrit Pandits (by whom everything with which they were acquainted was referred to a Brahmanical origin), and too hastily taken for granted by the earlier European scholars, that the Drâvidian languages, though differing in many particulars from the North-Indian idioms, were equally with them derived from the Sanscrit. They could not but see that each of the Drâvidian languages to which their attention had been drawn, contained a certain proportion of Sanscrit words, some of which were quite unchanged, though some were so much altered as to be recognized with difficulty; and though they observed clearly enough that each language contained also many Un-Sanscrit words and forms, they did not observe that those words and forms constituted the bulk of the language, or that it was in them that the living spirit of the language resided. Consequently they contented themselves with ascribing the Un-Sanscrit portion of these languages to an admixture of a foreign element of unknown origin. According to this view there was no essential difference between 'the Drâviḍas' and 'the Gauḍas;' for the Bengali and the other languages of the Gaura group contain also a small proportion of Un-Sanscrit words and forms, whilst in the main they are corruptions of the Sanscrit. This representation fell far short of the real state of the case, and the supposition of the derivation of the Drâvidian languages from the Sanscrit, though entertained in the past generation by a Colebrooke, a Carey, and a Wilkins, is now known to be entirely destitute of foundation. The orientalists referred to, though deeply learned in Sanscrit and well acquainted with the idioms of Northern India, were unacquainted, or but very slightly acquainted, with the Drâvidian languages. No person who has any acquaintance with the principles of comparative philology and who has carefully studied the grammars and vocabularies of the Drâvidian languages, and compared them with those of the Sanscrit, can suppose that the grammatical structure and inflexional forms of those languages and the greater number of their more important roots are capable of being derived from the Sanscrit by any process of corruption whatsoever.

The hypothesis of the existence of a remote original affinity between the Drâvidian languages and the Sanscrit, or rather between those languages and the Indo-European family of tongues, inclusive of the Sanscrit, of such a nature as to allow us to give the Drâvidian languages a place in the Indo-European group, is altogether different from the notion of the direct derivation of those languages from the Sanscrit. The hypothesis of a remote original affinity is favoured by some interesting analogies both in the grammar and in the vocabulary, which will be noticed in their place. Some of those analogies are best accounted for by the supposition of the retention by the Drâvidian family, as by the Finnish and the Turkish, of a certain number of roots and forms belonging to the Pre-Sanscrit period, the period which preceded the final separation of the Indo-European group of tongues from the Scythian. I think I shall also be able to prove, with respect to another portion of the analogies referred to, that instead of the Drâvidian languages having borrowed them from the Sanscrit, or both having derived them from a common source, the Sanscrit has not disdained to borrow them from its Drâvidian neighbours. Whatever probabilities may be in favour of the hypothesis now mentioned, the older supposition of the direct derivation of the Drâvidian languages from the Sanscrit, in the same manner as the Hindi, the Bengali, and the other Gaura dialects are directly derived from it, was certainly erroneous. (1.) It overlooked the circumstance that the Un-Sanscrit portion of the Drâvidian languages was nearly as much in excess of the Sanscrit, as in the North-Indian idioms the Sanscrit was in excess of the barbarian or Un-Sanscrit element. (2.) It overlooked the still more material circumstance that the pronouns and numerals of the Drâvidian languages, their verbal and nominal inflexions, and the syntactic arrangement of their words—everything, in short, which constitutes the living spirit of a language—were originally and radically different from the Sanscrit. (3.) The Orientalists who held the opinion of the derivation of the Drâvidian languages from the Sanscrit relied mainly on the circumstance that all dictionaries of Drâvidian languages contained a large number of Sanscrit words scarcely at all altered, and a still larger number which, though much altered, were unquestionably Sanscrit derivatives. They were not, however, aware that such words are never regarded by native scholars as of Drâvidian origin, but are known and acknowledged to be derived from the Sanscrit, and that they are arranged in classes, according to the degree in which they have been corrupted, or with reference to the medium through which they have been derived. They were also unaware that true Drâvidian words, which form the great majority of the words in the southern vocabularies, are placed by native grammarians in a different class from the above-mentioned derivatives from the Sanscrit, and honoured with the epithets 'national words' and 'pure words.' The Telugu grammarians specify even the time when Sanscrit derivatives were first introduced into Telugu; by which we are doubtless to understand the time when the Brahmans established themselves in the Telugu country. They say,—"The adherents of King Ândhra-râya, who then resided on the banks of the Godavery, spoke Sanscrit derivatives, many of which words in course of time became corrupted. That other class of words consisting of nouns, verbals, and verbs, which were created by the god Brahma before the time of this king, are called 'pure (Telugu) words.' The date of the reign of this King Andhra-râya, or King of the Ândhras (a division of the ancient Telugus), who is now worshipped at Chicacole as a deity, is unknown, but was probably several centuries anterior to the Christian era.

In general no difficulty is felt in distinguishing Sanscrit derivatives from the ancient Drâvidian roots. There are a few cases only in which it may be doubtful whether particular words are Sanscrit or Drâvidian, *e. g.*, 'nîr,' *water*, and 'mîn,' *fish*, are claimed as component parts of both languages; though I believe that both are of Drâvidian origin.

(4.) The Orientalists who supposed the Drâvidian languages to be derived from the Sanscrit were not aware of the existence of uncultivated languages of the Drâvidian family, in which Sanscrit words are not at all, or but very rarely, employed; and they were also not aware that some of the Drâvidian languages which make use of Sanscrit derivatives, are able to dispense with those derivatives altogether, such derivatives being considered rather as luxuries or articles of finery than as necessaries. It is true it would now be difficult for the Telugu to dispense with its Sanscrit: more so for the Canarese; and most of all for the Malayâlam:—those languages having borrowed from the Sanscrit so largely, and being so habituated to look up to it for help, that it would be scarcely possible for them now to assert their independence. The Tamil, however, the most highly cultivated *ab intra* of all Drâvidian idioms, can dispense with its Sanscrit altogether, if need be, and not only stand alone but flourish without its aid.

The ancient or classical dialect of the Tamil language, called the 'Shen-Tamil,' or correct Tamil, in which nearly all the literature has been written, contains exceedingly little Sanscrit; and differs from the colloquial dialect, or the language of prose, chiefly in the sedulous and jealous care with which it has rejected the use of Sanscrit derivatives and characters, and restricted itself to pure Drâvidian sounds, forms, and roots. So completely has this jealousy of Sanscrit pervaded the minds of the educated classes amongst the Tamilians, that a Tamil composition is regarded as refined, in accordance with good taste, and worthy of being called classical, not in proportion to the amount of Sanscrit which it contains, as would be the case in some other dialects, but in proportion to its freedom from Sanscrit! The speech of the very lowest classes of the people in the retired country districts accords to a considerable extent with the classical dialect in dispensing with Sanscrit derivatives. In every country it is in the poetry and in the speech of the peasantry that the ancient condition of the language is best studied. It is in Tamil prose compositions and in the ordinary speech of the Brahmans and the more learned Tamilians that the largest infusion of Sanscrit is contained; and the words that have been borrowed from the Sanscrit are chiefly those which express abstract ideas of philosophy, science, and religion, together with the technical terms of the more elegant arts. Even in prose compositions on religious subjects, in which a larger amount of Sanscrit is employed than in any other department of literature, the proportion of Sanscrit which has found its way into Tamil is not greater than the amount of Latin contained in corresponding compositions in English. Let us, for example, compare the amount of Sanscrit which is contained in the Tamil translation of the Ten Commandments (Prayer Book version) with the amount of Latin which is contained in the English version of the same formula, and which has found its way into it, either directly, from Ecclesiastical Latin, or indirectly, through the medium of the Norman-French. Of forty-three nouns and adjectives in the English version twenty-nine are Anglo-Saxon, fourteen Latin : of fifty-three nouns and adjectives in the Tamil (the difference in idiom causes this difference in the number) thirty-two are Dravidian, twenty-one Sanscrit. Of twenty verbs in the English, thirteen are Anglo-Saxon, seven Latin : of thirty-four verbs in the Tamil, twenty-seven are Drâvidian, and only seven Sanscrit. Of the five numerals which are found in the English, either in their cardinal or their ordinal shape, all are Anglo-Saxon : of the six numerals found in the Tamil, five are Drâvidian, one ('thousand') is probably Sanscrit. Putting all these numbers together, for the purpose of ascertaining the percentage, I find that in the department of nouns, numerals and verbs, the amount of the foreign element is in both instances the same, viz., as nearly as possible forty-five per cent. In both instances, also, all the pronouns, prepositions, adverbs, and conjunctions, and all the inflexional forms and connecting particles are the property of the native tongue.

Trench's expressions respecting the character of the contributions which our mother-English has received from Anglo-Saxon and from Latin respectively, are exactly applicable to the relation and proportion which the native Drâvidian element bears to the Sanscrit contained in the Tamil.

"All its joints, its whole *articulation*, its sinews and its ligaments, the great body of articles, pronouns, conjunctions, prepositions, numerals, auxiliary verbs, all smaller words which serve to knit together, and bind the larger into sentences, these, not to speak of the grammatical structure of the language, are exclusively Anglo-Saxon (Drâvidian). The Latin (Sanscrit) may contribute its tale of bricks, yea of goodly and polished hewn stones, to the spiritual building, but the mortar, with all that holds and binds these together, and constitutes them into a house is Anglo-Saxon (Drâvidian) throughout."

Though the proportion of Sanscrit which we find to be contained in the Tamil version of the Ten Commandments happens to correspond so exactly to the proportion of Latin which is contained in the English version, it would be an error to conclude that the Tamil language is as deeply indebted to the Sanscrit as the English is to the Latin.

The Tamil can readily dispense with the greater part or the whole of its Sanscrit, and by dispensing with it rises to a purer and more refined style ; whereas the English cannot abandon its Latin without abandoning perspicuity. Such is the poverty of the Anglo-Saxon that it has no synonymes of its own for many of the words which it has borrowed from the Latin; so that if it were obliged to dispense with them, it would, in most cases, be under the necessity of using a very awkward periphrasis instead of a single word. The Tamil, on the other hand, is peculiarly rich in synonymes; and generally it is not through any real necessity, but from choice and the fashion of the age, that it makes use of Sanscrit. If the Ten Commandments were expressed in the speech of the lower classes of the Tamil people, or in the language of every-day life, the proportion of Sanscrit would be very greatly diminished; and if we wished to raise the style of the translation to a refined and classical pitch, Sanscrit would almost entirely disappear. Of the entire number of words which are contained in this formula there is only one which could not be expressed with faultless propriety and poetic elegance in equivalents of pure Drâvidian origin: that word is 'graven image' or 'idol'! Both word and thing are foreign to primitive Tamil usages and habits of thought; and were introduced into the Tamil country by the Brahmans, with the Purânic system of religion and the worship of idols. Through the predominant influence of the religion of the Brahmans, the majority of the words expressive of religious ideas which are in actual use in modern Tamil are of Sanscrit origin; and though there are equivalent Drâvidian words which are equally appropriate, and in some instances more so, such words have gradually become obsolete, and are now confined to the poetical dialect; so that the use of them in prose compositions would sound affected and pedantic. This is the real and only reason why Sanscrit derivatives are so generally used in Tamil religious compositions.

In the other Drâvidian languages, whatever be the nature of the composition or subject-matter treated of, the amount of Sanscrit which is employed is considerably larger than in Tamil; and the use of it has acquired more of the character of a necessity. This is in consequence of the literature of those languages having chiefly been cultivated by Brahmans. Even in Telugu the principal grammatical writers and the most celebrated poets have been Brahmans. There is only one work of note in that language which was not composed by a member of the sacred caste; and indeed the Telugu Sûdras, who constitute *par excellence*, the Telugu people, seem almost entirely to have abandoned to the Brahmans the culture of their own language, with every other branch of literature and science. In Tamil, on the contrary, few Brahmans have written anything worthy of preservation. The language has been cultivated and developed with immense zeal and success by native Tamilian Sûdras; and the highest rank in Tamil literature which has been reached by a Brahman is that of a commentator. The commentary of Parimêlaṛagar on the Kuṟaḷ of Tiruvaḷḷuvar (a Pariar! but the acknowledged and deified prince of Tamil authors) is the most classical production which has been written in Tamil by a Brahman.

Professor Wilson observes that the spoken languages of the South were cultivated in imitation and rivalry of the Sanscrit, and but partially aspired to an independent literature; that the principal compositions in Tamil, Telugu, Canarese, and Malayalam are translations or paraphrases from Sanscrit works; and that they largely borrow the phraseology of their originals. This representation is not perfectly correct, in so far as the Tamil is concerned; for the compositions that are universally admitted to be the ablest and finest in the language, viz., the Cuṟaḷ and the Chintâmaṇi, are perfectly independent of the Sanscrit, and original in design as well as in execution; and though it is true that Tamil writers have imitated—I cannot say translated—the Râmâyana, the Mahâ-bhârata, and similar works, they boast that the Tamil Râmâyana of their own Kamban is greatly superior to the Sanscrit original of Vâlmîki.

(5.) Of all evidences of identity or diversity of languages the most conclusive are those which are furnished by a comparison of their grammatical structure; and by such a comparison the independence of the Drâvidian languages of the Sanscrit will satisfactorily and conclusively be established. By the same comparison (at the risk of anticipating a question which will be discussed more fully in the body of the work), the propriety of placing these languages in the Scythian group, rather than in the Indo-European, will be indicated.

The most prominent and essential differences in point of grammatical structure between the Drâvidian languages and the Sanscrit, are as follows:—

(i.) In the Drâvidian languages all nouns denoting inanimate substances and irrational beings are of the neuter gender. The distinction of male and female appears only in the pronouns of the third person; in the adjectives (properly appellative nouns) which denote rational beings, and are formed by suffixing the pronominal terminations; and in the third person of the verb, which, being formed by suffixing the same pronominal terminations, has three forms in the singular and two in the plural, to distinguish the several genders, and in accordance with the pronouns of the third person. In all other cases where it is required to mark the distinction of gender, separate words signifying 'male' and 'female' are prefixed; but, even in such cases, though the object denoted be the male or female of an animal, the noun which denotes it does not cease to be considered neuter, and neuter forms of the pronoun and verb are required to be conjoined with it. This rule presents a marked contrast to the rules respecting gender which we find in the vivid and highly imaginative Sanscrit, and in the other Indo-European languages, but it accords with the usage of all the languages of the Scythian group.

(ii.) Drâvidian nouns are inflected, not by means of case-terminations, but by means of suffixed post-positions and separable particles, as in the Scythian tongues. The only difference between the declension of the plural and that of the singular, is that the inflexional signs are annexed in the singular to the base, in the plural to the sign of plurality, exactly as in the Scythian languages. After the pluralising particle has been added to the base, all nouns, irrespective of number and gender, are declined in the same manner as in the singular.

(iii.) The Drâvidian dative 'ku,' 'ki,' or 'ge,' bears no analogy to any dative case-termination which is found in the Sanscrit or in any of the Indo-European languages; but it perfectly corresponds to the dative of the Oriental Turkish, to that of the language of the Scythian tablets of Behistun, and to that of several of the languages of the Finnish family.

(iv.) Wherever prepositions are used in the Indo-European languages, the Drâvidian languages, with those of the Scythian group, use post-positions instead,—which post-positions do not constitute a separate part of speech, but are real nouns of relation or quality, adopted as auxiliaries. All adverbs are either nouns or the gerunds or infinitives of verbs.

(v.) In Sanscrit and all the Indo-European tongues, adjectives are declined like substantives, and agree with the substantives to which they are conjoined in gender, number, and case. In the Drâvidian languages, as in the Scythian, adjectives are incapable of declension. When used separately as abstract nouns of quality, which is the original and natural character of Drâvidian adjectives, they are subject to all the affections of substantives; but when they are used adjectivally, *i.e.*, to qualify other substantives, they do not admit of any inflexional change, but are simply prefixed to the nouns which they qualify.

(vi.) It is also a characteristic of these languages, as of the Mongolian, the Manchu, and several other Scythian languages, in contradistinction to the languages of the Indo-European family, that, wherever it is practicable, they use as adjectives the relative participles of verbs, in preference to nouns of quality, or adjectives properly so called; and that in consequence of this tendency, when nouns of quality are used, the formative termination of the relative participle is generally suffixed to them, through which suffix they partake of the character both of nouns and of verbs.

(vii.) The existence of two pronouns of the first person plural, one of which includes, the other excludes the party addressed, is a peculiarity of the Drâvidian dialects, as of many of the Scythian languages; but is unknown to the Sanscrit and the languages of the Indo-European family.

(viii.) The situation of the governing word is characteristic of each of these families of languages. In Sanscrit and the Indo-European family it usually precedes the word governed: in the Drâvidian and in all the Scythian languages, it is invariably placed after it; in consequence of which the principal verb always occupies the last place in the sentence. The adjective precedes the substantive: the adverb precedes the verb: the substantive which is governed by a verb, together with every word that depends upon it or qualifies it, precedes the verb by which it is governed: the relative participle precedes the noun on which it depends: the negative branch of a sentence precedes the affirmative: the noun in the genitive case precedes that which governs it: the *pre*-position changes places with the noun and becomes a *post*-position in virtue of its governing a case: and finally the sentence is concluded by the one, all-governing, finite verb. In each of these important and highly characteristic peculiarities of syntax the Drâvidian languages and the Scythian are thoroughly agreed.

(ix.) The Drâvidian languages like the Scythian, but unlike the Indo-European, prefer the use of continuative participles to conjunctions.

(x.) The existence of a negative as well as an affirmative voice in the verbal system of these languages, constitutes another essential point of difference between them and the languages of the Indo-European family: it equally constitutes a point of agreement between them and the Scythian tongues.

(xi.) It is a marked peculiarity of these languages as of the Mongolian and the Manchu, and in a modified degree of many other Scythian languages, that they make use of relative participles instead of relative pronouns. There is not a trace of the existence of a relative pronoun in any Drâvidian language. The place of such pronouns is supplied, as in the Scythian tongues mentioned above, by relative participles, which are formed from the present, preterite, and future participles of the verb by the addition of a formative suffix; which suffix is in general identical with the sign of the possessive case. Thus, *the person who came*, is in Tamil 'vand-a âḷ,' literally, *the who-came person*; 'vand' the preterite *verbal* participle signifying *having come,* being converted into a *relative* participle, equivalent to *the-who-came,* by the addition of the old possessive and adjectival suffix 'a.'

Many other differences in grammatical structure will be pointed out hereafter, in the course of the grammatical analysis: but in the important particulars which are mentioned above, the Drâvidian languages evidently differ so considerably from the languages of the Indo-European family, and in particular from the Sanscrit (notwithstanding the predominance for so many ages of the social and religious influence of the Sanscrit-speaking race), that it cannot be doubted that they belong to a totally different family of tongues. They are neither derived from the Sanscrit, nor are capable of being affiliated with it: and it cannot have escaped the notice of the student of comparative philology, that in every one of those particulars in which the grammatical structure of the Drâvidian languages differs from the Sanscrit, it agrees with the structure of the Scythian languages, or the languages of Central and Northern Asia.

Is the Un-Sanscrit Element contained in the Vernacular Languages of Northern India Drâvidian?

The hypothesis of the direct derivation of the Drâvidian tongues from the Sanscrit, with the admixture of a proportion of words and forms from an unknown source, being now no longer entertained, some oriental scholars have adopted an opposite hypothesis, and attributed to the influence of the Drâvidian languages that corruption of the Sanscrit out of which the vernaculars of Northern India have arisen. It has been supposed by the Rev. Dr. Stevenson, of Bombay, Mr. Hodgson, of Nipaul, and some other orientalists, (1) that the North-Indian vernaculars have been derived from the Sanscrit, not so much by the natural process of corruption and disintegration, as through the over-mastering, re-moulding power of the Un-Sanscrit element which is contained in them; and (2) that this Un-Sanscrit element is identical with the Drâvidian speech, which they suppose to have been the speech of the ancient Nishâdas, and other aborigines of India.

The first part of this hypothesis appears to rest upon a better foundation than the second: but even the first part appears to me to be too strongly expressed, and to require considerable modification; for in some important particulars the corruption of the Sanscrit into the Hindi, the Bengali, &c. has been shown to have arisen from that natural process of change which we see exemplified in Europe, in the corruption of the Latin into the Italian and the French. Nevertheless, on comparing the grammatical structure and essential character of the Sanscrit, with that of the vernaculars of Northern India, I feel persuaded that those vernaculars have to a considerable extent been corrupted in a Scythian direction, and through the operation of Scythian influences.

The modifications which the grammar of the North-Indian languages have received, being generally of one and the same character, and in one and the same direction, it is obvious that there must have been a common modifying cause; and as the barbarian or Un-Sanscrit portion of those languages, which Professor Wilson styles 'a portion of a primitive, unpolished, and scanty speech, the relics of a period prior to civilization,' is generally calculated to amount to one-tenth of the whole, and in Marâthi, to a fifth, it seems reasonable to infer that it was from that extraneous element that the modifying influences proceeded.

It is admitted that before the arrival of the Âryans, or Sanscrit-speaking colony of Brahmans, Kshatriyas, and Vaisyas, the greater part of Northern India was peopled by rude aboriginal tribes, called by Sanscrit writers, Mlêchchas, Dasyus, Nishâdas, &c.; and it is the received opinion that those aboriginal tribes were of Scythian, or at least of Non-Âryan origin. On the irruption of the Âryans, it would naturally happen that the copious and expressive Sanscrit of the conquering race would almost overwhelm the vocabulary of the rude Scythian tongue which was spoken by the aboriginal tribes. Nevertheless, as the grammatical structure of the Scythian tongues possesses peculiar stability and persistency; and as the Pre-Âryan tribes, who were probably more numerous than the Âryans, were not annihilated, but only reduced to a dependent position, and eventually, in most instances, incorporated in the Âryan community, the large Sanscrit addition which the Scythian vernaculars received, would not necessarily alter their essential structure, or deprive them of the power of influencing and assimilating the speech of the conquering race. According to this theory, the grammatical *structure* of the spoken idioms of Northern India was from the first, and always continued to be, in the main, Scythian; and the change which took place when Sanscrit acquired the predominance, as the Âryans gradually extended their conquests and their colonies, was rather a change of vocabulary than of grammar, —a change not so much in arrangement and vital spirit as in the *matériel* of the language.

This hypothesis seems to have the merit of according better than any other with existing phenomena. Seeing that the northern vernaculars possess, with the words of the Sanscrit, a grammatical structure which in the main appears to be Scythian, it seems more correct to represent those languages as having a Scythian basis, with a large and almost overwhelming Sanscrit addition, than as having a Sanscrit basis, with a small admixture of a Scythian element.

Whichever proposition be adopted, there is not much room for difference of opinion respecting the *facts* that are involved in the dispute; the existence of a Scythian element in the colloquial dialects of Northern India having been pointed out many years ago by Sir W. Jones, and never since called in question.

The second part of the hypothesis of Dr. Stevenson, viz., the identity of the Un-Sanscrit or Scythian element which is contained in those languages with the languages of the Drâvidian family, rests on a different foundation, and appears to me to be less defensible.

According to the supposition in question, the Scythian or Drâvidian element is substantially one and the same in all the vernacular languages of India, whether northern or southern, but is smallest in amount in those districts of Northern India which were first conquered by the Âryans; greater in the remoter districts of the Dekhan, Telingana, and Mysore; and greatest of all in the Tamil country, at the southern extremity of the peninsula, to which the aggressions of the Brahmanical race had not extended in the age of Manu and the Râmâyana.

This hypothesis is certainly in accordance with the current of events in the ancient history of India: but whatever relationship, in point of blood and race, may originally have subsisted between the northern aborigines and the southern—whatever *ethnological* evidences of their identity may be supposed to exist,—when we view the question *philologically*, and with reference to the evidence which is furnishe by their languages alone, the hypothesis of their identity does not appear to me to have been established. It may be true that various analogies in point of grammatical structure appear to connect the Un-Sanscrit element which is contained in the North-Indian idioms with the Scythian or Tartar tongues. This connection, however, amounts only to a general relationship to the entire group of Scythian languages; and no special relationship to the Drâvidian languages, *in contra-distinction* to those of the Turkish, the Finnish, or any other Scythian family, has yet been proved to exist. Indeed I conceive that the Scythian substratum of the North-Indian idioms presents a greater number of points of agreement with the Oriental Turkish, or with that Scythian tongue or family of tongues by which the New Persian has been modified, than with any of the Drâvidian languages.

The principal particulars in which the grammar of the North-Indian idioms accords with that of the Drâvidian languages are as follows:—(1), the inflexion of nouns by means of separate post-fixed particles; (2), the inflexion of the plural by annexing to the unvarying sign of plurality the same suffixes of case as those by which the singular is inflected; (3), the use of a dative or dative-accusative in 'kô' or 'ku:' (4), the use in several of the northern idioms of two pronouns of the first person plural, the one including, the other excluding the party addressed; (5), the use of post-positions, instead of prepositions; (6), the formation of verbal tenses by means of participles; (7), the situation of the governing word after the word governed. In the particulars above-mentioned the grammar of the North-Indian idioms undoubtedly resembles that of the Drâvidian family: but the argument founded upon this general agreement is to a considerable extent neutralised by the circumstance that those idioms accord in the very same particulars, and to the very same extent, with the Turkish and several other families of the Scythian group. Not one of those particulars in which the Drâvidian languages differ from the Turkish or the Mongolian (and there are many such points of difference) has as yet been discovered in the North-Indian idioms. For instance, those idioms contain no trace of the relative participle which is used in all the Drâvidian tongues instead of a relative pronoun; they are destitute of the regularly inflected negative verb of the Drâvidian languages; and they contain not one of the Drâvidian pronouns or numerals—not even those which we find in the Scythic tablets of Behistun, and which still survive even in the languages of the Ostiaks and Lapps. If the Un-Sanscrit element contained in the northern vernaculars had been Drâvidian we might also expect to find in their vocabularies a few primary Drâvidian roots—such as the words for 'head,' 'hand,' 'foot,' 'eye,' 'ear,' &c.; but I have not been able to discover any reliable analogy in words belonging to this class. The only resemblances which have been pointed out are those which Dr. Stevenson has traced in a few words remote from ordinary use, and on which, in the absence of analogy in primary roots, and especially in grammatical structure, it is impossible to place any dependence.* The difference between the Drâvidian vocabulary and that of the languages of Northern India with respect to primary roots together with the essential agreement of all the Drâvidian vocabularies one with another, will appear from the following comparative view of

* In many instances Dr. Stevenson's lexical analogies are illusory, and disappear altogether on a little investigation. Thus, he supposes the North Indian 'peṭ,' *the belly, the womb*, to be allied to the first word in the Tamil compound 'peṭṭa piḷḷei,' *own child*. That word should have been written 'pettra' in English, to accord with the pronunciation of the Tamil word: the Tamil spelling of it, however, is 'peʀʀa.' It is the preterite relative participle of 'peʀ-u,' *to bear, to obtain*, signifying *that was borne*. 'Peʀ-u,' *to obtain*, has no connexion with any word which signifies *the womb*, and its derivative noun 'pêʀ-u,' means *a thing obtained, a birth, a favour*. The affinities of this root will be inquired into in the Comparative Vocabulary.

the pronouns of the first and second persons singular. It sometimes happens that where one form of the pronoun is used in the nominative, another survives in the oblique cases, and a third in the verbal inflexions: it also sometimes happens that the ancient form of the pronoun differs from the modern. Where such is the case I have given all extant forms a place in the list, for the purpose of facilitating comparison.

Pronoun of the first person singular:—

NORTH-INDIAN IDIOMS.

(Sanscrit primary form 'aham;' secondary forms, 'ma,' 'mi,' 'm;' Turkish primary form, 'man.')

Hindi,	mai*n*
Bengali,	mûi
Marathi,	mî
Gujarathi,	hu*n*
Sindhi,	ma*n*

DRÂVIDIAN IDIOMS.

Tamil,	nân, yân, ên, en
Canarese,	ân, nânu, en, êne
Tulu,	yân, en, e
Malayalam,	ñjân, ên, en, in
Telugu,	nênu, nâ
Tuda,	ôn, ân, en, ini
Kôta,	âne, en, e
Gônd	âna, ân
Ku	ânu, nâ, ênu, e
Rajamahal,	en
Uraon,	enan

Pronoun of the second person singular:—

NORTH-INDIAN IDIOMS.

(Sanscrit primary forms 'tvam,' 'tav,' 'te;' secondary form, 'si,' 's;' Turkish primary form, 'sen.')

Hindi,	tu*n*, tu, te
Bengali,	tûi, to
Marathi,	tû*n*, tu, to
Gnjarathi,	tû*n*, ta
Sindhi,	tu*n*, to

DRÂVIDIAN IDIOMS.

Tamil,	nî, nin, nei, i,
Canarese,	nîn, nînu, î, i
Tulu,	î, ni, nin
Malayalam,	nî, nin, nan
Telugu,	nîvu, nî, nin
Tuda,	nî, nin, i
Kota,	nî, nin, i
Gônd,	ima, nî, i
Ku	înu, nî, i
Uraon	nien
Rajamahal	nin
Brahui	nî
Scythic of the Behistun tablets,	nî

From the striking dissimilarity existing between the North-Indian pronouns and the Drâvidian it is obvious that, whatever may have been the nature and origin of the Scythic influences by which they were modified, those influences do not appear to have been Drâvidian. In the pronouns of almost all the North-Indian languages, the Scythian termination—the obscure '*n*' which forms the final of most of the pronouns—is at once observed: we cannot fail also to notice the entire disappearance of the nominative of the Sanscrit pronoun of the first person singular, and the substitution for it of the Turkish 'men' or 'man:' but in no connexion, in no number or case, in no compound or verbal inflexion do we see the least trace of the peculiar personal pronouns of the Dravidian family. Possibly, after all, further research may disclose the existence in the northern vernaculars of distinctively Drâvidian forms and roots: but their existence does not appear to me as yet to be proved; for most of Dr. Stevenson's analogies take too wide a range, and where they are supposed to be distinctively Drâvidian, they invariably disappear on examination. I conclude, therefore, that the Un-Sanscrit portion of the northern languages cannot safely be placed in the same category with the southern, except perhaps in the sense of both being Scythian rather than Indo-European.

With what Group of Languages are the Drâvidian Idioms to be affiliated?

Leaving the idioms of Northern India out of consideration for the present, as extraneous to the object of this work, and restricting our attention to the Drâvidian languages, and the question of their affiliation, the supposition of their Scythian relationship appears to me to be that which is most fully borne out by grammatical analysis and the comparison of vocabularies.

In using the word 'Scythian,' I use it in the wide general sense in which it was used by Professor Rask, who first employed it to designate that group of tongues which comprises the Finnish, the Turkish, the Mongolian, and the Tungusian families. All these languages are formed on one and the same grammatical system, and in accordance with the same general laws. Their formation of cases, moods, and tenses, by the simple agglutination of successive, unchangeable suffixes, determine them to be a distinct class of languages—a class distinct from the Semitic, which inflects dissyllabic roots by the variations of internal vowels, and also from the Indo-European idioms, which make so extensive a use of technical case-signs and other inflexions, of euphonic modification, and of composition. These languages have been termed by some the Tatar or Tartar family of tongues, by others the Finnish, the Ural-Altaïc, the Mongolian, or the Turanian; but as these terms have often been appropriated to designate one or two families, to the exclusion of the rest, they seem to be too narrow and too liable to misapprehension to be safely employed as common designations of the entire group. The term 'Scythian' having already been used in the Classics in a vague, undefined sense, to denote generally the barbarous tribes of unknown origin that inhabited the northern parts of Asia and Europe, it seems to be the most appropriate and convenient word which is available. Professor Rask, who was the first by whom this word was employed as a common generic designation, was also the first to suggest that the Drâvidian or Tamilian languages were probably Scythian. He has the merit of having *suggested* this relationship; but the evidence of it was left both by him, and by succeeding writers, in a very defective state. In the grammatical analysis and comparison of the Drâvidian languages on which we are about to enter I hope to help forward the solution of a problem which has often been stated, and which has been ingeniously elucidated up to a certain point, but which has never yet been thoroughly investigated.

The various particulars which were recently adduced to prove that the Drâvidian family is essentially different from and independent of the Sanscrit (each of which will be more fully considered in the sequel, under its appropriate head) may also be regarded as proving that those languages are intimately related to the Scythian group.

In this introductory part of the work, I shall content myself with adducing in proof of their Scythian relationship the evidence which was recently furnished by the translation of the Behistun tablets. The inscriptions discovered at Behistun record the political autobiography of Darius Hystaspes in the Old Persian, in the Babylonian, and also in the language of the Scythians of the Medo-Persian empire; and the translation of the Scythian portion of those inscriptions has thrown new light on the propriety of giving the Drâvidian languages a place in the Scythian group. The language of the Scythic tablets, at first supposed to be Median, has been shown in Mr. Norris's valuable paper (in the *Journal of the Royal Asiatic Society*, vol. XV.) to be distinctively Scythian. Consequently we are now enabled to compare the Drâvidian idioms with a fully developed, copious language of the Scythian family, as spoken in the fifth century, B.C.: and whilst the language of the tablets has been shown to belong generally to the Scythian group, it has been found to bear a special relationship to a particular family included in that group—the Ugro-Finnish—that very family to which the Drâvidian dialects have long appeared to me to be most nearly allied. The principal points of resemblance between the Drâvidian dialects and the language of the tablets are as follows:—

(1.) The language of the tablets appears to accord with the Drâvidian tongue in the use of consonants of the cerebral class, 'ṭ,' 'ḍ,' and 'ṇ.' These sounds exist also in the Sanscrit, but I have long been persuaded that the Sanscrit borrowed them from the indigenous Drâvidian languages (vide the section on "Sounds"); and I find that Mr. Norris has expressed the same opinion.

(2.) The language of the tablets agrees with the Tamil in regarding the same consonant as a surd in the beginning of a word, and as a sonant in the middle, and in pronouncing the same consonant as a sonant when single, and as a surd when doubled. (See in the section on "Sounds" illustrations of the Tamil rule.)

(3.) The genitive case of the language of the tablets is formed by suffixing the syllables 'na,' 'ni-na,' or 'inna.' The analogous forms of the Drâvidian languages are 'ni,' in the Telugu, 'na,' or 'a,' in the Gônd and Brahui, and 'ni,' in the Tamil.

(4.) The dative of the tablets is 'ikki' or 'ikka.' There are analogies to this both in the Tartar-Turkish and in the Ugrian families; but the form which is most perfectly in accordance with it is that of the Dràvidian dative suffix 'ku,' 'ki,' 'ka,' &c., preceded, as the suffix generally is in Tamil and Malayâlam, by an euphonic 'u' or 'i,' and a consequent doubling of the 'k.' Compare 'nî-ikka,' *to thee*, in the language of the tablets, with the corresponding Telugu 'nî-ku,' and the Malayâla 'nan-i-kka.'

(5.) The pronouns of the language of the tablets form their accusative by suffixing 'un,' 'in,' or 'n.' Compare the Telugu accusative inflexion 'nu' or 'ni,' and the Canarese 'am,' 'ann-u,' &c.

(6.) The only numeral which is written in letters in the Scythian tablets is 'kir,' *one*, with which appears to be connected the numeral adjective, or indefinite article, 'ra' or 'irra.' In Telugu, *one* is 'oka,' and in Tamil, 'or.' From a comparison of all the shapes which this numeral has assumed in the various Drâvidian dialects and in compounds, I had long ago come to the conclusion that both the Telugu and the Tamil forms were probably derived from a common and older form, 'okor' or 'kor,' which I regarded as identical with the Samoyede 'okur,' *one*. I can now compare it also with the 'kir' of the tablets. The Ku numeral adjective *one* is 'ra,' corresponding to the Tamil 'oru,' but more closely to the 'ra' or 'irra,' of the tablets.

In the language of the tablets all ordinal numbers end in 'im,' in Tamil in 'âm,' in Samoyede in 'im.'

(7.) The pronoun of the second person is exactly the same in the language of the inscriptions as in the Drâvidian languages and the Brahui: in all it is 'nî.' Unfortunately the plural of this pronoun is not contained in the tablet,—the singular having been used instead of the plural in addressing inferiors.

(8.) The language of the tablets, like the Drâvidian languages, makes use of a relative participle. A relative pronoun is used in addition to the relative participle; but Mr. Norris supposes the use of this pronoun to be owing to the imitation of the Persian original. The particular particle which is used in the tablets in forming the relative participle differs from that which is generally used in the Drâvidian languages; but the position and force of this particle, and the manner in which the participle formed by it is employed, are in perfect harmony with Drâvidian usage. Perhaps the use of this relative participle is the most remarkable and distinctive characteristic of the grammar of every unaltered dialect of the Scythian family.

(9.) The negative imperative, or prohibitive particle of the tablets is 'inni,' in Gônd, 'minni.'

(10.) The only verbal roots which appear to be analogous are the following:—

Language of the Tablets.		Drâvidian.	
to say,	nan		an or en
to make known,	uri	urei,	to explain; aRi, to know.
to go,	pori	pô,	
a king,	ko (the vowel considered uncertain)	kô or kôn	

The conjugational system of the language of the tablets accords with that of the Magyar, the Mordwin, and other languages of the Ugrian family, but differs considerably from the Drâvidian languages, which form their tenses in a simpler manner, by the addition of particles of time to the root, and which form the persons of their verbs by the addition of the ordinary pronominal terminations to the particles of time. Notwithstanding this discrepancy in the inflexions of the verbs, the resemblances shown to subsist between the language of the tablets and the Drâvidian idioms, most of which are in particulars of primary importance, fully establish the existence of a radical, though remote, connection. From the discovery of these analogies, we are enabled to conclude that the Drâvidian race, though resident in India from a period long prior to the commencement of history, originated in the central tracts of Asia—the seed plot of nations; and that from thence, after parting company with the rest of the Ugro-Turanian horde, and leaving a colony in Beluchistan, they entered India by way of the Indus.

Whilst I regard the grammatical structure and prevailing characteristics of the Drâvidian idioms as Scythian, I claim for them a position in the Scythian group which is independent of its other members, as a distinct family or genus, or at least as a distinct sub-genus of tongues. They belong not to the Turkish family, or to the Ugrian, or to the Mongolian, or to the Tungusian (each of which families differs materially from the others, notwithstanding generic points of resemblance), but to the group or class in which all these families are comprised. On the whole, the Drâvidian languages may be regarded as most nearly allied to the Finnish or Ugrian family, with special affinities, as it appears, to the Ostiak; and this supposition, which I had been led to entertain from the comparison of grammars and vocabularies alone, derives some confirmation from the fact brought to light by the Behistun tablets that the ancient Scythic race, by which the greater part of Central Asia was peopled prior to the irruption of the Medo-Persians, belonged not to the Turkish, or to the Mongolian, but to the Ugrian stock. Taking for granted, at present, the conclusiveness of the evidence on which this hypothesis rests, the result at which we arrive is one of the most remarkable that the study of comparative philology has yet realized.

How remarkable that the closest and most distinct affinities to the speech of the Drâvidians of inter-tropical India should be those that are discovered in the languages of the Finns and Lapps of Northern Europe, and of the Ostiaks and other Ugrians of Siberia! and, consequently, that the Pre-Âryan inhabitants of the Dekhan should be proved by their language alone, in the silence of history, in the absence of all ordinary probabilities, to be allied to the tribes that appear to have overspread Europe before the arrival of the Goths and the Pelasgi, and even before the arrival of the Celts! What a confirmation of the statement that 'God hath made of *one* blood all nations of men, to dwell upon the face of the whole earth!'

In weighing the reasons which may be adduced for affiliating the Drâvidian languages with the Scythian group, it should be borne in mind that whilst the generic characteristics of the Scythian languages are very strongly marked and incapable of being mistaken, in a vast variety of minor particulars, and especially in their vocabularies, the languages which are comprised in this family differ from one another more widely than the various idioms of the Indo-European family mutually differ. The Ugrian and the Turkish families can be proved to be cognate almost as certainly as the Gothic and the Sanscrit, or the Zend and the Greek; yet, apart from the evidence of structure and vital spirit, and looking only at the vocabulary, and the grammatical *materièl*, the agreement of any one of the Ugrian dialects with any one of the Turkish is found to be very far inferior even to the agreement of the Sanscrit and the Celtic,—the longest separated and most widely differing members of the Indo-European family. Thus, whilst in nearly all the Indo-European languages the numerals are not only similar but the same,—(the Sanscrit word for *one* and the Gaelic word for *five* are the only real exceptions to the rule of general identity),—not only do the numerals of every Scythian family differ so widely from those of every other as to present few points of connection, but even the numerals of any two dialects of the same family are found to differ very widely. Whilst the Sanscrit and the Gaelic agree in eight numerals out of ten, and differ in two only (*one* and *five*); the Magyar and the Finnish, though as closely allied in point of grammatical structure as the Gaelic and the Welsh, have now only the first four numerals in common, and perfectly coincide in two numerals only, *one* and *four* So great indeed is the diversity existing amongst the Scythian tongues, that, whilst the Indo-European idioms form but one family, the Scythian tongues are not so much a family as a group of families. The Indo-European languages may be regarded as forming but a single genus, of which each language—(Sanscrit, Zend or Persian, Greek, Latin, Gothic, Lithuanian, Slavonic, Armenian, Celtic)—forms a species; whilst the languages of the Scythian group, more prolific in differences, comprise at least five or six authenticated genera, each of which includes as many species as are contained in the solitary Indo-European genus; besides twenty or thirty isolated languages, which have up to this time resisted every effort to classify them. This remarkable difference between the Indo-European languages and those of the Scythian stock seems to have arisen partly from the higher mental gifts and higher capacity for civilisation, with which the Indo-European tribes appear to have been endowed from the beginning, and still more from the earlier literary culture of their languages, and the better preservation, in consequence, of their forms and roots: but, from whatever cause this difference may have arisen, it is obvious that in weighing evidences of relationship this circumstance must be taken into account; and that so minute an agreement of long separated sister dialects of the Scythian stock is not to be expected as in parallel cases amongst the Indo-European dialects.

Of late years some inquirers have been inclined to question the relationship of the Drâvidian languages to the Scythian, either in consequence of comparing them with the Tartar or Turkish languages alone, to the exclusion of the more nearly allied Ugrian family, or in consequence of observing in the Drâvidian languages certain Indo-European affinities which seemed inconsistent with the Scythian theory. A friend of mine, who is a good Tamil scholar, was so much struck with the latter class of analogies that he was led to adopt the supposition of the Indo-European relationship of the Drâvidian tongues. At the very outset of my own inquiries I observed those Indo-European analogies myself; and, rejecting affinities which are unreal and which disappear on investigation—(such as the connection of the Tamil numerals 'ondru' or 'onnu,' *one;* 'anju,' *five;* 'eṭṭu,' *eight;* with 'un-us,' 'pancha,' and 'ashṭa,'—a connection which looks very plausible, but is illusory (see section on 'Numerals'),—I think it capable of satisfactory proof that a small number of the grammatical forms of the Drâvidian languages, and a more considerable number of their roots, are to be regarded as of cognate origin with corresponding forms and roots in the Indo-European languages. Notwithstanding the existence of a few analogies of this character, the most essential parts of the grammar and vocabulary of the Drâvidian idioms are undoubtedly Scythian, and therefore I have no doubt of the propriety of placing those idioms in the Scythian group. Though the majority of Hebrew roots have been proved to be allied to the Sanscrit, yet the Hebrew language does not cease to be regarded as Semitic rather than Indo-European; so, notwithstanding some interesting analogies with the Sanscrit, the Greek, the Gothic, and the modern Persian, which may be discovered on a careful examination of the Drâvidian tongues, and which will be pointed out in each of the succeeding sections, the essential characteristics of those tongues are such as to require us to regard them as in the main Scythian.

In stating that the Drâvidian languages contain certain roots and forms allied to the Sanscrit, and to the Indo-European languages generally, it is necessary to preclude misapprehension. During the long period of the residence of the Drâvidian and Âryan races in the same country, the Drâvidian vocabularies have borrowed largely from the Sanscrit. It is necessary, therefore, to premise that the analogies to which I refer are not founded on the existence in the Drâvidian tongues of Sanscrit derivatives, but are such as are discoverable in the original structure and primitive vocabulary of those languages. Whilst the Drâvidian languages have confessedly borrowed much from their more wealthy neighbours, the Sanscrit, in some instances, has not disdained to borrow from the Drâvidian: but in general there is no difficulty in distinguishing and eliminating what the one language has borrowed from the other; and the statement which I have now made relates not to derivatives, or words which may be supposed to be derivatives, but to radical, deep-seated analogies which cannot be explained on any supposition but that of a partial or distant relationship. In most instances the words and forms in which analogies are discoverable are allied not to the Sanscrit alone, but to the entire Indo-European family: in not a few instances analogies are discoverable in the Greek and Latin, which are not found in the Sanscrit; and in many instances in which the Sanscrit appears to exhibit the closest analogy, it is not the euphonized, systematised Sanscrit (Samscrita) of written compositions, but the crude, original Sanscrit, which is discoverable by analysis and comparison, the 'Pre-Sanscrit' of W. von Humboldt.

I subjoin here a few illustrations of primitive, underived Indo-Europeanisms, which are discoverable in the Drâvidian languages.

I. Analogical grammatical forms.

(1.) The use of 'n,' as in Greek, to prevent *hiatus.*

(2.) The use of 'd' or 't' as the sign of the neuter singular of demonstrative pronouns.

(3.) The existence of a neuter plural, as in Latin, in short 'a.'

(4.) The formation of the remote demonstrative from a base in 'a,' the proximate from a base in 'i;' as in the New Persian, 'ân,' *that,* and 'în,' *this.*

(5.) The formation of most preterites, as in the Persian and the Germanic tongues, by the addition of 't' or 'd.'

(6.) The formation of some preterites by the reduplication of a portion of the root.

II. Analogical vocables.

The following are instances of roots which are much more nearly allied to the Greek, the Gothic, or some other western language of the Indo-European stock, than to the Sanscrit.

'Kâ-ÿ,' *to burn:* Greek 'καί-ω;' Sanscrit 'kâm.'

'ki,' 'gi,' or 'ge'—(Gônd and Can.), *to do:* Old Persic 'ki; Sanscrit 'kri.'

'mig-u,' *much*; related words 'migala' and 'mikkili:' Persian 'mih,' English 'migh-t,' Old High-German 'mih-hil,' Norse 'mikil;' Sanscrit 'mahâ.'

'mugil,' *a cloud:* Lithuanian 'migla,' Greek 'ὀ-μίχλ-η,' Gothic 'milh-ma;' Sanscrit 'mêgha.'

'pamp-u,' *to send:* Greek 'πέμπ-ω;' no allied word in Sanscrit.

The illustrations which are given above form only a small portion of the analogous forms and roots which will be adduced in the grammatical analysis and in the glossarial affinities: they will, however, suffice to prove that primitive, deep-seated Indo-European analogies are discoverable in the Drâvidian languages. They also serve to illustrate the statement, that, though the Sanscrit has long been the nearest neighbour of the Drâvidian tongues, there are not a few Drâvidian roots which are more nearly allied to the Western Indo-European idioms than to the Sanscritic or Eastern. Whilst, therefore, I classify the Drâvidian family of languages as essentially and in the main Scythian, I consider them as of all Scythian tongues those which present the most numerous, ancient, and interesting analogies to the Indo-European languages. The position which this family occupies, if not mid-way between the two groups, is on that side of the Scythian group on which the Indo-European appears to have been severed from it, and on which the most distinct traces of the original identity of the families still remain. If this view be correct (as I think it will be shewn to be), the Indo-Europeanisms which are discoverable in the Drâvidian languages carry us back to a period beyond all history, beyond all mythology, not only prior to the separation of the western branches of the Indo-European race from the eastern, but prior also to the separation of the yet undivided Indo-Europeans from the Scythian stock.

It is a remarkable circumstance, that in the vocabulary of the Drâvidian languages, especially in that of the Tamil, a few Semitic analogies may also be discovered. In some instances the analogous roots are found in the Indo-European family, as well as in Hebrew, though the Hebrew form of the root is more closely analogous. For example, though we find in Latin, 'ave-o,' *to desire*, and in Sanscrit, 'ava,' of which *to desire* is a subordinate meaning; yet the corresponding Tamil words 'ạvâ,' *desire*, and 'âval' (signifying also *desire*), a verbal noun from a lost verb 'âv-u,' *to desire*, seem still more directly allied to the Hebrew 'âvah,' *to desire*, and the verbal noun 'avvâh,' *desire*. In addition, however, to such general analogies as pervade several families of tongues, including the Drâvidian, there are roots discoverable both in the Drâvidian languages and in the Hebrew, to which I am not aware of the existence of any resemblance in any language of the Indo-European family. The following are illustrations of such special analogies :—

mâʀ-u	*to change*, or *exchange*, *to sell;* Hebrew 'mûr,' *to exchange;* Syriac 'môr,' *to buy*.
śuvar	*a wall;* Hebrew, 'shûr,' *a wall*.
kûr	*a sharp point;* Hebrew, 'kûr,' *to bore, to pierce*.
śev-(vei) . . .	*equal, level, right;* Chaldee, 'shev-â,' *to be equal, level,* &c.; Hebrew, 'shâv-âh,' the same.
al, il, lâ, lê . .	*no, not;* Hebrew, 'al,' 'lô,' *not;* Chaldee, 'lâ,' *not*. Compare also Chaldee 'lêth,' *it is not*, with Telugu 'lêdu,' *there is not*.

The Semitic analogies observable in the Tamil are neither so numerous nor so important as the Indo-European, nor do they carry with them such convincing evidence; but taking them in connexion with that more numerous and important class of analogous roots which are found in the Indo-European languages, as well as in the Hebrew, but of which the Hebrew form is more closely allied to the Drâvidian (see the Glossarial Affinities), these analogies, such as they are, constitute an additional element of interest in the problem of the origin and pre-historical connections of the Drâvidian race. I do not adduce these analogies for the purpose of endeavouring to prove the existence of any relationship between the Drâvidian language and the Hebrew, similar to that which subsists between the Drâvidian and the Indo-European languages. Aware of the danger of proving nothing by proving too much, I content myself with merely stating those analogies, without attempting to deduce any inference from them. The Indo-European analogies are so intimately connected with the individuality and vital essence of the Drâvidian languages, that it seems impossible to suppose them to be merely the result of early association, however intimate. It is only on the supposition of the existence of a remote or partial relationship that they appear to be capable of being fully explained. In the case of the Semitic analogies, the supposition of a relationship between the two families of tongues does not appear to be necessary. All the analogies that exist can be accounted for on the hypothesis—a very easy and natural one—that the primitive Drâvidian nomades were at some early period before their arrival in India, associated with a people speaking a Semitic language.

It seems proper here to notice the remarkable general resemblance which exists between the Drâvidian pronouns and those of the aboriginal tribes of Southern and Western Australia. In whatever way it may be explained or accounted for, the existence of a general resemblance (which was first pointed out by Mr. Norris), seems to be unquestionable; but it has not hitherto been observed that the Australian pronouns of the first person, are more nearly allied to the Tibetan than to the Drâvidian. This will appear from the following comparative view of the pronoun of the first person singular.

	Drâvidian.	Australian	Tibetan.	Chinese.
I	nân, nâ, ên	nga, ngaii, ngatsa, nganya	nga, nge, nged	ngo

Whilst the base of this pronoun seems to be closely allied to the corresponding pronoun in Tibetan, and in the Indo-Chinese family generally, the manner in which it is pluralised in the Australian dialects bears a marked resemblance to the Drâvidian, and epecially to the Telugu. The Telugu forms its plurals by suffixing 'lu' to the singular; the Australian dialects by a similar addition of 'lu,' 'li,' 'dlu,' 'dli,' &c. In this particular some of the dialects of the North-Eastern frontier of India exhibit also an agreement with the Telugu: *e. g.*, compare Dhimal 'nâ,' *thou*, with 'nyel,' *you*. In the Australian dialects I find the following plurals and duals of the pronoun of the first person—*we*, or *we two*, 'ngalu,' 'ngadlu,' 'ngadli,' 'ngalata,' &c. Compare this with the manner in which the Telugu forms its plural; *e.g.* 'vâḍ'-u,' *he*; 'vâḍlu,' *they*; and even with the colloquial Tamil plural of the pronoun of the first person; *e. g.*, 'nân,' *I*; 'nânggaḷ,' *we*.

The resemblance between the Australian pronouns of the second person, both singular and plural, and those of the Drâvidian languages is more distinct and special; and is apparent, not only in the suffixes, but in the pronominal base itself. The normal forms of these pronouns in the Drâvidian languages are—singular, 'nîn,' plural, 'nîm.' The personality resides in the crude root 'nî,' *thou*; which is the same in both numbers, with the addition of a singular formative 'n' (*e. g.* 'nî-n,' *thou*), and a pluralising formative 'm' (*e. g.*, 'nî-m,' *thous*, or *you*). In some cases the pluralising particle 'm' has been displaced, and 'r,' which I regard as properly the sign of the epicene plural of the third person, has been substituted for it; *e. g.*, 'nîr,' *you* (in Telugu 'mîr-u'). This abnormal form 'nîr' is most used in a separate form: the older and more regular 'nîm' retains its place in compounds, and in the imperative of the verb. Whilst 'i' is the vowel which is almost invariably found in the singular of the pronoun of the second person, in the plural, 'i' often gives place to 'u,' as in the classical Tamil 'numa,' *your*, and the Brahui 'num,' *you*. It is to be noticed also that the modern Canarese has softened 'nîm' into 'nîvu' or 'nîwu,' in the nominative.

It is singular, in whatever way it may be accounted for, that in each and all of the particulars now mentioned the Australian dialects resemble the Drâvidian. See the following comparate view. Under the Australian head I class the dual together with the plural, as being substantially the same.

	Drâvidian.	Australian.
thou,	nîn, nin	ninna, nginne, ngintoa, ningte
you,	nîm, nim, nîr, num, nîwu	nimedoo, nura, niwa, ngurle

Compare also the accusative of the first person singular in Tamil, 'ennei,' *me*, with the Australian accusative 'emmo.'

The grammatical structure of the Australian dialects exhibits a general agreement with the languages of the Scythian group. In the use of post-positions instead of prepositions; in the use of two forms of the first person plural, one inclusive of the party addressed, the other exclusive; in the formation of inceptive, causative, and reflective verbs by the addition of certain syllables to the root; and, generally, in the agglutinative structure of words and in the position of words in a sentence, the dialects of Australia resemble the Drâvidian—as also the Turkish, the Mongolian, and other Scythian languages: and in the same particulars, with one or two exceptions, they differ essentially from the dialects which are called Polynesian.

The brief vocabularies of the Australian dialects which have been compiled do not appear to give additional confirmation to the resemblances pointed out above: but it is difficult to suppose those resemblances to be unreal, or merely accidental; and it is obvious that the Australian dialects demand (and probably will reward) further examination.

What Dialect best represents the Primitive Condition of the Drâvidian Tongues?

Before entering upon the grammatical comparison of the Drâvidian dialects, it seems desirable to ascertain where we should look for their earliest characteristics. Many have been of opinion that the Shen-Tamil, or high dialect of the Tamil language, is to be regarded as the best representative of the primitive Drâvidian speech. Without under-estimating the great value of the Shen-Tamil, I am convinced that no one dialect can be implicitly received as a mirror of Drâvidian antiquity. A comparison of all the dialects that exist will be found our best and safest guide to a knowledge of the primitive tongue from which the existing dialects have diverged; and not only the Shen-Tamil, but every existing dialect, even the rudest, will be found to contribute its quota of help towards this end. The Tamil pronouns of the first and second person cannot be understood without a knowledge of the Ancient Canarese: and the Ku, one of the rudest dialects, and the grammar of which was reduced to writing only a few years ago, is the only dialect which throws light on the masculine and feminine terminations of the Drâvidian pronouns of the third person. Still it is unquestionable that the largest amount of assistance towards ascertaining the primitive condition of the Drâvidian languages will be afforded by the Tamil, and in particular by the Shen-Tamil; and this naturally follows from the circumstance that of all the Drâvidian idioms the Tamil was the earliest cultivated.

Priority of the Literary Cultivation of the Tamil.

The relatively high antiquity of the literary cultivation of the Tamil being a matter of interest considered in itself, irrespective of its important bearings on the question of Drâvidian comparative grammar, I shall here adduce a few of the evidences on which this conclusion rests.

1. The Shen-Tamil, which is the language of the poetry and of the ancient inscriptions, and which not only contains all the refinements which the Tamil has received, but also exhibits to a great extent the primitive condition of the language, differs more from the colloquial Tamil than the poetical dialect of any other Drâvidian idiom differs from its ordinary dialect. It differs from the colloquial Tamil so considerably that it might almost be considered as a distinct language: for not only is classical Tamil poetry as unintelligible to the unlearned Tamilian as the Æneid of Virgil to a modern Italian peasant, but even prose compositions written in the classical dialect might be read for hours in the hearing of a person acquainted only with the colloquial idiom, without his understanding a single sentence. Notwithstanding this, High Tamil contains less Sanscrit, not more, than the colloquial dialect. It affects purism and national independence; and its refinements are all *ab intra*. As the words and forms of the Shen-Tamil cannot have been invented by the poets, but must at some period have been in actual use, the degree in which the colloquial Tamil has diverged from the poetical dialect, notwithstanding the slowness with which language, like every thing else, changes in the East, is a proof of the high antiquity of the literary cultivation of the Tamil.

2. Another evidence consists in the extraordinary copiousness of the Tamil vocabulary, and the number and variety of the grammatical forms of the Shen-Tamil. The Shen-Tamil grammar is a crowded museum of obsolete forms, cast-off inflexions, and curious anomalies. A school lexicon of the Tamil language, published by the American missionaries at Jaffna, contains no less than 58,500 words; and it would be necessary to add several thousands of technical terms, besides provincialisms, in order to render the list complete. Nothing strikes a Tamil scholar more, on examining the dictionaries of the other Drâvidian dialects, than the paucity of their lists of synonyms in comparison with those of the Tamil. The Tamil vocabulary contains not only those words which may be regarded as appropriate to the language, inasmuch as they are used by the Tamil alone, but also those which may be considered as the property of the Telugu, the Canarese, &c. Thus, the

word used for *house* in ordinary Tamil is 'vîḍu;' but the vocabulary contains also, and often uses, the word appropriate to the Telugu, 'il' (Telugu, 'illu'), and the distinctive Canarese word, 'manei' (Canarese, 'mana); besides another synonym, 'kuḍi,' which it has in common with the whole of the Finnish languages. The grammar and vocabulary of the Tamil are thus to a considerable extent the common repository of Drâvidian forms and roots: and as the grammars and vocabularies of the other dialects contain only the words and forms which are now peculiar to themselves, we may conclude that the literary cultivation of the Tamil dates from a period prior to that of the other idioms, and prior to the final breaking up of the language of the ancient Drâvidians into lialects.

3. Another evidence of the antiquity and purity of the Tamil consists in the agreement of the Ancient Canarese, the Malayâlam, the Tulu, and also the Tuda, Gônd, and Ku, with the Tamil, in many of the particulars in which the modern Canarese and the Telugu differ from it.

4. The fact that in many instances the forms of the Telugu roots and inflexions have evidently been corrupted from the forms of the Tamil, is a strong confirmation of the higher antiquity of the Tamilian forms. Instances of this will be given in the section on the phonetic system of these languages. It will suffice now to adduce, as an illustration of what is meant, the transposition of vowels which we find in the Telugu demonstrative pronouns. The true Drâvidian demonstrative bases are 'a,' remote, and 'i,' proximate; to which are suffixed the formatives of the genders, with 'v' euphonic, to prevent *hiatus*. The Tamil demonstratives are 'avan,' *ille*, and 'ivan,' *hic*. The Telugu masculine formative answering to the Tamil 'an,' is 'ḍu,' or 'aḍu;' and hence the demonstratives in Telugu, answering to the Tamil 'avan,' 'ivan,' might be expected to be 'avaḍu' and 'ivaḍu instead of which we find 'vaḍû,' *ille*, and 'vîḍu,' *hic*. Here the demonstrative bases 'a' and 'i,' have shifted from their natural position at the beginning of the word to the middle; whilst by coalescing with the vowel of the formative, or as a compensation for its loss, their quantity has been increased. The altered, abnormal form of the Telugu is evidently the later one; but as even the high dialect of the Telugu contains no other form, the period when the Telugu grammar was rendered permanent by written rules and the aid of written compositions, must have been subsequent to the origin of the corruption in question, and therefore subsequent to the literary cultivation of the Tamil.

5. Another evidence of antiquity consists in the great cor-

ruption of many of the Sanscrit derivatives that are found in the Tamil.

The Sanscrit contained in Tamil may be divided into three portions of different dates, introduced by three different parties.

(1.) The most recent portion was introduced by the school of Sankara Achârya, the apostle of Advaita, or Vedantic Saivism, and by its chief rival, the school of Sri Vaishnava, founded by Râmânuja Achârya. The period of the greatest activity and influence of those sects extended from about the tenth century, A.D., to the fifteenth;* and the Sanscrit derivatives introduced by the adherents of these systems (with the exception of a few points wherein change was unavoidable) are pure, unchanged Sanscrit.

(2.) The school of writers, partly preceding the above and partly contemporaneous with them, by which the largest portion of the Sanscrit derivatives that are found in Tamil were introduced, was that of the Jainas, which flourished from about the eighth century, A.D., to the twelfth or thirteenth. The period of the predominance of the Jainas (a predominance in intellect and learning—rarely a predominance in political power) was the Augustan age of Tamil literature, the period when the Madura College, a celebrated literary association, flourished, and when the Cuṟaḷ, the Chintâmaṇi, and the classical vocabularies and grammars were written. Through the intense Tamilic nationalism of the adherents of this school, and their jealousy of Brahmanical influence, the Sanscrit derivatives which are employed in their writings are very considerably altered, so as to accord with Tamil euphonic rules. Thus 'lôka,' Sanscrit, *the world*, is changed into 'ulagu;' 'râjâ,' *a king*, into 'araśu;' and 'râ,' *night* (an abbreviation of 'râtri'), into 'iravu.'

Nearly the whole of the Sanscrit derivatives that are found in Telugu, Canarese, and Malayâlam belong to the periods now mentioned, or at least they accord on the whole with the derivatives

* Sankara Acharya is supposed by Professor Wilson to have lived in the eighth or ninth century, A.D.: but the statement which I have here made relates not to Sankara Acharya personally, but to the school of theology and philosophy which was founded by him. This school did not reach the acme of its influence in the Carnatic till the tenth or eleventh century, when it appears probable that the great temples of the Carnatic were erected. Those temples, the most stupendous works of the kind in the East, owe their existence to the enthusiasm and zeal of the adherents of the system of Sankara Acharya. I have not yet been able to ascertain the exact date when any of the more celebrated temples was *erected;* but from inscriptions in my possession recording donations and endowments made to them, I am able to state that the greater number of the Saiva temples were in existence in the twelfth century, many in the eleventh, and a few in the tenth. I have not ascertained the existence of any Vaishnava temple in the South before the twelfth century.

found in the Tamil of those two periods, especially the former or more recent. They are divided, according to the degree of permutation or corruption to which they have been subjected, into the two classes of 'tat-sama,' *the very same, i.e.,* words which are identical with Sanscrit, and 'tad-bhava,' *the same nature, i.e.,* words which are derived from a Sanscrit origin, but have been slightly corrupted or changed by local influences.

The former class, or 'tat-sama' words, are scarcely at all altered, and generally look like words which have been used only by Brahmans, or which had been introduced into the vernaculars at a period when the Sanscrit alphabetical and phonetic systems had become naturalised, through the predominance of the later forms of Hinduism. Those Sanscrit derivatives which have been altered more considerably, or 'tad-bhava' words, do not appear to have been borrowed directly from the Sanscrit, but are represented by Telugu and Canarese grammarians themselves as words that have been borrowed from the Prâcrits, or colloquial dialects of the Sanscrit, which were formerly spoken in the contiguous Gaura provinces.

(3.) In addition to the Sanscrit derivatives of the two periods now mentioned—the Jaina and the modern Vedantic Saiva periods—the Tamil contains many derivatives belonging to the very earliest period of the literary culture of the language,—derivatives which are probably of an earlier date than the introduction of Sanscrit into the other dialects. The derivatives of this class were not borrowed from the northern Prâcrits (though much more corrupted than even the Sanscrit which was borrowed from those Prâcrits by the Canarese and Telugu), but appear to have been derived from oral intercourse with the first Brahmanical priests, scholars, and astrologers; and probably remained unwritten for a considerable time. The Sanscrit of this period is not only greatly more corrupted than that of the period of the Jainas, but its corruptions are of an entirely different character. The Jainas altered the Sanscrit which they borrowed in order to bring it into accordance with Tamil euphonic rules; whereas in the Sanscrit of the period which is now under consideration—the earliest period—the changes that have been introduced are in utter defiance of rule. The following are instances of derivatives of this class:

(*a.*) The Sanscrit 'srî,' *sacred,* was altered into 'tiru;' whilst a more recent alteration of the Sanscrit word is into 'strî.'

(*b.*) The Sanscrit 'karmam,' *a work,* is in the Tamil of the more modern periods altered into 'karumam' and 'kanmam;' but in the older Tamil it was corrupted into 'kam,' a word which is now found only in the old compound, 'kam(m)-âḷan,' *an artificer.*

(*c.*) Several of the names of the Tamil months supply us with illustrations of early corruptions of Sanscrit. The Tamil months, though now solar-siderial, are named from the old lunar asterisms; the names of which asterisms, and still more the names of the months borrowed from them, are greatly corrupted. *E.g.*, the asterism 'pûrva-âṣhâḍam,' is changed into 'pûrâḍam:' 'aṣhâḍam,' also is changed into 'âḍam,' from which is formed 'âḍi,' the Tamil name of the mouth July—August. The name of the asterism 'aswini' has been corrupted into 'eippasi,' which is the Tamil name of the month October—November. The change of 'pûrva bhadra-pada,' the Sanscrit name of one of the asterisms, into 'puraṭṭâsi' is still more extraordinary. 'Pûrva-bhadra-pada' was first changed into 'pûraṭṭâdi,' the name of the corresponding asterism in Tamil; and this, again, by the shortening of the first syllable and the change of 'di' into 'si,' became 'pûraṭṭâsi,' the Tamil month September—October.

The corresponding names of the asterisms and months in Telugu, Canarese, &c., are pure, unchanged Sanscrit; and hence the greater antiqnity of the introduction of those words into Tamil, or at least the greater antiquity of their use in Tamil written compositions, may safely be concluded.

6. The higher antiquity of the literary cultivation of the Tamil may also be inferred from Tamil inscriptions. In Carnâtaka and Telingâna, every inscription of an early date, and the majority even of modern inscriptions, are written in Sanscrit. Even when the characters employed are the Ancient Canarese or the Telugu (characters which have been arranged to express the peculiar sounds of the Sanscrit), it is invariably found that Sanscrit is the language in which the inscription is written, if it is one of any antiquity. In the Tamil country, on the contrary, *all* inscriptions belonging to an early period are written in Tamil; and I have not met with, or heard of, a single Sanscrit inscription in the Tamil country which appears to be older than the fourteenth century, A.D., though I have obtained *fac-similes* of all the inscriptions that I could hear of in Tinnevelly and South Travancore—integral portions of the ancient Pândiyan kingdom. The number of inscriptions that I have obtained is about a hundred and fifty. They were found on the walls and floors of temples, and on rocks and pillars. The latest are written in Grantham, or the character in which Sanscrit is written by the Drâvida Brahmans; those of an earlier age in an old form of the existing Tamil character;* and the earliest in a

* I hope at some future period to make public the items of historical information which are contained in those inscriptions; not one of which is included in

still older character, which appears to have been common to the Tamil and the ancient Malayâla countries, and is the character in which the ancient Sâsanas in the possession of the Jews at Cochin and of the Syrian Christians in Travancore are written. This character presents some points of resemblance to the modern Telugu-Canarese character, and also to the character in which some undeciphered inscriptions in Ceylon and the Eastern Islands are written.

The language of all the more ancient of these inscriptions is Tamil; and the style in which they are written is that of the classical dialect, without any of those double plurals (*e.g.*, 'nînggal,' *yous*, instead of 'nîr,' *you*), and other unauthorized novelties by which modern Tamil is disfigured; but it is free also from the affected brevity and involutions of the poetical style.

As no inscription of any antiquity in Telingâna or Carnâtaca is found to be written in the Canarese or the Telugu *language*, whatever be the *character* that is employed, the priority of Tamil literary culture, as well as its national independence to a considerable extent, may fairly be concluded.

I may here remark that the Cochin and Travancore 'sâsanas' or tablets which are referred to above, and which have been translated by the Rev. Dr. Gundert, prove conclusively, not only the priority of Tamil to Malayâla literature, but also the derivation of the Malayâla idiom from the Tamil. The date of those documents is not certainly known, but is probably not later than the ninth century, A.D., nor earlier than the seventh; for the technical terms of solar-siderial chronology (derived from the Sûrya-Siddhânta of Ârya-bhaṭṭa) which are employed in these inscriptions were not generally introduced till the seventh century. The 'sâsanas' were written at a time when the

the inscriptions belonging to the Mackenzie collection of MSS. I may, however, mention here the following interesting items.—(1.) The generally fictitious character of the long lists of kings of Madura, each with a high-sounding Sanscrit name, which are contained in the local 'purânas' and other legends, and which have been published by Professor Wilson in his *Historial Sketch of the Pandiyan Kingdom*, and by Mr. Taylor in his *Oriental Historical MSS.* (2.) The veracity and accuracy of most of the references to the Pândiya and Chôla dynasties which are contained in the Mahâ-wanso and other historical records and compilations of the Singhalese Buddhists. (3.) The fact, or proof of the fact, of the conquest of the whole of the Pândiya country, including South Travancore, by the Chôlas in the eleventh century. (4.) The probable identification of Sundara Pândiyan, by whom the Jainas (sometimes erroneously termed Buddhists) were finally expelled from Madura, and whom Professor Wilson has placed in the eighth or ninth century A.D. with the 'Sender Bandi,' who is said by Marco Polo to have been reigning in the southern part of the peninsula during his visit to India in the middle of the thirteenth century. The same Sundara Pândiyan is placed by native Hindu authorities some millions of years before the Christian era!

Chêra or Kêrala dynasty was still predominant on the Malabar coast:* but though words and forms which are peculiar to the modern Malayâla language may be detected in them, the general style of the language in which they are written is Tamil; the inflexions of the nouns and verbs are Tamil, and the idiom is mostly Tamil; and we are therefore left to infer that at that period Tamil was the language at least of the court and of the educated classes in the Malayâla country, and that what is now called Malayâlam, if it then existed at all, was probably nothing more than a rustic patois that was current amongst the inhabitants of the hills and jungles in the interior. The fact that the 'sâsanas' which were given by the ancient Malayâla kings to the Jews and Syrian Christians, are in the Tamil language, instead of the Malayâlam, cannot be accounted for from the circumstance of the temporary conquest of any part of the Malayâla country by the ancient kings of Madura; for the kings in question were Kêrala, not Pâṇḍiya, kings, with Kêrala names, titles, and insignia; and it is evident from the Greek geographers themselves, from whom alone we know anything of this conquest, that it was only a few isolated places, on or near the Malabar coast, that were really under the rule of the Pândiyas. The only part of the Malayâla country which at that period could be regarded as belonging *bonâ fide* to the Pândiyas, was the southern part of 'Paralia,' *i.e.*, South Travancore, a district which has always been inhabited chiefly by Pândiyas, and where to the present day the language of the entire people is Tamil, not Malayâlam.

From the various particulars mentioned above it appears certain that the Tamil language was of all the Drâvidian idioms the earliest cultivated: it also appears highly probable, that in the endeavour to ascertain the characteristics of the primitive Drâvidian speech, from which the various existing dialects have been derived, most assistance will be furnished by the Tamil. The amount and value of this assistance will appear in almost every portion of the grammatical comparison on which we are about to enter. It must, however, be borne in mind, as has already been intimated, that neither the Tamil nor any other

* One of them is dated 'in the seventh year of King Ravi Varma, *opposite the second year*.' By this vexed expression, 'opposite the second year,' Mr. Whish supposed that a reference was made to the 'second cycle of a thousand years from the building of Quilon,' a calculation according to which the present year, 1856, would be the thirty-first of the third cycle; but the same expression is exceedingly common in the ancient Tamil inscriptions (*e.g.* 'the seventh year of King Kulasêkhara, *opposite* the fifteenth year'); and it denotes, I conceive, the year of 'the cycle of sixty' (which was formerly the prevailing calculation all over India and the East) to which the year of the king's reign stands 'opposite,' or answers.

single dialect, ancient or modern, can be *implicitly* adopted as a faithful representative of the primitive Drâvidian tongue. A careful comparison of the peculiarities of all the dialects will carry us up still further, probably up to the period of their mutual divergence, a period long anterior to that of grammars and vocabularies; and it is upon the result of such a comparison that most dependence is to be placed.

EARLIEST EXTANT WRITTEN RELICS OF THE DRÂVIDIAN LANGUAGES.

The Drâvidian words which are contained in the Râmâyana, the Mahâ-bhârata, and other Sanscrit poems of undoubted antiquity, are so few that they throw no light whatever upon the ancient condition of the Drâvidian languages, prior to the eighth or ninth centuries A.D., the earliest date to which any extant Tamil compositions can safely be attributed. The name 'Pâṇḍiya' being probably of Sanscrit origin, the only Drâvidian names which are contained in the poems referred to, are 'Chôla,' corrupted from the Tamilic 'Sôṛa' (commonly pronounced 'Chôḷa'), the collective name of the Tamilians of Tanjore, and 'Malaya,' the name of a mountain range, the Western Ghauts, which is probably derived from the Drâvidian 'mala,' *a hill.*

It is a remarkable circumstance, that the largest stock of primitive Drâvidian words which is contained in any authentic written document of ancient times—the earliest extant traces of the existence of the Drâvidian languages, as distinguished from the Sanscrit—are those which are contained in the notices of the Greek geographers, Ptolemy, Strabo, and the author of the *Periplus Maris Erythraei*; including also the *Natural History* of Pliny. Many of the names and places and tribes which are recorded by those geographers, not long after the commencement of the Christian era, are identical, letter for letter, with the names which are now in use. Several of those names have become obsolete, or cannot now be identified: but the signification of the compound words of which they consist cannot be mistaken; and in several of them we can detect the operation of some interesting dialectic peculiarity or euphonic rule which is still characteristic of these languages. I subjoin a few examples of Drâvidian words of this class which are recorded by the Greeks.

(1.) '*ὁ Πανδίων*' '*οἱ Πανδιόνες*,' 'Pâṇḍiya,' is probably a word of Sanscrit origin, but the masculine termination which is given by the Greeks is unmistakeably Tamil. The Tamilic sign of the masculine singular is 'an;' consequently '*ὁ Πανδίων*' (and still better the plural form of the word, 'Πανδιόνες,' which is applied to the subjects of the Pandiya monarchy), faithfully represents the Tamil nominative singular 'Pâṇḍiyan.'

The form of the masculine singular in Ancient Canarese which corresponds to the Tamil 'an,' is 'am:' in Telugu it is 'uḍu,' so that 'Pâṇḍiyuḍu' in Telugu, answers to 'Pâṇḍiyan' in Tamil. Consequently, we learn that, as early as the Christian era, the Tamil differed dialectically from the other Drâvidian idioms, and that its mode of forming the masculine singular was then the same as it is now. 'Pâṇḍiya' was not the name of any one king, but the titular name of the dynasty of Madura (Μόδουρα βασίλειον Πανδίονις). The race were 'Pâṇḍis,' or 'Pâṇḍiyas' (πανδιόνες); the king, *the* 'Pâṇḍiyan' (ὁ Πανδίων), or the 'Pâṇḍiya Dêva.' It is a proof of the advanced social position which was occupied by the Pâṇḍiyas, that after the termination of the political relations which subsisted between the Greeks of Alexander's time, and the princes of the Punjaub, the Pâṇḍiyas were the only Indian princes who perceived the advantages of an European alliance. Two embassies were sent by the Pâṇḍiyan king to Augustus: the first (which is mentioned in the Eusebian fragments) was received by Augustus at Tarragona; the second is mentioned by Strabo. The friendship of the Romans was sought by only one other Hindu prince, ὁ κηροβόθρος, the King of Chêra (or Kêrala), who was also a Drâvidian, and probably a Tamilian.

(2.) 'Κοττιάρα.' This is the name of a place in the country of the 'Aii,' or 'Paralia' (identical with South Travancore), which is called 'Kottiara Metropolis' by Ptolemy, 'Cottora' by Pliny. Undoubtedly the town referred to is 'Kôṭṭâʀa,' or, as it is ordinarily spelled by Europeans, 'Kotaur,' the principal town in South Travancore, and now, as in the time of the Greeks, distinguished for its commerce. The name of the place is derived from 'Kôd-u,' Tam., *a line of circumvallation, a fortification,* and 'âʀú,' *a river.* It is a rule in the Tamil and the Malayâlam, that when a word like 'Kôḍ' is the first member of a compound, the final 'ḍ' must be doubled for the purpose of giving the word the force of an adjective: it is another rule that sonants when doubled become surds. Consequently the compound 'kôḍ'-âʀa' becomes by rule 'kôṭṭ-âʀa.' It is interesting to perceive that in the time of the Greeks the same peculiar phonetic rules existed which are now in operation. It is also worth noticing that the Greek writers represent the last syllable of the name of the town, not as 'âʀu,' but as 'âʀa.' The Tamil has 'âʀu,' the Malayâlam 'âʀa.' At Kotaur, the dialectic peculiarities of the Malayâla language begin to supersede those of the

Tamil; and this appears to have been the case even in the time of the Greeks.

(3.) "Ἀρκάτου βασίλειον." The place referred to by this name was supposed by one of the editors of Ptolemy to be Bijnagar; which would accord well enough, it is true, with the position which Ptolemy gives it, midway between the sources of the Câvêri and Gondwana: but the resemblance of the name to that of Arcot, and the circumstance that the place is represented as the capital of 'the nomadic Sôras' (Σῶραι), indicate the propriety of identifying it with Arcot in the Carnatic: for not only was Arcot included in the ancient Sôra or Chôla Kingdom, but there is a distinct, uniform tradition, that the inhabitants of that part of the Carnatic which lies between Madras and the Ghauts, including Arcot, were 'Kurumbars,' or wandering shepherds—nomades—for several centuries after the Christian era. If this identification is correct, we have another instance of the antiquity of the existing dialectic peculiarities of the Tamil; for the second syllable of the name *Arcot*, (properly 'âʀu-kâḍu,' *the jungle on the river*), viz., 'kâḍ-u,' *a jungle*, is peculiar to the Tamil,—the corresponding word used in Telugu being 'aṭavi' or 'aḍavi.'

Ptolemy gives the name of the people of the neighbouring country more accurately than the Sanscrit writers. They are called in Tamil 'Sôṛas;'* Chôlas in Sanscrit; but Sôrae, and also Sôrigi, or Sôrigêti

* I am doubtful whether the eastern coast of India derived from this word ('Sôra') the name of the 'Coromandel' coast, by which it is styled by Europeans. Undoubtedly Fra Paolo à St. Bartolomaeo was wrong in supposing it to be derived from 'chôḷa-mandalam,' *the millet country.* 'Chôḷam' is not *millet*, but *maize;* and compounds of indigenous Drâvidian words like 'chôḷam' and Sanscrit words like 'mandaḷam' are ordinarily inadmissible; and this compound in particular is quite unknown. 'Sôṛa-mandaḷam,' *the country of the Sôras,* who are called 'Chôlas' in Sanscrit, is a compound which is in actual use, like 'Pâṇḍi-maṇḍalam,' *the country of the Pândiyas,* and 'Sêra-maṇḍalam,' *the country of the Sêras, or Kêrala:* and doubtless this is the word with which Paolo's informants had supplied him. This derivation of the word 'Coromandel,' viz. from 'Sôṛa-maṇḍalam,' has generally been accepted; but there is this serious objection to it, that the name of that part of the eastern coast—from Cuddalore to Madras —with which Europeans first became acquainted, is 'Toṇḍa-maṇḍalam,' not 'Sôṛa-maṇḍalam:' in addition to which, these terms are rarely used by the natives themselves: their use is restricted to classical compositions, and it is extremely unlikely that the first European mariners and factors ever heard of them. We have, therefore, to seek for some more trite, easy, and natural derivation of the word 'Coromandel;' and this I think we find in 'Karu-maṇal' (literally *black sand*), the name of a small village on the eastern coast near Pulicat (the first Dutch settlement), which is invariably up to the present day pronounced and written 'Coromandel' by the Europeans who are resident in Madras; some of whom annually take refuge in 'Karumanal' or 'Coromandel' during the hot land winds. Coromandel is often the first point which is sighted by ships from Europe bound to Madras; and the objects on which my own eyes first rested on approaching the coast in January, 1838, were the cocoa-nut trees of Coromandel and the distant Nagari hills.

by the Greeks. The two last names must have been applied by Ptolemy to the Sôṛas of the Tanjore delta; for the Câvêri flowed through the country of the Sôrigi, and 'Χαβήρος,' the emporium at the mouth of the Câvêri (which he calls 'Χάβηρις,'), belonged to them. The Sôṛas are sometimes in poetical Tamil called 'Sôṛagas' or 'Sôṛiyas,' and their country 'Sôṛagam,'—'g' being optionally added to many roots as an euphonic. The 'r' of the Tamil word 'Sôṛa,' is a peculiar sound, not contained in any of the other Drâvidian dialects; in which it is generally represented by 'ḷ' or 'ḍ;' in Sanscrit and in the Pâli of the 'Mahâ-wanso' by 'l.' The more accurate spelling of this word given by the Greeks shews that then, as now, the use of this peculiar vocalic 'ṛ' was a dialectic characteristic of the Tamil.

(4.) *Modogalingum.* Pliny observes, "Insula in Gange est .... Modogalingum nomine." The same island, country, or city (for the description of it is somewhat obscure) is called by Ptolemy, Triglyphum or Trilingum. Though the place referred to is said to be "on the Ganges," it may have been considerably to the south: for the Godâvery has always been considered by Hindus as a branch of the Ganges, or as mythologically identical with it; and the Greeks would most probably be taught to regard it in the same light. At all events, from the circumstance that the Ândhras and Calingas (the two ancient divisions of the Telugu people) are represented by the Greeks as Gangetic nations, and as living in or near Triglyphum, it may be considered as certain that Triglyphum, Trilingum, or Modogalingum, was identical with Telingâna, or Trilingam, 'the country of the three lingas;' from which word, indeed, the modern term 'Telinga' is ordinarily derived by native grammarians. The derivation of 'Telugu,' 'Telungu,' or 'Telinga', from 'Trilinga' is repudiated by Mr. C. P. Brown; who also states that the name 'Trilinga' is not contained in any of the ancient Sanscrit lists of countries. This statement is probably correct: nevertheless, the ancient use of the appellation 'Trilingam,' and the identity of the names Trilingam and Modogalingum, are proved by the evidence of Ptolemy and Pliny, as conclusively as if they had been mentioned by Sanscrit writers. This being the case, the Telugu name and language are fixed near the mouths of the Ganges, or at least between the Ganges and the Godavery, about the commencement of the Christian era: and not only so, but the existence of the dialectic peculiarities of the Telugu, as early as the time of the Greek geographers, may safely be inferred; inasmuch as 'modoga,' the word used by Pliny, is the ancient word for *three* ('moda,' or 'modoga'), answering to the Canarese 'mûru,' the Tamil 'mûnru' (pronounced mûndru), and the modern Telugu 'mûḍu.' The word used by Pliny being exclusively a Telugu word, we may conclude that at that early period the dialectic peculiarities of the Telugu, one of which is the use of 'ḍ' where the other dialects have 'r,' were already in existence.

(5.) Καροῦρα βασίλειον κηροβόθρου. The place referred to is evidently Karûr, a town in the Coimbatoor country, which was formerly the capital of the Chêra dynasty. 'Cerobothrus' is given as the titular name of the king of the country (ordinarily called by Tamilians 'the Chêran'), whose rule extended over Coimbatoor, part of Mysore, and a portion of the Malabar coast. Probably 'Cerobothrus' is identical with 'Chêra-putra,' *son of Chêra.* The Greek spelling of the word κηρο confirms the supposition of the identity of the Drâvidian title of the dynasty, Sêra or Chêra, with the Sanscrit 'Kêrala,' and the greater antiquity of the latter mode of spelling.

The name Καροῦρα, in Tamil 'Karûr,' is derived from 'kar,' *black,* and 'ûr,' *a town.* The exact agreement of the Greek word with the Tamil is remarkable.

It is deserving of notice that in Ptolemy's lists of names of places in India the termination ουρ or ουρα, equivalent to the Drâvidian 'ûr,' *a town,* (Anglicè, 'oor' or 'ore'), is frequently met with, not only in the southern part of the peninsula, but as far north as the mouths of the Ganges.

(6.) ὁι Καρέοι. The Careï of Ptolemy were a people who inhabited the southern part of Tinnevelly, in whose country part of the 'Paralia' of the author of the *Periplus* seems at one time to have been included. 'Kare' or 'karei' is the Tamil word for *coast* or *shore* (from the verbal root 'karei,' *to be melted down,—to be washed away*), and is obviously identical in meaning with the Greek Παραλία. Up to the present time part of the Tinnevelly coast—that part where I have myself resided and laboured for thirteen years—is called by the same name ('karei,' *the shore*) by which the whole southern coast of Tinnevelly and Travancore appears to have been known to the Greeks; and a caste of fishermen found farther north are called 'karei-(y)-âr,' *coast-people.*

(7.) Καλλίγικον. This is one of the names given by Ptolemy to the promontory of Κῶρυ. This promontory is supposed by some to be Cape Comorin; but as it is said to be situated opposite the most northern point of Ceylon, and to form the boundary between the 'Gangetic Gulf,' or Bay of Bengal, and the 'Orgalic' or 'Agaric Gulf,' the Gulf of Manaar, it is evidently Point Calimere. The Tamil name of this point, from which 'Calimere' has been corrupted, is 'kaḷḷi-mêḍu,' *the cactus eminence;* and it is evident that the first part of the Greek name Καλλίγικον is identical with the Tamil 'kaḷḷi,' *cactus*, the first part of the name by which the place is now called.

(8.) Amongst many words of less importance of which the Tamil signification can be easily recognised, I subjoin the following:—Παλοῦρα (obviously from 'pâl,' *milk*, and 'ûr,' *a town*), a place in the Bay of Bengal, possibly at the mouth of the 'Pâlâr,' *Milk-river*, a river which flows into the Bay of Bengal a little to the south of Madras: Τεννάγορα (from the Tamil 'ten,' *south*, and the Sanscrit 'nagara,' *a city*), a town in the Sôra country: also the word ὄρυζα, *rice*, which is obviously derived from the Tamil 'ariśi,' *rice deprived of the husk;* this being the state in which rice was then, as now, bought up in India for exportation to Europe.*

(9.) During the period in which the Greeks traded with India, the names of places and tribes recorded by them, and various circumstances which they have related, prove that the Brahmans had then established themselves in the Carnatic, and given names to some of the principal places. 'Μόδουρα' (Madura) is a Sanscrit word, signifying *the sweet city;* the name of the Câvêri, ''Χάβηρίς,' *the yellow river,* is claimed by the Sanscrit, though possibly Tamil; and

* The Hebrew word for *pea-fowl*, which is 'thuki' in the Book of Kings, 'thûki' in Chronicles, is certainly Drâvidian. The pea-fowl is an Indian bird. It was probably on the Malabar or Western coast of India that the pea-fowl was procured by (or for) Solomon's servants; and the old classical name of the fowl in Tamil is 'tôkei,' dialectically pronounced 'tôgei.' In *modern* Tamil 'tôkei' generally signifies only *the peacock's tail*, or any similar tail-feathers; but in old classical Tamil it signifies also *the peacock* itself. If this identification is correct, the Hebrew word referred to is the oldest specimen of the Drâvidian languages which is extant in any written document. The Arabic word for the peacock, 'tawas,' and the Armenian 'taus,' are probably derived from the same source; as also the Greek 'ταῶς,' with which, by the insertion of the digamma, some connect the Latin 'pavo.' I cannot connect the Tamil 'tôg-ei,' as Max Müller does, with the Sans. 'sikhin;' for it is regarded by Drâvidian lexicographers as a pure Tamilian word; and the Tamil corruption of 'sikhin' is 'sigi,' *a peacock*, which is a recognised Sans. derivative. 'tôg-ei' is not in Canarese or Telugu.

Huge old specimens of the Baobab, or Adansonia Digitata, an African tree, of which the Hindus do not know even the name, may still be seen in or near various sites of foreign commerce in the extreme south of the Indian peninsula: *e. g.*, in Kôttâr, near Cape Comorin, and near Tutocorin in Tinnevelly—possibly on the site of the ancient Kolkhi. By what race of foreign merchants were those trees planted? The great age to which they are known to grow (they are called by Humboldt 'some of the oldest specimens of organic life on the globe') will admit of the supposition that they were brought from the mouth of the Red Sea by the Grecian navigators, or even by the Phenicians and 'the servants of Solomon' themselves.

May it not have been by the same people that the Hebrew word 'sak,' a *sack* (in Tamil 'sâkk-u,' in Malayâlam 'châkka'), was introduced into Southern India? This word, though so long naturalised that it is considered by native scholars to be indigenous, is unknown to the Telugu and Canarese, as well as to the Sanscrit. It is found only where the Baobab is found, and where the Hebrew name for the peacock had its origin.

Κομάρια ἄκρον' (Cape Comorin) is certainly derived from the Sanscrit 'kumâri. *a virgin,* a name of the goddess Durgâ. This word is commonly pronounced in Tamil 'kumări; and in the vulgar dialect of the people residing in the neighbourhood of the Cape, *a virgin* is not 'kumâri,' or 'kumări,' but 'kumar,' pronounced 'komar.' It is remarkable that this vulgar corruption of the Sanscrit is identical with the name which is given to Cape Comorin by the author of the *Periplus.* He says, 'After this, there is another place called 'Κομάρ,' where there is a fort and harbour, where also people come to bathe and purify themselves: . . . . for it is related that a goddess was once accustomed to bathe there monthly.' This monthly bathing in honour of the goddess Durgâ or Pârvati, is still continued at Cape Comorin, but is not practised to the same extent as in ancient times. Cape Comorin formerly ranked as one of 'the five renowned sacred bathing places' (a representation which accords with the statement of the author of the *Periplus*), but the number of visitors to it now is extremely small.

Though the Greek geographers have not given us any information respecting the languages of India, beyond what is furnished by the names of places contained in their works, the information derived from those lists is exceedingly interesting. The earliest extant traces of the Drâvidian languages which possess reliable authority, are those with which we have been furnished by the ancient Greeks; and from an examination of the words which they have recorded, we seem to be justified in drawing the conclusion, not only that the Drâvidian languages have remained almost unaltered for the last two thousand years, but also that the principal dialects that now prevail had a separate existence at the commencement of the Christian era, and prevailed at that period in the very same districts of country in which we now find them. The art of writing had probably been introduced, the grammar of the Drâvidian languages had been arranged, and some progress made in the art of composition, several centuries before the arrival of the Greek merchants;* and the fixity with which those languages appear to have been characterised ever since that period is in perfect accordance with the history of all other Asiatic languages, from the date of the commencement of their literary cultivation.

* The arrival in India of those Grecian merchants, appears to have been contemporaneous with the conquest of Egypt by the Romans. The earliest Roman coins found in India are those of the reign of Augustus. A very large number of Roman imperial 'aurei' were lately found on the Malabar coast; upwards of thirty types of which, commencing with the earlier coins of Augustus, and including many of Nero, were described by me in a pamphlet published at Trivandrum in 1851 by the Rajah of Travancore, to whom the coins belonged.

If the Drâvidian family of languages is allied, as I believe it to be, to the Scythian families, it may justly claim to be considered as one of the oldest members of the group. With the exception of the language of the Behistun tablets, no words belonging to any other Scythian language can be traced up to the Christian era. Mr. Norris says, 'I know of nothing written in the Magyar language earlier than the fifteenth century, and of the other Ugrian languages we have nothing above fifty or sixty years old The great Finnish heroic poem, 'the Kalevala,' may be of any age, but as it appears to have been brought down to us only by word of mouth, it has naturally varied, like all traditional poetry, with the varying forms of the language.' The Uigurs, or Oriental Turks, acquired the art of writing from the Nestorian Christians, the Mongolians from the Uigurs; so that the literary cultivation of neither of those languages is to be compared in point of antiquity with that of the Drâvidian. Amongst the earliest records of Scythian tongues that have been discovered, is a brief list of words which are recorded by the Chinese as peculiar to the old Turks of the Altaï; and of eight words contained in this list, all of which are found in the modern dialects of the Turkish, probably three, certainly two, are Drâvidian. Those words, as given by the Chinese, are :—

Turkish of the Altaï.		Modern Turkish.	Tamil.
black,	koro	quarâ	kar-u
old,	kori	gori	kiṛa
chieftain,	kân	khân	kôn or kô

I am strongly inclined to consider the last Tamil word, 'kôn' or 'kô,' to be identical with the 'kân,' 'khân,' or 'khâgan' of the Turco-Mongolian languages. The Ostiak, an Ugrian dialect, has 'khon;' and the word signifying *king*, which is found in the Scythic version of the Behistun tablets, and which certainly commences with 'k,' or 'kh,' is conjecturally written by Mr. Norris 'ko.' In the old Tamil inscriptions I have invariably found 'kô' or 'kôn,' instead of the Sanscrit 'Râjâ:' but the word has become obsolete in modern Tamil, except in compounds, and in the honorific title 'kôn,' which is assumed by shepherds. This conjunction of meanings (*king* and *shepherd*) is very interesting, and reminds one of the Homeric description of kings as 'ποιμένες λαῶν.'

The Tamil literature now extant enables us to ascend, in studying the history of the language, only to the eighth or ninth century, A.D.: the Drâvidian words handed down to us by the Greeks carry us up, as we have seen, to the Christian era. Beyond that period, the comparison of existing dialects is our only available guide to a knowledge of the primitive condition of the Drâvidian language. The civilization of the Tamil people, together with the literary cultivation of their language, commenced probably about the sixth or seventh century, B.C., but the separation of the primitive Drâvidian speech into dialects must have taken place shortly after the arrival of the Drâvidians in the districts which they at present inhabit—an event of unknown, but certainly of very great antiquity.

The Irish and the Welsh dialects of the Celtic, the Old High and the Old Low dialects of the Teutonic, and the Finnish and Magyar dialects of the Ugrian, had probably become separate and distinct idioms before the tribes by which those dialects are spoken settled in their present habitations; but the various Drâvidian dialects which are now spoken appear to have acquired a separate existence subsequently to the settlement of the Drâvidians in the localities in which we now find them. Supposing that their final settlement in their present abodes in Southern India took place shortly after the Âryan irruption (though I think it probable that it took place before), every grammatical form and root which the various dialects possess in common, may be regarded as at least coeval with the century subsequent to the arrival of the Âryans. Every form and root which the Brahui possesses in common with the Drâvidian tongues may be regarded as many centuries older still. The Brahuic analogies enable us to ascend to a period anterior to the arrival in India of the Âryans (which cannot safely be placed later than 1600, B.C.); and they furnish us with the means of ascertaining, in some degree, the condition of the Drâvidian language before the Drâvidians had finally abandoned their original abodes in the central tracts of Asia.

Political and Social Relation of the Primitive Drâvidians to the Âryan and Pre-Âryan Inhabitants of Northern India.

The arrival of the Drâvidians in India was undoubtedly anterior to the arrival of the Âryans, but there is some difficulty in determining whether the Drâvidians were identical with the Scythian aborigines whom the Âryans found in possession of the northern provinces, and to whom the vernacular languages o Northern India are indebted for their Un-Sanscrit element, or whether they were a distinct and more ancient race. The question may be put thus:—Were the Drâvidians identical with the 'Dasyus' and 'Mlêchchas,' by whom the progress of the Âryans was disputed, and who were finally subdued and incorporated with the Âryan race as their 'Sûdras,' or serfs and dependents? or were they a race unknown to the Âryans of the first age, and which had already been expelled from Northern India, and driven southwards towards the extremity of the Peninsula before the Âryans arrived? This question of the relation of the Drâvidians to the primitive Sûdras, or Âryanised Mlêchchas, of Northern India is confessedly involved in obscurity, and can be settled only by a more thorough investigation than any that has yet been made of the relation of the Drâvidian languages to the Un-Sanscrit element contained in the northern vernaculars. We may, indeed, confidently regard the Drâvidians as the earliest inhabitants of India, or at least as the earliest race that entered from the North-West, or crossed the Indus; but it is not so easy to determine whether they were the people whom the Âryans found in possession, or whether they had already been expelled from the northern provinces by the pre-historic irruption of another Scythian race. Some recent inquirers hold the identity of the Drâvidians with the primitive Sûdras; and much may be said in support of this hypothesis. I am not competent to pronounce a decided opinion on a point which lies so far beyond my own province, but the differences which appear to exist between the Drâvidian languages and the Scythian under-stratum of the northern vernaculars induce me to incline to the supposition that the Drâvidian idioms belong to an older period of the Scythian speech—the period of the predominance of the Ugro-Finnish languages in Central and Higher Asia, anterior to the westward migration of the Turks and Mongolians. If this supposition is correct, it seems to follow that the progenitors of the Scythian portion of the Sûdras and mixed classes now inhabiting the northern and western provinces must have made their way into India subsequently to the Drâvidians, and also that they must have thrust out the Drâvidians from the greater part of Northern India, before they were in their turn subdued by a new race of invaders. By whomsoever the Drâvidians were expelled from Northern India, and through what causes soever they were induced to migrate southward, I feel persuaded that it was not by the Âryans that they were expelled. Neither the subjugation of the Chôlas, Pâṇḍiyas, and other Drâvidians by the Âryans, nor the expulsion from Northern India of the races who afterwards became celebrated in the South, as Pâṇḍiyas, Chôlas, Kêralas, Calingas, Ândhras, &c., is recognised by any Sanscrit authority, or any Drâvidian tradition. Looking at the question from a purely Drâvidian point of view, I am convinced that the Drâvidians never had any relations with the primitive Âryans but those of a peaceable and friendly character; and that if they were expelled from Northern India, and forced to take refuge in Gondwana and Daṇḍa-Kâraṇya, the great Drâvidian forest, prior to the dawn of their civilisation, the tribes that subdued and thrust them southwards must have been Pre-Âryans.

Those Pre-Âryan Scythians, by whom I have been supposing the Drâvidians to have been expelled from the northern provinces, are not to be confounded with the Kôles, Sontâls, Bhills, Dôms, and other aboriginal tribes of the North. Possibly these tribes had fled into the forests from the Drâvidians prior to the Pre-Âryan invasion, just as the British had taken refuge in Wales before the Norman conquest. It is also possible that the tribes referred to had never crossed the Indus at all, or occupied Northern India, but had entered it, like the Bhutân tribes, by the North-East, and had passed from the jungles and swamps of Lower Bengal to their present abodes,—taking care always to keep on the outside of the boundary line of civilisation. At all events, we cannot suppose that it was through an irruption of those forest tribes that the Drâvidians were driven southwards; nor does the Un-Sanscrit element which is contained in the northern vernaculars appear to accord in any degree with the peculiar structure of the Kole languages. The tribes of Northern India whom the Âryans gradually incorporated in their community, as Sûdras, whosoever they were, must have been an organized and formidable race. They were probably identical with the 'Æthiopians from the East,' who, according to Herodotus, were brigaded with other Indians in the army of Xerxes, and who differed from other Æthiopians in being 'straight-haired.'

I admit that there is a difficulty in supposing that the Drâvidians, who have proved themselves greatly superior to the Âryanised Sûdras of Northern India in mental power, independence, and patriotic feeling, should have been expelled from their original possessions by an irruption of the ancestors of those very Sûdras. It is to be remembered, however, that the lapse of time may have effected a great change in the warlike, hungry, Scythian hordes that rushed down upon the first Drâvidian settlements. It is also to be remembered that the dependent and almost servile position to which this secondary race of Scythians was early reduced by the Âryans, whilst the more distant Drâvidians were enjoying freedom and independence, may have materially altered their original character. It is not therefore so improbable as it might at first sight appear, that after the Drâvidians had been driven across the Vindhyas into the Dekhan by a newer race of Scythians, this new race, conquered in its turn by the Âryans and reduced to a dependent position, soon sank beneath the level of the tribes which it had expelled; whilst the Drâvidians, retaining their independence in the southern forests into which they were driven, and submitting eventually to the Âryans not as conquerors, but as colonists and instructors, gradually rose in the social scale, and formed communities and states in the Dekhan, rivalling those of the Âryans in the north.*

Mr. Curzon (*Journal of Royal Asiatic Society*, vol. 16) recently attempted to meet the difficulty which I have stated by supposing that the Tamilians were never in possession of Ârya-vartta, or Northern India, at all; but that they were connected with the Malay race, and came to Southern India by sea, from the opposite coast of the Bay of Bengal, or from Ceylon. This theory seems, however, perfectly gratuitous; for it has been proved that the languages of the Gônds and Kus are Drâvidian, equally with the Tamil itself; that the Rajmahal is also substantially Drâvidian; and that the Brahui partakes so largely of the same character (not to speak of the language of the Scythic tablets of Behistun), as to establish a connection between the Drâvidians and the ancient races west of the Indus. It has also been shewn that in the time of Ptolemy, when every part of India had long ago been settled and civilised, the Drâvidians were in quiet possession, not only of the south-eastern coast, but of the whole of the Peninsula, up nearly to the mouths of the Ganges.

It is undeniable that immigrations from Ceylon to the southern districts of India have occasionally taken place. The Teers (properly 'Tîvâr,' *islanders*) and the Iḷavars, 'Singhalese,' (from 'Iḷam,' *Ceylon*, a word which has been corrupted from the Sanscrit 'Si*m*halam,' or rather from the Pali 'Sihalam,' by the omission of the initial 's'), both of them Travancore castes, are certainly immigrants from Ceylon; but these and similar immigrants are not to be considered as Singhalese, in the proper sense of the term, but as offshoots from the Tamilian population of the northern part of the island. They were the partial reflux of the tide which peopled the northern and western parts of Ceylon with Tamilians. Bands of marauding Tamilians ('Sollies,' 'Pandis,' and other 'Damilos,' *i. e*, Chôlas, Pândiyas, and other

* 'Dekhan' is a corruption of the Sanscrit 'dakshiṇa,' *the south*, literally *the right* ('*dexter*'), an appellation which took its rise from the circumstance that the Brahman in determining the position of objects, looked towards the East, which he called 'pûrva,' *the opposite region*, when whatever lay to the southward was to the right. The South, as the region of freedom, safety, and peace, was to the primitive Drâvidian what the East was to the Brahman. He called it 'ten,' of which one meaning in Tamil is *opposite*, another, *sweet*: whence also 'tennei' is the Tamil name of the cocoa-nut, literally *the sweet nut*; whilst the North was 'vaḍa' (the north-wind 'vâḍei), which is probably connected with 'vâḍ-u,' *to wither*,—the north wind being regarded by Tamilians with as much dread as the south wind (mythologically the car of Kâma, the Indian Cupid) was associated with the idea of everything that was agreeable. Referring to the physical configuration of the Carnatic, the Drâvidians called the East *downward*; the West, the region of the Ghauts, *upward*.

Tamilians) frequently invaded Ceylon, as we are informed by the Mahâ-wanso, both before and subsequently to the Christian era. On several occasions they acquired the supreme power, and at length they permanently occupied the northern provinces of the island. There is no relation, however, between the Singhalese language—the language of the Singhalese, properly so called, who were Buddhists and colonists from Magadhâ or Behâr—and the language of the Tamilians; nor is there any reason for supposing that the natural course of emigration (viz., from the mainland to the island) was ever inverted to such a degree as to justify the supposition that the whole mass of the Drâvidians entered India from Ceylon.

Original Use and Progressive Extension of the Term 'Sûdra.'

The term 'Sûdra,' which is now the common appellation of the mass of the inhabitants of India, whether Gaudians or Drâvidians, seems originally to have been the name of a tribe dwelling near the Indus. Lassen recognises their name in that of the town Σύδρος on the Lower Indus; and especially in that of the nations of the Σύδροι in Northern Arachosia. He supposes them to have been, with the Abhiras and Nishâdas, a black, long-haired race of aborigines, not originally a component part of the Âryan race, but brought under its influence by conquest; and that it was in consequence of the Sûdras having been the first tribe that was reduced by the Aryans to a dependent condition, that the name 'Sûdra' was afterwards, on the conquest of the aborigines in the interior part of the country, extended to all the servile classes. Whatever may have been the origin of the name 'Sûdra,' it cannot be doubted that it was extended in course of time to all who occupied or were reduced to a dependent condition; whilst the name 'Mlêchcha' continued to be the appellation of the unsubdued, Un-Âryanised tribes.

Most writers on this subject, including Lassen and Max Müller, suppose that the whole of the Sûdras, or primitive, servile classes of Northern India, to whom this name was progressively applied, belonged to a different race from their Âryan conquerors. Whilst I assent to every other part of the supposition, I am unable to assent to this. It seems to me to be probable that a considerable proportion of the slaves, servants, dependents, or followers, of the high-caste Âryans belonged to the Âryan race. As the Slavonian serfs are Slavonians, and the Magyar serfs Magyars, there is no improbability in the supposition, that a large number of the Âryan serfs or Sûdras, perhaps the majority, were Âryans; and I cannot on any other supposition account for the fact that nine-tenths of the component materials of the northern vernaculars are Sanscrit.

The supposition of the Âryan origin of a large number of the Sûdras, seems also most in accordance with the very old mythological statement of the origin of the Sûdras from Brahmâ's feet; for though the Brahmans, Kshatriyas, and Vaisyas, the twice-born classes, are represented as springing from more honourable parts of Brahmâ's body, yet the Sûdras are represented to have sprung from the same divinity, though from an ignoble part; whereas the Nishâdas, or barbarian aborigines, are not represented to have sprung from Brahmâ at all, but formed a 'fifth class,' totally unconnected with the others. It appears from this mythological tradition that the Sûdras were supposed in the first ages to differ from the 'twice born' Âryas in rank only, not in blood. I regard as confirmatory of this view the statement of Manu that 'all who become outcasts are called Dasyus, whether they speak the language of the Mlêchchas or that of Âryas:' for in the same manner, all who enjoyed the protection of the Âryas, as their dependents and servants, would naturally receive a common appellation, probably that of Sûdras,—whether, as aborigines, they spoke 'the language of Mlêchchas,' the Scythian vernacular, or whether, as Âryas of an inferior rank in life, they spoke 'the language of Âryas,' a colloquial dialect of the Sanscrit. It is true, as Professor Max Müller says, that the three twice-born castes alone are called Âryas by the Satapatha-Brâhmana of the Rigveda: but as 'the four castes,' including the Sûdras, but excluding the Dasyus and Nishâdas, are distinctly referred to in the most ancient hymns; as outcaste Âryas are styled Dasyus by Manu; and as the higher classes of the Tamilians monopolize the national name in this very manner, and pretend that the lower classes of their race are not Tamilians, I think that we may safely attribute the statement in question to the pride of 'the twice-born.' Even the Vrâtyas, who are distinguished from the Sûdras and are regarded as an inferior class, did not differ from the Brahmans in language, and must, therefore, have been Âryas.

The aboriginal Scythian inhabitants of India seem to have been subdued, and transformed from Mlêchchas into Sûdras, by slow degrees. In the age of Manu, they retained their independence and the appellation of Mlêchchas in Bengal, Orissa, and the Dekhan; but in the earlier period which is referred to in the historic legends of the Maha-bhârata, we find the Mlechchas and Dasyus disputing the possession of Upper India itself with the Âryas. Sâgara, the thirty-fifth king of the Solar dynasty, is related to have laboured in vain to subdue the heterodox aborigines residing on or near his frontier: and in the reign preceding his, in conjunction with certain tribes connected with the Lunar line, those aborigines had succeeded in overrunning his territories.*

The introduction of the Drâvidians within the pale of Hinduism, and the consequent change of their appellation from Mlêchchas to that of Sûdras appears to have originated, not in conquest, but in the peaceable process of colonisation and progressive civilisation. There is no tradition extant of a warlike irruption of the Âryas into Southern India, or of the forcible subjugation of the Drâvidians; though if such an event ever took place, it must have been subsequent to the era of Manu and the Ramâyana, and therefore some remembrance of it would probably have survived. All existing traditions, and the names by which the Brahmanical race is distinguished in Tamil, viz., 'Eiyar,' *instructors, fathers*, and 'Pârppâr,' *overseers*, (probably the ἐπισκοποι of Arrian), tend to show that the Brahmans acquired their ascendency by their intelligence and their administrative skill.

The most adventurous immigrations from Northern India to the Dekhan were those of the offshoots of the Lunar dynasty, a dynasty which originated from the Solar, and whose chief city was Ayôdhyâ, Oude, the traditional starting point of most of their immigrations. The Pândiya kings of Madura were feigned to have sprung from the Lunar line. The title 'Pâṇḍiya,' is supposed to be derived from the

* Sâgara, finding himself unable to extirpate or enslave those heterodox tribes, entered into a compromise with them, by imposing upon them various distinguishing marks; by which, I think, we may understand their obstinate persistence in the use of the distinguishing marks to which they had been accustomed. One of those marks is worthy of notice in an inquiry into the relations of the early Drâvidians. 'The Pâradas,' it is recorded, 'wore their hair long in obedience to his commands.' Professor Wilson observes, with reference to this statement (in his notes on the *Vishnu Purana*), 'What Oriental people wore their hair long, except at the back of the head, is questionable; and the usage would be characteristic rather of the Teutonic and Gothic nations.' The usage referred to is equally characteristic of the Drâvidians, and it is even possible that the Pâradas may have been a Drâvidian tribe. Up to the present day the custom of wearing the hair long, and twisted into a knot at the back of the head, is characteristic of all the inferior castes in the southern provinces of the Tamil country, and also of the shepherds and Maravars. In ancient times this mode of wearing the hair was in use amongst all Drâvidian soldiers; and sculptured representations prove that at a still earlier period it was the general Drâvidian custom. The Kôtas of the Nilgherry Hills wear their hair in the same manner. The Tudas wear their hair long, but without confining it in a knot. Probably it was from the Drâvidian settlers in Ceylon that the Singhalese adopted the same usage; for as early as the third century A.D., Agathemerus, a Greek geographer, describing Ceylon, says, 'the natives cherish their hair as women among us, and twist it round their heads." The wearing of the hair long appears to have been regarded by the early Drâvidians as a distinctive sign of national independence: whilst the shaving of the hair of the head, with the exception of the 'kuḍumi,' or lock at the back of the head, corresponding to the tail of the Chinese, was considered as a sign of Âryanisation, or submission to Âryan customs, and admission within the palo of Âryan protection.

name of the 'Pâṇḍavas' of Northern India, the celebrated combatants in the great war of the Mahâ-bhârata, to whom every Cyclopean work of unknown antiquity is traditionally ascribed. Probably this derivation of the *name* of 'Pâṇḍiyas' is correct; but there is no reason whatever to suppose that the kings of Madura, by whom this name was assumed, sprang from any of the royal dynasties of Northern India. The Âryan immigrants to the South appear to have been Brahmanical priests and instructors, not Kshatriya soldiers; and the kings of the Pândiyas, Chôlas, Calingas, and other Drâvidians, appear to have been simply Drâvidian chieftains, or 'Poligars,' whom their Brahmanical preceptors and spiritual directors dignified with Âryan titles, and taught to imitate and emulate the grandeur and cultivated tastes of the Solar, Lunar, and Agni-kula races of kings.* In our own times we may see the progress of a similar process in Gondwana, where barbarous Gônd chieftains have learned from their Brahman preceptors, not only

* I find that a similar opinion respecting the relation that subsisted between the Âryans and the early Drâvidians, has been expressed by Professor Max Müller (*Report of British Association for* 1847). He says, 'Wholly different from the manner in which the Brahmanical people overcame the north of India, was the way they adopted of taking possession of and settling in the country south of the Vindhya. They did not enter there in crushing masses with the destroying force of arms, but in the more peaceful way of extensive colonisation, under the protection and countenance of the powerful empires in the north.

'Though sometimes engaged in wars with their neighbouring tribes, these colonies generally have not taken an offensive but only a defensive part; and it appears that, after having introduced Brahmanical institutions, laws, and religion, especially along the two coasts of the sea, they did not pretend to impose their language upon the much more numerous inhabitants of the Dekhan, but that they followed the wiser policy of adopting themselves the language of the aboriginal people, and of conveying through its medium their knowledge and instruction to the minds of uncivilised tribes. In this way they refined the rude language of the earlier inhabitants, and brought it to a perfection which rivals even the Sanscrit. By these mutual concessions, a much more favourable assimilation took place between the Arian and aboriginal race; and the south of India became afterwards the last refuge of Brahmanical science, when it was banished from the north by the intolerant Mahommedans. It is interesting and important to observe how the beneficial influence of a higher civilisation may be effectually exercised, without forcing the people to give up their own language and to adopt that of their foreign conquerors, a result by which, if successful, every vital principle of an independent and natural development is necessarily destroyed.'

I cannot see how this statement of the Professor can be reconciled with his identification of the old Drâvidians with the Nishâdas of Northern India. In his more recent *Results of Turanian Researches*, he interprets Siva's triumph over Tripura, and the Garuda's devouring of the Kirâtas, as traditions of the conquest of Nishâda races by the Aryans; and represents the same Nishâdas as retiring before the Âryas to the south of the Vindhyas, broken and scattered in the centre, and violently pressed together even in the south. If the Nishâdas who were thus dealt with had been Drâvidians, I think we should find some distinct notice of this in the Mahâ-bhârata, in which the peaceable, polished Chôlas, Kalingas, Pândiyas, and other Drâvidians of the South, are carefully distinguished from the Nishâdas of various races, whom the old Solar and Lunar kings are represented as subduing in Northern India.

to style themselves Râjâhs, but even to assume the sacred thread of the 'twice-born' Kshatriyas.

The only Drâvidian kings who are commonly believed to have been really Kshatriyas (though with what truth it is now impossible to say), were the kings of the Kêrala dynasty on the Malabar coast; from whom the modern Rajahs of Cochin claim to be descended.

It is proper to notice here that the title 'Sûdra' conveys a higher meaning in Southern than in Northern India. The primitive 'Sûdras' of Northern India were slaves to the Âryans, or in a condition but little superior to that of slaves. They had no property of their own, and no civil rights. In Southern India, on the contrary, it was upon the middle and higher classes of the Drâvidians that the title of 'Sûdra' was imposed; and the classes that appeared to be analogous to the servile Sûdras of Northern India, were not called 'Sûdras,' but 'Pallas,' 'Parias,' &c., names which they still retain. The application of the term 'Sûdra,' to the ancient Drâvidian chieftains, soldiers, and cultivators may prove that the Brahmans, whilst pretending to do them an honour, treated them with contempt; but it does not prove that they had ever been reduced by the Brahmans to a dependent position, or that they ever were slaves, like the Northern Sûdras, to any class of Âryans. The Brahmans, who came in 'peaceably, and obtained the kingdom by flatteries,' may probably have persuaded the Drâvidians, that in calling them Sûdras, they were conferring upon them a title of honour. If so, their policy was perfectly successful; for the title of 'Sûdra' has invariably been regarded by Drâvidians in this light: and hence, whilst in Northern India the Sûdra is a low caste man, in Southern India he ranks next to the Brahman, and the place which he occupies in the social scale is immeasurably superior, not only to that of the Pariars, or agricultural slaves, but also to that of the unenslaved low castes, such as the fishermen, and the cultivators of the cocoa-nut and palmyra palms.

Pre-Âryan Civilisation of the Drâvidians.

Though the Drâvidians were destitute of letters, and unacquainted with the higher arts of life, prior to the arrival of the Brahmans, they do not appear to have been so barbarous and degraded a people as the Purânic legends represent. They are represented to us by the Brahmans as uncouth 'râkshasas,' or giants; as monkeys (by an interesting anticipation of the theory of the author of the *Vestiges of the Natural History of the Creation,* who regards the monkeys of the Dekhan as the progenitors of the human race); or as vile sinners, who ate raw meat and human flesh, and disturbed the contemplations of holy Rishis. Even Hanumân, their king, and Rama's most useful ally, is half-praised, half-ridiculed, as a monkey-god.

This picture may in some few particulars have correctly enough represented the condition of the barbarous Kole, or Gônd tribes who inhabited the Vindyha forests; but it cannot be doubted that the Drâvidians, properly so called, had acquired, at least, the elements of civilisation prior to the arrival amongst them of the Brahmans.

If we eliminate from the Tamil language the whole of its Sanscrit derivatives, the primitive Drâvidian words that remain will furnish us with a faithful picture of the simple, yet not savage, life of the Un-Âryanised Drâvidians. Mr. Curzon holds that there is nothing in the shape of a record of the Tamil mind which can recall to us anything independent of an obvious Sanscrit origin; and that if the contrary supposition were tenable, we ought to find the remains of a literature embodying some record of a religion different from Hinduism. Unequivocal traces of the existence amongst the Un-Âryanised Drâvidians, both ancient and modern, of a religion different from Hinduism, will be pointed out in the Appendix. At present I will merely adduce those records of the primitive Tamil mind, manners, and religion which the ancient vocabularies of the language, when freed from the admixture of Sanscrit, will be found to furnish.

From the evidence of the words in use amongst the early Tamilians, we learn the following items of information. They had 'kings,' who dwelt in 'fortified houses,' and ruled over small 'districts of country:' they were without 'books,' and probably ignorant of written alphabetical characters, but they had 'minstrels,' who recited 'songs' at 'festivals:' they were without hereditary 'priests' and 'idols,' and appear to have had no idea of 'heaven' or 'hell,' of the 'soul' or 'sin;' but they acknowledged the existence of God, whom they styled 'kô,' or *king*—a realistic title which is unknown to orthodox Hinduism. They erected to his honour a 'temple,' which they called 'Kô-il,' *God's-house*; but I cannot find any trace of the 'worship' which they offered to him. The chief, if not the only actual worship which they appear to have practised was that of 'devils,' which they worshipped systematically by 'giving to the devil,' *i.e.* offering bloody sacrifices, and by the performance of frantic 'devil dances.' They were acquainted with all the ordinary metals, with the exception of 'tin' and 'zinc;' with the planets which were ordinarily known to the ancients, with the exception of 'Mercury' and 'Saturn.' They had numerals up to a 'hundred,'—some of them to a 'thousand;' but were ignorant of the higher denominations, a 'lakh' and a 'crore.' They had 'medicines,' but no 'medical science,' and no 'doctors;' 'hamlets' and 'towns,' but no 'cities;' 'canoes,' 'boats,' and even 'ships' (small 'decked' coasting vessels), but no foreign 'commerce;' no acquaintance with any people beyond sea, except in Ceylon, which was then accessible on foot at low water; and no word expressive of the geographical idea of 'island' or 'continent.' They were well acquainted with 'agriculture,' and delighted in 'war.' All the ordinary or necessary arts of life, including 'cotton weaving' and 'dyeing,' existed amongst them, but none of the arts of the higher class. They had no acquaintance with 'painting,' 'sculpture,' or 'architecture;' with 'astronomy,' or even 'astrology;' and were ignorant, not only of every branch of 'philosophy,' but even of 'grammar.' Their uncultivated intellectual condition is especially apparent in words that relate to the operations of the mind. Their only words for the 'mind' were the 'diaphragm' (the 'Φρῆν' of the early Greeks), and 'the inner parts' or 'interior.' They had a word for 'thought;' but no word distinct from this for 'memory,' 'judgment,' or 'conscience,' and no word for 'will.' To express 'the will' they would have been obliged to describe it as, 'that which in the inner parts says, 'I am going to do so and so.'

This brief illustration, from the primitive Tamil vocabulary, of the social condition of the Drâvidians, prior to the arrival of the Brahmans, will suffice to prove that the elements of civilisation already existed amongst them. They had not acquired much more than the elements; and in many things were centuries behind the Brahmans whom they revered as 'instructors,' and obeyed as 'overseers:' but if they had been left altogether to themselves, it is open to dispute whether they would not now be in a much better condition, at least in point of morals, than they are.

The mental culture and the higher civilisation which they derived from the Brahmans, have, I fear, been more than counterbalanced by the fossilising caste rules, the unpractical, pantheistic philosophy, and the cumbersome routine of inane ceremonies, which were introduced amongst them by the guides of their new social state.

The Probable Date of the Âryan Civilisation of the Drâvidians.

It would appear, from the unanimous voice of ancient legends, that the earliest Drâvidian civilisation was that of the Tamilians of the Pândiya kingdom, near the southern extremity of the Peninsula. This civilisation is traditionally, and with much show of reason, attributed to the influence of successive colonies of Brahmans from Upper India, who were probably attracted to the South by the report of the fertility of the rich alluvial plains that were watered by the Câvêri, and other Peninsular rivers; or as the legends relate, by the fame of Râmachandra's exploits, and the sacred celebrity of the emblem of Siva, which Râma discovered and worshipped at Ramisseram, or Râm-îsvaram, a holy place in the island of Paumben, between the mainland and Ceylon. The leader of the first, or most influential colony, is traditionally said to have been Agastya, a personage who is celebrated in Northern India as a holy 'rishi,' or *hermit*, but who is venerated in the South with greater reason as the first teacher of science and literature to the primitive Drâvidian tribes. It is very doubtful whether Agastya (if there ever were such a person) was really the leader of the Brahman immigration: more probably he is to be considered as its mythological embodiment. 'The Vindhya mountains,' it is said, 'prostrated themselves before Agastya;' by which I understand that they presented no obstacle to his resolute, southward progress; for he is said to have penetrated as far south as Cape Comorin. He is called by way of eminence the 'Tamiṛ muni,' or *Tamilian sage;* and is celebrated for the influence which he acquired at the 'court' of Kulasêkhara, according to tradition the first Pandiyan king, and for the numerous elementary treatises which he composed for the enlightenment of his royal disciple; amongst which his arrangement of the grammatical principles of the language has naturally acquired most renown. He is mythologically represented as identical with the star Canopus, the brightest star in the extreme southern sky in India, and is worshipped near Cape Comorin as Agast-îsvara. By the majority of orthodox Hindus he is believed to be still alive, though invisible to ordinary eyes, and to reside somewhere on the fine conical mountain, commonly called 'Agastya's hill,' from which the 'Porunei' or 'Tamraparni,' the sacred river of Tinnevelly, takes its rise.

The age of Agastya, and the date of the commencement of the Brahmanical civilisation of the Tamilians cannot now be determined with certainty; but data exist for making an approximate estimate. It was certainly prior to the Christian era: for then the whole country appears to have been already Brahmanised, and the Pândiya dynasty of kings had become known even in Europe. It was as certainly subsequent to the era of the Râmâyana and Manu: for then the whole

* The proper name of this mountain is 'Podeiyam' or 'Podeiya-mâ-malei,' *the great common mountain,* which has received this name from the circumstance that it is equally conspicuous on the Pândiya or Tinnevelly side of the Ghauts, and on the Chêra or Travancore side.

of the Coromandel coast was still inhabited by 'Mlêchchas,' who 'ate human flesh,' 'consorted with demons,' and 'disturbed the contemplations of holy hermits.' The age of Agastya is undoubtedly to be placed between those two eras. If we be could be sure that the references to the Chôlas, Drâviḍas, Kuntalas, Kêralas, Mushicas, and Karnâṭakas, which are contained in the present text of the Mahâbhârata, formed originally part of that poem, the era of the commencement of Tamilian civilisation, and the date of the Agastyan colony from which it proceeded, might be brought within a still narrower compass, and placed between the age of Manu and that of the Mahâbhârata. The genuineness of those references being as yet doubtful, and the era of Manu (in deference to an allusion to the Chinese, under the name of 'Chînas,' which, like similar allusions to the 'Chînas' and 'Yavanas' in the Mahâ-bhârata, is probably an interpolation) being generally placed I think too low, I am inclined to look to Ceylon for the best means of arriving at an approximate date. The immigration into Ceylon of the colony of Âryans from Magadhâ, probably took place about B.C. 550, or, at least, some time in the course of that century: and I think we may safely argue that the Âryas, or Sanscrit-speaking inhabitants of Northern India, must have become acquainted with, and formed establishments in, the Dekhan and the Coromandel coast, and must have taken some steps towards clearing the Daṇḍa-kâraṇya, or primitive forest of the Peninsula, before they thought of founding a colony in Ceylon. Wijeya, the leader of the expedition into Ceylon, is related in the Mahâ-wanso to have married the daughter of the king of Pândi; and though it may be doubtful enough whether he really did so (for on the same authority we must believe that he married also the queen of the Singhalese demons); this at least is certain, that it was the persuasion of the earliest Singhalese writers, who were, on the whole, the most truthful and accurate of oriental annalists, that the Pândi kingdom of Madura (the first kingdom which was established on Âryan principles in the Peninsula) existed prior to the establishment of the Magadhi rule in the neighbouring island.

Probably, therefore, we shall not greatly err in placing the era of Agastya, or that of the commencement of Tamilian civilisation and literature, in the seventh, or at least in the sixth century, B.C.

Relative Antiquity of Drâvidian Literature.

Notwithstanding the antiquity of Drâvidian civilisation, the antiquity of the oldest Drâvidian literature extant is much inferior to that of the Sanscrit. Indeed it is questionable whether the word 'antiquity' is a suitable one to use respecting the literature of any of the Drâvidian languages.

The earliest writer on Telugu grammar is said to have been a sage called 'Kaṇva,' who lived at the court of Ândhra-râya, the king in whose reign Sanscrit was first introduced into the Telugu country, according to the tradition which was formerly mentioned.

For this tradition there is probably a historical groundwork, the introduction of Sanscrit derivatives being necessarily contemporaneous with the immigration of the Brahmans; and the statement that the first attempt to reduce the grammatical principles of the language to writing proceeded from a Brahman residing at the court of a Telugu prince, is a very reasonable one.

Kaṇva's work, if it ever existed, is now lost; and the oldest extant work on Telugu grammar (which is composed, like all Telugu grammars, in Sanscrit) was written by a Brahman, called Nanniah Bhatta, or Nannappa, who was also the author of the greater part of the Telugu version of the Mahâ-bhârata, which is the oldest extant composition of any extent in Telugu. Nannappa lived in the reign of Vishnu Vardhana, a king of the Calinga branch of the Chalukya family, who reigned at Rajamundry. The reign of this king is placed by Mr. A. D. Campbell about the commencement of the Christian era; but Mr. C. P. Brown, in his Cyclic tables, places it, on better authority, in the beginning of the 12th century, A.D.

With the exception of a few other works, which were composed towards the end of the 12th century, nearly all the Telugu works that are now extant were written in the fourteenth and subsequent centuries, after the establishment of the kingdom of Bijnagar, or Vijaya-nagara; and many of them were written in comparatively recent times.

Though the Telugu literature which is now extant cannot boast of a high antiquity, the language must have been cultivated and polished, and many poems that are now lost must have been written in it, prior to the twelfth century—the date of Nannappa's translation of the Mahâ-bhârata: for as this translation is considered 'the great standard of Telugu poetry,' it cannot be supposed to have sprung into existence all at once, without the preparation of a previous literary culture.

Tamil literature is undoubtedly older than Telugu, though the high antiquity which is ascribed to some portions of it by the Tamilian literati cannot be admitted.

The sage Agastya occupies in Tamil literature a place of still greater eminence and importance than that of Kaṇva in Telugu.

Not only is the formation of the Tamil alphabet attributed to

Agastya, and the first treatise upon Tamil grammar, together with the original settlement of the grammatical principles of the language; but he is also said to have taught the Tamilians the first principles of medicine, of chymistry or alchymy, of architecture, astronomy, and law; and some of the most ancient and admired treatises on all these sciences, as well as many modern ones, are attributed to his pen. It is admitted by Tamilians that his grammar does not now exist; but they suppose him to have been the author of most of the extant treatises on medicine and other sciences which bear his name.

Though the literary cultivation of the Tamil language may have commenced, as the Tamilians believe, in the age of Agastya (premising however, that it is undecided whether he was a real personage, or is only to be regarded as the mythological representative of a class or period), I feel quite certain that none of the works which are commonly ascribed to Agastya, were written at so early an age. Probably there is not any one of them older than the tenth century, A.D.

Of the works which are attributed to him, those which advocate the system of the 'Siddhas' (Tamulice 'Sittar'), or the 'Siddhantam,' a mystical compound of alchymy and quietism, with a tinge of Christianity, were certainly written after the arrival of Europeans in India: and Agastya's name appears to have been used by the writers, as had been done by many successions of authors before, for the purpose of gaining the ear of the people for whose use the books were composed.

We cannot doubt that the substance of the following stanza, which is contained in the 'Njâna nûRu,' or *centum of wisdom*, a small poem attributed to Agastya, has been borrowed from statements of Christianity, notwithstanding that Christianity is not directly named in it, or in any other work of this class:—

> 'Worship thou the Light of the Universe; who is One;
> Who made the world in a moment, and placed good men in it;
> Who afterwards himself dawned upon the earth as a Guru;
> Who, without wife or family, as a hermit performed austerities;
> Who appointing loving sages (siddhas) to succeed him,
> Departed again into heaven:—worship Him.'

It is a striking illustration of the uncritical structure of the Hindu mind, that this stanza is supposed, even by Tamil literati, to have been written by Agastya himself many thousands of years ago. Heathens endeavour to give it a heathen meaning, and Hindu Christians regard it as a kind of prophecy.

Though there is not a single archaism in it; though it is written not only in the modern dialect, but in a vulgar, colloquial idiom, abounding in solecisms; neither party entertains any doubt of its antiquity.

Leaving out of account various isolated stanzas, of high but unknown antiquity, which are quoted as examples in the grammatical and rhetorical works, the oldest Tamil works now extant are those which were written, or are claimed to have been written, by the Jainas, or which date from the era of the literary activity of the Jaina sect. The Jainas of the old Pândiya country were animated by a national and anti-Brahmanical feeling of peculiar strength; and it is chiefly to them that Tamil is indebted for its high culture and its comparative independence of the Sanscrit. The Saiva and Vaishnava writers of a later period, especially the Saivas, imbibed much of the enthusiasm for Tamilic purity and literary independence, by which the Jainas were distinguished: in consequence of which, though Tamil literature, as a whole, will not bear a comparison with Sanscrit literature, as a whole, it is the only vernacular literature in India which has not been contented with imitating the Sanscrit, but has honourably attempted to emulate and outshine it. In one department, at least, that of ethical epigrams, it is generally maintained, and I think must be admitted, that the Sanscrit has been outdone by the Tamil.

The Jaina period extended probably from the eighth or ninth century, A.D., to the twelfth or thirteenth. In the reign of Sundara Pândiya, which appears to synchronize with Marco Polo's visit to India, the adherents of the religious system of the Jainas, were finally expelled from the Pândiya country: consequently, all Tamil works which advocate or avow that system must have been written before the middle of the thirteenth century, A.D., and probably before the decadence of Jaina influence in the twelfth.

It seems reasonable to conclude that the period in which Jaina literature chiefly flourished was that which preceded the enthusiastic propagation of the Vedantic doctrines of Sankara Âchârya. If this conclusion is correct, the most celebrated poem which was written by an avowedly Jaina author—the 'Chintâmaṇi,' a brilliant romantic epic, containing 15,000 lines—cannot be placed later than the tenth century.

The 'Nan-nûl,' a High Tamil grammar of great excellence, and the poetical vocabularies, which were all written by Jaina scholars, must be placed a little later than the 'Chintâmaṇi;' but yet anterior to the Chôla conquest of the Pândiya country, which took place in the eleventh century.

The 'Tol-kâppiyam,' or *ancient composition*, the oldest extant

Tamil grammar, is probably to be placed at the very commencement of the Jaina period. Though written by a Saiva, its Saivism is not that of the mystical school of Sankara; and in the chapters which are extant (for much of it has been lost), native grammarians have noticed the existence of various grammatical forms which are considered to be archaic. It is traditionally asserted that the author of this treatise, who is styled technically 'Tolkâppiyanâr,' was a disciple of Agastya himself, and that he embodied in his work the substance of Agastya's grammatical elements. This tradition is on a par with that which ascribes so many anonymous works to Agastya: nevertheless, if any relics of poems of the first age of Tamil literature still survive, they are to be found amongst the poetical quotations which are contained in this and similar works, and in commentaries which have been written upon them. Some of those quotations are probably the oldest specimens of the poetical style that are now extant.

The 'Kuṟaḷ' of Tiruvaḷḷuvar, a work consisting of 1330 distichs, or poetical aphorisms, on almost every subject connected with morals and political economy, and which is regarded by all Tamilians (and perhaps justly) as the finest composition of which the Tamil can boast, appears to be not only the best but the oldest Tamil work of any extent which is now in existence.

I think we should not be warranted in placing the date of the Kuṟal later than the ninth century, A.D.

The reasons which induce me to assign to it so high an antiquity are as follows:—

(1.) The Kuṟaḷ contains no trace of the distinctive doctrines of Sankara Âchârya. It teaches the old Sânkhya philosophy, but ignores Sankara's additions and developments; and would therefore appear to have been written before the school of Sankara had risen to notice, if not before Sankara himself, who lived not later than the ninth century.

(2.) There is no trace in the Kuṟaḷ of the mysticism of the modern Purânic system; of *Bhakti*, or exclusive, enthusiastic faith in any one deity of the Hindu Pantheon; of exclusive attachment to any of the sects into which Hinduism has been divided since the era of Sankara; or even of acquaintance with the existence of any such sects. The work appears to have been written before Saivism and Vaishnavism had been transformed from rival schools into rival sects; before the Purânas, as they now stand, had become the text books of Hindu theology; and whilst the theosophy of the early Vedânta and the mythology of the Mahâ-bhârata comprised the entire creed of the majority of Hindus.

(3.) The author of the Kuṛaḷ is claimed with nearly equal reason by Saivas, Vaishnavas, and Jainas. On the whole the arguments of the Jainas appear to me to preponderate, especially that which appeals to the Jaina *tone* that pervades the ethical part of the work:—*e.g.*, scrupulous abstinence from the destruction of life is frequently declared to be the chiefest excellence of the true ascetic. Nevertheless, from the indistinctness and undeveloped character of the Jaina element which is contained in it, it seems probable that in Tiruvaḷḷuvar's age Jainism was rather an esoteric ethical school, than an independent objective system of religion, and was only in the process of development out of the older Hinduism. This would carry back the date of the Kuṛaḷ to the eighth or ninth century.

(4.) It is the concurrent voice of various traditions that Tiruvaḷḷuvar lived before the dissolution of the Madura *Sangaṃ*; *i. e.*, the college of literati, or board of literary examiners, at Madura. It is asserted that the Kuṛaḷ was the very last work which was presented for the approval of that body; and that it was in consequence of their rejection of the Kuṛaḷ (on account of the low caste of its author) that the college ceased to exist. If any weight is to be attached to this tradition, which has the appearance of verisimilitude, the Kuṛaḷ must be the oldest Tamil composition of any extent that is now extant: for every composition which is attributed (with any show of reason) to the literati who constituted that college, who were in any way connected with it, or who lived prior to the abolition of it (some of whom were the traditional fathers of Tamil literature), has long ago perished.

(5.) The Kuṛaḷ is referred to and quoted in grammars and prosodies which were probably written in the tenth century.

For these reasons I think the Kuṛaḷ should be placed in the eighth or ninth century at least. It is admitted, however, as in almost every similar inquiry pertaining to Indian literature, that the reasons for this conclusion are rather negative than positive.

Certain poetical compositions are attributed to Auveiyâr, '*the Matron*,' a reputed sister of Tiruvaḷḷuvar, of which some, at least, do not belong to so early a period.

It is a remarkable circumstance that the author of the Kuṛaḷ is represented to have been a Pariar. A later legend represents him to have been the offspring of a Brahman father by a Pariar mother. His real name is unknown. The Vaḷḷuvars are the priestly division of the Pariars, and the author of the Kuṛaḷ is known only as 'Tiruvaḷḷuvar,' *the sacred Valluvan*, or Pariar priest. It is a still more remarkable circumstance that the poetical compositions which are now referred to (small works of universal use and popularity in the Tamil country, and of considerable merit) are ascribed to a sister of Tiruvaḷḷuvar, a Pariar woman! Auveyâr's real name, like that of her brother, is unknown,—'Auvei,' or 'Auveiyâr,' signifying *a mother, a venerable matron.*

The brief verses (each commencing with a consecutive letter of the Tamil alphabet) which are ascribed to Auveiyâr, appear to be of considerable antiquity: but the Advaita work which is called 'Auveiyâr's Kuṛaḷ' was written subsequently to the arrival of the Mahommedans in Southern India; and the collection of moral epigrams (most of them possessed of real poetic merit) which is called the 'Mûdurei,' or *proverbial wisdom,* was written after the arrival of Europeans, perhaps after the arrival even of the English.

The proof of the modern origin of the Mûdurei is contained in the following simile:—'As the turkey that had seen the forest peacock dance, fancied himself also to be a peacock, and spread his ugly wings and strutted, so is the poetry which is recited by a conceited dunce.'

As it is certain that the turkey is an American bird, which was brought to Europe from America, and introduced into India from Europe, there cannot be any doubt of the late origin of the Mûdurei, if this stanza was always an integral portion of it, as it is represented to have been. When I have mentioned this anachronism to native scholars, and have called their attention to the circumstance that the Tamil word for 'turkey' (like the words denoting 'tobacco,' 'potato,' &c.), is not an original root, but a descriptive compound, signifying 'the heavenly fowl,' *i. e.,* 'the great fowl,' they have courageously maintained that the turkey was always found in India.

The date which is commonly attributed to the Tamil translation, or rather the Tamil imitation, of the Ramâyana, a highly finished and very popular work, is considerably too high. In a stanza which is prefixed to the work, and which is always believed to have been written by the author himself, it is related that it was finished in the year of the Sâlivâhana era corresponding to A. D. 733. This date has been accepted as genuine, not only by natives, but by those few European scholars who have turned their attention to matters of this kind. If it were genuine, the Tamil version of the Râmâyana would be the oldest Tamil composition which is now extant—a supposition to which the internal evidence of style is opposed; and the author, Kamban (so called from 'Kamba nâḍu,' a district in the Tanjore country, to which he belonged), would claim to be regarded as the father of Tamil poetry.

This date, though it is the only one with which I am acquainted in the whole range of Tamil literature, is I fear a surreptitious addition to Kamban's poem, which was prefixed to it by some admiring editor, for the purpose of giving it a higher antiquity than it can justly claim.

It is generally stated that Kamban finished his poem in the reign of Kulôtunga Chôla: and as certain poetical riddles, purporting to have been given him by Kulôtunga Chôla to solve, have come down to the present time, there seems to be no reason to doubt the propriety of placing him in the reign of that king. Mr. Taylor, in his analysis of the MacKenzie MSS., mentions a tradition that Kamban presented his poem to Râjêndra Chôla. As Râjêndra, Kulôtunga's father, was the Augustus of the Chôla line, it may be supposed that the more celebrated name crept into the story, instead of the less celebrated. Mr. Taylor represents Râjêndra as Kulôtunga's father, not his son: but in an inscription in my possession procured from Kôttâr, in South Travancore, and which was written during the period of the occupation of the Pândiya country by the Chôlas, it is stated that the temple on which the inscription is cut was 'erected by Kulôtunga Chôla to the honour of the divinity of Rajêndra Chol-îsvara,' *i. e.*, to Râjendra Chôla, 'deified,' or considered as identified with Siva, after his death. I therefore conclude that Kulôtunga was Râjêndra's son, not his father. It makes little difference, however, whether he were father or son: for Kamban may be supposed to have lived in both reigns, and a single reign is of no importance to my present argument. The other premiss of my argument is founded upon the evidence of an inscription which is found on the walls of an old temple at Cape Comorin. That inscription is dated in the reign of Râjêndra Chôla, and celebrates a victory gained by Râjêndra over Âhava Malla (a Jaina king, of the Chalukya race), on the banks of the Tunga-bhadra. The date of the inscription is in the two hundredth year of the Quilon era (a popular local era), answering to 1025, A. D. Mr. Walter Elliot's inscriptions, found in the old Chalukya country, place Âhava Malla's battle with Râjêndra Chôla a little later than this, but in the same century; and they also claim the victory not for the Chôla, but for the Chalukya king. This discrepancy, however, is not of any importance: for it is clear, from both sets of inscriptions, that Râjêndra Chôla lived about the beginning of the eleventh century, and Kulôtunga Chôla about the middle of it; and, in consequence, it appears to be certain that the publication of Kamban's Râmâyana, which professes to have been in A.D. 733, has intentionally and mendaciously been ante-dated three hundred years.

This is not the proper place for attempting to furnish the reader with an estimate of the intrinsic value of Drâvidian poetry. Whilst an elevated thought, a natural, expressive description, a pithy, sententious maxim, or a striking comparison, may sometimes be met with, unfortunately elegance of style, or an affected, obscure brevity, has always been preferred to strength and truthfulness, and poetic fire has been quenched in an ocean of conceits.

Nothing can exceed the refined elegance and 'linked sweetness' of many Telugu and Tamil poems; but a lack of heart and purpose, and a substitution of sound for sense, more or less characterise them all: and hence, whilst an anthology composed of well-selected extracts would please and surprise the English reader, every attempt to translate any Tamil or Telugu poem *in extenso* into English, has proved to be a failure.

To these causes of inferiority must be added a slavery to custom and precedent at least equal to what we meet with in the later Sanscrit. Literature could never flourish where the following distich (contained in the 'Nan-nûl,' or classical Tamil grammar) was accepted as a settled principle :—

'On whatsoever subjects, in whatsoever expressions, with whatsoever arrangement,
Classical writers have written, so to write is denoted *propriety of style*.'*

For the last hundred and fifty years the Drâvidian mind appears to have sunk into a state of lethargy,—partly in consequence of the discouraging effect of foreign domination, but chiefly through the natural tendency to decay and death which is inherent in a system of slavery to the authority of great names.

With the exception of a small ethical poem, called the 'Nîti-neRi-viḷakkam,' the only Tamil poems or treatises of any real value which have been written within the period mentioned, have been composed

* It is deserving of notice that alliteration is of the essence of Drâvidian poetry, as of Welsh; and that the Drâvidians have as just a claim as the Welsh to the credit of the invention of rhyme. The rhyme of modern European poetry is supposed to have had a Welsh or Celtic origin; but Drâvidian rhyme was necessarily invented by Drâvidians. The chief peculiarity of Drâvidian rhyme consists in its seat being, not at the end of the line, but at the beginning—a natural result of its origin in a love of alliteration. The rule in each Drâvidian dialect is that the consonant which intervenes between the first two vowels in a line is the seat of *rhyme*. A single Tamil illustration must suffice:—

sîrei (t)têdil,
ôrei (t)têḍu.—AUVEI.

'If you seek for prosperity,
Seek for a plough.'

The agreement of those two consonants constitutes the minimum of rhyme which is admissible: but often the entire first foot of one line rhymes with the same foot in the second; sometimes the second feet in each line also rhyme; and the rhyme is sometimes taken up again further on in the verse, according to fixed laws in each variety of metre.

by European missionaries. At the head of compositions of this class, and high in the list of Tamil classics, stands the 'Têm-bâ-vaṇi,' of Father Beschi. This long and highly elaborated scriptural epic possesses great poetical merit, and exhibits an astonishing command of the resources of the language: but unfortunately it is tinged with the fault of too close an adherence to the manner and style of 'the ancients,' and is still more seriously marred by the error of endeavour-to Hinduize the facts and narratives of Holy Scriptnre, and even Scripture geography, for the purpose of pleasing the Hindu taste.

Now that native education has commenced to make real progress, and the advantages of European knowledge, European civilisation, and European Christianity are becoming known and felt by so many of the Hindus themselves, it may be expected that the Drâvidian mind will ere long be roused from its lethargy, and stimulated to enter upon a new and brighter career.

If the national mind and heart were stirred to so great a degree a thousand years ago by the diffusion of Jainism, and some centuries later by the dissemination of the Saiva and Vaishnava doctrines, it is reasonable to expect still more important results from the propagation of the grand and soul-stirring truths of Christianity, and from the contact of the minds of the youth with the ever-progressive literature and science of the Christian nations of the West.

It is a great and peculiar advantage of the English and vernacular education which so many Hindus are now receiving from European missionaries and from Government teachers, that it is communicated to all who wish to receive it, without distinction of caste. In former ages the education of the lower castes and classes was either prohibited or seduously discouraged, and female education was generally regarded as disgraceful; but now the youth of the lower classes, of both sexes, are generally admitted to the same educational advantages as those that are enjoyed by the higher castes. The hitherto uncultivated minds of the lower and far most numerous classes of the Hindu community, are now for the first time in history brought within the range of humanising and elevating influences. A virgin soil is now for the first time being ploughed, turned up to the air and light, and sown with the seed of life; and in process of time we may reasonably expect to reap a rich crop of intellectual and moral results.

In the Appendix I have endeavoured to answer the question, 'are the Pariahs and the Tudas Drâvidians?' I have also subjoined some remarks 'on the Drâvidian physical type,' and 'on the religion of the ancient Drâvidian tribes.'

COMPARATIVE GRAMMAR.

NOTE.

All foreign words, to whatever family of languages they may belong, are represented in this work in the Roman character, for the double purpose of preventing unnecessary expense and trouble, and of facilitating comparison.

Long vowels are invariably marked thus,—'â:' when no such accent is placed over a vowel, it is intended that it should be pronounced short.

All vowels are pronounced in the Continental manner.

The 'cerebral' consonants are denoted by a subscribed dot, *e.g.*, 'ṭ, ḍ, ṇ:' the peculiar vocalic 'r,' and the surd 'l,' of the South-Indian languages are denoted in a similar manner, *e.g.*, 'ṛ, ḷ:' the obscure, inorganic nasal 'n,' or 'm,' is italicized, *e.g.*, '*n*,' or '*m*:' and the hard, rough 'r,' is represented by a capital 'R.'

The dental 'd,' in Tamil, and the corresponding 't,' in Malayâlam, are pronounced in the middle of a word, or between two vowels, like the English 'th,' in *than*; and in Telugu, 'j' and 'ch,' when followed by certain vowels, are pronounced like 'dz' and 'ts:' but as these are merely peculiarities of *pronunciation*, and one consonant is not exchanged for another, no change has been made in the characters by which those sounds are represented.

In colloquial Telugu, a 'y' euphonic is generally written, as well as pronounced, before 'i' and 'e;' and a similar 'v' before 'o:' but as this is merely a colloquial corruption, and one which tends to hinder comparison with other dialects, all such words will be written without the 'y' or 'v,' and it will be left to the reader to pronounce them as usage requires. This is the rule in Tamil, in which 'evan,' *who?* is always pronounced, but never written, 'yevan.'

SECTION I.

SOUNDS.

It will be my endeavour in this section to elucidate the laws of sound by which the Drâvidian languages are characterized, and which contribute to determine the question of their affiliation. Special notice will be taken of those regular interchanges of sound in the different dialects which enable us to identify words under the various shapes that they assume, and to which it will frequently be necessary to allude in the subsequent sections of this work.

Drâvidian Alphabets.—Before entering on the examination of the Drâvidian sounds, it is desirable to make some preliminary observations on the alphabets of the Drâvidian languages.

There are three different Drâvidian alphabets at present in use, viz., the Tamil, the Malayâlam, and the Telugu-Canarese. I class the Telugu and the Canarese characters together, as constituting but one alphabet; for though there are differences between them, those differences are few and unimportant. The Tuḷu is ordinarily written in the Malayâla character: the Ku grammar of which I have made use, is written in the characters of the Uriya—characters which are much less appropriate than those of the Telugu would have been, for expressing the Ku sounds. The other uncultivated dialects of this family have hitherto been content to have their sounds expressed in the Roman character.

The three Drâvidian alphabets which have been mentioned above, viz., the Tamil, the Malayâlam, and the Telugu-Canarese, together with their older but now obsolete shapes, and the 'Grantham,' or character in which Sanscrit is written in the Tamil country, have all been derived, I conceive, from the early Dêva-nâgari, or from the still earlier characters that are contained in the cave inscriptions—characters which have been altered and disguised by natural and local influences, and especially by the custom, universal in the Dekhan, of writing on the leaf of the palmyra palm with an iron stylus.

It was supposed by Mr. Ellis, and the supposition has gained currency, that before the immigration of the Brahmans into the Tamil country, the ancient Tamilians were acquainted with the art of writing; that the Brahmans recombined the Tamil characters which they found in use, adding a few which were necessary for the expression of sounds peculiar to the Sanscrit; and that from this amalgamation, which they called 'Grantham,' or *the book*, the existing Tamil characters have been derived. There cannot be any doubt of the derivation of the Tamil character from the Grantham: for some characters are evidently identical with Grantham letters which are still in use; others with more ancient forms of the Grantham: but the other part of the hypothesis, viz., the existence of a Pre-Sanscrit Tamil character out of which the Grantham itself was developed, is very doubtful; and though it is true that there is a native Tamil word which signifies 'a letter;' yet there is no tradition extant of the eixstence of Tamil characters older than those which the first Brahman immigrants introduced. The Indian characters referred to by Iambulus, as quoted by Prinsep, evidently differed widely from the Tamil, and appear to have been identical with, or allied to, 'the cave character;' and the character called Haḷa Kannaḍa, or Old Canarese, and the various characters in which Tamil is found to be written in old inscriptions, are plainly founded on the basis of an alphabetical system which was originally intended for the use of the Sanscrit.

The modern Telugu-Canarese differs considerably from the modern Tamil, and departs more widely than the Tamil from the Dêva-nâgari type; but there is a marked resemblance between many of the Telugu-Canarese characters and the corresponding characters that are found in early Tamil inscriptions, such as the 'Sâsanas,' or royal grants, in the possession of the Jews of Cochin.* The modern Malayâla character is manifestly derived from the Tamilian Grantham. Thus, there is reason to conclude that all the alphabetical characters which are used or known in Southern India have a common origin;

* The Cochin inscriptions have been published and interpreted by the Rev. Dr. Gundert, in the *Journal of the Madras Literary Society*. They are written in the Tamil language, though in an idiom which is tinged with the peculiarities of the Malayâlam. The character in which they are written, was once supposed to be peculiar to the Malayâla country: but I have in my possession many fac similes of inscriptions in the same character, which were obtained in various districts of the Southern Tamil country, or Pândiyan kingdom; and it would appear to have been the character which was most generally used at an early period all over the South.

and that their origin is the same as that of all the existing alphabets of Northern India, namely, the system of characters in which Sanscrit was written by the ancient Brahmans.

The difference between the northern and the southern alphabets arises from the antiquity of the literary cultivation of the southern languages, as compared with the northern. The southern languages commenced to be cultivated in that early period when the cave character was used: the northern vernaculars were not cultivated till after the cave character had become obsolete, and had been superseded by the later Dêva-nâgari.

The Telugu and the Canarese alphabets correspond to the Dêva-nâgari in power and arrangement. The only difference is that a short 'e' and 'o,' and a hard 'r' which is unknown to the Sanscrit, are contained in those alphabets, together with a surd 'ḷ,' which is not used in the modern Sanscrit, but is found in the Sanscrit of the Vêdas, as well as in the Drâvidian languages.

In other respects the characters of those alphabets are convertible equivalents of the Dêva-nâgari. The Malayâla alphabet generally agrees with the Telugu-Canarese: it differs from them in having the vocalic 'ṛ,' of the Tamil, in addition to the other characters mentioned above; and in having only one character for long and short 'e,' and another for long and short 'o.' The aspirated letters and sibilants which all those alphabets have borrowed from the Sanscrit, are seldom used except in pronouncing and writing Sanscrit derivatives.

Those letters are not really required for native Drâvidian purposes; though, through the prevalence of Sanscrit influences, they have acquired a place in the pronunciation of a few words which are not derived from the Sanscrit.

The letters 'ch' and 'j,' are pronounced in Telugu in certain situations 'ts' and 'dj:' but no additional characters are employed to represent those sounds.

The Tamil alphabet differs more widely than the Malayâlam, or the Telugu-Canarese, from the arrangement of the Dêva-nâgari. The grammar of the Tamil language having, to a considerable degree, been systematised and refined independently of Sanscrit influences, and Sanscrit modes of pronunciation being almost unknown to Tamilians, the phonetic system of the Tamil demanded, and has secured for itself, a faithful expression in the Tamil alphabet. The materials of that alphabet are wholly, or in the main, Old Sanscrit; but the use which is made of those materials is Tamilian.

The following are the principal peculiarities of the Tamil alphabet,

In common with the Telugu and Canarese alphabets, the Tamil

alphabet possesses separate characters for long and short 'e,' and for long and short 'o.' Formerly it had but one character for the long and the short sounds of those vowels; and it is believed that the marks by which the long are now distinguished from the short were first introduced by Beschi. The Tamil has no characters corresponding to the liquid semi-vowels 'ri' and 'li,' which are classed amongst vowels by Sanscrit grammarians; and it has not adopted the 'anusvâra,' or obscure nasal of the Sanscrit. Much use is made of nasals in Tamil: but those nasals are firm, decided sounds, not 'echoes,' and are classed amongst consonants by native grammarians. 'm' is the natural sound of the Tamil nasal, and this sound is uniformly retained at the end of words and before labials: when followed by a guttural, 'm' is changed into 'ng,' the nasal of the guttural row of consonants; and it is changed in a similar manner into 'ñj,' 'ṇ,' or 'n,' according as it is followed by a palatal, a cerebral, or a dental. The Tamil alphabet has nothing to correspond with the 'half anuswâra' of the Telugu—a character and sound which is peculiar to that language: nevertheless, the tendency to euphonize hard consonants by prefixing and combining nasals, from which the 'half anuswâra' has arisen, is in full operation in Tamil.

The Tamil makes no use whatever of aspirates, and has not borrowed any of the aspirated consonants of the Sanscrit, nor even the isolated aspirate 'h.'

In arranging the consonants, the Tamil alphabet follows the Dêva-nâgari in respect of the 'vargas,' or rows, in which the Sanscrit consonants are classified and arranged. It adopts, however, only the first and the last consonant of each row, omitting altogether the intermediate letters. In the first or guttural row, the Tamil alphabet adopts 'k,' and its corresponding nasal 'ng,' omitting 'kh,' 'g,' and 'gh:' in the second or palatal row it adopts 'ch,' and its corresponding nasal 'nj,' omitting 'chh,' 'j,' and 'jh:' in the third or cerebral row it adopts 'ṭ,' and its nasal 'ṇ,' omitting 'ṭh,' 'ḍ,' and 'ḍh:' in the fourth or dental row it adopts 't,' and its nasal 'n,' omitting 'th,' 'd,' and 'dh:' in the fifth or labial row it adopts 'p,' and its nasal 'm,' omitting 'ph,' 'b,' and 'bh.'

Thus, the Tamil alphabet omits not only all the aspirated consonants of the Dêva-nâgari, but also all its soft or sonant letters. The *sounds* which are represented by the sonants of the Dêva-nâgari, are as commonly used in Tamil as in Sanscrit: but in accordance with a peculiar law of sound (to be explained hereafter) which requires the same letter to be pronounced as a surd in one position and as a sonant in another, the Tamil uses one and the same *character* for representing both sounds; and the character which has been adopted for this purpose by the Tamil alphabet, is that which corresponds to the first consonant, viz., the tenuis or surd, in each of the Dêva-nâgari 'vargas.'

In the 'varga' of the semi-vowels the Tamil follows the Dêva-nâgari; but it subjoins to that 'varga' a row of four letters which are not contained in the Déva-nâgari. Those letters are a deep liquid 'r,' which will always be represented in this work as 'ṛ;' a harsh, rough 'r,' which will be represented as 'R; 'ḷ,' a peculiar surd 'l,' with a mixture of 'ṛ;' and 'n,' a letter to which it is unnecessary to affix any distinctive mark, the difference between it and the 'n' of the dental 'varga' being one of form rather than of sound. This peculiar 'n' is that which is invariably used as a final; and it is also much used in combination with 'R,' to represent the peculiar Tamil sound of 'ndr.'

The Tamil alphabet is not only destitute of aspirated consonants, but it is also without the separate aspirate 'h,' which has a place in the alphabets of so many other languages. It is destitute also of the Sanscrit sibilants 'ś,' 'ṣh,' and 's.' The second and third of these sibilants are occasionally used in pronouncing and writing Sanscrit derivatives; but these letters are never found in the ancient dialect of the Tamil, or in the classics, nor have they a place in the Tamil alphabet: when used, they are borrowed from the Grantham, from which a few other letters also are occasionally borrowed to express Sanscrit sounds. The first of the three Sanscrit characters referred to above, namely, 'the ś of ´iva,' is never used at all in pure Tamil: the Tamil palatal or semi-sibilant which corresponds to the Sanscrit 'ch,' and which is pronounced as a soft 'ś' or 'sh,' when single, and as 'ch,' when doubled, is the letter which is used instead.

The following comparative view of the 'Dêva-nâgari' and the Tamil alphabets exhibits the relation which the one bears to the other.

VOWELS.

Sanscrit	a, â · i, î : u, û : ri, rî : lrî : — ê : aî : — ô : aû : *n* : ah
Tamil	a, â : i, î : u, û : — —: — : e, ê : eî : o, ô : aû : —: —

CONSONANTS.

Gutturals,	Sans.	k,	kh	:	g,	gh	:	ng
Ditto,	Tamil	k,	—	:	—	—	·	ng
Palatals,	Sans.	ch,	chh	:	j,	jh	·	ñj
Ditto,	Tamil	ch,	—	·	—	—	:	ñj
Cerebrals,	Sans.	ṭ,	ṭh	:	ḍ,	ḍh	.	ṇ
Ditto,	Tamil	ṭ,	—	:	—	—	:	ṇ
Dental,	Sans.	t,	th	·	d,	dh	:	n
Ditto,	Tamil	t,	—	:	—	—	:	n
Labials,	Sans.	p,	ph	:	b,	bh	·	m
Ditto,	Tamil	p,	—	.	—	—	:	m

CONSONANTS.

Semi-vowels,	Sans.	y,	ṛ,	l,	v			
Ditto,	Tamil	y,	r,	l,	v;	ṟ,	ḻ,	ʀ
Sibilants and aspirate,								
	Sans.	ś,	ṣh,	s,	h			
	Tamil	—	—	—	—			

DRÂVIDIAN SYSTEM OF SOUNDS.—We now proceed to inquire into the sounds of the Drâvidian letters, and the laws of sound, or phonetic system, of this family of languages; and in doing so, it will be found advantageous to adhere to the order and arrangement of the 'Dêva-nâgari' alphabet. It is not my object to explain in detail the pronunciation of each letter: but such observations will be made on each vowel and consonant in succession as seem likely to throw light on the principles and distinctive character of the Drâvidian system of sounds. Tamil grammarians designate vowels by a beautiful metaphor, as 'uyir,' or the *life* of a word; consonants as 'meў,' or the *body*; and the junction of a vowel and consonant as 'uyir meў,' or an *animated body*.

I. **Vowels.**—(1.) 'ă' and 'â.' The sound of these vowels in the Drâvidian languages corresponds to their sound in Sanscrit. In Tamil, 'ă' is the heaviest of all the simple vowels, and therefore the most liable to change, especially at the end of words. In the other dialects it maintains its place more firmly; but even in them it is ordinarily strengthened at the end of words by the addition of the euphonic syllable 'vu,' consisting of the enunciative vowel 'u,' and the euphonic formative 'v.' 'ă' has almost entirely disappeared from the end of nouns in Tamil, and has been succeeded by 'u' or 'ei.' This rule holds universally with respect to nouns singular. When the Greeks visited India, 'ûru,' *a town*, appears to have been invariably pronounced 'ûra:' it has now become in Telugu and Tamil either 'ûru,' or 'ûr,' but remains 'ûra,' in Malayâlam. Where final 'a' changes into 'ei,' in Tamil, it generally changes into 'e,' in Canarese, or else it is propped up by the addition of 'vu.' In Telugu, and especially in Malayâlam, this vowel is less subject to change. Neuter plurals of appellatives and pronouns, which originally ended in 'a' in all the dialects, and which still end in 'a,' in Malayâlam, now end in most instances in 'ei,' in colloquial Tamil, in 'i,' in Telugu, and in 'u,' in Canarese. Thus, 'ava,' *those* (things), has become 'avei,' in Tamil; 'avi,' in Telugu; 'avu,' in Canarese: in Malayâlam alone, it is still 'ava.'

In the same manner, the long final 'â' of Sanscrit feminine

abstracts, becomes in Tamil 'ei,'—*e.g.*, 'âśâ,' Sans., *desire,* Tamil, 'âśei;' 'Chitrâ,' Sans., *April—May*, Tamil Śittirei.' The same 'â' becomes 'e,' in Canarese, *e.g.*, 'Gangâ,' *the Ganges*, is in Canarese 'Gange' or 'Gange-yu.' The diphthong into which final 'a' and 'â' are weakened in Tamil, is represented more properly as 'ei' than as 'ai.' The origination of the Tamil 'ei' from 'a,' and the analogy of the Sanscrit diphthong 'ai,' which is equivalent to 'âï,' might lead us to regard the Tamil diphthong as 'ai,' rather than 'ei.' It is curious, however, that though it originated from 'a,' every trace of the sound of 'a' has disappeared. It is represented in Grantham by a double 'e,' and in Telugu-Canarese by a character which is compounded of 'e' and 'i:' it accords in sound also very nearly with the sound of 'ê' or 'ey,' in *Turkey*. It is also to be observed that the Tamil 'ei,' is the equivalent of the 'ê,' of the Malayâla accusative, and is the ordinary representative of the final 'ĕ,' of Canarese substantives and verbal nouns. I conclude, therefore, that it is best represented by the diphthong 'ei,' which corresponds to the 'εῖ' of the Greeks.

(2.) 'i' and 'î.' These vowels call for no remark.

(3.) 'u' and 'û.' In the Indo-European languages, and also in the Semitic, the vowels 'ŭ' and 'û,' are very decided, inflexible sounds, which admit of little or no interchange with other vowels, or euphonic softening. In the Drâvidian languages, long 'û' is sufficiently persistent; but short 'u' is of all vowels the weakest and lightest, and is largely used, especially at the end of words, for euphonic purposes, or as a help to enunciation.

In grammatical, written Telugu, every word without exception must end in a vowel; and if it has not naturally a vowel ending of its own, 'u' is to be suffixed to the last consonant. This rule applies even to Sanscrit derivatives; and the neuter abstracts ending in 'm,' which have been borrowed from the Sanscrit, must end in 'm-u,' in Telugu. Though this 'u' is always written, it is often dropped in pronunciation. In modern Canarese a similar rule holds, with this additional development, that 'u' (or, with the euphonic copula 'v,' 'vu') is suffixed even to words that end in 'a:' *e.g.*, compare the Tamil 'sila,' *few* (things), and 'pala,' *many* (things), with the corresponding Can. 'kela-vu' and 'pala-vu.' The Tamil rule, with regard to the addition of 'u' to words which end in a consonant, accords with the rule of the ancient Canarese. That rule is, that in words which end in any hard or surd consonant, *viz.*, in 'k,' 'ch,' 'ṭ,' 't,' or 'p,' (each of which is the leading consonant of a 'varga'), or in the hard, rough 'ʀ,' which is peculiar to these languages, the hard consonant shall be followed by 'u' (as 'q,' by 'sh'vâ,' in Hebrew), in consequence of its being impossible for Tamilian organs of speech to pronounce those letters without the help of a succeeding vowel. In most instances this enunciative 'u' is not merely short, but so very short that its quantity is determined by grammarians to be equal only to a fourth of the quantity of a long vowel. The Malayâlam uses invariably a short 'a,' in those connexions and for those purposes for which 'u' is used in the other dialects.

It often happens (though it is not an invariable rule) that the final surd, to which enunciative 'u' or 'a' has been appended, is doubled, apparently for the purpose of furnishing a fulcrum for the support of the appended vowel. Thus, the Sanscrit 'vâk,' *speech,* becomes in Tamil 'vâk(k)-u;' 'ap,' *water,* becomes 'ap(p)-u;' and so in all similar cases. The rule is further extended in Tamil so as to apply to the final consonants of syllables, as well as to those of words. If a syllable, though in the middle of a word, terminates in one of the hard consonants above-mentioned, and if the initial consonant of the succeeding syllable is one which cannot be assimilated to it, the final consonant is doubled, and 'u' is affixed. Thus, 'advaita,' Sans., *in-duality,* becomes in Tamil 'attuveida.' The rule by which 'd,' when thus doubled, becomes 't,' will be explained hereafter.

In modern colloquial Tamil, 'u' is suffixed to almost every final consonant,—to the semi-vowels and nasals, as well as the surds; and even in the ancient or classical Tamil it is sometimes suffixed to final 'l,' *e.g.,* 'śol(l)-u,' *speak,* instead of simply 'śol.'

The employment of 'u,' in the manner and for the purposes now mentioned, is obviously quite foreign to Indo-European usages. It is not derived from the Sanscrit, and is directly opposed to Sanscrit laws of sound. It will be termed the 'enunciative u,' and will generally be separated off by a hyphen.

(4.) 'e,' 'ê:' 'o,' 'ô.' The Drâvidian languages possess, and largely employ the short sounds of the vowels 'e' and 'o' (epsilon and omicron), and have different characters for those sounds, for the purpose of distinguishing them from the corresponding long vowels.

The Sanskrit is destitute of short 'e' and 'o.' The entire absence of those sounds from a language which attends so nicely as the Sanscrit to the minutest gradations of sound, cannot be the result of accident; and the important place which they occupy in the Drâvidian system of sounds, shows that the Drâvidian languages are independent of the Sanscrit.

In a few cases, both in Telugu and in Tamil, particularly in the instance of the interrogative base 'e,' the short vowel has sometimes been corrupted into a long one, or lengthened by becoming the seat of emphasis; but such cases are rare and exceptional, and in general the difference between short 'e' and 'o,' and the corresponding long vowels, is a difference which pertains, not to the euphony or inflexional form, but to the bases or roots of words, and is essential to the difference in the signification. *E.g.*, in Tamil, 'tĕḷ,' means *clear*, and 'têḷ,' *scorpion*; 'kăl,' *stone*, and 'kâl,' *foot*.

(5.) 'eî.' It has already been mentioned that 'ei,' unlike the Sanscrit diphthong 'aî,' is derived from 'e' and 'i,' not from 'a' and 'i.' The primitive Drâvidian 'a' changes into 'e,' and this again into 'eî.'

Thus, *the head*, is 'tala,' in Telugu and Malayâlam; 'tale,' in Canarese; and 'talei,' in Tamil.

When 'ei' is succeeded in Tamil by another 'ei,' with only a single consonant between them, the first 'ei,' though naturally long, is considered short by position, and is pronounced short accordingly; *e.g.*, 'uḍeimei,' *property*, is regarded in prosody as 'uḍeĭmei.' In such cases 'ei' is an equivalent to its original 'ă' or 'ĕ.'

(6.) 'au.' This diphthong has a place in the Tamil alphabet; but it is not really a part of any of the Drâvidian languages, and it has been placed in the alphabets solely in imitation of the Sanscrit. It is used only in the pronunciation of Sanscrit derivatives; and when such derivatives are used in Tamil, they are more commonly pronounced without the aid of this diphthong. Ordinarily the diphthong is separated into its component elements: that is, the simple vowels 'a' and 'u,' from which it is derived, are pronounced separately, with the usual euphonic 'v' of the Tamil between them to prevent hiatus. *E.g.*, the Sanscrit noun 'saukhyam,' *health*, is ordinarily pronounced and written in Tamil, 'savukkiyam.'

It is a peculiarity of the Tamil system of sounds, as distinguished from that of the other languages of the family, that the vowels 'i,' 'î,' 'e,' 'ê,' and 'u,' acquire before certain consonants a compound, diphthongal sound, which is different from the sound which they have as simple vowels. Thus, 'i' before 'ṭ,' 'ṇ,' 'r,' 'ṛ,' 'ʀ,' 'l,' and 'ḷ,' acquires something of the sound of 'e:' 'î' before the same consonants, with the exception of the first 'r' and the first 'l,' takes a sound resembling 'û:' 'û' remains always unchanged; but 'ŭ,' not only before the above-mentioned seven consonants, but before all single consonants, when it is not succeeded by 'i,' 'u,' or 'e,' is pronounced nearly like 'o;' and in Telugu, 'o' is generally used in writing those words. 'e,' before the consonants above mentioned, with the exception of the semi-vowels, loses its peculiarly slender sound, and is pronounced nearly as it would be if the succeeding consonant were doubled. 'ê,' with the same exceptions, acquires a sound similar to 'ô.'

The circumstance which is most worthy of notice, in connection with these changes, is that each of the short vowels 'i,' 'u,' and 'e,' retains its natural sound, if it is succeeded by another 'i,' 'u,' or 'e.' Thus, 'uRa,' Tamil, infinitive, *to have, to be,* is pronounced 'oRa,' but the imperative 'uRu' is pronounced as it is written.

This rule discloses a law of sound which is unlike anything that is discoverable in Sanscrit. So far as it goes, it is evidently connected with the Scythian law of harmonic sequences, which will be referred to hereafter.

The vowel 'ă,' occurring in the last syllable of a word ending in 'n,' 'ṇ,' 'r,' 'ṛ,' 'l,' or 'ḷ,' acquires a slender sound resembling that of *e; e.g.,* 'avar,' Tamil, *they,* (honorifically, *he*) is pronounced 'aver.' This change corresponds to the weakening of the sound of heavy vowels, in the ultimate or penultimate syllables of words, which is sometimes observed in the Sanscrit family of tongues.

II. **Consonants.**—Tamil grammarians divide all consonants into three classes:—(1.) Surds, which they call 'vallinam,' or *the hard class,* viz., 'k,' 'ch,' 'ṭ,' 't,' 'p,' 'R.' (2.) Nasals, which they call 'mellinam,' or *the soft class,* viz., 'ng,' ñj,' 'ṇ,' 'n,' 'm,' with final 'n;' and (3.) semi-vowels, which they call 'iḍeiyinam,' or *the medial class,* viz., 'y,' 'r,' 'l,' 'v,' 'ṛ,' 'ḷ.'

In this enumeration, as I have already observed, the sonant equivalents of the surd consonants (viz., 'g,' the sonant of 'k'; 'ś,' the sonant of 'ch;' 'ḍ,' the sonant of 'ṭ;' 'd,' the sonant of 't;' and 'b,' the sonant of 'p') are omitted. In the other Drâvidian dialects the difference between surds and sonants is generally expressed by the use of different characters for each sound, in imitation of the system of the Dêva-nâgari; but in Tamil, and in part in Malayâlam, in accordance with the peculiar Drâvidian law of the convertibility of surds and sonants, one set of consonants serves for both purposes, and the difference between them is expressed in the pronunciation alone.

It is desirable before proceeding further to enquire into this law, viz.:

The Convertibility of Surds and Sonants.—We have seen that the Tamil alphabet adopts the first and last of each of the Devâ-nâgari 'vargas,' or rows of consonants, viz., the un-aspirated surd and the nasal of each 'varga;' we have also seen that the Tamil has not separate characters for surds and sonants, but uses one and the same character—that which, properly speaking, represents the surd only—to express both. This rule does not apply merely to the written characters of the language, but is the expression of a law of sound which is inherent in the language itself.

There are distinct traces of the existence of this law in all the Drâvidian dialects; but it is found most systematically and most fully developed in Tamil, next in Malayâlam. The law, as apparent in the Tamil system of sounds, is as follows: 'k,' 'ṭ,' 't,' 'p,' the first, unaspirated consonants of the first, third, fourth, and fifth 'vargas,' are always pronounced as tenues or surds (*i.e.*, as 'k,' 'ṭ,' 't,' 'p,') at the beginning of words, and whenever they are doubled. The same consonants are always pronounced as medials or sonants (*i.e.*, as 'g,' 'ḍ,' 'd,' 'b,') when single, in the middle of words. A sonant cannot commence a word, neither is a surd admissible in the middle, except when doubled; and so imperative is this law, and so strictly is it adhered to in Tamil, that when words are borrowed from languages in which a different principle prevails, as the Sanscrit or the English, the consonants of those words change from sonants to surds, or *vice versâ*, according to their position: *e.g.*, 'dantam,' Sanscrit, *a tooth*, becomes in Tamil, 'tandam;' 'bhâgyam,' Sanscrit, *happiness*, becomes 'pâkkiyam.' This rule applies also to the case of compounds. The first consonant of the second word, though it was a surd when it stood independent, is regarded as a sonant when it becomes a medial letter in a compounded word. This difference is marked in Telugu by a difference in the character which is employed; *e.g.*, 'anna-dammulu' (for 'anna-tammulu'), *elder and younger brothers*; 'koṭṭa-baḍu' (for 'koṭṭa paḍu'), *to be beaten*; but in Tamil, and generally in Malayâlam, the difference appears in the pronunciation alone. This rule applies to all compounds in Telugu: but in Tamil, when the words stand in a case relation to one another, or when the first is governed by the second, the initial surd of the second word is not softened, but doubled and hardened, in token of its activity; *e.g.*, instead of 'koṭṭa-baḍu,' *to be beaten*, it prefers to say, 'koṭṭa-(p)paḍu.' In 'dwanda' compounds the Tamil agrees with the Telugu.

A similar rule applies to the pronunciation of 'ch' (the Tamil 'ś'), the first consonant of the second 'varga.' When single it is pronounced as a soft, weak sibilant, with a sound midway between 'sh' and 'ch.' This pronunciation is unchanged in the middle of words, and in all cases in which the letter is single; but when it is doubled it is pronounced exactly like 'ch.' The principle involved in this instance is the same as in the cases previously mentioned; but the operation of the rule is in some degree different. The difference consists in the pronunciation of this consonant in the beginning of a word, as well as in the middle, as a sonant, *i.e.*, as 'ś.' By theory it should be pronounced as 'ch' at the beginning of a word,—and it is worthy of notice that it always receives this pronunciation at the beginning of a word in vulgar colloquial Tamil; and in Telugu it is written as well as pronounced 'ch.' A somewhat similar rule prevails with respect to the rough 'R' of the Tamil, which is pronounced as 'R' when single, and like 'ttr' when doubled.

The Tamilian rule which requires the same consonant to be pronounced as 'k' in one position and as 'g' in another—as 'ṭ,' 't,' 'p,' in one position, and as 'ḍ,' 'd,' 'b,' in another—is not a mere dialectic peculiarity, the gradual result of circumstances, or a modern refinement invented by grammarians; but is essentially inherent in the language, and has been a characteristic principle of it from the beginning.

The Tamil characters were borrowed from the earlier Sanscrit, and the language of the Tamilians was committed to writing on, or soon after, the arrival of the first colony of Brahmans, probably more than six centuries before the Christian era. Yet even at that early period the Tamil alphabet was arranged, not in accordance with Sanscrit laws of sound, but in such a manner as to embody the peculiar Drâvidian law of the convertibility of surds and sonants. The Tamil alphabet systematically passed by the sonants of the Sanscrit, and adopted the surds alone, considering one character as sufficient for the expression of both classes of sounds. This circumstance clearly proves that *ab initio* the Drâvidian phonetic system, as represented in the Tamil, its most ancient exponent, differed essentially from that of the Sanscrit.*

In none of the Indo-European languages do we find surds and sonants convertible; though Hebrew scholars will remember the existence in Hebrew of a rule which is somewhat similar to the Tamilian respecting 'k,' 't,' 'p,' and their equivalents. The Hebrew consonants composing the memorial words, 'begad kephath,' are pronounced in two different ways, according to their position. When any of those consonants begins a word, or in certain cases a syllable, it is to be pronounced hard, that is, as a surd or tenuis; and if it be an aspirated letter, it is then deprived of the aspirate which it naturally possesses. To denote this, such consonants have a point, called a 'dagesh,' inscribed in them. When those consonants are found in any other position

* See also the evidence which is furnished in the Introduction respecting the existence of this law of the convertibility of surds and sonants in the names of places in Southern India that are recorded by the Greek geographers; *e.g.*, Cottora (Kôṭṭâr), where the 'ḍ' of 'kôḍ,' the first part of the compound, being doubled, has become 'ṭ.'

they are pronounced as sonants, and two of them, 'ph' and 'th,' as aspirates.

This rule resembles the Tamilian in some particulars; but the resemblance which will be found to exist between the Tamilian rule and the law of sounds which prevails in some of the languages of the Scythian family, amounts to identity.

In the Finnish and Lappish there is a clearly marked distinction between surds and sonants: a sonant never commences a word or syllable in either tongue. But in the oldest specimen of any Scythian language which is extant—the Scythic version of the inscription at Behistun—Mr. Norris has ascertained (*Journal of the Royal Asiatic Society* for 1853) the existence of a law of convertibility of sonants and surds which is absolutely identical with the Tamilian. He has ascertained that in that language, in the middle of a word, the same consonant was pronounced as a sonant when single and as a surd when doubled.

We now enter upon an examination of the Drâvidian *consonants* in detail.

(1.) *The guttural 'varga:'* 'k,' 'g,' and their nasal, 'ng.'—These consonants are pronounced in the Drâvidian language precisely as in Sanscrit. 'g,' the sonant of 'k,' which is expressed by the same character in Tamil, is pronounced in Tamil in a peculiarly soft manner. Its sound resembles that of the Irish 'gh,' and is commonly used to express the 'h' of other languages. Thus, the Sanscrit adjective 'mahâ,' *great*, is written in Tamil 'magâ;' but so soft is the 'g' that it may be considered as an equivalent to 'h,' pronounced with less roughness than is usual with that aspirate.

(2.) *The palatal 'varga:'* 'ch,' 'j,' and 'ñj.'—It has been observed that the Tamil rejects the Sanscrit sibilants 'ś,' 'ṣh,' and 's.' The consonant which it adopts instead is 'ch,' which is pronounced in Tamil in a manner somewhat similar to the soft aspirated 'ś of Śiva,' or as a very soft 'sh,' with as little sibilation or aspiration as possible. In fact, it should be regarded as a palatal, not as a sibilant; and when it is doubled it takes precisely the sound of the Sanscrit palatal 'ch,' or its English equivalent in 'which.' To distinguish the Tamil letter from the sibilant 's' of the Sanscrit, it will be denoted, when single, by an accent, thus—'ś.'

In Telugu the sound of 'ch' is that with which this consonant is pronounced, not only when doubled, but also when single; and a similar pronunciation prevails in the lowest colloquial dialect of the Tamil, in which 'śeÿ,' *to do*, is pronounced 'cheÿ,' as in Telugu.

'j,' the second un-aspirated consonant of this row, is not used in correct Tamil; but in Telugu it is both written and pronounced: in vulgar Tamil also 'ch' is sometimes pronounced like 'j.' The same sound of 'j' is sometimes admitted in the use of those Sanscrit derivatives in which the letter 'j' is found in Sanscrit; but ordinarily the Tamil sound of 'ch,' or 'ś,' is used instead.

'ñj,' the nasal of this row of consonants, is pronounced as in Sanscrit, in all the Drâvidian languages. It is frequently used in Malayâlam as an initial where the Tamil uses 'n,' *e.g.* 'ñjân,' *I*, instead of the Tamil 'nân.'

It is necessary here to notice the existence in Telugu of a peculiarly soft pronunciation of 'ch' and 'j,' with their aspirates, which is unknown in Sanscrit and the northern vernaculars, and is found only in Telugu and in Marâthi. 'ch' is pronounced as 'ts,' and 'j' as 'dz,' before all vowels except 'i,' 'î,' 'e,' 'ê,' and 'ei.' Before these excepted vowels, the ordinary sounds of 'ch' and 'j' are retained. Whether the Telugu borrowed these sounds from the Marâthi, or the Marâthi from the Telugu, I will not venture to express an opinion; but this is not the only particular in which those languages are found to agree.

(3.) *The cerebral 'varga:'* 'ṭ,' 'ḍ,' 'ṇ.'—The pronunciation of the consonants of the cerebral 'varga' in the Drâvidian languages does not differ from their pronunciation in Sanscrit. In expressing these consonants, with their aspirates, in Roman characters in this work, a dot will be placed under each, to distinguish them from the 't,' 'd,' and 'n,' of the dental row.

Though 'ṭ' is the surd consonant of the cerebrals, it is not pronounced at the beginning of any word in Tamil, like the other surds. Its sound is too hard and rough to admit of its use as an initial; and therefore, in those few Sanscrit derivatives which commence with this letter, 'ṭ' is preceded in Tamil by the vowel 'i,' as a help to enunciation. When 'ṭ' is thus proceeded by a vowel, it is no longer an initial, and therefore no longer a surd; and hence it becomes 'ḍ' by rule: so that the sound of 'ṭ' is never heard in Tamil, except when 'ḍ' is doubled. In the other Drâvidian dialects 'ṭ' is sometimes pronounced singly, as in Sanscrit.

The Tamil differs from the other dialects in refusing to combine 'ṭ' with 'ṇ,' and changing it into 'ḍ' when 'ṇ' is combined with it.

This peculiarity is founded upon a general Tamilian law of sound, which is that nasals will not combine with surds, but coalesce with sonants alone. In consequence of this peculiar law, such combinations as 'ṇṭ,' 'nt,' and 'mp,' which are admissible in Telugu and Canarese, are inadmissible in Tamil; in which 'ṇḍ,' 'nd,' and 'mb,' must be used instead. This rule applies also to 'k' and 'ch;' which, when combined with the nasals corresponding to them, become 'g' and 'j.' Thus, 'manṭapam,' Sans., *a porch,* becomes in Tamil 'maṇḍabam;' 'antam,' Sans., *end,* becomes 'andam.' Probably the difference between the Tamil and the other Drâvidian languages in this point, arises from the circumstance that the Tamil has remained so much freer than its sister idioms from Sanscrit influences. A similar rule respecting the conjunction of nasals with sonants alone, is found in the Finnish; and is possibly owing to that delicacy of ear which both Finns and Tamilians appear to possess.

I reserve to the close of this examination of the Drâvidian consonants, some observations on the circumstance that the consonants of the cerebral class are found in Sanscrit as well as in the languages of the Drâvidian family.

(4.) *The dental 'varga:'* 't,' 'd,' 'n.'—The letters of the dental 'varga' have the same sound in the Drâvidian languages as in Sanscrit. The only exception consists in the peculiarly soft pronunciation of 't,' in Tamil and Malayâlam, when used as a sonant: it is then pronounced not as 'd,' but with the sound of the soft English 'th,' in 'that.' It is only when it is combined with a nasal (as in the word which was cited above 'andam,' *end,*) that the sonant of 't' is pronounced in Tamil as 'd;' the sound of 'd' being, in such a conjunction, more natural and easy than that of 'th.'

As this peculiar sound of 'th' is found only in Tamil, and in the Malayâlam, a daughter of the Tamil, it is doubtful whether 'th' is to be considered as the original sound of the sonant equivalent of 't,' or whether it is to be regarded as a corruption or further softening of 'd.' On the whole the latter supposition seems the more probable: and as the 'th' of the Tamil corresponds to the 'd' of the Telugu and of the other dialects, in position and power, I will always write it as 'd,' even when quoting Tamil words, except where it is used as an initial, and is therefore a surd, when it will be written as 't.'

(5.) *The labial 'varga:'* 'p,' 'b,' 'm.'—The pronunciation of 'p,' and its sonant 'b,' requires no remark. With regard to the use of 'm' in combination, I have only to observe that though it changes into 'ng,' 'ñj,' 'ṇ,' or 'n,' when immediately succeeded by a guttural, a palatal, a cerebral, or a dental, it is not to be confounded with the 'anusvâra' of the Sanscrit alphabet. The true 'anusvâra, *i.e.,* the sound which 'm' takes in Sanscrit before the semi-vowels, the sibilants, and the letter 'h,' is unknown to the Drâvidian languages. A character called by the name of 'anusvâra,' but of a different power from the 'anusvâra' of the Sanscrit, is in use in Telugu and Canarese; but it is used merely as the equivalent of the consonantal 'm,' in euphonic combinations, and even as a final. The Telugu has also a vocalic nasal, the half 'anusvâra,' which, though it is used merely for euphony, bears a close resemblance to the true 'anusvâra' of the Sanscrit. There is nothing in any of the Drâvidian languages which corresponds to the use of the obscure nasal 'anuswâra' as a final, in Hindi and in the other northern vernaculars.

The euphonic use of 'm' and its modifications, and also the use of 'n' and its equivalents, to prevent *hiatus*, will be considered at the close of this section.

(6.) *The 'varga' of the semi-vowels*: 'y,' 'r,' 'l,' 'v:' 'ṛ,' 'ḷ,' 'R.'—In classical Tamil neither 'r' nor 'l' can commence a word: each of them requires to be preceded by an euphonic auxiliary vowel; 'r' by 'i,' and 'l' by 'u.' Thus, the Sanscrit 'râ,' *night*, abbreviated from 'râtri,' is written and pronounced 'irâ;' and this again is softened into 'irăvu.' In like manner 'lôkam,' Sans., *the world*, becomes 'ulôgam,' and by a further corruption 'ulăgu.' The same rule applies to the second set of semi-vowels, 'ṛ,' 'ḷ,' 'R,' which are the exclusive property of the Drâvidian languages, and none of which can be pronounced without the help of preceding vowels.

Of these distinctively Drâvidian semi-vowels, 'ṛ' is found in the Tamil alone. Its sound resembles that of the English 'r' after a long vowel, as in the word 'farm;' but it is pronounced farther back in the mouth, and in a still more liquid manner. It is sometimes expressed in English books as 'zh,' or 'rzh;' but this is merely a local pronunciation of the letter, which is peculiar to the northern district of the Tamil country: it is at variance with its affinities and its interchanges, and is likely to mislead the learner. 'ṛ' is the only Drâvidian consonant which is pronounced differently in different districts. In the southern districts of the Tamil country, it is pronounced by the mass of the people, exactly in the same manner as 'ḷ,' which is the letter invariably used instead of 'ṛ' in Canarese. Between Tanjore and Pondicherry, it is softened into 'rzh,' or 'zh;' and in Madras and the neighbourhood, this softening process has been carried to such a length, that in the speech of the vulgar, 'ṛ' has become a silent letter.

The Telugu, which commences to be spoken about two days' journey north of Madras, has lost this letter altogether. Generally it uses 'ḍ' instead, as the Canarese uses 'ḷ;' but sometimes it uses no substitute, after the manner of the vulgar Tamil of Madras. Looking at such Telugu words as 'kinda,' *below*, answering to the Tamil 'kîṛnda,' and 'vingu,' *to swallow*, answering to the Tamil 'viṛungu,' we cannot but suppose, that the Telugu had this letter originally, like the Tamil, and that it lost it gradually through the operation of that softening process which, in the colloquial Tamil of Madras, converts 'kîṛê,' *below*, to 'kîê.'

'ḷ' is a peculiar heavy 'l,' with a mixture of 'ṛ,' which is found in the Vêdic Sanscrit, as well as in the Drâvidian languages. It may be styled the cerebral 'l;' and it is probably derived from the same source, whatever that source may be, from which the cerebral consonants 'ṭ,' 'ḍ,' and 'ṇ,' have proceeded.

The hard rough 'r' of the Drâvidian languages is not found in Sanscrit, and is not employed in pronouncing Sanscrit derivatives. It is found in Telugu poetry, and the grammarians insist upon using it; but in the modern dialect of the Telugu it has fallen into disuse. In Canarese also, the use of this letter is confined to the poets. It is evident that it was originally contained in all the dialects; though, through the influence of the Sanscrit, it has now ceased to be used except in the Tamil and Malayâlam, in which it has as firm footing as ever. In some of the older Tamil alphabets I have found this letter appropriately expressed by a double 'r;' and to distinguish it from the softer letter, it will be represented in this work by a capital 'R,' emblematical of its greater strength.

In the use of this hard 'R' in Tamil, there are two peculiarities which are worthy of notice.

(i.) 'R,' when doubled, is pronounced as 'ttr,' though written 'RR.' The 't' of this compound sound differs both from the soft dental 't' of the fourth 'varga,' and from the cerebral 'ṭ,' and corresponds very nearly to the emphatic final 't' of our English interrogative 'what?' This sound of 't' is not expressed in writing, but in pronunciation it is never omitted; and it is one of those peculiar Drâvidian sounds which are not derived from the Sanscrit, and are not found in it.

(ii.) The letter 'n' (not the dental 'n,' but the final 'n' of the Tamil), a letter which is not found in the Telugu or Canarese, is often prefixed in Tamil to the rough 'R' for the sake of euphony; when the compound 'nR' acquires the sound of 'ndr'—a sound of which the Tamil, like the language of Madagascar, is exceedingly fond. In another class of words, the 'n' which is prefixed to 'R' is radical, and should be followed by 'd,' according to rule (*e.g.*, in the preterites of verbs whose root ends in 'n'); but 'R' is suffixed to 'n' instead of 'd,' in consequence of which the sound of 'ndr' is substituted for that of 'nd.'

The 'R' is radical, and the 'n' euphonically prefixed, in 'mûnRu' (mûndru), Tam., *three,* (for 'mûru,' Can., the more ancient form of the word), and in 'onRu,' (ondru), Tam., *one,* (for 'oru.') The 'n' is radical (or an euphonised form of the radical), and the 'R' is used euphonically instead of 'd,' in the following examples; 'enRu' (endru), *having spoken,* instead of 'endu;' 'śenRu' (śendru), *having gone,* for 'śendu,' (which is instead of the less euphonic 'śeldu.') In the speech of the vulgar in the Tamil country, and in the Malayâlam, this compound 'ndr,' is further altered into 'nn' or 'ṇṇ.' In Telugu and Canarese 'nd' is always found instead of 'ndr.'

(7.) *The sibilants and the aspirate*: 'ś,' 'ṣh,' 's,' 'h.'—It has already been mentioned that the Tamil is destitute of sibilants. The other Drâvidian idioms freely use the sibilants and aspirates of the Sanscrit, in writing and pronouncing Sanscrit derivatives, and to some extent, through the prevalence of Sanscrit influences, in the pronunciation even of pure Drâvidian words. In Tamil 'the ś of Śiva,' occurring in Sanscrit derivatives, is represented by the peculiar palatal which answers to the 'ch' of the Sanscrit, and the sound of which, when single, closely resembles that of 'ś.' The other sibilants, 'ṣh,' and 's,' are altogether excluded from pure classical Tamil. In later Tamil books, and in the speech and letters of the better educated Tamilians of the present age, those sibilants are freely employed in writing and pronouncing words which have been borrowed from the Sanscrit; and in such cases, the characters which are used to express them are taken from the Grantham. By the mass of the people, however, those letters are rarely pronounced aright; and in the remoter districts the vulgar substitute for them, in accordance with the genius of the language, those letters which the ancient grammars enjoin, and the use of which is exemplified in the Sanscrit derivatives that are employed in the Tamil classics. The substitutions are as follows:—'ṣh,' the cerebral sibilant of the Sanscrit is represented in general by the cerebral 'ḍ;' sometimes by the liquid 'ṛ;' sometimes even by the dental 't' or 'd.' 's,' the sharp sibilant of the Sanscrit, is sometimes represented by 't;' sometimes it is omitted altogether; sometimes it is changed into the Tamil 'ch,' the equivalent of 'ś.' When this sibilant stands at the beginning of a Sanscrit derivative, and when it is desired in accordance with modern usage, to pronounce it with the unmodified Sanscrit sound, it is preceded (at least in pronunciation) by the vowel 'i,' without which it cannot be enunciated, in that connexion, by Tamil organs.

Thus, 'strî,' Sans., *a woman*, is always pronounced and generally written 'istiri.'

The Tamil is destitute of the sound of 'h,' and of aspirated consonants, as well as of sibilants. Aspirates are plentifully used in the other dialects of the Drâvidian family; and in Canarese, 'h' is regularly used as a substitute for 'p.'

Origin of the Cerebral Consonants.—In all the languages and dialects of India, whether they beloug to the Sanscrit or to the Drâvidian families, much use is made of a series of consonants—'ṭ,' 'ḍ,' with their aspirates, and 'ṇ'—which are called by Hindu grammarians 'cerebrals,' because they are pronounced far back in the mouth, with a hard, ringing sound. I have reserved to this place some observations on the existence of this peculiar class of sounds in two families of tongues which are so widely different from one another as the Drâvidian and the Sanscrit.

It seems natural to suppose, and it will readily be admitted, that one of those families must have borrowed the sounds in question from the other; but it remains to be determined which was the borrower, and which was the original proprietor.

The Hindi, the Bengali, and the other vernaculars of Northern India may be conceived to have borrowed the cerebral consonants from the Sanscrit, from the decomposition of which those languages have mainly arisen: but it is very difficult to suppose that they have been borrowed in this manner from the Sanscrit by the Drâvidian languages. On the contrary, I have long been persuaded that they were borrowed from the Drâvidian languages by the Sanscrit, after the arrival of the Sanscrit-speaking race in India. The reasons which lead me to adopt this view are these:—

(1.) The cerebral consonants are essential component elements of a large number of primitive Drâvidian roots, and are often necessary, especially in Tamil, for the discrimination of one root from another; whereas in most cases in Sanscrit, the use of cerebral consonants instead of dentals, and especially the use of the cerebral 'ṇ,' instead of the dental 'n,' is merely euphonic.

(2.) None of the cerebral consonants has ever been discovered in any of the primitive languages which are related to the Sanscrit. They are not found in the Classical languages, the Gothic, or the Celtic, in the Lithuanian, the Slavonian, or the modern Persian: they are not found in the Cuneiform Persian, or the Zend—those lannuages, or rather sister dialects, with which the Sanscrit finally shook hands on crossing the Indus and settling in Ârya-vartta. On the other hand, the Drâvidian languages, which claim to have had an origin independent of the Sanscrit, and which appear to have been spoken throughout India prior to the arrival of the Brahmans, possess the cerebral sounds in question, and for aught that appears, were in possession of them always. They are found even in the Brahui. There is no trace of these sounds in the Âryan family of tongues, west of the Indus: but no sooner does a member of that family cross the Indus, and obtain a lodgment in the ancient seats of the Drâvidians and other Scythians in India, than the cerebral sounds make their appearance in their language. It is worthy of notice also, that the Prâcrit, a local dialect or vernacular of the Sanscrit, makes a larger use of the cerebrals than the Sanscrit itself.*

(3.) Those consonants which the Tamil has borrowed from the Sanscrit within the period of the existence of Drâvidian literature, have been greatly modified to accord with the Tamilian laws of sound and delicacy of ear. Thus, the Tamil omits the aspirates even of Sanscrit derivatives, and omits or changes all the sibilants. It systematically softens down all harsh sounds. Even the Sanscrit cerebral-sibilant 'ṣh' cannot be pronounced by Tamil organs. Hence it seems improbable that a series of harsh, ringing sounds, like the cerebral 'ṭ,' 'ḍ,' and 'ṇ,' should have been borrowed by the Tamil from the Sanscrit without change, and used in the pronunciation, not only of Sanscrit derivatives, but also of a large number of the most essential Drâvidian roots.

(4.) Though the Telugu has been more exposed to Sanscrit influences than the Tamil, yet larger use is made of those sounds in Tamil than in Telugu,—a circumstance which is incompatible with the supposition of the derivation of those sounds from the Sanscrit.

Putting all these considerations together, it appears probable that instead of the Drâvidian languages having borrowed the cerebral consonants from the Sanscrit, the Sanscrit has borrowed them from the Drâvidian languages; and it will, I think, be demonstrated in the 'Glossarial Affinities,' that the Sanscrit has not disdained to borrow from the Drâvidian languages words as well as sounds.

After the foregoing observations were written, I met with Mr. Norris's paper on the language of the 'Scythic tablets' of Behistun, and found a similar opinion expressed therein respecting the

* The Vêdic Sanscrit possesses a peculiar 'l'—the cerebral 'ḷ' of the Drâvidian languages—which has disappeared from the more modern Sanscrit. This 'ḷ' is one of the most distinctive features of the Drâvidian languages, especially of the Canarese and the Tamil; and its origin is probably the same as that of the other cerebrals. It has nearly disappeared from the Telugu, apparently through the influence of the more modern Sanscrit.

Drâvidian origin of the Sanscrit cerebrals. Mr. Norris says, 'I will here express my conviction that the sounds called cerebral are peculiar to the Tartar or Finnish class of languages; that the really Indian languages are all of Tartar origin, or, at least, that their phonetic and grammatical affinities are Tartar; and that the writers of Sanscrit adopted the sound from their Indian neighbours, in the same way that the Scandinavians appear to have adopted a similar sound from their neighbours, the Lapps, who are undoubtedly Tartars; the Icelanders who retain the old Scandinavian language, pronouncing the words 'falla' and 'fullr,' as though written 'fadla' and 'fudlr.'

"It is certainly the case that this peculiar articulation has not been noticed as cerebral, so far as I know, by the writers who have treated of those languages; but this may be accounted for from the fact that Tartars have had few, if any, native grammarians; that generally speaking, their languages are unwritten; and that, where written, the alphabet, not having been adopted by themselves, but given to them by nations more civilized than themselves, the difference between the dentals and cerebrals was not striking enough to a foreigner to induce him to invent new characters to designate the sounds new to him. But the existence of a 't' or 'd,' convertible into 'l,' is well-known to Finnish philologers. Castrén, a Finnlander, in his *Ostiak Grammar*, uses distinct characters for the cerebral and dental 'd' and 't,' though not giving them these denominations, and directs that the former should be pronounced somewhat aspirated, with the addition of 'l,' as 'dhl' or 'dl,' and 'thl' or 'tl;' observing that similar sounds occur in the Lappish and Finnish tongues."

These observations undoubtedly strengthen the supposition of the Drâvidian origin of the cerebral consonants of the Sanscrit, as well as of the Scythian relationship of the Drâvidian languages.

It is remarkable that the Drâvidian 'ḷ' (as will be seen under the next head) is interchangeable with the cerebral 'ḍ,' through their middle point, the vocalic 'ṛ.' All these letters appear to have a cognate origin; and the supposition of the existence of a remote connection between the Drâvidian and the Ugrian families evidently grows in strength as we proceed.

Dialectic Interchange of Consonants.—Under this head I intend to consider, not the euphonic refinements which have been invented by grammarians, but those natural, unintentional mutations and interchanges which are brought to view by a comparison of the various Drâvidian dialects. These dialectic interchanges will be found to throw much light on the Drâvidian laws of sound, whilst they enable us to identify many words and inflexional forms contained in the various dialects which appear at first sight to be unconnected, but which are in reality the same.

Following as before the order of the Dêva-nâgari alphabet, I proceed to point out the dialectic changes to which each Drâvidian consonant appears to be liable. I omit the aspirated consonants, as not really Drâvidian.

1. *The gutturals.*—'k,' 'g,' 'ng.'

'g' being merely the sonant of 'k,' in the changes now to be enquired into, 'k' and 'g' will be regarded as identical.

(i.) 'k,' when used as a sonant, that is, as 'g,' changes into 'v.' Where we have 'g,' in Tamil, we sometimes find 'v,' in Telugu; *e.g.*, 'âgu,' Tam., *to become;* 'avu,' Tel. In 'kâ,' the infinitive of this verb in Telugu, which corresponds to the Tamil 'âga,' 'k' (or 'g') reappears. It is especially in the middle of words that this consonant evinces a tendency to be changed into 'v.' This tendency constantly appears in the spoken language of the lower classes of the Tamil people in the southern provinces; and has found a place even in the poets; *e.g.*, 'nôva,' *to be pained,* instead of the more common 'nôga.'

In Telugu 'v' is often not only pronounced, but written, instead of 'g;' *e.g.*, 'pagaḍamu,' *coral,* corrupted into 'pavaḍamu.'

Compare with this the change of the Sanscrit 'laghu,' *light,* into the Latin 'levis.' It will be seen that, *per contra,* 'v' sometimes becomes 'g' in Telugu.

(ii.) 'k' changes into 'ch' or 'ś.' As the Tamil 'ś' becomes 'ch,' when doubled, and is represented in the alphabet by the equivalent of the Dêva-nâgari 'ch,' the change of 'k' into 'ch,' is identical with that of 'k' into 'ś.' The former change appears in the Telugu, the latter in the Tamil. Compare the change of the Greek and Latin 'k,' into the Sanscrit 'ś;' *e.g.*, 'δέκα' and 'decem,' softened into 'daśa,' *ten.*

The Canarese retains 'k,' the older pronunciation of this consonant, and where 'k' is found in the Canarese, we generally find 'ch' in Telugu, and 'ś' in Tamil; *e.g.*, 'kinna,' Can., *small;* 'chinna,' Tel.; 'śinna,' Tam. 'kevi,' Can., *the ear;* 'chevi,' Tel.; 'śevi,' Tam.

'Gêÿ,' Can., *to do;* 'chêy,' Tel.; 'śeÿ,' Tam. Sometimes the older 'k' is retained by the Tamil as well as by the Canarese, and the softening appears in the Telugu only; *e.g.*, 'kei,' Tamil, *the hand;* 'kyê,' or 'keiyyi,' Can.; 'chêy,' Tel. 'Keḍu,' Tam. and Can., *to spoil;* Tel., 'cheḍu,' or 'cheṟu.'

A similar change of 'k' into 'ch,' appears even in Sanscrit; *e.g.*, 'vâch-as,' *of speech*, from the crude nominative 'vâk,' *speech*.

(iii.) 'kk' change systematically into 'ch.' This change may be regarded as the rule of the pronunciation of the lower classes of the Tamil people in the southern districts. Further north, and in grammatical Tamil, it is rarely met with, but in the Telugu country the rule re-appears; and in a large class of words, especially in the formatives of verbs, the double 'k' of the Tamil is replaced regularly by 'ch' in Telugu. The following instances of this change are contained even in grammatical Tamil: 'kây̆chu,' *to boil*, for the more regular 'kây̆kku,' and 'pây̆chu,' *to irrigate*, for 'pây̆kku.'

A single illustration will suffice to illustrate the perfect conformity in this point between the vulgar pronunciation of Tamil in the extreme south and the regular, grammatical use of 'ch' for 'kk' in Telugu. 'veikka,' Tamil, *to place* (infinitive), is pronounced 'veicha,' by the illiterate in the southern Tamil districts; and in grammatical Telugu the same word is both written and pronounced 'veicha.'

(iv.) 'k' appears sometimes to have changed into 't.' I cannot adduce a good instance of this change in the Drâvidian languages; but I suspect that the 't' of some inflexional terminations in Gônd (*e.g.*, the nominative plural of the personal pronouns) has been derived from the Tamil 'k.' Compare also 'vâkili,' *a doorway*, Telugu, with the Malayâla form of the same word, 'vâtal.' I am doubtful, however, whether this illustration can be depended upon, because the Tamil form of the same word is 'vâśal,' classically 'vây̆il,' apparently from 'vây̆-il,' literally *mouth-house*.

In other families of languages the interchange between 'k' and 't' is not uncommon; *e.g.*, Doric 'τᾶνος,' *he*, instead of 'ε-κεῖνος.'

2. *The palatals*:—'ch' or 'ś,' 'j,' 'nj.'

I class the changes of 'ch,' 'ś,' and 'j,' together, those letters being in reality but one in the Drâvidian languages.

The only change to which this letter, 'ś' or 'j,' is liable is that of being softened into 'y.' On comparing the Tamil with the Canarese, many instances of this process are brought to light; *e. g.*, 'heśar,' Can., *a name* (ancient Canarese, 'peśar'), has been softened in Tamil into 'pey̆ar,' 'pey̆r,' or 'pêr.' In words borrowed by the Tamil from the Sanscrit, 'y' is optionally used instead of 'ś,' and very commonly instead of 'j.' Thus 'râjâ,' Sans., *a king* (in Tamil 'râśâ,' and with the masculine formative, 'râś-an'), becomes 'rây-an.' In the southern provinces of the Tamil country this change of 'ś' into 'y' has become a characteristic of the pronunciation of the lower classes. In those provinces in all words in which this letter occurs, whether Sanscrit or Tamil, the 'ś' is changed into 'y;' *e. g.*, they say 'ariyi,' *rice*, instead of 'ariśi.'

3. *The cerebrals* :—'ṭ,' 'ḍ,' 'ṇ.'

(i.) The cerebral 'ṭ,' when used as a sonant and pronounced as 'ḍ,' is sometimes changed into the vocalic 'ṛ' in Tamil: *e.g.*, 'nâḍi,' Sans., *a measure*, is commonly written and pronounced in Tamil 'nâṛi;' and this is colloquially pronounced 'nâḷi' in the southern districts, by a further change of 'ṛ' into 'ḷ.' The counterpart of this change, *viz.*, the change of 'ṛ' into 'ḍ,' is much more common in the Drâvidian languages. (See 'ṛ.') In Telugu there are some instances of the change of 'ḍ' into the hard rough 'ʀ,' *e.g.*, 'cheḍu,' *to spoil* (Tamil and Canarese, 'keḍu'), should have for its transitive form 'cheḍuchu,' answering to the Tamil 'keḍukku;' whereas 'cheʀuchu' is used instead.

(ii.) 'ṇ' This cerebral nasal is frequently softened in Telugu into 'n,' the nasal of the dental row. The Tamil, the most correct representative of the ancient speech of the Drâvidians, makes much use of 'ṇ,' as well as of the other cerebrals; and the colloquial Tamil and the Malayâlam go beyond the grammatical Tamil in preferring 'ṇ' to 'n.' The Telugu, on the other hand, whilst it uses the other cerebrals freely enough, often prefers 'n' to 'ṇ.' Thus, it softens the Tamil (and old Drâvidian) words 'kaṇ,' *eye*, 'viṇ,' *heaven*, 'maṇ,' *earth*, into 'kannu,' 'vinnu,' and 'mannu.' It softens even some Sanscrit words in a similar manner; *e. g.*, 'guna,' *quality*, instead of 'guṇa.' Sometimes, both in Tamil and in the other idioms, 'ṇ' is first euphonized into 'ṇḍ,' and then converted into 'ḍ,' which when doubled becomes 'ṭ;' *e. g.*, 'eṇ,' *eight*, has first become in Canarese 'eṇṭu,' and then in Tamil 'eṭṭu:' 'peṇ,' *a female*, has become 'peṇḍu;' and in the equivalent Tamil word, 'peḍei,' *a hen*, the 'ṇ' has disappeared and left no substitute.

4. *The dentals* :—'t,' 'd,' 'n.'

(i.) 't,' or its sonant equivalent 'd,' changes into 'r' in Tamil. In the interchange of the cerebral 'ḍ' and 'ṛ,' 'ṛ' sometimes appears to have been the original sound, and 'ḍ' the corruption; but in the change which is now referred to, it is 'd' that is the original sound, and which is changed into 'r.' This change may arise from the circumstance that the 'r' into which 'd' is altered is pronounced very like a dental, and bears a considerable resemblance to 'd.' In the southern districts of the Tamil country the change of 'd' (when preceded and followed by a vowel) into 'r' is exceedingly common in the pronunciation of the lower classes: but the same change has in some instances found its way into the written language; *e. g.*, 'virei,' *seed*, or *to sow*, instead of the more correct 'videi.' In Canarese 'ad,' the inflexional increment, or basis of most of the oblique cases of certain singular nouns, changes in some instances into 'ar;' *e. g.*, compare 'id-ar-a,' *of this*, from 'id-u,' *this*, with 'mar-ad-a,' *of a tree*, from 'mara,' *a tree*. In this instance the change from 'd' to 'r,' or some equivalent change, was obviously required by euphony: 'id-ad-a' would have been intolerably monotonous, and 'mar-ar-a' not less so. This change of 'd' into 'r' is not unknown to the North Indian languages; and in that family it is often followed up by a further change of 'r' into 'l.' Bopp has pointed out some instances in the Hindustani and Bengali; *e. g.*, 'des,' *ten*, becomes 'reh' in the compound numbers, as 'bâ-reh,' *twelve*. An instance of the change of 'r' into 'l' is furnished by another compound numeral, *sixteen*, which is not 'sô-reh,' but 'sô-leh.' The Prâcrit also changed 'd' into 'r,' as is seen in the instance of the word 'raha,' *ten*, which has superseded 'daha,' a softened form of the Sanscrit 'daśa,' and which is used instead of 'daha' at the end of compound numerals.

It seems to me not improbable that in these cases, and also in the use in Bengali and Marathi of 'l' instead of 'd' or 't,' as a sign of the preterite and passive participle, we see an evidence of the ancient prevalence of Drâvidian influences in Northern India.

It may be noticed here that the Umbrian also regularly changed 'd' into 'r;' *e. g.*, 'sedes' was written 'seres.' As in Tamil, however, this change took place only when 'd' came between two vowels.

(ii.) 'd' sometimes changes into 'ś.'

This change appears in Tamil in the optional use of 'ś' in the formatives of nouns instead of 'd.' Thus, 'vayadu,' *age*, becomes 'vayaśu;' and 'periśu,' *large*, or *that which is large*, is commonly used instead of 'peridu,' the more correct form. In Telugu, 'd' is still more frequently subject to this change. We have a remarkable instance of the softening of 'd' into 's,' of 's' into 'y,' and finally of the obliteration of the 'y' itself in the Drâvidian word signifying *a name*. This in Tulu is 'pudar,' in ancient Canarese 'peśar,' in classical Tamil 'peÿar;' and finally in modern Tamil 'pêr.'

(iii.) 'nd' changes in Tamil into 'ñj.' In this change 'j' must be considered as identical with 'ś,' being the sound which 'ś' takes when preceded by a nasal; and it is always expressed by 'ś' in Tamil. In this conjunction the dental 'n' changes into 'ñ,' which is the dental of the palatal row. The change of 'nd' into 'nj' especially takes place after the vowels 'i' or 'ei' In general it is heard in the pronunciation of the lower classes only; but in a few instances it has found its way into grammatical compositions; *e. g.* 'eindu,' *five,* has changed into 'einju,' and this again into 'anju,' a form which is found even in the Tamil classics.

(iv.) 'tt' change into 'ch' in Tamil after the vowels 'i' and 'ei.' The change to which I refer appears to be one of 'dd' into 'śś,' if the form of the Tamil letters is regarded: but it has already been explained that sonants become surds when doubled; and hence 'dd' must be expressed as 'tt,' and 'śś' as 'ch,' this being their pronunciation when in juxtaposition. The corruption of the double, soft dentals 'tt' into the palatals 'śś,' which are represented by 'ch,' is peculiarly easy and natural. This 'ch' which arises out of 'tt,' though almost universally characteristic of the pronunciation of the mass of the Tamil people, as distinguished from the literati, is rarely found in grammatical compositions, except in the formatives of derivative nouns, after the semi-vowel 'r;' *e. g.*, 'uṇar-chi,' *sensation, knowledge,* instead of 'uṇar-tti,' which is more in accordance with analogy. In Malayâlam this change not only appears in the pronunciation of the vulgar, but is the rule of the language after the vowels 'i' and 'e;' and 'ch' is written as well as pronounced: *e. g.*, compare 'siricha,' *that laughed,* with the corresponding Tamil 'śiritta.'

(v.) 'n,' the nasal of the dental 'varga,' changes or is softened into 'y.' This change rarely occurs; but we have an indubitable instance of it in the change of 'nu,' the Telugu copulative conjunction *and,* into 'yu.' 'yu' has been still further softened in Canarese into 'û.' We have also an instance of this in the softening in classical Tamil of 'na,' the termination of certain preterite relative participles into 'ya;' *e. g.*, 'śolli-ya,' *that said,* instead of the more regular 'śolli-na.'

(vi.) 'n' also changes, though still more rarely, into 'm:' *e.g*, 'mîru,' *you,* in Telugu, must have been altered from 'nîru,' the form which answers to the Tamil 'nir,' and which Telugu analogies would lead us to expect. See the section on The Pronoun.

5. *The labials:—*'p,' 'b,' 'm.'

(i.) 'p' changes in Canarese into 'h.' This remarkable rule applies to the initial 'p' of nearly all words in modern Canarese, whether they are pure Drâvidian words or Sanscrit derivatives; *e. g.* 'pattu,' Tam., *ten* ('padi,' Tel.), is in Canarese 'hattu.' In like manner, 'paṇa,' *money,* a Sanscrit derivative, is in modern Canarese 'haṇa.' This change of 'p' into 'h' has taken place in comparatively recent times; for in the old Canarese, and in the dialect of the Badagars of the Nilgherries, 'p' maintains its ground. A change similar to this is occasionally apparent in the Marâthi, the neighbour of the Canarese on the north: the Sansc. participle 'bhûta-s,' *one who has been*, being altered in Marâthi to 'hôtô;' *e. g.*, 'hôtô-n,' *I was*. Compare also the Prâkrit 'hô-mi,' *I was*, from 'bhûta-smi.' A similar change of 'p' into 'h' appears in Armenian; *e.g.*, *foot* is in Armenian 'het' (for 'pet'), and *father*, 'hayr' (for 'payr').

(ii.) 'b,' the sonant of 'p,' sometimes changes into 'm;' *e.g.*, 'padi,' Tel., *ten*, becomes 'midi' in 'tom-midi,' *nine*, a compound which the analogy of both the Tamil and the Telugu would require to be 'tom-badi: 'enbâr,' *they will say*, is often in poetical Tamil 'enmar.' 'b' is also euphonically added to 'm' in vulgar Tamil. I do not refer to such words as 'pâmbu,' Tam., *a snake*, as compared with 'pâmu,' Telugu; for in those instances the 'm' itself is euphonic, and 'bu' (in Can., 'vu') is the real formative. Cases in which the 'm' is radical and the 'b' euphonic occur plentifully in colloquial Tamil; *e.g.*, 'kôdumei,' *wheat*, commonly pronounced 'kôdumbei.'

(iii.) 'b' is often softened into 'v' in Tamil. Most transitive verbs in Tamil form their future tense by means of 'p' or 'pp;' and in the corresponding intransitives we should expect to find the future formed by 'b,' the sonant of 'p.' Where the root ends in a nasal consonant, this 'b' appears; but where it ends in a vowel, 'b' is ordinarily changed into 'v.' See the section on The Verb. In some instances in the Tamil poets this 'b' of the future is changed, not into 'v' but into 'm,' according to the previous rule.

(iv.) 'm' changes into 'n.' This change is often apparent in the nominatives of neuter nouns in Tamil, the natural termination of many of which is 'm,' but which optionally terminate in 'n:' *e.g.*, 'pala-n,' *profit*, a derivative from 'phala.' Sans., is more commonly used than 'pala-m.' In Telugu 'kola-nu,' *a tank*, answers to the Tamil 'kuḷa-m.' In the same manner 'um,' the Tamil aoristic future formative, has become 'nu' in Telugu; and 'um,' the Tamil copulative particle, has in Telugu been changed into 'nu.'

(v.) 'm' changes into 'v;' *e.g.*, 'nâm,' *we*, and 'nêm,' *you*, in ancient Canarese are softened in the modern dialect to 'nâv-u' and 'nîv-u.'

6. *The semi-vowels*:—'y,' 'r,' 'l,' 'v:' 'ṛ,' 'ḷ,' 'ʀ.'

(i.) 'y' changes into 'ś.' It has been shown that 'ch,' 'ś,' and 'j' are softened into 'y' in Tamil. Notwithstanding this, and in direct opposition to it, we find in the colloquial Tamil, especially in that of the southern districts, a tendency also to harden 'y' into 'ś.'

Through some peculiar perversity, where 'ś' ought to be, it is pronounced as 'y,' and where 'y' ought to be, it is pronounced as 'ś;' *e.g.*, 'paśi,' *hunger*, is mispronounced by the vulgar 'payi;' whilst 'vayaṟu,' *the belly*, is transformed into 'vaśaṟu.' This change of 'y' into 's' is not confined to the South, though it is more frequently met with there. Even in Madras, 'payangal,' *boys*, is pronounced 'paśangaḷ,' and 'ayal,' *near*, is not only pronounced but written 'aśal.' In Telugu 'y' is invariably converted into 'ś,' after the participial 'i;' *e.g.*, 'chêyi,' *having done*, becomes 'chêsi.' When 'y' is used euphonically to prevent hiatus, it invariably retains its proper sound.

(ii.) 'r' changes into 'd.' A change of 'd' into 'r' has already been mentioned. This is sometimes met by a counter-change of 'r' into 'd;' *e.g.*, 'per-u,' or 'per-iya,' Tam., *large*, becomes in Telugu 'pedd-a.'

(iii.) 'r' changes into 'l.' 'r' and 'l' are found to be interchangeable in many families of languages; and in the Drâvidian family this interchange is one of very common occurrence. Sometimes 'l' is corrupted into 'r;' but in a larger number of cases 'r' appears to be the original, and 'l' the corruption. In the case of the distinctively Drâvidian 'ṛ' and 'ḷ,' the change is uniformly of the latter nature; and the change of the ordinary semi-vowel 'r' into the corresponding 'l,' though not uniform, is an exceedingly common one; and one which may be regarded as a characteristic of colloquial Tamil. It is especially at the beginning of words that this change occurs, and it takes place as frequently in the case of derivatives from the Sanscrit, as in the case of Drâvidian roots; *e.g.*, 'rakṣhi,' *to save* ('rakṣh-a,' Sans.), is pronounced by the vulgar 'lakṣhi,' or 'laṭchi.'

In the middle of words 'r' is less frequently changed into 'l;' nevertheless where the Tamil uses 'r' we sometimes find 'l' in the Telugu; *e.g.*, 'teri,' *to appear*, in Tamil, becomes 'teli-yu' in Telugu.

Seeing that a tendency to change 'r' into 'l' still exists and operates in the Drâvidian languages, especially in Tamil, it may be concluded that in those ancient roots which are the common property of several families of language, and in which an interchange appears to exist between 'r' and 'l,' 'r' was the original, and 'l' the altered sound: *e.g.*, if the Drâvidian 'kar-u,' or 'kâr,' *black*, is connected, as it probably is, with the Sanscrit 'kâl-a,' *black*, it may be concluded that the Sanscrit form of the root is less ancient than the Drâvidian; and this supposition is confirmed by the existence of this root 'kar,' *black*, in many of the Scythian languages.

The fact of the frequency of the interchange between 'r' and 'l,' (irrespective of the question of priority), would lead us to suspect a remote connection between several sets of Drâvidian roots, which are now considered to be independent of each other; *e.g.*, compare 'siR,' Tam., *small*, with 'sil,' *few*;' and 'par' (another form of 'per'), *large*, with 'pal,' *many*.

(iv.) 'l' changes into 'r.' Whilst the ordinary change is that of 'r' into 'l,' the change of 'l' into 'r' is occasionally met with, and forms one of the peculiarities of the Tuḷu. The Tuḷu generally changes the final 'l' of the other Drâvidian languages into 'r;' *e.g.*, 'vil,' Tam., *a bow*, ('billu,' Can.), becomes in Tuḷu 'bir.' In this instance it cannot be doubted that 'l' was the original termination of the word; for we find the same root west of the Indus in the Brahui 'billa,' *a bow*. A similar interchange between 'l' and 'r' takes place in Central Asia. The 'l' of the Manchu is converted into 'r' in the Mongolian.

In Zend and Old Persian 'l' was unknown, and 'r' was systematically used instead.

In Telugu, 'lu,' the pluralising suffix of nouns, is sometimes changed into 'ru.' This change, however, of 'l' into 'r' is not systematic as in the Tulu, but exceptional. In Tamil, 'l' is euphonically changed, not into 'r,' but into 'R' before 'p;' *e.g.*, 'palpala,' *various*, becomes in written compositions 'paRpala.' This proves that a change of 'l' into 'r' is not contrary to Tamil laws of sound.

(v.) 'l' changes in the language of the Kus to 'ḍ.' The change of 'ḍ' into 'ḷ' is common enough; but the regular change of 'l' into 'ḍ' is peculiar to this idiom; *e.g.*, 'pâlu,' Telugu, *milk*, is in Ku 'pâḍu;' 'illu,' *house*, is 'iḍḍu.'

(vi.) 'v' is generally hardened in Canarese into 'b' in the beginning of a word; *e.g.*, 'vâṛ,' Tamil, *to flourish*, becomes in Canarese 'bâḷ.' Where 'v' is not changed into 'b,' viz., in the middle of words, the Canarese generally softens it into 'w.' The same softening is sometimes observed in the pronunciation of the lower classes of Tamilians. In Malayâlam, 'v' is always 'w.'

(vii.) The 'v' euphonic of the Tamil is sometimes changed into 'g' in Telugu. Both 'y' and 'v' are used euphonically to prevent *hiatus* in Tamil; so in Telugu 'g' is sometimes used not only instead of 'v,' but also instead of 'y.' Compare Tam. 'âRu-(v)-ar,' *six persons*, with the Tel. 'âRu-(g)-uru,' and the Tam. honorific singular 'tandei-(y)-âr,' *father*, with the corresponding Tel. 'tandri-(g)-âr-u.' This will, perhaps, explain the occasional use of 'g' instead of 'v' as the sign of the future tense in High Tamil; *e.g.*, 'śeÿgên,' instead of 'śeÿvên,' *I will do*.

(viii.) 'ṛ' (the peculiar vocalic 'ṛ' of the Tamil) interchanges with three different consonants. Sometimes it becomes 'ṇ;' *e.g.*, 'miṛugu,' Tamil, *to sink*, is changed in Telugu to 'muṇagu;' and 'kuṛi,' Tam., *a hole*, becomes in Canarese 'kuṇi.' Ordinarily 'ṛ' is changed in Telugu into 'ḍ.' Neither the Telugu nor the Canarese possesses the Tamil 'ṛ.' In a very few instances the Telugu uses 'ṇ' or 'ḷ' instead: sometimes it omits the consonant altogether, without using a substitute; but in a vast majority of instances it converts 'ṛ' into 'ḍ.' 'ṛ' is ordinarily converted in Canarese into 'ḷ:' the same change characterises the pronunciation of the mass of the Tamil people in the southern districts of the country, and prevails in the Malayâlam also.

This change of 'ṛ' into 'ḷ,' and the previous one of 'ṛ' into 'ḍ,' form the constituents of an important dialectic law. That law is that the same consonant which is 'ṛ' in Tamil, is generally 'ḍ' in Telugu, and always 'ḷ' in Canarese. Thus, *to caress*, is 'taṛ-u' in Tamil; 'taḍ-u,' in Telugu; and 'taḷ-u,' in Canarese. The numeral *seven* is 'êṛ-u,' in Tamil; 'êḍ-u,' in Telugu; and 'êḷ-u,' in Canarese. In the compound numeral 'êḷnûru,' *seven hundred*, the Telugu 'êḍ-u' is found to change, like the Canarese, into 'êl-u.' The word signifying *time*, which is included in the adverbial nouns *then* and *now* (literally *that time* and *this time*), is in Tamil 'poṛu-du,' in Telugu 'puḍ-u,' or 'podd-u,' and in Malayâlam 'pôḷ.' In this instance the Canarese uses a different word. It thus appears that 'ḷ' and 'ḍ' are as intimately allied as 'ḍ' and 'ṛ.' This is a point of some importance in the affiliation of languages; for an interchange of 'd' and 'l' is characteristic of the Ugrian family of languages, as well as of the Drâvidian family and the North-Indian vernaculars. The same word is written with 't' or 'd' in the Ostiak, and with 'l' in the Magyar and Finnish.

A corresponding interchange is occasionally observed even in the Indo-European languages; *e.g.*, compare 'δακρυμα,' *a tear*, with *lachryma:* but in those languages it is rarely met with, whereas it is a characteristic dialectic sign of several families of tongues belonging to the Scythian group.

(ix.) It may be added that 'ḷ' changes, though rarely, into 'r;' *e.g.*, 'kammâḷan,' Tamil, *an artificer*, from 'kam,' *work*, and 'âḷ,' *to exercise*, becomes in Canarese 'kammâran-u,' though 'âḷi,' a suffix equivalent to 'âḷau,' is used in Canarese as well as in Tamil.

(x.) 'R' (the strong, rough R of the Tamil), is frequently changed in Tuḷu into 'j;' *e.g.*, 'muRu' (the original form of 'mûndru'), Tam. *three*, becomes 'mûji;' 'âRu,' *six*, 'âji.'

This change of 'R' into 'j,' the equivalent of 'ś,' is directly the converse of the change of 's' into 'r,' which is so common in the Indo-European tongues.

Having now finished the consideration of the dialectic changes which pure Drâvidian consonants undergo, it remains to point out the changes which take place in the Sanscrit sibilants, when words in which they occur are borrowed from the Sanscrit by the Tamil.

(1.) 'ṣh.' The hard, cerebral sibilant of the Sanscrit is unknown to the classical Tamil. Sometimes it is changed into 'ś,' a change which ordinarily takes place at the present day in the pronunciation of the lower classes in the southern districts: sometimes, though more rarely, it is changed into 'ṛ;' but most commonly it is converted into 'ḍ.' This 'ḍ' is sometimes softened down into the dental 'd.' Thus, 'manuṣhya,' Sans., *man,* becomes in classical Tamil 'mâniḍa-n;' and this by a further change becomes 'manida-n.' A very old example of the change of the Sanscrit 'ṣh' into 'ḍ' in Tamil, can be adduced. The month 'Âṣhâda,' Sans., *July—August,* has become in Tamil 'Âḍi:' and this change dates probably from the earliest period of the cultivation of the Tamil language. In 'Teiṣha,' *January—February,* the hard 'ṣh,' instead of being changed, has been discarded altogether: the Tamil name of this month, as far back as the literature reaches, has been 'Tei.'

2. 's.' The hissing sibilant of the Sanscrit, answering to our English 's,' is ordinarily in Tamil converted into 'd,' the sonant of 't,' which is pronounced as 'th' in *that; e.g.,* 'mâsam,' Sans., *a month,* becomes in classical Tamil 'mâdam;' and 'manas,' *the mind,* becomes 'manad-u.' In this conversion of the Sanscrit 's' into 'd' in Tamil, there is a change from the sibilant to the dental, which is exactly the reverse of that change from the dental to the semi-sibilant which has already been described. It may be compared with the weakening of 's' into 'h' which we find in several of the Indo-European languages.

When 's' happens to be the first consonant of a Sanscrit derivative, it is sometimes omitted in Tamil altogether; *e.g.,* 'sthânam,' *a place,* becomes 'tânam.' More commonly in modern Tamil, an effort is made to pronounce this 's' with the help of the vowel 'i,' which is prefixed to it in order to assist enunciation; *e.g.,* 'istiri' ('strî,' Sans.), *a woman.*

The Sanscrit sibilant never changes into 'r' in Tamil. This change, though very common in languages of the Indo-European family, rarely, if ever, appears in the Drâvidian.

The only instances in which it may be conjectured to have taken place, are the following. The Tamil-Canarese root 'ir,' *to be*, in Brahui 'ar,' may be allied to the Indo-European substantive verb, as represented by the Sanscrit 'as:' the Canarese 'mûr-u,' *three*, is identical with the Brahui 'mus-it,' and the Tulu 'mûj-i:' the Tamil plural of rational beings 'ar,' resembles the Sanscrit epicene plural 'as:' and perhaps, though more doubtfully still, the Tamil 'iru,' *iron*, euphonized into 'iru-mbu,' may be compared with the Sanscrit 'ayas,' and the English word 'iron'—which is allied to 'ayas,' through the change of 's' into 'r.' The instances, however, which I have now cited, are not by any means decisive; for the only reliable affinity amongst them is that of 'mûr-u' and 'mus-it;' and in that instance 'r' was probably the original letter, and 's' or 'j' the corruption.

Euphonic permutation of Consonants.—The permutation of consonants for euphonic reasons, though it throws less light on the laws of sound than dialectic interchange, includes a few points of considerable interest. Drâvidian grammarians have bestowed more attention and care on euphonic permutation than on any other subject; and the permutations which the grammar of the Tamil requires or allows, are at least twice as numerous, and more than twice as perplexing to beginners, as those of the Sanscrit. On examining the permutations of consonants prescribed in the grammar of the Tamil, the Telugu, and the Canarese—the three principal languages of this family—it is evident that a considerable proportion of them are founded upon Sanscrit precedents: another class in which Sanscrit rules of euphony have been, not imitated, but emulated and surpassed, may be regarded rather as prosodial than as grammatical changes: but after these have been eliminated, a certain number of euphonic permutations remain, which are altogether peculiar to these languages, and which proceed from, and help to illustrate, their laws of sound. It will suffice to notice a few of those permutations; for the subject is too wide, and at the same time not of sufficient importance, to allow of our entering on a minute investigation of it.

(1.) In 'dwanda' compounds, *i.e.*, in nouns which are united together, not by copulative conjunctions, but by a common sign of plurality (in the use of which common sign the Drâvidian languages resemble, and perhaps imitate, the Sanscrit), if the second member of the compound commences with the first or surd consonant of any of the five 'vargas' (*viz.*, 'k,' 'ch' or 'ś,' 'ṭ,' 't,' 'p'), the surd must be changed into the corresponding sonant or soft letter. In those Drâvidian languages which have adhered to the alphabetical system of the Sanscrit, as the Telugu and the Canarese, this conversion of the surd into the sonant is carried into effect and expressed by the employment of a different character. In Tamil, in which the same character is used to represent both surds and sonants, a different character is not employed, but the softening of the first consonant of the second word is always apparent in the pronunciation.

This peculiar rule evidently proceeds from the Drâvidian law, that the same consonant which is a surd at the beginning of a word, should be regarded as a sonant in the middle; for the first consonant of the second word, being placed in the middle of a compound, has become a medial by position. The existence of this rule in the Telugu and Canarese, notwithstanding the Sanscrit influences to which they have been subjected, proves that the law of the convertibility of surds and sonants is not confined to the Tamil.

All the Drâvidian dialects agree in softening the initial surd of the second member of 'dwanda' compounds: but with respect to compounds in which the words stand to one another in a case relation, *e.g.*, substantives, of which the first is used adjectivally or to qualify the second, or an infinitive and its governing verb, the Telugu pursues a different course from the Tamil. The rule of the Telugu is that when words belonging to the 'druta' class, including all infinitives, are followed by any word commencing with a surd consonant, such consonant is to be converted (as in 'dwanda' compounds) into its soft or sonant equivalent. The rule of the Telugu on this point resembles that of the Lappish, and still more the rule of the Welsh; and it has been observed that the Welsh, possibly through the pre-historic influence of the Finnish, is the most Scythic of all the Indo-European languages.

It is curious that in combinations of words which are similar to those referred to above, and uniformly after infinitives in 'a,' the Tamil, instead of softening, doubles and hardens the initial surd-sonant of the succeeding word. The Tamil also invariably doubles, and consequently hardens, the initial surd of the second member of 'tat-purusha' compounds, *i.e.*, compounds in which the words stand in a case-relation to each other. In such combinations, the Canarese, though it is less careful of euphony than either the Tamil or the Telugu, requires that the initial surd of the second member of the compound should be softened: it requires, for instance, that 'huli togalu,' *a tiger's skin*, shall be written and pronounced 'huli dogalu.' The Tamil, on the contrary, requires the initial surd in all such cases to be hardened and doubled; *e.g.*, the same compound in Tamil, viz., 'puli tôl,' *a tiger's skin*, must be written and pronounced, not 'puli dôl,' but 'puli-(t)tôl.' This doubling and hardening of the initial is evidently meant to symbolize the transition of the signification of the first word to the second; and it will be seen that this expedient has been very generally resorted to by the Tamil.

When the first word is used not as a noun or adjective, but as a verb or relative participle, the initial surd of the second word becomes a sonant in Tamil also, as in Telugu; *e.g.*, compare 'kâÿ gombu,' *a withering branch*, with 'kâÿ-(k)kombu,' *a branch with fruit.*

(2.) The Tamil system of assimilating, or euphonically changing, concurrent consonants, is in many particulars almost identical with that of the Sanscrit, and has probably been arranged in imitation of it. Nevertheless, there are some exceptions which may be regarded as distinctively Drâvidian, and which are founded upon Drâvidian laws of sound; *e.g.*, the mutation of 'l' into 'n' in various unexpected combinations. Through this tendency to nasalisation, 'pôl-da,' *like*, becomes 'pôn-da,' or rather 'pôn-dra;' 'koḷ-ḍa,' *taken, bought*, becomes 'koṇ-ḍa;' and the latter euphonic mutation has found its way in Telugu into the root itself, which is 'kon-u,' *to buy*, instead of the older Tamil 'koḷ.' It does not appear to have been noticed even by Tamil grammarians, that 'l,' in a few instances, has been converted into 'n' before 'k.' Thus 'nân-ku,' or 'nân-gu,' *four*, is derived from 'nâl-ku,' an older form of the word; and 'Panguni,' the Tamil name of the month of *March-April*, has been altered from the Sanscrit 'Phalguna.' In Telugu a corresponding tendency appears in the change of 'l' into 'ṇ' before 'ṭ;' *e.g.*, 'ilṭi,' *of a house*, is softened into 'iṇṭi.' In all these cases 'l' is undoubtedly the original; and these proofs of the priority of 'l' to 'n,' corroborate the suspicion that the Latin 'alius' is older than its Sanscrit equivalent 'anyas.'

Euphonic Nunnation, or Nasalization.—Much use is made in the Drâvidian languages, especially in the Tamil and Telugu, of the nasals 'ng,' 'ñj,' 'ṇ,' 'n,' and 'm' (to which should be added 'n' or 'm,' the 'half anuswâra' of the Telugu), for the purpose of euphonising the harder consonants of each 'varga.' All the nasals referred to, with the exception of the 'half anuswâra,' which is an inorganic sound, are regarded by native grammarians as modifications of the sound of 'm;' the nature of each modification being determined by the manner in which 'm' is affected by succeeding consonants. In Tamil, as in Sanscrit, all those modifications are expressed by the nasal consonants which constitute the final characters of each of the five 'vargas.' In Telugu and in Canarese one and the same character, which is called 'anuswâra,' but which possesses a greater range of power than the 'anusvâra' of the Sanscrit, is used to represent the whole of the nasal modifications referred to. The pronunciation of this character, however, varies so as to accord with the succeeding consonant as in Tamil.

The 'nunnation,' or nasalization, of the Drâvidian languages is of three kinds.

1. The first kind of 'nunnation' is used to a greater extent in Tamil than in any other dialect. It consists in the insertion of a nasal before the initial consonant of the formative suffix of many nouns and verbs. The formative syllable or suffix, the nature of which will be explained more particularly in the succeeding section, is added to the crude root of the verb or noun, and constitutes the inflexional theme, to which the signs of inflexion are annexed. The nasalised formative is used in Tamil by the intransitive form of the verb and by the isolated form of the noun. When the verb becomes transitive, and when the noun becomes adjectival, or is placed in a case-relation to some other noun, the nasal disappears, and the consonant to which it was prefixed—the initial consonant of the formative—is hardened and doubled.

The nasal is modified in accordance with the nature of the initial consonant of the formative suffix: it becomes 'ng' before 'k' or 'g;' 'ñj' before 'ś' or 'ch;' 'ṇ' before 'ṭ' or 'ḍ;' 'n' before 't' or 'd;' and 'm' before 'p' or 'b.' The Telugu uses the 'anuswâra' to express all these varieties of sound; and the 'half anuswâra' in certain other cases.

(i.) Of the use of the first nasal, 'ng,' to emphasize and euphonize the formative suffix 'k-u' or 'g-u,' the Tamil affords innumerable examples. One verb and noun will suffice; *e.g.*, 'aḍa-ngu,' *to refrain oneself, to keep in,* is formed from the root 'aḍa' by the addition of the formative, intransitive suffix 'gu,' which is euphonized into 'ngu:' 'kâ-nggei,' *heat,* is from 'kâ' or 'kây̆,' *to burn* (in Telugu 'kâ-gu'); with the addition of the suffix 'gei,' euphonized into 'nggei.'

(ii.) Instances of the euphonic use of the nasal of the second 'varga,' 'ñ,' are more common in Telugu than in Tamil. Thus, 'pañch-u,' Tel., *to divide,* is derived from 'pag-u,' Tamil (changed into 'pach-u,' and then nasalized into 'pañch-u'); and is analogous to the Tamil noun 'pang-u,' *a share,* which is derived from the same verbal root: 'reṭṭi-ñchu, Tel., *to double,* is an example of the use of the euphonic nasal by verbs of the transitive class; a class in which that nasal is not used by any other dialect but the Telugu.

(iii.) The cerebrals 'ṭ' and 'ḍ' are not used as formative suffixes of verbs, though some verbal roots end in those consonants; but they are not unfrequently used as formatives of neuter nouns; *e.g.*, 'ira-ḍ-u,' the original of the Tamil numeral *two*, corresponding to the Canarese 'era-ḍu,' has been euphonised to 'ira-ṇḍ-u.' The Tamil adverbial nouns 'â-ṇḍ-u,' *there*, 'î-ṇḍ-u,' *here*, 'yâ-ṇḍ-u,' *where*, are derived from 'â' and 'î,' the demonstrative bases, and 'yâ,' the interrogative base, with the addition of the usual neuter formative 'ḍ-u,' euphonised to 'ṇḍ-u.' In Telugu a large number of masculine formatives in 'ḍ-u' receive in pronunciation the obscure nasal '*n*;' *e.g.*, for 'vâḍu-lu' or 'vâḍ-lu,' *they*, 'vâ*n*ḍ-lu' is commonly used. On comparing the Tamil 'karaṇḍi,' *a spoon*, with 'gariṭe,' the Telugu form of the same word, we find that sometimes the nasal is used of one dialect and rejected by another.

(iv.) We see an example of the euphonic use of 'n,' the nasal of the dental 'varga,' in the intransitive verb 'tiru-nd-u,' Tamil, *to become correct*, from 'tiru,' the radical base, and 'du,' the formative, euphonised into 'ndu:' the transitive form of the same verb is 'tiru-ttu,' *to correct*. We find the same euphonic insertion in the Tamil demonstrative adjectives 'anda,' 'inda,' *that, this*, which are derived from the demonstrative pronouns 'ad-u,' *that*, 'id-u,' *this*, by the addition of the adjectival or relative participial 'a,' and the insertion of the euphonic nasal before 'd,' the neuter formative. An example of the nasalisation of a noun of this class is found in 'maru-ndu,' Tamil, *medicine*, which is derived from 'maru,' *fragrant*, with the addition of the formative 'du,' euphonised to 'ndu.'

(v.) Many examples of the euphonic insertion of 'm' before the suffix in 'b' might be adduced; but the following will suffice. 'tiru-mbu,' *to turn* (intransitively), of which the root is unquestionably 'tiru,' as appears from the corresponding Telugu 'tiru-gu' and Canarese 'tiru-vu.' The Tamil form of the transitive of the same verb is 'tiru-pp-u,' *to turn*. An example of a similar insertion of euphonic 'm' before the formative 'b' of a noun, is seen in 'eʀu-mbu,' Tamil, *an ant*, when compared with the equivalent Canarese word 'iru-ve.' The formatives 'nd-u' and 'mbu,' are extremely common terminations of Tamil nouns; and with few if any exceptions, wherever those terminations appear, they will be found on examination to be euphonized suffixes to the root.

2. The second use to which the euphonic nasal is put is altogether peculiar to the Tamil. It consists in the insertion of an euphonic 'n,' between the verbal theme and the 'd' which constitutes the sign of the preterite of a very large number of Tamil verbs. The same 'd ordinarily forms the preterite in ancient Canarese, and it is not

unknown to the Telugu; but in those languages the nasal, 'n,' is not prefixed to it.

The following are examples of this nasalisation of the sign of the preterite in Tamil: 'vâṛ-nd-ên' (for 'vâṛ-d-ên'), *I flourished,* from the root 'vâṛ,' in Canarese 'bâḷ:' compare Old Canarese preterite, 'bâḷ-d-en.' So also, 'viṛu-nd-u' (for 'viṛu-d-u'), *having fallen,* from the root 'viṛu' or 'vîṛ:' High Tamil, 'vîṛ-d-u;' Canarese equivalent, 'bidd-u.' The corresponding Malayâla 'vîṇ-u,' is an example of the absorption of the dental in the nasal.

In colloquial or vulgar Tamil, this euphonic insertion of 'n' is carried further than the grammatical Tamil allows. Thus, 'śey̆-d-a,' *done,* and 'pey̆-d-a,' *rained,* are vulgularly pronounced 'śey̆-nj-a' and 'pey̆-nj-a.'

3. A third use of the euphonic nasal, is the insertion, in Tamil, of 'ṇ' or 'n,' before the final 'ḍ' or 'd,' of some verbal roots.

The same rule sometimes applies to roots and forms that terminate in the rough 'R,' or even in the ordinary semi-vowel 'r.' Thus, 'kar-u,' Can., *a calf,* is 'kanR-u' in Tamil (pronounced 'kandr-u'); and 'mûr-u,' Can., *three,* is in Tamil 'mûnR-u' (pronounced 'mûnd-u').

In the first and second classes of instances in which *nunnation* is used for purposes of euphony, the Drâvidian languages pursue a course of their own, which is different from the usages of the Scythian, as well as of the Syro-Arabian and Indo-European families of languages. In the Syro-Arabian languages, especially in Talmudic Hebrew, euphonic 'n' is always a final, and is often emphatic as well as euphonic.

In the Turkish, 'n' is used between the bases of words and their inflexions, in a manner similar to its use in Sanscrit. In the North-Indian vernaculars an obscure nasal, '*n*,' is often used as a final. But none of these usages perfectly corresponds to the Drâvidian nasalisation referred to under the first and second heads. In the third class of instances, the Drâvidian usage bears a close resemblance to the Indo-European. In the seventh class of Sanscrit verbal roots, a nasal is inserted in the special tenses, so as to coalesce with a final dental, *e.g.*, 'nid,' *to revile,* becomes 'nindati,' *he reviles.* Compare also the root 'uda,' *water,* with its derivative root 'und,' *to be wet.* A similar nasalisation is found both in Latin and Greek. In Latin we find the unaltered root in the preterite, and a nasalised form in the present: *e.g.*, compare 'scidi' with 'scindo;' 'cubui' with 'cumbo;' 'tetigi' with 'tango;' 'fregi' with 'frango.' Compare also the Latin 'centum,' with the Greek 'ἑ-κατόν.' In Greek, compare the roots 'μαθ' and 'λαβ,' with the nasalised forms of those roots found

K

in the present tense, *e.g.*, '*μανθ-άνω*,' *to learn*, and '*λαμβ-άνω*,' *to take.* The principle of euphonic nasalisation contained in these Sanscrit, Greek, and Latin examples, though not perfectly identical with the Drâvidian usage, corresponds to it in a remarkable degree. The difference consists in this, that in the Indo-European languages the insertion of 'n' is purely euphonic, whereas in Tamil it contributes to grammatical expression. The consonant to which 'n' is prefixed by neuter verbs, is deprived of the 'n,' and also hardened and doubled, by transitives.

PREVENTION OF 'HIATUS.'—An examination of the means employed in the Drâvidian languages to prevent *hiatus* between concurrent vowels, will bring to light some analogies with the Indo-European languages, especially with the Greek.

In Sanscrit, and all other languages in which negation is effected by the use of 'alpha privative,' when this 'a' is followed by a vowel, 'n' is added to it to prevent *hiatus*, and 'a' becomes 'an,' 'in,' or 'un.' In the Latin and Germanic languages, this 'n,' which was used at first euphonically, has become an inseparable part of the privative particles, 'in' or 'un.' In the greater number of the Indo-European languages, this is almost the only conjuncture of vowels in which *hiatus* is prevented by the insertion of an euphonic 'n.' In Sanscrit and Pâli, 'n' is also used for the purpose of preventing *hiatus* between the final base-vowels of nouns or pronouns and their case terminations, in order that the vowels of the base may escape elision or corruption, and be preserved pure. In some instances (a probably older) 'm' is used for this purpose, instead of 'n.' This usage is unknown in the cognate languages, with the exception of the use of 'n' between the vowel of the base and the termination of the genitive plural in the Zend and the Old High German.

It is in Greek that the use of 'n,' to prevent *hiatus*, has been most fully developed: for whilst in Sanscrit contiguous vowels are combined or changed, so that *hiatus* is unknown, in Greek, in which vowels are more persistent, 'n' is used to prevent *hiatus* between contiguous vowels, and that not only when they belong to the same word, but also, and still more, when they belong to different words.

On turning our attention to the Drâvidian languages, we may chance at first sight to observe nothing which resembles the system now mentioned. In Tamil and Canarese, and generally in the Drâvidian languages, hiatus between contiguous vowels is prevented by the use of 'v' or 'y.' Vowels are never combined or changed in the Drâvidian languages, as in Sanscrit, except in the case of compounds which have been borrowed directly from the Sanscrit itself; nor are final vowels elided in these languages before words commencing with a vowel, with the exception of some short finals, which are considered as mere vocalisations.

In Telugu and Canarese, a few other unimportant vowels are occasionally elided. Ordinarily, however, for the sake of ease of pronunciation, and in order to the retention of the agglutinative structure which is natural to these languages, all vowels are preserved pure and pronounced separately: but as 'hiatus' is dreaded with peculiar intensity, the awkwardness of concurrent vowels is avoided by the interposition of 'v' or 'y,' between the final vowel of one word and the initial vowel of the succeeding one. The rule of the Tamil, which in most particulars is the rule of the Canarese also, is that 'v' is used after the vowels 'a,' 'u,' and 'o,' with their long vowels, and 'au,' and that 'y' is used after 'i,' 'e,' with their long vowels, and 'ei.' Thus in Tamil, 'vara illei,' *not come*, is written and pronounced 'vara-(v)-illei,' and 'vaṛi-alla,' (it is) *not the way*, becomes 'vaṛi-(y)-alla.'

This use of 'v,' in one conjunction of vowels, and of 'y,' in another, is doubtless a result of the progressive refinement of the language. Originally, we may be sure that one consonant alone was used for this purpose. These euphonic insertions of 'v' and 'y' between contiguous vowels are observed in the common conversation of Drâvidians, as well as in written compositions; and they are found even in the barbarous dialects: *e.g.*, in the Ku, which was reduced to writing only a few years ago, 'v' may optionally be used for euphony, as in Tamil. Thus in Ku, one may say either 'ââlu,' *she*, or 'â(v)âlu.' This insertion of 'v' or 'y,' takes place, not only when a word terminating with a vowel is followed by a word beginning with another vowel, but also (as in Sanscrit) between the final vowels of substantives and the initial vowels of their case terminations: *e.g.*, 'puḷi-(y)-il,' *in the tamarind*, 'pilâ-(v)-il,' *in the jack*. The use of 'alpha privative' to produce negation being unknown to the Drâvidian languages, there is nothing in any of them which corresponds to the use of 'an,' 'in,' or 'un' privative, instead of 'a,' in the Indo-European languages, before words beginning with a vowel.

Hitherto the only analogy which may have appeared to exist between the Drâvidian usage and the Greek, in respect of the prevention of *hiatus*, consists in the use of 'v' or 'y,' by the Drâvidian languages as an euphonic copula.

As soon as we enter upon the examination of the means by which *hiatus* is prevented in Telugu, a real and remarkable analogy comes to light; for in many instances, where the Tamil uses 'v,' the Telugu, like the Greek, uses 'n.' By one of the two classes into which all words are arranged in Telugu for euphonic purposes, 'y' is used to prevent *hiatus* when the succeeding word begins with a vowel; by the other, a very numerous class, 'n' is used, precisely as in Greek. Thus, instead of 'tinnagâ êgenu,' *it went slowly,* the Telugu requires us to say 'tinnagâ-(n)-êgenu.' When 'n' is used in Telugu to prevent hiatus, it is called 'druta,' and words which admit of this euphonic appendage are called 'druta prakrits,' words of the 'druta' class. 'Druta' is used in the sense of *extra*, and 'the druta n' may be interpreted as 'the *extra* n,' or 'the n which has no meaning of its own.' The other class of words consists of those which use 'y' instead of 'n,' or prevent elision in the Sanscrit manner, by 'sandhi,' or combination. Such words are called the 'cala' class, and the rationale of their prefering 'y' to 'n' was first pointed out by Mr. Brown. Whenever 'n' (or its equivalent, 'ni' or 'nu') could have a meaning of its own, *e.g.*, wherever it could be supposed to represent the copulative conjunction, 'ni' or 'nu,' or the case sign of the accusative or the locative, there its use is inadmissible, and either 'y' or 'sandhi' must be used instead. Hence, there is no difference in principle between 'n' and 'y;' for the latter is used in certain cases instead of the former, merely for the purpose of preventing misapprehension; and it can scarcely be doubted that both letters were originally identical in origin and in use, like 'v' and 'y,' in Tamil. The Telugu 'n' directly corresponds to the Tamil 'v.' Compare the Tel., 'râ-(n)-ê lêdu,' (he, she, or it) *has not come indeed,* with the Tam., 'vara-(v)-ê illei.'

Even in Tel., 'n' is replaced by 'v,' after the emphatic 'ê: *e.g.*, 'â-âst'-ê-(v)-ê,' *that very property.* After 'e,' the Tamil requires 'y' instead of 'v.' An euphonic peculiarity of the Telugu may here be noticed. 'ni' or 'nu,' the equivalents of 'n,' are used euphonically between the final vowel of any word belonging to the 'druta' class (the class which uses 'n' to prevent hiatus) and the hard, surd initial consonant of the succeeding word—which initial surd is at the same time converted into its corresponding sonant. They may also be optionally used before any initial consonant, provided always that the word terminating in a vowel to which they are affixed, belongs to the class referred to. It is deserving of notice, that in this conjunction 'ni' or 'nu' may be changed into that form of 'm' (the Telugu 'anuswâra') which coalesces with the succeeding consonant.

I regard 'n' as the original form of this euphonic copula of the Telugu, and 'y,' as a softening of the same. An undoubted and independent instance of this softening process is seen in the change of the Telugu copulative particle, 'nu,' *and,* into 'yu,' in certain conjunctions in the higher dialect of the language. This word has been softened still further in Canarese into 'û.'* In the Sanscrit of the Vedas also, 'y' is often used euphonically instead of 'n,' between base vowels and case terminations. That 'nu' was the original of 'yu,' not conversely 'yu' the original of 'nu,' appears from the connection of 'nu' with its Tamil equivalent 'um.' Another instance of this interchange of 'um' and 'nu,' has already been pointed out in the identity of the 'nu' of the Telugu aorist, and the 'um' of the Tamil aoristic future.

It has been mentioned that 'v' and 'y' are the letters which are used in Tamil for preventing hiatus, where 'n' and 'y' are used by the Telugu. On examining more closely the forms and inflexions of the classical Tamil, we shall find reason for advancing a step farther; inasmuch as in Tamil also 'n' is used instead of 'v' in a considerable number of instances, especially in the pronominal terminations of verbs in the classical dialect. Thus, the neuter plural demonstrative being 'avei' (for 'a-(v)-a,' from 'a-a'), we should expect to find the same 'a-(v)-ei,' or the older 'a-(v)-a,' in the third person plural neuter of verbs: but we find 'a-(n)-a' instead; *i.e.*, we find the hiatus of 'a-a' filled up with 'n' instead of 'v:' *e.g.*, 'irukkindra(n)a,' *they are* (neuter), instead of 'irukkindra(v)a.' So also, whilst in the separate demonstratives 'avan,' *he*, and 'avar,' *they* (epicene), the hiatus is filled up with 'v' ('a-(v)-au,' 'a-(v)-ar'), in the pronominal terminations of verbs in the classical dialect we find 'a-(n)-an' often used instead of 'a-(v)-an,' and 'a-(n)-ar' instead of 'a-(v)-ar:' *e.g.*, 'irunda-(n)an,' *he was*, instead of 'irunda(v)an,' or its ordinary contraction 'irundân.' We sometimes also find the same 'n' in the neuter plural of appellative nouns in the classical dialect; *e.g.*, 'poruḷa(n)a,' *things that are real, realities*, instead of 'poruḷa(v)a,' or simply 'poruḷa.' We find the same use of 'n' to prevent hiatus in the preterites and relative past participles of a large number of Tamil verbs; *e.g.*, 'kâṭṭi(n)ên,' *I showed*, 'kâṭṭi(n)a,' *which showed:* in which forms the 'n' which comes between the preterite participle 'kâṭṭi' and the terminations 'ên' and 'a,' is clearly used (as 'v,' in ordinary cases) to prevent hiatus. The euphonic character of the 'n' of 'na,' whatever be its origin (respecting which see the section on Verbs,—Preterite tense), is conformed by the circumstance that 'n' optionally changes in classical Tamil into 'y;' *e.g.*, we may say, 'kâṭṭi(y)a,' *that showed*, instead of 'kâṭṭi(n)a.

* According to this view of the case, the connection between the Canarese particle of conjunction, 'û,' and the copulative conjunction, 'u,' which is found in the Vêdas, and also the 'û' of the Semitic languages, will appear to be accidental rather than real; for we have no reason to suppose the 'u' of the Sanscrit and the 'û' of the Hebrew to be softened forms of 'um,' 'mu,' or 'nu.'

Another instance of the use of 'n' in Tamil for the prevention of *hiatus*, is furnished by the numerals. The compound numerals between 'ten' and 'twenty' are formed by the combination of the word for 'ten' with each numeral in rotation. The Tamil word for *ten* is 'pattu;' but 'padu' is used in the numerals above twenty, and 'padi,' identical with the Telugu word for 'ten,' is used in the numerals from eleven to eighteen inclusive. Between this 'padi' and the units which follow, each of which, with the exception of 'mûndru,' *three*, and 'nâlu,' *four*, commences with a vowel, 'n' is inserted for the prevention of hiatus, where the modern Tamil would have used 'v.' The euphonic character of this Tamil 'n' will appear on comparing the Tamil numerals with those of the Telugu, in most of which 'h' is used instead of 'n:'—*e.g.*,

	TELUGU.	TAMIL.
15	padi-(h)-ênu	padi-(n)-eindu
16	padi-(h)-âru	padi-(n)-âṛu
17	padi-(h)-êḍu	padi-(n)-êṛu

In the Tamil compound numeral, 'padi-(n)-mûndru,' *thirteen*, we find the same 'n' used as in the previous examples, though there is no hiatus to be prevented. The Telugu has here 'pada-mûḍu;' the Canarese, 'hadi-mûru;' and as the Canarese uses 'n,' like the Tamil, in all the other compound numbers between 'eleven' and 'eighteen' inclusive, and dispenses with it here, I think it is to be concluded, that in the Tamil 'padi(n)mundru,' the 'n' has crept in through the influence of the numerals on each side of it, and in accordance with the euphonic tendencies of the language in general.

We have an indubitable instance of the use of 'n,' even in common Tamil, to prevent hiatus, in appellative nouns ending in 'ei:' *e.g.*, when an appellative noun is formed from 'iḷei,' *youth*, or *young*, by annexing 'an,' the sign of the masc. sing., the compound is not 'iḷei-(y)-an,' but 'iḷei-(ñj)-an' or even 'iḷei-(n)-an.' 'ñj' is merely a more liquid form of 'n,' and in Malayâlam regularly replaces 'n' in the pronoun of the first person. Probably also 'manâr,' the epicene plural of the future tense of the Tamil verb in some of the poets, is for 'ma-ar;' *e.g.*, 'enma-(n)-âr,' *they will say*, for 'enmâr,' and that for 'enbâr,' the more common form.

There is thus reason to suppose, that originally the Tamil agreed with the Telugu in using a nasal instead of a semi-vowel, to keep contiguous vowels separate. It may be objected that 'n' evinces no tendency to change into 'v.' I admit this; but if we suppose 'm,' not 'n,' to have been the nasal which was originally employed for this purpose, every difficulty will disappear, for 'm' readily changes on the one hand to 'v,' and on the other to 'n.' Nor is it a merely gratuitous supposition that the Telugu may have used 'm' at a former period instead of 'n,' for we have already noticed that 'ni' or 'nu,' the euphonic equivalents of 'n,' are interchangeable in certain conjunctions with the 'anuswâra' or assimilating 'm;' that in two important instances (the copulative particle and the aorist formative) the 'n' of the Telugu replaces an older 'm' of the Tamil; and that in Sanscrit also, instead of the 'n' which is ordinarily inserted between certain pronominal bases and their case-terminations, an older 'm' is sometimes employed. It may also be noticed that the 'ni' or 'nu,' which may be considered as the euphonic suffix of the accusative in Telugu, is replaced in Old Canarese by 'm.'

The reader cannot fail to have observed that whilst the Drâvidian languages accord to a certain extent with the Sanscrit in the point which has now been discussed, they accord to a much larger extent, with the Greek, and in one particular (the prevention of hiatus between the contiguous vowels of *separate words*) with the Greek alone.

It is impossible to suppose that the Drâvidian languages borrowed this usage from the Sanscrit, seeing that it occupies a much less important place in the Sanscrit than in the Drâvidian languages, and has been much less fully developed.

It should be mentioned here that the letter 'r' is in some instances used to prevent hiatus in each of the Drâvidian idioms.

In Tamil, 'kâ,' the imperative singular of the verb *to preserve*, becomes in the plural, not 'kâ-(v)-um,' but 'kâ-(r)-um.' The Canarese in certain cases inserts 'r' or 'ar' between the crude noun and the case terminations, instead of the more common 'v,' 'n,' or 'd;' *e.g.*, 'karid'-ar-a,' *of that which is black*. The Telugu inserts 'r' in a more distinctively euphonic manner between certain nouns and 'âlu,' the suffix by which the feminine gender is sometimes denoted; *e.g.*, 'sundaru-(r)-âlu,' *a handsome woman*. Compare the latter with the Tamil 'soundariya-(v)-aḷ,' in which the same separation is effected by the use of the more common euphonic 'v.'

The 'd' which intervenes between the 'i' of the preterite verbal participle and the suffixes of many Canarese verbs (*e.g.*, 'mâḍi-(d)-a,' *that did*), though probably in its origin a sign of the preterite, is now used simply as an euphonic insertion. 'This 'd' becomes invariably 'n' in Telugu and Tamil; and in Tamil it is sometimes softened further into 'y.' 'ṭ' is stated to be used in Telugu for a similar purpose, viz., to prevent hiatus between certain nouns of quality and the nouns which are qualified by them; *e.g.*, 'kaṇaku-ṭammu,' *a sharp arrow*, but I have no doubt that this 'ṭ' is identical with 'ṭi,' and originally an inflexional particle. 'g' is, in some instances, used by the Telugu to prevent hiatus, or at least as an euphonic formative, where the Tamil would prefer to use 'v;' *e.g.*, the 'rational' plural noun of number, *six persons*, may either be 'âru(g)ur-u,' or 'âru(v)ur-u:' probably 'kâḍu,' *he*, for 'vâḍu,' is another instance of the optional use of 'g' for 'v' in Telugu. It is used euphonically, instead of the 'y' euphonic of the Tamil, in such words as 'tandri-(g)-âr-u,' *fathers* (used honorifically to signify *father*), compared with the Tamil 'tandei-(y)-âr.'

Harmonic Sequence of Vowels.—In all the languages of the Scythian group (Finnish, Turkish, Mongolian, Manchu), but especially in Manchu, a law has been observed, which may be called 'the law of harmonic sequence.' The law is, that a given vowel occurring in one syllable of a word, or in the root, requires an analogous vowel, *i.e.*, a vowel belonging to the same set (of which sets there are in the Turkish four) in the following syllables of the same word or in the particles appended to it, which, therefore, alter their vowels accordingly. This rule, of which some traces remain even in the modern Persian, appears to pervade all the Scythian languages; and has been regarded as a confirmation of the theory that all those languages have sprung from a common origin.

In Telugu a similar law of attraction, or harmonic sequence, is found to exist. The range of its operation is restricted to two vowels 'i' and 'u;' but in principle it appears to be identical with the Scythian law, 'u' being changed into 'i,' and 'i' into 'u,' according to the nature of the preceding vowel. Thus the copulative particle is 'ni' after 'i,' 'î,' 'ei;' and 'nu' after 'u' and the other vowels. 'ku,' the sign of the dative case, becomes in like manner 'ki' after 'i,' 'î,' and 'ei.'

In the above mentioned instances it is the vowels of the appended particles which are changed through the attraction of the vowels of the words to which they are suffixed: but in a large number of cases the suffixed particles retain their own vowels, and draw the vowels of the verb or noun to which they are suffixed, as also the vowels of any particles that may be added to them, into harmony with themselves. Thus, the Telugu pluralising termination or suffix being 'lu,' the plural of 'katti,' *a knife*, would naturally be 'kattilu;' but the vowel of the suffix is too powerful for that of the base, and accordingly the plural becomes 'kattulu.' So also, whilst the singular dative is 'katti-ki,' the dative plural is, not 'kattila-ki,' but 'kattula-ku;'

for 'la,' the plural inflexion, has the same power as the pluralising particle 'lu' to convert 'katti' into 'kattu,' besides being able to change 'ki,' the dative post-position of the singular, into 'ku.'

In the inflexion of verbs, the most influential particles in Telugu are those which are marks of time, and by suffixing which the tenses are formed. Through the attraction of those particles, not only the vowels of the pronominal fragments which are appended to them, but even the secondary vowels of the verbal root itself, are altered into harmony with the vowel of the particle of time. Thus, from 'kalugu,' *to be able*, 'du,' the aorist particle, and 'nu,' the abbreviation of the pronoun 'nênu,' *I*, is formed the aorist first person singular 'kalugu-du-nu,' *I am able*. On the other hand, the past verbal participle of 'kalugu,' is not 'kalugi' but 'kaligi,' through the attraction of the final 'i'—the characteristic of the tense; and the preterite of the first person singular is not 'kalugi-ti-nu,' but 'kaligi-ti-ni.' Thus the verbal root 'kalu' becomes 'kali;' 'nu,' the abbreviation of 'nênu,' becomes 'ni;' and both have by these changes been brought into harmony with 'ti,' an intermediate particle, which is probably an ancient sign of the preterite.

This remarkable law of the Telugu phonetic system evidently accords with the essential principles of the law of harmonic sequence by which the Scythian languages are characterised, and differs widely from the prevailing usage of the Indo-European languages. The change which is apparent in the pronominal terminations of the various tenses of the Telugu verb (*e.g.*, 'nu' in the first person of the present tense, 'ni' in the preterite), have been compared with the variation in Greek and Latin of the pronominal terminations of the verb according to the tense: but the change in Greek and Latin arises merely from euphonic corruption; whereas the Drâvidian change takes place in accordance with a regular fixed phonic law, the operation of which is still apparent in every part of the grammar.

Though I have directed attention only to the examples of this law which are furnished by the Telugu, in which it is most fully developed, traces of its existence could easily be pointed out in the other dialects. Thus in the Canarese verbal inflexions, the final euphonic or enuntiative vowel of the personal pronouns is 'u,' 'e,' or 'i,' according to the character of the preceding vowel; *e.g.*, 'mâḍut-têv-e,' *we do*, 'mâḍuttîr-i,' *ye do*, 'mâḍidev-u,' *we did*. If in the means employed to prevent hiatus between contiguous vowels, the Drâvidian languages appeared to have been influenced by Indo-European usages, still more decided traces of Scythian influences and a Scythian relationship may be noticed in the phonetic law now mentioned.

PRINCIPLES OF SYLLABATION.—The chief peculiarity of Drâvidian syllabation is its extreme simplicity and dislike of compound or concurrent consonants; and this peculiarity characterizes the Tamil, the most early cultivated member of the family, in a more marked degree than any other Drâvidian language.

In Telugu, Canarese, and Malayâlam, the great majority of primitive Drâvidian words, *i.e.*, words which have not been derived from Sanscrit or altered through Sanscrit influences, and in Tamil all words without exception, including even Sanscrit derivatives, are divided into syllables on the following plan. Double or treble consonants at the beginning of syllables, like 'str' in 'strength,' are altogether inadmissible. At the beginning not only of the first syllable of every word, but also of every succeeding syllable, only one consonant is allowed. If in the middle of a word of several syllables, one syllable ends with a consonant, and the succeeding one commences with another consonant, the concurrent consonants must be euphonically assimilated, or else a vowel must be inserted between them. At the conclusion of a word, double and treble consonants, like 'gth' in 'strength,' are as inadmissible as at the beginning: and every word must terminate, in Telugu and Canarese, in a vowel; in Tamil, either in a vowel or in a single semi-vowel, as 'l' or 'r,' or in a single nasal, as 'n' or 'm.' It is obvious that this plan of syllabation is extremely unlike that of the Sanscrit.

The only double consonants which can stand together in the middle of a word in Tamil without an intervening vowel, are as follows. The various nasals, 'ng,' 'ñj,' 'ṇ,' 'n,' and 'm,' may precede the sonant of the 'varga' to which they belong; and hence, 'ng-g,' 'ñj-ś,' 'ṇ-ḍ,' 'n-d,' 'm-b,' may concur; also 'ngng,' 'ṇjnj,' 'ṇṇ,' 'nn,' 'mm,' 'ṇm,' and 'nm:' the doubled surds 'kk,' 'chch,' 'ṭṭ,' 'tt,' 'pp,' 'ḷḷ,' 'RR' (pronounced 'ttr'): also 'ṭk' and 'ṭp;' 'Rk,' 'Rch,' and 'Rp;' 'ÿÿ,' 'll,' 'vv;' and finally 'nR,' pronounced 'ndr.' The only treble consonants which can coalesce in Tamil under any circumstances, are the very soft, liquid ones, 'ṛnd' and 'ÿnd.' Tamilian laws of sound allow only the above mentioned consonants to stand together in the middle of words without the intervention of a vowel. All other consonants must be assimilated, that is, the first must be made the same as the second, or else a vowel must be inserted between them to render each capable of being pronounced by Tamilian organs. In the other Drâvidian dialects, through the influence of the Sanscrit, nasals are combined, not with sonants only, but also with surds; *e.g.*, 'pamp-u,' Tel., *to send*, 'eṇṭ-u,' Can., *eight*. The repugnance of the Tamil to this practice is so very decided, that it must be concluded to be Un-Drâvidian.

Generally 'i' is the vowel which is used for the purpose of separating unassimilable consonants, as appears from the manner in which Sanscrit derivatives are Tamilised. Sometimes 'u' is employed instead of 'i.' Thus the Sanscrit preposition 'pra' is changed into 'pira' in the compound derivatives which have been borrowed by the Tamil; whilst 'Krishna' becomes 'Kiruṭṭina-n' ('ṭṭ' instead of 'ṣh'), or even 'Kiṭṭina-n.' Even such soft conjunctions of consonants as the Sanscrit 'dya,' 'dva,' 'gya,' &c., are separated in Tamil into 'diya,' 'diva,' and 'giya.'

Another rule of Tamil syllabation is, that when the first consonant of an unassimilable double consonant is separated from the second and formed into a syllable by the intervention of a vowel, every such consonant (not being a semi-vowel) must be doubled before the vowel is suffixed. Thus, 'tatva,' Sans., *nature*, becomes in Tamil 'tat(t)uva;' 'aprayôjana,' *unprofitable*, 'ap(p)irayôśana.'

In consequence of these peculiarities of syllabation and the agglutinative structure of its inflexions, the Tamil language appears very verbose and lengthy when compared with the Sanscrit and the languages of Europe. Nevertheless, each syllable being exceedingly simple, and the great majority of the syllables being short, rapidity of enunciation is made to compensate for the absence of compression.

The mental physiology of the different races may be illustrated, perhaps, by their languages. The languages of the Indo-European class are fond of combining clashing consonants, and welding them into one syllable by sheer force of enunciation; and it is certain that strength and directness of character and scorn of difficulties are characteristics not only of the Indo-European languages, but of the races by which those languages are spoken. On the other hand, the Drâvidian family of languages prefers softening difficulties away to grappling with them; it aims at ease and softness of enunciation rather than impressiveness: multiplying vowels, separating consonants, assimilating differences of sound, and lengthening out its words by successive agglutinations, it illustrates the characteristics of the races by which it is spoken by the soft, sweet, garrulous effeminancy of its utterances.

Whilst the syllabation of the Drâvidian languages differs widely from that of the Indo-European and Semitic families of tongues, it exhibits many points of resemblance to the system of the Scythian group, and especially to that of the Finnish or Ugrian family.

The Finnish, the Hungarian, and other languages of the same stock, allow of only one consonant at the beginning of a syllable. When foreign words which begin with two consonants are pronounced by a Magyar, the consonants are separated by the insertion of a vowel; *e.g.*, 'krâl' becomes 'kirâly.' Where the first consonant is a sibilant, it is formed into a distinct syllable by a prefixed vowel; *e.g.*, 'schola' becomes 'iskôla.' How perfectly in accordance with Tamil this is, is known to every European resident in Southern India who has heard the natives speak of establishing, or sending their children to, an English 'iskool." The same peculiarity has been discovered in the language of the Scythic tablets of Behistun. In rendering the word 'Sparta' into Scythian, the translator is found to have written it with a preceding 'i; *e.g.*, 'Isparta,' precisely as it would be written in the present day in Magyar or in Tamil.

I do not suppose the Tamilian system of separating contiguous consonants by a vowel to be older than the Indo-European system of combining them into one syllable. On the contrary, many of the lexical affinities which will be found in the section of 'Roots' and in the 'Glossarial Affinities,' appear to me to prove that the Drâvidian roots were originally monosyllabic, and that the tendency to separate consonants by the insertion of a vowel, was not a characteristic of the older speech, whatever it may have been, from which the Drâvidian family branched off. The inference which I draw is, that as a similar phonetic peculiarity appears in the Ugrian family of languages, and is found in the Behistun tablets to have been a characteristic of the oldest Scythian tongue of which written records survive, the Drâvidian languages probably claim kindred rather with the Scythian group than with the Indo-European.

MINOR DIALECTIC PECULIARITIES.—

1. *Euphonic displacement of Consonants.*

In the Drâvidian languages, consonants are sometimes found to change places, through haste or considerations of euphony.

We have an example of this in the Tamil 'taśei,' *flesh*, which by a displacement of consonants, and a consequent change of the surd into the sonant, has become 'śadei. 'kudirei,' *a horse*, is in this manner often pronounced by the vulgar in the Tamil country 'kuridei:' and looking at the root-syllable of the Telugu word, 'gur-ram,' it is hard to decide whether 'kuridei' or 'kudirei' is to be regarded as the true Drâvidian original. In many instances, through the operation of this displacement, we find one form of a word in Tamil, and another, considerably different, in Telugu or Canarese. Thus, 'koppuḷ,' Tam., *the navel*, is in Telugu 'pokkili;' and 'paḍar,' Tam., *to spread as a creeper*, is in Canarese 'paraḍ-u.' In comparing words in the different dialects, it is always necessary to bear in mind the frequent recurrence of this displacement.

2. *Euphonic displacement of Vowels.*

In Telugu we find many instances of a still more curious displacement of vowels. This displacement occurs most commonly in words which consist of three short syllables beginning with a vowel; and when it occurs, we find that the second vowel has disappeared, and that the first vowel has migrated from the beginning of the word to the second syllable, and at the same time been lengthened to compensate for the vowel that is lost. I take as an example the Drâvidian demonstrative pronouns, remote and proximate; and I select the plural, rather than the singular, to get rid of the disturbing element of a difference which exists in the formatives. In Tamil those pronouns are 'avar,' *they*, remote; and 'ivar,' *they*, proximate, corresponding to '*illi*' and '*hi*.' The Canarese adds 'u' to each word, so that they become 'avaru' and 'ivaru.' By analogy this is the form we should expect to find in Telugu also; but on examination, we find in Telugu 'vâru' instead of 'avaru,' and 'vîru' instead of 'ivaru;' a change which has evidently been produced by the rejection of the second vowel, and the substitution for it of a lengthened form of the first. The neuter demonstrative pronouns of the Telugu being dissyllables, there is no displacement in their nominatives ('adi,' *that*, 'idi,' *this*, corresponding closely to the Tamil 'adu,' 'idu'); but when they become trisyllables by the addition of the inflexional suffix 'ni,' we find a displacement similar to that which has been described: *e.g.*, 'adini,' *it* or *of it*, becomes 'dâni,' and 'idini' becomes 'dîni.'

Many ordinary substantives undergo in Telugu a similar change; *e.g.*, 'ural,' Tamil, *a mortar*, pronounced 'oral,' should by analogy be 'oralu' in Telugu; but instead of 'oralu' we find 'rôlu.'

As soon as this peculiar law of the displacement of vowels is brought to light, a large number of Telugu words and forms which at first sight appear to be widely different from the Tamil and Canarese, are found to be the same or but slightly altered. Thus 'kâdu,' Tel., *it will not be*, or *it is not*, is found to be the same as the Tamil 'âgâdu;' 'lêdu,' *there is not*, corresponds to the Tamil 'illadu;' and by an extension of a similar rule to monosyllables, we find 'lô,' Tel., *within*, to be identical with 'uḷ,' Tam.; and 'nu,' Tel., the copulative particle, to be identical with 'um,' Tam.

A similar rule of displacement appears in the Tuḷu, though in a less degree.

3. *Rejection of Radical Consonants.*

The Telugu evinces a tendency to reject or soften away consonants in the middle of words, even though such consonants should belong to the root, not to the formative. Thus, 'neruppu,' Tamil, *fire*, is softened into 'nippu;' 'elumbu,' *a bone*, into 'emmu;' 'uḍal' (pronounced 'oḍal'); *body*, into 'oḷḷu;' 'poṛudu,' *time*, into 'poddu;' 'erudu,' *an ox*, into 'eddu;' 'marundu,' *medicine*, into 'mandu.'

Something similar to this process takes place, but not so systematically, in vulgar colloquial Tamil.

In a few instances, on the other hand, the Telugu appears to have retained a radical letter which has disappeared from the Tamil. For example, if we search for the origin of 'ôḍu,' *with, together with*, the suffix of the Tamil conjunctive case, no trace of its origin is apparent in Tamil. On examining the Telugu, we find that the corresponding suffix is 'tôḍa.' It has already been shown that 'ḍ' in Telugu corresponds to 'ṛ' in Tamil; and consequently 'tôḍa' would become in Tamil 'tôṛa.' 'tôṛa' (tôṛa-mei) is actually contained in Tamil, and means *companionship;* and thus by the help of the Telugu we find that the Tamil 'ôḍu' and 'tôṛa' are virtually identical; that the meaning of the suffix 'ôḍu' exactly accords with its use; and that there is also reason to conclude another pair of similar words to be allied, viz., 'uḍan,' *with*, a suffix of the conjunctive case in itself a noun signifying *connection*, and 'tuḍar,' a verbal root, *to follow, to join on.*

4. *Accent.*

It is generally stated that the Drâvidian languages are destitute of accent, and that emphasis is conveyed by the addition of the 'ê' emphatic alone. Though, however, the Drâvidian languages are destitute of the Indo-Greek system of accents, the use of accent is not altogether unknown to them; and the position of the Drâvidian accent, always an accute one, accords well with the agglutinative structure of Drâvidian words. The accent is upon the first syllable of the word, that syllable alone, in most cases, constituting the base, prior to every addition of formatives and inflexional forms, and remaining always unchanged. The first syllable of every word may be regarded as the natural seat of accent; but if the word is compounded, a secondary accent distinguishes the first syllable of the second member of the compound.

As in other languages, so in the Drâvidian, accent is carefully to be distinguished from quantity; and in enunçiation an accented short vowel is more emphatic than an unaccented long one. Thus in the intransitive Tamil verb, 'aḍangugiʀadu,' *it is contained*, the second syllable 'ang' is long by position; yet the only accent is that which is upon the first syllable 'aḍ,' which, though shorter than the second, is more emphatic. Another example is furnished by the compound verb 'uḍeind'-irukkiʀadu,' *it is broken*, literally *having been broken it is*. Though in this instance the second syllable of the first word of the compound is long, not only by position, but by nature, and the second syllable of the auxiliary word is long by position, yet the principal accent rests upon the first syllable of the first word, 'uḍ,' the most emphatic portion of the compound, and the secondary accent rests upon 'ir,' the first syllable and crude base of the auxiliary; hence it is pronounced 'úḍeindírukkiʀadu,' every syllable, except the two accented ones, being enunciated lightly and with rapidity.

The general rule of the Drâvidian languages which fixes the accent in the first or root-syllable, admits of one exception. In poetical Tamil one and the same form is used as the third person of the verb (in each tense, number, and gender) and as a participial noun; *e.g.*, 'ôduvân,' means either *he will read*, or *one who reads*, *i.e. a reader*. Even in the colloquial dialect, the third person neuter singular, especially in the future tense, is constantly used in both senses; *e.g.*, 'ôduvadu,' means either *it will read*, or *that which will read*, or abstractedly, yet more commonly still, *a reading*, or *to read*.

The same form being thus used in a double sense, Tamil grammarians have determined that the difference in signification should be denoted by a difference in accent. Thus when 'ôduvân' is a verb, meaning *he will read*, the accent is left in its natural place, on the root syllable, *e.g.*, 'óduvân; but when it is an appellative or participial noun, meaning *he who reads*, the pronominal termination is to be pronounced more emphatically, that is, it becomes the seat of accent, *e.g.*, 'ôduván.'

SECTION II.

ROOTS.

Before proceeding to examine and compare the grammatical forms of the Drâvidian languages, it is desirable to examine the characteristics of Drâvidian roots, and the nature of the changes which are effected in them by the addition of the grammatical forms. The manner in which various languages deal with their roots is strongly illustrative of their essential spirit and distinctive character; and it is chiefly with reference to their differences in this particular, that the languages of Europe and Asia admit of being arranged into classes.

Those classes are as follows:—(1.) The monosyllabic, uncompounded, or isolative languages, in which roots admit of no change or combination, and in which all grammatical relations are expressed either by auxiliary words or phrases, or by the position of words in a sentence. (2.) The Semitic or intro-mutative languages, in which grammatical relations are expressed by internal changes in the vowels of dissyllabic roots. (3.) The agglutinative languages, in which grammatical relations are expressed by affixes or suffixes added to the root or compounded with it. In the latter class I include both the Indo-European and the Scythian groups of tongues. They differ, indeed, greatly from one another in details, and that not only in their vocabularies, but also in their grammatical forms; yet I include them both in one class, because they appear to agree, or to have originally agreed, in the principle of expressing grammatical relation by means of the agglutination of auxiliary words. The difference between them is rather in degree than in essence. Agreeing in original construction, they differ considerably in development. In the highly cultivated languages of the Indo-European family, post-positional additions have gradually been melted down into inflexions, and sometimes even blended with the root; whilst in the less plastic languages of the Scythian group, the principle of agglutination has been more faithfully retained, and every portion and particle of every compound word has not only maintained its original position, but held fast its separate individuality. In this particular the Drâvidian languages agree in general with the Scythian; and hence in each dialect of the family, there is, properly speaking, only one declension and one conjugation.

I here proceed to point out the most notable peculiarities of the Drâvidian root-system, and of the manner in which roots are affected by inflexional combinations.

ARRANGEMENT OF DRÂVIDIAN ROOTS INTO CLASSES.—Drâvidian roots, considered by themselves, apart from formative additions of every kind, may be arranged into the three classes of—(1.) verbal roots, capable of being used also as nouns, which constitute by far the most numerous class; (2.) Nouns which cannot be traced up to any extant verbs; and (3.) Particles of which the origin is unknown.

1. *Verbal Roots.*—The Drâvidian languages differ from the Sanscrit and Greek, and accord with the languages of the Scythian group, in generally using the crude root of the verb, without any addition, as the imperative of the second person singular. This is the general rule, and the few apparent exceptions that exist are to be regarded either as corruptions, or as euphonic or honorific forms of the imperative. In a few instances, both in Tamil and in Telugu, the second person singular of the imperative has cast off its final consonant, which is generally in such cases a soft guttural or a liquid; but in those instances the unchanged verbal theme is found in the less used second person plural, or in the infinitive.

A considerable proportion of Drâvidian roots are used either as verbal themes or as nouns, without addition or alteration in either case; and the class in which they are to be placed, depends solely on the connection. The use of any such root as a noun may be, and probably is, derived from its use as a verb, which would appear to be the primary condition and use of every word belonging to this class; but as such words, when used as nouns, are used without the addition of formatives or any other marks of derivation, they can scarcely be regarded as derivatives from verbs; but in respect of grammatical form, the verb and the noun must be considered either as twin sisters or as identical. The following will suffice as examples of this two-fold condition or use of the same root:—'karei,' Tam., as a verb, means *to melt, to be washed away;* as a noun, *a bank, a shore;* 'alei,' Tam., as a verb, *to wander;* as a noun, *a wave.* In these instances it is evident that the radical meaning of the word is unrestrained, and free to take either a verbal or a nominal direction. Moreover, as the Drâvidian adjective is not separate from the noun, but is generally identical with it, each root may be said to be capable of a three-fold use; viz., (1) as a noun, (2) as an adjective, and (3) as a verb. Thus, in Tamil, 'kaḍ-u,' if used as the nominative of a verb, or followed by case terminations, is a noun, and means *pungency* or *sharpness:* if it is placed before another noun for the purpose of qualifying it, it becomes an adjective; *e.g.*, 'kaḍu naḍei,' *a sharp walk;* 'kaḍu vây̆,' *the tiger*, literally *sharp mouth:* and when it is followed by verbal suffixes, it becomes a verb; *e.g.*, 'kaḍu-kkum,' *it is or will be sharp or pungent.* With the formative addition 'gu,' the same root becomes 'kaḍu-gu,' *mustard.*

In these and in all similar instances, the quantity of the root vowel remains unchanged; whereas in those few instances in which the Sanscrit root is not tied to a single condition, the nominal and verbal forms differ in the quantity of their root vowel; *e.g.*, compare 'vâch-as' (for 'vâk-as'), *of speech,* with 'văk-mi,' *I speak.*

It would appear that originally there was no difference whatever in any instance between the verbal and the nominal form of the root in any Drâvidian dialect; gradually, however, as the dialects became more cultivated, and as logical distinctness was felt to be desirable, a separation commenced to take place. This separation was effected by modifying the theme by some formative addition, when it was desired to restrict it to the one purpose alone, and prevent it from being used for the other also.

In many instances the theme is still used in the poetry, in accordance with ancient usages, indifferently either as a verb or as a noun; but in prose more commonly as a noun only, or as a verb only.

(2.) *Nouns.*—In Sanscrit and the languages allied to it, all words, with the exception of a few pronouns and particles, are derived by native grammarians from verbal roots. In the Drâvidian languages the number of nouns which are incapable of being traced up or resolved into verbs, is more considerable. Still such nouns bear but a small proportion to the entire number; and not a few which are generally considered to be underived roots, are in reality verbal nouns or verbal derivatives.

Many Drâvidian dissyllabic nouns have for their second syllable 'al,' a particle which is a commonly used formative of verbal nouns in

Tamil, and a sign of the infinitive in Canarese and Gônd. All nouns of this class may safely be concluded to have sprung from verbal roots. In some instances their themes are discoverable, in others no trace of the verb from which they have been derived is now apparent. I cannot doubt that the following Tamil words, generally regarded as primitives, are derived from roots which are still in use: viz., 'viral,' *a finger*, from 'viri,' *to expand;* 'kaḍal,' *the sea*, from 'kaḍa,' *to pass beyond;* 'maṇal,' *sand*, from 'maṇ,' *earth;* 'kuḍal,' *a bowel*, and 'kuṛal,' *a pipe*, from 'kuḍei,' *to hollow out*. I cannot discover the derivation of 'niṛal,' *shade*, 'sêval,' *a cock*, and a few similar nouns; nevertheless, judging of them by analogy, I have little doubt that they also have been derived from verbal themes.

There are many nouns denoting primary objects, which in most languages are primitive words, but which in the Drâvidian languages are evidently derived from, or are identical with, extant verbal roots. Thus, 'nilam,' Tam., *the ground*, is from 'nil,' *to stand;* 'mâḍu,' *an ox*, is from 'mâḍu,' Can., *to do, to work;* 'âḍu,' *a sheep*, is identical with 'âḍu,' *to frisk;* 'kurangu,' *a monkey*, is from 'kura,' *to make a noise;* 'pagal,' *day*, as distinguished from *night*, is from 'pagu,' *to divide;* 'kaṇ,' *the eye*, is identical with 'kâṇ,' *to see;* 'mûkku,' *the nose*, is from 'mûgu,' Can., *to smell*. Probably also, 'kei,' *the hand*, bears the same relation to 'gê,' Can., *to do*, which 'kara,' Sans., *hand*, bears to 'kri' or 'kar,' the Sanscrit verb *to do*.

Though the greater number of Drâvidian nouns are undoubtedly to be regarded as verbal derivatives, a certain proportion remain which appear to be underived and independent. In this class are to be included the personal pronouns; most of the nouns of relation which are used as post-positions, answering to the prepositions of other languages, such as 'mêl,' *above*, 'kîṛ,' *below;* and a considerable number of common nouns, including names of objects, *e.g.*, 'kâl,' *foot*, 'maṇ,' *earth*, 'viṇ,' *the sky*, and nouns of quality, *e.g.*, 'kar,' *black*, 'veḷ,' *white*, 'se,' *red*, &c. A suspicion may be entertained that some of the apparently simple nouns belonging to this class are derived from verbal roots which have become obsolete. Thus, 'mun,' *before*, a noun of relation, appears at first sight to be an underived radical, yet it is evident that it is connected with 'mudal,' *first;* and this word, being a verbal noun in 'dal,' is plainly derived from a verb in 'mu,' now lost; so that after all 'mun' itself may be a verbal derivative.

(3.) *Particles.*—A large majority of the Drâvidian post-positions and adverbs, and several of the particles employed in nominal and verbal inflexions are in reality verbs or nouns adapted to especial uses. Every word belonging to the class of adverbs and prepositions in the Drâvidian languages is either the infinitive or the participle of a verb, or the nominative case of a noun used in a locative sense; and even of the inflexional particles which are employed in the declension of nouns and in conjugating verbs, several are easily recognized to be derived from nouns. Thus, in Telugu, the signs of the instrumental ablative, 'chê' and 'chêta,' are the nominative and locative of the word *hand;* and the same case in Tamil is formed by the addition of 'âl,' which is probably a corruption of 'kâl,' in the sense of *a channel.* So also the Tamil 'locative of rest' may be formed by the addition of any noun which signifies 'a place;' and the 'locative of separation,' a case denoting 'motion from a place,' or rather 'the place from whence motion commences,' is formed by the addition of 'il' or 'in,' which means *a house.*

The same suffix added to the crude aoristic form of the verb, constitutes the subjunctive case in Tamil, *e.g.*, 'var-il,' *if* (he, she, it, or they) *come,* literally *in* (his or their) *coming*, that is, *in the event of* (his or their) *coming.*

Whilst all the post-positional adverbs and some of the inflexional particles are certainly derived either from verbs or nouns, there are several particles in use in the Drâvidian languages which do not appear to be connected with any nouns or verbal roots that are now extant, and of which the origin is unknown; *e.g.*, the copulative particle, 'um' in Tamil, 'nu' in Telugu, and 'û' in Canarese; the suffixes of present time, which form the present tense of verbs; viz. 'giR,' in Tamil; 'dap,' in ancient, 'utta,' in modern Canarese; and 'chu' or 'tu,' in Telugu; 'd' or 'i,' the suffix of past time, and 'v' or 'b,' the sign of the future.

Of the post-positions, or suffixes, which are used as signs of case, some distinctly retain their original meaning; in some, the original meaning shines more or less distinctly through the technical appropriation; but no trace whatever remains of the original meaning of 'ku,' 'ki,' or 'ge,' the sign of the dative, or of 'ei,' 'e,' 'annu,' or 'am,' the sign of the accusative.

The Drâvidian dative and accusative have, therefore, assumed the character of real grammatical cases; and in this particular the Drâvidian languages have been brought into harmony with the genius of the Indo-European grammar by the literary cultivation which they have received. It is impossible, I believe, to identify or connect any of the above-mentioned particles with any verbal or nominal roots which are now discoverable in the Drâvidian languages, as will be shown respecting each of them in order; yet it is not only possible but probable that some of them may have sprung from some such origin.

DRÂVIDIAN ROOTS ORIGINALLY MONOSYLLABIC.—It may appear at first sight scarcely credible that the Drâvidian roots were originally monosyllabic, when it is considered that the majority of the words in every Drâvidian sentence are longer than those of (perhaps) any other language in Asia or Europe (*e.g.*, compare 'irukkiRadu,' Tamil, *it is*, with the Latin 'est'), and are inferior in length only to the words of the poly-synthetic languages of America.

The great length of Drâvidian words arises partly from the separation of clashing consonants by the insertion of euphonic vowels, but chiefly from the successive agglutination of formative and inflexional particles and pronominal fragments. A considerable number of Drâvidian verbal themes, prior to the addition of inflexional forms, are trisyllabic; but it will generally be found that the first two syllables have been expanded out of one by the euphonic insertion or addition of a vowel; whilst the last syllable of the apparent base is in reality a formative addition, which appears to have been merely euphonic in origin, but which now serves to distinguish transitive verbs from intransitives. In some instances the first syllable of the verbal theme contains the root, whilst the second is a particle anciently added to it and compounded with it for the purpose of expanding or restricting the signification. The syllables that are added to the inflexional base are those which denote case, tense, person, and number.

Hence, whatever be the length and complication of Drâvidian words, they may invariably be traced up to monosyllabic roots, by a careful removal of successive accretions. Thus, when we analyse 'perugugiRadu,' Tam., *it increases*, we find that the final 'adu,' represents the pronoun 'it;' 'giR,' is the sign of the present tense; and 'perugu,' is the base or verbal theme. Of this base, the final syllable 'gu,' is only a formative, restricting the verb to an intransitive or neuter signification; and by its removal we come to 'peru,' the real root, which is used also as an adjective or noun of quality, signifying *greatness* or *great*. Nor is even this dissyllable 'peru,' the ultimate condition of the root: it is an euphonized form of 'per,' which is found in the adjectives 'per-iya' and 'per-um,' *great*; and a lengthened but monosyllabic form of the same is 'pêr.' Thus, by successive agglutinations, a word of six syllables has been found to grow out of one. In all these forms, and under every shape which the word can assume, the radical element remains unchanged, or is so slightly changed, that it can readily be pointed out by the least experienced scholar.

The root always stands out in distinct relief, unobscured, unabsorbed, though surrounded by a large family of auxiliary affixes. This distinctness and prominence of the radical element in every word is a characteristic feature of all the Scythian tongues (*e.g.*, of the Turkish and the Hungarian); whilst in the Semitic and Indo-European tongues the root is frequently so much altered that it can scarcely be recognised.

It is desirable here to explain in detail the manner in which Drâvidian roots, originally monosyllabic, have been lengthened by the insertion or addition of euphonic vowels, or by formative additions, or in both ways.

Euphonic Lengthening of Roots. — There are two modes in which the crude Drâvidian root is euphonically lengthened.

First, by the insertion of an euphonic vowel between the two initial consonants of the original base. It has already been shown that in the Tamilian or oldest Drâvidian system of sounds, a double consonant cannot stand at the beginning of any word or syllable. A vowel must be inserted, or one of the consonants must be omitted. This is invariably the rule in Tamil, and generally so in Telugu; and in the event of a vowel being inserted in the double initial, it is obvious that the root, if a monosyllable, will become a dissyllable. Thus, 'viri,' Tam., *to expand*, the origin of 'viral,' *a finger*, was probably at first 'vri.' The double consonant 'vr,' was incapable of being pronounced by Tamil organs, and was, therefore, converted into a dissyllable by the insertion of a vowel. The probability of the change in this instance is strengthened by the circumstance that where the Tamil has 'viral,' *a finger*, the Telugu has first 'vrêlu,' and finally 'vêlu.' In the same manner, where the Tamil has 'maram,' *a tree* (Canarese 'mara'), the Ku has 'mrânu,' softened in Telugu into 'mânu;' and where most of the Drâvidian languages have 'tala,' *head*, the Ku has 'tlâva;' the final 'vu' being an euphonic addition to 'tlâ.' The best proof that in the Drâvidian languages dissyllables were in this manner lengthened from monosyllables, is furnished by the circumstance that all Sanscrit words and particles which commence with a double consonant, are altered on this very plan when they are borrowed by the Tamil; *e.g.*, 'tripti,' *satisfaction*, is converted into 'tirutti,' and 'pra,' the preposition *before*, into 'pira.' This euphonic lengthening out of the crude base by the insertion of an euphonic vowel, is apparent also in those bases which become polysyllabic by the further addition of formatives. Thus, 'tirumbu,' *to turn*, is compounded of 'tiru,' the original base, and 'bu' (euphonized in the intransitive into 'mbu'), a formative. 'tiru' itself, however (answering to 'tiri,' *to wander*, and to several other related words), was doubtless originally a monosyllable, probably 'tri.' We find this very form in the Telugu transitive verb, which is 'tri-ppu,' corresponding to the Tamiḻ 'tiru-ppu;' with which we may compare the Greek 'τρέπε,' a word which is almost identical in sound as well as in signification.

The *second* mode in which crude Drâvidian roots are lengthened, is by the addition of an euphonic vowel to the base. This euphonic addition to the final consonant takes place in grammatical Telugu and Canarese in the case of all words ending in a consonant, whatever be the number of syllables they contain.

Vowel additions to roots which contain two syllables and upwards, are made solely for the purpose of helping the enunciation; but when the additions which have been made to some monosyllabic roots are examined, it is found that they are intended not merely for vocalisation, but rather for euphonization.

When it is desired merely to help the enunciation of a final consonant, 'u' is the vowel that is ordinarily employed for this purpose (in Malayâlam 'a'), and this 'u' is uniformly elided when it is followed by another vowel: but 'u' is not the only vowel which is added on to monosyllabic roots, though perhaps it is most frequently met with; and in some of the instances under consideration, it becomes so intimately blended with the real base, that it will not consent to be elided; *e.g.*, 'aḍu,' Tamil, *to be near*, the final 'u' of which does not admit of elision, though the crude base is probably 'aḍ.' Next to 'u,' the vowel which is most commonly employed is 'i;' then follows 'a;' then 'e' or 'ei.' Verbal roots borrowed from the Sanscrit, have generally 'i' added to the final consonant in all the Drâvidian languages; to which the Telugu adds 'nchu,' and the Canarese 'su,' formatives which will be noticed afterwards. Thus, 'sap,' Sans., *to curse*, is in Tamil 'śabi;' in Telugu, 'sabinchu;' in Can., 'sabisu.' On comparing the various Drâvidian idioms, it is found that all these auxiliary or enunciative vowels are interchangeable. Thus, of Tamil verbs in 'a,' 'kaḍa,' *to pass*, is in Telugu, 'gaḍachu;' 'maṛa,' *to forget*, is in Canarese 'mare:' of Tamil verbs in 'i,' 'kaḍi,' *to bite*, is in Telugu 'kara-chu;' 'geli,' *to win*, is in Canarese 'gillu.' Of Tamil verbs in 'ei,' 'muḷei,' *to sprout*, is in Telugu, 'moluchu.' These final vowels being thus interchangeable equivalents, it is evident that they are intended merely for the promotion of euphony, and as helps to enunciation, that they are not essential parts of the themes to which they are suffixed, and do not add anything to their meaning.

Formative Additions to Roots.—Formative suffixes are appended to the crude bases of nouns, as well as to those of verbs. They are added not only to verbal derivatives, but to nouns which appear to be primitive; but they are most frequently appended to verbs properly so called, of the inflexional bases of which they form the last syllable, generally the third. Whatever may have been the origin of these particles, they now serve to distinguish transitive verbs from intransitives, and the adjectival form of nouns from that which stands in an isolated position and is used as a nominative. In Tamil, in which these formatives are most largely used and most fully developed, the initial consonant of the formative is single when it marks the intransitive or neuter signification of the verb, or that form of the noun which governs verbs or is governed by them: when it marks the transitive or active voice of the verb, or the adjectival form of the noun, viz., that form of the noun which is assumed by the first of two nouns that stand in a case relation to one another, the initial consonant of the formative is doubled, and is at the same time changed from a sonant into a surd. The single consonant, which is characteristic of the intransitive formative, is often euphonised by prefixing a nasal, without, however, altering its signification or value. The Tamilian formatives are—(1.) 'gu' or 'ngu,' and its transitive 'kku,' answering to the Telugu 'chu' or 'nchu;' (2.) 'śu' and its transitive 'śśu' or 'chu;' (3.) 'du' or 'ndu,' and its transitive 'ttu;' and (4.) 'bu' or 'mbu,' with its transitive 'ppu.'

Though I call these particles 'formatives,' they are not regarded in this light by native grammarians. They are generally suffixed even to the imperative, which is supposed to be the crude form of the verb; they form a portion of the inflexional base, to which all signs of gender, number, and case, and also of mood and tense, are appended; and hence it was natural that native grammarians should regard them as constituent elements of the root. I have no doubt, however, of the propriety of representing them as formatives, seeing that they contribute nothing to the signification of the root, and that it is only by means of a further change, *i.e.*, by being hardened and doubled, that they express a grammatical relation, viz., the difference which subsists between the transitive and the intransitive forms of verbs, and between adjectival and independent nouns.

In this particular perhaps more than in any other, the high

grammatical cultivation of the Tamil has developed a tendency to imitate the Indo-European tongues by retaining syllables of which it has lost the original distinctive meaning, and combining such syllables after a time with the radical element of the word, or using them for a new purpose.

I proceed to consider the various formatives more particularly, with examples of their use and force.

(1.) 'gu' or 'ngu,' with its transitive 'kku.' Tamil examples; 'peru-gu,' intrans., *to become increased,* 'peru-kku,' trans., *to cause to increase;* 'aḍa-ngu,' *to be contained,* 'aḍa-kku,' *to contain.* So also in the case of dissyllabic roots, *e.g.*, 'â-gu,' *to become,* 'â-kku,' *to make;* 'nî-ngu,' *to quit,* 'nî-kku,' *to put away.* There is a considerable number of nouns, chiefly trisyllabic, in which the same formative is employed. In this case, however, there is no difference between the isolated shape of the noun and the adjectival shape. Whatever particle is used, whether 'gu,' 'ngu,' or 'kku,' it retains its position in all circumstances unchanged. Examples: 'paḍa-gu,' *a boat,* 'kura-ngu,' *a monkey,* 'sara-kku,' *any article of merchandize.* From a comparison of the above examples, it is evident that 'ng' is equivalent to 'g,' and euphonized from it; and that 'ng,' equally with 'g,' becomes 'kk' in a transitive connection.

In a few instances, 'kku,' the transitive formative, is altered in colloquial Tamil usage to 'chu,' according to a law of interchange already noticed; *e.g.*, 'kâÿkku,' *to boil* (crude root 'kâÿ'), is generally written and pronounced 'kâÿchu.' This altered form of the sign of the transitive, which is the exception in Tamil, is in Telugu the rule of the language, 'kku' being regularly replaced in Telugu by 'chu.'

In Telugu the intransitive formative 'gu' is not euphonically altered into 'ngu' as in Tamil; but an obscure nasal, the half 'anuswâra,' often precedes the 'gu,' and shows that in both languages the same tendency to nasalisation exists. It is remarkable, that whilst the Tamil often nasalises the formative of the neuter, and never admits a nasal into the transitive formative, the Telugu, in a large number of cases, nasalises the transitive, and generally leaves the neuter in its primitive, un-nasalised condition. Thus in Telugu, whenever the base terminates in 'i' (including a large number of Sanscrit derivatives), 'chu' is converted into 'nchu;' though neither in this nor in any case does the 'kku' of the Tamil change into 'ngku.' *E.g.*, from 'raṭṭi,' *double,* the Tamil forms 'raṭṭi-kka' (infinitive), *to double;* whilst the Telugu form of the same is 'reṭṭi-ncha.' 'manni-ncha,' *to forgive,* in Telugu, corresponds in the same manner to the Tamil 'manni-kka.' In some cases in Telugu the euphonic nasal is prefixed to 'chu,' not after 'i' only, but after other vowels besides. Thus, 'perugu,' *to increase*, neut., is the same in Tamil and in Telugu. but instead of finding 'peru-chu' to be the transitive or active (corresponding to the Tamil transitive 'peru-kku'), we find 'penchu,' corrupted from 'peru-chu:' so also instead of 'pagu-kku,' Tam., *to divide*, we find in Telugu 'panchu,' for 'pagu-nchu.'

The identity of the Tamil 'k' and the Telugu 'ch' appears also from the circumstance that in many cases 'vu' may optionally be used in Telugu instead of 'chu.' This use of 'vu' as the equivalent of 'chu' points to a time when 'gu' was the formative in ordinary use in Telugu as in Tamil; for 'ch' has no tendency to be converted into 'v,' 'b,' or 'p,' whilst 'k' or 'g,' constantly evinces this tendency to change into 'v,' not only in Telugu, but also in colloquial Tamil; and 'v' is regularly interchangeable with 'b' and its surd 'p.'

I conclude, therefore, that 'gu' was the original shape of this formative in the Drâvidian languages; and that its doubled, surd shape, 'kku,' the formative of transitives, was softened in Telugu into 'chu,' and in Canarese still further softened into 'śu.'

(2.) 'śu,' and its transitive 'śśu,' pronounced 'chu.'—This formative is very rare in Tamil, and the examples which the Telugu contains, though abundant, are not to the point, inasmuch as they are apparently altered from the older 'ku' and 'kku,' by the ordinary softening process by which 'k' changes into 'ś,' and 'kk' into 'ch.' A Tamil example of this formative is seen in 'aḍei-śu,' *to take refuge*, of which the transitive is 'aḍei-chu,' *to enclose, to twine round.*

(3.) 'du' or 'ndu,' with its transitive form 'ttu.'—There appears to be no difference whatever between this formative and the other three, 'gu,' 'śu,' or 'bu,' in meaning or grammatical relation; and as 'gu' is euphonized in the intransitive to 'ngu,' so is 'du,' to 'ndu;' whilst in the transitive the doubled 'd' (and its equivalent 'nd') changes by rule into 'tt.' The euphonic change of 'du' to 'ndu,' has so generally taken place, that 'ndu' is invariably used instead of 'du' in the formatives of verbs; and it is only in the formatives of nouns that 'du,' the more primitive form, is sometimes found to have survived.

The formative 'gu' remains unaltered in the adjectival form of nouns; but 'du' changes into 'ttu,' when used adjectivally, in the same manner as in the transitive voice of verbs. Tamil examples of this formative;—'tiru-ndu,' *to become correct*, 'tiru-ttu,' *to correct;* 'maru-ndu,' *medicine*, adjectival form of the same, 'maru-ttu,' *e.g.*, 'maruttu-(p)pei,' *a medicine bag*. The primitive unnasalised 'du' and its adjectival 'ttu,' are found in such words as 'eru-du,' *a bull, an ox,* and 'eru-ttu-(p)pûṭṭu,' *the fastening of an ox's traces.* Nearly all the verbs which take 'du,' or 'ndu,' as a formative are trisyllabic. Of the few dissyllabic verbs of this class in Tamil, the most interesting is 'nîndu,' *to swim,* of which I consider 'nî' as the crude form. 'Nîndu,' is evidently an euphonized form of 'nîdu,' ('du' changed into 'ndu'); for the verbal noun derived from it, 'nîttal,' *swimming,* is without the nasal, and the Telugu uses 'nîdu,' for the verb itself, instead of 'nîndu.' I have little doubt that the 'du,' or 'ndu' of this word, is simply a formative, and that the crude primitive base is 'nî,' answering to the Greek *νέ-ω*, the Latin 'no,' 'nato' and also to 'nau,' Sans. *a boat,* of which the Sanscrit does not contain the root.

Derivative nouns formed from verbs which have formative suffixes always prefer as their formative the transitive suffix, or that which doubles and hardens the initial consonant. Thus from 'tiru-ndu,' *to become correct,* is formed 'tiru-ttam,' *correction;* and from 'tû-ngu,' *to sleep,* 'tû-kkam,' *sleep.*

In some instances the crude root of a verb is used as the intransitive, whilst the transitive is formed by the addition of 'ttu' to the root. *E.g.* 'paḍu,' *to lie down,* 'paḍu-ttu,' *to lay;* 'tâṛ,' *to be low,* 'tâṛ-ttu,' *to lower;* 'nil' (Telugu 'nilu'), *to stand,* 'niru-ttu' (for 'nilu-ttu'), *to establish.* In such cases the Canarese uses 'du' instead of the Tamil 'ttu,' *e.g.,* 'tâḷ-du,' *to lower,* instead of 'tâṛ-ttu.' This transitive formative is sometimes represented as a causal; but it will be shown in the section on 'The Verb,' that 'vi' (euphonically 'bi,' or 'ppi') is the only real causal in the Drâvidian languages. In all the cases now mentioned, where 'ttu' is used as the formative of the transitive by the Tamil, the Telugu uses 'chu' or 'pu.'

I class under the head of this formative all those nouns in which the 'cerebral' consonants 'ḍ,' 'ṇḍ,' and 'ṭṭ,' are used in the same manner and for the same purpose as the dentals 'd,' 'nd,' and 'tt;' *e.g.* 'kuru-ḍu,' *blindness,* adjectival form of the same, 'kuru-ṭṭu,' *blind;* 'ira-ṇḍu,' *two,* adjectival form, 'ira-ṭṭu,' *double.* The Telugu hardens but does not double the final 'ḍ' of such nouns; *e.g.,* 'ôḍ-u,' *a leak,* 'ôṭi,' *leaky.*

In some instances in Tamil, the hard rough 'ʀ,' when used as a final, seems to be equivalent to 'du,' or 'ḍu,' and is doubled and pronounced with a 't;' *e.g.,* 'kiṇa-ʀu,' *a well,* 'kiṇa ʀʀu' (pronounced 'kiṇattru'), *of a well.* On this point, however, see Section on Nouns.—Increment 'ṭi,' or 'attu.'

(4.) 'bu' or 'mbu,' with its transitive 'ppu.'—In Canarese, 'bu,' the original form of this intransitive suffix, has been softened into 'vu,' and in Tamil 'bu,' has universally been euphonized into 'mbu.' This Tamilian formative 'mbu,' is in some instances softened in Telugu nouns into 'mu.' The 'bu' or 'mbu' of Tamil verbs is superseded by 'vu' or 'gu' in Telugu; and the forms answering to the Tamil transitive 'ppu' are 'pu' and 'mpu,' rarely 'ppu.'

Example of the use of this formative by a verb:—'nira-mbu,' Tam. *to be full*, 'nira-ppu,' *to fill;* of which the crude base 'nir,' re-appears in the related verb 'niʀ-ei,' *to be full*, or *to fill*. The Telugu has 'niṇḍu' instead of 'nirambu;' but the transitive 'nimpu,' answers very nearly to the Tamil 'nirappu.' Example of a noun in 'mbu' and 'ppu;'—'iru-mbu,' Tam., *iron*, adjectival form, 'iru-ppu,' *of iron, e.g.*, 'iruppu-(k)kôl,' *an iron rod*. In Telugu 'irumbu' is softened into 'inumu,' adjectival form 'inupa.' The Canarese still adheres to the original form of this suffix, generally softening 'b' into 'v,' but leaving it always unnasalised; *e.g.*, Canarese 'hâvu,' *a snake*, properly 'pâvu:' Tamil 'pâmbu,' nasalised from 'pâbu;' adjectival form 'pâppu,' *e.g.*, 'pâppu-(k)koḍi,' *the serpent banner:* Telugu, still further altered, 'pâmu.' This example clearly illustrates the progress of the formative in question, and confirms the supposition, that it was merely euphonic in its origin, and that it was by degrees that it acquired the character of a formative.

It has been mentioned that the Telugu uses 'pu' or 'mpu' as a formative of transitive verbs, where the Tamil uses 'ppu.' It should be added that even in those cases where the Tamil uses the other formatives previously noticed, viz., 'kku' and 'ttu,' the Telugu often prefers 'pu.' Compare the following infinitives in Tamil and in Telugu, *e.g.* 'mêykka,' Tam. *to feed cattle*, 'mêpa,' Tel.; 'nirutta,' Tam. *to establish*, 'nilupa,' Tel. Where 'kku' in Tamil, and 'pu' in Telugu are preceded by 'i,' this formative becomes in Telugu either 'mpu' or 'nchu;' *e.g.*, compare 'oppuvi-kka,' Tamil, *to deliver over*, with the corresponding Tel. infinitive, 'appavi-mpa,' or 'appavi-ncha.'

It appears from the various particulars now mentioned, that transitive verbs, and nouns used adjectivally, must have been regarded by the primitive Tamilians as possessing some quality in common. The common feature possessed by each, is doubtless the quality of transition; for it is evident that when nouns are used adjectivally there is a transition of the quality or act denoted by the adjectival noun to the noun substantive to which it is prefixed, which corresponds to the transition of the action denoted by the transitive verb to the accusative which it governs.

It is manifest that the various particles which are used as formatives do not essentially differ from one another either in signification, in the purpose for which they are used, in the manner in which they are affixed, or in the manner in which they are doubled and hardened. It was euphony only that determined which of the sonants 'g,' 'ś,' 'ḍ,' 'd,' or 'b,' should be suffixed as a formative to any particular verb or noun.

Possibly, indeed, the use of these formatives originated altogether in considerations of euphony. The only point in which a grammatical principle appears to exist, is the doubling of the initial consonant of the formative to denote or correspond with the putting forth of energy which is inherent in the idea of active or transitive verbs, as distinguished from intransitives.

From the statements and examples given above, it may be concluded that wherever Drâvidian verbs or nouns are found to terminate in any of the syllables referred to there is reason to suspect, that the first part of the word alone constitutes or contains the root. The final syllables 'gu,' 'ngu,' 'kku;' 'śu,' 'chu;' 'ḍu,' 'ṇḍu,' 'ṭṭu;' 'du,' 'ndu,' 'ttu;' 'bu,' 'mbu,' 'mpu,' 'pu,' 'ppu;' 'mu,' 'vu;' may, as a general rule, be rejected as formative additions.

This rule will be found on examination to throw unexpected light on the derivation and relationship of many nouns which are commonly supposed to be primitive and independent, but which, when the syllables referred to above are rejected, are found to be derived from or allied to verbal roots which are still in use. I adduce, as examples, the following Tamil words:—'kombu,' *a branch, a twig;* 'vêmbu,' *the Margosa tree;* 'vambu,' *abuse;* 'pâmbu,' *a snake.* As soon as the formative final, 'mbu,' is rejected, the verbs from which these nouns are derived are brought to light. Thus, 'ko-mbu,' *a twig,* is plainly derived from 'ko-ÿ,' *to pluck off, to cut;* 'vê-mbu,' *the Margosa tree,* is from 'vê-ÿ,' *to be umbrageous, to screen or shade* (the shade of this tree being peculiarly prized); 'va-mbu,' *abuse,* is from 'vei,' properly 'va-ÿ' (corresponding to the Canarese 'vayyu'), *to revile;* 'pâ-mbu,' *a snake,* is from 'pâ-ÿ,' *to spring.* In these instances, the verbal base which is now in use ends in 'y,' a merely euphonic addition, which does not belong to the root, and which disappears in the derivatives before the consonants which are added as formatives.

The same principle applied to nouns ending in the other formative syllables will be found to yield similar results; *e.g.,* 'par-andu,' *a hawk,* from 'para,' *to fly;* and 'kiṛangu,' *a root,* from 'kiṛ,' *to be beneath,* the 'i' of which, though long in Tamil, is short in the Telugu 'kinda,' *below.*

REDUPLICATION OF THE FINAL CONSONANT OF THE ROOT.—The principle of employing reduplication as a means of producing grammatical expression is recognized by the Drâvidian languages, as well as by those of the Indo-European family; though the mode in which the reduplication is effected and the objects in view are different. It is in Tamil that this reduplication is most distinctly apparent, and it should here be borne in mind, that when a Tamil consonant is doubled, it is changed from a sonant into a surd. The final consonant of a Tamil root is doubled—(1) for the purpose of changing a noun into an adjective, showing that it qualifies another noun, or putting it in the genitive case, *e.g.*, from 'mâḍu,' *an ox*, is formed 'mâṭṭ-u (t)tôl,' *ox-hide*; (2) for the purpose of converting an intransitive or neuter verb into a transitive, *e.g.*, from 'ôḍ-u,' *to run*, is formed 'ôṭṭu,' *to drive*; (3) for the purpose of 'forming the preterite,' *e.g.*, 'tag-u,' *to be fit*, 'takk-a,' *that was fit*; and (4) for the purpose of forming derivative nouns from verbal themes, *e.g.*, from 'eṛud-u,' *to write*, is formed 'eṛutt-u,' *a letter*. [See this subject further elucidated in the sections on 'The Noun' and 'The Verb.'] It is remarkable, that whilst the Indo-European tongues mark the perfect tense by the reduplication of the *first* syllable, it is by the reduplication of the *last* letter that the Drâvidian languages effect this purpose; and also, that whilst the Tibetan converts a *noun* into a *verb* by doubling the last consonant, this should be a Drâvidian method of converting a *verb* into a *noun*. The rationale of the Drâvidian reduplication is, that it was felt to be a natural way to express the idea of *transition* both in the act and in the result.

Up to this point it has been found that all Drâvidian polysyllabic roots are traceable to a monosyllabic base, lengthened either by euphonic additions and insertions, or by the addition of formative particles. An important class of dissyllabic bases remains, of which the second syllable is neither an euphonic nor a formative addition, but an inseparable particle of specialisation, into the nature and use of which we shall now inquire.

Particles of Specialisation.—The verbs and nouns belonging to the class of bases which are now under consideration, consist of a monosyllabic root or stem, containing the generic signification, and a second syllable, perhaps the fragment of a lost root or lost post-position, by which the generic meaning of the stem is in some manner modified. The second syllable appears sometimes to expand and sometimes to restrict the signification, but in some instances, through the absence of synonyms, its force cannot now be ascertained. As this syllable is intended in some manner to specialise the meaning of the root, I call it 'the particle of specialisation.'

The principle which is involved in the use of this particle, and the manner in which it is carried into effect, remarkably correspond to a characteristic feature or law of the Semitic languages, which it appears to be desirable to notice here somewhat particularly. As far back as the separate existence of the Semitic family of languages can be traced, every root is found to consist of two syllables, comprising generally three consonants. When Semitic bi-literal roots are compared with their synonyms, or corresponding roots, in the Indo-European languages, and especially with those which are found in Sanscrit, a simpler and more primitive root-system has been brought to light. It has been ascertained, in a large number of instances, that whilst the first syllable of the Hebrew root corresponds with the Sanscrit, the second syllable does not in any manner correspond to any Indo-European synonym. It is found also, that the second syllable has not any essential connection with the first, and that a considerable number of families of roots exist in which the first syllable is the same in each case, whilst the second continually varies. It is therefore inferred that in such cases the first syllable alone (comprising two consonants, the initial and the final, together with the vowel used for enunciation) contains the radical base and generic signification, and that the second syllable, perhaps the fragment of an obsolete word, has been appended to the first and afterwards compounded with it, for the purpose of giving the generic signification a specific and definite direction. According to this view, which appears to be in the main correct, Hebrew roots are to be regarded not singly and separately, as independent monads, but as arranged generically in clusters or groups, exhibiting general resemblances and special differences. The family likeness resides in the first syllable, the radical base; the individuality or special peculiarity in the second, 'the particle of specialisation.'

It is true that in some instances the second syllable of Semitic roots meets with its counterpart in the Indo-European languages, as well as the first, or even instead of the first; but the peculiar rule or law now referred to is found to pervade so large a portion of the Hebrew roots, that it justly claims to be considered as a characteristic of the language.

Thus, there is a family of Hebrew roots signifying generally 'to divide,' 'to cleave,' 'to separate,' &c. The members of this family are 'pâlâh,' 'pâlaḥ,' 'pâlag,' 'pâlâ,' 'pâlal;' and also (through the dialectic interchange of 'l' with 'r'), 'pârash,' 'pâras;' Chaldee 'peras.' It cannot be doubted that in all these instances the first syllable 'pâl' or 'par,' or rather 'p-r,' 'p-l' (for the vowel belongs not to the root, but to the grammatical relation), expresses merely the general idea of 'division;'

whilst the second syllable (which is in some instances a reduplication of the final consonant of the bi-literal) expresses, or is supposed to express, the particular mode in which the 'division' or 'partition' is effected. The first syllable, which is the same in all the members of this group of roots, is that which is to be compared with synonyms in other languages, whilst the second syllable is merely modal. In this instance we not only observe a distinct analogy between the Hebrew roots, 'p-r,' 'p-l,' and the Greek '*πόρ-ω*,' the Latin 'par-s,' 'par-tis,' and the Sanscrit 'phal,' *to divide*, but we also discover the existence of a distinct and remarkable analogy with the Drâvidian languages. Compare with the Hebrew 'p-r,' 'p-l,' the Tamil 'piri,' *to divide*, and 'pâl,' *a part*; 'piḷa' and 'pôṛ,' *to cleave*; as also 'pagir' and 'pagu,' *to portion out, to divide*. See also the 'Glossarial Affinities.'

On turning our attention to the root-system of the Drâvidian languages, we are struck with the resemblance which it bears to the Semitic root-system referred to above. We find in these languages groups of related roots, the first syllables of which are nearly or wholly identical, whilst their second syllables are different in each instance, and in consequence of this difference produce the required degree of diversity in the signification of each member of the group. We also find in these languages, as in Hebrew, that the generic particle or common base, and the added particle of specialisation, are so conjoined as to become one indivisible etymon. The specialising particle, which was probably a separable suffix or post-position at first, has become by degrees a component part of the word,—and this word, so compounded, constitutes the base to which all formatives and all inflexional particles are appended.

This root-system exists in all the languages of the Drâvidian family, but its nature and peculiarities are especially apparent in the Tamil. Out of many such groups of related Tamil roots, I select as illustrations two groups which commence with the first letter of the alphabet.

1. Roots which radiate from the syllable 'aḍ:'

aḍu	*to come near*; also 'aḍu,' transitive, *to unite.*
aḍa	*to join, to join battle.*
aḍa-ngu aḍa-kku	*to be contained, to enclose*; verbs formed from 'aḍa,' the preceding verb, by the addition of the formatives 'ngu' and 'kku.'
aḍei	*to attain, to get in, to roost*: transitive, *to enclose.*
aḍeiśu	*to take refuge*, from 'aḍei,' with the addition of the formative 'śu;' also 'adeigu.'
aḍar	*to be close together, to be crowded.*
aḍuk-(ku)	*to place one thing upon another, to pile up.* This verb is properly

'aḍuk,' but final 'k' in Tamil is always vocalised by the help of 'u,' and often doubled, as in this instance, before receiving the 'u.'

aṇḍu (Telugu aṇṭu), *to approach.* This verb seems to be identical with 'aḍu,' the first in the list, and euphonized from it by the insertion of the nasal.

It is obvious that all these roots are pervaded by a family resemblance. All contain the generic notion of 'nearness,' expressed by the first or base syllable 'aḍ;' whilst each, by means of the second syllable, or particle of specialisation, denotes some particular species of nearness.

2. Roots which radiate from the base syllable 'aṇ:'—

aṇu *to touch.*
aṇi *to put on, to adorn.*
aṇei *to connect, to embrace;* as a noun, *a weir, a dam.*
aṇavu *to cleave to.* ('vu' is probably an euphonic addition.)
aṇṇu *to lean upon.* (From this verb is derived 'aṇṇal' or 'aṇṇan' *an elder brother, one to lean upon,* a derivation as poetical as it is reliable).

The generic idea signified by the base syllable 'aṇ' is evidently that of 'contact;' and this group differs from the previous one as actual 'contact' differs from 'contiguity' or 'nearness.' Probably 'âṇi,' *a nail, a fastening,* is derived from the same verb, and it appears probable also that this is the origin of the Sanscrit 'aṇi' or 'âṇi,' *the pin of an axle.* At all events it seems a more natural derivation than that which is given by the Sanscrit grammarians, viz., from 'aṇa,' *to sound.*

The illustrations given above prove, that the second syllables of the various verbs now adduced have not been added merely for purposes of euphony, but have been appended in order to expand, to restrict, or in some manner to modify and specialise the signification. It was shown in a previous part of this section, that the vowels 'a,' 'i,' 'u,' 'e,' and 'ei' are sometimes added euphonically to monosyllabic roots. It is obvious, however, that this is not the only purpose for which those vowel additions are used; and it is of importance to know that when they are merely euphonic they are found to be interchangeable with other vowels, whereas when they are used as particles of specialisation they retain their individual character more firmly.

The examples already given may suffice to illustrate the use of appended *vowels* as specialising particles. Syllables ending in consonants, especially in 'l' and 'r,' are also used very frequently for this purpose; and it seems desirable here to adduce examples of the use of particles of this class. The following examples are mostly from the Tamil, in which 'l' and 'r' may stand as finals. The other dialects add 'ŭ' to the final consonant of each of these particles. The Tamil requires this euphonic addition of 'u' when a word ends in the hard, rough 'ʀ,' or in any consonant besides the nasals and semi-vowels.

Each root being considered either as a verb or as a noun according to circumstances, I give examples of nouns as well as of verbs. Some of the following roots, though used as verbs, are more commonly used as nouns, and some, though used as nouns, are more commonly used as verbs. Some of the examples, again, are used either as nouns only or as verbs only:—

Final Particles.	Verbs.	Nouns.
ar	vaḷar, *to grow*	suvar, *a wall*
ir	tuḷir, *to sprout*	ugir, *a finger nail*
ur		nudur-u, Tel., *the forehead*
aṛ	pugaṛ, *to praise*	idaṛ, *a flower leaf*
iṛ	magiṛ, *to rejoice*	tamiṛ, *sweetness, Tamil.*
aʀ-u	iḍaʀ-u, *to trip*	kiṇaʀ-u, *a well*
iʀ-u		muyiʀ-u, *the red ant*
al	suṛal, *to whirl*	îral, *the liver*
il	kuyil, *to utter a sound*	tigil, *a fright*
ul	pagul-u, Tel., *to break*	
aḷ	tuvaḷ, *to bend*	tinggaḷ, *the moon*
iḷ		madiḷ, *a fort wall*
uḷ	uruḷ, *to roll*	iruḷ, *darkness*
uk-(ku)	kaḍuk-(ku), *to suffer pain*	koḍuk-(ku), *a sting*

Of all the fourteen specialising particles ending in consonants, of which examples have now been adduced, only one appears occasionally to be used as an equivalent for a vowel addition. 'ar' alternates with 'ei;' *e.g.*, 'amar,' Tam., *to rest*, and 'amei,' are apparently equivalent. The verb *to grow*, also, is in Tamil 'vaḷar,' and in Canarese 'baḷe,' which in Tamil would be 'vaḷei.' Similar instances, however, abound in Hebrew, without invalidating the general principle; and even with respect to the latter of the two Drâvidian illustrations, there is a marked distinction in Tamil between 'vaḷar,' and a related theme, 'viḷei,' 'vaḷar' meaning *to grow* 'upwards, as a man or a tree,' whilst 'viḷei,' means *to grow* 'as a crop;' hence as a noun 'viḷei' means *a field*.

I here subjoin an example of another peculiar and interesting set of groups of roots which are found in the Drâvidian languages, and which are formed upon a plan differing considerably from that which has now been explained.

The roots referred to are dissyllabic, but they contain only one consonant, which is preceded and followed by a vowel. This consonant appears to represent the ultimate or radical base, whilst the initial and final vowels alter in accordance with the particular shade of signification which it is desired to convey. When we compare 'iḍu,' Tam., *to press* or *crush*, 'oḍu,' *to squeeze, to bring into a smaller compass*, and 'iḍi,' *to bruise, to beat down*, as also 'aḍi,' *to beat*; or 'oḍi,' *to break in two*, and 'uḍei' (pronounced 'oḍei'), *to break open*; we cannot avoid the conclusion that the first four roots are closely related members of the same family or group; that the last two roots are in like manner mutually related; and that possibly the whole of them have an ulterior relationship, in virtue of their possessing in common the same nucleus or radical base, the central consonant 'ḍ,' and the same generic signification.

DRÂVIDIAN ROOTS SUSTAIN NO INTERNAL CHANGE ON RECEIVING FORMATIVE OR INFLEXIONAL ADDITIONS, OR IN COMPOSITION.—In general this rule is so strictly adhered to, and the deviations from it are so few and unimportant, that it may be regarded as a characteristic of the Drâvidian root-system, and a counterpart of the rigid unchangeableness which characterizes Scythian roots.

The vowels of Drâvidian roots belong as essentially to the radical base as the consonants. They neither belong, as in the Semitic languages, to the system of means by which grammatical relations are expressed, nor are they modified, as in the Indo-European languages, by the addition of inflexional forms.

In the Semitic languages the radical base is destitute of vowels, and by itself unpronounceable. The insertion of vowels not only vocalises the consonants of the root, but constitutes it a grammatically inflected verb or noun, the signification of which varies with the variation of the interior vowels.

In the Indo-European languages grammatical modifications are produced by additions to the root; and though in the earliest period of the history of those languages, the root, generally monosyllabic, is supposed to have remained unaltered by additions and combinations, yet the existence of that rigidity is not capable of direct proof; for on examining the Sanscrit, Greek, Latin, and German, the most faithful representatives of the early condition of those languages, we find that the root vowels of a large proportion of the words are modified by the addition of the suffixes of case and tense; and in particular, that the reduplication of the root, by which the perfect appears usually to have been formed, is often found either to alter the quantity of the root-vowel, to change one vowel into another, or entirely to expunge it.

In the Scythian family of tongues, not only does the vowel belong essentially to the root, but it remains unalterable under all circumstances. Neither the vowel nor the consonant (or consonants) of which the root is composed, sustains any change or modification on the addition of the signs of gender, number, and case, or of person, tense, and mood; which are successively agglutinated to the root, not welded into combination with it.

This rigidity or persistency is characteristic also of the roots of the Drâvidian languages, with a few exceptions which will shortly be mentioned. In general, whatever be the length or weight of the additions made to a Drâvidian root, and whether it stands alone or is combined with other words in a construct state, it is represented as fully and faithfully in the oblique cases as in the nominative, in the preterite and future as in the present tense or in the imperative.

I proceed to point out the principal exceptions to this rule.

1. *Euphonic Exceptions.*

(1.) Some exceptions are purely enunciative, and consist only in such changes as are necessary to enable Drâvidian organs to enunciate double consonants. See the portions of this section in which the lengthening of roots by the euphonic insertion or addition of vowels is explained.

(2.) A second class of euphonic exceptions is connected with one of the 'minor dialectic peculiarities' noticed at the end of the section on Sounds. It consists in the occasional omission or mutation of the final consonant of a root when it is followed by a formative or inflexional particle. Most of the instances which I have noticed, occur in Canarese or Telugu, especially in the latter. They are such as the following, viz., 'eddu,' Tel., *an ox*, instead of 'erdu' (in Tamil 'erudu'); 'penchu,' Tel., *to increase*, instead of 'perunchu' (in Tamil 'perukku'); 'biddu,' Canarese, *having fallen*, for 'bildu' (Tamil 'virdu'); and 'tiddu,' Can., *to correct*, for 'tirudu' (in Tamil 'tiruttu'). This omission, or softening, has no relation to grammatical expression, and appears to have arisen chiefly from haste in pronunciation. A few examples of this change are found even in Tamil; *e.g.* 'vandu,' *having come*, instead of 'varndu' or 'varundu.' In this case the omitted 'r' has not a place in the imperative of the second person singular, which is 'vâ,' *come*, not 'var;' and hence it might be doubted whether the 'r' really belongs to the root, or whether it is only an euphonic addition. I suspect, however, that this 'r' is radical, for the Telugu imperative singular is 'râ,' not 'vâ,' as if from 'vara;' and we find in the Rajmahal dialect that *to come* is 'bârâ.' In Tamil also the imperative of the second person *plural* is 'vâr-um.' Hence 'vandu,' *having come,* seems really to be a softened form of 'varndu.' Another example appears to be furnished by a Tamil verb meaning *to give,* which is 'tar,' in the infinitive, the present, and the future; 'tâ,' in the imperative singular; and 'tă' in the preterite, *e.g.* 'tandêu' (for 'tarndên'), *I gave.* The resemblance or identity of the Tamil 'ta' and the Sanscrit 'da,' *to give,* might lead us to suppose 'ta' to be a Sanscrit derivative, in which case the 'r' referred to would be an euphonic addition. It is difficult, however, to suppose that this 'r' has been added euphonically, and the difficulty is increased by the circumstance that in every part of this verb, with the exception of the imperative, the form of the root which we find to be used, is not 'tâ' but 'tar-u.' Hence it seems open to conjecture that 'tar-u' is not derived from the present shape of the Sanscrit, though related to it, but that it springs from an older source, of which a trace remains in the Greek 'δῶρ-ον,' and possibly also in the Hebrew base, 'tan.'

(3.) A third class of euphonic exceptions to this rule is connected with another of the 'minor dialectic peculiarities' referred to. It consists in the occasional softening or rejection of the medial consonant of a dissyllabic root or verbal noun, together with the coalescence of the vowels that preceded and followed it. It has been shown that 'g' has a tendency to be softened into 'v' and then to disappear, and that 'ś' changes in the same manner into 'y,' when it sometimes become absorbed. When either of these consonants is a medial, it is apt to be thus softened down and rejected. Thus, 'dogal-u,' Canarese, *skin,* becomes in Tamil 'tôl;' 'peśar,' Canarese, *a name,* becomes in Tamil first 'peÿar' and then 'pêr.' So in Tamil, 'togup-pu,' *a collection,* is softened into 'tôp-pu,' which has the restricted meaning of *a collection of trees, a tope.*

(4.) The most important class of euphonic exceptions to the general rule of the unchangeableness of the root appears at first sight to correspond to a characteristic usage of the Indo-European languages, and especially of the Sanscrit. In those languages the quantity of the root vowel is sometimes altered when the crude or abstract noun is changed into an adjective. Thus in Sanscrit 'Draviḍa,' a gentile appellation, becomes 'Drâviḍa,' *pertaining to the Dravidas,* the 'a' changing into 'â;' and if the vowel is naturally long, as the 'ê' in 'Vêda,' it becomes a diphthong when the word is changed to an adjective; *e.g.,* 'Vaidika,' *pertaining to the Vêdas.* In Tamil we discover a class of changes which, though in reality they are purely euphonic and unconnected with grammatical relations, appear at first sight to resemble the above-mentioned Indo-European usage. Drâvidian roots, though originally monosyllabic, have very generally taken a dissyllabic form by the insertion or addition of a vowel which is intended to facilitate enunciation. In such cases the first syllable, always a short one, represents the crude root, the added vowel constitutes the euphonic suffix; *e.g.*, 'per-u,' *great;* 'kar-u,' *black;* 'ar-u,' *precious.* In Tamil, especially in the old poetical dialect and in the speech of the peasantry, such dissyllabic adjectives, or nouns of quality, are often found to sustain a further change. The final euphonic vowel is rejected, and to compensate for its loss, the interior vowel of the root is lengthened. Thus 'per-u' becomes 'pêr;' 'kar-u,' 'kâr;' and 'ar-u,' 'âr.' In the same manner 'or-u,' *one*, becomes 'ôr;' and 'ir-u,' *two*, 'îr.' This lengthened monosyllabic form is considered to be peculiarly elegant, and is much used in combinations. It is also used more frequently than the dissyllabic form as a concrete noun of quality. Thus 'kâr,' *black*, is much used by itself to denote 'the rainy season,' or 'Coromandel monsoon,' or 'the rice grown at that season.' This euphonic lengthening of the root vowel and rejection of the final will be found to throw light in the derivation of some nouns of quality; *e.g.*, 'pâṛ,' *desolate, a wilderness*, is evidently derived from 'paṛa,' *old*.

When the final consonant of the crude root belongs to the class of hard letters ('k,' 'ś,' 'ṭ,' 't,' 'p,' 'ʀ') it cannot be enunciated by Tamilians without the help of an appended vowel; and in such cases, though the interior vowel of the root is lengthened, the final 'u' remains: *e.g.*, 'paś-u,' *green*, becomes in poetical and vulgar usage, not 'pâś,' but 'pâś-u.' This final 'u,' however, being retained solely for the sake of enunciation, is considered like the Hebrew 'sh'vâ,' as only half the length of an ordinary short vowel.

At first sight the change in the interior vowels of Drâvidian roots now pointed out may appear to resemble the usage of the Sanscrit; but on further examination the resemblance is found to disappear. It is evident that the Drâvidian increase of quantity is wholly euphonic, and not, like that of the Sanscrit, a means of producing grammatical modification: for though that form of the Drâvidian noun of quality, or adjective, in which the root vowel is lengthened, is more frequently employed as a concrete noun than the older dissyllabic form, yet the dissyllabic form is also used as a concrete, and both forms are used indiscriminately as adjectives; from which it is obvious that the difference between them pertains, not to grammatical relation, but only to considerations of euphony. Thus, though 'âr,' *precious*, is more often used than 'ar-u,' to signify *preciousness*, or *that which is precious*, yet 'ar-u' also is used by the poets in the same sense; and either 'ar-u' or 'âr' may optionally be used in composition as an adjective.

2. *Real Exceptions.*

It has been stated as a general rule that the internal vowels of Drâvidian roots sustain no internal change on receiving formative or inflexional additions or in composition; it has also been stated that deviations from this rule exist, but that they are few and unimportant. The apparent exceptions mentioned above have been shown to be merely euphonic. I proceed to notice the few real exceptions which are observed.

(1.) In most of the Drâvidian languages the quantity of the root-vowels of the pronouns of the first and second persons, both singular and plural, is shortened in the oblique cases. The nominatives of those pronouns are long; *e.g.*, 'nân,' Tamil, *I*, 'nâm,' *we;* 'nî,' *thou*, 'nîr,' *you*. But in Tamil, Canarese, Malayâlam, and Tulu, in all the oblique cases the vowels are shortened before receiving the suffixed inflexional particles. Thus, in Canarese, *to me* is not 'nân-a-ge,' but 'năn-a-ge;' *to thee* is not 'nîn-a-ge,' but 'nĭn-a-ge.' The Telugu, Gônd, and Ku generally retain the quantity of the root-vowel unaltered: *e.g.*, in Telugu we find 'nî-ku,' *to thee*, as well as 'nî,' *thou;* but in the accusative, 'nin-u,' *thee*, the quantity is altered in the same manner. The only other instance of a similar shortening of the root-vowel of a Drâvidian word is that which is supplied by the numerals. The radical portion of the Tamil numeral 'mûndru,' *three*, is 'mû;' but this becomes 'mŭ,' when used as an adjectival prefix, as in 'muppattu,' *thirty*, and 'munnûʀu,' *three hundred*. In like manner when 'âʀ-u,' *six*, is used adjectivally, it is shortened to 'aʀ-u;' and 'ê̤r-u,' *seven*, to 'e̤ru;' *e.g.*, 'aʀubadu,' *sixty*, 'e̤rubadu,' *seventy*. The oblique case of a noun or pronoun is identical with that form which the same noun or pronoun takes when it is used adjectivally; and hence both these classes of instances fall under the same rule.

The shortening of the root-vowel takes place in the personal pronouns and numerals alone. All other pronominals and nouns substantive adhere to the general rule of the Drâvidian languages of preserving the root-vowels unaltered.

Singularly enough, this exception from the general rigidity of the root-vowels is a Scythian exception, as well as a Drâvidian one. In the

Scythian version of the Behistun tablets, whilst the nominative of the pronoun of the second person is 'nî,' *thou*, as in the Drâvidian languages, the possessive case is 'nĭ,' *thy*, and the accusative 'nin,' *thee*, corresponding in quantity to the Drâvidian oblique cases; *e.g.*, Telugu and Tulu, 'nin-u,' *thee*, High Tamil 'nĭn,' *thy*, and 'nĭnnei,' *thee*.

(2.) Another class of exceptions appears in those few instances in which the Tamil shortens the quantity of the long vowel of the root in the preterite. This shortening is occasionally observed in the Canarese, but the best illustrations are those which are furnished by the Tamil: *e.g.*, 'vêgu,' properly 'vê,' *to burn*, has for its preterite participle, not 'vêgundu' or 'vêndu,' but 'vendu;' 'nôgu,' *to be in pain*, properly 'nô,' has in the preterite, not 'nôgundu' or 'nôndu,' but 'nondu;' and 'kâṇ,' *to see*, not 'kâṇḍu,' but 'kaṇḍu.'

The two classes of exceptions mentioned above evidently accord, as far as they go, with a prevalent usage of the Indo-European languages, inasmuch as they are examples of the shortening of the interior vowels of the root on receiving the addition of the inflexional particles, to make compensation for the additional weight which is thus imposed on the root-vowel.

(3.) A third class consists of instances in which the quantity of a vowel is lengthened when a verbal root is formed, directly and without any extraneous addition, into a noun. The alteration which the root vowel sustains is prior to any inflexional additions being made. If any formative particle is added to a verbal root to convert it into a noun, the quantity of the root-vowel remains unchanged. The lengthening of the root-vowel to which I refer takes place only in (some of) those cases in which the verbal base itself is used as a noun. Thus, the verb 'keḍ-u,' *to destroy* or *to become destroyed*, may become a verbal noun by the addition of the formative 'di,' *e.g.*, 'keḍudi, *destruction*, in which event the root-vowel remains unaltered; but the verbal base may also be used without addition as a verbal noun, in which case 'keḍ-u' is lengthened into 'kêḍ-u.'

The following Tamil examples of the lengthening of each of the five primary vowels will suffice to illustrate this usage:

From 'paḍ-u,' *to suffer*, is formed 'pâḍ-u,' *a suffering;* from 'min,' *to shine*, 'mîn,' *a star;* from 'śuḍ-u,' *to burn*, 'śûḍ-u,' *heat;* from 'peṟ-u,' *to obtain*, 'pêṟ-u,' *a benefit obtained;* and from 'koḷ,' *to receive*, 'kôḷ,' *reception*.

I am not aware of the existence of a similar rule in any of the Scythian languages, but it is well known to the Sanscrit (*e.g.*, comp. 'vach,' *to speak*, with 'vâch,' *a word;* 'mar' ('mri'), *to die*, with 'mâra,' *death*). Nevertheless, I can scarcely think it likely that it is from the

Sanscrit that the Drâvidian languages have derived a usage which prevails among them to so great an extent, and which has every appearance of being an original feature of their own. It may here be added, that in two instances in Tamil the root vowel has been lengthened in the imperative of verbs : *e.g.*, 'tara,' *to give*, is in the imperative plural 'târ-um,' *give ye;* and 'vara,' *to come*, 'vâr-um,' *come ye.* I consider this change as euphonic, not pertaining to the grammatical expression, for in the parallel forms in Telugu the vowel is short, *e.g.*, 'ra-(m)mu,' *come ye.*

In concluding this section it seems desirable to notice an apparent change of interior vowels occurring in Tamil, which has been supposed to accord with the Sanscrit change of a short vowel into a long one, and of a naturally long vowel into a diphthong, on a noun being changed into an adjective. It consists in the change of 'paśum,' *green*, in certain conjunctions, into 'peim ;' *e.g.*, 'peim-pon,' *excellent* (literally *green*) *gold.* It is certain, however, that this is merely an euphonic change, in no way affecting grammatical relations. 'pasum,' *green*, is not derived, as Beschi supposes, from 'pasumei,' *greenness*, by the omission of the final 'ei ;' for 'mei,' not 'ei,' is the particle by which abstracts are formed, and the 'm' is the most essential part of that particle. It is derived from 'paś,' *green*, the crude adjective or noun of quality, with the addition of 'um,' the sign of the aorist, commonly called 'the future,' by which it is made an aoristic relative participle, a class of participles which all Scythian tongues delight to use as adjectives. It has already been shown that 'ś,' when medial, has a tendency to be softened into 'y,' and then to disappear altogether; and in consequence of this tendency, 'paśum' naturally became 'paỹum,' and this again, by an easy change, and one which in pronunciation is almost imperceptible, 'peim.' We have a parallel instance of this change in the noun 'kaśuppu,' *bitterness*, which may optionally be written and pronounced 'keippu ;' 'kaśuppu' changing first into 'kaỹuppu,' and then into 'keippu.'

It should also be observed that 'peim' has not superseded 'pasum,' though it may optionally be used instead of it, for 'pasum' also is still in use ; and this proves that both forms are grammatically equivalent.

SECTION III.

THE NOUN.

In this section it will be my endeavour to investigate the nature and affections of the Drâvidian noun, with the view of ascertaining its method of expressing the relations of gender and number, and the principles on which that method proceeds, together with the characteristics and origin of its case-system, or system of means for expressing the relationship of nouns with other parts of speech. It will be shown at the close of the section on 'The Verb,' how derivative nouns are formed from verbal roots; and the various classes of participial nouns will then also be investigated.

Part I.—Gender and Number.

1. Gender.

When the Indo-European laws of gender are compared with those of the Scythian group of tongues, it will appear that in this point, as in many others, the Drâvidian languages accord more closely with the Scythian than with the Indo-European family.

In all the more primitive Indo-European languages, not only are words that denote rational beings and living creatures regarded as masculine or feminine, according to the sex of the objects referred to, but also inanimate objects and even abstract ideas have similar sexual distinctions attributed to them; so that many nouns which are naturally destitute of gender, and which ought therefore to be regarded as neuters, are treated by the grammars of those languages as if the objects they denote were males and females, and are fitted not with neuter, but with masculine or feminine case-terminations, and with pronouns of corresponding genders. This peculiar system is a proof of the highly imaginative and poetical character of the Indo-European mind, by which principles of resemblance were discerned in the midst of the greatest differences, and all things that exist were not only animated, but personified. A similar remark applies to the Semitic languages also, in which the same or a similar usage respecting gender prevailed.

In the progress of the corruption of the primitive Indo-European languages, a less imagiuative but more natural usage gained ground: nevertheless, in a majority of the modern colloquial dialects of this family, both in Europe and in India, the gender of nouns is still an important and difficult section of the grammar, and a standing impediment in the way of the idiomatic use of those languages by foreigners.

On the other hand, in the Manchu, Mongolian, Turkish, and Finnish families of tongues—the principal families of the Scythian group—a law or usage respecting the gender of nouns universally prevails, which is generically different from that of the Indo-European and the Semitic idioms. In those families, not only are all things which are destitute of reason and life denoted by neuter nouns, but no nouns whatever, not even nouns which denote human beings, are regarded as in themselves masculine or feminine. All nouns, as such, are neuter, or rather are destitute of gender. In those languages there is no mark of gender inherent in, or inseparably annexed to, the nominative of any noun (the crude root being generally the nominative); and in none of the oblique cases, or post-positions used as case-terminations, is the idea of gender at all involved. The unimaginative Scythians reduced all things, whether rational or irrational, animate or inanimate, to the same dead level, and regarded them all as impersonal. They prefixed to common nouns, wherever they found it necessary, some word denoting sex, equivalent to 'male' or 'female,' 'he' or 'she;' but they invariably regarded such nouns as in themselves neuters, and generally they supplied them with neuter pronouns. The only exceptions to this rule in the Scythian languages consist in a few words, such as 'God,' 'man,' 'woman,' 'husband,' 'wife,' which are so highly instinct with personality that of themselves, and without the addition of any word denoting sex, they necessarily convey the signification of masculine or feminine.

When our attention is turned to the Drâvidian languages we find that whilst their rules respecting gender differ generally from those of the Indo-European group, they are not quite identical with those of the Scythian. It seems probable, however, that the particulars in which the Drâvidian rules respecting gender differ from those of the Scythian languages, and evince a tendency in the Indo-European direction, are not the result of Sanscrit influences, of which no trace is perceptible in this department of Drâvidian grammar, but have arisen from the progressive mental cultivation of the Drâvidians themselves.

Drâvidian nouns are divided into two classes, which Tamil grammarians denote by the technical terms of 'high caste' and 'caste-less' nouns, but which are called by Telugu grammarians 'mahât,' *majors* and 'a-mahât,' *minors.* 'High-caste' nouns, or 'majors,' are those which denote 'the celestial and infernal deities and human beings,' or, briefly, all things that are endowed with reason; and in all the Drâvidian dialects (with a peculiar exception which is found only in the Telugu and the Gônd) nouns of this class are treated in the singular as masculines or feminines respectively, and in the plural as epicenes, that is, without distinguishing between masculines and feminines, but distinguishing both from the neuter. The other class of nouns, called 'caste-less,' or 'minors,' includes everything which is destitute of reason, whether animate or inanimate. This classification of nouns, though not so imaginative as that of the Indo-European and Semitic tongues, is decidedly more philosophical; for the difference between rational beings and beings or things which are destitute of reason, is more momentous and essential than any difference that exists between the sexes. The New Persian, which uses one pluralising particle for nouns that denote animated beings and another and different one for things that are destitute of life, is the only Un-Drâvidian language in which nouns are classified in a manner which is in any degree similar to the Drâvidian system.* The peculiar Drâvidian law of gender which has now been described would appear to be a result of grammatical cultivation; for the masculine, feminine, and epicene suffixes which form the terminations of Drâvidian 'high-caste' nouns, are properly fragments of pronouns or demonstratives of the third person, as are also some of the neuter formatives. It may, indeed, be stated as a general rule that all primitive Drâvidian nouns are destitute of gender, and that every noun or pronoun in which the idea of gender is formally expressed, being a compound word, is necessarily of later origin than the uncompounded primitives. The technical term by which such nouns are denoted by the grammarians is 'pagu-padam,' *divisible words, i.e.,* compounds. Hence the poetical dialects, which retain many of the primitive land-marks, are fond of discarding the ordinary suffixes of gender or rationality, and treating

* This is not the only particular in which the Drâvidion idiom attributes greater importance than the Indo-European, to reason and the mind. *We* make our bodies the seat of personality. When we are suffering from any bodily ailment, we say '*I* am ill;' whereas the Drâvidians denote the mind—the conscious *self* or 'âtmâ'—when they say *I*, and therefore say, more philosophically, 'my body is ill.'

all nouns, as far as possible, as abstract neuters. Thus in poetical Tamil 'Dêv-u,' *God*, a crude noun destitute of gender, is reckoned more classical than 'Dêv-an,' the corresponding masculine noun. This word is a Sanscrit derivative, but the same tendency to fall back upon the old Scythian rule appears in the case of many other words which are primitive Drâvidian nouns; *e.g.*, 'iʀei,' *a king*, a word which is destitute of gender, is more classical than 'iʀei-(v)-an,' the commoner form, which possesses the masculine singular termiuation.

In the modern Tamil which is spoken by the educated classes, the words which denote 'sun' and 'moon' ('sûriy-an' and 'śandir-an,' derived from the Sanscrit 'sûrya' and 'chandra,') are of the masculine gender, in accordance with Sanscrit usage and with the principles of the Brahmanical religion; but in the old Tamil of the poets and the peasants, 'ñjâyiʀu,' *the sun*, and 'tinggaḷ,' *the moon*, both pure Drâvidian words, are neuters. All true Drâvidian names of towns, rivers, &c., are in like manner destitute of every mark of personality or gender. In some few instances the Malayâḷam and the Canarese retain the primitive laws of gender more faithfully than the Tamil. Thus, in the Tamil word 'peiyan,' *a boy*, we find the masculine singular termination 'an;' whereas the Malayâlam (with which agrees the Canarese,) uses the older word 'peital,' a word (properly a verbal noun) which is destitute of gender; to which it prefixes in a thoroughly Scythian manner words that signify respectively 'male' and 'female,' to form compounds signifying 'boy' and 'girl;' *e.g.*, 'âṇ peital,' *a boy*, 'peṇ peital,' *a girl*.

The nature and origin of the terminations which are used to signify gender in the various Drâvidian dialects, will be enquired into under the head of 'Number,' with the consideration of which this subject is inseparably connected. Under this head I restrict myself to a statement of the general principles respecting gender, which characterize the Drâvidian languages.

A peculiarity of the Telugu, which appears also in the Gônd, should here be mentioned. Whilst those dialects agree with the other members of the Drâvidian family in regarding masculines and feminines and both combined as constituting in the plural a common or epicene gender; they differ from the other dialects in this respect, that they are wholly or virtually destitute of a feminine singular, and instead of the feminine singular use the singular of the neuter.

This rule includes in its operation pronouns and verbs as well as substantives, and applies to goddesses and queens, as well as to ordinary women. The Telugu possesses, it is true, a few forms which are appropriate to the feminine singular, but they are rarely used, and that only in certain rare combinations and conjunctures. 'He' and 'it,' are the only pronouns of the third person singular, which are ordinarily made use of by fourteen millions of the Telugu people; and the colloquial dialect does not even possess any pronoun, equivalent to our pronoun 'she,' which is capable of being applied to women of the lower as well as of the higher classes. Ordinarily every woman is spoken of in Telugu as a chattel or a thing, or as we are accustomed to speak of very young children (*e.g.*, '*it* did so and so'), apparently in the supposition either that women are destitute of reason, or that their reason, like that of infants, lies dormant. Whilst each woman taken singly is treated by Telugu grammar as a chattel or as a child, women taken collectively are regarded with as much respect as by the other Drâvidian dialects. In the plural they are honoured with the same 'high-caste' or 'rational' suffixes and pronouns that are applied to men and gods.

The Canarese and Malayâlam agree in this point with the Tamil, and regard women, not in the plural only, but also in the singular, as pertaining to the class of 'rationals:' accordingly in those languages there is a feminine singular pronoun equivalent to 'she,' which corresponds in the principle of its formation to the masculine 'he.' With those languages agrees the Ku, which, though the near neighbour of the Telugu and the Gônd, pursues in this respect a politer course than either.

In the idioms of the Tudas and Kôtas, the rude aborigines of the Nilgherry hills, there is no pronoun of the feminine singular; but instead of the feminine, those dialects appear to use not the neuter but the masculine. This extraordinary usage reminds one of the employment in the Old Hebrew of the same pronoun, 'hû,' to signify both 'he' and 'she.'

2. Number.

The Drâvidian languages recognize only two numbers, the singular and the plural. The dual, properly so called, is unknown, and there is no trace extant of its use at any previous period. Several of the languages of this family contain two plurals of the pronoun of the first person, one of which includes the party addressed as well as the party of the speaker, and which may therefore be considered as a species of dual, whilst the other excludes the party addressed. As, however, this peculiarity is restricted to the personal pronouns, it will be examined in that connexion. Under the head of 'Number,' we shall enquire into the Drâvidian mode of forming the masculine, feminine, and neuter singular, and the epicene and neuter plural.

(1.) *Masculine Singular.*—It has already been intimated that the formatives by which the gender of nouns is occasionally expressed, are identical with the terminations of the demonstrative pronouns. From a very early period of the history of these languages, particles or formatives of gender were suffixed to the demonstrative bases, by the addition of which suffixes demonstrative pronouns were formed. Those formatives of gender were not originally appended to or combined with *substantive* nouns; but their use was gradually extended as their utility was perceived, and nouns which included the idea of gender, learned to express that idea by suffixing the gender-terminations of the pronouns, whereby they became appellative nouns. The manner in which all these suffixes are added will be sufficiently illustrated by the instance of the masculine singular.

The masculine singular suffix of the Tamil is 'an,' 'ân,' or 'ôn.' 'An,' the shorter formative, is that which appears in the demonstrative pronoun 'avan' ('a-(v)-an'), *he;* and by suffixing any of these formatives to an abstract or neuter noun, the noun ceases to be abstract, and becomes a concrete masculine-singular appellative. Thus 'mûpp-u,' *age,* by the addition of 'an' becomes 'mûpp-an,' *an elder,* literally *age-he,* or *age-man;* and from 'Tamiṛ' comes 'Tamiṛ-an,' *a Tamilian, a Tamil-man.*

These and similar nouns are called generically 'compound or divisible words' by Tamil grammarians. They are obviously compounded of a noun—generally a noun of quality or relation—and a suffix of gender, which appears also to have been a noun originally.

In the instances which have been adduced, the suffix of gender is annexed to the nominative or *casus rectus;* but in many cases it is annexed to the oblique case or inflexional base, viz., to that form of the noun to which the case signs are suffixed, and which when used by itself has the meaning of the genitive. When the inflexion, or oblique case, is employed instead of the nominative in compounds of this nature, it generally conveys a genitival or possessive signification: *e.g.* 'maleiy*in*an' ('malei-(y)-*in*-an'), *a mountaineer,* literally *a man of the mountain;* 'paṭṭin*att*ân' ('paṭṭin'-*att'*-ân'), *a citizen,* literally *a man of the city.* Sometimes, however, the genitival 'in' is merely added euphonically; *e.g.,* there is no difference in meaning between 'villau,' *a bowman,*' and 'vill*in*an' ('vill'-*in*-an'), which is considered a more elegant form.

Words of this description are in some grammars called 'adjectives;' but they are never regarded as such by any native grammarians: they cannot be simply prefixed for the purpose of qualifying other words;

and it is evident from their construction that they are merely appellative nouns.

A subdivision of appellatives consists of words in which the suffixes of gender are annexed to adjectival forms; *e.g.*, 'koḍiya-n,' *a cruel man.* I regard words of this class as participial nouns, and they will be investigated in the section on 'The Verb,' under the head of 'Appellative Verbs;' but whatever be the nature of 'koḍiya' (the first part of the compound), 'koḍiya-n,' is certainly not an adjective; for before it can be used adjectivally we must append to it the relative participle 'âna,' *that is; e.g.* 'koḍiyan-âna,' *that is a cruel man,* and as the compound *cruel man,* cannot be called an adjective in English, neither is 'koḍiyan' an adjective in Tamil: it is properly an appellative noun. It may be said that the neuter plural of this word, viz., 'koḍiya,' may be prefixed adjectivally to any substantive: but 'koḍiya,' *cruel things,* the neuter plural of 'koḍiyan,' is not identical with the adjective 'koḍiya,' *cruel,* but totally distinct from it, though so similar in appearance. The 'a' of the former word is the neuter suffix of plurality; whereas the 'a' of the latter is that of the possessive case and of the relative participle, as will be shown at the close of this section (see 'Adjectival Formatives') and in the section on 'Verbs.'

Another species of Tamil appellative nouns is said by Beschi to be formed by annexing suffixes of gender to verbal roots, *e.g.*, 'ôduvân,' *a reader,* from 'ôdu,' *to read;* but this, I believe, is an error. Those words are to be regarded as *participial* nouns, and 'ôduvân,' is liṭerally *he who will read, i.e., he who is accustomed to read.*

In the same manner 'ôdinan,' is the participial noun of the preterite tense, and means *he who read or is accustomed to read:* 'ôdugindravan,' the corresponding present participial noun, *he who reads,* belongs to the same class; and these forms are not to be confounded with appellative nouns properly so called. On the other hand, such words as 'kâppan,' *a protector,* are true appellatives; but 'kâppan' is not formed from the future tense of the verb (though 'kâppân' means *he will protect*), but from 'kâppu,' *protection,* a derivative noun, of which the final and formative 'ppu' is from the same origin as the corresponding final of 'mûppu,' *old age.* See the concluding part of the section on 'The Verb.'

The suffixes of gender which form the terminal portion of appellative nouns vary somewhat in form; but they are one and the same in origin, and their variations are merely euphonic. It is the vowel only that varies, never the consonant.

When a neuter noun ends with a vowel which is essential to it, and is incapable of elision, and also when a noun happens to be a long monosyllable, 'ân,' or in poetry 'ôn,' is more commonly suffixed than 'an.' In some cases 'avan,' *he*, the full demonstrative pronoun, is suffixed instead of its termination only; and this mode is thought peculiarly elegant. Thus from 'vill-u,' *a bow*, we may form 'vill-an,' 'vill-ân,' and 'vill-ôn,' *an archer, a bowman*, and also 'vill-avan.' Indeed 'ân' and 'ôn,' have possibly been formed, not from 'an,' but from 'a-(v)-an,' by the softening of the euphonic 'v,' and the coalescence of the vowels. This corruption of 'avan' into 'ân,' appears systematically in the third person masculine singular of the colloquial Tamil verb; *e.g.*, 'pôn-ân' (not 'pôn-avan'), *he went*.

The Canarese masculine singular suffix 'anu,' is identical with the Tamil 'an,' the addition of 'u' being a phonetic necessity of the modern dialect. In the older Canarese, the termination which was used was 'am;' a particle which is to be regarded as the equivalent of 'an,' 'n' and 'm' being interchangeable nasals. The Malayâlam is, in this particular, perfectly identical with the Tamil.

The Telugu masculine singular formative is 'ḍ-u,' 'uḍ-u,' or 'aḍ-u;' *e.g.*, 'vâḍu' ('va-aḍu'), *he;* and by suffixing the same formative to any substantive noun, it becomes a masculine singular; *e.g.*, 'mag-aḍu,' *a husband*, a word which is identical in origin with the Tamil 'mag-an,' *a son* (the primitive and proper meaning of each word being *a male*). The masculine singular suffix of the Telugu often takes the shape of 'uḍ-u,' and in like manner the epicene plural suffix, which is in Tamil 'ar-u,' is often 'ur-u' in Telugu; but in these instances 'a' changes into 'u' through attraction.

As the Tamil forms masculine appellatives by suffixing the demonstrative pronoun 'avan,' so does the Telugu sometimes suffix its full demonstrative pronoun 'vâḍu;' *e.g.*, 'chinna-vâḍu,' *a boy* (Tamil, 'śinna-(v)-an'), literally *he who is little*. It is probable that the Telugu masculine singular suffix was originally 'an' or 'an-u,' as in Tamil-Canarese. 'aḍu,' 'uḍ-u,' or 'ḍu,' is found only in the nominative in correct Telugu, and it is replaced in all the oblique cases by 'ani' or 'ni;' and that this 'ni' is not merely an inflexional increment, but the representative of an old masculine singular suffix, appears on comparing it with 'ri,' the corresponding oblique-case suffix of the masculine-feminine plural, which is certainly formed from 'ar-u.' When 'vâniki,' *to him*, is compared with its plural 'vâriki,' *to them*, it is evident that the former corresponds as closely to the Tamil 'avanukku' as the latter to 'avarukku;' and consequently the 'ni' of 'vâniki,' must be significant of the masculine singular. Probably the same termination survives in the demonstrative, 'âyana,' *he*, a form which is more rarely used than 'vâḍu.'

That the Tamil-Canarese masculine suffix 'an,' and the Telugu 'aḍ-u' or 'uḍ-u,' were originally one and the same, will, I think, appear when the derivation and connections of both are inquired into. The Ku, though one of the most barbarous of the Drâvidian dialects, throws more light than any other upon this point. It forms its demonstrative pronouns in a simple and truly primitive manner by prefixing 'â,' the demonstrative base, to common nouns, which signify *man* and *woman*. Those nouns are 'âñj-u,' *a man*, and 'âl-u,' *a woman;* and 'ââñj-u' (compare Tam., 'a(v)an'), literally *that man*, is used to signify *he*, and 'ââlu' (compare Tam. 'a(v)aḷ') *that woman*, to signify *she*. The Ku 'âñj-u,' *a man*, is certainly identical with the Tamil noun 'âṇ,' *a male:* and we see the same root in the Ancient Can. 'âṇma,' *a husband, a ruler*, and 'âṇmu,' *to be brave* (compare the Tamil abstract noun 'âṇ-mei,' *strength*). In the use to which this primitive root is put in the Ku word 'â-âñj-u,' we cannot but see the origin of 'an,' the suffix of the masculine singular in most of the Drâvidian dialects. The final 'ñ,' and probably the entire termination 'ñju,' of the Ku word 'âñ-ju,' being merely euphonic, the root appears to be 'ân;' and as 'ṇ' and 'n' have been shown to be interchangeable, 'ân' must be regarded as only another form of 'âṇ.' 'ṇ,' again, is not only often euphonised by suffixing 'ḍu' (*e.g.*, 'peṇ,' Tam., *a female*, colloquially and poetically 'peṇḍ-u'), but it is also sometimes directly changed into 'ḍ,' of which we have an instance in the classical Tamil 'peḍ-ei,' *a hen*, a word which is derived by this process from, and is identical with, 'peṇ,' *a female*. Hence, the Telugu suffix 'aḍ-u,' might naturally be derived from an older form in 'aṇ,' if it should appear that that form existed; and that it did exist, appears from the vulgar use to the present day of 'ṇ' instead of 'n' in some of the oblique cases (*e.g.*, 'vâṇṇi,' *him*, instead of 'vâni'), and from the 'half anuswâra,' or obscure nasal, which precedes 'ḍu' itself in the speech of the vulgar and in the written compositions of the pedantic; *e.g.*, 'vânḍu,' for 'vâḍu,' *he*. A close connection is thus established between the Tamil-Canarese 'an' and the Telugu 'aḍ-u,' through the middle point 'aṇ.'

The only difficulty in the way of the perfect identification of the formative 'an' with the Ku, 'âñj-u,' *a man*, and with the Tamil 'âṇ,' *a male*, lies in the length of the vowel of the latter words. Here again the Ku comes to our assistance; for we find that the vowel was euphonically shortened in some instances in the very dialect in which the origin of the word itself was discovered. In Ku the 'â' of 'âñj-u' is long, both when it is used as an isolated word and in the demonstratives, 'ââñj-u,' *he*, and 'ââl-u,' *she;* but when the demonstrative pronoun is appended to, and combined with, the relative participle of the verb, so as to form with it a participial noun, the 'â' of 'âñj-u' is shortened into 'a,' and in this shortened form the connection of the Ku formative with the Tamil-Canarese is seen to be complete. Compare the Ku participial noun 'gităñj-u,' *he who did*, with the corresponding Canarese 'gêyidăn-u; 'gitâr-u,' Ku, *they who did*, with 'gêyidar-u,' Can., and also 'gital-u,' Ku, *she who did*, with 'gêyidaḷ-u,' Can.

(2.) *Feminine Singular.*—Though the Telugu and the Gônd generally use the neuter singular to supply the place of the feminine singular, the other Drâvidian dialects possess and constantly use a feminine singular formative which is quite distinct from that of the neuter. This formative is 'aḷ,' in Tamil and Malayâlam, 'aḷ-u,' in Canarese; and by suffixing the sign of gender to the demonstrative base, the feminine singular demonstrative pronoun 'avaḷ' (a-(v)-aḷ'), *she*, is formed—a word which perfectly corresponds to 'avan' (a-(v)-an'), *he*.

A numerous class of feminine singular appellative nouns is formed by suffixing the same particle to abstract or neuter nouns in their crude state; *e.g.*, compare 'mag-aḷ,' Tam., *a daughter*, with 'mag-an,' *a son;* and (with an euphonic lengthening of the vowel) 'ill-âḷ,' *a house-wife, a wife*, with 'ill-ân,' *a husband.*

The Telugu, in some few connexions, uses a feminine singular formative which appears to be identical with that of the Tamil-Canarese. That formative is 'âl-u,' which is used by the Ku more largely than by the Telugu; and its identity with the Tamil-Canarese 'aḷ,' will be found to furnish us with a clue to the origin and literal meaning of the latter. As 'aŭj-u,' in Ku, means *a man*, so 'âl-u,' means *a woman :* 'ââḷ-u,' *she*, is literally *that woman.* The same word 'âl-u,' means *a woman, a wife*, in poetical and vulgar Telugu also; and in Gônd there is a word which is apparently allied to it, 'âr,' *a woman.* Even in Sans. we meet with 'âli,' *a woman's female friend.* It is evident that 'âl-u,' would be shortened into 'al,' as easily as 'âñj-u' into 'an,' and the constant occurrence of a cerebral 'ḷ' in Tamil and Canarese, where the Telugu has the medial 'l,' fully accounts for the change of the one semi-vowel into the other. The unchanged form of this suffix appears in Telugu in such words as 'manama-(r)-âlu,' *a grand-daughter*, compared with 'manama-ḍu,' *a grand-son.* The abbreviation of the vowel of the feminine suffix, which is characteristic of the Tamil and Canarese, is exemplified in Telugu also, in the words 'maradal-u,' *a niece*, and 'kôḍal-u, *a daughter-in-law;*' in which words the feminine suffix 'al-u,' is evidentical identical both with the Tamil-Canarese 'aḷ' or 'aḷ-u,' and also with 'âl-u,' the older and more regular form of this suffix, which is capable of being used by itself as a noun.

Probably the Tel. 'âḍ-u,' adj., *female*, is identical in origin with 'âl-u,' through the very common interchange of 'ḍ' and 'ḷ;' an illustration of which we have in 'kei-(y)-âḷu,' Tam., *to use*, which is converted in the colloquial dialect to 'kei-(y)-âḍu.'*

The feminine singular suffix, 'aḷ' or 'aḷ-u,' appears in Tamil and Canarese in the terminations of verbs as well as in those of pronouns. The Telugu, on the other hand, which uses the neuter demonstrative instead of the feminine singular, uses the final fragment of the same demonstrative as the termination of the feminine singular of its verb.

It may be remarked that in some of the Caucasian dialects, 'n' and 'l' are used as masculine and feminine terminals, exactly as in Tamil: *e.g.*, in Awar, 'emen,' is *father*, 'evel,' is *mother*.

There is another mode of forming the feminine singular of appellative nouns, which is much used in all the Drâvidian dialects, and which may be regarded as especially characteristic of the Telugu. It consists in suffixing the Telugu neuter singular demonstrative, its termination, or a modification of it, to any abstract or neuter noun. The neuter singular demonstrative being used by the Telugu instead of the feminine singular (*it* for *she*), this neuter suffix has naturally in Telugu supplied the place of a feminine suffix; and though in the other dialects the feminine pronouns are formed by means of feminine suffixes, not by those of the neuter, yet the less respectful Telugu usage has crept into the department of their appellative nouns.

In Tamil, this neuter-feminine suffix is 'atti' or 'tti.' This will appear on comparing 'veḷḷâḷ-atti,' *a woman of the cultivator caste*, with

* It is more doubtful whether the Gônd-Telugu, 'âl-u,' *a woman*, is allied to the Tamil common noun 'âḷ,' *a person;* and yet the existence of some alliance seems probable. 'âḷ,' means properly *a subject person, a servant—male or female, a slave.* It is derived from 'âḷ' (Tel. 'êl-u'), *to rule*, and this seems a natural enough origin for a word intended to signify a Hindu woman. The ordinary Tamil word which signifies a woman is 'peṇ,' the literal signification of which is *desire*, from the verbal root 'peṇ,' *to desire;* but the word is generally restricted to mean *a young woman, a bride.* Hence, taking into consideration the subject position of women in India, the word 'âḷ,' *one who is subject to rule, a person whose sole duty is to obey*, is as natural a derivation for a word signifying *a woman, a female*, as 'peṇ;' and perhaps more likely to come into general use as a suffix of the feminine singular.

'veḷḷâḷ-an,' *a man of the same caste;* 'oru-tti,' *one woman,* '*una,*' with 'oru-(v)-an,' *one man,* '*unus;*' and 'vaṇṇâ-tti,' *a washerwoman,* with 'vaṇṇâ-n,' *a washerman.* 'tt,' a portion of this suffix, is erroneously used in vulgar Tamil as a component element in the masculine appellative noun 'oruttan,' *one man,* instead of the classical and correct 'oruvan.' With this solitary exception its use is exclusively feminine.

The same suffix is 'iti' or 'ti' in Canarese, *e.g.,* 'arasiti,' *a queen* (corresponding to the Tamil 'râsâtti'), 'okkalati,' *a farmer's wife.*' The Telugu uses 'adi' or 'di,' *e.g.,* 'kômaṭi-(y)-adi' or 'komaṭi-di,' *a woman of the Komti caste;* 'mâla-di,' *a Pariar woman;* 'chinna-di,' *a girl.*

It seems to me evident, not only that all these suffixes are identical, but that the Telugu form of the demonstrative neuter singular, viz. 'adi,' *it,* which is used systematically by the Telugu to signify *she,* is the root from whence they have all proceeded.

Another feminine singular suffix of appéllatives which is occasionally used in the Drâvidian languages, has been derived from the imitation of the Sanscrit. It consists in the addition of 'i' to the crude or neuter noun; and it is only in quantity that this 'i' differs from the long 'ī,' which is so much used by the Sanscrit as a feminine suffix. In the majority of cases it is only in connexion with Sanscrit derivatives that this suffix is used; but it has also come to be appended to some pure Drâvidian nouns; *e.g.,* 'manei-(v)-i,' Tam., *a house-wife,*' from 'manei,' *a house;* and 'talei-(v)-i,' Tam., *a lady* (compare 'talei-(v)-an,' *a lord*), from 'talei,' *a head:* compare also the Gônd 'perdgal,' *a boy,* with 'perdgi,' *a girl.* This feminine suffix is not to be confounded with 'i,' a suffix of agency, which is much used in the formation of nouns of agency and operation, and which is used by all genders indiscriminately. See 'Verbal Derivatives,' at the close of the section on 'The Verb.'

(3.) *Neuter Singular.*—There is but little which is worthy of remark in the singular forms of neuter Drâvidian nouns. Every Drâvidian noun is naturally neuter, or destitute of gender, and it becomes masculine or feminine solely in virtue of the addition of a masculine or feminine suffix. When abstract Sanscrit nouns are adopted by the Drâvidians, the neuter form of those nouns (ending in 'am') is generally retained; and there are also some neuter nouns of pure Drâvidian origin which end in 'am,' or take 'am' as their formative. The Drâvidian termination 'am' is not to be regarded, however, as a sign of the neuter, or a neuter suffix, though such is undoubtedly its character in Sanscrit. It is merely one of a numerous class of formatives, of which much use is made by the Drâvidian dialect, and by the addition of which crude verbal roots become derivative nouns. Such formatives are to be regarded as forming a part of the noun itself, not of the inflexional additions. See 'Verbal Derivatives,' at the close of the section on 'The Verb.'

All animated beings that are destitute of reason are placed by Drâvidian grammarians in the 'caste-less,' or neuter class, and the nouns that denote such animals, both in the singular and in the plural, are uniformly regarded as neuter or destitute of gender, irrespective of the animal's sex.

If it happens to be necessary to distinguish the sex of any animal that is included in this class, a separate word, signifying 'male' or 'female,' 'coḳk' or 'hen,' is prefixed. Even in such cases, however, the pronoun with which the noun stands in agreement is neuter, and notwithstanding the specification of the animal's sex, the noun itself remains in the 'caste-less' or neuter class.

For this reason, suffixes expressive of the neuter gender, whether singular or plural, were not much required by Drâvidian substantive nouns. The only neuter singular suffix of the Drâvidian languages, which is used in the same manner as the masculine 'an' or 'aḍu,' and the feminine 'aḷ,' is that which constitutes the termination of the neuter singular of demonstrative pronouns and appellative nouns. This pronoun is in Tamil-Canarese 'adu,' *that,* 'idu,' *this;* in Telugu 'adi,' 'idi;' in Malayâlam 'ata,' 'ita;' in Gônd 'ad,' 'id.'

The same neuter demonstrative, or in some instances its termination only, is used in the conjugation of Drâvidian verbs as the sign of the neuter singular of each tense, and in Telugu as the sign of the feminine singular also. The bases of the Drâvidian demonstratives being 'a' and 'i' ('a' remote, 'i' proximate), that part of each pronoun which is found to be annexed to those demonstrative vowels is evidently a suffix of number and gender; and as the final vowels of 'ad-u,' 'ad-i,' 'at-a,' 'id-u,' 'id-i,' 'it-a,' are merely euphonic, and have been added only for the purpose of helping the enunciation, it is evident that 'd' or 't' alone constitutes the sign of the neuter singular. This view is confirmed by the circumstance that 'd' or 't' never appears in the neuter plural of this demonstrative, but is replaced by 'ei,' 'u,' 'i,' or short 'a,' with a preceding euphonic 'v' or 'n;' *e.g.,* compare 'adu' ('a-d-u'), Tam., *that,* with 'ava' ('a-(v)-a'), Malayâlam, *those.* It will be shown afterwards that this final 'a' is a sign of the neuter plural.

Appellative nouns which form their masc. singular in Tamil in 'an,' and their feminine sing. in 'aḷ,' form their neuter sing. by annexing 'du,' with such euphonic changes as the previous consonant happens to require; *e.g.*, 'nalla-du,' *a good thing;* 'al-du,' euphonically 'andru,' *a thing that is not;* 'periya-du' or 'peri-du,' *great, a great thing.*

This neuter singular suffix 'd,' is largely used in all the dialects in the formation of verbal nouns, *e.g.*, 'pôgiṉa-du,' Tam., *the act of going,* 'pôna-du,' *the having gone,* 'pôva-du,' *the being about to go.* This form has been represented by some, but erroneously, as an infinitive: it is a concrete verbal or participial noun of the neuter gender, which has gradually come to be used as an abstract.

The affinities of the neuter singular suffix in 'd' or 't,' are exclusively Indo-European, and they are found especially in the Indo-European pronouns and pronominals. We may observe this suffix in the Sanscrit 'tad' or 'tat,' *that;* in 'tyad,' *that;* in 'adas,' a weakened form of 'adat,' *that;* in 'êtad,' *this.* We find it also in the Latin 'illud,' 'id,' &c. (compare the Latin 'id,' with the Tamil 'i-du,' *this*); and in our English demonstrative neuter 'it' (properly 'hit'), the neuter of 'he,' as also in 'what,' the neuter of 'who.' Compare also the Vedic 'it,' an indeclinable pronoun, described as 'a petrified neuter,' which combines with the negative particle 'na' to form 'nêt,' *if not,* apparently in the same manner as in Telugu the aoristic neuter 'lêdu,' *there is not,* is compounded of the negative 'la' and the suffix 'du.'

Though the Drâvidian languages appear in this point to be allied to the Sanscrit family, it would be unsafe to suppose that they borrowed this neuter singular suffix from the Sanscrit. The analogy of the Drâvidian neuter plural in 'a,' which though Indo-European, is foreign to the Sanscrit, and that of the remote and proximate demonstrative vowels 'a' and 'i,' which though known to the Indo-European family, are used more systematically and distinctively by the Drâvidian languages than by any other class of tongues, would lead to the supposition that these particles were inherited by the Drâvidian family, in common with the Sanscrit, from a primitive, Pre-Sanscrit source.

THE PLURAL: PRINCIPLES OF PLURALISATION.—In the primitive Indo-European tongues, the plural is carefully distinguished from the singular; and with the exception of a few nouns of quantity which have the form of the singular but a plural signification, the 'number' of nouns is always clearly denoted by their inflexional terminations. Nouns whose number is indefinite, like our modern English 'sheep,' are unknown to the older dialects of this family. In the languages of the Scythian group a looser principle prevails, and number is generally left indefinite, so that it is the connexion alone which determines whether a noun is singular or plural. The Manchu restricts the use of its pluralising particle to words which denote animated beings: all other words are left destitute of signs of number. Even the Tartar, or Oriental Turkish, ordinarily pluralises the pronouns alone, and leaves the number of other nouns indeterminate. In the Brahui also, the number of nouns is generally left undefined; and when it is desired to attach to any noun the idea of plurality, a word signifying 'many' or, 'several' is prefixed to it. Notwithstanding this rule, Brahui verbs are regularly pluralised; and the number of an indeterminate noun may often be ascertained from the number of the verb with which it agrees.

With respect to principles of pluralisation, the Drâvidian tongues differ considerably from the Indo-European family, and accord on the whole with surprising exactness with the languages of the Scythian stock. The number of Drâvidian nouns, especially of neuter nouns, is ordinarily indefinite; and it depends upon the connexion whether any noun is to be regarded as singular or as plural. It is true that when more 'persons' than one are referred to, the 'high-caste' or 'rational' pronouns that are used are almost invariably plural; and that even neuter nouns themselves are sometimes pluralised, especially in polished prose compositions: but the poets and the peasants, the most faithful guardians of antique forms of speech, rarely pluralise the neuter, and are fond of using the singular noun in an indefinite singular-plural sense, without specification of number, except in so far as it is expressed by the context. This rule is adhered to with especial strictness by the Tamil, which in this, as in many other particulars, exhibits most faithfully the primitive condition of the Drâvidian languages. Thus in Tamil, 'mâḍu,' *ox*, means either *an ox* or *oxen*, according to the connexion; and even when a numeral is prefixed which necessarily conveys the idea of plurality, idiomatic speakers prefer to retain the singular or indefinite form of the noun. Hence they will rather say 'nâlu mâḍu mêygiʀadu,' literally *four ox is feeding*, than 'nâlu mâḍugaḷ mêygindrana,' *four oxen are feeding,*' which would sound clumsy and pedantic.

Even when a neuter noun is pluralised by the addition of a pluralising particle, the verb is rarely pluralised to correspond; but the singular form of verb is still used for the plural,—the number of the neuter singular being naturally indeterminate. This is invariably the practice in the speech of the lower classes; and the colloquial style of even the best educated classes exhibits a similar characteristic. The Tamil language contains, it is true, a plural form of the third person neuter of the verb, and the existence of this form is a clear proof of the high cultivation of the Tamil; but the use of the neuter plural verb is ordinarily restricted to poetry, and even in poetry the singular number both of neuter nouns and of the verbs that correspond is much more commonly used than the plural. It should be remarked also, that the third person neuter of the Tamil future, or aorist, is altogether destitute of a plural. In this particular, therefore, the Tamil verb is more decidedly Scythian in character than the noun itself. Max Müller supposes that a Drâvidian neuter plural noun, with its suffix of plurality, is felt to be a compound (like 'animal-mass' for 'animals,' or 'stone-heap' for 'stones'), and that it is on this account that it is followed by a verb in the singular. The explanation which I have given seems to me preferable. The number of all Drâvidian nouns, whether 'high-caste' or 'caste-less,' was originally indefinite: the singular, the primitive condition of every noun, was then the only number which was or could be recognized by verbal or nominal inflexions, and plurality was left to be inferred from the context. As civilization made progress, the plural made its formal appearance, and effected a permanent settlement in the department of high-caste or masculine-feminine nouns and verbs; whilst the number of caste-less or neuter nouns, whether suffixes of plurality were used or not, still remained generally unrecognized by the verb in the Drâvidian languages. Even where the form exists it is little used. It is curious, that in this very point the Greek verb exhibits signs of Scythian influences, viz., in the use of the singular verb for the plural neuter.

The Drâvidian languages ordinarily express the idea of singularity or oneness, not by the addition of a singular suffix to nouns and pronouns, or by the absence of the pluralising particle (by which number is still left indeterminate), but by prefixing the numeral adjective 'one.' Thus, 'mâḍu,' Tam., *ox*, does not mean exclusively either *an ox* or *oxen*, but admits of either meaning according to circumstances; and if we wish distinctly to specify singularity, we must say 'oru mâdu,' *one* or *a certain ox*. Europeans in speaking the Drâvidian dialects use this prefix of singularity too frequently, misled by their habitual use of an indefinite article in their own tongues. They also make too free a use of the distinctively plural form of neuter nouns, when the objects to which they wish to refer are plural. Occasionally, when euphony or usage recommend it, this is done by Drâvidians themselves, but as a general rule the neuter singular is used instead of the neuter plural, and that not in the Tamil only, or in the Drâvidian languages only, but also in almost all the languages of the Scythian group

Another important particular in which the Indo-European languages differ from the Scythian is, that in the former the plural has a different set of case-terminations from the singular, by the use of which the idea of plurality is not separately expressed, but is conjoined with that of case-relation; whilst in the latter family the plural uses the same set of case-terminations as the singular, and plurality is expressed by a sign of plurality common to all the cases, which is inserted between the singular or crude form of the noun and the case-terminations. In the Indo-European languages, each inflexion includes the twofold idea of number and of case. Thus there is a 'genitive singular' and a 'genitive plural,' each of which is a complex idea; but there is no inflexion which can be called 'genitive,' irrespective of number; and in many instances (this of the genitive being one) there is no apparent connexion between the case-termination of the singular and that which is used in, and which constitutes, the plural.

In those few cases in which the sign of number and the sign of case seem to have been originally distinct, and to have coalesced into one, the sign of case seems to have preceded that of number: *e.g.*, the Gothic plural accusative 'ns,' is derived from 'n' or 'm,' the sign of the accusative singular, and 's,' the sign of plurality. When the Scythian family of languages is examined, it is found that each of their case-signs is fixed and unalterable. It expresses the idea of 'case' and nothing more, and is the same in the plural as in the singular, with the exception of those few trivial changes which are required by euphony. The sign of plurality also is not only distinct from the case-sign, but is one and the same in all the cases. It is an unalterable post-position—a fixed quantity; and it is not post-fixed to the case-sign, much less compounded with it, as in the Indo-European languages, but is prefixed to it. It is attached directly to the root itself, and followed by the variable signs of case.

In the Drâvidian languages a similar simplicity and rigidity of structure characterizes the use of the particles of plurality. They are added directly to the crude base of the noun (which is equivalent to the nominative singular), and are the same in each of the oblique cases as in the nominative. The signs of case are precisely the same in the plural as in the singular, the only difference being that in the singular they are suffixed to the crude noun itself, in the plural to the pluralising particle, after the addition of that particle to the crude noun.

For example, in Hungarian 'hâz,' *a house*, is declined as follows:

Singular.		Plural.	
Nominative,	hâz	Nom.	hâz-ak
Genitive,	hâz-nak	Gen.	hâz-ak-nak
Dative,	hâz-nak	Dat.	hâz-ak-nak
Accusative,	hâz-at	Acc.	hâz-ak-at

In Tamil 'manei,' *a house*, is declined as follows:

Singular.		Plural.	
Nominative,	manei	Non.	manei-gaḷ
Accusative,	manei-(y)-ei	Acc.	manei-gaḷ-ei
Instrumental,	manei-(y)-âl	Instr.	manei-gaḷ-âl
Conjunctive,	manei-(y)-ôḍu	Conj.	manei-gaḷ-ôḍu
Dative,	manei-kku	Dat.	manei-gaḷ (u)-kku
Ablative,	manei-(y)-il-irundu	Ablat.	manei-gaḷ-il-irundu
Genitive,	manei-(y)-in	Gen.	manei-gaḷ-in
Locative,	manei-(y)-iḍatt-il	Locat.	manei-gaḷ-iḍatt-il
Vocative,	manei-(y)-ê	Voc.	manei-gaḷ-ê

The particular signs which are used to express plurality and as exponents of case, are taken from the resources of each language; but the manner in which they are used in both languages is precisely the same.

The neuter of Drâvidian nouns being identical with the crude base, when the pluralising particle is attached to a neuter noun, it is attached to it not as a substitute for any suffix of the singular, but directly and without any change: it is attached to it pure and simple. In the case of masculine and feminine nouns, including pronouns, a somewhat different method of pluralisation is necessary. The singular of the masculine and feminine is formed, as has already been pointed out, by the addition to the root of particles denoting 'a male,' or 'a female.' Hence to pluralise those nouns, it is necessary either to add a pluralising particle to the masculine and feminine suffixes, or to substitute for those suffixes an epicene pluralising particle.

In all the Drâvidian languages the primitive plan of pluralising these two classes of nouns was that of substituting for the masculine and feminine singular suffixes a suffix of plurality which applied in common to men and women, without distinction of sex. This is the mode which is still used in most of the dialects; but in Telugu it retains its place only in connexion with pronouns and verbs, and has disappeared from substantives, which form their plural by means of a neuter suffix.

The classification of Drâvidian nouns into 'rationals' and 'irrationals,' has already been explained: it has also been shown that in the singular, the masculine of 'rational' nouns is distinguished from the feminine. In the plural both those genders are combined; the high caste particle of plurality, or plural of rational beings, is the same for both genders, and includes men and women, gods and goddesses, without distinction of sex.

'Irrational' or neuter nouns have a particle of plurality different from this and peculiar to themselves. Hence the Drâvidian languages have one form of the plural which may be called 'epicene' or 'masculine-feminine,' and another which is ordinarily restricted to the neuter; and by means of these pluralising particles, gender and number are conjointly expressed in the plural by one and the same termination. The masculine-feminine plural expresses the idea of plurality conjointly with that of rationality; the neuter plural, the idea of plurality conjointly with that of irrationality.

Arrangements of this kind for giving combined expression to gender and number, are very commonly observed in the Indo-European family; and even the plan of classing masculines and feminines together in the plural, without distinction of sex, is also very common. Thus the Sanscrit plural in 'as' is masculine-feminine; so is the Latin plural in 'es,' and the Greek in 'ες.'

The chief difference with respect to this point between the Drâvidian system and the Indo-European one lies in this, that in the Drâvidian languages, the masculine-feminine particle of plurality is carefully restricted to rational beings; whereas in the Indo-European languages irrational and even inanimate objects are often complimented with inflexional forms and pluralising particles which imply the existence, not only of vitality, but even of personality, that is, rational self-consciousness.

A still closer analogy to the Drâvidian system is that which is exhibited by the New Persian. That dialect possesses two pluralising particles of which one, 'ân,' is suffixed to nouns denoting living beings,* the other, 'hâ,' to nouns denoting inanimate objects. The particles which are employed by the Persians are different from those which

* Bopp derives 'ân,' the New Persian plural of animated beings, from the Sanscrit 'ân,' the masculine-plural accusative. I am inclined with Colonel Rawlinson to connect this particle with the Chaldaic and Cuthite plural 'ân,' allied to 'îm' and 'în' (*e.g.*, 'anân,' Chald., *we*); the New Persian being undoubtedly tinged with Chaldaco-Assyrian elements, through its connection with the Pehlvi. One is tempted to connect with this suffix our English plural suffix 'en,' in *brethren;* a suffix which is regularly used by the Dutch as a particle of plurality. Bopp, however, holds that this 'en,' is an ancient formative suffix, which was originally used by the singular as well as the plural.

are used in the Drâvidian languages, but the principle is evidently analogous. The Persians specialise *life*, the Drâvidians *reason;* and both of them class the sexes together indiscriminately in the plural.

In Telugu some confusion has been introduced between the epicene sign of plurality 'ar-u,' and the neuter 'lu.' The pronouns pluralise their masculines and feminines regularly by substituting 'ar-u' for their masculine and feminine singular suffixes, whilst the substantives and some of the appellative nouns append 'lu,' which is properly the neuter sign of plurality, instead of the more correct 'ar-u.' Thus the Telugu demonstrative pronoun 'vâr-u,' *they* (the plural of 'vâḍu,' *he*), corresponding to the Canarese 'avar-u,' exhibits the regular epicene plural; whilst 'magaḍu,' *a husband* (in Tamil 'magan'), takes for its plural not 'magaru,' but 'magalu;' and some nouns of this class add 'lu' to the masculine or feminine singular suffix; *e.g.*, 'alluḍu,' *a son-in-law*, makes in the plural not 'alluru,' nor even 'allulu,' but 'allu*n*ḍlu,' nasalised from 'alluḍ'-lu; and instead of 'vâru,' *they*, 'vâṇḍlu,' is colloquially used, a word which is formed on the same plan as the low Madras Tamil 'avan-gaḷ,' *they*, instead of 'avargaḷ' or the higher and purer 'avar.'

Perhaps the only case in which the 'irrational' pluralising particle is used in the higher dialect of the Tamil instead of the 'rational' epicene, is that of 'makkaḷ' (mag-gaḷ'), *mankind, people.* The singular of this word being 'mag-an,' the plural ought by rule to have been 'mag-ar;' and it is interesting to notice that there is in the higher dialect a rarely used plural, 'magâr,' in addition to the ordinary 'makkaḷ.'

The Ku rational plural is 'ngâ,' which is properly an irrational one, but the pronouns and participial nouns form their rational plural by the addition of 'âru,' which is identical with the 'aru' of the other dialects.

The modern colloquial Tamil has been influenced in some degree by the usage of the Telugu, and has adopted the practice of adding the irrational plural to the rational one, thereby systematically forming a double plural 'ar-gal,' instead of the old rational plural 'ar:' *e.g.*, 'avan,' *he*, and 'avaḷ,' *she*, properly take 'avar,' *they*, as their plural; but the plural which is preferred by the modern Tamil, is the double one 'avar-gaḷ.' So also the plural of the second person is properly 'nîr;' but the plural which is most commonly used as 'nîng-gaḷ' (from 'nîm,' an older form of 'nîr,' and 'gaḷ'), which is a double plural like 'avar-gaḷ.' Two forms of the epicene plural being thus placed at the disposal of the Tamil people (the classical 'nîr' and 'avar,' and the colloquial 'nîng-gaḷ' and 'avar-gaḷ'), they have converted the former, in colloquial usage and in prose compositions, into an honorific singular, and the same practice has been adopted in Canarese. This usage, though universally prevalent now, was almost unknown to the poets. I have not observed in the poets, or in any of the old inscriptions in my possession, any instance of the use of the epicene plural as an honorific singular, except in connection with the names and titles of the divinities, whether those names and titles are applied to the gods themselves, or are conferred honorifically upon kings. Even in those cases, however, the corresponding pronoun follows the ordinary rule, and is very rarely honorific. In modern Telugu a double plural, similar to that of the Tamil, has gained a footing; *e.g.*, 'vâru-lu' (for 'vâr-u'), *they*, and 'mîru-lu' (for 'mîr-u'), *you*.

The Telugu, as has been observed, pluralises masculine and feminine substantive nouns by the addition, not of the rational, but of the neuter or irrational sign of plurality: by a similar inversion of idiom, the Gônd sometimes uses the rational plural to pluralise neuter nouns; *e.g.*, 'kâwâlor,' *crows*. Such usages, however, are evidently exceptions to the general and more distinctively Drâvidian rule, according to which the neuter pluralising particle is restricted to neuter nouns, and the epicene particle to rational or personal nouns, *i.e.*, masculines and feminines.

We shall now consider in detail the pluralising particles themselves.

1. *Epicene Pluraisling Particle.*—This particle is virtually one and the same in all the dialects, and the different forms which it has taken are owing merely to euphonic peculiarities. In Tamil nouns, pronouns, and verbs, it assumes the forms of 'ar,' 'âr;' 'ôr;' 'ir,' 'îr:' in Canarese and Telugu, 'aru,' 'uru; 'âre,' 'êru;' 'ri,' 'ru:' in Ku, 'âru;' in Gônd, 'ôr.' The Brahui also forms the second person plural of its verb in 'ere,' 'ure,' &c., the third person in 'ur' or 'ar.' I regard 'ar' (not simply 'r') as probably the primitive shape of this pluralising particle, from which the other forms have been derived by euphonic mutation. It is true that 'nî,' *thou*, forms its plural in modern Tamil by simply adding 'r;' but this does not prove that 'r' alone was the primitive form of the epicene plural, for an older form of 'nîr,' *you*, is 'nî-(v)-ir' or 'nî-(y)-ir,' from which 'nîr' has evidently been derived. It might naturally be supposed that in this case 'ir' is used instead of 'ar,' through the attraction of the preceding long vowel, 'î;' but we also find 'ir' used as a pluralising particle in 'magaḷir,' High Tam., *women*, and also a longer form, 'îr,' in 'magaḷîr:' consequently 'ir' has acquired a position of its own in

the language, as well as 'ar.' All that we can certainly conclude respecting the original shape of this particle is that the final 'r,' which is plainly essential, was preceded by a vowel, and that that vowel was probably ' a.'

The Canarese rational plural suffix 'andar,' *e.g.*, 'avandar-u,' (for 'avar-u '), '*illi*,' and 'ivandar-u' (for 'ivar-u '), '*hi*,' seems to be identical with the Tel. indefinite plural 'andar-u, indar-u,' *so many*, the final 'ar' of which is the ordinary suffix of the epicene plural.

The Tamil and Malayâlam have another particle of plurality which is applicable to rational beings, *viz.*, 'mâr,' or in High Tamil 'mar,' which has a considerable resemblance to 'ar,' and is probably allied to it. 'mâr' is used to pluralise rational nouns substantive alone, and is not like 'ar' used by pronouns and verbs. It is suffixed to the noun which it qualifies in a different manner also from 'ar;' for whilst 'ar' is substituted for the masculine and feminine suffixes of the singular, not added to them, 'mâr' is generally added to the singular suffix by idiomatic writers and speakers. Thus in Tamil, 'puruṣhan ' (a Sans. derivative), *a man, a husband*, when pluralised by suffixing 'ar' becomes ' puruṣhar;' but if 'mâr' is used instead of 'ar,' it is not substituted for 'an' the masculine singular suffix, but appended to it, *e.g.*, ' puruṣhan-mâr,' not ' puruṣha-mar.' 'Mâr,' it is true, is sometimes added to 'ar,' *e.g.*, ' puruṣhar-mâr;' but this is considered unidiomatical. 'Mâr' is also sometimes used as an isolated particle of plurality in a peculiarly Scythian manner, *e.g.*, ' tâÿ - tagappan - mâr,' Tam., *mothers and fathers, parents;* in which both *mother* and *father* are in the singular, and 'mâr' is separately appended to pluralise both.

Probably there was originally no difference in signification between 'ar' and 'mar,' whatever difference there may have been in their origin. In modern Tamil, 'mâr' is suffixed to nouns signifying *parents, priests, kings*, &c., as a plural of honour, like the Hungarian 'mek;' but it may be suffixed, if necessary, to any class of nouns denoting rational beings. In Malayâlam it is used with a wider range of application than in Tamil, and in cases in which an honorific meaning cannot be intended, *e.g.*, 'kaḷḷan-mâr,' *thieves*. The antiquity of many of the forms of the Malayâla grammar, favours the supposition that in ancient Tamil, which was probably identical with ancient Malayâlam, 'mâr' may generally have been used instead of 'ar,' as the ordinary pluralising particle of 'high caste' nouns. A few traces of this use of the particle 'mâr' survive in classical Tamil; 'măr,' which is evidently equivalent to 'mâr,' and probably older, being sometimes used in poetry instead of 'ar,' *e.g.*, 'eṇ-mar' (from 'eṇ,' *to count*), *accountants*.

We have now to inquire whether 'ar' and 'mâr,' the Drâvidian plurals of rationality, sustain any relation to the plural terminations, or pluralising suffixes, of other languages.

It might at first sight be supposed that the formation of the plural by the addition of 'r' to the singular which characterises some of the Teutonic tongues, is analogous to the use of 'r' or 'ar' in the Drâvidian languages. In the Icelandic the most common plural is that which terminates in 'r'—sometimes the consonant 'r' alone, sometimes the syllables 'ar,' 'ir,' 'ur,' *e.g.*, 'konungur,' *kings*. A relic of this plural may be traced in the vulgar English 'childer,' for 'children.' The same plural appears in the Old Latin termination of the masculine plural in 'or' which is found in the Eugubian tables, *e.g.*, 'subator' for 'subacti,' and 'screhitor' for 'scripti.'

Compare also 'mas,' the termination of the first person plural of verbs in Sanscrit, with 'mar,' the corresponding termination in Irish, answering to the Doric μες and the ordinary Greek μεν.

In these cases, however, the resemblance to the Drâvidian plural 'ar' is rather apparent than real; for the final 'r' of these forms has been hardened from an older 's;' whilst there is no evidence of the existence of a tendency in the Drâvidian languages to harden 's' into 'r,' and therefore nothing to warrant the supposition that the Drâvidian epicene 'ar' has been derived from, or is connected with, the Sanscrit masculine-feminine 'as.'

It should also be noted that the Irish 'mar' is a compound of two forms, 'ma,' the representative of the singular of the personal pronoun '*I*,' and 'r,' the hardened equivalent of the plural suffix 's;' and that, therefore, it has no real resemblance to the Drâvidian 'mar,' which is entirely and exclusively a plural suffix of the third person.

There is more probability of the Drâvidian plural suffixes being related to the pluralising particles of some of the Scythian languages. The Turkish plural suffix, which is inserted, as in the Drâvidian languages, between the crude noun and each of the case terminations, is 'lar' or 'ler,' *e.g.*, 'ân-lar,' *they*. Dr. Logan says, but on what authority does not appear, that 'nar' is a plural suffix in Kôl. Mongolian nouns which end with a vowel, are pluralised by the addition of 'nar' or 'ner,' a particle which is evidently related to, or identical with, the Turkish 'lar' or 'ler:' and the resemblance of this Mongol suffix 'nar' to the Drâvidian 'mar,' both in the final 'ar' and in the nasal prefix is remarkable. It is well known that 'm' evinces a tendency to be softened into 'n' (witness the change of the Sanscrit 'mama,' *my*, into 'maña' in Zend); and in this manner it seems not improbable that the Drâvidian 'mar' may be allied to, or even the origin of, the High Asian 'nar.' Again, in the Scythian tongues 'n' is often elided or dropped, and the same peculiarity characterises the Drâvidian languages. Thus, 'nu,' the conjunctive particle of the Telugu, becomes 'û' in Canarese. In this manner the Drâvidian plural suffix 'ar,' may have been softened from 'mar; and if both forms continued to be occasionally used, 'mar,' the older of the two, would naturally and regularly acquire an honorific signification. The Tamil 'iḷeiñjar' ('iḷei-ñjar'), *young people*, a plural appellative noun, formed from 'iḷei,' *youth*, exhibits a form of pluralisation which at first sight seems very closely to resemble the Mongolian 'nar.' Nay, 'nar' is actually used in this very instance instead of 'ñjar' by some of the poets, and it is certain that 'ñj' and 'n' often change places. Unfortunately we find this 'nj' or 'n' in the singular, as well as the plural; which proves it to have been inserted merely for euphony in order to prevent hiatus, and therefore 'ileiñjar' must be re-divided, and represented not as 'iḷei-ñjar,' but as 'iḷei-(ñj)-ar' or 'iḷei-(n)-ar,' equivalent to 'iḷei-(y)-ar.'

Probably the same explanation should be given of 'manâr,' the epicene plural termination of the future tense in some of the poets, especially Tolkâppiyan, the most ancient Tamil grammarian; *e.g.*, 'enmanâr,' *they will say*, instead of the more common 'enbâr.' 'm' is in this connection used as the sign of futurity, and is equivalent to 'b,' and 'enmâr' is equivalent to 'enmanâr.'

The insertion of an euphonic 'n' between the sign of tense and the pronominal suffix is exceedingly common in the present and preterite; *e.g.*, 'naḍanda-(n)-em' (for 'naḍand'-êm'), *we walked;* and if so, there seems no reason why the same 'n' should not make its appearance in the future also, converting 'enmâr' (for 'enba-ar' or 'enbâr') into 'enma-(n)-âr.' If this explanation does not suffice, 'nâr' must, in this instance, be regarded as the equivalent of 'mâr,' and therefore as directly allied to 'nar,' the Mongolian plural suffix. It is deserving of notice that the Turkish, besides its ordinary plural 'lar' or 'ler,' uses 'z' as a plural suffix of the personal pronouns, as may be observed in 'biz,' *we*, and 'siz,' *you;* and that the Turkish terminal 'z' corresponds to the 'r' of some other Scythian languages. Thus 'yâz,' Turkish, *summer*, is in Magyar 'yâṛ' or 'nyâr' (compare the Tamil 'nyâyiR,' *the sun*). It would almost appear, therefore, that the Turkisk suffix of plurality has undergone a process of change and comminution which is similar to that of the Tamil, and that the

Turkish 'z' and the Tamil 'r' are remotely connected, as the last remaining representatives or relics of 'mar,' 'ñar,' and 'lar.'

2. *Pluralising Particles of the Neuter.*—There are two neuter pluralising particles used by the Drâvidian languages.—

(1.) *The neuter plural suffix* 'gaḷ,' *with its varieties.*—It has already been noticed that 'gaḷ' is occasionally but improperly used in Tamil and Canarese as the plural suffix of 'rational' nouns and pronouns; and that the corresponding Telugu 'lu' is still more systematically used in this manner. Nevertheless, I have no doubt that it was originally and is essentially a suffix of the neuter plural.

This suffix is in both dialects of the Tamil 'gaḷ,' *e.g.*, 'kei-gaḷ,' *hands,* with only such changes as are required by Tamilian rules of euphony. In accordance with one of those rules, when 'g,' the initial consonant of 'gaḷ,' is doubled, or preceded without an intermediate vowel by another consonant, 'gaḷ' is regularly hardened into 'kaḷ' or 'kkaḷ.' Thus 'kal-gaḷ,' *stones,* is changed by rule into 'kaʀ-kaḷ.' 'gaḷ' is occasionally lengthened in Tamil poetry into 'gâḷ.' In Malayâlam this particle is generally 'kaḷ' or 'kkaḷ,' but sometimes the initial 'k' coalesces with a preceding nasal and becomes 'ng,' *e.g.*, 'ning-ngaḷ,' *you,* instead of 'nim-kaḷ,'—in Tamil 'nîng-gaḷ.' In modern Canarese we have 'gaḷ-u,' in ancient 'gaḷ,' as in Tamil. The three southern idioms are in perfect agreement with respect to this particle, but when we advance further north we shall find its shape considerably modified.

In Telugu, the corresponding neuter plural suffix is 'lu,' of which the 'l' answers, as is usual in Telugu, to the cerebral 'ḷ' of the other dialects: 'l-u,' therefore, accords with the final syllable of the Canarese 'gaḷ-u' The only real difference between the Telugu and the Tamil-Canarese consists in the omission by the former of the initial consonant 'k' or 'g.' Traces, however, exist in Telugu, of the use of a vowel before 'lu.' Thus, in 'guʀʀâlu,' *horses,* the long 'â' is derived from the combination of the short final 'a' of the inflexional base 'guʀʀa' and a vowel, evidently 'a,' which must have preceded 'lu.' We thus arrive at 'al-u,' as the primitive form of the Telugu plural; and it is obvious that 'al-u' could easily have been softened from 'gal-u.' Conjecture, however, is scarcely needed, for in some nouns ending in 'n-u,' of which the Tamil equivalents end in 'm,' the old Drâvidian pluralising particle in 'gaḷ,' is exhibited in Telugu almost as distinctly as in Tamil. Thus, 'kolan-u,' *a tank* (Tamil 'kuḷam'), takes as its plural 'kolan-kul-u' (Tamil 'kuḷang-gaḷ'), and 'gon-u,' the name of a species of tree, forms its plural in 'gon-gul-u.' When 'kul-u' and 'gul-u' are compared with the Tamil-Canarese forms 'kaḷ,' 'gaḷ,' and 'gaḷ-u,' it is obvious that they are not only equivalent but identical.

An illustration of the manner in which the Telugu 'lu' has been softened from 'gal-u,' may be taken also from colloquial Tamil, in which 'avar-gal,' *they*, is commonly pronounced 'avâḷ.' 'k' or 'g' is dropped or elided in a similar manner in many languages of the Scythian family.

The Tulu, though locally remote from the Telugu, follows its example in many points, and amongst others in this. It rejects the 'k' or 'g' of the plural, and uses merely 'ḷu' or 'ḷ,' like the Telugu; rarely 'kulu.'

The same form of the pluralising particle appears in the languages of some of the tribes of the north-eastern frontier—languages which possibly form a link of connection between the Drâvidian and the Tibetan families. In the Miri or Abor-Miri dialect, 'nô,' *thou*, forms its plural in 'nôlu, *you*; and in the Dhimâl, 'nâ,' *thou*, is pluralised into 'nyêl,' *you*. The pronoun of the Mikir is pluralised by adding 'li,' *e g.*, 'na-li,' *you*, whilst substantives have no plural form. In the Dhimal, substantive-nouns are pluralised by the addition of 'galai,' which is possibly the origin of the pronominal plural 'l,' though this particle or word, 'galai,' is not compounded with, or agglutinated to, the noun, but placed after it separately. Though it is used as a separate word it does not seem to retain any signification of its own independent of its use as a post-position. The resemblance of 'galai' to the Tamil-Canarese 'gaḷ' or 'gaḷu,' is distinct and remarkable. The pluralising particle of the Naga also is 'khala.'

It is not an uncommon occurrence to find one portion of a much used prefix or suffix in one language or dialect of a family, and another portion of it in another member of the same family. Seeing, therefore, that the Telugu has adopted the latter portion of the particle 'kaḷ,' 'gaḷ,' or 'gaḷu,' and omitted the initial 'ka,' 'ga,' or 'k,' we may expect to find this 'k' used as a pluralising particle in some other Drâvidian dialect, and the final 'ḷu' or 'ḷ' omitted. Accordingly in Gônd we find that the plural neuter is commonly formed by the addition of 'k' alone, *e.g.*, 'nai,' *a dog*, 'naik,' *dogs* (compare Tamil 'nâŷkaḷ,' pronounced 'nâŷgaḷ.') The Seoni-Gônd forms its plural by adding 'nk,' *e.g.*, 'neli,' *a field*, 'nelnk,' *fields*. The Ku dialect uses 'ngâ,' and also 'skâ,' of all which forms 'k' or 'g' constitutes the basis.

'k' is sometimes found to interchange with 't,' especially in the languages of High Asia. This interchange appears also in the Gônd pluralising particle; for whilst 'k' is the particle in general use, the pronouns of the first and second persons form their plurals, or double plurals, by the addition of 't' to the nominative, *e.g.*, 'amat,' *we*, 'imat,' *you*. The same interchange between 'k' and 't' appears in the Brahui. Though a separate word is usually employed by the Brahui to denote plurality, a suffix in 'k' is also sometimes used; but this 'k' is found only in the nominative plural, and is replaced by 't' in the oblique cases.

When we turn to the grammatical forms of the Finnish family of languages, we find some tolerably distinct analogies to this Drâvidian plural suffix. Compare with the Drâvidian forms noticed above the Magyar plural in 'k' or 'ak;' the Lappish in 'k,' 'ch,' or 'h;' also the 't' by which 'k' is replaced in almost all the other dialects of the Finnish family: and observe the re-appearance of the sound of 'l' in the Ostiak plural suffix 'tl.' In Ostiak the dual suffix is 'kan' or 'gan;' in Samoïed-Ostiak 'ga' or 'ka;' in Kamass 'gai.' Castren supposes these suffixes to be derived from the conjunctive particle 'ka' or 'ki,' *also;* but their resemblance to the Drâvidian signs of plurality renders this derivation doubtful. Even the Armenian forms its plural in 'k,' *e.g.*, 'tu,' *thou*, 'tuk,' *you;* 'sirem,' *I love*, 'siremk,' *we love.* In the Turkish also, 'k' is the sign of plurality in some forms of the first person plural of the verb, *e.g.*, 'îdum,' *I was*, 'îduk,' *we were.* 't,' on the other hand, is the sign of the plural in Mongolian, and in the Calmuck is softened into 'd.' Even in Zend, though a language of a different family, there is a neuter plural in 't.' Thus, for 'imâni,' Sans., *these things*, the Zend has 'imat.'

In those instances of the interchange of 't' and 'k,' in which it can be ascertained with tolerable clearness which consonant was the one originally used and which was the corruption, 't' appears to be older than 'k.' Thus the Doric 'τῆνος' is in better accordance with related words, and therefore probably older, than the Æolian 'κῆνος,' the origin of 'ε-κεῖνος.' The Semitic pronoun or pronominal fragment 'ta,' *thou* (preserved in 'attâ' and 'antâ'), is also, I doubt not, a more accurate and older form than the equivalent or auxiliary suffix 'kâ.' In several of the Polynesian dialects, 'k' is found instead of an undoubtedly earlier Sanscrit or Pre-Sanscrit 't.' If, in accordance with these precedents, where 'k' and 't' are found to be interchanged, 't' is to be regarded as older than 'k,' it would follow that 'kaḷ,' the Drâvidian plural suffix now under consideration, may originally have been 'taḷ.' I cannot think that the Drâvidian 'gaḷ' has been derived, as Dr. Stevenson supposes, from the

Sanscrit 'sakala' (in Tamil 'sagala'), *all.* 'kal,' the base of 'sa-kala,' has been connected with 'ὅλ-ος;' but the root signifying *all*, which the Drâvidians have preferred to retain, viz., 'ell,' is connected, not with 'ὀλ,' *whole*, the Hebrew 'kol,' &c., but with the Saxon 'eal,' English *all.* This being the case, it is unlikely that they would have preserved the other root also. The Drâvidian 'taḷ-a' or 'daḷ-a,' *a host, a crowd*, would give a good meaning; but even this derivation of 'kaḷ' or 'taḷ,' is altogether destitute of evidence. The supposititious Drâvidian 'taḷ' may be compared with the Ostiak plural suffix 'tl;' but in the absence of evidence it is useless to proceed with conjectural analogies.

The New Persian neuter plural, or plural of inanimate objects, which corresponds generally to the Drâvidian neuter plural, is 'hâ,' a form which Bopp derives with much probability from the Zend. It may here be mentioned, though I do not attach any importance to a resemblance which is certainly accidental, that the Tamil plural 'gaḷ' sometimes becomes 'ha' in the pronunciation of the peasantry, *e.g.*, 'irukkiṟârgaḷ,' *they are*, is vulgarly pronounced 'irukkiṟâha.'

(2.) *Neuter Plural Suffix in* 'a.'—In addition to the neuter plural in 'gaḷ,' with its varieties, we find in nearly all the Drâvidian languages a neuter plural in short 'a,' or traces of the use of it at some former period.

'gaḷ,' though a neuter plural suffix, is occasionally used, especially in the modern dialects, as the plural suffix of rationals; but in those dialects in which 'a' is used, its use is invariably restricted to neuters, and it seems therefore to be a more essentially neuter form than 'gaḷ' itself.

We shall first examine the traces of the existence and use of this suffix which are contained in the Tamil.

'gal' is invariably used in Tamil as the plural suffix of uncompounded neuter nouns; but 'a' is preferred in the classical dialect for pluralising neuter compounds, that is, appellative nouns, or those which are compounded of a base and a suffix of gender, together with demonstrative pronouns, pronominal adjectives, and participial nouns. Even in the ordinary dialect, 'a' is generally used as the suffix of the neuter plural in the conjugation of verbs.

The second line in one of the distichs of Tiruvaḷḷuvar's 'Kuṟal,' contains two instances of the use of 'a' as a neuter plural of appellative nouns; *e.g.*, 'âgula nîra piṟa,' *vain shows (are all) other (things).* The first of these three words is used adjectivally; and in that case the final 'a' is merely that which remains of the neuter termination 'am,' after the regular rejection of 'm;' but the next two words 'nîra' and 'piʀa,' are undoubted instances of the use of 'a' as a suffix of the neuter plural of appellatives. The much used Tamil words 'pala,' *several*, or *many* (*things*), and 'sila,' *some*, or *some* (*things*) (from 'pal' and 'sil'), though commonly considered as adjectives, are in reality neuter plurals; *e.g.*, 'piṇi pala,' *diseases* (*are*) *many*; 'pala-(v)-in pâl,' *the neuter plural gender*, literally, *the gender of the many* (*things*). The use of these words adjectivally, and with the signification, not of the collective, but of the distributive plural, has led some persons to overlook their origin and real meaning, but I have no doubt that they are plurals. So also 'alla,' *not*, is properly a plural appellative: it is formed from the root 'al,' *not*, by the addition of 'a,' the plural suffix, and literally means *things that are not*, and the singular that corresponds to 'alla' is 'al-du,' *not*, euphonically 'andru,' literally *a thing that is not*. In the higher dialect of the Tamil, all nouns of quality and relation may be, and very frequently are, converted into appellatives and pluralised by the addition of 'a;' *e.g.*, 'ariya,' (Kuʀaḷ), *things that are difficult*, '*difficilia*.' We have some instances in High Tamil of the use of 'a' as the plural suffix even of substantive nouns, *e.g.*, 'poruḷa,' *substances, things that are real, realities* (from the singular 'poruḷ,' *a thing, a substance*); also 'poruḷana' and 'poruḷavei,'—with the addition of 'ana' and 'avei' (for 'ava'), the plural neuters of the demonstrative pronouns.

The neuter plural of the third person of the Tamil verb, a form which is used occasionally in ordinary prose as well as in the classical dialect, ends in 'ana;' *e.g.*, 'irukkindrana,' *they* (neut.) *are*. 'ana' is undoubtedly identical with 'ava' (now 'avei'), the neuter plural of the demonstrative pronoun, and is probably an older form than 'ava.' It is derived from the demonstrative base 'a,' with the addition of 'a' the neuter plural suffix, and an euphonic consonant ('n' or 'v') to prevent hiatus; *e.g.*, 'a-(n)-a' or 'a-(v)-a.' Sometimes in classical Tamil this 'a,' the sign of the neuter plural, is added directly to the temporal suffix of the verb, without the addition of the demonstrative base of the pronoun, *e.g.*, 'mîṇḍa,' *they* (neut.) *returned*, instead of 'mîṇḍana.' This final 'a' is evidently a sign of the neuter plural and of that alone.

Possibly we should also regard as a sign of the neuter plural, the final 'a' of the high Tamil possessive adjectives 'ena,' *my* (*things*), *mea*; 'nama,' *our* (*things*), *nostra*. The final 'a' of 'ena' would, on this supposition, be not only equivalent to the final 'a' of the Latin 'mea,' but really identical with it. These possessive adjectives are regarded by Tamil grammarians as genitives; and it will be shown hereafter that 'a' is undoubtedly one of the forms of the genitive in the Drâvidian languages. The real nature of 'ena' and 'nama' will be discussed when the genitive case-terminations are inquired into. It should be stated, however, under this head, that Tamil grammarians admit that 'ena' and 'nama,' though, as they say, genitives, must be followed by nouns in the neuter plural; *e.g.*, 'ena keigaḷ,' *my hands;* and this, so far as it goes, constitutes the principal argument in favour of regarding the final 'a' of these words, not as a genitive, but as the ordinary neuter plural suffix of the high dialect.

In Malayâlam, the oldest daughter of the Tamil and a faithful preserver of many old forms, the neuter plurals of the demonstrative pronouns are 'ava,' *those (things)*, and 'iva,' *these (things)*. The existence, therefore, in Tamil and Malayâlam of a neuter plural in short 'a,' answering to a neuter singular in 'd,' is clearly established.

The Canarese appears to have originally agreed with the Tamil in all the particulars and instances mentioned above: but the neuter plural in 'a' is now generally hidden in that dialect by the addition of a formative or euphonic syllable. Thus 'piʀa,' Tam., *other (things)*, is in Canarese 'peravu,' of which the final syllable 'vu' is undoubtedly an euphonic addition—an addition of which the Canarese is very fond. The neuter plural of the demonstrative pronoun is not 'ava' in Canarese, as it is in Malayâlam, and as it must have been in primitive Tamil, but 'avu.' Though, however, the nominative is 'avu,' all the oblique cases in the ancient Canarese reject the final 'u' before receiving the case suffixes, and must have been formed from the base of an older 'ava;' *e.g.*, 'avara' ('ava-ra'), *of those things*.

The Telugu plural neuters of the demonstratives are 'avi,' *those*, 'ivi,' *these*, answering to the singular neuters 'adi' and 'idi.' The oblique forms of the same demonstratives, to which the case-terminations are suffixed, are 'vâ' remote, and 'vî' proximate, which are evidently formed (by that process of displacement which is peculiar to the Telugu) from the primitive bases 'ava' and 'iva,' like 'vâru' from 'avaru,' and 'vîru' from 'ivaru.'

The neuter plural of the Telugu verb is formed by suffixing 'avi' or 'vi.'

In Gônd the singular demonstratives are 'ad' and 'id;' the corresponding plurals 'av' and 'iv.'

If the Telugu and the Gônd were the only extant dialects of the Drâvidian family, we should naturally conclude that as 'd' is the sign of the neuter singular, so 'v' is the sign of the neuter plural. When the other extant dialects, however (the Tamil, Malayâlam, and Canarese), are examined, we perceive that this 'v' is not a sign of plurality, nor a sign of anything but of abhorrence of hiatus; and that it is merely an euphonic link between the preceding and succeeding vowels. The Telugu and Gônd must therefore yield to the overpowering weight of evidence which is adducible in proof of this point from their sister dialects. Nor is there anything opposed to analogy in the supposition that the Telugu has changed the 'a,' which was the sign of the neuter plural of its pronouns and verbs, into 'i,' and then adopted to represent the idea of plurality a consonant which was used originally merely to prevent hiatus. In the case of 'avaru,' *they*, '*illi*,' converted into 'vâru,' and 'ivaru,' *they*, '*hi*,' converted into 'vîru,' 'v,' though only euphonic in its origin, has become an initial and apparently a radical; and the old initial and essentially demonstrative vowels 'a' and 'i,' have been thrust into a secondary place. The conversion, therefore, of 'ava' into 'vâ,' and of 'iva' into 'vî,' the oblique forms of the Telugu plural demonstratives, is directly in accordance with this analogy; and thus the Telugu cannot be considered as opposed to the concurrent testimony of the other dialects, which is to the effect that 'v' is merely euphonic, and that 'a' is the sign of the neuter plural of the demonstrative pronouns.

It may here be remarked as a curious irregularity, that in Tulu 'v' has become the sign of the neuter singular instead of 'd,' *e.g.*, 'avu,' *it*. The Tulu 'atu,' corresponding to the Tamil-Canarese 'adu,' which should have been used to signify *it*, has come to be used for *yes*.

If short 'a' be, as it has been shown to be, a sign of the neuter plural which is inherent in the Drâvidian languages, and most used by the oldest dialects, we have now to inquire into the relationship which it evidently sustains to the neuter plural suffix of some of the Indo-European languages. I know of no neuter plural in any of the Scythian tongues with which it can be compared; and we appear to be obliged to attribute to it, as well as to 'd,' the suffix of the neuter singular, an origin which is allied to that of the corresponding Indo-European forms. In the use of 'a' as a neuter plural suffix, it is evident that the Drâvidian family has not imitated, or been influenced by, the *Sanscrit*, and that it was not through the medium of the Sanscrit that Indo-European influences made their way into this department of the Drâvidian languages; for the Drâvidian neuter plural 'ă,' differs widely from the Sanscrit neuter plural 'âni,' and it is as certainly unconnected with the masculine-feminine plural 'as' (softened in modern Sanscrit into 'ah'). It is with the short 'a' which constitutes the neuter plural of the Zend, the Latin, and the Gothic, that the Drâvidian neuter plural 'a' appears to be allied. Compare also the Old Persian neuter plural 'â.'

Part II.—Formation of Cases.

Principles of Case-Formation.—The Indo-European and the Scythian families of tongues originally agreed in the principle of expressing the reciprocal relations of nouns by means of post-positions or auxiliary words. The difference between those families with respect to this point consists chiefly in the degree of faithfulness with which they have retained this principle.

In the Scythian tongues, post-positions or appended auxiliary words have rigidly held fast their individuality and separate existence. In the Indo-European tongues, on the contrary, the old post-positions or suffixes have been welded into combination with the roots to which they were appended, and converted into mere technical case-signs or inflexional terminations; whilst in the later corruptions to which those languages have been subjected, most of the case-terminations have been abandoned altogether, and prepositions, as in the Semitic tongues, have generally come to be employed instead of the older case-signs. It cannot reasonably be doubted, that the case-terminations of the primitive dialects of the Indo-European family were originally post-positions, which were added on to the root to express relation, and at length blended into an inseparable union with it, through that love of composition by which every member of the family was characterised. In most instances the root and the original signification of those post-positions are now unknown, or they are ascertained with difficulty by means of analogy and comparison.

Both in Greek and in Latin some post-positions are used in a manner which illustrates the conversion of a portion of this class of words into case-endings; *e.g.*, in Latin 'nobiscum,' and in Greek such words as 'ἀγρόθι,' *in the country;* 'ἅλαδε,' *to the sea;* and 'οὐρανόθεν,' *from heaven.* The post-positional auxiliary words which are used in those instances are appended to their bases in a truly Scythian manner. If there is any difference between them and the usage of the Scythian post-positions, it consists in this—that in the Scythian tongues, 'θι,' 'δε,' 'θεν,' would be appended to the nominative; whereas in Greek, they are suffixed either to a crude form of the noun differing from the nominative or to the accusative; and also, that in most of the languages of the Scythian group they would be written as separate words.

One of the Greek post-positions quoted above, 'δε,' signifying *direction to a place,* has been supposed to be allied to 'de,' the dative of the Manchu; and the Greek 'θεν' has been conjectured to be allied to the Tartar ablative 'din' or 'den.' I am doubtful whether any such connexion can be established; but in the manner in which the particles are appended to their bases a distinct analogy may be observed.

On turning our attention to the Drâvidian languages, we find that the principle on which they have proceeded in the formation of cases is distinctively Scythian. All case-relations are expressed by means of post-positions, or post-positional suffixes. Most of the post-positions of the Telugu are, in reality, separate words; and in all the Drâvidian dialects most of the post-positions retain traces of their original character as auxiliary nouns. Several case-signs, especially in the more cultivated dialects, have lost the faculty of separate existence, together with their original signification, and can only be treated now as case-terminations; but there is no reason to doubt that they were all post-positional nouns originally.

There is another point in which the Scythian principles of case-formation differ materially from the Indo-European. In the Indo-European family the case-endings of the plural differ from those of the singular. It is true, that on comparing the case-terminations of all the members of the family, some traces have been discovered of the existence of an original connexion between the singular and the plural terminations of some of the cases; but in several instances, *e.g.*, in the instrumental case, no such connexion between the singular and the plural has been brought to light by any amount of investigation; and it may be stated as a general rule, that the languages of this family appear to have acted from the beginning upon the principle of expressing the case-relations of the singular by one set of forms, and the case-relations of the plural by another set. On the other hand, in all the languages of the Scythian group, the same case-signs are employed both in the singular and in the plural, without alteration, or with only such alterations as euphony is supposed to require. In the singular, the case post-positions are appended directly to the nominative, which is identical with the base: in the plural they are appended, not to the nominative or base, but to the particle of pluralisation which has been suffixed to the base. In general, this is the only difference between the singular case-signs and those of the plural. The only exception of importance is, that in some of the Scythian tongues, especially in the languages of the Finnish family, the included vowel of the case-sign differs in the two numbers: it is generally 'a' in the singular and 'e' in the plural—a change which arises from the 'law of harmonic sequences' by which those tongues are characterized, and which re-appears, but little modified, in the Telugu.

When the Drâvidian languages are examined, it is found that they differ from those of the Indo-European family, and are in perfect accordance with the Scythian group, in their use of the same signs of case in the plural as in the singular. The only exception is the truly Scythian one which is apparent in the Telugu, in which the dative case-sign is either 'ki' or 'ku,' according to the nature of the vowel by which it is preceded or influenced; in consequence of which it is generally 'ki' in the singular and 'ku' in the plural.

This identity of the singular and plural case-endings in the languages of the Scythian group, including those of the Drâvidian family, will be found greatly to facilitate the comparison of the case-signs of one language of either of those families with those of the other.

Number of Declensions.—There is only one declension, properly so called, in the Drâvidian languages, as in the Scythian family generally.

Those varieties of inflexional increments which have been called 'declensions' by some European scholars, especially with reference to the Canarese and Telugu, are considered by native grammarians to constitute but one declension; and in truth they do constitute but one, for there is no difference between one so called declension and another with respect to the signs of case. Those signs are precisely the same in all: the difference which exists relates solely to suffixes of gender, or to the euphonic and inflexional increments which are added on to the bases before the addition of the case-signs.

On proceeding to analyse the case-formation of the Drâvidian languages, we shall follow the order in which they have been arranged by Drâvidian grammarians, which is the same as that of the Sanscrit. The imitation of the Sanscrit in this particular was certainly an error; for whilst in Sanscrit there are eight cases only, the number of cases in Tamil, Telugu, &c., is indefinite. Every post-position annexed to a noun constitutes, properly speaking, a new case; and therefore the number of such cases depends upon the requirements of the speaker and the different shades of meaning which he wishes to express. Notwithstanding this, the usage of Drâvidian grammarians has restricted the number of cases to eight; and though there are disadvantages in this arrangement, it will conduce to perspicuity to adhere to the ordinary usage in the analysis on which we are about to enter. Tamil grammarians, in following the order of the Sanscrit cases, have also adopted or imitated the Sanscrit mode of denominating them—not by descriptive appellations, as 'dative' or 'ablative,' but by numbers. They have affixed a number to each case in the same order as in Sanscrit, *e.g.*, 'first case,' 'second case,' &c., to 'eighth case.' Though a nominative, or 'first case,' stands at the head of the Drâvidian list of cases, the only cases, properly so called, which are used by these languages are the oblique cases. Instead, therefore, of proceeding to examine the Drâvidian nominative, the particular which now falls to be noticed is—

The absence of Nominative Case-Terminations.—The Drâvidian nominative singular is simply 'peÿr-ĕ,' '*the noun itself*'—the inflexional base of the noun—without addition or alteration; but it necessarily includes the formative, if there be one. The nominative plural differs from the nominative singular only by the addition to it of the pluralising particle.

There are three apparent exceptions to this rule, or instances in which the nominative might appear to have terminations peculiar to itself, which it is desirable here to inquire into.

(1.) The neuter termination 'am' might at first sight be supposed to be a nominative case-sign. In Sanscrit 'am' is the most common sign of the nominative neuter; and in Tamil also, all nouns ending in 'am' (in Telugu 'am-u'), whether Sanscrit derivatives or pure Drâvidian words, are neuter abstracts. In Sanscrit the accusative of the neuter is identical with the nominative, but in the other cases 'am' disappears. In Tamil, 'am' is discarded by all the oblique cases of the singular without exception: every case retains it in the plural, but in the singular it is used by the nominative alone. This comprises the sum total of the reasons for regarding 'am' as a termination of the nominative. On the other hand, though 'am' disappears in Tamil from the oblique cases in the singular, it retains its place in every one of the cases in the plural. The particle of plurality is regularly suffixed to 'am,' and the signs of case are then suffixed to the particle of plurality; which is a clear proof that, whatever 'am' may be, it is not a mere termination or case-sign of the nominative. The Telugu regards 'am' or 'am-u,' as part of the inflexional base, retains it in each case of *both* numbers alike, and suffixes to it in the singular the case-signs, in the plural the particle of plurality.

The modern Canarese makes no use whatever of this termination 'am,' in any case, or in either number. The ancient Canarese uses it, like the Tamil, in the nominative singular, but discards it, not only in the oblique cases of the singular, but in every case of the plural also. In that dialect *a tree* is 'maram,' as in Tamil, but the plural nominative, *trees*, is not 'maṛanggaḷ' ('maram-gaḷ'), but 'mara-gaḷ.'

Neuter nouns borrowed from the Sanscrit by the Tamil ordinarily retain (in the nominative alone, in the singular) the 'am' of the Sanscrit nominative singular: this 'am' is used in every one of the cases in the plural; so that even in Sanscrit derivatives, 'am' is regarded in Tamil, not as a case-sign, but as a portion of the inflexional base.

Whatever be the origin of the Tamil 'am,' considered (as I think we must consider it) as a formative, it does not appear to have been borrowed from the Sanscrit, in which it is used for so different a purpose; and I question whether it does not spring from a source altogether independent of the Sanscrit. At all events we find it added to many of the purest Drâvidian roots, and by the addition of it many verbs of that class are converted into nouns.

Thus 'kuḷam,' Tam., *a tank*, is from 'kuḷi, *to bathe*; and 'nil-am,' Tam., *the ground*, is from 'nil,' *to stand*. See 'Derivative Nouns,' in the section on 'The Verb.'

(2.) In Canarese the crude form of the personal pronouns is occasionally used instead of the nominative, *e.g.*, 'nâ,' instead of 'nânu,' *I*, and 'tâ,' instead of 'tânu,' *self*; and hence it might be supposed that the final 'n' or 'nu' of those pronouns constitutes a nominative termination. This supposition, however, is inadmissible; for in all the oblique cases, without exception, the final 'n' or 'nu' retains its place, and it is to it that the signs of case are added. Consequently it is evident that 'n' is not a sign of the nominative, but a formative, which has been compounded with the inflexional base, or annexed to it, though it is capable of occasional separation from it.

(3.) In all the Drâvidian languages, the quantity of the included vowels of the personal pronouns in some of the oblique cases (and in Tamil-Canarese in all the oblique cases), differs from the quantity of the same vowels in the nominative. In the nominative the vowel is invariably long, in the oblique cases generally short: *e.g.*, in Canarese we find 'nânu,' *I*, 'nanna,' *my*; 'nînu,' *thou*, 'ninna,' *thy*; 'tânu,' *self*, 'tanna,' *of one's self*. This is the only instance contained in these languages in which there is a difference between the nominative and the oblique cases of such a nature as almost to constitute the nominative a case by itself. In this instance, however, the nominative is the true, unchanged, inflexional base, and the shortening of the quantity of the vowel in the oblique cases, prior to the addition of post-positions, has arisen from the euphonic tendencies of the language. The Telugu shortens the root-vowel in the accusative only. In Tamil the shortened form, without any inflexional addition, is often used as a possessive; *e.g.*, 'nĭn,' *thy*, from the obsolete 'nîn,' *thou*—a usage which is in accordance with the ordinary Drâvidian rule that the inflected form of every noun, or the basis of the oblique cases, is to be regarded as of itself a possessive or adjective.

Before proceeding to consider the oblique case-signs seriatim, it is necessary to enquire into the changes which the base sustains prior to receiving the suffixes.

Inflexional base of the oblique cases.—In the majority of instances that form of the Drâvidian noun which constitutes the crude base, and which is used as the nominative, constitutes also the inflexional base. The nominative of this class of nouns and the base of the oblique cases are identical; and the case-signs are added to the base or nominative without any link of connexion, whether inflexional or euphonic, beyond the ordinary 'v' or 'y,' which is inserted to prevent hiatus between concurrent vowels.

In a smaller number of instances (a number which constitutes, however, a very large minority), the base or nominative undergoes some alteration before receiving the addition of the terminations, or case-signs of the oblique cases.

In the solitary instance of the Tamil-Canarese personal pronouns, as pointed out under the preceding head, the nominative sustains a curtailment (viz., by the shortening of the quantity of the included vowel) on becoming the inflexional base, or base of the oblique cases: but in all other instances the alteration which the base sustains consists in an augmentation, which is sometimes optional and sometimes necessary; and it is to this augmented form (augmented by the addition of some inflexional increment) that the case-signs are attached. This Drâvidian rule may be illustrated by the Hebrew. In Hebrew the personal and other suffixes of substantives and verbal nouns are attached, not to the base or nominative, but to the 'construct state,' *i.e.*, the state in which a noun stands when it is qualified by a subsequent noun. Just so in the Drâvidian languages, in that large class of nouns in which the inflexional base of the noun, or its adjectival form, differs from the crude form or nominative, the signs of case are attached not to the crude, natural form of the noun, but to the altered, inflected form, viz., to that form which a Drâvidian noun assumes when it qualifies or is qualified by a subsequent noun, or when it stands to such noun in the relation of an adjective. This inflected form of the noun is frequently used by itself, without the addition of any case-termination, and when so used it has a possessive or adjectival force. Tamil grammarians hold that the 'inflexion' is not a possessive, though they cannot but admit that for every purpose for which the possessive or genitive is used, the 'oblique case,' or inflected form of the noun may be used instead. They admit that it is used adjectivally: but it appears to me that its use as an adjectival formative is a secondary one, and that it was originally, like many other adjectival formatives in various languages, a sign of the genitive. Its use eventually as the inflexional basis of all the cases is in perfect harmony with this view of its origin, and testifies to the existence of a period in the history of the language when each of the post-positions of case was known and felt to be a substantive, which required to be united to its base by a sign of possession or adjectival relationship.

At present, however, it is our object to seek out and arrange the various increments which are used for forming the inflexional base of the oblique cases, without reference to the other uses to which those increments are put.

(1.) *The inflexional increment* 'in,' *with its varieties.*—The particle 'in' constitutes the inflexion of certain classes of nouns in Tamil-Canarese; and the corresponding Telugu particles are 'ni' and 'na.' All these particles are, I believe, virtually one and the same. The Tamil uses 'in' in the singular and in the plural alike; and its original signification has been forgotten to such a degree that it is now often used merely as an euphonic link of connexion between the base and its case-signs. For this reason its use both in Tamil and in Canarese is optional. In Telugu the corresponding particles are used only in the singular; and where they are used, their use is not euphonic merely, but is intended to constitute the 'inflexion.'

The Ku, which in this respect is more nearly allied than the Telugu is to the Tamil, and more regular, uses 'ni' as the inflexion of the plural as well as of the singular of all classes of nouns.

When 'in' is used in Tamil as the inflexion of the neut. sing. demonstratives 'adu,' *that,* 'idu,' *this,* it is apt to be confounded with 'an,' a termination which those pronouns often take, especially in the oblique cases, instead of 'u.' Instead of 'adu' and 'idu,' we may say in Tamil 'adan' and 'idan.' In the nominative these forms are very rarely used; but the accusative, 'adan-ei,' is more common, and the dative, 'adaʀku' ('adan-ku'), still more so. 'id-in-âl,' *through this,* 'ad-in-âl,' *through that,* and cases similarly formed, must therefore be carefully distinguished from 'idan-âl' and 'adan-âl.' The 'an' of the latter is a formative, which is probably of the same origin as the 'am' of many neuter nouns (that 'am' being almost always convertible into 'an'); whereas 'in' is an inflexional increment, and was originally a case-sign of the genitive.

The use of 'in' as an inflexional increment effects no alteration whatever in the meaning of the case-sign which is suffixed to it. Where it is not followed by a case-sign, it becomes of itself a mode of expressing the genitive; but where a case-sign follows, it is merely euphonic, and its use is optional. Thus, we may say either 'keiyal' ('kei-(y)-âl'), *with the hand,* or 'keiyin-âl' ('kei-(y)-in-âl); either 'kâlâl,' *with the foot,* or 'kâlinâl' ('kâl-in-âl').

In the first of these instances ('kei-(y)-in-âl'), 'y' is used to keep the initial vowel of 'in' pure, in accordance with the ordinary rule of the language; from the use of which, in this instance, it is evident that 'in,' though merely euphonic in its present application, was in its origin something more than a mere euphonic expletive.

'in' is not only attached as an inflexional increment to the crude base of Tamil nouns, but it is appended also to other inflexional increments, viz., to 'attu,' and to the doubled final 'ḍ' and 'ʀ' of certain classes of nouns. Thus, by the addition of 'attu' to 'mara-m,' *a tree.* we form 'marattu,' the inflexional base of the oblique cases, by suffixing to which 'âl,' the sign of the instrumental case, we form 'marattâl,' *by a tree*: but we may also attach 'in' to 'attu,' forming 'attin' ('att-in'), a doubled and euphonized increment, *e.g.*, 'marattinâl' ('mara-attu-in-âl'). As 'in' when standing alone, without the suffix of any case-sign, has the force of the genitive, so also has the double increment, 'attin;' *e.g.*, 'marattin' signifies *of a tree.* In Tamil, 'in' is the 'inflexion' of all nouns, except those which end in 'am,' or in 'ḍ-u' or 'ʀ-u:' in Canarese 'in' is much more rarely used than in Tamil; but where it is used, its use is rather euphonic and optional, than inflexional, and it cannot be used by itself to express the force of the genitive. As in Tamil 'guruvil,' *in a priest,* and 'guruvinil' are identical, so we may say in Canarese either 'guruvalli' or 'guruvinalli.'

In Telugu the corresponding particles 'ni' and 'na' constitute the inflexion, or natural genitive of certain classes of nouns, and are also attached as inflexional increments to the base before suffixing the case-signs; *e.g.*, 'dîniki' ('dî-ni-ki'), *to it,* 'tammuniki' ('tammu-ni-ki'), *to a younger brother,* 'guru-na-ku,' *to a spiritual teacher.* These increments are attached only to the singular in Telugu: they constitute the singular 'inflexion,' *i.e.*, the genitival or adjectival base of the noun, and are not merely euphonic; nor are they to be regarded as the inflexion of masculine nouns and pronouns alone, though they are chiefly used by them, for 'dâniki,' *to that,* 'dîniki,' *to this,* are neuters.

The Telugu 'ni,' and the Tamil-Canarese 'in,' are doubtless identical in origin. The change in the position of the vowel is in accordance with the change of 'il,' Tam., *the negative particle,* into 'lê,' in Telugu, and of 'uḷ,' Tam., *within,* into 'lô,' in Telugu. It also corresponds to the change of the position of the vowel which is apparent when 'in,' the Latin preposition, is compared with the corresponding Sanscrit preposition 'ni.'

(2.) *The inflexional increments* 'ad' *and* 'ar.'—The particles 'ad' and 'ar,' are extensively used by the Canarese as inflexional increments. Their use exactly resembles that of 'in' in the same language, though each is restricted to a particular class of words. 'in' is used as an increment of the base solely in connexion with nouns which end in 'u,' *e.g.*, 'guru,' *a priest*; and 'ad' and 'ar' are used in connexion with neuter nouns and demonstratives, and with those alone.

In the Canarese genitive case-endings, 'ara,' 'ada,' 'ina,' and 'a,' it will be seen that the real and only sign of the genitive is 'a,' the final vowel of each; and therefore Dr. Stevenson has erred in comparing 'ara' or 'ra' (properly 'ar-a' or 'ad-a') with the New Persian 'râ.' 'ad' and 'ar' are prefixed to the signs of case, not by the genitive only, but by three cases besides, viz., by the accusative, the instrumental, and the locative. Thus we may say not only 'idaṛa' ('id-ar-a'), *of this,* and 'marada' ('mar-ad-a'), *of a tree,* but also 'idaralli' ('id-ar-alli'), *in this,* and 'maradinda' ('mar-ad-inda'), *by a tree.* Consequently 'ad' and 'ar,' whatever be their origin, are not signs of case, in so far as their use is concerned, but are used merely as increments of the base, or inflexional bonds of conjunction between the base and the case-signs, like 'in,' 'ni,' &c. Moreover, the Canarese differs in its use of these increments from the Telugu and the Tamil in this, that it never suffixes them alone without the addition of the case-signs, and never gives them the signification of genitives or adjectival formatives.

'ad' and 'ar' are not only related, but are, I believe, really identical. Both are increments of the neuter alone; and where the Canarese uses 'ar,' the Tulu uses 'ad.' 'd' and 'r' are known to change places dialectically, as in the southern provinces of the Tamil country, in which 'adu,' *it,* is pronounced 'aRu;' and the Canarese increment 'ad' or 'ar' is, I have no doubt, identical with that very word, viz., with the Tamil-Canarese demonstrative 'adu' or 'ad,' *it.*

Though the Tamil has not regularly adopted the unchanged form of this demonstrative, 'adu,' as an inflexional increment of the base in the declension of nouns, it makes use of it occasionally in a manner which perfectly illustrates the origin of the Canarese use of it.

In classical Tamil the neuter demonstrative may optionally be added to any neuter noun in the singular, not for the purpose of altering the signification, but merely for the improvement of the euphony, and for the purpose of meeting the requirements of prosody. 'adu may thus be added even to the nominative; *e.g.*, we may not only write 'pon,' *gold*, but also poetically 'ponnadu,' *gold*, or etymologically *gold-that*, *i.e.*, *that (which is) gold*. It is much more common, however, and more in accordance also with the Canarese usage, to use 'adu' in the oblique cases; in which event it is inserted between the base and the case-sign, so as to become virtually (yet without losing its proper character) an inflexional increment; *e.g.*, instead of 'ponnei,' the accusative of 'pon,' *gold*, we may write 'ponnadei' ('ponn-ad-ei').

I connect with the Canarese 'ar,' and therefore with 'ad,' and ultimately with the neuter demonstrative itself, the euphonic consonant 'r,' which is used by the Telugu in certain instances to separate between a Sanscrit noun of quality used as an adjective and the feminine suffix 'âlu,' *e.g.*, 'sundaru-r-âlu,' *a handsome woman*. This would be quite in accordance with the peculiar Telugu usage of employing the neuter demonstrative singular in place of the feminine singular.

(3.) *The inflexional increment* 'ṭi.'—In Telugu 'ṭi' or 'ti' is the most common and characteristic inflexional increment of neuter singular nouns, and it is used in Telugu, like the corresponding 'attu' in Tamil, not merely as an increment of the base, but as the 'inflexion,' with the signification of the possessive case or of that of an adjective, as the context may require. Two instances of the use of this increment will suffice out of the very numerous class of neuter nouns which form their singular inflexion by the addition of 'ṭi' or 'ti' (or rather by the substitution of that particle for their last syllable); *e.g.*, 'vâgili,' *a door way*, inflexion 'vâgiṭi;' 'nuduru,' *the forehead*, inflexion 'nuduṭi.' In these instances of the use of 'ṭi' or 'ti,' the inflexional increment is substituted for the last syllable; but it is certainly to be considered as an addition to the word—as a particle appended to it; and the blending of the increment with the base, instead of merely suffixing it, has arisen from the euphonic tendencies of the language.

I have no doubt that the suffixed particle which constitutes the Telugu inflexional increment was originally 'ti,' not 'ṭi'—the dental, not the cerebral. This would account for the circumstance that 'ṭ' alone follows words of which the final consonant is 'r' or 'l;' for on the addition of the dental 't' to 'r' or 'l' both consonants dialectically coalesce and become 'ṭ;' the hard cerebral being regarded as euphonically equivalent to the two soft letters. In no case in Telugu is there a double 'ṭ' in the inflexional increment. It is sometimes, however, euphonised by prefixing a nasal, *e.g.*, 'tolli,' *antiquity*, forms its inflexion in 'toṇṭi' (instead of 'tolṭi), or 'tolliṇṭi.' The dental 'ti' is used instead of the cerebral 'ṭi,' as the inflexion of nouns ending in 'yu' after a pure vowel, *e.g.*, 'vâyu,' *the mouth*, inflexion 'vâti.' This circumstance proves that it was the dental 'ti' which was originally used in all cases. The dental 't' on being appended to consonants changes naturally into the cerebral; whereas the cerebral rarely, if ever, changes into the dental.

If we now conclude, as I think we undoubtedly may, that the Telugu inflexion was originally 'ti,' not 'ṭi,' this inflexional increment may at once be connected with the Telugu neuter demonstrative, 'adi,' in the same manner as the Canarese 'ad,' and the Tamil 'attu,' are connected with the Tamil-Canarese neuter demonstrative 'adu.' This identification is confirmed by the circumstance that 'aṭṭi' is sometimes used for 'adi' in Telugu, and 'iṭṭi' for 'idi,' just as 'attu' is sometimes used for 'adu' in colloquial Tamil. Though the identification of the inflexion and the neuter sing. demonstrative could not easily be established from the Telugu alone, or from any one dialect alone, yet the cumulative argument derived from a comparison of all the dialects has irresistible force. An important link of evidence is furnished by the inflexion which follows.—

(4.) *The inflexional increment* 'attu' *or* 'attru.'—All Tamil nouns which end in 'am,' whether Sanscrit derivatives or pure Tamil roots, reject 'am' in the oblique cases in the singular, and take 'att-u' instead; and it is to this increment that the various case-signs are suffixed: *e.g.*, the locative case-sign 'il' is not added to 'âṛam,' *depth*, but to the inflexional base 'âṛ-attu,' so that, *in the depth* is not 'âṛam-il,' but 'âṛ-att-il.' This rule admits of no exception in the ordinary dialect of the Tamil; but in the poetical dialect, which represents more or less distinctly an older condition of the language, 'attu' is sometimes left unused, and the case-sign is added directly to the crude base: *e.g.*, instead of 'kay-attu-kku,' *to the depth* (from 'kayam,' *depth*'), 'kaya-kku' is used in the Chintâmaṇi. When the increment 'attu' is not followed by any sign of case, but by another noun, like the other inflexion 'in' and like the corresponding Telugu inflexion 'ṭi,' it has the force either of the genitive or of an adjective; *e.g.*, 'mar-attu koppu, *the branch of a tree*, 'kuḷ-attu mîn,' *tank fish*. This inflexion, like 'ad' and 'ar' in Canarese, and 'ṭi,' or 'ti' in Telugu, is used in connexion with the singular alone. 'am,' the formative of the base, which is used only by the nominative in the singular, is retained in the plural, not in the nominative only, but in all the oblique cases. To it the sign of plurality is appended, and the case-sign follows the sign of plurality; *e.g.*, 'maranggaḷil' ('maram-gaḷ-il'), *in trees*.

There are in Tamil a few naturally plural (neuter) pronominals and nouns of relation (*e.g.*, 'avei,' *those* (*things*); 'sila,' *few;* 'pala,' *many;* 'ellâ,' *all*), which receive in their oblique cases the inflexional increment 'aʀʀu,' pronounced 'attru.' Thus, from 'ellâm,' *all*, which is properly 'ellâ-um' ('um' being the conjunctive and intensitive particle *even*, and 'ellâ-um' or 'ellâm' signifying *even all, all together*), the locative which is formed by the Tamil is 'ellâvattrilum, (ellâ-(v)-attr'-il-um), *in all*, literally *even in all*. So also 'avei,' *they* (neut.), forms its accusative not by adding 'ei,' the accusative case-sign, to 'avei,' but by inserting 'attru,' and adding 'ei' thereto, *e.g.*, 'avattrei' ('av-attr-ei'), *them;* in which instance 'ei' (for 'a'), the sign of the plural, is rejected, and its place is supplied by 'attru,' the inflexional increment of this class of plurals.

It is evident that the Tamil increments, 'attu' and 'attru,' are virtually identical. The difference in use is slight, and in pronunciation still slighter; and in general 'attru' is pronounced exactly like 'attu' by the vulgar. We may, therefore, conclude that they are one and the same, and on examining the Telugu we find additional confirmation of their identity. In Telugu, avi, *they* (neut.), answering to the Tamil 'avei,' forms its inflexion in 'vâṭi' (for 'avaṭi'). This Telugu (supposititious) 'avaṭi' is evidently identical with the Tamil 'avattru.' The 'ṭi' of this inflexion is certainly the same as the 'ṭi' of Telugu nouns substantive: and if there is no difference in Telugu between the 'ṭi' which forms the inflexional increment of neuter singular nouns and demonstratives and the plural inflexion 'ṭi' of such words as 'vâṭi,' we may also conclude that there is no real difference between the singular 'attu' and the plural 'attru' of the Tamil.

Whence did the 'r' which is included in 'aʀʀu,' or 'attr-u,' take its rise? We see its origin clearly enough in Canarese; for in the ancient dialect 'ar,' or 'r,' forms the inflexional increment of every one of the plural pronominals which take 'aʀʀu' in Tamil: *e.g.*, 'avara' (corresponding Tam. 'avaʀʀu'), *of those things;* 'ellavara' (Tam. 'ellâvaʀʀu'), *of all things;* 'kelavara' (Tam. 'silavaʀʀu'), *of some* (*things*). The Canarese 'r' is, as we have seen, derived from, and originally identical with, 'd,' or 't;' and hence the Tamil in doubling 'ʀ' gives it the sound 'ttr.' Thus, not only the Tamil increment 'att-u,' but also 'aʀʀ-u,' is clearly derived from the same origin as the Canarese 'ad' or 'ar,' and the Telugu 'ṭi,' viz., from the neut. sing. demonstrative. Both these inflexions have been formed also by the same process; for 'ar,' when doubled, becomes 'aRR-u' ('attr-u'), as naturally as 'ad,' when doubled, becomes 'att-u;' and in each case the doubling arises from the adjectival use to which the suffixed pronoun is put. It is a recognized rule of the Tamil that when a noun ending in 'd-u' is used adjectivally, the 'd-u' may either become 'd-in' or 'tt-u;' *e.g.*, from 'erud-u,' *an ox*, is formed either 'erud-in' or 'erutt-u,' *of an ox*. So also 'ad-u,' *it*, which is now generally inflected by the addition of 'in,' seems to have been inflected formerly as 'att-u.' 'adu' is vulgarly pronounced in the oblique cases as 'attu' by the bulk of the northern Tamilians. The majority of the natives of Madras, for instance, use 'attei' ('attu-ei') as the accusative of 'adu,' *that*, instead of 'adei;' and in the neuter singular pronominal suffixes to the verb the same pronunciation is not only commonly heard, but is often written: *e.g.*, instead of 'irukkiRadukku,' *to its being* (the dative of 'irukkir-adu,' *it is, the being*, or *that which is*), Madras Tamilians invariably write 'irukkiRattukku; in which compound 'attu' is evidently used as the neuter demonstrative singular instead of 'adu.' It is also deserving of notice, that the feminine singular suffix of a large class of appellative nouns, which is 'di' or 'adi' in Telugu, and which has been shown to be identical with the neuter demonstrative, is in Tamil 'tti' or 'atti,' *e.g.;* 'râsâtti,' *a woman of the Râjâ caste, a queen*. Even in the nominative 'aṭṭi' is sometimes used in Telugu instead of 'adi,' *that*, and 'iṭṭi' instead of 'idi,' *this*.

Two instances will suffice to prove the identity of the Tamil 'attu' and the Canarese 'ad,' and thus supply the only link that is wanting to the perfect identification of 'attu' with the Telugu 'ti,' and of both with 'adu.' The Tamil 'pûrv-att-il,' *in ancient times*, is compounded of 'pûrv-am' (Sans. deriv.), *antiquity*, 'att-u,' the inflexional increment, and 'il,' the sign of the locative. Compare this with the corresponding Canarese 'pûrv-ad-alli,' in which it is evident that 'ad' is used in the same manner as 'att-u,' and perfectly agrees with it in signification. Again, the Tamil 'âyirattondru,' *a thousand and one*, is formed from 'âyiram,' *a thousand* (the inflexion of which is 'âyir-attu'), and 'ondru,' *one*. When this is compared with the corresponding Canarese word 'sâviradondu,' from 'sâvir',' *a thousand* (equivalent to the Tamil 'âyir'') - inflexional form 'sâvir ad' - to which 'ondu,' identical with 'ondru,' is appended, it is evident that the Canarese increment 'ad'' and the Tamil 'att'' are one and the same; and also that in this instance the Canarese 'ad'' is used for precisely the same purpose as the Tamil 'att',' viz., as an inflexional increment with an adjectival signification.

(5.) *The formation of the inflexion by means of doubling and hardening the final consonant.* — Tamil nouns ending in 'ḍ-u' and 'ʀ-u' form the basis of their oblique cases by doubling the final 'ḍ' and 'ʀ;' and the doubled 'ḍ' becomes by rule 'ṭṭ,' and the doubled 'ʀ,' 'ttr' (though spelled 'ʀʀ'): *e.g.*, from 'kâḍ-u,' *a jungle*, is formed 'kâṭṭ-(u)-kku,' *to a jungle;* from 'âʀ-u,' *a river*, 'âttr-il' ('âʀʀ-il'), *in a river*.

This doubling of the final consonant of such nouns places them in an adjectival relation to the succeeding noun. It is to be regarded as a sign of transition, for when intransitive or neuter verbs ending in 'ḍ-u' or 'ʀ-u' double their finals, they acquire a transitive signification; *e.g.*, from 'ôḍ-u,' *to run*, is formed 'oṭṭ-u,' *to drive;* from 'têʀ-u,' *to become clear*, comes 'têttr-u' ('têʀʀ-u'), *to clarify, to comfort.* Properly speaking, therefore, this doubling of the final is an adjectival formative, rather than an inflexion or case-sign basis: but in this, as in many other cases, the same form is used in both connections, in consequence of the case-sign which is appended to the doubled final having originally been a noun, and still retaining in compounds the force of a noun.

In Telugu the final consonant of nouns of this class is hardened, but not doubled, to form the inflexion or basis of the oblique cases; *e.g.*, the inflexion of 'êʀ-u,' *a river*, is not 'êttri' ('êʀʀi'), but 'êṭi,' *of a river;* and that of 'nâḍu,' *a country*, is 'nâṭi,' *of a country.* In some instances the Telugu corresponds more closely to the Tamil in forming the inflexion of nouns in 'ʀʀ' by changing that into 'ʀt:' *e.g.*, 'aʀʀ-u,' *the neck;* inflexion of the same 'aʀti.' If we regarded the Telugu alone, we should consider these examples, not as instances of the doubling of a final 'd' or 'ʀ,' but rather as instances of the incorporation of 'ṭi,' the usual inflexional suffix with those finals; and we should suppose this view to be confirmed by the circumstance that the Telugu does not, like the Tamil, double the final 'ḍ-u' or 'ʀ-u' of intransitive verbs on converting them into transitives, but adds a formative 'chu.' Nevertheless, the Tamil rule is so clear and express and so evidently founded upon grammatical reasons, and the Telugu words in question, 'nâṭi,' &c., so exactly agree with the Tamil, that we cannot but recognise in them the operation of the same principle, though somewhat disguised. In other and parallel instances, though the Telugu hardens, it does not double: *e.g.*, from 'pâḍ-u,' Tam. and Tel., *to sing*, the Tamil forms 'pâṭṭ-u,' *a song*, the Telugu 'pâṭ-a.' The final 'i' of such Telugu inflexions as 'nâṭi,' *of a country* (from 'nâḍ-u'), instead of 'nâṭ-u,' which the Tamil would lead us to expect, is owing, I have no doubt, to the influence of 'ṭi,' which is the ordinary suffix of the inflexion of neuter nouns.

7. *The inflexional increment* 'i.'—The inflexion of the plural of the Telugu epicene demonstrative pronoun consists in 'i,' *e.g.*, 'vâru' (from 'avaru'), *those persons;* inflexion 'vâri,' *of them, their.*

The final 'u' of 'vâr-u' is merely euphonic, but the 'i' of 'vâri' is certainly an inflexional increment; and possibly the final 'i' of the singular masculine demonstrative inflexional 'vâni' is not to be regarded as a portion of 'ni,' the ordinary inflexional increment of Telugu masculine nouns, but is identical with the final 'i' of 'vâri.' A small class of Telugu nouns form their singular inflexion also in 'i,' *e.g.*, 'kâl-i,' *of a foot,* 'têr-i,' *of a car.* What is the origin of this 'i?' I think we are guided to a true idea of its origin by comparing it with the possessive pronoun 'vâridi,' Tel., *that which is theirs,* which in Ku also is 'êvâridi.' When 'vâridi' is compared with the Tamil possessive 'avaradu,' the meaning of which is exactly the same, we see that in each language the termination is that of the neuter demonstrative pronoun, which is 'adu' in Tamil, 'adi' in Telugu; and we also see that the penultimate 'i' of 'vâridi' is derived by attraction, according to Telugu usage, from the succeeding 'i,' which is that of the neuter demonstrative singular 'adi.' The final 'i' of 'vâri' may therefore be regarded as an abbreviation of 'adi,' or at least as derived from it.

(8.) *Telugu plural inflexional increment in* 'a.'—In Telugu 'a' constitutes the plural inflexion of most colloquial pronominals, and of all substantive nouns without exception. 'l-u,' properly 'l,' is the pluralising particle of all neuter nouns in Telugu, and of the majority of 'rational' ones: the inflexion is effected by changing this 'l-u' into 'la,' or to speak more correctly, by suffixing 'a' to 'l'—the final vowel of 'lu' being merely euphonic; and it is to this incremental 'a,' as to 'ni' and 'ṭi,' the singular inflexions, that all the case-signs are appended, *e.g.*, 'kattulu,' *knives;* inflexion 'kattula;' instrumental 'kattula-chêta,' *by knives.*

I have no doubt that this inflexional increment 'a' is identical with 'a,' one of the Tamil-Canarese signs of the genitive, and of the use of which as a genitive, in the singular as well as in the plural, we have an illustration even in Telugu, in the reflexive pronouns 'tan-a,' *of self,* 'tam-a,' *of selves.* This increment also, therefore, is to be regarded as a genitive in origin, though in actual use merely an inflexion; and I have no doubt that each of the Drâvidian inflexions proceeds from some genitive case-sign.

Before leaving this subject, I should briefly refer to one which bears some relation to it, viz.:—

Euphonic links of connection between the base and the inflexion, the base and the case-signs, or the inflexion and the case-signs.

In Tamil the dative case-sign 'ku' is generally preceded by an euphonic 'u,' and through the influence of this 'u' the 'k' is doubled. Thus, from 'avan,' *he*, is formed not 'avanku,' *to him*, but 'avanukku' ('avan-u-kku'). The personal pronouns, both in the singular and in the plural, make use of an euphonic 'a' in this connection, instead of 'u;' *e.g.*, from 'nân' (or rather from an older 'ên'), *I*, is formed the inflexion 'en;' and this takes as its dative not 'enku' or 'enukku,' *to me*, but 'enakku' (en-a-kku).

In Malayâlam the personal pronouns require the insertion of an euphonic 'i' between the inflexion and the case-sign, *e.g.*, 'inikka,' *to me*, 'nanikka,' *to thee.* In some instances in Tamil the euphonic vowel which is made use of in this connection is not 'u' or 'a,' but 'ei.' Thus 'nâḷ,' *a day*, forms its dative not in 'nâḷku,' 'nâḷukku.' or 'nâḷakku,' but in 'nâḷeikku.' In the higher dialect of the Tamil the dative case-sign 'ku' is often directly attached to the noun, especially in those instances in which the noun terminates in a liquid or semi-vowel; *e.g.*, we find in that dialect not 'avarukku' ('avar-u-kku'), *to them*, but 'avarku.' In ancient Canarese also, the dative case-sign was invariably attached in this manner.

Whenever concurrent vowels meet in Tamil 'v' and 'y' are used, as has already been shown, to prevent hiatus; and accordingly they are used between the final vowel of nouns and those inflexions or case-signs which begin with vowels; *e.g.*, 'naḍuvil' ('naḍu-(v)-il'), *in the middle;* 'vaṛiyil' ('vaṛi-(y)-il'), *in the way.* Compare this with the use of 'v' for a similar purpose in Magyar: *e.g.*, from 'lô,' *a horse*, and 'at,' the sign of the objective case, is formed not 'lôät,' but 'lôvat,' precisely as would be done in Tamil. 'v' and 'y' are used by the Canarese in the same manner as by the Tamil; but in Telugu, as has already been shown, 'n' is used as a preventive of hiatus instead of 'v.'

The way has now been prepared for the investigation of the Drâvidian oblique cases, and of the signs of case properly so called.

The accusative or 'second' case.—In the Indo-European languages the case-sign of the accusative of neuter nouns is identical with that of the nominative case. This identity has arisen, I conceive, not from the nominative being used as an accusative, but *vice versâ* from the accusative being used as a nominative. The accusative case-suffix is a sign of passivity, or of being acted upon; and it was suffixed to masculine and feminine nouns to denote that in that instance they were to be regarded not as agents, but as objects. Subsequently, I conceive, it was adopted, because of this signification, as a general characteristic of the neuter, objective, or dead class of nouns, and so came to be used as the nominative, or normal case-ending of nouns of that class.

In the Drâvidian languages also an accusative case-sign seems to have been adopted as a formative termination of abstract neuter nouns. The Old Canarese accusative case-sign 'am' seems to be identical with, and is probably the origin of, the 'am' which is so largely used by Drâvidian neuters. Notwithstanding this, the use of the nominative, or rather of the simple, unformed base, as the accusative of neuter nouns, is the ordinary and almost universal colloquial usage of the Drâvidians, and is often found even in their classical compositions. The accusative case-termination may be suffixed whenever it appears to be desirable to do so, either for the sake of euphony or to prevent ambiguity; but it is rarely employed except when it is required for those purposes. When this case-termination is used without necessity, it sounds stiff and unidiomatic; and this is one of the peculiarities by which the Tamil of foreigners is marked. Drâvidian masculine and feminine nouns and their corresponding pronouns invariably take the accusative case-suffix when they are governed by active verbs. This probably proceeds from the principle that it is more natural for rational beings to act than to be acted upon; and hence when they do happen to be acted upon—when the nouns by which they are denoted are to be taken objectively—it becomes necessary, in order to avoid misapprehension, to suffix to them the objective case-sign. On the other hand, the difference between the nominative and the accusative of neuter nouns is often allowed to pass unnoticed, because such nouns, whether they act or are acted upon, are alike destitute of personality and inert. Whether the accusative is used as the nominative, as in the Indo-European languages, or whether, as is often the case in the Scythian tongues, the nominative is used for the accusative, the principle involved appears to be one and the same.

The use of the nominative of neuter nouns for the accusative is not unknown to the North-Indian vernaculars, and is one of those particulars in which those vernaculars appear to be allied to the Drâvidian family. Ordinarily, however, the North-Indian vernaculars are distinguished from the southern by their use of the dative case-sign for the accusative. In the Drâvidian family, with the solitary exception of the Gônd, the dative case-sign is always quite distinct from the accusative; whereas in the Gauḍa or North-Indian family, there is generally little or no difference between those two cases. In most instances, the case-sign which is allied to the Drâvidian dative suffix, and which appears to be essentially a dative, is that which is used for both cases indiscriminately; and it is the connexion which determines whether the dative or the accusative is to be understood.

(1.) *Accusative case-signs* 'ei,' 'ê,' *and* 'a.'—The only sign of the accusative which the Tamil recognizes is 'ei,' which is suffixed to both numbers and to all genders; though, as has been mentioned, the accusative of neuter nouns is often identical with the nominative or base. Examples,-'avan-ei,' *him*, 'avaḷ-ei,' *her*, 'ad-ei,' *it*. The accusative case-sign of the Malayâlam is 'ê;' and this is evidently a primitive form of the Tamil 'ei.' The Canarese ordinarily uses either 'a' or 'annu,' as its accusative case-sign; but in some instances (*e. g.*, 'nanna,' *me*, 'ninna,' *thee*,) it appears to make use of 'na,' instead of 'a.' This 'a' seems to be equivalent to the Malayâla 'ê' and the Tamil 'ei,' into which the Canarese short 'a' is often found to change by rule.

The Tamil-Malayâla accusative case-sign 'ê' or 'ei,' may be compared with 'hê' or 'ê,' the dative-accusative of Hindi pronouns; with the Gujarathi dative-accusative singular 'ê;' and with the preponderance of the vowel 'ê' which is observed in the dative-accusatives of the Bengali and Sindhi. Compare also the Brahui dative-accusative 'ne' or 'e,' and the Malay 'e.'

On pushing the comparison amongst the Scythian tongues, not a few of their accusative case-signs are found to resemble the Tamil accusative. Thus the Wotiak accusative is formed by adding 'â' to the root, *e.g.*, 'ton,' *thou*, 'ton-â,' *thee*. The Turkish accusative is 'î' or 'yî;' the Mongolian 'î' after a consonant: 'djî,' instead of the Turkish 'yî,' after a vowel.

The Turkish 'î' is doubtless a softened form of the Oriental Turkish accusative case-sign 'nî,' from which it has been derived, by the same process by which the Turkish dative case-sign 'eh' or 'yeh,' is undoubtedly derived from the old Oriental Turkish 'gâ' or 'ghâh.' It would therefore appear that the Scythiau accusative originally contained a nasal; and in accordance with this supposition we find in the Calmuck pronouns an accusative case-sign corresponding to the Oriental Turkish 'nî,' *e.g.*, 'bida-nî,' *us*, from 'bida,' *we*, and also 'na-maï,' *me*, and 'dzi-maï,' *thee*, from the bases 'na' and 'dzi.' With this we may again compare the Brahui dative-accusative 'ne' or 'e.' That the Oriental Turkish 'nî' could easily aud naturally be softened into 'yî' or 'î,' appears from the Drâvidian languages themselves; in which, for instance, the personal pronoun 'nân,' Tam., *I*, has been softened first into 'yân,' and then, in the oblique cases and the verbal terminations, to 'ên' and 'en.' 'nî' being evidently the basis of the Turkish and Mongolian sign of the accusative, if the Drâvidian 'ei' or 'ê' is allied to it, as we have supposed to be probable, this 'ei' or 'ê' must originally have been preceded or followed by a nasal; and in investigating the other Drâvidian accusative case-signs we shall discover some reasons for concluding this to have been actually the case.

(2.) *Accusative case-signs* 'am,' 'annu,' 'anna,' 'nu,' &c.—'am' is the characteristic sign of the ancient Canarese accusative, and is used in connexion with nouns and pronouns alike, *e.g.*, 'avaḷ-am,' *her*. The more modern form of the Canarese accusative is 'annu,' *e.g.*, 'avaḷ-annu,' *her;* and this 'annu' is certainly identical with the older 'am.' 'am' has in other instances besides this evinced a tendency to change into 'an;' for *he* is 'avam' in ancient Canarese, though 'avan' in Tamil. The change of the old Indo-European 'm,' the sign of the accusative in Latin and Sanscrit, into the Greek 'ν' is also a parallel case. The ancient Canarese case-sign 'am' no sooner changed into 'an,' than it would irresistibly be impelled to euphonise 'an' by the addition of 'nu.' Even in Tamil 'viṇ,' *the sky*, is commonly pronounced 'viṇṇu,' and in Telugu it is 'vinnu' by rule. Hence we seem to be quite safe in deriving 'annu' directly from 'an,' and 'an' from 'am.'

Another form of the Canarese accusative case-sign is 'anna,' instead of 'annu,' or simply 'nna' or 'na,' *e.g.*, 'na-nna,' *me*. The final 'u,' has in this instance been changed into 'a,' through the attractive force of the primitive 'an:' or rather, perhaps, the entire euphonic appendage 'nu,' has been rejected, and the original case-sign 'an' been softened to 'a,' whilst the final 'n' of the base has been doubled to augment or express the objectivity of the signification.

The Tulu accusatives 'nu' and 'n' (*e.g.*, 'yanu' or 'yannu,' *me*) are evidently identical with the Canarese, and also with the Telugu; and they are peculiarly valuable as tending to show the connection of the Telugu accusative suffix 'nu' or 'ni,' with the older Canarese 'an' and the still older 'am.' The Tuda accusative of the pronoun of the first person singular ends in 'ama,' *e.g.*, 'en-ama,' *me:* when the Gônd accusative differs from the dative it is denoted by 'ûn.'

In Telugu the neuter accusative is ordinarily the same as the nominative, as in the other Drâvidian dialects; but when the noun belongs to the class of 'rationals' or 'majors,' the accusative must be expressed by the addition of a sign of case. The accusative case-sign may optionally be suffixed, as in Tamil, to neuter nouns; but whether the noun be a 'major' or a 'minor,' singular or plural, the sign of case must be suffixed to the inflexion, genitive, or oblique-case basis, not to the nominative. When the inflexion is the same as the nominative, the noun to which the case-sign is attached is still regarded as the inflexion, so that in theory the rule admits of no exceptions.

The sign of the accusative in Telugu is 'nu' or 'ni:' when preceded by 'i' it is 'ni,' *e.g.*, 'iṇṭi-ni,' '*dom-um;*' where it is preceded by any other vowel it is 'nu,' *e.g.*, 'biḍḍa-nu,' '*puer-um.*'

A similar 'ni' or 'na' is used in Telugu (but not so systematically as the corresponding 'in' in Tamil) as an euphonic inflexional increment; and 'na' or 'ni' is also a sign of the locative in Telugu. Probably those locative and genitive suffixes were originally, and are still to be regarded, as one and the same; but the sign of the accusative, though nearly identical in sound, proceeds apparently from a different source. Comparing it with the Canarese and especially with the Tulu accusative, we can scarcely avoid the conclusion that, though in sound it is identical with the ordinary inflexional augment, it is to be regarded as a relic of the Canarese accusative case-sign 'annu' or 'am.' The suffixes of the accusative of the Telugu personal pronouns can be explained on this supposition alone. The 'inflexions' of those pronouns are essentially different from their accusatives, and incapable of being confounded with them; and the accusatives of those pronouns take of necessity, and not merely for euphony, the nasal suffixes 'nu' or 'nnu' in the singular, and 'mu' or 'mmu' in the plural. Thus, whilst 'nâ,' *of me*, is the inflexion of 'nênu,' *I*, its accusative is 'nanu' or 'nannu,' *me;* the accusative of the second person is 'ninu' or 'ninnu,' *thee*, and their plurals are 'mamu' or 'mammu,' *us*, 'mimu' or 'mimmu,' *you*, whilst the inflexions of those plurals are 'mâ' and 'mî.'

When these accusatives are compared with the Canarese and Tulu, especially with 'yanu,' *me*, and 'ninu,' *thee*, in the latter, their virtual identity, and therefore the origin of them all from the ancient Canarese 'am,' can scarcely be doubted.

We may now proceed to compare this accusative case-sign 'am,' 'an,' 'annu,' 'nu,' or 'na' with the Gujarathi dative-accusative 'nê,' with the Panjâbi 'nu' or 'num,' and also with the Brahui 'nê' or 'ê,' and the Turkish and Mongolian 'nî' or 'î.' In the Finnish tongues the greater number of singular accusatives are formed by suffixing 'en,' 'an,' &c., which are also used as signs of the genitive: in the plural there is rarely any difference between the nominative and the accusative. Ascending further towards the source of the Scythian tongues, we find in the language of the Scythian tablets at Behistun an unquestionable link of connexion with the Drâvidian. The pronoun of the second person singular in that language is 'nî,' *thou,* of which 'nin' is the accusative; and when this is compared with the Tulu 'nin-u,' *thee,* we cannot fail to be struck with the closeness of the resemblance.

We should also notice the extensive use of 'm' or 'n' as an accusative case-sign in the languages of the Indo-European family. In Sanscrit, Latin, and Gothic, 'm' predominates, in Greek, 'n;' but these consonants are virtually identical, like the 'm' of the ancient Canarese, and the 'n' of the modern.

A similar form of the accusative being extensively prevalent, as we have seen, in the Scythian tongues, it would be unreasonable to derive the Drâvidian case-sign from the Indo-European. In this instance it is better to conclude that both families have retained a relic of their original oneness.

It only remains to inquire whether the Tamil-Malayâlam accusative case-sign 'ei' or 'e' cannot be connected with the Canarese 'am,' 'annu,' and 'na.' On comparing the ancient Canarese accusative 'ninnam,' *thee,* with the more modern 'ninna,' it can scarcely be doubted that the latter is derived from the former by the ordinary process of the softening away of the final nasal. Through this very process the final 'am' of many substantive nouns has been softened to 'a,' *e.g.,* 'maram,' Ancient Can., *a tree,* 'mara' or 'mara-vu,' modern Can. If then the sign of the accusative in 'ninna,' *thee,* is not 'na' but 'a' (instead of 'am'), as is probably the case, there cannot be any difficulty in deriving from it the Tamil accusative case-sign 'ei', for the change of 'a' into 'ei,' takes place so frequently that it may almost be considered as a dialectic one, *e.g.,* compare Old Tamil 'ila,' *not,* with the modern Tamil 'illei.'

The instrumental, or 'third' case.—Different particles are used by different Drâvidian dialects as suffixes of the instrumental case. In Telugu the most classical instrumental is identical with the inflexional locative, and consists in changing 'ṭi' or 'ti,' the 'inflexion,' into 'ṭa' or 'ta;' *e.g.,* 'râ-ta,' *with a stone,* from 'râ-yi,' *a stone,* the inflexion of which is 'ṛâ-ti.'

This form of the instrumental was probably a locative in its original signification, and at all events it is identical with an old form of the locative; *e.g.,* 'iṇṭa,' *in a house,* from 'illu,' *a house,* of which the inflexion is 'iṇṭi.' The more commonly used instrumental of the Telugu is formed by the addition to the inflexion of any noun of 'chê' or 'chêta,' which is itself the instrumental form of 'chê-yi' (Tam., 'kei'), *the hand*, signifying *by the hand (of)*; *e.g.*, 'nibbu-chêta,' *by fire*, literally *by the hand of fire*.

The inflexion, or genitive, without the addition of any special suffix, is also occasionally used in Telugu, as in High Tamil, to denote the instrumental case, as well as the ablative of motion and the locative.

The particle 'na' is also sometimes suffixed to neuter nouns to denote all three ablatives.

In Ancient Canarese the instrumental case-sign is 'im;' in the modern dialect 'inda,' an euphonised, adjectival form of the same suffix. The suffix of the Tulu is 'd'da.'

I consider 'im,' the old Canarese instrumental suffix, to be identical in origin with 'in,' the suffix of the Tamil 'ablative of motion,' or 'locative.' It has already been seen how easily 'm' changes into 'n:' and both in Canarese and in Tamil there is so close a connexion between the ablative of motion and the instrumental, that the case-sign of the former is very often used for the latter, especially by the poets; *e.g.*, 'vâḷ-in âya vaḍu,' Tam., *a wound inflicted 'by' a sword*, not *'from' a sword*. In Canarese also the ablative of motion is denoted more frequently by the suffix of the instrumental than by its own suffix. Through a similar tendency to confound these cases, the case-sign of the instrumental has disappeared from the Latin, Greek, &c., and the sign of the ablative has come to be used instead. Even in English, 'by,' originally a locative (*e.g.*, 'close by'), has lost this meaning altogether, and is used at present to form the ablative, or more properly the instrumental.

In Tamil and Malayâlam the suffix of the instrumental is 'âl;' in High Tamil 'ân' also. 'âl' is the case-sign of the ablative or instrumental in Gônd, though in Telugu, which is spoken between the Tamil country and the country of the Gônds, a different case-sign is used. This suffix 'âl' is possibly derived from, or allied to, 'kâl,' Tam., *a channel*, a noun which is contained not only in the Drâvidian dialects, but also in Bengali.

In some dialects '*channel*' is a compound word (Tam., 'kâlvây̆;' Tel., 'kâlava;' Can., 'kâlive'), and the only meaning of 'kâl' is *a foot*. This meaning is contained in the Tamil, but that of a 'channel,' which the Tamil contains also, suits better the supposed use which is made of 'kâl,' as a sign of the instrumental case. 'kâl' may have lost its initial 'k' in the same manner as 'kaḷ,' the neuter sign of plurality, is known to have done in Telugu and Tulu, in which it has become 'l-u,' by corruption from 'kal-u' or 'gal-u.'

In the Indo-European family of languages there are no signs of the instrumental case which at all resemble those that we have noticed in the Drâvidian family. The only analogies which I have noticed (and probably they are illusory) are those which exist between the case-sign of the Tamil-Malayâlam and the corresponding case-signs of the Finnish tongues. Compare 'âl' with the instrumental suffix of the Magyar, which is 'al' in the singular, 'el' in the plural; and with 'alla,' 'ella,' &c., the instrumental suffixes of the Finnish proper, and which are euphonically augmented forms of 'al' and 'el.'

A secondary or periphrastic mode of forming the instrumental case, which obtains in the Drâvidian languages, as also in the northern vernaculars, is by means of the preterite verbal participle of the verb 'to take,' and the accusative or abstract nominative of any noun; *e.g.*, 'kattiyei (k)koṇḍu,' Tam., *with a knife*, literally *having taken a knife:* compare the corresponding Bengali 'churi diyâ,' *with* (*i.e.*, *having taken*) *a knife.*

This has arisen from the repugnance of the Drâvidian (as of all the Scythian) languages to continue to make use of any inflexional form after it has ceased to express its original meaning, and has become a mere technical sign. When that has taken place, as in the instance of the Tamil 'kâl' or 'âl,' those languages are often found to abandon the old form, or let it fall gradually into disuse, and to adopt some word or phrase instead which has a distinct meaning of its own, and the use of which recommends itself at once to the intelligence of the speaker.

Under this head it is desirable to enquire into the force of the Drâvidian CONJUNCTIVE CASE, and the suffixes by which it is denoted.

Drâvidian grammarians have arranged the case system of their nouns in the Sanscrit order, and in doing so have done violence to the genius of their own grammar. It is very doubtful whether the Drâvidian 'ablative of motion' and the 'locative' are not one and the same case, though represented as different by grammarians, in deference to Sanscrit precedents; and the Drâvidian 'social ablative,' as some have called it, or rather, as it should be termed, 'the conjunctive case,' has been omitted in each dialect from the list of cases, or added on to the instrumental, simply because it is a case of which the Sanscrit knows nothing.

The only reason why the case-signs of the conjunctive are classed in Tamil with that of the instrumental is that the fact of their being destitute of a proper place of their own is less obvious in that position than it would be in any other. Notwithstanding this, the difference between those two cases is considerable.

The instrumental is best rendered in English by the preposition 'by,' 'by means of;' the force of the conjunctive is that of the preposition 'with,' in the sense of the Latin 'cum,' or *together with*. Sometimes the English preposition 'with' is used in either sense; *e.g.*, 'I cut it *with* a knife'—'I went *with* him:' but in the Drâvidian languages the former 'with' would be represented by the sign of the instrumental case, the latter by that of the conjunctive; *e.g.*, 'katti-(y)-âl,' Tam., *by a knife*, 'avan-ôḍu,' *with him*.

Though the Sanscrit and the Indo-European languages generally are destitute of this case, the Latin evinces a tendency towards it in such forms as 'nobiscum;' whilst most of the Scythian tongues have a regularly formed conjunctive case equally with the Drâvidian: and 'den,' the conjunctive case-sign of the Calmuck, may even be compared (though probably the resemblance is accidental) with the Tamil conjunctive case-sign, 'uḍan.'

The Tamil conjunctive case-signs are 'uḍan,' 'oḍu,' and 'ôḍu;' of which the two last have now no meaning of their own, and the first is occasionally used as a noun signifying 'conjunction' or 'continuity.' It is also capable of being combined with another word as an adjective, *e.g.*, 'uḍan âḷ,' *a fellow servant;* and with the addition of the emphatic 'ê' ('uḍan-ê'), it is used also as an adverb to signify *immediately*.

The final 'an' of 'uḍan' (Tel., 'tôḍan-u'), is probably a formative addition to the root-syllable, for 'udam' is another and equivalent Tamil form; and the first syllable can scarcely be doubted to be allied to 'oḍu,' the other sign of the same case in High Tamil.

'u' is always pronounced as 'o' before 'ḍ,' and other cerebrals, whenever the word in which it appears has a second syllable. Hence 'uḍan' is invariably pronounced 'oḍan;' and in the Canarese postposition 'oḍane' (Tel., 'tôḍane'), this pronunciation is written as well as heard. 'ôḍu' (emphatically "ôḍ-ê'), the third suffix of this case in Tamil, and the most common in the colloquial dialect (in Malayâlam 'ôṭa'), is evidently allied to 'oḍu,' and through it to 'uḍan.' As neither 'oḍu' nor 'ôḍu' has any meaning of its own in Tamil, it is evident that they have undergone some alteration, and it is desirable to trace their connexions in the other dialects.

On turning to the Telugu, we find that its conjunctive case-signs, which are evidently allied to those of the Tamil, have the consonant 't' prefixed to each of them, *e.g.*, 'tôḍa' and 'tô.' Supposing 'tôḍa,' Tel., *with*, to be identical with the Malayâlam 'ôṭa' and the Tamil 'ôḍu' (and its identity is put beyond a doubt by comparing the Tamil adjective 'uḍan' with the Tel. 'tôḍan-u,' and the Tam. adverb 'uḍanê' with the Tel. 'tôḍanê'), the conjunctive suffixes of the Tamil-Malayâlam, which were destitute of meaning by themselves, are now found to acquire a very appropriate meaning; for the Tamil 'tôṛa' (in the abstract 'tôṛa-mei'), which is phonetically equivalent to 'tôḍa' ('ḍ' in Telugu corresponding by rule to 'ṛ' in Tamil), means *companionship.* 'tôḍu' itself also is found, with the related signification of *a congeries, a collection*; and though 'uḍan' has by itself the meaning of *conjunction,* or *continuity,* yet when 't' is prefixed to it, we can immediately detect its relationship to 'tuḍar' or 'toḍar,' *to follow,* and ultimately to 'tôḍu' and 'tôṛa.' Thus it appears highly probable that all these words and forms are virtually identical.

The dative or "fourth" case.—In the North-Indian dialects one and the same post-position or suffix is used as a sign of case both by the dative and by the accusative. In the Drâvidian languages, not only is the difference between the dative and the accusative essential and strongly marked, but there is less discrepancy amongst the various Drâvidian dialects with respect to the particular suffix which is used to denote the dative, than with respect to any other case-sign. The accusatives, instrumentals, ablatives, and genitives, of the various dialects, exhibit material differences; but in all the dialects of this family—in the rudest as well as in the most polished—there is but one suffix of the dative.

The dative is formed in Tamil by suffixing 'ku' (in construction 'kku'); in Malayâlam 'kka'; in Telugu 'ku' or 'ki,' according to the nature of the preceding vowel,—properly and naturally 'ku;' in Old Canarese 'ge' or 'ke;' in the modern dialect 'ge' or 'kke,' and in construction 'ige.' From a comparison of these forms it is obvious that the guttural 'k' or 'g' (followed by a vowel) constitutes the only essential part of this suffix; and that, as the vowel seems to have been added chiefly for the purpose of helping the enunciation, it is of little moment what vowel in particular is used for this purpose.

In the primitive Indo-European tongues we discover no trace of any such dative suffix or case-sign as the Drâvidian 'ku;' but on turning to the Scythian family, interesting analogies meet us at every step.

In the vernaculars of Northern India, which are deeply tinged with Scythian characteristics, we find a suffix which appears to be not only similar to the Drâvidian, but the same.

The dative-accusative in the Hindi and Hindustani is 'kô,' or colloquially 'ku;' in the language of Orissa 'ku;' in Bengali 'kô;' in Sindhi 'khê;' in Singhalese 'ghai;' in the Uraon, a Semi-Drâvidian Kole dialect, 'gai;' in the language of the Bodos, a Bhutân hill-tribe, 'khô;' in Tibetan 'gya.'

The evident existence of a connexion between these suffixes and the Drâvidian dative case-sign 'ku' is very remarkable. Of all the analogies between the North-Indian dialects and the Southern, this is the clearest and most important; and it cannot but be regarded as betokening either an original connexion between the Northern and Southern races, prior to the Brahmanic irruption, or the origination of both races from one and the same primitive Scythian stock.

The dative-accusatives of the North-Indian vernaculars have commonly been supposed to be accusatives in their original signification, and datives in a secondary application alone. This is the opinion of Dr. Max Müller, who attempts to derive 'kê,' the Bengali dative-accusative, from the Sanscrit adjectival formative 'ka.' I need not here criticize the Professor's arguments; for the extensive use of this particle, or its equivalent, as a distinctively and exclusively dative suffix in the Drâvidian languages, and also, as will be shown, in the Scythian tongues, appears to me to prove, beyond reasonable doubt, that it was a dative, not an objective suffix, originally; and that its origin was far earlier and more remote than the late Sanscrit genealogy which is attributed to it by the Professor. Dr. Kay is, I believe, right, in holding that the dative has a better claim than the accusative to the use of 'kô' even in the Northern vernaculars, and in directing attention to the parallel use of the Semitic preposition 'la.'

The suffix of the dative in the various languages of the Turkish family perfectly corresponds to the Drâvidian dative and to the North-Indian dative-accusative. The forms of this suffix which are found in the Oriental Turkish are 'ke,' 'ka,' 'ge,' 'ga,' 'ghah,' and also 'a.' The Osmanli Turkish dative is 'eh' or 'yeh,' the initial 'k' or 'g' of the older dialect having been softened into 'y,' and then discarded.

The Manchu 'de' and the Mongolian 'dou' are possibly allied to the Tartar 'ke;' for it has already been remarked that the change of 'k' into 't' or 'd,' or *vice versâ*, is not an uncommon one in this group of tongues, and that even amongst sister dialects belonging to the same family or sub-genus, the pluralising particle in one dialect is 'ek,' and in another 'et.' Perhaps, therefore, we may venture to connect with 'ke' not only the Mongolian 'de,' but even the Uriya 'te' and the Singhalese 'ta,' which are commonly supposed to have a different origin from 'ku' and 'ghai.'

In the Finnish family of languages the Turko-Drâvidian dative re-appears;—though the Finnish proper has 'le,' not 'ke.'

In the Irtish and Surgutish dialects of the Ostiak the suffix of the dative is 'ga,' corresponding to the Oriental Turkish 'ga' or 'ge.' The ordinary Ostiak has also 'a,' softened, as in the Oriental Turkish itself, from 'ga.' Compare also the Mordwin *adessive* suffix 'va' or 'ga.'

The most interesting and remarkable analogies are those which have been brought to light by the Scythian tablets of Behistun. We learn from those tablets that a dative suffix, which is almost identical with the Drâvidian, and also with the Turkish and Ostiak, was used by the oldest Scythian dialect of Central Asia of which any remains are extant. The dative case-sign or suffix which is most largely used in the Scythic tablets is 'ikki' or 'ikka.' Mr. Norris noticed the resemblance of this suffix to the Magyar genitive-dative 'nek' and the Telugu genitive post-position 'yokka;' but its resemblance to the dative suffix of the Telugu and of the other Drâvidian dialects is closer and more reliable.

The 'Tamil 'ku' becomes, as we have seen, 'akku' or 'ukku' in construction; the Canarese 'ge' becomes 'ige,' and the Malayâla 'kka' becomes 'ikka;' which last form of the suffix is identical, letter for letter, with the Scythian of Behistun. Compare, *e.g.*, the Cuneiform Scythian 'nî-ikka' or 'nî-ikki,' *to thee*, with the corresponding Malayâla 'nani-kka,' and the Telugu 'nî-ku.'

It has thus been shown that the principal languages of the Scythian family accord very exactly with the Drâvidian languages in the use of 'ka,' 'ki,' 'ku,' or some related particle, as the suffix of the dative.

It may be noticed also, that in the language of the Malays there is a prefix, 'ko' or 'ka,' which signifies *to* or *for*, and that there is a similar preposition even in Russian.

It is difficult to determine whether the Finnish dative suffix 'le' has any connexion with 'ke.' It certainly seems much more closely connected with the Tibetan, Pushtoo, and Marathi dative suffix 'lâ;'—which 'lâ' is evidently equivalent to the New Persian 'râ.' [Compare, *e.g.*, the Marathi 'tu-lâ,' *to thee, thee*, with the corresponding New Persian 'to-râ.']

The Malayâlam alone of all the Drâvidian dialects appears to possess two suffixes of the dative, viz., 'kka,' which is the suffix most largely used, and 'inna,' 'na,' or 'a,' which is occasionally used in the dative singular only. This 'inna' is a compound form; and is evidently euphonized and softened from 'in-ka.' The Tamil is fond of adding to the base of nouns which are to be declined the euphonic increment 'in' (originally a genitive), before suffixing the signs of case. The same practice prevails in Malayâlam also. Consequently, this exceptional Malayâla dative is not 'inna' or 'na,' but is simply 'a;' and the doubled 'n' which sometimes precedes it (*e.g.*, 'awanna,' *to him*) is an euphonic compensation for the loss of the 'k.' The 'k' or 'g' of 'ka' or 'ga' has been softened away in some dialects of the Turkish and Ostiak, precisely as in Malayâlam.

The ablative of motion or 'fifth' case.—This case appears to have been included in the list of cases by Drâvidian grammarians out of deference to the grammatical principles of the Sanscrit.

It is true, that if we look at the construction and meaning of a Drâvidian sentence, the *signification* of an 'ablative of motion' will be found to exist; and it will be found to be expressed much more clearly even than in Sanscrit: but a distinction is to be drawn between the existence of a case and the existence of a case-sign, or regular, technical suffix of case. The Drâvidian languages have undoubtedly an 'ablative of motion,' and a great many other ablatives besides; but I doubt whether they have any case-suffix which belongs exclusively to the ablative of motion.

On comparing the suffixes of the ablatives of motion (which are also used sometimes in an instrumental sense) with those of the locatives in the various dialects of this family, no real difference is apparent between the one class and the other; or at least, no adequate reason appears for regarding them as distinct and independent suffixes; for whatever difference does exist is to be attributed, not to the signs of case, but to the verbs or verbal participles which are annexed to them. The object of the *ablative of motion* is to furnish an answer to the question, *whence?* and this answer is obtained in the Drâvidian tongues by suffixing to a noun of place the sign of the locative, and annexing to that sign a verb of motion. By this means the locative is converted into what is called the ablative, without changing its case-suffixes, and the idea of change of place is thus naturally and necessarily educed. Native Tamil grammarians appear to hold that 'il,' the ordinary suffix of the ablative, and 'il,' the most largely used sign of the locative in the colloquial dialect, though written and pronounced alike, are different particles with different significations. I am persuaded, however, that this view is erroneous; and that a natural system of case classification would determine that the Drâvidian languages have no ablative, properly so called, but only a variety of locative and instrumental suffixes, which are capable of becoming ablatives by the addition of appropriate verbs.

In Tamil, the suffixes which are used in forming the 'fifth' case, or ablatives of motion, are 'il' and 'in.' 'il' (Tel. 'illu') signifies by itself *a house, a place, e.g.*, 'kô-(v)-il,' *a temple, God's house;* and it is therefore well suited for becoming a sign of the locative. Accordingly it has a place in the list of locative suffixes, as well as in those of the ablative; and in the colloquial dialect it is used as a sign of the locative far more frequently than any other particle.

The other suffix, 'in,' is identical, I conceive, with 'im,' the Old Canarese sign of the instrumental: it is used as an instrumental in Tamil also; but probably both that 'im' and 'in' were previously locative suffixes, and were originally suffixes of the genitive. In Canarese the proper suffix of the ablative is 'attaṇim,' which is itself formed from the demonstrative adverb 'aṭṭaṇa' (identical with 'attal-u' or 'atta,' *there*, or 'attal,' *that side*), by the addition of 'im,' the old instrumental suffix, from which 'inda,' the more modern suffix, is derived; and this 'inda,' though the ordinary sign of the instrumental, is also ordinarily used, with the addition of a verb of motion, as the sign of the ablative. Whilst I think that not only 'il,' but also 'in' and 'im,' were originally locative suffixes, it is more difficult to determine whether 'il' and 'in' were originally identical in sound and signification, as well as in application.

In every instance in which 'il' is used in Tamil, 'in' may be substituted for it poetically; and it is almost exclusively by the poets that 'in' is used. Moreover, in Telugu, 'illu,' *a house*, identical with 'il,' is euphonized into 'in,' in the inflexion 'inṭi,' *of a house*. On the other hand, 'il' and 'im' do not seem to have been regarded by the Canarese as identical; for 'il' is in that dialect 'li,' the base of the demonstrative local suffixes 'alli' and 'illi,' which are used as signs of the locative exclusively, whilst 'in' is in Canarese 'im' (modernized into 'inda), and though possibly a locative in its origin, is used not as a locative, but as an instrumental and ablative. Besides this, if we regard 'in' as originally a locative, it will be found to have a far wider range of analogies than 'il,' and may therefore be concluded to have sprung from a different root. In Finnish and Magyar we find 'an,' 'en,' and still more frequently 'in,' used as signs of the locative. Even in Sanscrit we find 'in' used as a locative case-sign of pronouns of the third person, *e.g.*, 'tasmin,' *in him;* and though this 'in' may have been euphonized from 'i,' yet in the Latin locative preposition 'in' and the Greek 'ἐν,' corresponding to the Sanscrit 'ni,' we find the existence of a very remarkable analogy. 'il,' on the other hand, has no apparent affinities out of the pale of the Drâvidian family.

It seems probable that 'in,' one of the signs of the locative in Tamil, is identical with 'in,' a sign of the genitive, or inflexional increment, in Tamil-Canarese: and if so, a new and very wide range of affinities is disclosed, as will be seen when the case-signs of the genitive are inquired into. 'attu,' which is often used in Tamil as a locative, is undoubtedly a genitive suffix, and this shows the possibility of the use of 'in' as a locative being derived from its use as a genitive.

The Tamil 'il' and 'in' agree in this, that when they are used as suffixes of the ablative, they both require to be followed by verbs of motion. In the spoken dialect of the Tamil, the verb of motion is preceded by the verbal participles 'nindru,' *standing*, or 'irundu,' *being*. The use of these participles strengthens the supposition that 'il' and 'in' are properly to be regarded as locatives. In the higher dialect, however, they are ordinarily dispensed with, and 'il' or 'in' is followed by a verb of motion alone; *e.g.*, 'malei-(y)-in viṛum aruvi,' *the cataract which falls from the mountain.* In this expression the idea of 'motion from a place' is plainly implied in the aoristic relative participle 'viṛum,' *which falls;* and hence 'in,' whatever it may have been in origin, acquires the force of a sign of the ablative of motion.

In Canarese the compound ablative suffixes 'attaṇim' and 'adeseyinda' are not so commonly used as 'inda,' the terminal member of the second compound suffix; and though 'inda' is described to be the sign of the instrumental, I have no doubt that it is identical with 'im' and 'in,' and a locative in its origin. 'inda' is not only used by itself to form the ablative, but is also added to 'alli' or 'illi,' the sign of the locative, for the purpose of denoting the ablative. Compare the Canarese 'alliṇda' or 'illinda,' *from*, with the corresponding Tamil compound 'il-irundu' or 'il-nindru.'

In Telugu the particle 'na,' which corresponds to the Tamil 'in' and the Old Canarese 'im,' is more distinctively a locative than an ablative of motion. This particle is 'ni' after 'i;' and if this is its normal form it may at once be identified with the Tamil 'in.'

The Telugu ablative of motion is ordinarily formed by means of the verbal participle 'nuṇḍi' or 'nunchi' alone, without the aid of any such suffix as 'na' or 'ni,' 'il' or 'in;' consequently this ablative has still less of the character of an independent case than in Tamil and Canarese. A locative particle, however, viz., 'lô,' which corresponds to the Tamil 'il' or 'uḷ' and the Canarese 'ôḷ,' is often suffixed in Telugu to the noun of place (precisely as 'il' or 'in' is in Tamil), before the addition of the verbal participle 'nuṇḍi.' This participle is properly 'unchi,' from a verb signifying *to place*, which has been euphonised by prefixing to it the nasal 'n.' It corresponds in use, though not in origin, to the participle 'nindru,' from 'nil,' *to stand*, which is used by the Tamil.

The genitive, or 'sixth' case.—The genitive or possessive case is formed in the Drâvidian languages in various ways and by means of various suffixes, each of which requires to be examined separately.

(1.) *The abbreviated pronominal genitive.*—The personal pronouns of the Tamil form their 'inflexion,' or ordinary genitive, by shortening the included vowel of the root; *e.g.*, 'nî' (properly 'nîn'), *thou*, 'nĭn,' *thy*; 'nâm,' *we*, 'năm,' *our*. This shortened form has the force of a genitive in Tamil without any suffix or addition whatever, though it is often strengthened by the addition of a suffix in the other dialects: *e.g.*, in the Canarese it requires to have a genitive suffix appended to it, and of itself is merely an inflexional basis. It may be worth noticing that in the Scythian of the Behistun tablets the nominative of the pronoun of the second person is long, viz., 'nî,' whilst the inflexional form and enclitic possessive 'nĭ' is short, precisely as in Tamil-Canarese.

We shall best understand the origin and force of this peculiar form of the genitive of personal pronouns, by considering it as a pronominal adjective. Every Drâvidian noun of quality or relation becomes an adjective on being prefixed to a noun-substantive for the purpose of qualifying it; and ordinarily the only changes which it undergoes on becoming an adjective are such petty euphonic changes as are intended to facilitate the combined enunciation of the two words. The change in the quantity of the personal pronoun, to which I have now referred, appears to have this origin alone: it is simply euphonic, and euphony is certainly promoted by this conversion of a long vowel into a short one prior to the addition of the case-suffixes, or of the governing substantive. We find a similar euphonic shortening of the quantity of the vowel of the root, on the conversion of the abstract noun into an adjective, in the section on 'Numerals;' *e.g.*, 'âṟu,' Tam., *six*, 'ăṟu-badu,' *sixty*; 'êṛu,' *seven*, 'ĕṛubadu,' *seventy*. The principle which is involved in both classes of instances is precisely the same.

(2.) *The neuter inflexional genitive.*—The neuter inflexions 'attu,' 'attru,' 'ṭi,' 'ti,' &c., are largely used in forming the genitive in Tamil and Telugu.

The various suffixes which are used to form the 'inflexion' were originally, I conceive, signs of the possessive case: but in process of time they have come to convey either a possessive or an adjectival signification, according to the connexion; and in many cases, as has been shown, they have shrunk into inflexional increments of the base, or become mere euphonic links of connexion between the base and the case-suffix. The inflexion which is now under consideration is in

Tamil 'attu,' and is used by the singular of neuter nouns alone. 'aRRu,' pronounced 'attru,' is occasionally used by neuter pronominal plurals. The same inflexion, for I believe I have shown it to be the same, is in Telugu 'ṭi' or 'ti.'

The inflexional suffixes being, as I conceive, genitive or possessive suffixes in their origin, their adjectival use naturally flowed from their use in forming possessives. There is little difference in signification between the genitive and the adjective (*e.g.*, 'a mountain of gold' and 'a golden mountain' come to the same thing); and in several languages besides the Drâvidian, the adjectival formative either appears to have been derived from the possessive suffix, or to be identical with it. Thus, in Tamil, it matters little whether 'kuḷattu mîn' (from 'kuḷam,' *a tank*, and 'mîn,' *fish*) be translated adjectivally *tank fish*, or genitivally *the fish of the tank;* whether we render 'âttru maṇal' (from 'âRu,' *a river*, and 'maṇal,' *sand*), *the sand of the river* or *river sand;* or whether 'mâṭṭu-(t)-tôl' (from 'mâḍu,' *an ox*, and 'tôl,' *hide*'), be translated *ox hide* or *the hide of an ox*. The adjectival rendering is ordinarily the more natural one, but if a few words be added to the compound expression, so as to bring out the full force of the inflexional suffixes, it will be evident that those suffixes must have been signs of case, or genitives, originally, and that their adjectival use is secondary to their use as signs of the possessive.

Thus, when we say in Tamil, 'i-(k)kuḷattu mîn perugittru,' to render the sentence *this tank fish has increased*, would not only be barbarous, but would partly fail to express the meaning, which is, *the fish of this tank have increased.* In this instance it is evident that the suffix 'attu,' has in itself the force of a sign of the genitive, though capable of acquiring in certain connexions the force of an adjectival formative. So also, 'marattu (k)koppu,' can only be rendered *the branch* of *a tree*, and *a tree-branch* would be as barbarous as it is unnecessary. Moreover, this same suffix 'attu,' has sometimes in Tamil (as 'atta' in Malayâlam) the force of a sign of the locative, like the corresponding inflexional suffixes in Telugu; and when used as a suffix of the locative, it is governed by a verb not by a noun; from which it is absolutely certain that it is a case-suffix in origin.

I have already mentioned the connexion which subsists between the inflexional suffix 'attu' and 'adu,' *it*, the neuter singular demonstrative pronoun. It is deserving of notice in this place that 'adu' (the very same demonstrative, I doubt not) is one of the recognized suffixes of the possessive case in Tamil, and is occasionally used as a possessive in the other dialects also. Thus we may say in Tamil either 'marattu (k)koppu' (from 'maram,' *a tree*, and 'koppu,' *a branch*), *the branch of a tree,* or 'marattinadu koppu' ('mar-attin-adu'). 'mar-amadu' may also be used, though not in ordinary use, because in-euphonic; but the possessive case-sign 'adu' is quite as frequently suffixed to the crude form of the noun, or the nominative, as to the oblique form: *e.g.*, 'vâṛei-(y)-adu paṛam,' *the fruit of the plaintain,* is as common as 'vaṛei-(y)-in-adu paṛam,' and is even more elegant.

I have no doubt of the identity of the 'adu' of 'vâṛei-(y)-adu' and the 'attu' of 'marattu' in origin. The old crude base of 'maram,' *a tree,* is 'mara,' as found in Canarese, the final 'am' or 'm' being a formative; and on 'adu,' the sign of the possessive (originally a demonstrative) being added to 'mara,' we shall have 'maradu,' *of a tree* (in Canarese 'marada'); of which the 'd' has only to be doubled (as it is colloquially by the Tamil people, many of whom say 'attu' for 'adu'), when the word becomes 'marattu,' the very form in which we now find it.

In Telugu, the inflexional suffixes 'ṭi' and 'ti' are used without any additional particle as signs of the possessive or genitive, even more frequently than in Tamil. The post-position 'yokka' is but seldom added to it, and needs not ever be added. In Telugu also the connexion subsisting between this suffix and the neuter demonstrative pronoun is still more obvious than in Tamil. 'adi,' *it,* is systematically suffixed in Telugu to nouns and pronouns, to convert them into possessives (*e.g.*, 'vâridi,' *their* or *their's*), and the relation subsisting between 'adi' (or 'di,' as it is in some instances) and 'ṭi' or 'ti,' is very close.

In Canarese the corresponding particles 'ad' and 'ar,' though used as inflexional increments of the base, prior to the addition of several of the signs of case to certain classes of nouns, have not now of themselves a possessive signification. Their present use is purely euphonic, and does not contribute to grammatical expression.

Nouns in which 'ad' and 'ar' are introduced form their possessives in 'ada' and 'ara;' and in these forms the final 'a' is that which contains and conveys the possessive signification. 'ad' and 'ar' have only the same incremental or euphonic force in 'ad-a' and 'ar-a,' that 'in' has in 'in-a,' which is a corresponding Canarese possessive.

(3.) *The neuter-demonstrative genitives.*—'adu,' *it,* and its euphonically lengthened equivalent 'âdu,' are often used, especially in classical Tamil, as signs of the possessive, and they are ranked by native grammarians amongst genitive case-signs. 'adu' is the neuter singular demonstrative (derived from 'a,' the remote demonstrative base, and 'd,' the sign of the neuter singular). Its meaning when standing alone is invariably that of a demonstrative pronoun, but by usage it has acquired the signification of a genitive or possessive, when annexed to any noun as a suffix. 'avan-adu,' is literally *he—that*, but by usage it means *his*. This use of 'adu,' as a possessive suffix, is derived from its use as the formative of nouns of possession.

By the addition of this demonstrative to any noun or pronoun (generally it is added to the inflexion,—in the case of pronouns it is always to the inflexions that it is added) a compound noun of possession or relation is formed, which, like all Drâvidian nouns of relation, is capable of being used as an adjective; and it is the use of nouns with this termination as possessive adjectives which has led to 'adu,' and its equivalents, being regarded as signs of the possessive case. The noun to which 'adu' is appended may be used, and often is used, without any addition or modification, as the nominative of a verb or a sentence. Thus, 'enadu,' Tam. (from 'en,' *my*, and 'adu,' *that*), signifies properly *that (which is) mine;* and this compound possessive may either be used adjectivally, *e.g.*, 'enadu kei,' *my hand*, literally *the hand that is mine* (in which instance 'adu' is called by grammarians a genitive case-sign); or it may be used as a possessive noun, and as such it becomes the nominative of a verb, *e.g.*, 'enadu pôyittru,' *mine (or my property) is gone.* Thus 'adu,' which at first meant *that*, became secondly the formative of a possessive noun ('avan-adu,' *that which is his*, literally *he—that*), thirdly the formative of a possessive adjective ('avan-adu,' *his*), and lastly a sign of the possessive case generally, signifying *of* or *belonging to*. Another reason for regarding the genitive case-sign 'adu' as originally and properly the formative of a noun or adjective of possession, is that it cannot be followed indiscriminately by any kind of noun, but by neuter nouns alone, and properly by the neuter singular alone. Thus we may say 'enadu kei,' *my hand*, but not 'enadu keigaḷ,' *my hands;* except indeed in the colloquial dialect, in which the singular is used for the plural more frequently than in the higher dialect, or by the poets.

The higher dialect would prefer in this instance 'ena keigaḷ,'—'ena' instead of 'enadu,' *i.e.*, '*mea*' instead of '*meum*.' 'adu' is not only a formative, therefore, but is distinctively a neuter singular formative, employed to give a possessive signification to the noun to which it is suffixed. Like all other nouns, these possessive nouns in 'adu' are capable of being used as adjectives, by being prefixed without alteration to other nouns; and when so prefixed, 'adu' came to be used and regarded as a possessive case-sign. This explanation seems to account for all the phenomena, and therefore to be the true explanation.

A similar use of the neuter singular of the demonstrative as a possessive suffix obtains in Telugu also; *e.g.*, 'nâdi,' *mine*, literally *that* (*which is*) *mine*, from 'nâ,' *my*, and 'adi,' *that*, a form which is exactly equivalent to the Tamil 'enadu.' The Telugu uses a similar suffix to form a plural possessive to correspond with 'enadu' or 'nâdi,' viz., 'vi,' which bears the same relation to 'avi' *those* (*things*), which 'di' does to 'adi,' *that* (*thing*); *e.g.*, 'vârivi,' *theirs* or *the* (*things which are*) *theirs*. In this respect the Telugu acts more systematically than the spoken Tamil. It is not so fond, however, of using these possessive nouns adjectivally as the Tamil, and therefore 'di' and 'vi' have not in Telugu come to be regarded as case-signs of the genitive.

The Canarese and the Tamil not only form neuter possessive nouns and adjectives by adding to them the neuter demonstrative, but they form also masculine and feminine possessives, or possessive appellatives, of both numbers, by adding the masculine and feminine formatives to the genitive case or 'inflexion' of nouns and pronouns.

All the Drâvidian dialects agree in appending the demonstrative-possessive suffixes to the inflexion not to the nominative, as a general rule, wherever the nominative differs considerably from the inflexion. When nouns receive in Tamil a double inflexional increment, *e.g.*, 'attu' and 'in' (in combination 'attin'), the possessive suffix is added to this double increment, *e.g.*, 'mar-attin-adu koppu,' *the branch of a tree*.

(4.) *The possessive suffix* 'in,' *and its varieties*.—'in,' in Tamil, and 'ni,' in Telugu, and corresponding particles in the other dialects, are not only used as inflexional augments of the base and euphonic bonds of connexion between the base and the case-signs, but also as suffixes of the possessive and as adjectival formatives. I have no doubt that 'in' and 'ni,' of themselves and originally, were genitive or possessive suffixes, and that every other use to which they have been applied grew out of their use as signs of the genitive. Native Tamil grammarians do not include 'in' amongst their genitive suffixes, but describe it as a formative augment or adjectival increment alone: but on comparing its use in Tamil with its use in the other dialects, I am convinced that it was originally and distinctively a sign of the genitive, and that it is still to be regarded, notwithstanding its subsidiary uses, as one of the most characteristic of the genitive suffixes.

In Tamil, of all genitive case-signs, 'in' is that which is most frequently used. 'attu' is used in the neuter singular alone, and 'aRRu' ('attru') in the neuter plural alone; but 'in' is used in connexion with both numbers and with all genders. A similar use of 'in' appears in the Malayâlam. In Canarese, on the other hand, 'in' is used only as an inflexional augment, not as a sign of case. One of the so-called declensions of the Canarese is said by grammarians to take 'ina' as its genitive case-sign; but in this instance the final 'a' is the real sign of the genitive, as it invariably is in Canarese; and this genitive 'a' is found to be preceded by various euphonic increments—'in,' 'ad,' 'ar,' or 'v,' according to circumstances.

Doubtless, the 'in' of 'in-a,' was a genitive suffix originally, but it has long ceased to contribute to grammatical expression, and therefore cannot now be regarded as a sign of case. In Telugu, 'na' or 'ni,' the dialectic equivalent of 'in,' is used as a possessive suffix, as in Tamil, though not so frequently. The only difference in principle is that 'ni' is used in Telugu in connexion with the singular alone, and might be called a genitive singular case-sign, if the Telugu stood in an isolated position; whereas in Tamil it is used in connexion with plural nouns as frequently as with the singular. In Ku, which has special resemblances to the Telugu, 'ni' constitutes the inflexion (in reality the genitive) of all classes of nouns, whether singular or plural, precisely like the Tamil 'in.' The Gônd uses as genitive case-signs 'na' and 'nâ,' 'da' and 'â'—forms which are probably allied one to another, as well as to the Brahui 'nâ,' and to the Telugu and Gônd 'ni,' and the Tamil 'in.'

Though 'in' is not regarded by Tamil grammarians as a sign of the genitive, yet when those particles which are regarded as genitive case-signs are suffixed to any noun, 'in' is ordinarily inserted between the noun and those case-signs; so that all auxiliary or additional particles are appended to this incremental 'in,' not to the noun itself; *e.g.*, from 'adu,' *it*, is formed not 'ad'-uḍeiya,' but 'ad-in-uḍeiya,' *of it*; from 'tambi,' *a younger brother*, is formed not 'tambi-(y)-adu,' but more commonly 'tambi-(y)-in-adu,' *of a younger brother*: and this rule seems to indicate that 'in' is more essentially a genitive case-sign than the genitive particles which have subsequently been suffixed to it. The same inference is still more clearly deducible from the circumstance that in a large number of instances, both in the singular and in the plural, each of the case-suffixes in succession is appended, not to the crude form of the noun, but to the increment 'in.' These case-suffixes are not mere post-positional fragments, but were, or are still, nouns of relation; and 'in,' the particle by which they are united to the base, serves as a bond of connexion, in virtue, as I conceive, of its own original and natural signification as a suffix of the genitive. Thus, in the colloquial Tamil, 'kalliniḍattil ('kal(l)-in-iḍattil'), *in a stone*, 'iḍattil, the local ablative or locative suffix, literally means *in the place*;

and this suffix evidently requires, or at least desires, the possessive 'in' (with the signification *of*) to connect it with the base. Hence 'kal(l)-in-iḍattil,' literally signifies *in the place of* (*or occupied by*) *a stone.*

The adjectival meaning of 'in,' though not its only or original meaning, is one which is recognised by native grammarians, and which they prove by examples; *e.g.*, 'ponnin' ('pon(n)-in') kuḍam, *a golden vessel.* This adjectival use of 'in' is not only allied to, but is derived from, its use as a sign of the genitive, and in the illustration which has now been adduced it is evident that 'ponnin kuḍam,' might be rendered with equal propriety, *a vessel of gold.* It will be found also in the Indo-European analogies which will presently be adduced, that the similarity or identity of the adjectival formative, and the genitive case-sign which is apparent in this instance, has a wider range than that of the Drâvidian languages.

There is another particle resembling 'in,' and possibly identical with it in origin, viz., 'am,' which is occasionally used in Tamil for both those purposes, and, like 'in,' it is sometimes appended to the noun itself, and sometimes to the neuter inflexion. We see this fusion of the adjectival and the genitive signification of 'am,' in such forms as 'âlam ('âl-am') pû,' *the banyan flower* or *the flower of the banyan,* and 'âttrang karei' ('âttru,' the inflexion of 'âṟu,' *a river*), *the river-bank* or *the bank of the river.* Evidently 'attram' (before the 'k' of 'karei' 'am' changes into 'ang') is equivalent to 'âttr-in' (a form which is also commonly used), and 'am' to 'in;' and as 'am' or 'an' and 'in,' are identical in meaning, though not used with equal frequency, and so nearly alike in sound, I think we may safely regard them all as sprung from one and the same origin. 'am,' indeed, changes by rule into 'an,' when it is followed by a dental, *e.g.*, 'panan' ('panei-am') tôppu,' *a palmyra tope.* The same adjectival formative is much used in Malayâla also; *e.g.*, 'mal-am puli' ('mala-am puli'), *a mountain tiger* or *a tiger of the mountain, a royal tiger.*

We have now to inquire whether any trace of the genitive case-sign or adjectival formative in 'in,' 'an,' 'ni,' or any related form, can be found beyond the circle of the Drâvidian dialects.

Of all the North-Indian vernaculars the Gujarathi is the only one which contains a form of the genitive resembling that which we have been examining. That language has a genitive suffix in 'n' ('nô,' 'nî,' 'nun'), which cannot but be regarded as allied to the Telugu 'ni,' 'nu,' &c. In the language of the Bodos, a Himalayan tribe, the pronominal genitive is regularly formed by suffixing 'ni,' *e.g.*, 'ang-ni,' *of me,* 'nang-ni,' *of thee,* 'bi-ni,' *of him.*

In Sanscrit the 'n' which precedes the 'ah' or 'as,' of certain genitives is undoubtedly euphonic; but both in Sanscrit and in other members of the Indo-European family, we may observe distinct traces of the adjectival or genitival use of a particle of which the consonant 'n' is the most essential element. Compare with the Drâvidian particle 'an-a,' the Sanscrit adjectival formative, and 'an,' the suffix of appellatives; the Greek possessive suffix 'ων;' the adjectival use of 'ιν' in Greek words like 'λίθ-ιν-ος,' and of 'en,' in the Germanic 'wood*en*; and also 'in,' the Sanscrit suffix of agency, which is preserved in the adjectives of the New Persian. These forms are, it is evident, reciprocrally related; and it also appears probable that there is some ulterior relationship between them and the Tamilian 'in.' There are also traces in the Indo-European family of languages of the use of 'in' as a distinctively genitival suffix. The Celtic forms its genitive systematically by means of 'n,' 'an,' 'en,' &c.: nor is it the genitive plural only of the Celtic dialects which uses this case-sign (as in the Sanscrit family), but it is employed to form the genitive singular also. It should be noticed too that in the ancient Egyptian 'n' (alternating with 'm') was used to express all case-relations, but particularly that of the genitive. Compare also the Sanscrit genitive or possessive 'mama' ('ma-ma') *of me, my*, with the Zend 'mana,' the Old Persian 'manâ,' and the Gothic 'meina,' *mine*, 'theina,' *thine*, 'seina,' *his;* in each of which examples the final 'na,' or its Sanscrit equivalent 'ma,' resembles the Drâvidian 'in' or 'ni,' not only in sound, but also in the union of an adjectival signification with that of the possessive or genitive case.

The Lithunian goes further than any other Indo-European tongue in resemblance to the Tamil in this point, for it not only uses 'n' as a sign of the pronominal possessive (of the first person), but it adopts this genitival 'man' as the inflexional base of all the rest of the oblique cases of the same pronoun.

In the languages of the Scythian stock we find a large number of still more essential analogies with the Drâvidian genitival suffix 'in' or 'ni.'

Compare both with the Drâvidian and with the Indo-European possessives the Mongolian and Manchu 'mini' ('mi-ni'), of *me, my;* and the Mongolian 'tchini' and the Manchu 'sini' ('si-ni'), *of thee, thy.*

In the languages of the Finnish family, the prevailing form of the genitive is that which corresponds to the Drâvidian: it is 'n,' 'an,' 'en,' 'un,' &c., not only in pronominal inflexions, but universally. Thus in Mordwin and Cheremiss, the genitive is formed by suffixing 'n' or 'en;' *e.g.*, 'kudo,' *a house*, 'kudo-n,' *of a house*. The genitive plural of the Mordwin is 'nen,' possibly a reduplication of 'n,' intended to symbolise the plural; *e.g.*, 'kudot-nen,' *of houses.* The Lappish genitive takes 'n' or 'en' in the singular, and 'i' in the plural. 'ê' forms the ordinary possessive suffix of the Măgyar. The Finnish proper forms the genitive by suffixing 'n,' 'un,' 'in,' 'an,' &c., *e.g.*, 'minâ' ('min-â'), *I*, 'min-un,' *of me, my.*

The prevailing form of the genitive in the Tartar or High Asian families, corresponds to 'nen,' the reduplicated suffix of the Mordwin plural, and to its equivalent reduplication in the Old Scythian of the Behistun tablets; but whilst the reduplicated suffix is very frequently used, it systematically alternates with the simpler suffix 'un' or 'in.'

The Oriental Turkish forms its genitive by suffixing 'ning' or 'nin,' or 'nîng' or 'nîn.' In the Ottoman Turkish the initial nasal is only occasionally used: the genitive plural is uniformly 'u*n*;' the singular takes 'u*n*' or 'nu*n*,' according as the noun to which it is suffixed ends in a consonant or in a vowel. In the Mongolian, the sign of the genitive is 'û' after the consonant 'n;' after every other consonant, 'ûn;' and after a vowel, 'yin.' The personal pronouns, as has already been observed, from their possessive by suffixing 'ni,' *e.g.*, 'mi-ni,' *my.* Compare the Mongolian 'kôl-ûn,' *of the foot*, with the ordinary Tamil genitive of the corresponding noun 'kâl-in,' *of a foot.*

The Calmuck dialect of the Mongolian forms its genitive by suffixing 'i' to nouns ending in 'n,' and 'yin' to all other nouns. The Tibetan postfixes in like manner 'i' or 'yin.'

The Manchu makes much use of a possessive relative suffix 'ngge,' or 'ningge,' signifying *which has;* but it also forms genitives, properly so called, by suffixing 'ni' or 'i.'

In the language of the Scythian tablets of Behistun, the genitive was ordinarily formed by suffixing 'na:' the first personal pronoun formed its genitive by suffixing a reduplicated form of this particle, 'ni-na,' *e.g.*, 'hu-ni-na,' *of me;* whilst the genitive plural was generally formed by means of the addition of 'inna,' probably softened from 'ni-na.' The nearest direct resemblance to the Behistun-Scythian genitival 'na,' is the Brahui 'nâ,' and the Gônd 'nâ' or 'â.'

This interesting record of the speech of the ancient Scythians, furnishes us, I think, with a clue to the origin of 'nu*n*' or 'ni*n*,' the Tartar genitive suffix. In the Tartar tongues 'nu*n*' is interchangeable with and equivalent to 'u*n*;' and 'un' or 'in' is also interchangeable with 'ni' or 'nu;' in Mongolian, 'yin' and 'un' are suffixed to substantives, 'ni' to the personal pronouns. It appears from the Behistun tablets that 'na,' the ordinary genitive suffix, was sometimes euphonically changed into 'ni-na,' and that this again was softened into 'inna.' I conceive that the Tartar '*un*,' was in this same manner, by the reduplication of the nasal, converted into '*nun*;' which in Manchu became 'ngge' or ningge.' Possibly also 'ni' or 'nu' was nasalised by the addition of a final '*n*' or 'ng,' of the use of which we have an instance in point in the final euphonic 'n' of the first and second personal pronouns in most of the Scythian languages. A parallel instance of the reduplication of a nasal is apparent in the Telugu itself, in the conjunctive or copulative particle. This particle is 'um' in Tamil, 'û' in Canarese, and 'nu' in Telugu; but this Telugu 'nu' becomes euphonically 'nnu,' and by reduplication 'nunnu' in particular instances.

(5.) *The genitival suffix* 'a.'—This sign of the genitive or possessive claims to be regarded as equally with 'in' or 'ni,' a distinctively Drâvidian suffix. It is little used in Tamil, though placed first in the list of genitive case-signs by Tamil grammarians; but if we take all the Drâvidian idioms into consideration, it is perhaps more largely used than any other suffix of the genitive—a proof of the accuracy of the Tamil classification.

I conceive this suffix to be identical with 'a,' the formative of the most frequently used Drâvidian relative participles (see the section on 'The Verb'), but totally distinct from 'a,' the neuter particle of pluralisation, which has already been investigated.

In Canarese 'a' is the only sign of the genitive which is ever used. It is sometimes preceded by an euphonic consonant, which is inserted between it and the base, to form a link of connection between them, viz., by 'v' or 'y,' the use of which is purely of an euphonic nature, and by 'in,' 'ad',' or 'ar',' which are inflexional increments of the base, and old petrified genitives; *e.g.*, 'guru-(v)-a,' *of a priest;* 'kuri-(y)-a,' *of a sheep;* 'kûs-in-a,' *of a child;* 'mar-ad-a,' *of a tree;* 'ad-ar-a,' *of that* (*thing*), or *of it.* When this genitive 'a' is added to the abbreviated inflexional form of the Canarese personal pronouns, the final nasal of those pronouns is doubled, *e.g.*, 'nanna' (from 'nân,' *I*), *of me;* 'namma' (from 'nâm,' *we*), *of us.* A comparison of these forms with the Tamil and Tulu 'nama,' *of us*, *our*, proves that the doubling of the final nasal arises from an euphonic source. 'a' forms the genitive suffix not only of the singular of Canarese nouns and pronouns, but also of the plural, whether the noun belongs to the 'rational' or to the 'irrational' class, *e.g.*, 'avar-a,' *of them* (epicene), 'avugaḷ-a,' *of them* (neuter).

These examples prove that 'a' is the true Canarese genitive case-sign: and it is also to be noted that this case-sign is never used, like 'in' in Tamil, as the common fulcrum of the suffixes of all the oblique cases, but is used solely as the case-sign of the genitive.

In Tulu 'a' forms the genitive of by far the larger proportion of nouns. In many instances it is preceded by 'd' or 't:' but this consonant is merely the equivalent of the Canarese 'ad,' which has already been referred to; and in the genitive of the personal pronouns 'a' is preserved purer in Tulu than in Canarese. Thus, instead of the Canarese 'nanna,' *of me,* the Tulu has 'yan-a' (for 'nan-a'), and instead of 'ninna,' *of thee*, it has 'nin-a.'

The language of the Kotas of the Nilgherry hills forms all its genitives by suffixing 'a.'

In Telugu 'a' forms the plural inflexion or genitive of all substantive nouns without exception. 'lu,' the pluralising particle, is changed into 'la;' and as the 'u' of 'lu' is added merely to facilitate enunciation, and 'l' alone constitutes the suffix of the plural, it is evident that the 'a' of 'la' is a suffix of case. As the plural inflexion, 'a' constitutes the fulcrum to which the other case-signs, or suffixes of the oblique cases, are added; and as the genitive plural, it expresses the signification of the genitive, without any auxiliary or additional particle. The Telugu personal pronouns use their crude bases adjectivally as their inflexion and genitive. The pronouns of the third person, or the demonstratives, generally form their genitives both in the singular and in the plural by adding 'i' to the root: in the singular a few of them suffix 'ni,' as is done by the greater number of nouns in the singular. One of the Telugu pronouns uses 'a' both in the singular and in the plural, as the sign of the genitive, in complete accordance with the Canarese and Tulu. The genitive of the reflexive pronouns 'tân-u,' *self,* 'tâm-u,' *selves,* is formed in Telugu by shortening the quantity of the radical vowel and suffixing 'a,' as in Canarese; *e.g.*, 'tan-a,' *of self,* 'taṃ-a,' *of selves.* The adjectival 'a' of some Telugu substantives is evidently identical with this genitival 'a;' *e.g.*, 'ûr-a kavi,' *a village poet* or *a poet of the village.*

In Tamil, though 'a' is placed first in the list of genitive suffixes, it is less used than any other sign of the genitive, and indeed is used only as the classical genitive of the personal and reflexive pronouns; *e.g.*, 'nam-a,' *our* (from 'nâm,' *we*), like the Sanscrit 'mama,' *my,* and 'tava,' *thy.*

It is difficult, indeed, to determine whether this suffix has retained in Tamil any genitival signification whatever. Whether it be attached to a singular or to a plural pronoun, it must be followed by, and be in agreement with, a neuter plural noun; and this circumstance would lead to the conclusion that in Tamil it is a suffix of plurality, not a sign of the genitive. On this supposition, in the words 'ena keigaḷ,' *my hands*, 'ena' would signify not '*mei*,' *of me*, but '*mea*,' (*the things that are*) *mine*. It would be a pronominal adjective or possessive plural, not a genitive; and the fact that 'a' is largely used in classical Tamil as a sign of the neuter plural (*e.g.*, 'sila,' *few*, literally *a few things*, 'pala' *many*, literally *many things*), proves that this supposition would be a very natural one.

On the other hand, 'a' is classed with genitive suffixes by Tamil Grammarians themselves, and those grammarians, who are remarkably well acquainted with the principles of their own language, are perfectly aware that 'a' is also a sign of the plural of 'irrationals'. Moreover, though it is stated by Tamil grammarians that the genitive in 'a' must always be in agreement with a plural noun, yet they admit that the noun with which it agrees is sometimes singular in *form* though plural in signification; *e.g.*, the expression 'nun-a śîṟ'aḍi,' *thy small foot;* occurs in the Chintâmaṇi. They say that *foot* is here used for *feet*, and this is certainly true; but it does not follow that 'nun-a' is determined thereby to be a plural, for the use of the singular with a plural signification, yet with the declensional and conjugational forms of the singular, is a fixed usage of these languages. I think, therefore, that we may confidently regard this 'nun-a' as an illustration of the use of 'a,' even in Tamil, in connection with the singular. In Tamil, it is true, 'a' is ordinarily followed by the neuter plural alone; but in Canarese and Telugu it may be followed by any gender or number; and the 'a' of the Tamil 'tan-a,' *of self*, is evidently identical with that of the corresponding Telugu 'tan-a;' whilst the 'a' of 'nam-a,' *of us, our*, is evidently identical with the Canarese 'namm-a.' Hence, as the one 'a' is unquestionably a genitive, so must the other have been originally; and thus we are led to the supposition that the Tamil rule which requires 'a' to be followed by the neuter plural is merely a secondary, recent, dialectic peculiarity, which has arisen from the influence of its accidental resemblance to the sign of the plural of 'irrationals.' This peculiarity of the genitival 'a' in Tamil may be compared with the somewhat parallel case of the use in Hindustani of one possessive suffix rather than another, out of the three that exist in it, according to the gender of the noun which follows and governs that to which it is suffixed.

Though in grammatical Tamil 'a' is always followed by the plural, yet the vulgar in the rural districts commonly use it without discrimination of number, as in Canarese and Telugu. Thus, they will say 'nama' (or more commonly, as in Canarese, 'namma') 'ûr,' *our village;* and this confirms the supposition that in Tamil, as in the other dialects, the original use of this 'a' was simply that of a suffix of the genitive.

We have now to inquire with what language or family of languages this genitive suffix should be affiliated. There is no direct Scythian analogy for it, and the only affinities which I have observed are Kole and Indo-European. In the Ho, a Kole dialect, 'a' is a common possessive suffix; and it is also, as in Tamil, an adjectival formative. The most direct and reliable Indo-European analogy is that which is presented by the personal pronouns, which in some of the Indo-European dialects have a possessive in 'a,' strongly resembling this Drâvidian possessive. If we look only at the Gothic 'meina,' *my;* 'theina,' *thy;* 'seina,' *his* or *its;* we should naturally conclude the sign of the possessive in these words to be, not 'a,' but 'na' (answering to the Old Scythian and Brahui 'na' and to the Telugu 'ni'); but on comparing the forms which this sign of the possessive assumes in various languages, it appears probable that 'a' alone conveys the signification of the possessive; and that the nasal which precedes it in the Sanscrit 'mama,' the Zend 'mana,' and the Gothic 'meina,' may merely have been inserted euphonically for the purpose of keeping the contiguous vowels pure. Compare 'mama,' Sans. *my,* (from 'ma,' *I*), with 'tava,' *thy,* (from 'tva,' *thou*); and especially compare the Gothic 'meina,' 'theina,' 'seina,' with the corresponding Lithuanian possessives 'mana-s,' 'tava-s,' 'sava-s.' In these instances 'v' euphonic is used as the equivalent of 'n.' The Indo-European pronominal possessive in 'a' is exceptional: for the primitive languages of that family evince an almost perfect agreement in the use of 'as,' or some closely related form, as the sign of the genitive singular, and of 'sâm' or 'âm,' as the sign of the genitive plural. In the later Teutonic dialects, however, a genitive case-sign in 'a' becomes exceedingly common, and is found in the plural as well as in the singular. Thus in the Frisian all plural substantives and such singulars as end in a vowel form their possessive by suffixing 'a': in the Icelandic all plurals and all masculine and neuter singulars use 'a' as their case-sign; and in the Anglo-Saxon all plurals. Though the oldest Gothic possessives accorded with the ordinary Sanscrit forms, 'as' and 'âm;' yet the resemblance between the possessives of some of the Teutonic vernaculars and the Drâvidian possessive is deserving of notice. The use of 'a' as a sign of the possessive by all *plural* substantives in Telugu is especially remarkable. Has the Drâvidian 'a' under consideration been softened from 'as' (of which, however, there is not the smallest trace or analogical probability)? or has it

R 2

been softened from 'na,' the old Scythian suffix? The latter supposition, though unsupported by direct evidence, is not an improbable one; for we have seen that the Gônd 'nâ' alternates with 'â;' the Scythian 'ni-na' with 'inna;' the Turkish 'nu*n*' with 'u*n*;' and 'nu,' the Telugu particle of conjunction, with 'û,' its Canarese equivalent.

(6.) *The Malayâla genitive singular suffix*, 're' *or* 'de.'—In most cases this Malayâla genitive takes the shape of 'indre' or 'inde,' of which 'in' is the genitival suffix and inflexional increment, which has already been described. In 'en-de,' *my*, the inflexional base is of itself a genitive, and the addition of 'in' is not required; hence it appears that 'de' or 'dre' is an auxiliary genitive suffix, like the 'adu' which is so often added to 'in' in Tamil, and is probably from the same origin. This suffix is written 'ʀe;' but it is always added to 'n,' and when it is thus added, the compound is regularly pronounced, not as 'nʀe,' but as 'ndre' or 'nde.' Neither the Tamil nor the Malayâlam possesses any other method of producing the sound which is indicated by these letters (a peculiarly euphonic 'nd'), but that of conjoining the final 'n' of those languages and the hard 'ʀ;' which, when pronounced in combination, have the sound of 'ndr' or, as some pronounce it, 'ndz,' or more commonly still 'nd.' Thus, from 'en,' *to say*, and 'du,' the regular formative of the preterite participle, the Canarese forms 'endu,' *saying* or *having said;* and this in Tamil is written 'enʀu;' but it would be erroneous to suppose 'ʀu' to be the sign of the preterite in Tamil instead of 'du,' for 'enʀu' is intended to be, and is pronounced 'endu' or 'endru,' nearly as in Canarese.

Hence some analogies to the Malayâla 'ʀe' (in reality 'de') which might be suggested, appear at once to be illusory. The Malayâla 'ʀe,' has been connected by Dr. Stevenson with 'the Canarese genitive' 'ra.' It has been shown that 'a,' not 'ra,' is the genitive suffix of the Canarese, and that the 'ʀ' which precedes it is properly 'ar,' an inflexional increment (like 'ad' and 'in'), which is inserted between the root and the case-signs of three cases, besides the genitive, of certain classes of nouns. The Malayâla 'ʀe' (de), on the other hand, is suffixed exclusively to the genitive, and no other suffix of case is ever appended to it. Nevertheless, as I connect 'de' with the Tamil 'adu,' *it;* and as with this I connect also the Canarese 'ad'' and its hardened form 'ar',' it may be admitted that in this modified and remote manner, the Malayâla and the Canarese forms are allied.

Still more illusory is the apparent resemblance of this Malayâla 'ṟe' or 'de' to the adjectival possessive suffixes of the Hindustani personal pronouns, 'râ' and 'rî' (*e.g.*, 'mêrâ,' *meus*, 'mêrî,' *mea*); to the corresponding New Persian inflexion 'râ,' (*e.g.*, 'to-râ,' *thy, thee*); and to 'ra,' the Gothic genitive plural suffix of the personal pronouns (*e.g.*, 'unsara,' *our*, 'izvara,' *your*), from which the final 'r' of our English 'our' and 'your' has been derived.

The Hindustani 'r,' is supposed by Bopp to be derived from 'd;' 'mêrâ,' *meus*, being derived from the Sanscrit 'madîya,' *my;*' but I cannot suppose that the Malayâla form has any connexion whatever with the Hindustani and the Persian, except on the supposition that the 'd' of the Tamil demonstrative neuter singular, 'adu,' is remotely connected with the formative 'd' of the Sanscrit possessive adjective.

The Malayâla 'de,' like the Tamil 'adu,' is used as a genitive suffix of the singular alone, a confirmation of the opinion that it is derived from 'adu,' which in its original signification is the neuter singular of the demonstrative. In the genitive plural, the Malayâlam uses 'uṭe,' answering to the colloquial Tamil 'uḍeiya' (from 'uḍei'), *belonging to, of.* Compare the Malayâla 'enre,' 'endre,' or 'ende,' *of me*, with the corresponding Tamil 'enadu,' *of me, that which is mine.* The Malayâla possessive noun *mine*, or *that which is mine* is 'endeta,' from 'en-de,' *my*, and 'ata,' *it*, corresponding to the Tamil 'enadu.' This latter 'enadu,' however, is not the genitive 'enadu,' *my*, with which I have compared 'en-de,' but a possessive noun in the nominative case; and though I suppose the Malayâla 'de' to be itself a corruption from 'aḍa' or 'ata,' *it*, yet the demonstrative suffix would be appended a second time, on the origin and true meaning of 'de' being forgotten. We see illustrations of this repetition of an ancient suffix in many languages; *e.g.*, 'malei-(y)-in-in,' High Tam. *from a mountain;* and this very demonstrative 'adu,' *it*, is twice used in the Tamil negative participial noun 'illâdadu,' *the thing which is not;* in which the first 'd,' though a representative originally of the neuter singular demonstrative, has lost its proper signification, and become a mere euphonic link of connection, or technical sign, in consequence of which 'd' is required to be repeated,

In Tulu the genitive of neuter nouns is commonly formed by suffixing 'd,' 'da,' or 'ta,' *e.g.*, 'katti-da,' *of a knife*, 'kei-ta,' *of a hand.* The 'd' of this 'da,' or 'ta,' is not, however, as in the Canarese, used as the inflexional base of any other case; but is restricted to the genitive alone: hence it bears a close resemblance to the Malayâla genitive suffix.

(7.) *Auxiliary suffixes of the genitive in Telugu and Tamil.*

(i.) In Telugu, 'yokka,' or 'yoka,' is sometimes appended to the inflexion, or natural genitive, as an auxiliary suffix of case; *e.g.*, from the ordinary possessive 'nâ,' *my*, is formed optionally, the equivalent form 'nâ-yokka,' *my, of me.*

This suffix is rarely used, and seems foreign to the idiom of the language; for no other pure Drâvidian dialect possesses any suffix resembling it.

A suffix somewhat resembling 'yokka,' is found in the Râjmahal and Ûrâon languages, which contain an overwhelming preponderance of Kôl elements, though formed probably upon a Drâvidian basis.

The possessive suffix of the Râjmahal is 'ki,' that of the Ûrâon 'ghi.' If these particles are at all connected with the Telugu 'yoka,' which seems doubtful, we should be warranted in connecting the whole with the ordinary possessive or adjectival suffix of the Hindustani, the feminine of which is 'kî' (masculine 'kâ'), and through that suffix with the formative 'ka,' of the Sanscrit possessive adjectives 'mâmaka,' *my*, 'tâvaka,' *thy*, 'asmâkam,' *of us, our*, &c. A closer analogy to 'yoka,' is that of the dative post-fix of the Mikir, which is 'yok' or 'ayok.'

(ii.) In Tamil, 'uḍeiya' is commonly appended to the inflexion of nouns and pronouns, as an auxiliary possessive suffix. 'uḍeiya' ('uḍei-(y)-a') means *belonging to*, or, literally *which is the property of*, and is derived from the noun 'uḍei,' *property, possession*, by the addition of 'a,' the sign of the relative participle, on the addition of which to any noun it is converted into an adjective. Thus, 'enuḍeiya kei,' *my hand*, means literally *the hand which is my property*, for 'en' of itself signifies *my*. Through usage, however, there is no difference in signification, or even in emphasis, between 'en' and 'en-uḍei-(y)-a.' The Malayâlam dispenses with 'ya' or 'a,' the sign of the relative participle, and uses 'uṭe' (in Tamil 'uḍei'), the uninflected noun itself, as its auxiliary suffix of the genitive.

'uḍeiya' is very largely used as an auxiliary genitival suffix in colloquial Tamil; and in some grammars written by foreigners it is classed with the signs of the genitive; but, properly speaking, it is not a case-sign, or suffix of case at all, but the relative participle of an appellative verb used adjectivally, and it is to be compared not with our preposition *of*, but with the phrase *belonging to.*

Locative or 'seventh' case.—Drâvidian grammarians state that any word which signifies 'a place' may be used to express the locative.

In each dialect, however, some words or post-positions are so frequently and systematically used for this purpose that they may be regarded as distinctively locative suffixes.

In Tamil, 'kaṇ,' *an eye,* which has also the signification of *a place,* is given in the grammars as the characteristic suffix of the locative. As a verbal root 'kaṇ' means *to see :* its secondary signification was *look!* its third *there,* its fourth *a place;* and in consequence of the last meaning it came to be used as a sign of the locative. It is very rarely used; and I have no hesitation in saying that the most distinctive sign of the Tamil locative is 'il,' *a place,* literally *a house.* In colloquial Tamil the most commonly used sign of the locative is 'iḍattil,' a compound suffix, which is derived from 'iḍam,' the ordinary word for *a place,* 'attu,' the inflexion or basis of the oblique cases ('iḍ-attu'), and 'il,' an older, purer word for *a place,* which is added to 'id-attu' ('iḍ-att'-il'), as the real sign of the locative, with the meaning of our preposition *in.* The signification of the whole suffix is literally *in the place of* or *in the place occupied by;* but it is evident that what really distinguishes the locative in this compound is 'il,' *in*—the suffix of a suffix; and that the meaning which the entire compound receives in actual use is simply *in.* In the lowest patois of colloquial Tamil the locative suffix which is most used is 'kiṭṭa,' *near,* the infinitive of a verb.* The higher dialect of the Tamil uses also 'uḷ' and 'uṟi,' *within, among,* as signs of the locative.

The ancient Canarese used 'ôḷ,' corresponding to the Tamil 'uḷ,' as its locative suffix ; whilst the modern dialect uses 'alli' or 'illi,' an adverbial form which answers to the Tamil 'il.' 'alli' is properly an adverb of place, compounded of 'li' and the remote demonstrative 'a ;' and its fellow is 'illi,' compounded of the same root and 'i,' the proximate demonstrative. These words mean literally *that place* and *this place,* or *there* and *here ;* and their use as locative suffixes betokens a later state of the language than the use of 'il' and 'uḷ' in Tamil, and of 'ôḷ' in Canarese. Compare the change of 'il' in Tamil to 'li' in Canarese, with the similar change of 'in' in Latin into 'ni' in Sanscrit.

* I cannot forbear noticing the remarkable (though doubtless accidental) resemblance between the double meaning of 'il' in Tamil (which is, perhaps, identical with 'in' the sign of the ablative of motion) and of 'in' in Latin. Each is used as a locative suffix or affix, with the meaning of *in ;* and each is used also as a particle of negation. The Latin 'in' not only means *in,* but has also the additional meaning of *not* in such compounds as 'indoctus' (like the Gothic 'un' and the Greek and Sanscrit 'a' or 'an' privative); and in like manner the Tamil 'il' means not only *in,* but also *not.* Moreover, as the Latin 'in' privative is 'an' in some other dialects, so the Tamil 'il,' *not,* takes also the shape of 'al,' with a very slight difference, not in the meaning, but only in the application.

In Telugu the sign of the locative, which is most commonly used, is 'lô:' another form frequently employed is 'andu.' 'lô' is more intensely locative in its signification than 'andu:' it means *within*, and is obviously identical with the Canarese 'ôḷ' and the Tamil 'uḷ.' 'andu' means simply *in*, and like the Canarese 'alli' is properly an adverb; and is derived in a somewhat similar manner from 'a,' the remote demonstrative, with the addition of a formative 'd,' whilst 'indu,' its correlative adverb of place, is derived from 'i,' the proximate demonstrative. The Canarese also possesses adverbs corresponding to these, viz., 'anta' and 'inta,' 'antalu' and 'intalu;' but uses them chiefly to express comparison, like our adverb *than*. The Telugu locative suffix 'andu' (meaning *in*) bears some apparent resemblance to the Sanscrit 'antar,' *among*, but this resemblance is wholly illusory: for 'andu' is derived from 'a,' *that*, by the addition of the neuter formative 'du,' which becomes euphonically 'ndu,' and corresponds not to the Sanscrit, but rather to 'anda,' *that*, the demonstrative adjective of the Tamil.

In Telugu the post-position 'na,' which becomes 'ni' after 'i,' is used as a locative suffix in connexion with neuter nouns. 'ni' (and hence its equivalent 'na' also) is evidently identical with 'in,' the sign of the ablative of motion in High Tamil, which I have supposed to be properly a sign of the locative; and probably both are identical with 'in,' the Tamil, and 'ni' and 'na,' the Telugu, genitival or inflexional suffixes. The locative is more likely to be derived from the genitive, than the genitive from the locative. With this Telugu locative 'na,' we may compare the Ostiak locative 'na,' 'ne;' and the Finnish and Magyar locatives 'an' and 'en.'

In Telugu, and in the higher dialect of the Tamil, the inflexion or basis of the oblique cases, which has naturally the force of a genitive, is sometimes used to denote the locative also. In Tamil the inflexion which is chiefly used in this manner is 'attu;' *e.g.*, 'nilattu,' *upon the earth.* The Malayâlam uses 'atta' in a similar manner: and in Telugu a corresponding change from 'ti' to 'ta' converts the inflexion or obsolete genitive into a locative; *e.g.*, 'iṇṭi,' *of a house*, 'iṇṭa,' *in a house.* The same inflexion in 'ta' denotes the instrumental in Telugu, as well as the locative; *e.g.*, compare 'chêti,' *of a hand*, with 'chêta,' *by a hand*, but this form seems to have been a locative originally. This fusion of the meaning of the genitive and locative suffixes corresponds to a similar fusion of the signs of those cases which a comparison of the various Indo-European tongues brings to light. The genitive and locative case-signs are often identical in the Finnish family of languages also. Bearing this in mind, may we not conclude that 'in, the Tamil sign of the ablative of motion, probably a locative, and which is identical with 'im,' the Canarese sign of the instrumental, was originally a genitive, and identical with 'in,' which we have seen to be so exceedingly common as a genitival suffix?

In all the Drâvidian idioms the locative suffixes are used like our *than*, to express comparison. Sometimes the locative alone is used for this purpose: oftener the conjunctive particle is added to it; *e.g.*, 'il-um,' in Tamil, 'lô-nu,' in Telugu, which compound has the signification of our *even than*.

None of the Drâvidian suffixes of the locative bears any resemblance to the locative case-signs of the Sanscrit, of any other of the Indo-European languages, or of the North-Indian vernaculars.

The vocative or 'eighth' case.—In the Drâvidian languages there is nothing which properly deserves to be styled a suffix or case-sign of the vocative. The vocative is formed merely by affixing or suffixing some sign of emphasis, or in certain instances by suffixing fragments of the personal pronouns.

The most common vocative in Tamil is the emphatic 'ê,' which is simply appended to the noun. Sometimes, also, the vocative is formed by substituting 'â' for the formative of gender, *e.g.*, from 'kartan,' *Lord*, is formed 'kartâ,' *O Lord;* by converting the final vowel into 'ây̆' (a fragment of the old pronoun of the second person singular), *e.g.*, from 'tangei,' *sister*, is formed 'tangây̆,' *O sister;* or by lengthening the vowel of the pluralising particle, *e.g.*, from 'pâvigaḷ,' *sinners*, is formed 'pâvigâḷ,' *O sinners*. Sometimes, again, especially in poetry, rational plurals are put in the vocative by appending to them 'îr,' a fragment of 'nîr,' *you*, *e.g.*, 'ellîr,' literally 'ell-îr,' *all ye*.

In the Indo-European languages the nominative is often used for the vocative, and what appears to be a vocative case-ending is often only a weakened form of the final syllable. In the Drâvidian languages, in like manner, the crude-root, deprived of all increments, is often used as the vocative.

In Telugu the vocative singular is ordinarily formed by lengthening the final vowel of the nominative (and all Telugu words end in some vowel), or by changing the final 'u' into 'a' or 'â.' 'ara' or 'arâ,' from the same root as the Tamil pronominal fragment 'îr' (viz. 'nîr,' *ye*), is post-fixed as the vocative of masculine-feminine plurals. In addition to these suffixes, various unimportant vocative particles, or particles of exclamation, are prefixed to nouns; some to one number only, some to both. In Canarese the vocative is ordinarily formed by appending 'â,' by lengthening the final vowel of the nominative, or by adding 'e' or 'ê.' Masculine-feminine plurals form their vocative not only by means of 'e' or 'ê,' but also by suffixing 'ira' or 'irâ,' from the same source as the Telugu 'arâ,' viz., the old 'nîr,' *ye.*

Such being the origin and character of the Drâvidian signs of the vocative, it is evident that we cannot expect to find allied forms in any other family of languages.

Compound case-signs.—As in the Hungarian and other Scythian tongues, and in some of the languages of the Eastern islands, so in Drâvidian, two or more case-signs are occasionally compounded together into one. We have already noticed the custom of annexing the various signs of the oblique cases to the inflexion or sign of the genitive; but other combinations of case-signs are also in use. Thus, there is a combination of the dative and locative, *e.g.*, 'vîṭṭukkuḷ' ('vîṭṭu-kk'-uḷ'), colloquial Tam., *within the house,* in which the locative 'uḷ' is combined with the dative or directive 'kku,' for the purpose of intensifying *in,* and educing the meaning of *within.* The higher dialect would in this instance prefer 'vîṭṭuḷ,' the simple locative; but 'vîṭṭukkuḷ' is also idiomatical. The ablative of motion in each of the Drâvidian dialects is generally a compound case, being formed of the locative and a verbal participle, or even of two locatives; *e.g.*, 'mane-(y)-ill-inda,' Can., *out of the house,* from 'illi' or 'alli,' the sign of the locative, and 'inda,' a sign of the instrumental, which is used also as a sign of the ablative, but which was, I conceive, a locative originally, and identical with 'im,' the Canarese form of the Tamil 'in.'

The Malayâla 'inikkulla' ('in-i-kka' and 'uḷḷa'), *my,* is a compound of the dative of the personal pronoun (which is itself a compound), and a relative-participial form of 'uḷ,' *within*; in colloquial Tamil also a similar form is used as a possessive.

Such compounds may indeed be formed in these languages at pleasure, and almost *ad infinitum.* Another instance of them in Tamil is seen in the addition of the dative to the locative (*e.g.*, 'iḍattiʀ-ku' or 'kaṭ-ku'), to constitute the locative-directive, which is required to be used in such expressions as *I sent to him.*

Possessive compounds.—The Drâvidian languages are destitute of that remarkable and very convenient compound of nouns and pronominal or possessive suffixes which is so characteristic of the Turkish, Ugrian, and other Scythian families.

In Hungarian they form the following compounds of 'ur,' *master*, with the pronominal fragments, used as possessives :—

ur-am,	*my master*	ur-aim,	*my masters*
ur-ad,	*thy master*	ur-aid,	*thy masters*
ur-a,	*his master*	ur-ai,	*his masters*
ur-un-k,	*our master*	ur-ain-k,	*our masters*
ur-at-ok,	*your master*	ur-ait-ok,	*your masters*
ur-ok,	*their master*	ur-ai-k,	*their masters*

These compounds are regularly declined like uncompounded nouns, in the usual way, *e.g.*—

uramnak (ur-am-nak), *to my master*
urunknak (ur-un-k-nak), *to our master*
uraimnak (ur-aim-nak), *to my masters*
urainknak (ur-ain-k-nak), *to our masters*

The entire absence of compounds of this nature in the Drâvidian languages, notwithstanding their agreement with the Scythian group in so many other points, is very remarkable: it is the only point, however, in which any structural difference of a generic, or class type, appears to exist.

In all the Drâvidian languages the possessive pronouns are prefixed to nouns, as in the Indo-European tongues, never post-fixed as in the Scythian.

Part III.—Adjectives, or Nouns used Adjectivally.

The difference between the Indo-European languages and those of the Scythian group, with respect to the formation and use of adjectives, is very considerable.

The agreement of adjectives with the substantives which they qualify, in gender, number, and case, forms an invariable characteristic of the languages of the Indo-European family; whilst in the Scythian languages adjectives have neither number, gender, nor case, but are mere nouns of relation or quality, which are prefixed without alteration to substantive nouns. In this particular the Drâvidian languages present no resemblance to the Sanscrit, or to any other member of the Indo-European stock, but are decidedly Scythian in character. Drâvidian adjectives, properly so called, like those of the Scythian tongues, are nouns of quality or relation, which acquire the signification of adjectives merely by being prefixed to substantive nouns without declensional change; and, in virtue of that acquired signification, they are called by Tamil grammarians 'uri chol,' *qualitative words.* Participles of verbs, and nouns with the addition of participial formatives, are also largely used as adjectives in the Drâvidian, as in the Scythian, family.

Such being the simplicity of the construction of Drâvidian adjectives, it will not be necessary to occupy much time in the investigation of this department of grammar. It may suffice to state, *seriatim*, the various modes in which words are used as adjectives, and the formative or euphonic modifications which they undergo on being prefixed to the substantives which they qualify: nor will it be necessary to state *all* the modifications which are discoverable in each dialect, but only those which appear to be most characteristic, or which are peculiarly worthy of remark.

1. The majority of adjectives in all the Drâvidian dialects, as in the dialects of the Scythian group, are nouns of quality or relation which become adjectives by position alone, without any structural change whatever, and without ceasing to be, in themselves, nouns of quality. Thus, in the Tamil phrases, 'pon aridu,' *gold (is) scarce,* and 'pon muḍi,' *a golden crown,* 'pon,' *gold,* is precisely the same in both instances, whether used as a substantive, in the first, or as an adjective, in the second.

In a similar manner in English and the other *modern* Indo-European dialects the same word is often used as a noun in one connexion, and as an adjective, without addition or change, in another connexion; *e.g.*, '*gold' is more ductile than silver; a 'gold' watch:* but this is contrary to the original genius of languages of this family, and is the result of a process of corruption. Whilst adjectival nouns of this class undergo in the Drâvidian languages no structural change, their combination with the nouns to which they are prefixed is facilitated in certain instances by unimportant euphonic changes, such as the assimilation of the final consonant of the adjective and the initial consonant of the substantive, in accordance with the requirements of Drâvidian phonetics (*e.g.*, 'poṟ chilei' (for 'pon chilei), *a golden image*'); the softening, hardening, or doubling of the initial of the substantive; or the optional lengthening of the included vowel of the adjectival word, to compensate for the abandonment of the euphonic final 'u,' *e.g.*, 'kâr,' *black,* in place of 'karu,' or *vice versâ.* These changes are purely euphonic; they differ in the different dialects; and they contribute to grammatical expression only in so far as they serve to indicate the words which are to be construed together as adjective and substantive. It is only on the ground of the repugnance of the Drâvidian ear to certain classes of concurrent sounds that the changes referred to are required by Drâvidian rules; and in the majority of instances nouns sustain no change whatever on being used adjectivally.

In the poetial dialects, adjectival formatives are less used than even in the colloquial dialects; and it is generally the crude ultimate form of the noun of quality which performs the functions of the adjective in classical compositions. Thus, whilst 'nalla,' *good*, and 'pala,' *many*, are commonly used in spoken Tamil, the higher idiom prefers, and almost invariably uses, the crude nouns of quality and relation 'nal' and 'pal;' *e.g.*, 'nal vaṛi,' *the good way*, and 'pan' (for 'pal') 'malar,' *many flowers.*

2. Sanscrit derivatives (neuter nouns of quality) ending in 'am' in Tamil, and in 'amu' in Telugu, become adjectives when prefixed to other nouns by rejecting the final 'm' or 'mu;' *e.g.*, 'subam,' *goodness*, and 'dinam,' *a day*, become 'suba dinam,' *a good day.* This, however, is a Sanscrit rather than a Drâvidian rule; and it flows from the circumstance, that when two Sanscrit nouns are formed into a compound, the crude form of the first of the two nouns is used instead of the nominative,—'subha' instead of 'subham.'

Pure Drâvidian nouns ending in 'am' or 'amu' rarely become adjectives in this manner; and when they do, it is through imitation of Sancrit derivatives. In Telugu, final 'amu' is sometimes hardened into 'ampu; *e.g.*, from 'andamu,' *beauty*, is formed 'andápu' or 'andampu,' *beautiful.*' In Tamil, when a noun of this class is used as an adjective; 'am' is generally rejected, and 'attu,' the inflexion, suffixed instead; *e.g.*, from 'puʀam,' *externality*, is formed 'puʀattu,' *external.* Sometimes also the Tamil deals in this manner with Sanscrit derivatives, converting them into adjectives by means of the inflexional 'attu:' but in all instances of nouns ending in 'am' or 'amu,' the most common method of using them adjectivally is that of appending to them the relative participle of the verb *to become* ('âna,' Tam., 'áyana,' Tel., or 'âda,' Can.), without any change, whether structural or euphonic, in the nouns themselves.

3. Many Tamil nouns ending in 'ś-u,' 'ḍ-u,' 'ṇḍ-u,' or 'ʀ-u,' double their final consonants when they are used as adjectives, or when case-signs are suffixed to them: *e.g.*, compare 'nâḍ-u,' Tam., *the country*, with 'nâṭṭ-u vaṛakkam,' *the custom of the country*, or 'nâṭṭ-il,' *in the country.* From the corresponding Telugu 'nâḍ-u,' *the country*, is formed 'nâṭi,' *of the country.* In these instances the final consonant of the root is doubled and hardened (or in Telugu hardened only), for the purpose of conveying the signification of an adjective: but in

another class of instances the root remains unchanged, and it is the consonant of the formative addition that is doubled.

When Tamil nouns ending in the formative 'mbu' are used adjectivally, 'mbu' changes into 'ppu;' *e.g.*, from 'irumbu,' *iron*, and 'kôl,' *a rod*, is formed 'iruppu (k)kôl,' *an iron rod.* A similar change sometimes takes place in Telugu, in which 'inumu,' *iron*, becomes 'inupa,' *e.g.*, 'inupa pette,' *an iron box.*

Tamil nouns ending in the formative 'ndu' and 'du' change in the same manner to 'ttu' on being used as adjectives. *E.g.*, compare 'marundu,' *medicine*, and 'erudu,' *an ox*, with 'maruttu (p)pei,' *a medicine bag*, and 'eruttu (p)podi,' *an ox load.*

Nouns ending in the formative 'ngu' do not, as might have been expected, change into 'kku' on becomming adjectives. Both these classes of changes precisely resemble those which neuter or intransitive verbs ending in 'd-u' or 'R-u' (or with the formative additions of 'mb-u,' 'ng-u,' 'nd-u,' &c.) undergo on becoming active or transitive, and a similar principle is in each instance apparent in the change; for when nouns of quality are prefixed to other nouns adjectivally, there is a *transition* of their signification to the nouns which they are intended to qualify, which is analogous to the *transition* of the action of a transitive verb to the object which it governs. (See the Section on 'Roots,' and also that on 'The Verb').

4. Each of the inflexional increments, or petrified case-signs of the genitive, is used for the conversion of substantives into adjectives. These are 'in' in Tamil and 'ni' in Telugu, 'attu' in Tamil and 'ṭi' or 'ti' in Telugu. In those instances in which 'in' in Tamil and 'ni' in Telugu are used as adjectival formatives, their use is optional; *e.g.*, in Telugu we can say either 'tella,' *white*, or 'tella-ni;' and in Tamil either 'niṛal,' *shady* (literally *shade*, a noun used adjectivally), or (but in the poetical dialect only) 'niṛal-in.' So also, we may say either 'mara (k)koppu,' Tam., *the branch of a tree*, or 'mara-ttu (k)koppu.' In Tamil 'am,' an inflexional increment which is apparently equivalent to 'in,' is often used as an adjectival formative; *e.g.*, 'panan tôppu' ('panei-am tôppu'), *a palmyra tope.* The same formative is used in Malayâlam also; *e.g.*, 'malam pâmbu' ('mala-am pâmbu'), *a rock snake.*

It has been shown that the inflexions or inflexional augments, 'attu' and 'ṭi,' are in reality genitive or possessive case-signs; and that they are used to convert substantives into adjectives through the ultimate relation subsisting between genitives, *e.g.*, *of gold*, and adjectives, *e.g.*, *golden.* In consequence of the frequency of their use in this connexion, they have come to be appended even to adverbial forms for the purpose of giving to them an adjectival meaning. Thus, from 'monna,' Tel., *before*, is formed the adjective 'monna-ṭi' (*e.g.*, 'monna-ṭi tîrpu,' *the former decision*'); and in Tamil from 'vaḍakku,' *north*, (properly a dative) is formed the adjective 'vaḍakk'-att-u,' *northern* (*e.g.*, 'vaḍakkattiyân, *a northern Tamilian*').

5. Relative participles of verbs, and nouns of quality converted into relative participles by the addition of participial formatives, are largely used as adjectives in all the Drâvidian languages. Much use is made of relative participles as adjectives by the languages of High Asia also.

It often happens that the same root is used, or at least is capable of being used, both as a verb and as a noun; and hence, in many instances of this kind in the Drâvidian languages, two methods of forming adjectives are practicable, viz., either by prefixing the noun to the substantive which we wish to qualify, or by using one of the relative participles of the related and equivalent verb. The colloquial dialect of the Tamil prefers the latter method: the former is preferred by the poets on account of its greater simplicity and brevity. Thus, in Tamil either 'uyar,' *height* (adjectivally *high*), or the relative participle 'uyarnda,' *high*, literally *that was high* (from 'uyar' considered as a verb signifying *to be high*), may be used to expres *high* or *lofty*; *e.g.*, 'uyar malei' or 'uyarnda malei,' *a lofty hill*: but 'uyar' would be preferred in poetical compositions, whilst 'uyarnda' is better suited to prose and colloquial purposes, and is consequently the form which is commonly used by the Tamil people. This usage is not unknown to the Indo-European tongues also, but it constitutes a special characteristic of the Scythian group.

6. The past verbal participle of Telugu verbs is sometimes used adjectivally in Telugu; hence when Sans. neuter nouns in 'am' are used as adjectives 'ayi,' *having become* (the verbal participle), is often annexed to them instead of 'ayi-na' (Tam. 'âna,' Can. 'âda'), *that became, that is* (the relative participle). It is evident, therefore, that the final 'i' of many Telugu adjectives is that by which the past participles of verbs are formed; *e.g.*, 'kindi,' *low*, from 'kiṇda,' adverb, *below*; *e.g.*, 'kindi illu,' *the lower part of the house*. The addition of this 'i' converts substantives also into adjectives; *e.g.*, from 'kûn-u,' *a hump*, is formed 'kûni,' *hump-backed*.

7. A very numerous class of Drâvidian adjectives is formed by the addition to crude nouns of quality of the suffixes of the relative participles, more or less modified. 'uyarnḍa' is a perfectly formed preterite relative participle, comprising, in addition to the verbal root, 'nd,' the sign of the preterite tense, and 'a,' the sign of the relative;

and though the idea of time is in this connexion practically lost sight of, yet that idea is included and expressed. On the other hand, in the class of words now to be considered, the signs of tense are modified or rejected, to correspond with their use as adjectives, and the idea of time is entirely merged in that of relation. It is words of this class which are commonly adduced by native grammarians as specimens of *qualitative words*, or *adjectives;* and if the name can correctly be used at all in the Drâvidian family of tongues, it is to this class that it is applicable. I am convinced, however, that it is more correct to regard these words simply as relative participles; and I class them under this head, immediately after the investigation of the noun, because in most instances, the root to which the relative signs are suffixed is used by itself not as a verb, but only as a noun of quality or relation, or as an appellative.

(1.) Many Tamil adjectives of this class are formed by the addition of 'iya' to the root, *e.g.*, 'periya,' *great*, 'siṟiya,' *small.* The roots of those words are 'per-u' and 'siṟ-u;' and as 'u' is merely a help to enunciation, I do not say that 'u' is changed into 'i,' but prefer to say that 'iya' is added to the root. I have no doubt that we shall be able to explain each part of this addition grammatically, without having recourse to arbitrary mutations. 'iya' ('i-y-a'), is, I conceive, compounded of 'i,' a sign of the preterite tense, and 'a,' the sign of the relative participle. It has probably been originally softened from 'ida,' the suffix of the preterite relative participle in ancient Canarese, to which 'ina' corresponds in colloquial Tamil. In Telugu, the past-participle alone is often used adjectivally without the suffix of the relative, as we have already seen; and the 'i' with which that participle terminates, explains the 'i' which precedes the final 'a' of such Tamil adjectives as 'peri-(y)-a.' 'i' is the sign of the verbal participle, and the addition of 'a' or 'ya,' transforms it into a relative participle. In classical Tamil compositions 'iya' is generally used instead of 'ina,' as the sign of the preterite relative participle of ordinary verbs; *e.g.*, 'paṇṇiya,' instead of 'paṇṇina,' *that made.* When the same suffix is added to a noun of quality like 'per-u,' *great*, it converts it into a relative participle, which, with the form of the preterite, contains in it no reference to time, and which may therefore be called an adjective. The suffix 'iya,' being somewhat archaic, readily loses the idea of time; whereas that idea is firmly retained by 'ida,' 'ina,' and the other preterite relative suffixes which are in ordinary use. A good illustration of the adjectival use of 'iya' is furnished by the very roots to which we have referred, viz., 'peru,' *great*, 'siṟu,' *small.*

When these roots are regarded as verbs, their preterite relative participles are 'perutta,' *that was or became great*, 'siRutta,' *that was or became small;* in which participles the ideas of time and change are always included: whereas, when 'peru' and 'siRu' are regarded as nouns of quality, they are adapted for general use as adjectives by having 'iya' suffixed to them, *e.g.*, 'periya,' 'siRiya,' ('per'-iya,' 'siR'-iya.') In this shape they mean simply *great* and *small*, without any reference to time; and in consequence of 'iya' being so purely aoristic, adjectives of this mode of formation are largely used. 'periya,' *great*, 'koḍiya,' *cruel*, may properly be styled adjectives, seeing that they are used as such; but it is a mistake to regard 'periya-(v)-an,' or 'periya-n,' *a great man*, 'koḍiya-n,' *a cruel man*, and similar words as adjectives. They are compounds of adjectives and suffixes of gender; and are properly appellative nouns, as has been shown under the head of 'Gender,' and as appears from the manner in which they are used.

It is remarkable that 'a' or 'ia' is post-fixed in Kole also to many adjectives; and that the same participle is a sign of the possessive, as 'a' is in Drâvidian.

(2.) Some adjectives are formed by simply suffixing 'a,' the sign of the relative participle, without the preterite 'i,' or any other sign of tense whatever; *e.g.*, 'nalla,' Tam. *good;* 'doḍḍa,' Can. *great;* 'pedda,' Tel. *great*. The examples here given may be, and doubtless are, derived from preterite relative participles ('nalla'* from the high Tamil 'nalgiya' and 'doḍḍa' from the ancient Canarese 'doḍḍida'); but in some instances, 'a,' the sign of the relative participle, is appended directly to nouns, without borrowing any portion of the sign of the preterite. We have an instance of this even in colloquial Tamil, viz., 'uḍeiya' ('uḍei-(y)-a'), the ordinary colloquial suffix of the genitive, which literally signifies *that belongs to, that is the property of*, from 'uḍei,' *property*, to which 'a,' the sign of the relative participle, is simply suffixed. This mode of forming adjectives from substantives by directly suffixing 'a' is very common in the classical dialect of the Tamil, especially in connexion with substantives ending in 'ei' or 'î;' *e.g.*, from 'malei,' *a hill*, comes 'malei-(y)-a,' adj., *hilly*, or *of a hill;* from 'sunei,' *a spring*, comes 'sunei-(y)-a,' *that relates to a spring*. So also from 'tî,' *evil*, is formed 'tî-(y)-a,' adj., *evil*. The circumstance

* 'Nalla' is generally considered to be a primitive word, and a *bonâ fide* adjective: but if 'keṭṭa,' *bad*, is admitted to be a relative participle, from 'keḍ-u,' *to become bad*, it is reasonable to suppose that 'nalla,' *good*, has also some such origin. Accordingly we find a root, 'nal,' *goodness*, which is capable of being used adjectivally, and then signifies *good;* and connected with the same root we find also the verb 'nalg-u,' *to be bountiful, to be good*. The preterite relative participle of this verb is 'nalgiya,' *that was, or is, bountiful;* and from this, I believe, that the much-used adjective 'nalla,' *good*, has been derived.

that in most of these examples, the signification of the genitive is as natural as that of the adjective, shows how intimately the genitive and the adjective are allied. Nevertheless, as used in these examples, I regard 'a' as an adjectival termination, rather than as a sign of the genitive, and as acquiring this force from its being the sign of the relative participle. Indeed I would define these qualitative words ('malei-(y)-a,' &c.) to be the relative participles of 'appellative verbs.' See that class of words investigated in the section on 'The Verb.'

This usage, perhaps, explains the origin of the Tamil adjectives 'pala,' *many*, and 'sila,' *few*, viz., from the roots 'pal' and 'sil' (which are used in their crude state in the poets), and 'a,' the sign of the relative participle. It is true that these words are also regarded as neuters plural,—and that in some instances they are correctly so regarded appears from the phrase 'palavin' ('pala-v-in') 'pâl,' the Tamil designation of *the neuter plural*, literally *the gender of the many (things)*. But when we look also at such phrases as 'pala arasar,' *many kings*—phrases of constant occurrence, not only in the colloquial dialect, but in the classics—it is evident that the 'a' of this latter 'pala' is used, not as a suffix of the neuter plural, or as a sign of plurality of any sort, but as a sign of the relative participle, by the use of which 'pal-a' becomes an adjective.

(3.) Many adjectives of this class are formed by the addition to nouns of quality of the sign of the relative participle of the future or aorist, which is 'um' in Tamil, *e.g.*, 'perum,' *great*. Beschi supposes this adjective to be derived from the abstract noun 'perumei,' *greatness*, by the rejection of the final 'ei;' and to all other adjectives of this class he attributes a similar origin. 'mei,' however, not 'ei,' is the suffix by which abstract nouns are formed (*vide* the section on 'The Verb'), and as such it is one and indivisible. It is much better to derive 'perum' from 'per',' the un-euphonised form of the root 'peru,' *greatness, great*, and 'um,' the ordinary relative participle of the aorist; in the same manner as 'periya' has been seen to be derived from 'per' and 'iya,' the relative participle of the preterite. 'um' is ordinarily called the relative participle of the future, but this future will be shown, in the section on 'The Verb,' to be properly an aorist, and as such to be used very indeterminately, with respect to time. 'Viṇṇil minang-um śuḍar,' Tam., means, not *the stars that* will *shine in the sky*, but *the stars that shine in the sky*, this tense being especially fitted to denote continued existence: and in consequence of this looseness of reference to time, 'um,' the sign of the relative participle of this tense is better fitted even than 'iya' to be suffixed to nouns of quality, as an adjectival formative. Hence 'perum,' literally *that is was or will be great,* is a more expressive and more classical word for *great* than 'periya.'

It has already been shown, in the section on 'Sounds,' that 'peim,' Tam., *green,* is not a distinct form of adjective, but is softened from 'paśum' ('payum') by a dialectic rule, whilst 'paśum' is derived regularly from 'paś-u,' *greenness, green,* and 'um,' the particle which is now under consideration.

7. Drâvidian nouns of every description may be used adjectivally by appending to them the relative participles of the verb signifying *to become,* which are in Tamil 'âna' and 'âgum' (also 'uḷḷa,' an equivalent word), in Telugu 'agu' and 'ayana,' in Canarese 'âda:' *e.g.,* 'uyarvâna' ('uyarv'-âna'), Tam., *lofty,* literally *that was or has become high or a height.* This mode of forming adjectives is especially used in connexion with Sanscrit derivatives, on account of their greater length and foreign origin. Such adjectives, however, are phrases not words; and they are incorrectly classed amongst adjectives by Europeans who have treated of Drâvidian grammar.

I may here also again remark, that certain words have been styled adjectives by some European writers, which in reality are appellative nouns, not adjectives, and which acquire the force of adjectives merely from the addition of the relative participles of the verb *to become,* which have been referred to above. Thus, the Tamil words 'nallavan,' *a good (man),* 'nallavaḷ,' *a good (woman),* 'nalladu,' *a good (thing),* are appellative nouns formed by the suffix to a noun of quality of the formatives of the three genders; and the addition of 'âna,' *that has become,* to any of these words, though it constitutes them adjectives in effect, leaves them in grammatical form precisely what they were before. *Bonus* may either qualify another noun, *e.g., bonus vir,* when it is an adjective, or it may stand alone and act as nominative to a verb, when it is a qualitative noun, *e.g., bonus virtutem amat.* The Tamil 'nallavan,' *a good (man),* can only be used in the latter sense, and therefore is not an adjective at all.

Comparison of adjectives.—In all the Drâvidian dialects comparison is effected, not as in the Indo-European family by means of comparative or superlative particles suffixed to, and combined with, the positive form of the adjective, but by a method closely resembling that in which adjectives are compared in the Semitic languages, or by the simpler means which are generally used in the languages of the Scythian group. When the first of these methods is adopted, the noun of quality or adjective to be compared is placed in the nominative, and the noun or nouns with which it is to be compared are put in the locative and prefixed. It is generally stated in Tamil grammars that it is the ablative of motion which is thus used, but I am persuaded that even when the case-sign is that of the ablative of motion, the signification is purely that of the locative; and that in Tamil 'il' and 'in,' have in this connexion the meaning of *in* (*i.e.*, are locatives), rather than that of *from*: *e.g.*, 'avattr'-il idu nalladu,' Tam., *this is better than those,* literally *in those things this is good.*

The conjunctive particle 'um,' *and, even,* is often added, especially in the colloquial dialect, as an intensitive, *e. g.*, 'avattr'-il-um idu nalladu,' Tam., *this is better than those,* literally *even-in-those this is good.* Sometimes the noun with which comparison is to be made is put in the dative instead of the locative. Sometimes, again, comparison is effected by means of an auxiliary verb. The noun with which comparison is to be made is put in the accusative; it is followed and governed by the subjunctive or infinitive of a verb signifying *to see, to show,* or *to leave;* and the phrase is concluded by the subject of the preposition, with the adjective to be compared. Thus, in Tamil we may say 'adei-(p)pârkkilum idu nalladu,' literally *even though looking at that this* (*is*) *good,* or 'adei viḍa idu nalladu,' *quitting that this* (*is*) *good, i.e., this is so good as to induce one to abandon that.*

Such modes of comparison, however, are stiff, cumbrous, and little used except by Europeans; and in the Drâvidian dialects, as in those of the Scythian group, direct comparison of one thing with another is ordinarily left to be understood, not expressed. The effect which is aimed at is secured in a very simple manner by prefixing to the positive form of the adjective some word signifying *much* or *very,* or by appending to the subject of the proposition a sign of emphasis, or a word signifying *indeed, e.g.*, 'id-ê' (or 'idu tân') nalladu,' Tam., THIS *indeed is good.*

In Telugu and Canarese the conjunctive particles 'nu' and 'û' are not necessarily required to help forward the former method of comparison, like the Tamil 'um;' nor is this particle generally used in the higher dialect of the Tamil itself. The Canarese makes use also of the particles 'anta' and 'inta,' 'antalu' and 'intalu' (which, in their origin, are compounds of locatives and demonstratives), to assist in effecting comparison.

In all these dialects the superlative is generally expressed by means of prefixed adverbs signifying *much* or *very,* or by the primitive Scythian plan of doubling of the adjective itself, *e.g.*, 'periya-periya,' *very great,* literally *great-great.* If greater explicitness is required, the method by which it is effected is that of putting the objects with which comparison is made in the plural and in the locative-case. Thus the phrase, *the tiger is the fiercest animal*, would be expressed in Tamil as follows,—'vilangugaḷil puli koḍidu,' *amongst animals* (literally *in animals*) *the tiger is cruel.* Sometimes, for the purpose of increasing the intensity of the superlative signification the adjectival noun 'ellâ,' *all*, is prefixed to the plural noun which denotes the objects compared, *e.g.*, *in* (*i.e.*, *amongst*) *all animals the tiger is cruel.*

It is evident that the modes of forming the comparative and superlative degrees of adjectives which have now been described, differ greatly and essentially from those which characterize the Indo-European family of tongues. If Drâvidian adjectives had ever been compared like those of the Sanscrit, it is inconceivable that so convenient and expressive a plan should so completely have been abandoned. The Drâvidian modes of comparison agree, up to a certain point, with those of the Semitic tongues; but they are in most perfect accordance with the Turkish method, and with the modes of comparison which are employed in the languages of Tartary generally.

Robert de Nobilis and the Jesuit writers endeavoured to naturalise in Tamil the Sanscrit superlative particle 'tama;' but the Tamil adhered resolutely to its own idiom, and the attempt failed.

Prepositions or Post-Positions.—It has already been stated that all the Drâvidian post-positions are, or have been, nouns. When suffixed to other nouns as post-positions, they are supposed to be in the locative case; but they are generally suffixed in their un-inflected form, or in the nominative; and the locative case-sign, though understood, is rarely expressed. It seems quite unnecessary to enter into an investigation of the post-positions in a work of this kind, inasmuch as they are sufficiently explained in the ordinary grammars, and are to be regarded simply as nouns of relation.

SECTION IV.

THE NUMERALS.

In the Drâvidian languages, each of the cardinal numbers presents itself to us in a two-fold shape. The first and more primitive form is that of numeral adjectives: the second and more largely used is that of neuter nouns of number. The numeral adverbs ('twice,' 'thrice,' &c.) and also the distributive numerals ('by twos,' 'by threes,' &c.) are formed from the numeral adjectives; whilst the ordinal numbers ('second,' 'third,' &c.) are formed from the abstract numeral nouns.

In the colloquial dialects the neuter nouns of number are often used, without change, as numeral adjectives: *e.g.*, in Tamil, we may say 'iraṇḍu pêr,' *two persons;* though 'iru pêr,' or the still more classical appellative noun, 'iruvar,' might have been expected to be used. This use of the noun of number instead of the numeral adjective is not ungrammatical; but is in accordance with the characteristic Drâvidian rule that every noun of quality or relation, though in itself neuter and abstract, becomes an adjective by being prefixed to a substantive noun in direct apposition. The numeral noun 'ondru,' Tam., 'okaṭi,' Tel., *one,* is the only numeral which is never used in this manner even in the colloquial dialects; the adjectival numerals, 'oru,' 'oka,' &c., being invariably prefixed to substantive nouns as numeral adjectives: the same forms are employed also as indefinite articles.

The abstract or neuter nouns of number are sometimes elegantly post-fixed, instead of being pre-fixed to the substantive nouns which they are intended to qualify. *E.g.*, instead of 'nâl' erudu,' Tam., *four oxen,* we may say, not only 'nâng' erudu' (using the noun of number 'nângu,' instead of the numeral adjective 'nâlu'), but also 'erudu nângu;' a phrase which literally means *a quarternion of oxen.* This phrase affords an illustration of the statement that the Drâvidian nouns of number are properly abstract neuters.

The primitive radical forms of the Drâvidian numerals, will be found to be those of the numeral adjectives. In investigating the numerals one by one, it will be seen that the neuter or abstract nouns of number have been formed from the shorter and simpler numeral adjectives by the addition of neuter formatives and euphonic increments. It is, therefore, the numeral adjectives of the Drâvidian languages, not their numeral nouns, which are to be compared with the numerals of other families of languages.

The compound numbers between 'ten' and 'twenty,' and especially the higher compounds ('twenty,' 'thirty,' 'two hundred,' 'three hundred,' &c.), afford much help towards ascertaining the oldest forms of the Drâvidian numeral roots; seeing that the numeral adjectives which are employed in those compounds exhibit the numerals in their briefest, purest, and most ancient shape.

It is the adjectival form of the numerals which is used in forming appellative nouns of number, such as 'iruvar' ('iru-(v)-ar'), Tam., *two persons.* The basis of this word is not 'iraṇḍu,' the noun of number *two*, but the numeral adjective 'iru,' with the addition of 'ar,' the usual suffix of the epicene or masculine-feminine plural. In the colloquial dialects, adjectival or appellative nouns of number are formed in this manner from the first three numeral adjectives alone; *e.g.*, 'oruvan,' Tam., *one person*, (masc.), '*unus*;' 'orutti,' *one person* (fem.), '*una*;' 'iruvar,' *two persons;* 'mûvar,' *three persons* (both epicene): but in the higher or poetical dialects, almost all the numeral adjectives are converted in this manner into appellative nouns.

From these circumstances it is evident that the Drâvidian numeral adjectives are to be regarded as the only essential portion of the roots of the cardinal numbers, and probably as the very roots themselves.

One.—Two forms of the cardinal numeral 'one' are found in the Drâvidian languages, which will appear, I think, to be remotely allied. The first, 'oru,' is that which is used in all the dialects except the Telugu; the latter, 'oka,' is used in the Telugu alone.

(1.) The basis of the first and most commonly used form of this numeral is 'or,' to which 'u' is added for euphonisation; and this constitutes the numeral adjective 'one,' in all the dialects which make use of this base. 'or-u,' in colloquial Tamil, becomes 'ôr' in the poetical dialect; the essential vowel 'o' being lengthened to 'ô' to compensate for the rejection of the euphonic addition 'u.' The adjectival form used in Tulu is 'ori,' in Ku 'ra;' with which the Behistun numeral adjective 'irra' or 'ra' may be compared. The Canarese numeral adjective is identical with the Tamil, though its true character is somewhat concealed. Instead of 'oruvan,' Tam., '*unus*,' the Canarese has 'obban-u' (or-b-an'), and instead of 'oruvaḷ,' '*una*,' 'obbaḷ-u' ('or-b-al'). The ancient Canarese, however, uses 'ôrvvam' for the former, and 'ôrval' for the latter; the base of which, 'ôr,' is the numeral root, and is identical with the Tamil 'or-u' or 'ôr.'

The abstract neuter noun 'one,' meaning literally *one thing*, or *unity*, is in Canarese 'ondu;' in grammatical Tamil 'onʀu' (pronounced 'ondru' or 'ondu,' and in vulgar Tamil 'oṇṇu); in Malayâlam 'onna;' in Tulu 'onji;' in Gônd 'undî;' in Tuda 'voḍḍa,' 'od,' 'ood,' or 'vood;' in Ûrâon 'ûntâ.'

'or' being the adjectival form of this numeral, it claims by rule to be the representative of the crude root, as well as the basis of the abstract or neuter nouns of number signifying 'one' or 'unity,' which are used in the various dialects. It remains to be seen whether the derivation of each of those nouns of number from 'or' can be clearly made ont.

At first sight the Canarese 'ondu,' and especially the Malayâla 'onna,' appear to resemble the most common form of the Indo-European numeral 'one,' which is in Latin 'un-us' (in an older form 'oin-os'), in Greek 'ἕν,' in Gothic 'ain'-s.' In the Koibal, a Samoïede dialect, there is a similar word for 'one,' viz., 'unem:' and we find in the Tungusian 'um,' in the Manchu 'emu.' Even in Sanscrit, though 'êka' is invariably used for *one*, a form has been noticed which appears to be allied to the first numeral of the Western languages, viz., 'ûna-s,' *less*, which is prefixed to some of the higher numerals to express *diminution by one* (*e.g.*, 'ûnavinshati,' *nineteen*), like the corresponding prefix 'un' in the Latin 'undeviginti.' It would be an interesting circumstance if the Malayâla 'onn-a' and the Latin 'un-us' were found to be allied; but the resemblance is altogether illusory, and vanishes on the derivation of 'onna' from 'or' being proved.

It is reasonable to suppose that the numeral adjective of the Tamil, 'oru,' and its numeral noun 'onʀu,' must somehow be related. Now, whilst it is impossible on Drâvidian principles to derive 'oru' from 'onʀu,' it will be shown that the derivation of 'onʀu' from 'oru' is in perfect accordance with Drâvidian rules: and if the Malayâla 'onna' be simply an euphonised form of the Tamil 'onʀu,' as it certainly is, every idea of the existence of a connection between any of these forms and the Latin 'un-us' must be abandoned.

It was shown in the section on 'Sounds' that the Drâvidian languages delight to euphonise certain consonants by prefixing nasals to them. If the 'r' of 'oru' is found to have been converted in this manner into 'nr,' the point under discussion will be settled. What analogy, then, is there for this conversion? 'mûru,' Canarese, *three*, has through this very process become in Tamil, 'mûnʀu' (pronounced 'mûndru,' 'mûndu,' or 'mûṇu'); in Malayâlam, 'mûnna. 'karu,' Can., *a calf*, becomes in Tamil, 'kanʀu' (pronounced 'kandru' or 'kandu,' and vulgarised in colloquial Tamil into 'kaṇṇu'); in Malayâla 'kanna.' Again, 'kiʀu,' the verbal suffix denoting present time in Tamil, has become in the poetical dialect 'kinʀu,' pronounced 'kindru;' and this, in the Malayâlam present tense, is found to be still further softened into 'kunnu,' and even 'unnu.' In all these instances we perceive that very euphonic alteration by which 'oru' has become progressively 'onʀu,' 'ondru,' 'ondu,' 'oṇṇu,' and 'onna;' and thus the derivation of 'onna' from 'oru' is found to be strictly in accordance with analogy.

It may be objected that the illustrations which have been given above exhibit a change of the hard 'ʀ' into 'ndr,' whereas the 'r' of 'oru' is the soft medial; and that, therefore, the analogy, though very remarkable, is not complete. I answer that, though the 'r' of our present Tamil 'oru' is certainly the medial semi-vowel, not the hard 'ʀ,' yet originally the hard 'ʀ' must have been the very 'ʀ' employed. This appears from the Tamil adjective, *odd, single*. That adjective is 'oʀʀei' (pronounced 'ottrei'); and it is derived from the numeral adjective, *one*. It has been derived, however, by the usual process of doubling the final consonant, not from 'or-u,' but from 'oʀ,'—evidently a more ancient form of the word, in which the 'r' was the hard, rough 'ʀ,'—that very 'ʀ' which is usually euphonised into 'ndr.'

It appears, therefore, that the origin which I have ascribed to 'onru' is in complete accordance with analogy. Moreover, if the 'n' of 'ondru,' 'ondu,' or 'onna,' were part of the root of this numeral, the 'du' which is suffixed to it could only be a neuter formative; and in that event 'on' should be found to be used as the numeral adjective. 'on,' however, is nowhere so used; and therefore both the use of 'or-u,' instead of 'on,' as the numeral adjective, and the existence of the derivative 'oʀ(ʀ)eî' ('ottr-ei'), *single*, prove that the root of this numeral must have been 'or,' not 'on.'

Though 'or,' in its primitive, unnasalised shape, is not now found in the cultivated Drâvidian dialects as the first abstract neuter noun of number for *one*, or *unity*; yet it appears in one of the ruder dialects of the family, viz., in the Rajmahal or Male; in which the numeral noun *one* is 'art,' or 'ort,' which is evidenly formed directly from 'ar' or 'or.' If it is true, as has been asserted, that the Male 'art' is *appropriated to human beings*, it must be identical with the Tamil 'orutt-an,' *one man*, 'orutt-i,' *one woman;* the 'tt' of which is a formative, and is derived from the pronoun of the third person. See 'The Noun.' Compare also this form with the Brahui 'asit,' *one*, of which 'as,' the crude root, seems to bear as close an analogy to 'or-u' as 'mus,' the crude root of 'musit,' the Brahui for *three*, undoubtedly does to the Canarese 'mûr-u.' If in the latter case the 's' and 'r' are mutually convertible, it cannot be considered improbable that 'asit' and 'art,' and consequently 'as' and 'or,' bear a similar relation one to the other.

(2.) The basis of the Telugu numeral signifying *one* seems to be essentially different from that which is used in the other Drâvidian dialects. There is nothing extraordinary in the discovery in any language or family of languages of two roots for *one*. This would naturally arise from the very concrete character of this numeral, and the variety of uses to which it is put. Even in Sanscrit we find both 'êka' and 'prathama.' *Two* also is represented in Latin by 'duo,' 'ambo,' and 'secundus.'

The Telugu neuter noun of number for *one* is 'okaṭi,' literally *one thing*, of which the adjectival form is 'oka.' 'okaṭi' is formed from 'oka' by the addition of the neuter and inflexional formative, 'ṭi:' and by annexing the usual masculine and feminine suffixes, the Telugus form 'oka*n*ḍu' or 'okaḍu,' *one man*, and 'okate,' *one woman.* 'oka' being found to be the crude root of this numeral, we have now to inquire into its affinities.

Is the Telugu 'oka' derived, as has sometimes been supposed, from the Sanscrit 'êka,' *one?* It seems not improbable that the Telugu word has some ulterior connexion with the Sanscrit one, to which it bears so great a resemblance: but it is impossible to suppose it to have been directly derived from the Sanscrit, like the Bengali 'ok,' or even the Persian 'yak;' for the Telugu has borrowed and occasionally uses the Sanscrit numeral 'êka,' in addition to its own 'oka;' and it never confounds 'oka' with 'êka,' which Telugu grammarians regard as altogether independent one of another. It will be seen also that words closely analogous to 'oka' are used in the whole of the Finnish languages, by which they cannot be supposed to have been borrowed from the Sanscrit. Thus the numeral *one* is in Wotiak 'og,' 'odyg;' in Samoïede 'okur,' 'ookur,' 'ookur;' in Vogoul 'ak,' 'aku;' in Magyar 'egy;' in Lappish 'akt;' in Finnish 'yxi' ('yk-si);' in Tcheremiss 'ik,' 'iktä; in the Scythian of the Behistun tablets 'ir.' In the Sub-Himalayan languages, we find 'ako' in Miri, 'akhet' in Naga, and 'katka' in Kuki.

These remarkable analogies to the Telugu 'oka' prove that it has not necessarily, or even probably, been derived from the Sanscrit 'êka:' and if the two roots are allied, as they appear to be, it must be in consequence of the relation of both the Sanscrit and the Lappo-Drâvidian families to an earlier form of speech.

The Tamil infinitive 'okka,' which is used adverbially to mean *in one, all together*, and which forms the ordinary Malayâla word for *all*, (with which compare Mordwin 'wok,' *all*), is supposed by the grammarians to be derived from the obsolete verbal root 'o,' *to be one*. This root 'o' is sometimes used adjectivally in Canarese instead of 'or-u,' in which case it doubles the succeeding consonant; *e.g.*, 'ottaleyu' ('o-(t)tale'), *one head;* 'okkaṇṇanu' ('o-(k)kaṇṇan'), *a one-eyed man.* It is evident from this, that 'o' was originally followed by a consonant; and that it must have been derived by abbreviation either from the Tamil 'or,' or the Telugu 'ok'.'

Can 'oka' and 'or' be in any way allied? It appears very doubtful whether there is any relation between them; and yet some few traces of affinity may be discovered. On examining the Telugu word for *eleven*, 'padakoṇḍu,' the latter part of this compound numeral presents some peculiarities which are deserving of notice. We should have expected to find 'okaṭi' used for *one* in this connexion; instead of which we find 'koṇḍu,' a form which is found in this compound alone. 'koṇḍu' is here used as a neuter noun of number, and like all such nouns is formed from a crude base by the addition of some formative. If the 'k' is euphonic and intended to prevent hiatus, like the 'h' of 'padihêḍu' ('padi-(h)-êḍu,') *seventeen*, 'koṇḍu' is identical with 'k-oṇḍu,' and 'oṇḍu' is allied to the Canarese 'ondu,' from the root 'or:' but if, as appears more likely, the 'k' is radical, the crude adjectival form from which it was derived may have been 'kor:' and if we are at liberty to adopt this supposition, we may at once conclude that 'kor' was the original form of the Tamil-Canarese 'or;' for the initial 'k' might easily be softened off (and there are several instances of the disappearance of an initial 'k'), whilst it could not have been prefixed to 'or,' if it had not stood before it originally.

Supposing 'kor' to be an older form of 'or,' it is not difficult to suppose 'kor' and 'oka' to be allied, by the corruption of both from a common root. If the old Scythian word for *one* was 'okor,' corresponding to the Samoïede 'okur,' both 'kor' and 'or,' and also 'oka,' would naturally be derived from it. A change analogous to this appears in the Behistun tablets, in which we find that the numeral for *one* which is used in the oldest extant specimen of the language of the ancient Scythians was 'kir' (corresponding to our supposititious

Telugu 'kor'), and that the numeral adjective derived from it was 'irra' or 'ra.' Here we have an ancient and authentic illustration both of the existence of a word for *one* containing both 'k' and 'r,' and of a derived numeral adjective from which the 'k' had been softened off: and it deserves special notice that 'ra,' the Behistun numeral adjective, is identical with 'ra,' the numeral adjective of the Ku, a Drâvidian dialect. In the Turkish, *one* is represented by 'bir,' which seems to be allied rather to the Persian 'bâr' in 'bâri,' *once* (and ulteriorly to the Sanscrit 'vâr,' *time*), than to the Tamil 'or.' The Caucasian numerals for *one* exhibit a closer resemblance to the Drâvidian, viz., Lazian 'ar,' Mingrelian 'arti,' Georgian 'erthi;' and it may be noticed that as in the Drâvidian 'or,' *one*, and 'ir,' *two*, so in those Caucasian dialects, 'r' forms an essential part of *both* those numerals.

Drâvidian indefinite article.—The Drâvidian numeral adjectives, 'oru' and 'oka,' are used like similar numerals in most languages, as a sort of indefinite article. The Turkish uses 'bir,' *one*, in a similar manner; and a corresponding usage prevails in the modern European languages, as well as in the colloquial dialects of Northern India.

The only thing which may be considered as distinctive or peculiar in the use of the Drâvidian numeral adjective *one*, as an indefinite article, is the circumstance that it is not used in the loose general way in which in English we speak of *a man*, or *a tree*, but only in those cases in which the singularity of the object requires to be emphasized, when it takes the meaning of *a certain man, a particular kind of tree*, or *a single tree*. Europeans in speaking the native languages make in general too large and indiscriminate a use of this prefixed numeral, forgetting that the Drâvidian neuter noun, without prefix or addition, becomes singular or plural, definite or indefinite, according as the connexion requires.

Two.—The abstract or neuter noun of number signifying *two*, or *duality*, is in Canarese 'eraḍu,' in Tamil 'iraṇḍu,' in Telugu 'renḍu,' in Tulu 'eraḍ-u,' 'raḍḍha,' or 'ranḍu;' in Malayâlam 'renḍa;' in Gônd 'rend' or 'ranu;' in Seoni Gônd 'rund;' in Tuda 'aeḍ' or 'yeḍa.' The Singhalese word for *double* is 'iruntata.' In all the Drâvidian dialects the corresponding numeral adjective is 'ir,' with such minor modifications only as euphony dictates. This numeral adjective is in Tamil 'iru;' in the higher dialect 'îr,' the increase in the quantity of the radical 'i,' compensating for the rejection of the final euphonic 'u.' The 'r' which constitutes the radical consonant of 'ir,' is the soft medial semi-vowel; and it evinces in consequence of its softness a tendency to coalesce with the succeeding consonant, especially in Canarese and Telugu. Thus, for 'iruvar,' Tam., *two persons*, the modern Canarese uses 'ibbar-u' (ancient dialect 'irvar'), and the Telugu 'iddar-u.' Instead, also, of the correct 'irunûṟu,' *two hundred*, of the Tamil, both the Telugu and the Canarese have 'innûṟu;' and the Canarese word for *twenty* is 'ippattu,' instead of 'irupattu,' which would be in correspondence with the Tamil 'irubadu' and the Telugu 'iruvei.'

In the Canarese neuter noun of number 'eraḍu,' *two*, 'e' is used instead of 'i' as the initial vowel; but in this point the Canarese stands alone, and in all the compound numerals, even in the Canarese, the 'i' re-appears. Were it not for the existence of the numeral adjective 'ir-u' or 'ir,' we might naturally suppose the 'i' of the Tamil 'iraṇḍu' and of the obsolete Canarese 'iraḍu' to be, not a component element of the root, but an euphonic prefix, intended to facilitate pronunciation. 'i' is very commonly so prefixed in Tamil; *e.g.*, 'râ,' *night* (from the Sanscrit 'râtri'), becomes 'irâ,' and by a further change 'iravu.' This supposition with respect to the euphonic character of the 'i' of 'iraṇḍu,' might appear to be confirmed by the circumstance that it disappears altogether from the numeral nouns of the Telugu, the Malayâlam, and several other dialects. The existence, however, of the numeral adjective 'iru' or 'ir,' in every one of the Drâvidian dialects, and its use in all the compound numbers (such as 'twenty' and 'two hundred'), suffice to prove that the 'i' of the Tamil-Canarese numeral noun 'iraḍu' is not merely euphonic, but is a part of the root itself, and that 'iraḍu,' the neuter noun of number, has been formed from 'ir' by the addition of a formative suffix. A comparison of the various forms shows clearly that 'ir,' euphonised into 'iru,' was the primitive form of the numeral adjective *two:* and we have now only to inquire into the characteristics of the numeral noun.

The Canarese 'eraḍu' (or rather 'iraḍu,' as it must have been originally) is the earliest extant form of the noun of number. The Tamil is 'iraṇḍu,' 'ḍ' having been euphonically changed to 'ṇḍ.' Though there is a nasal in the Tamil word which is now in use, the Tamil noun-adjective *double* bears witness to the existence of an earlier form, which was destitute of the nasal, and which must have been identical with the Canarese. The Tam. word 'iraṭṭ-u,' *double*, is formed directly from 'iraḍ-u,' by the doubling of the 'ḍ,' as is usually done when a noun is converted into an adjective; and the euphonic change of 'ḍḍ' into 'ṭṭ' is according to rule. 'du' or 'ḍu' is a very common termination of neuter nouns, especially of appellative neuters, in all the Drâvidian languages. Thus, from the root 'kiṛa,' Tam., *old*, is formed 'kiṛaḍu, *that which is old*.' The 'ṇ' which is inserted before 'ḍ' in the Tamil 'iraṇḍu' is evidently euphonic, and is in perfect accordance with the ordinary phonetic usages of the Drâvidian languages. In Telugu every word ending in 'ḍu,' receives in pronunciation an obscure nasal, whether it has a place in the written language or not; and there are many instances in Tamil also of the insertion of this nasal before a final 'ḍu' for the sake of euphonisation, when it is quite certain that there was no such nasal originally in the word in which it is found: *e.g.*, 'âṇḍu,' *there*, 'îṇḍu,' *here*, and 'yâṇḍu,' *where?*' are euphonised forms of 'âḍu,' 'îḍu,' and 'yâḍu.' Compare also 'karaṇḍi,' *a spoon*, Tamil, with the more primitive Telugu 'gariṭe.' The Tamil noun of number, signifying *two*, must, therefore, have been 'iraḍu' originally. In the Gônd 'ranu,' the 'ḍ' of 'iranḍu' has disappeared altogether; a change which is in accordance with the Malayâla corruption of 'ondu,' *one*, into 'onna.' The Ûrâon word for *two*, 'enotan,' is probably Drâvidian. In Ûrâon 'otan' (from the Hindi 'gotan') is a suffix of each of the first three numerals; consequently 'en' is to be regarded as the Ûrâon root, and this seems to be analogous to the Drâvidian 'er.'

There are no analogies to 'ir,' *two*, in any of the Indo-European languages, and I am doubtful whether any real analogies to it are discoverable even in the Scythian group, except perhaps in the Caucasian.

The Brahui vindicates its claim to be regarded as in part Drâvidian, or at least as the inheritor of an ancient Drâvidian element, by the close affinity of its second and third numerals to those of the Drâvidian tongues. In Brahui *two* is 'irat;' and when this word is compared with the Brahui 'asit,' *one*, and 'musit,' *three*, it is evident that in each of these instances the final 'it' or 'at,' is a formative suffix which has been appended to the root. Consequently 'ir,' the root of 'ir-at,' is absolutely identical with the Drâvidian 'ir.' Even the Brahui formative evinces Drâvidian affinities; *e.g.*, compare 'irat' with the Canarese noun of number 'eraḍu,' and especially with the Tamil derivative 'iraṭṭ-u,' *double*.

The nearest analogies to the Drâvidian 'ir' which I have noticed in other families of tongues, are in the Caucasian dialects; *e.g.*, in the Georgian 'ori;' in the Suanian (a dialect of the Georgian) 'eru' or 'ieru;' in the Lazian 'zur;' and in the Mingrelian 'shiri:' compare also the Armenian 'ergov.'

In the Samoïede family of tongues, several words are found which bear at first sight some resemblance to the Drâvidian 'ir.' These are 'sit,' 'side,' and especially 'sire' or 'siri.' It seems improbable, however, that the Drâvidian 'ir' arose from the softening off of the initial 's' of these words; for in the Finnish family this same 's' appears as 'k;' whence *two* is in some dialects of that family 'kit;' in Magyar 'ket,' 'ketto;' and in Lappish 'quekt.' It has also been shown that an initial 'k' is a radical element in the majority of the Scythian words for *two;* and hence, though the Mongolian 'kur-in' (for 'kuyar-in'), *twenty,* becomes in Manchu 'or-in,' in Turkish 'igirmi;' we cannot venture to compare this Manchu 'or' with the Drâvidian 'ir' or 'er;' for it is certain that the latter was never preceded by 'k,' or any other consonant, so far back as the Drâvidian languages can be traced.

Three.—The neuter noun of number signifying *three* or *a triad,* is in Canarese 'mûru;' in Telugu 'mûḍu;' in ancient Telugu, as quoted by Pliny, and testified to by native grammarians 'moḍoga;' in Tamil 'mûnRu' (pronounced 'mûndru,' 'mûndu,' and 'mûṇu'); in Malayâlam 'mûnna;' in Tulu 'mûji;' in Gônd 'mûnd;' in Tuda 'mûd';' in Ûrâon 'man-otan.'

The numeral adjective *three,* which is employed in *three persons, thirty, three hundred,* and similar compounds, is either 'mû' or 'mŭ.' The long 'mû' is found in the Tamil and modern Canarese epicene nouns, 'mûvar,' 'mûvar-u,' *three persons,* and in the Canarese 'mûpattu,' *thirty.* The shorter form 'mu,' is used in *three hundred;* which in every one of the Drâvidian dialects is 'mŭnnûru; and we see it also in the Tamil 'muppattu,' and the Telugu 'mupphei,' *thirty,* and in the Telugu 'muggar-u,' *three persons.*

The primitive and most characteristic form of the neuter noun of number is evidently that of the Canarese 'mûr-u,' from which it is clear that the Tamil 'mûnR-u' ('mundr-u') has been derived, by the same nasalizing process as that by which 'oRu,' *one,* was converted into 'onRu.'

It was shown in the section on 'Sounds,' that the Tamil 'r' is often changed into 'ḍ' in Telugu: hence 'mûr-u' and 'mûḍ-u,' are identical; and it is more probable that 'mûḍ-u' has been altered from 'mûr-u,' than that 'mûr-u' was altered from 'mûḍ-u. 's' and 'r,' evince in many languages a tendency to interchange, generally by the hardening of 's' into 'r;' consequently the Brahui 'mus' ('mus-it'), *three,* is closely allied to the Canarese 'mûr' (possibly it was the original form of the word), and still more closely to the Tulu 'mûji.'

It is doubtful whether the 'r' of 'mûr-u,' should be considered as a formative, or as a part of the ancient root. On the whole, it seems probable that the 'r' is radical, for I have not met with any reliable instance of the use of a final formative in 'r-u.' The final consonants of 'âʀu,' Tam., *six*, and of 'êṛu,' *seven*, belong unquestionably to the roots of those numerals; and the existence in the Brahui word for *three* of an 's,' corresponding to the Tamil-Canarese 'r,' would seem to decide the question, especially seeing that this 's' is followed by the particle 'it,' which is itself a formative. Moreover, when we compare 'mun-nûʀu,' *three hundred* (the same in all the dialects), with 'in-nûʀu,' *two hundred*, in Telugu and Canarese; and when it is remembered that the latter has certainly been softened from 'ir-nûʀu' (in Tamil 'iru-nûʀu'), it seems to be probable that 'mun-nûʀu' has been formed in a similar manner from 'mur-nûʀu,' and consequently that 'mur,' not 'mu,' was the original root of this numeral. The same conclusion is indicated by a comparison of the Telugu 'iddaru,' *two persons*, and 'muggaru,' *three persons.*

It seems probable, therefore, that 'mu' originally was followed by a consonant; and the softening off of this consonant would naturally account for the occasional lengthening of 'mu' into 'mû.'

I have not been able to discover any analogy to this numeral, either in the Scythian or in the Indo-European tongues. The only Extra-Indian resemblance to it is that which is found in the Brahui; and this circumstance is a striking proof of the existence in the Brahui of a distinctively Drâvidian element. The total absence of analogy to the Drâvidian 'mur,' in other families of languages, leads me to suppose that it must have been derived directly from some Drâvidian verbal root. The Latin 'secundus,' is undoubtedly derived from 'sequor;' and Bopp connects the Indo-European 'tri,' *three*, with the Sanscrit root 'tri,' *to pass over, to go beyond*, signifying *that which 'goes beyond' two*. If this derivation of 'tri' be not regarded as too fanciful, a similar derivation of 'mur,' from a Drâvidian verbal root, may easily be discovered. In those languages there are two verbal roots which present some points of resemblance, viz., 'mîʀ-u,' Tam. and Can., *to go beyond, to pass, to exceed, to transgress;* and 'muʀ,' *to turn*, an obsolete root, which is contained in 'muʀ-ei,' Tam., *order, succession, a turn* (*e.g.*, 'idu un muʀei,' *this is your turn*). 'mâʀ-u,' Tam., Tel., and Can. *to change*, and the Tel. noun 'mâr-u,' *a time, a course*, seem to be correlative roots.

Four.—The Drâvidian noun of number signifying *four*, or *a quaternion*, is in Canarese 'nâlku;' in Telugu 'nâlugu;' in Tamil 'nâu-gu;' in Tuda 'nonku' or 'nonk;' in Gônd 'nâlû;' in Ûrâon 'nâkh-otan.'

The adjectival or crude form of this numeral is 'nâl' or 'nal.' In Tamil it is 'nâl-u,' in Malayâlam 'nâl-a,' in some Telugu compounds 'nal;' and this adjectival form is often used as a noun of number instead of 'nâlku,' &c. In composition 'nâl' undergoes some changes. The quantity of the included vowel, which is long in all the rest of the dialects, is short in Telugu compound numbers: *e.g.*, compare the Tamil 'nâʀpadu,' the Canarese 'nâlvattu,' and the Malayâlam 'nâlpadu,' *forty*, with the Telugu 'nălubhei;' and the Tamil 'nân-nûʀu,' and the Canarese 'nâl-nûʀu, *four hundred*, with the Telugu 'năn-nûru.'

The final 'l' also is subject to change. In Tamil it is changed into 'ʀ' before 'p,' as in 'nâʀpadu,' *forty;* and before 'n' it is assimilated and becomes 'n,' in both Tamil and Telugu; *e.g.*, 'nânnûʀu' (in the one), and 'nannûʀu' (in the other), *four hundred.* These changes of 'l,' however, are purely euphonic.

It is evident from a comparison of the above forms, that 'nâl' (or, as the Telugu seems to prefer it, 'năl') was the primitive shape of this numeral; to which 'ku' or 'gu' was subsequently added as a formative, in order to constitute it a neuter noun of number. This formative 'ku' (pronounced 'gu') is a very common one in the Drâvidian languages; *e.g.*, 'kaḍu-gu,' Tam., *mustard*, from 'kaḍu,' *pungent.* In Tamil the only numeral to which 'ku' or 'gu' is appended is 'nâl:' but in Telugu we find it used not only by 'nâlu-gu,' *four*, but also by *five, six, seven, eight*, and *nine*, in forming *rational* plurals; *e.g.*, from 'aru,' *six*, is formed 'ârugur-u,' *six persons.* In such connexions the Tamil uses 'v' euphonic instead of 'g' (*e.g.*, 'aʀu-(v)-ar),' which proves that 'gu' does not add to the grammatical expression, but is a mere euphonic formative. Even in Telugu 'âruvur-u' may be used instead of 'ârugur-u.'

The change of 'l,' in Tamil, into 'n,' before the 'k' of this appended formative, 'ku,' is an euphonic peculiarity which requires to be noticed. In modern Tamil 'l,' in this conjunction, would be changed into 'ʀ;' but the change of 'l' into 'n,' before 'k' or 'g,' which we find in the Tamil noun of number, 'nân-gu,' is one which, though now obsolete, appears to have been usual at an earlier period of the history of the language; *e.g.*, compare 'Pang-guni,' the Tamil name of the month *March — April*, with the Sanscrit name of that month, 'Phalguna,' from which it is known to have been derived. This change of 'l' into 'n,' in 'nân-gu,' must have been made at a very early period, seeing that we find it also in the Tuda 'nonk.'

In the entire family of the Indo-European languages there is not one language which contains a numeral signifying *four*, which in the smallest degree resembles the Drâvidian 'nâl.' Here the Brahui also fails us; for it is only in the first three Brahui numerals that we find traces of Drâvidian influences, and the rest of the numerals of that language from *four* to *ten* inclusive, are derived from the Sanscrit.

Though other analogies fail us, in this instance Ugrian affinities are more than usually distinct. The resemblance between the Finnish tongues and the Drâvidian, with respect to the numeral *four*, amounts to identity, and cannot have been accidental. Compare with the Drâvidian 'nal,' the Tcheremiss 'nil;' the Mordwin 'nile,' 'nilen;' the Vogul 'nila;' the Ostiak 'nül,' 'nel,' 'njedla,' 'nieda,' 'njeda;' the Finuish proper 'neljâ;' the Lappish 'nielj,' 'nelje,' 'nellâ;' the Magyar 'nêgy' (pronounced 'neidj'). The root of all these numerals is evidently 'nil' or 'nel,' the analogy of which to the Drâvidian 'nâl' or 'nal,' is very remarkable. The Magyar 'negy,' has lost the original 'l,' through the tendency, inherent in the Finnish idioms, to regard 'l' and 'd' as interchangeable. The Ostiak 'njedla' or 'nedla,' in which 'd' and 'l' form but one letter, a cerebral, constitutes the middle point of agreement. A similar softening down of the 'l' of 'nal,' appears in the Tulu, in which *fourteen* (ten-four) is 'pad'nâji.'

Five.—The Drâvidian numeral noun *five*, is in Canarese and Telugu 'eid-u;' in Tamil 'eind-u;' in the poetical and colloquial dialects of the Tamil 'anj-u;' in Malayâlam 'añjcha;' in Tulu 'ein-u' or 'ein-i;' in Tuda 'ûtsh' or 'ûj.' The Gônd has 'seighan' or 'seiyan,' —a word which is derived like 'sârûn,' *six*, from the use of 's' as an euphonic prefix: 'eiyan' is to be regarded as the correct form of the Gônd numeral. The Ûrâon, and other rude dialects of the North-Drâvidian family, exhibit no analogy to any of the Drâvidian numerals above *four*. In Telugu compounds, the word for *five* is not 'eid-u,' but 'hên-u;' *e.g.*, 'padihên-u,' *fifteen*. In this case the initial 'h' is purely euphonic, and used for the prevention of *hiatus*, as in the parallel instances of 'pada(h)âʀu,' *sixteen*, and 'padi(h)êḍu,' *seventeen*. The Telugu possesses, therefore, two forms of *five*, 'eid-u' and 'ên-u;' and the Tamil 'eindu' shows how 'eidu' was converted into 'ênu,' viz., by the insertion of an euphonic nasal and the subsequent assimilation to it of the dental.

The numeral adjective *five*, is in most of the Drâvidian dialects 'ei,' in Telugu 'ê.' In Tamil, and also occasionally in Canarese, 'ei' is in combination converted into 'ein' or 'eim,' by the addition of an euphonic nasal. Thus *fifty* (five tens) is in Canarese 'eivatt-u;' in

Tamil 'eimbad-u' ('ei-m-pad-u);' in Telugu 'êbhei' ('ê-bhei).' *Five hundred* is in Canarese 'ein-nûR-u,' in Tamil 'eiñ-ñjûRu,' in Telugu 'ê-nûR-u.' We see the numeral adjective *five,* and the noun of number *five,* in juxta-position in the Tamil 'ei-(y)-eind-u,' *five times five.* 'ei' remains also in its pure, unnasalised form in the Tamil 'eivar' ('ei-(v)-ar'), *five persons.* The nasal 'n' or 'm,' which follows 'ei,' in the compounds 'eimbad-u,' *fifty,* and 'eiññjûR-u,' *five hundred,* is not to be confounded with the 'n' of the Tamil 'eind-u,' or the Telugu 'ên-u,' but proceeds from a different source. It is an euphonic adjectival increment; and is added by rule, not only to this numeral adjective 'ei,' *five,* but to many similar words which consist of a single syllable, of which the final is a long open vowel, when such words are used adjectivally. Thus, we find in Tamil not only such compounds as 'eintiṇei' ('ei-n-tiṇei'), *the five conditions,* and 'eimpulan' ('ei-m-pulan'), *the five senses;* but also 'keinnoḍi' ('kei-n-noḍi'), *a snap of the finger,* and 'mângkai' ('mâ-ng-kai'), *a mangoe,* literally *the fruit of the* 'mâ.'

This adjectival, euphonic addition is an abbreviation of 'am' (or 'an' before a dental), and is probably from the same origin as the inflexional increment 'in' or 'an.' See the section on 'Nouns.'

It may be doubted whether the Tamil-Canarese 'ei,' or the Telugu 'ê' is the better representative of the original numeral; but the evidence of the various dialects preponderates in favour of 'ei.'

A remarkable resemblance must have been noticed between the Sanscrit 'panchan,' *five* (in Tamil 'panja'), and the true Tamil 'anju,' and the Malayâla 'añjcha.' The resemblance is so great that it has been supposed by some that the Drâvidian word was derived from the Sanscrit; but instead of this supposition being confirmed by a comparison of the various Drâvidian idioms, and of the various forms under which this numeral appears, as would be the case if the analogy were real, it is utterly dissipated by comparison, like the apparent analogy which has already been observed between the Malayâla 'onna,' *one,* and the Latin 'un-us.'

The primitive, radical form of the Drâvidian numeral *five* is 'ei' or 'ê,' as appears from its use as a numeral adjective. The abstract or neuter noun of number is generally formed from the numeral adjective by the addition of some formative. The formative suffix which is added to 'ir-u,' *two,* is 'ḍu;' and by the addition of 'd-u,' a corresponding formative, 'ei' becomes 'ei-du, *five,* or *five things;* which is in itself a neuter noun, though, like all such nouns, it is capable of being used without change as an adjective. This formative suffix 'd-u' is an exceedingly common formative of neuter appellative nouns in the Drâvidian languages, particularly in the Tamil; and is doubtless borrowed from, or allied to, the termination of 'ad-u,' *it*, the neuter singular of the demonstrative pronoun. 'eid-u,' the numeral noun of both the Canarese and the Telugu, is evidently the original and most regular form of this word. 'eid-u' could not have been corrupted from 'anj-u,' or even from 'eind-u,' but the corruption of 'eind-u' and 'anj-u' from an original 'eid-u' will be shown to be in perfect accordance with usage.

The first change was from 'eid-u' to 'eind-u,' by the insertion of an euphonic nasal, as in the former instances of 'iraḍ-u,' *two*, changed into 'iranḍ-u.' This euphonic insertion of 'n,' after certain vowels, is so common in Tamil, that it may almost be regarded as a rule of the language; and hence preterite participles which end in Canarese in 'ed-u,' always end in Tamil in 'n-du;' *e.g.*, compare 'aled-u,' Can., *having wandered*, with 'aleind-u,' Tam. When 'eid-u' had been changed into 'eind-u,' Tamil usages of pronunciation necessitated a further change into 'einj-u' or 'anj-u.' It is a rule of the colloquial Tamil that when 'nd' is preceded by 'ei' or 'i' it is changed in pronunciation into 'nj.' This change is systematically and uniformly practised in the colloquial dialect; and it has found its way into the classical and poetical dialect also.

Moreover, in changing 'eind' into 'einj,' there is a further change of the vowel from 'ei' to 'a,' in consequence of which 'einj' becomes 'anj.' This change is almost always apparent in the Malayâlam, and also in the pronunciation of the mass of the people in Tamil. Thus, 'paʀeindu,' Tam., *having spoken*, becomes in Malayâlam 'paʀaññju;' and in this instance we see illustrated the change both of 'ei' into 'a,' and of 'nd' into 'ñj:' consequently the perfect regularity of the change of 'eind-u,' *five*, into 'anj-u' and 'añjch-a' is established. Where the Malayâlam does not change 'nd' into 'ññj,' it changes it into 'nn;' *e.g.*, 'naḍandu,' Tam. *having walked*, is in Malayâlam 'naṭannu.' This illustrates the process by which 'eind-u' became 'ein-u' in Tulu, and 'ên-u' in the Telugu compound, 'padi(h)ên-u,' *fifteen*.

It is thus evident that the apparent resemblance of the Drâvidian 'anju' to the Sanscrit 'panchan' is illusory. It entirely disappears on examination, and the slight resemblance which does exist is found to arise from the operation of Drâvidian principles of sound. Consequently 'ei' or 'ê,' must be regarded as the sole representative of the Drâvidian numeral, and with this it is evident that neither 'panchan,' nor any other Indo-European form has any analogy whatever.

In some of the Finnish tongues the word for *five* has some slight resemblance to the neuter Drâvidian numeral 'eid-u.' The Vogoul is 'at;' the Ostiak 'uut' or 'wet;' the Magyar 'öt' (pronounced somewhat like 'êt.' I am doubtful, however, whether this resemblance is not merely accidental; for the final 't' of the Ugrian words for *five* appears to be radical; whereas the final 'd' of the Drâvidian noun of number, 'eid-u,' is simply a neuter formative. The Chinese 'u' may, perhaps, be compared with the Drâvidian numeral adjective 'ei.'

In some languages the word used to signify *five* properly means *a hand*, or is derived from a word which has that meaning,—the number of fingers in each hand being five. In Lepsius's opinion, the word for *ten* which is used in all the Indo-European dialects, had its origin in the Maeso-Gothic 'tai-hun,' *two hands.* Applying this principle to the Drâvidian languages, 'ei,' *five,* might be presumed to be derived from 'kei,' Tam., *a hand,* by the very common process of the softening away of the initial consonant. On the other hand, I do not consider 'kei,' *a hand,* to be itself a primitive, underived word. I have little doubt but that it is derived from 'ki,' 'gê,' 'gêy,' or 'chey,' *to do,* like the corresponding Sanscrit word 'kara,' *a hand,* from 'kri' *to do*; and in accordance with this opinion, I find that 'kei,' Tam., *a hand,* has in Telugu become 'chê,' just as the Canarese 'gêy,' *to do,* has become 'chey,' in both Tamil and Telugu.

Hence the derivation of 'ei,' *five,* from 'kei,' *a hand,* becomes impeded by the previous question, is not 'kei' itself a derivative?

Possibly 'ei' may be more nearly allied to the High Tamil abstract noun 'ei-mei,' *closeness, nearness, a crowd,* from an obsolete verbal root 'ei,' *to be close together.* In this case the use of 'ei' as a numeral, would take its origin from the *close* juxta-position and relation of the five fingers of the hand.

Six.—In all the Drâvidian dialects, the difference which is found to exist between the neuter noun of number *six* and the numeral adjective is extremely small. The numeral noun is 'âʀu' in Tamil, Telugu, and Canarese; 'âʀa' in Malayâlam; and 'âr' or 'ôr' in Tuda; in Gônd 's-ârûn.' In Tulu it is 'âji,' a form which bears the same relation to 'âʀu' that 'mûji,' Tulu, *three,* does to the Canarese 'mûru.'

The numeral adjective differs from the noun of number with respect to the quantity of the initial vowel alone; and in some cases even that difference does not exist. In all Tamil compounds in which 'âʀ-u' is used adjectivally, it is shortened to 'ăʀ-u;' *e.g.*, 'aʀubadu,' *sixty.* The vowel is short in the Can. 'aravattu,' and the Telugu 'aʀuvei,' *sixty;* whilst it is long in the higher compound 'ârunûru,

Can., and 'ÂRNÛRU,' Tel., *six hundred*. In Tamil it is short in *six hundred*, but long, as in the other dialects, in *six thousand*. Probably 'ÂR-u' was the primitive form of this numeral, the initial vowel of which, like the included vowel of the personal pronouns, was euphonically shortened in composition.

No analogy whatever can be traced between this Drâvidian numeral and any word for *six* that is contained in the Indo-European languages; and I am very doubtful whether any Scythian analogies are discoverable. In Magyar *six* is 'hat;' in the Turkish languages 'álty,' 'âlte,' &c. It may be supposed to be possible that the first syllable of the latter word, 'âl,' is allied to the Drâvidian 'ÂR',' in virtue of that interchange of 'l' and 'r,' which is so common in the Scythian tongues. It may be conceived also, that the Turkish 'alt,' and the Magyar 'hat' are allied. I have no faith, however, in these indistinct resemblances of sound; for the Magyar 'at' seems originally to have had an initial consonant. 'kot' is the corresponding numeral in Lappish, and 'kûsi' in Finnish; in Tcheremiss 'kut;' whereas, there is no reason to suppose that the Drâvidian 'ÂR' ever commenced with a consonant; nor do I suppose it very likely that in the rude Scythian tongues, in which even the numerals of cognate dialects differ from one another so widely, any real analogy with the Drâvidian numerals above *four* or *five* would be discoverable.

Seven.—The Drâvidian noun of number *seven* is 'êṛ-u' in Tamil, 'èṛ-a' in Malayâlam, 'êḷ-u' in Canarese and Tulu, 'êḍ-u' in Telugu. These differences are in accordance with the rule that the Tamil deep, liquid, semi-vowel 'ṛ' becomes 'ḍ,' in Telugu, and 'ḷ,' in Canarese. In the Tuda this numeral is 'êr' or 'üd;' in Mahadeo Gônd 'y-ênû' or 'y-êtû;' in Seoni Gônd 'êro.'

The numeral adjective *seven*, which is used in the compound numbers *seventy*, *seven hundred*, &c., exhibits a few trivial differences from the noun of number. In Tamil 'êṛ-u' is shortened to 'eṛ-u' when used adjectivally, like 'âR-u,' *six*, which is similarly shortened to 'aR-u.'

In Canarese *seventy* is 'eppattu,' in which not only is 'ê' shortened to 'e,' but the radical consonant 'ḷ,' answering to the Tamil 'ṛ,' has been assimilated to the initial consonant of the succeeding word.

In 'êḷnûru,' Can., *seven hundred*, this assimilation has not taken place. In Telugu, the 'ḍ' of 'êḍ-u' does not appear to be very persistent. In 'êḷnûRu,' *seven hundred*, 'ḍ' becomes 'ḷ' as in the Canarese; and in 'ḍebbei,' *seventy* (for 'eḍubhei'), the initial vowel 'e' has been displaced, according to a peculiar usage of the Telugu, which was explained in the section on 'Sounds.'

This displacement of the initial vowel shows that the 'e' of the suppositious 'edubhei' was short, as in the corresponding Tamil and Canarese compounds.

It cannot be determined with perfect certainty which of the three consonants, 'ṛ,' 'ḍ,' or 'ḷ,' was the primitive one in this numeral; but as the Tamil 'ṛ' changes more easily into 'ḷ' or 'ḍ,' than either of those consonants into 'ṛ,' and could also be changed more easily than they into the 'n' of the Gônd, probably 'êr-u,' as in Tamil, is to be regarded as the primitive form of this numeral; from which 'êḍ-u' and 'êḷ-u' were derived.

No resemblance to this Drâvidian numeral is to be found in any of the Indo-European languages; and the slight apparent resemblances which may perhaps be traced in some of the Scythian tongues, are not I fear, trustworthy. Compare with the Telugu 'êḍ-u,' the Turkish 'yedi;' the Turkish of Yarkand 'yettah' (the root of which appears in the Ottoman Turkish 'yet-mish,' *seventy*); and the Magyar 'het.'

In Armenian, *seven* is 'yotn,' in Tahitian 'hetu.' The 'h' of the Magyar numeral and the 'y' of the Turkish seem to be identical; but both have been derived from a harder sound, as will appear on comparing the Magyar 'het' with the Lappish 'kietya,' and with the corresponding Finnish 'seit,' in 'seitzemân.'

Eight.—The Tamil numeral noun 'eṭṭu,' *eight*, bears a remarkable resemblance to the corresponding numeral of the Indo-European family, which is in Latin 'octo,' in Gothic 'ahtau; and especially to 'aṭṭa,' the manner in which 'ashṭan,' Sans. *eight*, is written and pronounced in classical Tamil, in which it is occasionally used in compounds; hence it has naturally been supposed by some, that the Tamil 'eṭṭu' has been derived from, or is identical with, this Sanscrit derivative 'aṭṭa.' It will be found, however, that this resemblance, though so close as to amount almost to identity of sound, is accidental; and that it disappears on investigation and comparison, like the resemblance between 'onna' and 'unus,' 'anju' and 'pancha.'

The Drâvidian noun of number *eight* is in Tamil 'eṭṭu,' in Malayâlam 'eṭṭ-a,' in Canarese 'eṇṭ-u,' in Telugu 'enimidi' or 'enmidi,' in Tulu 'eṇuma,' in Gônd 'anumâr' or 'armûr,' in Tuda 'etthu,' 'vet,' 'oet' or 'yeṭa.'

The corresponding numeral adjective, which should by rule exhibit the primitive form of the word, is generally 'eṇ.' In Tamil 'eṇ' is used adjectivally for *eight* in all compound numerals; *e.g.*, 'eṇ-badu, *eighty*, 'eṇ-nûru,' *eight hundred*, as also in miscellaneous compounds, such as 'eṇ-kaṇan,' *he who has eight eyes*. The same form is used adverbially in 'eṇ-êṛu,' *eight times seven*. In Canarese, in which the numeral noun is 'eṇṭu,' 'eṇ' is used as the numeral adjective in 'eṇvar-u,' *eight persons;* whilst in 'embattu,' *eighty*, 'n' is changed into 'm,' through the influence of the labial initial of the second member of the compound. In 'eṇṭu-nûru,' *eight hundred*, the numeral noun is used adjectivally instead of the numeral adjective. The Telugu noun of number 'enimidi,' *eight*, differs considerably from the Tamil 'eṭṭu,' and the Canarese 'eṇṭu;' but the difference diminishes when the numeral adjectives are compared. The Telugu numeral adjective used in 'enabhei,' *eighty*, is 'ena,' which is obviously identical with the Tamil-Canarese 'eṇ.' In 'enamaṇḍru,' or 'enamaṇḍugur-u,' *eight persons*, and 'yenamannûru,' *eight hundred*, the 'm' of 'enimidi,' *eight*, evinces a tendency to assume the place of an essential part of the root. It will be shown, however, that 'midi' is not a part of the root of this numeral, but a suffix; and consequently 'eṇ' or 'en,' without the addition of 'm,' may be concluded to be the true numeral adjective and also the root itself.

Thus, the apparent resemblance of the Tamil 'eṭṭu' to the Sanscrit derivative 'aṭṭa' (euphonised from 'ashṭa'), disappears as soon as the various forms under which it is found are compared.

The primitive form of the neuter noun of number derived from 'en,' is evidently that which the Canarese has retained, viz, 'eṇṭu,' which is directly formed from 'eṇ' by the addition of 'ṭu,' the phonetic equivalent of 'ḍu'—a common formative of neuter nouns, and one of which we have already seen a specimen in 'eraḍu,' *two*. The Tamil 'eṭṭu' has been derived from 'eṇṭu' by a process which is in accordance with many precedents. It is true that in general, the Tamil refrains from assimilating the nasal of such words as 'eṇṭu,' and oftentimes it inserts a nasal where there is none in Canarese; *e.g.*, 'iraṇḍu,' Tam., *two*, compared with the Can. 'eraḍu:' still this rule, though general, is not universal, and is sometimes reversed. Thus, 'peṇṭe,' Can., *a hen*, (in modern Canarese 'heṇṭeyu,') has in Tamil become 'peṭṭei'—a change exactly parallel to that of 'eṇṭu' into 'eṭṭu.'

Some difficulty is involved in the explanation of 'enimidi,' the Telugu noun of number which corresponds to 'eṇṭu.' 'eni' or 'ena' (as in 'enabhei,' *eighty*), is evidently identical with the Tamil-Canarese 'eṇ:' but what is the origin of the suffix 'midi?' This 'midi' becomes 'ma' in some instances; *e.g.*, 'enama-ṇḍru,' *eight persons;* and the Tuḷu noun of number, *eight*, is 'eṇuma.' Shall we consider 'midi' to be synonomous with 'padi,' *ten;* and 'enimidi,' *eight,* to be a compound word, which was meant to signify *two from ten?*

It will be shown under the next head that in the Telugu 'tommidi,' *nine,* 'midi' is without doubt identical with 'padi,' *ten.* If so, there would seem to be a valid reason for supposing that the 'midi' of 'enimidi,' *eight,* is also derived from the same source, and appended to 'en' with the same intent.

It will be shown in our examination of the Drâvidian numeral *ten* that 'padi' has become greatly corrupted in compounds, especially in Telugu; in which the second syllable has disappeared in compounds above *twenty.* If 'midi,' identical with 'padi, were liable to a similar corruption, as is probable enough, we may see how 'enimidi' would be softened into 'enama' (in 'enamaṇḍru), and also into 'eṇuma' in Tulu.

It is a characteristic of the Scythian languages that they use for *eight* and *nine* compounds which signify *ten minus two* and *ten minus one.* In some instances an original uncompounded word is used for eight: but *nine* is always a compound. The Drâvidian word for *nine* is, I have no doubt, formed in this very manner; and this seems to be a rational explanation of the origin of the Telugu word for *eight.*

On the other hand, in the Tamil-Canarese idioms, 'eṇ' by itself is used to signify *eight,* without any trace of the use in conjunction with it of the word 'pattu' or 'padi,' *ten.* It is also deserving of notice that in the Telugu 'enabhei,' *eighty,* the second member of 'enimidi' has disappeared.

It is difficult to determine whether the disuse of *ten* as a component element in the numeral *eight* of the Tamil and Canarese is to be regarded as a corruption, or whether the use of *ten* by the Telugu in the construction of *eight* is itself a corruption, arising from the influence and attraction of the principle which was adopted in the formation of the next numeral *nine.* On the whole, I consider the latter supposition as the more probable, and therefore regard the Tamil-Canarese 'eṇ' (in Telugu 'ena,') as the primitive shape of this Drâvidian numeral. Max Müller's supposition that 'en' is identical with 'er,' properly 'ir,' *two,* is quite inadmissible.

'eṇ' has no resemblance to any numeral belonging to any other language, whether Indo-European or Scythian; and it cannot, I think, be doubted, that it was first adopted into the list of numerals by the Drâvidian people themselves. We have not to go far out of our way to seek for a derivation. 'eṇ' is a primitive and very common Drâvidian root, signifying either *to reckon* or *a number,* according as it is used as a verb or as a noun. In Tamil it is 'eṇ,' in Telugu 'enn-u,' in Canarese 'eṇ-usu.' We have an instance of its use as a noun in 'eṇ-suvaḍi,' Tam., *a book of Arithmetic,* literally *a number book.* After the Drâvidians of the first age had learned to count *seven,* they found they required a higher numeral, which they placed immediately above *seven* and called 'eṇ,' *a number*—an appropriate enough term for perhaps the highest number which they were then accustomed to reckon.

A similar mode of seizing upon a word which denotes properly *a number* or *any number,* and using it restrictively to denote some one number in particular—generally a newly invented, high number—is found in other languages besides the Drâvidian. Thus, in Lappish, 'lokke,' *ten,* means literally, *a number,* from 'lokket,' *to count.*

Nine.—In all the Drâvidian idioms the numeral *nine* is a compound word, which is used indifferently, and without change, as a noun of number and as a numeral adjective.

The second member of the compound numeral *nine* is identical with, or evidently derived from, the numeral *ten,* the differences between it and that numeral being such as can be accounted for by the phonetic tendencies of the various Drâvidian dialects.

The principal forms which this numeral assumes are the following: in Tamil it is 'onbad-u,' in Canarese 'ombhatt-u,' in Telugu 'tommidi,' in Tulu 'ormbo,' 'orambu,' or 'worambu,' in Tuda 'yenbot,' in Kota 'worpatthu:' in each of which instances the second member of the compound plainly represents *ten.*

In Tamil *ten* is 'patt-u;' *nine* is 'onbad-u' ('on-pad-u,' euphonically, 'on-badu'): and not only is it evident that 'patt-u' and 'pad-u' are allied, but the resemblance becomes identity when 'pad-u,' the second member of 'onbad-u,' is compared with the representative of *ten* in 'irubad-u,' *twenty'*—literally *twice ten*—and similar compound numerals. Moreover 'onbad-u' itself becomes 'onbatt-u' when used adverbially, *e.g.,* 'onbatt'—êṛ-u,' *nine times seven.'* In ancient Canarese *ten* was 'patt-u,' as in Tamil. In modern Canarese it changes by rule into 'hatt-u;' nevertheless the original labial retains its place in the compounds 'ombhatt-u,' *nine,* and 'embatt-u,' *eighty;* from which it is evident that in Canarese *nine* is formed from *ten,* by means of an auxiliary prefix, as in Tamil. In Telugu alone there is some difference between the word which separately signifies *ten* and the second member of 'tommidi,' the compound numeral *nine. Ten* is in Telugu 'padi,' whilst *nine* is not 'tompadi,' or 'tombadi,' but 'tommidi;' and *nine persons* is 'tommaṇḍugur-u.' It can scarcely be doubted, however, that 'tommidi' has been euphonised from 'tompadi.' In the other compound numerals of the Telugu (*twenty, thirty,* &c.,) in which 'padi' forms of necessity the second member, the corruption of 'padi' into 'bhei' or 'vei' is still greater than in the instances now before us. It may be regarded, consequently, as certain that the second member of the various Drâvidian words for *nine* is identical with *ten.* We have, therefore, now to inquire only into the origin and signification of the first member of the compound.

In the Tamil 'onbad-u,' 'on' is the auxiliary prefix by which 'padu' is specialised; and this 'on' is evidently identical with the Canarese 'om,' in 'ombhatt-u.' Max Müller, naturally enough, concluded it to be derived from 'on,' the first portion of the Tamil 'ondru,' *one*:' but this derivation, though plausible, is inconsistent with many facts which will be adduced. In Telugu the auxiliary prefix of 'tommidi,' *nine,* is 'tom,' which is undoubtedly equivalent to 'om' in Canarese, and 'on' in Tamil; and as it is more likely that the 't' of 'tom' should have been softened away in the other idioms than arbitrarily added by the Telugu, it seems probable, *à priori* that the original form of this numeral prefix was 'tom,' as in Telugu, rather than 'om,' or 'on.'

The Tulu appears to have preferred a different prefix; *nine* being expressed in that language by 'wormbu' or 'orambu'—a word which is probably identical with the Kota 'worpatthu,' and of which the first member 'wor' or 'or' seems to be allied to 'or,' *one,* so as to give the compound the meaning of *one from ten.*

When the various compounds into which *nine* enters, and the various shapes in which it presents itself in the different Drâvidian idioms are compared, it is evident that the first member of the Telugu compound 'tommidi,' of the Canarese 'ombhatt-u,' and of the Tamil 'onbad-u,' must originally have commenced with 't.' Though this 't' is not found in the Tamil 'ombadu,' yet it has retained its place in the higher and less used members, viz., 'toṇṇûʀ-u,' *ninety,* and 'toḷ-âyiram,' *nine hundred.* In Telugu it is found not only in *nine,* but in *all* compound numerals into which *nine* enters: and in Canarese, though it has disappeared from *nine* and *nine hundred,* it retains its place in 'tombatt-u,' *ninety.*

Additional light is thrown upon this prefix by the Tamil 'toḷ-âyiṛam,' *nine hundred,* in which 'toḷ' is used as the equivalent of 'ton' or 'tom;' and this is evidently the most primitive shape in which the prefix appears. Even in the Tamil 'toṇṇûʀ-u,' *ninety,* the prefix to 'nûʀu is not 'tom' or 'ton,' but is really 'toḷ,' as every Tamil scholar knows. The 'ḷ' is assimilated to the 'n' of 'nûʀ-u,' and both nasals are changed into the nasals of the cerebral row, by a recognized Tamil law of sound. The operation of the same law is apparent in the trite word 'eṇṇey,' Tam., *oil;* which is properly 'eḷ ney,' *the oil or ghee of the* 'eḷ' *or sesame,* and in which the concurrent consonants 'ḷ' and 'n' are converted by rule into 'ṇṇ.'

Seeing that the 'toṇ' of the Tamil compound 'toṇṇûru,' *ninety,* thus resolves itself into 'toḷ,' in accordance with the higher number 'toḷ-âyiram,' *nine hundred,* it is evident that 'on,' 'om,' 'tom,' and 'toṇ,' are but different forms of the same word; and that 'toḷ,' being the most distinctive form, must be the parent of the rest, and the truest representative of the root. In composition 'toḷ' will become 'toṇ,' or 'tom,' without difficulty; but none of those forms can be converted into 'toḷ' under any circumstances whatever. A final 'ḷ' is constantly and regularly euphonised in Tamil, through the influence of the initial consonant of the succeeding syllable or word; and this rule especially applies to the final 'ḷ' of the first syllable of compounds. When 'ḷ' is followed by 'd,' it is changed by rule into 'n,' *e.g.,* 'koḷ-du,' *having taken,* becomes 'koṇḍu in Tamil; and this euphonised form of 'ḷd' occupies in the Telugu 'konu' the position of the root of the verb. When 'ḷ' is followed by 'p' or 'b,' it is ordinarily changed into the cerebral 't;' and this is the consonant which we should expect to find in the compound numeral *nine,* viz., 'oṭpad-u' or 'ṭoṭpad-u,' instead of 'onbad-u,' 'ombhatt-u,' and 'tommidi.' The true explanation of the change of 'toḷpad-u' into 'tonbad-u' is furnished by the poetical dialect of the Tamil, in which there are traces of the existence of a system of euphonic changes, somewhat different from those which are now in use. Thus, from 'nal,' a verbal root, the ordinary Tamil even of the poets forms 'naṭpu,' *friendship;* but we also occasionally meet in the poets with 'naṇbu,' a rarer and older form; and this shows the possibility of 'toḷpad-u' becoming, by the earlier euphonic process, 'toṇbad-u.' The possibility becomes a certainty when we find in the Tamil classics a word for *nine* of which the basis is actually not 'on,' but 'toṇ,' viz., 'toṇḍu,' *nine,* a word which is unquestionably and directly derived from 'ṭoḷ,' and which shows, not only that 'onbadu' must originally have been 'toṇbadu,' but also that 'toḷ' is the basis of the first member of every Drâvidian form of this compound numeral.

When the Telugu and Canarese compounds *ninety, nine hundred,* &c., are compared with their equivalents in Tamil, we cannot fail to be struck with the great simplicity and regularity of the Tamil compounds. In Telugu and Canarese, *ninety* is 'tombei' and 'tombattu' (literally *nine tens*), in each of which compound numerals 'tom' is used to signify *nine,* though properly it does not represent *nine,* but is only the first member of the numeral *nine,* which is itself a compound. In like manner *nine hundred* is in Telugu 'tommannûʀu,' in Canarese 'ombaynûʀu;' compounds which are formed on the same plan as *ninety,* though with a fuller representation of both parts of the compound *nine,* which they adopt as their first member. In Tamil, on the other hand, the composite numeral *nine* is altogether lost sight of in the construction of the compounds *ninety* and *nine hundred;* and those compounds are formed (by means of the same expedient, it is true, as *nine,* but independently of it) by prefixing 'toḷ' to the word *a hundred* in order to form *ninety,* and the same 'toḷ' to *a thousand* in order to form *nine hundred.* In these instances 'toḷ' must be regarded as an adjective, not signifying any one numeral in particular, but having some such general signification as *defect, diminution,* or *minus;* and thus we arrive at the conclusion that it must have had the same meaning in *nine* also. As 'toṇṇûʀ-u' ('toḷ-nûʀ-u'), *ninety,* means *the* 'toḷ' (or *defective*) *hundred,* and as 'toḷ-âyiram,' *nine hundred,* means *the* 'toḷ' (or *defective*) *thousand;* so 'onbad-u' ('toṇbadu'), *nine* must mean *the* 'toḷ' (or *defective*) *ten.*

We have here, doubtless, the primitive Drâvidian mode of forming the higher compounds of which *nine* is the first member. The absence of this idiom in the higher compound numerals of the Telugu and Canarase is an illustration of the greater antiquity of the Tamil; whilst the formation of *nine* on this peculiar plan in both Telugu and Canarese shows that originally it was the common property of all the dialects. Its mode of forming the higher compounds corresponds to the Scythian mode of forming *eight* and *nine,* as has already been pointed out. The higher as well as the lower compounds are formed in this manner in Ostiak; *e.g.,* from 'nît,' *eight,* and 'sôt,' *a hundred,* is formed 'nît sôt,' not only *eight hundred,* but also *eighty.* It corresponds also to the use of 'ûn' to denote *diminution by one* in the Sanscrit 'ûnavinshati,' *nineteen,* and the parallel Latin 'undeviginti.'

It only remains to inquire into the origin and meaning of the prefix 'toḷ.' It is not to be confounded with 'tol,' *ancient,* the 'l' of which belongs to a different 'varga:' and yet that 'l' also supplies us with several good derivations. Though *ancient* is the meaning of 'tol' in Tamil, it is used to signify *first* in Telugu; *e.g.,* 'toli-vâram,' *the first day of the week,* and the meaning, *first,* might naturally flow from an earlier meaning, *one,* of which however no trace remains. Another possible derivation is from 'tol-a,' Tel. and Can., *a bit,* or *division* (as in an orange or jack-fruit); and a better one still is 'tolaga,' Tel., an infinitive, which is used adverbially to signify *off; e.g.,* 'tolaga tîyu,' *to take off.* The objection to all these derivations is that the Tamil numeral prefix is not 'tol,' but 'toḷ;' and that those consonants are most carefully discriminated in all Tamil dictionaries. There are two similar roots containing the surd 'ḷ' in Tamil, viz., 'toḷ,' *loose, lax,* and 'tuḷ-ei' or 'toḷ-ei' (Can., 'toḷḷ-u'), *to hollow, to perforate;* as an adjective, *perforated; e.g.,* 'toḷḷei kâdu,' a long, pendent, *perforated ear.* These meanings do not harmonize very well with the use of 'toḷ' as a diminuent prefix to the higher numerals, and yet it appears probable that the word is the same. We must, therefore, take refuge in the supposition that originally 'toḷ' conveyed the meaning of *deficient* or *diminished.*

It seems scarcely necessary now to add that there is no affinity whatever, as some have surmised, between the initial portion of the Tamil 'onbadu' and the Greek '*ἐννέα.*' The Manchu 'onyan,' *nine,* has not only some resemblance to the Drâvidian word, but seems to be a compound formed on similar principles. Nevertheless the ultimate component elements of the Manchu word—'emu,' *one,* and 'juan,' *ten*—have no resemblance whatever to the Drâvidian.

Ten.—In all the Drâvidian languages the words used for *ten* are virtually the same; in Tamil 'patt-u,' in Canarese 'hatt-u,' in Telugu 'padi,' in Tuda 'pota,' in Gônd 'pudth.'

In those Tamil compound numerals in which *ten* is the second member; *e.g.,* 'irubadu,' *twenty,* 'pattu' becomes 'padu' (euphonically 'badu'), which is apparently the oldest extant form of this numeral, and in close agreement with the Telugu 'padi.'

In the Tamil compound numerals under *twenty,* in which *ten* constitutes the first number, *e.g.,* 'padin-âṟu,' *sixteen,* literally *ten + six;* 'pad-u' becomes converted into 'pad-in,' the 'in' of which I consider to be either an adjectival formative used as an euphonic augment, or an euphonic augment used as an adjectival formative. In 'pattonbadu,' *nineteen,* 'pattu,' which I regard as an adjectival form of 'padu,' is used instead of 'padin'—the prefix of all the rest of the *teens* in Tamil, except 'panniraṇḍu,' *twelve.* That is simply a corruption of 'padin-iraṇḍu.'

The Telugu 'padi,' *ten,* is evidently identical with the Tamil 'padu;' as 'adi,' Tel., *it,* is identical with the Tamil 'adu.' The Telugu 'padi' undergoes more changes in composition than its equivalents in the other idioms. In the compounds under *twenty,* in which *ten* is represented by 'pad,' 'padi,' 'pada,' or 'padd,' the changes are trifling; the principal being in 'pandhommidi' ('pan,' for 'padin,' *ten,* and 'tommidi,' *nine*), *nineteen;* but in the compounds from *twenty* upwards, in which *ten* is the second member of the compound and is a numeral noun, 'padi' is materially changed. In *twenty* and *sixty* it is altered to 'vei;' in *thirty* to 'phei;' in *seventy* to 'bbhei;' and in the other numbers to 'bhei.' This change is effected by the softening of the 'd' of 'padi,' after which 'pa-i' or 'ba-i' would naturally become 'bei,' and then 'vei.'

In Canarese, *ten* is 'hatt-u,' by the change of 'p' into 'h,' which is usual in the modern dialect: in the ancient dialect, as in Tamil, it is 'patt-u.' In the compounds from *eleven* to *nineteen* inclusive, in which *ten* is used adjectivally, and is the first portion of the word, 'hatt-u' is represented by 'hadin,' as 'patt-u' in Tamil by 'padin.' In the compounds in which *ten* is placed last, and is used as a noun of number (from *twenty* and upwards), 'patt-u' is found in *twenty* and *seventy*, 'batt-u' in *eighty* and *ninety*, and 'vatt-u' in all the remainder.

The Tulu uses 'patt'' for the noun of number, and 'pad'' as the numeral adjective.

The vocabulary of the Drâvidian languages throws no light on the derivation of 'pad',' the normal form of this numeral. It is quite unconnected with 'paRRu,' Tam. (pronounced 'pattru'), *to receive*, the 'R' of which is radical, and connected with 'paRi,' *to catch*. Etymologically, the nearest Tamil root to 'pad-u' is 'padi,' *to be fixed in, to be imprinted.* The noun 'padi' hence may mean *anything that is noted down, imprinted, or recorded;* and the numeral *ten* might have received this name from the use to which it has always been put in decimal calculation. Another possible derivation is the Telugu 'padu-vu' or 'padu-pu,' *a collection, a crowd; e.g.*, 'kukka padu-pu,' *a pack of hounds.* This word, however, is not recognised by the Tamil. The only analogy or resemblance to this numeral which I have observed in any other language, is in the 'Koibal,' a Samoïede dialect, in which *ten* is 'bet.' It seems improbable, however, that the resemblance is other than accidental, seeing that none of the other numerals of that language, with the exception of 'okur,' *one*, bears any resemblance to the Drâvidian. It is only in the lower numerals, from *one* to *four*, that any real affinity is to be found or looked for in that rude and distant Scythian dialect.

A Hundred.—The only cardinal number above *ten* which requires to be noticed in a Drâvidian Comparative Grammar is that of *a hundred.* In all the Drâvidian dialects, without exception, this word is 'mûR-u.'

I have not been able to discover any resemblance to this numeral in any other family of tongues. In no two Scythian stems do we find the same word used to express this high number; nor indeed amongst such rude tribes could we expect to find it otherwise.

One and the same word for *hundred*, slightly modified, is used in every language of the Indo-European family, a remarkable proof of the unity and ancient intellectual culture of the race; and the Finnish word for *a hundred*, 'sata,' has evidently, like some other Finnish words, been borrowed from that family of tongues.

The Tamil has a verbal root 'nûRu,' *to destroy*, which is identical in sound with 'nûRu,' *a hundred;* and there is also a related root 'nîR-u' (in Tel., 'nûr-u'), *to reduce to powder;* but it cannot be supposed that the numeral 'nûR-u' proceeded from either of these roots. A word which may be supposed to be the origin of it is 'nûṛ,' *to heap up*, the suppositious verbal root of 'nûṛil,' Tamil, *a heap.*

A Thousand.—The Drâvidian words for *thousand* are 'âyiram,' Tam. and Mala.; 'sâvira,' and also 'savara,' Can.; 'vêlu,' softened into 'veyyi,' Tel.; 'sâra,' Tulu. 'sâvira' or 'savara,' and 'sara,' are evidently identical; and we may safely derive both from the Sans. 'sahasra.' Probably also the Tam 'âyira-m' was originally 'âsira-m' or 'âsra-m,' and therefore an old corruption of the Sans. *A priori* we might have expected to find the Drâvidian languages borrowing from the Sanscrit a word for expressing this very high numeral. The Telugu word for *thousand*, 'vêl-u,' is a purely Drâvidian word, and is the plural of 'veyi' or 'veyyi' ('veyu-lu'). The origin of 'veyi' does not appear; but I am inclined to connect it ultimately with the Tamil root 've,' *to be excessive, to be hot, harsh,* &c.

Ordinal Numbers. — It is unnecessary in this work to devote much attention to the Ordinal numbers of the Drâvidian languages, seeing that they are formed directly, and in the simplest possible manner, from the cardinal numbers, by means of suffixed verbal participles or participial forms.

The only exception is that of the first ordinal, viz., the word signifying *first*, which in most of the Drâvidian languages, as in the Indo-European, is formed, not from the cardinal number *one*, but from a prepositional root. In the Canarese and Malayâlam, the numeral *one* is the basis of the word used for *first.*

The base of the first ordinal in Tamil and Telugu is 'mudal,' a verbal noun, signifying *priority*—in time or place, or *a beginning.* This, like all other Dravidian nouns, may be used adjectivally without any addition or change; and therefore 'mudal' alone, though signifying *a beginning*, is often used as an ordinal number in the sense of *first*. More frequently, however, it receives the addition in Tamil of 'âm,' which is the usual suffix of the ordinal numbers, and is in itself an aoristic relative participle of the verb 'âg-u,' *to become*. When 'mudal' is used in Telugu without the usual ordinal or participial suffix, it requires to be put in the inflected form; *e.g.*, not 'modal,' but 'modaṭi.' The verbal noun 'mudal' is connected with the post-position 'mun,' Tam., *before;* so that there is the same connexion between the ordinal number *first* in the Drâvidian languages, and the post-position *before*, which is observed to exist in the Indo-European languages between the preposition 'pra,' Sans., *before*, and 'prathama,' 'πρῶτος,' &c., *first*. Though the Tamil 'mun,' *before*, is allied to 'mudal,' *first*, yet neither of those words exhibits the ultimate root. The 'n' of 'mun' appears in the verb 'mundu,' Tam., *to get before;* but it does not appear to have had any place in 'mudal;' of which 'dal' is a formative termination belonging to a numerous class of verbal nouns, and 'mu' alone is the (suppositious) root. 'Mudal,' though itself, I believe, a verbal noun, is also used as the root of a new verb, signifying *to begin*. I have no doubt that all these words and forms spring from 'mu,' as their ultimate base. 'mu' is evidently a word of relation, signifying like the Sanscrit 'pra,' *priority;* and with it I would connect 'mû,' Tam., *to be old*, properly 'mu,' as found in 'mudu,' *antiquity*, which is a species of *priority*, viz., *priority in time*.

In all the Drâvidian idioms, the other ordinal numbers from *two* upwards, are formed directly from the cardinal numbers by the addition of formative suffixes. The same suffix is added to every numeral in succession, without change either in the cardinal number or in the suffix itself.

The ordinal suffix of the grammatical Telugu is 'va' or 'ava,' *e.g.*, 'mûḍava,' *third:* the Canarese adds 'nî' or 'anî' to the cardinal numbers, *e.g.*, 'mûranî,' *third:* the ordinal of the Tamil is formed by adding 'âm' to the cardinal; *e.g.*, 'mûndrâm,' *third*. The clear and certain origin of the Tamil suffix 'âm' from 'âgum,' poetically and vulgarly 'âm,' the aoristic relative participle of 'âgu,' *to become*, illustrates the origin of the suffixes of the Telugu and Canarese, which, though considerably changed, are undoubtedly identical with the Tamil in origin.

The adverbial forms of the Drâvidian numerals are formed by means of another class of suffixes from the same auxiliary verb 'âgu,' *to become*. In this instance the suffixes which are used by the Tamil, 'âvadu,' &c., are neuter participial nouns used adverbially. Oftentimes, however, adverbial numerals are formed by the addition of nouns signifying *succession*, &c., to the cardinal or ordinal numbers; *e.g.*, 'iru-muʀei,' Tam. *twice*, literally *two times*.

The multiplicative numbers, as has already been stated, are the same as the numeral adjectives.

It only remains to inquire what evidence respecting the affiliation of the Drâvidian family of tongues is furnished by the preceding investigation of the numerals of that family.

The evidence is not only decidedly opposed to the supposition that the Drâvidian languages are derived from the Sanscrit, but is equally inconsistent with the supposition of the connexion of those languages with the family to which the Sanscrit belongs, either as a member of that family, or even as a remote offshoot.

Not the smallest trace of resemblance has been discovered between the Drâvidian numerals and those of any Indo-European language, with the exception of the resemblance of the Telugu 'oka,' *one*, to the Sanscrit 'êka,' as well as to the Ugrian 'og,' 'ak,' and 'okur;' and in that instance I have no doubt that the Sanscrit itself has inherited a Scythian numeral, the numeral for *one* of the Greek, Gothic, Celtic, &c., being derived from a different base.

All the other numerals of the Indo-European languages spring from one and the same root, and are virtually identical; with the solitary exception of the Gaelic word for *five*; and hence, when we find in the Drâvidian numerals no resemblance to those of the Indo-European tongues, with the exception of the abnormal Sanscrit 'éka,' we are compelled to conclude that the Drâvidian languages belong to a different stock from the Indo-European.

On the other hand, a comparison of the Drâvidian numerals with those of the Scythian tongues appears to establish the fact of the existence of Scythian, and especially of Ugrian, or Finnish, analogies in the Drâvidian family. The resemblance between the Drâvidian *one* and *four*, and the corresponding numerals in the Ugrian languages is so complete, that we may justly regard, and cannot but regard, those numerals as identical.

The same statement applies to the word for *one*, which is found in the Scythian version of Darius's Cuneiform inscriptions at Behistun. The numeral *four*, and the other numerals above *one*, are not contained in that unique relic of the ancient Scythian speech of Central Asia; and in this case the negative argument concludes nothing.

It may perhaps be thought that the resemblance of only two numerals (*one* and *four*) out of ten, cannot be considered to prove much; but it is to be borne in mind that this resemblance is all, or nearly all, that is observed in the Scythian languages themselves between the numerals of one language of a family and those of other languages belonging to the same family.

Thus, it cannot be doubted that the Magyar and the Finnish are sister tongues, essentially and very closely allied; and yet with respect to four numerals, *seven*, *eight*, *nine*, and *ten*, no distinct trace of resemblance between them survives; and it is only in the case of the numerals *one*, *two*, and *four*, that it can be said, without hesitation, that the same root appears to be used in both languages. The Drâvidian numerals are therefore almost as closely allied to the Finnish as are those of the Magyar itself.

SECTION V.

THE PRONOUN.

Much light is thrown by the pronouns on the relationship of languages and families of languages; for the personal pronouns, and especially those of the first and second person singular, evince more of the quality of permanence than any other parts of speech, and are generally found to change but little in the lapse of ages. They are more permanent even than the numerals, the signs of case, and the verbal inflexions: and though, like every thing else, they are liable to change, yet their connexions and ramifications may be traced amongst nearly all the languages of mankind, how widely soever sundered by time or place.

In some instances the personal pronouns constitute the only appreciable point of contact or feature of relationship between languages which belonged originally to one and the same family, but which, in the lapse of time, and through the progress of corruption, have become generically different.

This remark especially applies to the pronoun of the first person, which of all parts of speech is the most persistent.

I.—Personal Pronouns.

1. Pronoun of the First Person Singular.

Comparison of dialects.—Our first inquiry must be 'What was the primitive form of this pronoun in the Drâvidian languages?'

In Tamil the form which is used in the colloquial dialect is 'nân,' the inflexion of which is not 'nan,' as might have been expected, but 'en;' and this inflexion 'en' indicates the original existence of a nominative in 'ên.' Though 'ên' is no longer found in a separate shape, it survives in the inflexions of verbs; in which the sign of the first person singular is 'ên,' sometimes poetically shortened into 'en.'

In the higher dialect of the Tamil 'yân' is more commonly used than 'nân,' the inflexion of which is uot 'yan,' but 'en,' as in the colloquial dialect.*

From the examples which have been adduced above, it would appear that there are three forms of the pronoun of the first person singular recognized in Tamil, viz., 'nân,' 'yân,' and 'ên.' The first of these forms, though the most common, was probably the primitive one: its initial 'n' was first, I think, softened into 'y,' and finally abandoned. It is not so easy to determine whether the included vowel of this pronoun was originally 'â' or 'ê.' A comparison of the corresponding plurals 'nâm,' 'yâm,' and 'em' (the inflexion of 'êm'), and of the plural terminations of the verb, 'ôm,' 'âm,' 'am' and 'em,' leads to the conclusion that 'â' was most probably the original vowel.

In the singular, 'en' is the only *inflexion* of this pronoun which is extant in Tamil; but in the plural we find not only 'em,' but also 'nam' and 'yam.' Though 'nam' is most frequently used as the inflected form of the isolated pronoun (*e.g.*, 'namar,' *they who are ours*, '*nostrates*'), the initial 'n' has altogether disappeared from the corresponding form in the pronominal terminations of the verb. At first sight we might suppose 'nam' and 'nem' to be the pronominal terminations of the High Tamil 'naḍandanam,' or 'nadandanem,' *we walked*; but the 'n' of these terminations is merely euphonic, and is used to prevent hiatus. When it is omitted, the vowels which it had kept separate immediately coalesce; *e.g.*, 'naḍanda-am' becomes 'naḍandâm' and 'naḍanda-em' becomes 'naḍandêm;' a more common form than either of which, but not so correct, is 'naḍandôm.' The final 'ôm' of this word could not well have been corrupted from 'êm,' but would spring naturally enough from 'âm;' and of this we have a proof in the circumstance that 'âm' (from 'âgum,' *it is, yes*) is also sometimes converted into 'ôm.' Moreover, whilst there are many instances of the change of 'a' into 'e' or 'ei,' there is not any of the converse. It is deserving of notice also, that in this change from the heavier 'a' to the lighter 'e,' the Drâvidian dialects exhibit the counterpart of the change of the corresponding Sanscrit pronominal root 'ma' into 'ἐμέ,'

* In explanation of the abbreviated form of the pronoun called 'the inflexion,' which has been referred to above, it may here be repeated that in the personal and reflexive pronouns of the Tamil, Canarese, Malayâlam, and Tulu, and in the reflexive pronoun of the Telugu, the 'inflexion,' or basis of the oblique cases (which by itself denotes the genitive, and to which the signs of all other cases are suffixed), is formed by simply shortening the long included vowel of the nominative. The included vowel of each of the personal pronouns is naturally long; and if in any instance the nominative has disappeared whilst the inflexion remains, we have only to lengthen the short vowel of the 'inflexion,' in order to discover the nominative from which it was derived.

me, &c., in other dialects of the same family. I conclude, therefore, that 'â' was originally the included vowel of the Tamil pronoun of the first person, and that 'nân,' the ordinary colloquial form of the pronoun, is the most faithful representative of the primitive Tamil *I*. As we proceed in our comparison of the various dialects, it will be found that the evidence is cumulative and gathers strength as we proceed. It might appear, indeed, at first sight that 'yân' was an older form than 'nân;' but before our investigation is concluded, we shall be convinced, I think, that the 'n' is radical. 'n' is known to change into 'y;' but 'y' evinces no tendency to be changed into 'n.'

In Malayâlam, the nominative is 'ñjân' ('ny,' 'jñ,' or 'ñj,' the nasal of the palatal 'varga,' is to be pronounced as one letter, like the 'ni' of *onion*); but the oblique form, or inflexion, is 'en' as in Tamil, except in the dative 'inikka,' in which 'en' is altered to 'in.' The ordinary Malayâla verb is destitute of personal endings: but in the poetry an inflected form of the verb is occasionally used, in which the pronominal termination of the first person singular is 'ên,' precisely as in Tamil.

The compound sound of 'ñj' or 'ny,' in the Malayâla 'ñjân' or 'nyân,' is a middle point between the 'n' of 'nân,' and the 'y' of 'yân.' It is a softened and nasalized form of 'n,' from which the change to 'y' is easily made. In like manner, 'nîn,' the original form of the pronoun of the second person singular in all the Drâvidian dialects, has become in Tamil, first 'nîy,' then 'nî;' and in the verbal terminations 'aiy,' 'i,' and 'ei.'

In Canarese, the nominative of this pronoun which is used in the colloquial dialect is 'nân-u,' as in Tamil, the inflexion of which (as seen in 'nanna,' *my*) is 'nan.' The ancient dialect uses 'ân,' the inflexion of which is 'en'—identical with that of the Tamil. 'ân' is evidently softened from the Tamil 'yân,' as 'yân' from 'nyân,' or 'ñjân,' and that from 'nân'; and the same softening is apparent in the Canarese plural 'âm' (instead of 'yâm' or 'nâm'), *we*. The crude form of this pronoun ('nâ') is sometimes used in Canarese as a nominative, instead of 'nânu;' *e.g.*, 'nâ bandenu,' *I came;* and in the same manner in Tamil, 'nî,' the crude form of 'nîn,' *thou*, has altogether superseded 'nîn.' The pronominal terminations of the first person singular of the Canarese verb are 'en' in the ancient dialect, and 'êne,' 'ênu,' and 'enu' in the modern.

The Tulu nominative is 'yân,' the inflexion 'yân,' the pronominal ending of the verb 'e,' which is probably softened from 'en.'

The Tuda nominative is 'ôn' (plural 'ôm'), of which 'en' is the inflexion; the singular terminations of the verb are 'ên' and 'ini.'

In the dialect of the Kôtas the nominative is 'âne,' the inflexion 'en,' and the pronominal ending of the verb 'e,' as in Tulu.

In Telugu the nominative of this pronoun is 'nên-u;' in the higher dialect 'ên-u' (answering to 'ên,' the Tamil-Canarese pronominal ending of the verb, and 'en,' the Tamil and Ancient Canarese inflexion); and this preference of 'ê' to 'â' appears also in the plural, which is 'mêm-u,' and in the higher dialect 'êm-u.' 'nê' may be used at pleasure instead of 'nên-u,' like 'nâ' in Canarese; and in the higher dialect 'ên-u' is sometimes represented by 'ê' alone.

The verbal inflexions of the Telugu, use only the final syllable of the nominative of each of the pronouns, viz., 'nu' (from 'nênu,' *I*), 'vu' (from 'nîvu,' *thou*), and 'ḍu' (from 'vâḍu,' *he*). The most important and essential part of each pronoun has thus been omitted; and the fragments which have been retained are merely formatives, or at most signs of gender and number.

'nênu,' *I*, takes 'nâ' for its inflexion or oblique form; and this shows that 'â' not 'ê' was originally the included vowel in Telugu, as well as in Tamil and Canarese. This view is corroborated by the accusative of this pronoun in Telugu, which is 'nanu' or 'nannu,' *me*, (compare the Canarese accusative 'nanna' or 'nannu'), and which has evidently been derived from a nominative, 'nân' or 'nâ.'

The Ku nominative is 'ân-u,' which is identical with that of the Ancient Canarese. In the inflexion, which is 'nâ' as in Telugu, the old initial 'n' retains its place.

The verbal terminations of the Ku are 'in' or 'in,' in the present tense, and 'e' in the past; *e.g.*, 'mâin,' *I am*, 'mâsse,' *I was*.

In Gônd the nominative is 'anâ,' and the inflexion is 'nâ,' as in Ṭelugu and Ku. In the verbal inflexions 'ân' is commonly found, more rarely 'na.' The Seoni Gônd nominative is 'nâk,' which is properly a dative.

In the Rajmahali the nominative is 'en;' in Ûrâon 'enan.' The Brahui nominative is 'î;' but in the oblique cases (*e.g.*, 'kanâ,' *of me*; 'kane,' *me, to me*), the personal base is 'ka' or 'kan,' a root which is totally unconnected with the Drâvidian 'nâ,' and which is to be compared rather with the Cuneiform, Scythian, Babylonian, and Gujarathi 'ku,' 'hu,' &c.

From this comparison the weight of evidence appears to be in favour of our regarding 'nâu,' the Tamil nominative, as the best existing representative of the old Drâvidian nominative of this pronoun, and 'nâ,' the crude form of the Canarese, as the primitive, unmodified root. This conclusion will be found to gain strength from the investigation of the pronoun of the second person, the root of which will appear to be not 'î' or 'yî,' but 'nî.'

Each consonant of 'nân' evinces a tendency to be softened away. The initial 'n,' though the more essential of the two, has been softened first into 'dñj' or 'ny,' then into 'y,' and finally has disappeared; and in none of the dialects has it, or any relic of it, been retained in the personal terminations of the verb.

The final 'n,' though not a part of the root, has shown itself more persistent, especially in the verbal terminations; but in the Telugu and Ku inflexion 'nâ,' in the Canarese crude nominative 'nâ,' and in the corresponding Telugu 'nê,' it has disappeared altogether.

The origin of the final 'n' of 'nân' is doubtful; but whatever were its origin, it does not appear to belong to the root. In the plural, it is uniformly rejected, and 'm,' the sign of plurality which is used in connexion with the personal pronouns, is not added to it, but substituted for it. In Tamil the singular is 'nâ-n,' the plural 'nâ-m;' and a similar change from 'n' in the singular to 'm' in the plural, takes place in the other dialects also. This appears to prove that 'nâ' alone forms the pronominal base of both numbers of the pronoun of the first person; that it denotes either *I* or *we* according to the singularity or plurality of the suffixed particle ('nâ-n,' *I alone*, 'nâ-m,' *Is*); and that the final 'n' of 'nân,' no less than the final 'm' of 'nâm,' is a sign, not of personality, but merely of number.

Is the final 'n' of 'nân' a sign of gender as well as of number?—Is it a sign of the masculine singular, and connected with 'an' or 'n,' the ordinary masculine singular suffix of the Tamil? The pronouns of the first and second persons are naturally epicene; but it is not unusual to find them assuming the grammatical forms of the masculine. Thus, in Sanscrit, the terminations of the oblique cases of the pronouns of the first and second persons are those which are characteristic of the masculine gender. The analogy of the Scythian pronouns, however, inclines me to the supposition that the final 'n' of the Drâvidian 'nân' was not in its origin a sign of gender or a means of grammatical expression, but was merely euphonic, like the final nasal of the Tartar 'man,' *I*. Whatever were its origin, it must have had a place in the personal and reflexive pronouns from a very early period, for we find it in the Brahui 'ten,' *self* (Compare Tam. 'tân'), and in the Ostiak 'nyn,' *thou* (Compare Old Drâvidian 'nîn).'

If, as we have seen, 'nâ' is to be regarded as the primitive form of the Drâvidian pronoun of the first person, and the final 'n' as merely a sign of number, or as an euphonic formative, it might appear extraordinary, that in the pronominal terminations of the verb, the initial 'n,' the primitive sign of personality, has invariably and altogether disappeared; whilst the first person singular is represented by the final 'n' alone. We might almost be led to suppose the initial 'n' to be a formative prefix, and the succeeding vowel to be the real pronominal base. Formative and definitive *pre*-fixes, however, are utterly unknown to the Drâvidian languages; and the anomaly referred to accords with similar anomalies which are discovered in other languages. In Hebrew, 'anachnu,' *we*, from 'anach' (in actual use 'anôkî'), *I*, with the addition of 'nu,' a sign of plurality, is the full form of the plural of the first personal pronoun; yet in the verbal terminations, 'anachnu' is represented solely by 'nu,' the final fragment, which originally was only a suffix of number. Another and still more reliable illustration of this anomaly is furnished by the Telugu itself. The pronoun of the second person singular in Telugu is 'nîvu,' *thou*, from 'nî,' the radical base, and 'vu' an euphonic addition. This 'vu' is of so little importance that it totally disappears in all the oblique cases. Nevertheless, it forms the regular termination of the second person singular of the Telugu verb; and it has acquired this use simply through the accident of position, seeing that it is not even a sign of number, much less of personality, but is merely an euphonisation.

Extra-Drâvidian relationship.—We now enter upon a comparison of 'nâ,' the Drâvidian pronoun of the first person, with the pronouns of the same person which are contained in other families of tongues, for the purpose of ascertaining its relationship. As 'nâ' constitutes the personal element in 'nâm,' *we*, as well as in 'nân,' *I*, it is evident that our comparison should not be exclusively restricted to the singular, but that we are at liberty to include in the comparison, the plurals of this pronoun in the various languages which are compared; for it is not improbable *à priori* that some analogies may have disappeared from the singular, which have been retained in the plural.

All pronouns of the first person singular that have been used at any time in Asia, Europe, or Northern Africa, whether it be in connexion with the Indo-European, the Semitic, or the Scythian family of tongues, are traceable, I believe, to two roots only. Each of those roots has been preserved in the Sanscrit, and in the more primitive members of the Indo-European family—one ('ah') in the nominative, the other and by far the more widely prevalent one ('ma') in the oblique cases. In order, therefore, to investigate thoroughly the affiliation of the Drâvidian pronoun of the first person, it will be necessary to extend our inquiries over a wider area than usual.

(1.) *Semitic analogies.* — The Semitic pronoun presents some remarkable analogies to the Drâvidian. This will appear on comparing the Drâvidian 'nâ' (Gônd. 'anâ,') with the corresponding Hebrew 'anî;' with the prefix 'an' of the Hebrew 'ânôkî,' of the Egyptian 'anuk,' and of the Babylonian 'anaku,' 'anaka,' or 'anku;' and especially with the Jewish-Syriac 'anâ,' the Christian-Syriac 'euo,' and the Æthiopic and Arabic 'anâ.' The plural of the Aramaic 'anâ' is formed by suffixing 'n' (the final consonant of 'în' or 'ân'): we may therefore compare the Tamil 'nâm,' *we,* with the Aramaic plural 'anân,' and also with the Egyptian plural 'anen.'

Notwithstanding this remarkable resemblance between the Semitic pronoun and the Drâvidian, it is doubtful whether the resemblance is not merely accidental. The Semitic initial syllable 'an,' in which the resemblance resides, is not confined to the pronouns of the first person. We find it not only in 'ana' (from 'anah,' and that again from 'anaḥ,') *I;* but also in the Arabic and Old Hebrew 'antâ' and the Aramaic 'ant,' *thou,* (Egyptian 'en-tek,' 'en-ta'). The prefix being precisely the same in both cases, the pronoun of the second person seems to have as good a claim to it as that of the first. It does not seem, moreover, to be an essential part of either pronoun; for we find a similar prefix in the third person in some of the Semitic dialects, *e.g.,* in the Egyptian 'entuf,' *he,* 'entus,' *she,* and the Chald. and Heb. suffix 'enhu,' *he.* Moreover, the alliance of the Semitic pronouns of the first and second persons with the Indo-European comes out into more distinct relief when this prefix is laid aside. When the initial 'an' is removed from the pronoun of the first person, we cannot doubt the connexion of the remaining syllable ('oki,' 'ah,' 'aḥ,' 'uk,' 'aku,' or 'ak,') with the Sanscrit 'ah,' the Gothic 'ik,' and the Greek-Latin 'eg:' and it is equally evident that when 'an' or 'en' is rejected from the pronouns of the second person ('antâ,' 'anti,' 'ant,' 'entek,' 'enta,') the 'ta,' 'ti,' 'te,' or 't,' which remains is allied to the Sanscrit 'tva' and the Latin 'tu.'

It has sometimes been supposed that this Semitic prefix 'an' is simply euphonic—a sort of initial *nunnation* like that which is admitted to exist in the Talmudic 'înhû,' *he,* when compared with the ordinary and undoubtedly more ancient Hebrew 'hû.' On this supposition, it is allied, in nature and origin, to the euphonic suffixes or *nunnations* which may be observed in the Greek 'ἐγώ-νη,' in the Finnish 'mi-nâ,' *I*, and in the final nasal of the North-Indian 'mai*n*,' *I*, and 'tai*n*' or 'tu*n*,' *thou*.

If this be the origin of the Semitic prefix 'an,' it must certainly be unconnected with the Drâvidian 'nâ' or 'anâ.'

Colonel Rawlinson supposes 'an' to be a particle of specification, a sort of definite article; and he also considers it to be identical with 'am,' the termination of the Sanscrit personal pronouns 'ah-am,' *I*, 'tv-am,' *thou*, 'va-y-am,' *we*, 'yu-y-am,' you. The only difference, he says, is that the particle is prefixed in the one family of languages, and suffixed in the other, with a change of 'm' into its equivalent nasal 'n.' I am unable, however, to adopt this supposition, and prefer to regard the Sanscrit termination 'am' as the ordinary termination of the nominative of the neuter singular, and as used instead of the masculine and feminine, simply because of the intense personality which is inherent in the first and second personal pronouns, especially in their nominatives, and which renders the terminations of those genders unnecessary.

The only remaining argument which can be adduced in favour of regarding the Drâvidian 'nâ' and the Semitic 'an' as ultimately allied, is the following. In the Semitic languages the first and second personal pronouns have one element in common, the prefix 'an.' In like manner, when we compare the Drâvidian 'nâ,' *I*, and 'nî,' *thou*, we find that they also have one element in common, the initial and *ultimate* base 'n.' If it can be supposed that this initial consonant denotes personality in general, and that it is the office of the succeeding vowel to inform us whether the person referred to is the first or the second, then an ultimate connexion may be conceived to exist between the Drâvidian 'n' and the Semitic 'an:' for whatever may have been the origin of the latter particle, it appears to be *used* like the Drâvidian 'n,' as a sign of personality in general, and to constitute the basis to which 'aḥ,' the sign of person No. 1, and 'ta,' the sign of person No. 2, are suffixed. Probably, however, the resemblance between the Semitic and the Drâvidian languages in this point, though remarkable, is altogether accidental.

(2.) *Indo-European analogies.*—It has already been remarked that there are but two pronouns of the first person singular known to the Indo-European family of tongues, as to the Semitic and Scythian, one of which appears in the nominative of the older Indo-European languages, the other in the oblique cases. The nominative of this pronoun is 'ah-am' in Sanscrit, 'ad-am' in Old Persian, 'az-em' in

Zend, 'eg-o' in Latin and Greek, 'ik' in Gothic, 'ih' in the Old German, 'az' in the Old Sclavonic, 'asz' in Lithuanian, and 'gâ' in Bohemian. We find substantially the same root in the Semitic 'âh,' 'aḥ,' 'uk,' 'aku,' 'ôkî,' &c., and in several languages of the Malayo-Polynesian group; *e.g.*, Malay 'âkû,' Tagala 'aco,' Tahitian 'au.' It is evident that there is not the smallest resemblance between any of these and the Drâvidian 'nâ.' But though the Indo-European *nominative* has no connexion with the Drâvidian pronoun, we shall probably be able to establish the existence of some connexion between the Drâvidian pronoun and the base of the *oblique* cases in the Indo-European languages.

The oblique cases of this pronoun in the Indo-European family are formed from a totally different base from that of the nominative; and of this oblique base the best representative is the Sanscrit 'ma.' 'm' forms the most prominent and essential portion of 'ma;' and this 'm' is followed either by 'a' or by some vowel which appears to have been derived from it. In the oblique cases of the Sanscrit, this pronoun has the form of 'ma,' whenever the nature of the succeeding syllable allows 'a' to remain unchanged; *e.g.*, 'ma-yi,' *in me*, 'ma-ma,' *of me*. In the secondary forms of the dative and the genitive it becomes 'mâ.' In Zend and Old Persian, 'ma' preponderates; whilst compounded and abbreviated vowels appear in the Zend dative-genitives 'mê,' 'môi;' and a pronominal base in 'ama' is found in some of the Old Persian prepositional compounds. In the Greek 'με,' 'ἐμέ,' 'μοί,' 'μοῦ,' &c., the vowel which is employed librates between 'e' and 'o,' each of which is naturally derived from 'a;' whilst the initial 'e' of 'ἐμέ' is in accordance with the tendency of the Greek to prefix a vowel to certain words beginning with a consonant, *e.g.*, 'ὄνομα' for 'νῶμα.' The Latin has 'me,' except in the dative, which is 'mihi.' The Gothic has 'mi' and 'mei.' The Lithuanian uses 'man' as the basis of its oblique cases; though possibly the final 'n' of this form belongs properly to the sign of the genitive.

In the pronominal terminations of the verb in the Indo-European languages, the first person singular almost invariably makes use of this oblique pronominal base, in preference to the base of the nominative, with such modifications as euphony may require. The termination of the first person singular is 'mi', or 'm' in Sanscrit and Zend, in all primary and secondary verbs. We have the same ending in Greek verbs in 'μι,' and in the 'μαι' of the middle voice; in the 'm' of the Latin 'sum' and 'inquam;' in the Lithuanian 'mi;' in the Polish 'am;' in the Armenian 'em;' in the New Persian 'am.' It becomes 'm' in the Old High German 'gâm,' *I go;* 'tuom,' *I do;*

and 'bim' or 'pim' (Sansc. 'bhavâmi'), *I am;* converted in Modern German to 'bin.'

On comparing the pronominal terminations which have now been cited, it is evident that the preponderance of use and authority is in favour of 'mi;' and that 'm' has been derived from 'mi' by abbreviation. It is equally clear, however, that 'mi' itself has been derived from 'ma,' the normal base of the oblique cases; for in all languages 'a' evinces a tendency to be converted into some weaker vowel, 'i,' 'e,' or 'o;' whereas no instance is adducible of the opposite process. Perhaps the best illustration of the regularity of this change from 'ma' to 'mi' is that which is furnished by the Esthonian, a Finnish dialect, in which each of the personal pronouns has two forms, the one primitive, the other euphonised; *e.g.*, 'ma' or 'minna,' *I;* 'sa' or 'sinna,' *thou.*

We have now to inquire whether any analogy is discoverable between the Drâvidian 'na' and the ultimate Indo-European base 'ma.'

I am inclined to believe that these forms are allied, and that 'na' is derived from 'ma.' A change of 'm' into 'n'—of the stronger nasal into the weaker—is in accordance both with Drâvidian and Indo-European precedents. Thus 'am,' the accusative case-sign of the Ancient Canarese is weakened into 'an' ('annu'), in the modern dialect; 'um,' the conjunctive or copulative particle of the Tamil, is 'nu' in Telugu; and even in Tamil itself, 'am,' the formative termination of a large class of nouns, is optionally converted into 'an;' *e.g.*, 'uran,' *strength*, is used by the poets instead of 'uram.' In the Indo-European family, in like manner, the change of 'mama,' Sans., *my*, into 'mana' in Zend, and 'mene' in Old Slavonian, has already been noticed; but proofs exist also of the special change of the 'm' of 'ma' itself—the most radical part of 'ma'—into 'n.' The final 'm' of the first person of Sanscrit and Latin verbs (the abbreviation and representative of 'mi' or 'ma') has in some instances degenerated into 'n' in Greek; *e.g.*, compare the Sanscrit 'âsam,' *I was*, and the corresponding Latin 'eram,' with the Greek ''ἦν;' and 'adadâ-m' with 'ἐδί-δω-ν.' We see a similar change of 'm' into 'n,' on comparing the Irish 'chanaiM,' *I sing*, with the Breton 'kanaNN;' the modern German 'biN,' *I am*, with the Old High German 'biM' or 'piM;' and the Persian 'hastaM,' *I am*, with the Beluchi 'hastjaN.' Compare also the Laghmani 'pâkaN,' *I go.*

The 'n' which alternates with 'v,' as the initial and radical consonant of the plural of the pronoun of the first person in many of the Indo-European languages, has been derived, I conceive, from the same 'm.' It was shown in the section on 'Sounds,' that the Drâvidian 'm' is sometimes euphonically degraded either into 'n' or into 'v;' and that whenever 'n' and 'v' are found to alternate, we have reason to consider both to be derived from an older 'm.' In like manner the 'va' of the Sanscrit 'va-(y)-am,' *we*, and the 'na' of 'nas,' the secondary, oblique form of the same pronoun, appear to be mutually connected; and both have probably been derived from 'ma.' The oldest form of the plural of this pronoun is that which is employed in the verbal inflexions, and which in Sanscrit is 'mas,' in Latin 'mus,' in Greek 'μεν' (for the more ancient and more correct Æolic 'μες'): the most natural explanation of which pronominal ending is to consider it as derived from 'ma,' the old first person singular, by the addition of 's,' the sign of plurality. The 'm' of this primeval 'mas' sometimes becomes 'v,' *e.g.* in the Sanscrit 'vayam,' the Zend 'vaêm,' and the Gothic 'veis;' and sometimes also it becomes 'n,' *e.g.* in the Latin 'nos,' the Welsh 'ni,' the Greek 'νῶι;' and also in the Sanscrit secondary forms, 'nas' and 'nau,' the Zend 'nô,' and the Old Slavonic 'nas.' This 'n' is evidently a weakening of 'm,' and represents the personality of the pronoun of the first person, irrespective of the idea of number; which is expressed by the subsequent portion of the word. This being the case, we seem to be warranted in considering it as identical in origin with the 'n' of the Drâvidian 'na' (as apparent in the singular 'nâ-n,' and the plural 'nâ-m').

It has been suggested by Col. Rawlinson that the Sanscrit 'nas,' the Latin 'nos,' and the Greek 'νῶι' (like the 'nu' of the Hebrew 'anachnu'), were originally signs of plurality, which have made themselves independent of the bases to which they were attached. I am unable, however, to adopt this view: for the 'n' of these forms naturally interchanges with 'm,' and evidently conveys the idea of personality; and the 's' of the Latin 'nos' (as of the corresponding 'vos') is more likely to be a sign of plurality than an abbreviation (as Bopp conjectures it to be) of the syllable 'sma.'

It may here be mentioned, as some confirmation of the supposition that the Drâvidian 'na' is derived from an older 'ma,' that in Telugu 'm' is used as the equivalent of 'n,' and as the representative of the personality of the pronoun of the first person in the plural 'mêm-u,' *we*. The second 'm' of this word is undoubtedly a sign of plurality; and though the first 'm' may possibly be derived from 'n,' through the attraction of 'm,' the sign of the plural, yet this change would more naturally take place, if an initial 'm' had originally been used. On this supposition 'mêm-u' corresponds to the Sanscrit 'mas;' and has been weakened into 'nêm-u' or 'nâm,' in the same manner as 'mas' has been weakened into 'nas.' On the whole, therefore, I think we are warranted in coming to the conclusion that the Drâvidian 'na' and the old Indo-European 'ma' are allied, and, if so, that the former has been derived from the latter.

(3.) *Scythian analogies.*—When we examine the personal pronouns of the Scythian group of tongues, the views which have been expressed above are found to be corroborated: in addition to which, some independent and very interesting analogies to the Drâvidian pronoun are brought to light.

The pronominal root which constitutes the basis of the oblique cases in the Indo-European languages is adopted in the languages of the Scythian family, not only in the oblique cases, but also in the nominative itself. Whilst in both families the oblique cases are substantially the same, the Indo-European uses as its nominative the base in 'ah;' the Scythian, the base in 'ma.' There are a few languages even in the Indo-European family in which 'ma' has found its way into the nominative; *e.g.*, the Celtic has 'mi,' the New Persian 'man,' the North-Indian vernaculars 'mai*n*.' It is observeable, however, that in each of these exceptional cases Scythian influences have been in operation. The New Persian has been influenced by the Oriental and Turkish, the Celtic by the Finnish, and the idioms of Northern-India by the Scythian vernacular which preceded the Sanscrit. In some cases also, especially in the later dialects of this family, the accusative has come to be used instead of the nominative, in violation of existing grammatical rules. Thus, the Singhalese 'mama,' the Kawi 'mami,' and the later Cuneiform Persian 'mâm,' are probably accusatives in their origin, like the Italian 'mi' and the French 'moi.' On the other hand, we are met by one, and only one, exceptional case in the Scythian tongues. The Scythian of the Behistun Inscriptions makes use of 'hu' as its nominative; but in 'mi,' the corresponding possessive suffix, the ordinary Scythian base re-appears.

The nominative (as well as the oblique cases) of the first personal pronoun in all existing languages of the Scythian group, is derived from a base in 'ma;' and it will be shown that this 'ma' not unfrequently comes into perfect accordance with the Drâvidian pronoun, by changing into 'na.'

In those languages 'ma' is very generally euphonised or nasalised by the addition of a final 'n,' or of an obscure nasal resembling the Sanscrit; 'anusvâra:' in consequence of which, not 'ma,' but 'man,' may be stated to be the normal form of the Scythian pronoun, and this bears a closer resemblance than 'ma' to the Drâvidian 'nân.'

The addition of this euphonic nasal is not unknown even to the

Indo-European languages. It may be seen in the Persian 'man,' the Sindhian mân,' and the Belûchî 'menik;' and a similar inorganic addition is apparent in the Old Greek 'ἐγών' and 'ἐγῶνη,' as also in 'τύνη' and 'τούν.' The first nasal is much more common, however, and more characteristic in the Scythian tongues. On examining the Turkish family of tongues, we find 'men' in Oriental Turkish; 'mân' in Turkoman; 'mâm' in Khivan; 'ben' ('m' degraded to 'b') in Ottoman Turkish. In the Finnish family, the Finnish proper has 'minâ;' the Lappish 'mon;' the Esthonian 'ma' or 'minna;' the Mordwin and Votiak 'mon;' the Ostiak 'ma' (dual 'mîn,' plural 'men'). The Samoïede dialects have 'man,' 'mani.' In both Mongolian and Manchu the nominative of this pronoun is 'bi;' but this is evidently corrupted from 'mi' (like the Ottoman 'ben' from the Uigur 'men'); and it is 'mi,' with a final nasal, which forms the basis of the oblique cases. In both languages the genitive is 'mini:' and the dative is 'men-dou' in Mongolian, 'min-de' in Manchu. The Tibetan pronoun is 'gnya,' 'gna,' or 'nga' (identical doubtless with 'ma'); the Chinese 'ngo;' the sub-Himalayan 'gna;' the Avan 'nga;' the Mikir 'ne;' the Corean 'nai.'

It is evident from the above comparison (1), that the true and essential representative of the personal of this pronoun in the Scythian tongues is 'ma;' and (2) that as 'ma' has been euphonised in the Western families of that group into 'man,' so it also evinces a tendency in the eastern stems to change into 'nga' or 'na.' In many of those idioms 'ma' still retains its place unchanged, or may optionally be used instead of the later 'man.' The Mingrelian has 'ma,' the Suanian 'mi,' the Lasian 'ma,' the Georgian 'me.' The Finnish has both 'me' or 'ma' and 'minâ,' and also 'mia:' the Ostiak both 'min' and 'ma.'

It is found also in those languages in which 'man' constitutes the isolated pronoun, that 'm' is used as its equivalent in the personal terminations of the verbs, and generally in all inflexional compounds. We see this usage illustrated in the colloquial languages of Northern India and in the Persian. For example, whilst 'man' is the nominative of the Persian pronoun, the basis of the oblique cases is not 'man' but 'ma' (*e.g.*, 'ma-râ,' *me, of me*); and the pronominal ending of the verb in the first person singular is 'm.' In a similar manner, in the Turkish family of languages, 'm' is used in composition as the equivalent of 'man' or 'men.' Thus, in Oriental Turkish, whilst 'men' is retained in the present tense; *e.g.*, 'bôlâ-men,' *I am;* the preterite is contented with 'm' alone; *e.g.*, 'bôldî-m,' *I was.*

The same suffix is used to denote the first person singular in the possessive compounds of the Turkish, a class of words which is peculiar to the Scythian family; *e.g.*, 'bâbâ-m,' *my father*, from 'bâbâ,' *father*, and 'm,' the representative of the first person singular. In the Magyar also, though the isolated pronoun of the first person singular is 'ên,' yet 'm' is used instead of 'n' in the possessive compounds and determinate inflexional terminations: *e.g.*, from 'atya,' *father*, is formed the possessive compound 'atya-m,' *my father;* and the first person singular of *definite* or *determinate* verbs ends in 'm;' *e.g.*, 'szeretem,' *I love (some one)*. It is also to be noticed, that whilst the Magyar has 'ên' as the the singular of the isolated pronoun, its plural is 'mi' or 'mink;' the former of which is evidently pluralised from 'ma' or 'me,' the latter from 'min.'

It was shown that the initial and radical 'm' of the Indo-European pronoun was occasionally converted in 'n:' we have now to show that a similar change from 'm' to 'n' is apparent in the Scythian languages also, and that in some of those languages 'n' has become as distinctive of the first person as in the Drâvidian family itself.

In Finnish, though the isolated form of this pronoun is 'ma' or 'minâ,' yet in all inflexional additions and compounds 'm' is represented by 'n;' *e.g.*, from 'isâ,' *father*, is formed 'isâ-ni,' *my father*, and from 'ôl,' *to be*, is formed 'ôl-en,' *I am.*

This final 'n' is not derived from the euphonic 'n' of 'minâ;' but from a direct conversion of 'm' into 'n;' for though we see the same euphonic addition of 'n' in 'sinâ' (from 'se' or 'sia'), *thou*, yet we have 't' alone (the equivalent of 's.') in 'ôl-et,' *thou art.* 'n' has, therefore, become in Finnish, as in Drâvidian, the ordinary sign of the first person singular of the verb, by conversion from an older 'm.'

The Magyar 'ên,' *I*, appears to be still more nearly allied to the Drâvidian pronoun; and in this case 'n' is certainly derived from 'm,' for whilst 'n' is found in the nominative, 'm' is used instead in all possessive compounds and verbal inflexions. With the Magyar nominative 'ên,' compare not only the Tamil-Canarese 'ên' or 'en,' but also 'ân' or 'awn,' *I*, in the Lar, a Sindhian dialect. A similar form of this pronoun is found in the Mordwin, another idiom of the Finnish or Ugrian family, in which, whilst 'mon' is the isolated nominative, 'an' is used instead in verbal inflexions;' *e.g.*, 'paz-an,' *I (am) the Lord.*

In the Olet or Calmuck dialect of the Mongolian tongue, there are distinct traces of the same change of 'ma' into 'na.'

The nominative of this pronoun in Calmuck is 'bi' (from 'mi'), and the same base appears in the genitive 'mini:' but the rest of the oblique cases are formed not from 'bi' or 'mi,' but from 'na;' *e.g.*, 'na-da,' *to me*, 'na-da-edze,' *from me*, and also 'na-maï,' *me*. We here discover the existence of a pronominal base in 'na' (probably derived from 'ma'), which is in perfect agreement with the Drâvidian.

In a few of the Scythian languages the isolated pronoun, including its nominative, seems to be absolutely identical with that of the Drâvidian family; *e.g.*, 'na' in the Quasi Qumuk, a Caucasian dialect, and 'ne' in Motor, a dialect of the Samoïede. Compare also the East-Asian forms; *e.g.*, Avan, 'na' or 'nga;' Tetenge, an Assam dialect, 'ne;' Corean, 'nai;' Tibetan, 'nga;' Chinese, 'ngo.' I doubt not that the 'nga,' *I*, and 'nge,' *we*, of the Tibetan, are identical with the 'ma' and 'me' of the other languages of High Asia; and as 'nga' is plainly identical with 'na,' as well as with 'ma,' the supposition that the Drâvidian 'na' is derived from the Indo-European and Scythian 'ma' is confirmed. We may here also compare the Australian pronouns of the first person, viz., 'nga,' 'nganya,' *I*; its dual 'ngalee,' *we two*; and the plurals 'ngadlu' and 'nadju,' *we*.

On the whole we appear to have reason to conclude that the various forms of the pronoun of the first person singular which have now been compared, 'ma,' 'nga,' and 'na,' are identical; and that this word was the common property of mankind prior to the separation of the Indo-European tribes from the rest of the Japhetic family.

2. Pronoun of the Second Person Singular.

Comparison of dialects. — In Canarese the nominative of this pronoun is 'nîn' or 'nîn-u;' and in the oblique cases the included vowel of 'nîn' is shortened by rule; *e.g.*, 'ninna,' *thy*. The plural differs from the singular only in the use of 'm' as a final, instead of 'n:' it may therefore be concluded that those finals are marks or formatives of number, not of personality; a conclusion which is converted into a certainty by the circumstance which has already been pointed out that in the pronoun of the first person also the final 'n' of the singular is converted in the plural into 'm.'

In Canarese not only are 'nâ' and 'nî' regarded as the crude bases of the pronouns of the first and second persons, but they are occasionally used also as nominatives of verbs instead of 'nân' and 'nîn.'

In the personal terminations of the verb, this pronoun is much changed in all the Drâvidian dialects. It not only loses its initial 'n,' like the pronoun of the first person; but its final 'n' also disappears. Generally nothing remains in the verbal inflexions but the included vowel, and that also is more or less modified by use. In the Canarese verb it appears as 'i,' 'î,' 'îye,' and 'e:' in the ancient dialect of the Canarese it is 'âÿ,' as in Tamil.

In Tamil 'nî,' which is properly the crude base, is invariably used as the isolated nominative, instead of 'nîn'—the form which would correspond by rule to 'nân,' the nominative of the first person singular. That 'nîn' originally constituted the nominative even in Tamil, appears from this that the oblique cases in the higher dialect agree in using 'nin' (shortened by rule from 'nîn') as the base to which the case-suffixes are attached. Another form which is occasionally used by the poets is 'nîÿ,' in which the final 'n' is softened to 'y'—in the same manner as the initial 'n' of 'nân.' The final 'n' of this pronoun, though totally lost in the nominative, is invariably retained in the oblique cases; in which it is the initial 'n' that becomes liable to alteration. In the colloquial obliques the initial 'n' entirely disappears, and does not leave even a 'y' behind it, as the initial 'n' of the first personal pronoun generally does. When the initial is discarded, the included vowel changes from 'i' to 'u.' 'u,' however, constitutes the included vowel of this pronoun, not only when the initial 'n' is lost, but sometimes, in the higher dialect, even when it is retained. 'nin,' nun,' and 'un' are severally used as the basis of the oblique cases. In the personal terminations of the Tamil verb, this pronoun is represented by the suffixes 'âÿ,' 'ei,' or 'i:' from each of which suffixes the final 'n,' as well as the initial, has disappeared. In the poetical dialect of the language the initial 'n' at first sight appears to have retained its place in such forms as 'naḍandanei,' *thou didst walk*, and in the corresponding plural, 'naḍandanir,' *ye walked:*' but the 'n' of these pronominal terminations ('nei' and 'nir') is merely euphonic, and is inserted for the purpose of keeping separate the contiguous vowels of 'naḍanda-ei' and 'naḍanda-ir. In the same manner, in the first person, 'naḍandanen, *I walked,* is used poetically for 'naḍanda-en;' and when its vowels are allowed to coalesce, instead of being kept separate, they become 'naḍandên,' which is the more ordinary form.

The root of the verb is regularly used in Tamil as the second person singular of the imperative, without any pronominal suffix, and even without any euphonic addition: but the second person plural of the imperative in the colloquial dialect is formed by the addition of 'um' (the ordinary plural base of the oblique cases); which 'um' is derived from a singular form in 'un,' one of the bases of the oblique cases already referred to. In the higher dialect 'âÿ' and 'îr,' the ordinary representatives of these pronouns in the verbal inflexions, are often added to the root to form the singular and plural imperative;

e.g., 'kêḷây,' *hear thou*, 'kêḷîr,' *hear ye*. [These forms are apparently identical with 'kêḷâÿ,' *thou hearest not*, and 'kêḷîr,' *ye hear not:* but they are not really identical, as Beschi supposed, for it will be shown in the Section on the 'Negative Verb' that 'a,' a relic of 'al,' *not*, is an element in all negative forms; though in these and in some other instances it has been absorbed in the succeeding long vowel.]

With respect to the consonantal elements of the pronoun of the second person, there is little room to doubt that they consisted in an initial and final 'n,' the former essential, the latter formative: but there seems to be some doubt with respect to the included vowel. Authority preponderates in favour of 'i;' 'u' ranks next, and 'â' next to that; but 'ei' and 'e' are also found. Sometimes in Tamil, 'î' is converted in pronunciation into a sound resembling 'û;' whilst the converse never takes place. It may therefore perhaps be concluded that 'i' constituted the included vowel of the original base of this pronoun.

Beschi, in his grammar of the High Tamil, represents 'di' as being used occasionally by the Tamil poets as a suffix of the second person singular of the imperative; and if this representation were correct, it would be necessary to regard 'di' as a pronoun, or as the fragment of a pronoun, of the second person singular. It is founded, however, on a mistake: for the word which Beschi cites in proof ('âdi,' *become thou*, from 'âgu,' abbreviated into 'â,' *to become*') is not really an imperative, but is the second person singular of the preterite; and 'di' is compounded of 'd,' the sign of the preterite tense, and 'i,' the usual fragment of 'nî,' *thou*. 'Âdi' means properly *thou hast become*, and it is used as an imperative by the poets alone to convey an emphatic prediction of a result which is regarded as already certain. We find the same suffix in such poetical preterites as 'varu-di' (for 'vandâÿ') *thou camest*, and 'keḍu-di' (for 'keṭṭâÿ') *thou art ruined*.

In Malayâlam the nominative of this pronoun is 'nî;' but 'nin' is used, as in classical Tamil, in the oblique cases. The dative has 'nan,' instead of nin; *e.g.*, 'nanikka,' *to thee* — as if from a nominative in 'nan,' with 'a' as the included vowel. This use of 'a' is in accordance with the colloquial Tamil personal termination of the verb, which is 'âÿ,' instead of 'îÿ.'

In Tulu the nominative is 'î;' but the oblique cases are formed upon the base of 'ni' or 'nin.' In the personal terminations of the verb the second person singular is represented by 'a.' The Tulu nominative 'î' illustrates the fact already stated that each of the nasals of 'nîn' (both the radical initial and the formative final) has sometimes been worn off.

The Tuda has 'nî' as its nominative, 'nin' as the base of its oblique cases, and 'i' as the personal termination of the verb.

The Telugu nominative is 'nîvu,' expanded from 'nî' by the addition of the euphonic particle 'vu:' 'nîvu,' Tel., *thou*, is identical in form, though not in meaning, with the modern Canarese plural of the same pronoun, viz., 'nîvu,' *you*. In the oblique cases the Telugu rejects the euphonic addition of 'vu,' and uses 'nî' as its inflexional base, and also as its possessive. The objective alone follows the example of the other dialects in abbreviating the included vowel, and appending a final nasal. That case is 'ni-nu,' 'nin-u,' or 'nin-nu,' and is evidently formed from a nominative 'nîu-u.' In the higher dialect of the Telugu, 'îvu,' from an old nominative 'î,' which is identical with the Tulu, is occasionally used instead of 'nîvu.'

The Telugu plural of this pronoun has 'mîru' as the nominative, 'mî' as the inflexion, and 'mimu' as the accusative. Both 'mîru' and 'mimu' indicate a base in 'mî' from which they have been formed by the addition of signs of plurality; and 'mî' bears the same relation to the 'nî' of the other dialects that 'mâ,' the Telugu plural of the first person, does to the ordinary Dravidian 'nâ.' How this change from 'n' to 'm' has taken place will be inquired into under the head of 'The Plurals.'

In the personal terminations of the verb, the Telugu rejects every portion of the pronominal root, and employs only the euphonic addition 'vu' or 'vi.'

In Gônd the nominative is 'ima;' but 'ni' is used in the oblique cases, 'n' or 'i' in the personal terminations of the verbs.

The Ku corresponds on the whole to the Telugu. Its nominative is 'îuu;' its inflexion 'nî;' the personal termination of its verb 'i.'

The Rajmahal nominative is 'nîn;' the Ûrâon, 'nien.'

The Brahui nominative is 'nî,' as in most of the Drâvidian languages; and its nominative plural is 'num'—a form which is much used in the higher dialect of the Tamil.

On a comparison of the various Drâvidian dialects we arrive at the conclusion that the primitive form of this pronoun was 'nî,' 'nû,' or 'na;'—most probably the first. The only essential part of the pronoun appears to be the initial consonant 'n;' just as in the Indo-European languages 't' is the only essential part of the corresponding pronoun. In each family the vowel by the help of which the initial consonant is ennunciated varies considerably, but evinces, on the whole, a preference for 'i' in the Drâvidian languages, for 'u' in the Indo-European.

Supposing 'nî' to be the primitive form of the Drâvidian pronoun of the second person, and comparing it with 'nâ,' which we have seen to be the primitive form of the Drâvidian pronoun of the first person, it is deserving of notice that the only difference between the two is the difference between the two included vowels, 'a' and 'i.' The consonant 'n' seems to be the common property and the common sign of both pronouns, and the means by which their personality is expressed; whilst the annexed 'a' restricts the signification to the first person, or that of the speaker; 'i,' to the second person, or that of the person addressed. The only resemblance to this arrangement with which I am acquainted is that which is found in the personal pronouns of the Hebrew, in which *I* is 'an-ôkî;' *thou*, 'an-tâ' (corrupted into 'at-tâ'). The method adopted by the Drâvidian languages of expressing the difference between the first person and the second by means of the vowels 'a' and 'i,' used as auxiliaries, does not appear to be the result of accident. It is probably founded on some ultimate principle; though it may be difficult or impossible now to discover what that principle is.

If 'a' and 'i' be considered as identical with the demonstratives, an idea which would suit the signification, and which is corroborated by the circumstance that 'u' is also a demonstrative, we are met by the apparently insurmountable difficulty that in all the Drâvidian tongues, and (as far as the use of these demonstrative vowels extends) in all the tongues of the Indo-European family, 'a' is not the proximate, but the remote, demonstrative; and 'i' is not the remote, but the proximate; whilst 'u' is used in Tamil as an intermediate between those two.

Is any weight to be attributed to the circumstance that 'a' has naturally the first place in all lists of vowels, and 'i' the second?

Extra-Drâvidian relationship.—It has been shown that the Drâvidian pronoun of the first person has affinities with each of the great Japhetic groups, with some special Scythian affinities. It will be found that the relationship of the pronoun of the second person is less extensive, but more distinctive: it is specifically Scythian.

Throughout the Scythian as well as the Indo-European group, the most prevalent form of the pronoun of the second person singular is that which is formed from the consonant 't' (*e.g.*, 'tu'), or its euphonised equivalent 's' (*e.g.*, 'σύ'); and the only other form which is found to be used in any family of either of those groups is that which is formed from the consonant 'n,' and of which the Cuneiform-Scythian and the Drâvidian 'ni' is the best representative.

These roots appear to have been always perfectly independent. I cannot discover any reliable trace of a connexion between them, or of a gradual change in any instance of the one form into the other.

In order to place this point in a clear light, it is desirable, in the first place, to trace out the connexions and alliances of the pronominal root 'tu.'

It has been conjectured that this pronoun had its origin in the demonstrative base 't;' but the investigation of this point is beyond our purpose, which is merely that of tracing its relationship.

In Sanscrit the pronoun of the second person singular is 'tva-m;' in Zend 'tû-m, and also 'thw'' as included in the accusative 'thwâ,' *thee.* Connected with the Sanscrit 'tva,' there is a simpler form, 'ta,' which is apparent in 'tava,' *thy;* and we have analogies to this in the Kawi 'ta' and the Semitic 'tâ' (included in 'antâ,' *thou*'). The Semitic 'tâ' is changed in the inflexions to 'kâ,' a change which resembles that of the Kawi, which has 'ta' as its nominative and 'ko' as its possessive. Bopp supposes that 'yu,' the base of the most common form of the plural of this pronoun, is derived from 'tu,' and that 'va,' the base of the Sanscrit secondary plural 'vas' and of the Latin 'vos,' is derived from 'tva.' 'v,' however, is more frequently derived from 'm' than from any other letter. 'tva-m' becomes 'tuva-m' in the Old Persian; and from 'tu' (itself derived from 'tv') proceeds the Sanscrit dative 'tu-bhayam:' the base of which is allied to, or identical with, the Latin, Armenian, and Pehlvi 'tu;' the Æolic and Doric 'τύ;' the Persian, Afghan, and Singhalese 'to;' and the Gothic 'thu.' The 'th' of the Gothic and Zend points out the path by which the Old Greek 'τύ' was converted into 'σύ.'

In the personal terminations of the verbs, in Sanscrit and most other languages of the same family, the earlier 't' of this pronoun has very generally been weakened into 's' in the singular, whilst in most of the plural terminations, 't,' with some trivial modifications, and with a sign of plurality annexed, has succeeded in retaining its place. In our investigation of the pronoun of the first person it was found that 'ma' was converted in the personal terminations of the verb into 'mi,' and 'mi' still further weakened into 'm:' so also 'su' (for 'tu') generally becomes 'si' in the verbal terminations; and 'si' in like manner afterwards becomes 's.'

In the Scythian group of tongues, the pronoun of the second person which is in general use is substantially the same as in the Indo-European—another evidence of the primeval identity of both groups: but in the Scythian tongues the weaker 's' has obtained wider prevalence than the older 't;' and the vowel by which 's' is enunciated is more frequently 'i' or 'e,' than 'u' or 'a.'

The Magyar has 'te' in the singular, 'ti' or 'tik' in the plural, with which we may compare the Armenian 'tu,' *thou*, and 'tuk,' *you*.

The Mongolian 'tchi' or 'dzi,' *thou*, exhibits the progress of 'ti' towards softening into 'si.' In Finnish proper, the isolated pronoun of the second person singular, is 'se' or 'sina;' but 't' retains its place in the plural; and the personal termination of the verb even in the singular is 't.'

The chief peculiarity apparent in the Scythian form of this pronoun is, that it has generally been euphonised by the addition of a final nasal—the consonant 'n,' precisely in the same manner as the pronoun of the first person singular.

In the older Greek 'τύνη' and 'τούν,' correspond to 'ἐγώνη' and 'ἐγών;' and in like manner, in the languages which belong to the Scythian family, or which have been subject to Scythian influences, where the pronoun of the first person is found to be nasalised, the pronoun of the second person generally exhibits the same feature.

In the vernaculars of Northern India, we see this euphonic addition to the pronoun of the second person in the Hindi, Panjabi, and Sïndhi, 'tu*n*,' and in the Marathi and Gujarathi 'tû*n*.' In some of those idioms, especially in the Gujarathi and Panjabi, the euphonic nasal appears in the oblique cases as well as in the nominative, but more commonly it is found in the nominative alone.

In the Turkish family of tongues, 'sin' or 'sen' is the usual form of the pronoun of the second person singular. The 'n' retains its place in the oblique cases, but is lost in 'siz' the plural. Compare also the Georgian 'shen;' the Samoïede 'tan,' 'tani;' the Lappish 'don;' the Votiak and Mordwin 'ton' (plural 'tin'); and the Finnish 'sinâ,' which alternates with 'se,' 'sia,' and 'sie.'

The euphonic origin of this 'n' is most evident in the Esthonian dialect of the Finnish, which uses indifferently 'sa' or 'sinna' for the second person, and 'ma' or 'minna' for the first.

In the Mongolian and Manchu, 'n' appears in the oblique cases only. In Mongol the nominative is 'tchi,' in Manchu 'si;' but the genitive in the former is 'tchini,' in the latter 'sini,' and the corresponding datives are 'tchim-dou' and 'sin-de.'

In Calmuck the nominative is 'dzi' or 'dzima,' genitive 'dzini,' dative 'dzimadou,' accusative 'dzimaï.' In the pronouns of this language we may observe several instances of 'm' being used as an euphonic, instead of 'n.'

It is evident that there is no resemblance whatever between any of the pronouns compared above and the Drâvidian 'nî.' The final 'nâ' of the Finnish 'sinâ,' and its equivalent, the final 'νη' of the Greek 'τύνη,' are separable, euphonic, inorganic additions, and can have no real connexion with 'nî,' which is an ultimate root.

We have seen that the Indo-European and Scythian 'm'—the initial of the pronoun of the first person—was probably the origin of the 'n' of the Drâvidian 'nâ.' Is it possible that the radical 't' of the pronoun of the second person in both those families of tongues was changed in like manner into 'n,'—so as that 'tu' or 'ti' was the origin of the Drâvidian 'nî?' I think not. This is supposed, indeed, by Castrén, a very high authority, to be the history of the 'n' by which the second person singular is often represented in the personal affixes of the Finnish and Turkish families. It may also be mentioned here, that a change of 't' into 'n' is not quite unknown even in the Indo-European languages. It is somewhat frequently found to take place in Pali; *e.g.*, 'tê,' *they*, masculine, becomes optionally 'nê;' 'tâ,' *they*, feminine becomes 'nâ;' and 'tâni,' *they*, neuter, becomes 'nâni.' In Sanscrit also 'êtam,' *him*, is sometimes changed into 'ênam.' There is no evidence, however, that the 'n' now under consideration—the initial of the Drâvidian 'nî'—arose from any such process of change; the supposition would be wholly a gratuitous one; and the discovery of 'nî' in languages of such high antiquity as the Cuneiform-Scythian of the Behistun Inscriptions and the Chinese, shows that 'nî' claims to be regarded as independent of 'tva,' or 'tu,' and as an ultimate pronominal root. It thus appears that there are probably two Japhetic bases of the second personal pronoun, as well as two of the first.

There are traces, more or less distinct, in various languages of the Scythian group, of the existence of a pronoun of the second person identical with, or evidently allied to, the Drâvidian 'nî.'

I begin with the most remarkable and decisive analogy, because the most ancient which is capable of direct proof, viz., the second personal pronoun in the Scythian tablets at Behistun. This is 'nî,' precisely as in the Drâvidian idioms; and the possessive which is used in compounds is 'nĭ,' which is identical with the similarly abbreviated basis of the Drâvidian oblique cases of this pronoun. The plural of this pronoun is, unfortunately, unknown. The personal termination of the verb is not 'ni,' but 'nti;' which I suspect to be a compound of 'ni' and 'ti,' like the 'antâ,' 'anti,' of the Semitic languages.

The antiquity and distinctively Scythian character of the Drâvidian pronoun of the second person is thus clearly proved; and this proof of its antiquity entitles us to regard as allied to the Drâvidian 'nî' certain resemblances to it which otherwise might be thought to be accidental.

In the Ostiak, the most Drâvidian of the Finnish dialects, in that compound of nouns with possessive suffixes which is so characteristic of the Scythian group, the first personal pronoun is represented by 'm;' the second, as in the Drâvidian languages, by 'n;' *e.g.*, 'ime-m,' *my wife*, 'ime-n,' *thy wife*. In the Syrianian, another Finnish idiom, the second person of the verb, both singular and plural, is formed by annexing a pronoun of which 'n' is the initial and radical; *e.g.*, 'kery-n,' *thou hast done* (from 'kery,' *to do*), 'kery(n)nyd,' *you have done*. In 'nyd,' *you*, we see indication of a singular 'ny,' *thou*, which has been pluralised, as is usual in these languages, by suffixing to it 'd' or 't.'

In addition to the allied forms discoverable in these compounds, we find in the Ugrian tongues several instances in which the isolated pronoun of the second person which is used as a nominative is plainly allied to the Drâvidian. In the Ugro-Ostiak, or that dialect of the Ostiak which is treated of in Castrén's grammar, *thou* is 'neṇ;' *you two*, 'nîṇ;' *you* (indefinitely plural) 'nen.' Here 'ne' or 'ni' constitutes the pronominal base; and the final 'n' of the singular 'neṇ,' is a formative or euphonic addition like that which has converted the Drâvidian 'nî' into 'nîn.' The strong pronunciation of this Ostiak final 'n' reappears, as we shall see, in the Turkish. In other Ostiak dialects we find 'num' and 'ma,' and also (which is more deserving of notice) 'nyn,' with a plural 'nynt.' In the Vogoul we find analogies which are no less remarkable than the above; *e.g.*, 'nei,' 'ny,' 'nan,' 'nyngi,' and 'nank.' Compare also the Vogoul plurals 'nen' and 'non.'

In the Finnish proper, the only trace of this pronoun which we observe is one which, but for the existence of such express analogies in other members of the family, we should probably have overlooked. In the plural of the second person of the Finnish verb (*e.g.*, 'olette,' *ye are*, pluralised from 'olet,' *thou art*), the suffixed pronoun corresponds to that of which 't' or 's' is the initial; but in the possessive compounds, in which we should expect to find precisely the same form, we find instead of it a plural possessive of which the initial and radical is 'n.' Thus, the expression *thy hand*, being 'kâtes,' we should expect to find *your hand*, 'kâtesse,' or, more primitively, 'kâtette,' like the corresponding Magyar 'kezetek,' (from 'tek,' *you*, another form of 'te'); whereas the form actually used in Finnish is 'kâtenne.' It thus appears that two pronouns of the second person retain their place in the Finnish; one, the singular of which is 'si,' or more properly 'ti,' the plural 'te;' and another, hidden in the ancient compounds, the plural of which is 'ne,' and of which, by dialectic rules, the singular must have been 'ni.'

Even in the Turkish, we shall find traces of the existence of a similar pronoun. In the possessive compounds, the second person singular is not represented, as we should have expected it to be, by 'sen,' as the first person singular is by 'm;' but '*n*' or 'ng' is used instead (a nasal which corresponds to that of the Ostiak 'neṇ'); *e.g.*, 'bâbâ-*n*,' *thy father;* and as the final 'm' of 'bâbâ-m' is derived from 'mi' or 'me,' *I*, we seem to be obliged to deduce also the final '*n*' of bâbâ-*n*,' from an obsolete '*ni*' or '*ne*,' *thou*, which is allied to the corresponding forms that have been pointed out in other Scythian tongues. We find this possessive '*n*' or 'ng' not only in the Osmanli Turkish, but even in the Yakute, the Turkish of Siberia.

The same '*n*' makes its appearance in the personal terminations of the Turkish verb. 'sen' is more commonly used than '*n*;' but '*n*' is found as the representative of the second person in those verbal forms which must be considered as of greatest antiquity; *e.g.*, in the preterite of the auxiliary substantive verbs, 'îdum,' *I was*, 'îdu*n*,' *thou wast*, 'îdî,' *he was.* In the Oriental Turkish the forms corresponding to these are 'bôldîm,' 'bôldû*n*,' 'bôldî;' and the same termination of the second person singular—the nasal '*n*'—appears in all the preterites of that language. We may compare also the plural forms of this pronominal suffix. The Turkish pronouns are pluralised by changing the final formative 'n' into 'z,' or rather by adding 'z' to the crude base. Thus, *we* is 'biz' (for 'miz'), and *you* is 'siz.' In possessive compounds 'i' changes into 'u;' and hence *our father* is 'bâbâ-muz.' In the same manner, *your father* is 'bâbâ-*n*uz,' indicating a supposititious, isolated pronoun, '*n*iz,' *you*, corresponding to 'miz,' *we*. Whilst 'u' is used instead of 'i' in Osmanli Turkish, the older and more regular 'i' retains its place in the Oriental Turkish; *e.g.*, 'uzû-*n*îz,' *you yourselves;* in which *you* is '*n*îz' or 'ngîz,' and from which, when 'z,' the sign of plurality, is rejected, we deduce the singular '*n*î' or 'ngî.' The same mode of forming the plural termination of the second person appears in all regular Turkish verbs; *e.g.*, compare 'ḳôrḳdu-*n*uz,' *ye feared*, with 'ḳôrḳdu-*n*,' *thou fearedst.* We see it also in the imperative 'ḳôrḳu-*n*uz,' *fear ye.* In all these instances, I consider the Turkish '*n*' or 'ng' to be dialectically equivalent to the Finnish 'n;' and the pronominal root which is thus found to underlie so many Turkish and Ugrian compounds of the second person may, I think, be regarded as identical with the Drâvidian and Behistun-Scythian pronoun. Even the libration between 'i' and 'u,' which we noticed in considering the Drâvidian forms of this pronoun, meets us again in the Turkish.

In the Himalayan dialects, though Tibetan or Indo-Chinese influences generally seem to preponderate over Drâvidian, we cannot fail to see Drâvidian analogies in the Dhimal 'nâ,' in the Miri 'no,' in the Garo 'nââ;' and in the 'n' which forms the first and most essential radical of the pronoun of the second person in all the rest of the Lohitic dialects.

Still more remarkable is the Chinese 'ni,' which is absolutely identical both with the Drâvidian and with the Behistun-Scythian pronoun: so also is the 'ni' of the Horpa, a dialect of Tibetan nomades. Compare also the pronouns of the second person in various Australian dialects: *e.g.*, 'ninna,' 'nginnee,' 'nginte;' the duals 'niwa,' 'nura;' and the plural 'nimedoo.'

On a comparison of the various forms of this pronoun which have been adduced above, it must be evident that the affinities of the Drâvidian 'nî' are wholly Scythian; and this important circumstance, taken in conjunction with the predominance of Scythian influences over Indo-European in the formation of the first personal pronoun, contributes largely to the establishment of the Scythian relationship of the Drâvidian family.

3. The Reflexive Pronoun 'Self.'

The Drâvidian pronouns of the third person are, properly speaking, demonstratives, not personal pronouns; and they will, therefore, be investigated under a subsequent and separate head. The pronoun, which is now under consideration is entitled to a place amongst personal pronouns, because it possesses all their characteristics, and is declined precisely in the same manner. It corresponds in meaning to the Sanscrit 'svayam,' and to the defective Greek 'ἕ' and the Latin 'sui,' 'sibi,' 'se;' with a range of application which is more extensive than theirs.

In Tamil the nominative singular of this pronoun is 'tân;' the plural of which (by the usual pronominal change of 'n' into 'm') is 'tâm:' and the *inflexion*, or basis of the oblique cases (which, taken by itself, has the force of a possessive), is formed, as in the case of the other personal pronouns, by simply shortening the included vowel; *e.g.*, 'tăn,' *of self*, '*sui*,' or (adjectivally) '*suus*,' '*sua*,' '*suum*.' In all its cases and connexions 'tân' is found to be more regular and persistent than any other pronoun.

The Canarese nominative is 'tân' in the ancient, 'tân-u' in the modern dialect: the inflexion is formed, as usual, by the shortening of the included vowel; and the crude root 'tâ' (without the formative 'n') is sometimes used instead of 'tân-u,' just as 'nâ,' of the first person, and 'nî,' of the second, are occasionally used instead of 'nân-u' and 'nîn-u.'

In Telugu the reflexive pronoun is more regularly declined, and is more in accordance with the Tamil-Canarese, than any other pronoun of the personal class. The nominative is 'tân-u;' the inflexion and possessive 'tăn-a;' the plural nominative 'tâm-u' or 'târ-u:' 'tâ' may be used at pleasure, as in Canarese, for 'tân-u.'

A similar regularity of formation and of declension is apparent in all the Drâvidian dialects, so that further comparison of the forms of this pronoun seems to be unnecessary. The root or base is evidently 'tâ,' *self*. The final 'n' of the singular, though probably only a formative addition (like the final 'n' of 'nâ-n,' *I*, and 'nî-n,' *thou*), is one of great antiquity, for we find it even in the Brahui: *e.g.*, the nominative singular is 'tenat' (compare with this the inorganic 't,' which is suffixed to the personal pronouns in Gônd); gen, 'tena;' dat. 'tene.'

'tân,' *self* (like 'nân,' *I*, and 'nîn,' *thou*), is of no gender, and is used in connexion with each personal gender indiscriminately; so that this final 'n' has evidently a different origin from the 'n' or 'an,' which constitutes the sign of the masculine of rationals. The 'n' of the singular of the personal pronouns has nothing to do with gender, and is a sign of the singular number alone.

The *use* of this pronoun agrees with the use of the corresponding Indo-European reflexive. It always agrees with the principal nominative of the sentence, and with the governing verb, or that which is in agreement with the principal nominative. It is also used as an emphatic addition to each of the personal and demonstrative pronouns, like the Latin 'ipse,' or like the English *self*, in the compounds *myself*, *yourself*, &c.: *e.g.*, we say in Tamil 'nân-tân,' *I myself*; 'nî-tân,' *thou thyself*; 'avan-tân,' *he himself*; 'avaḷ-tân,' *she herself*; 'adu-tân,' *itself* or *that itself*: and 'tâm,' the plural of 'tân' (or, in the colloquial dialect, its double plural 'tâng-gaḷ'), is in like manner appended to the plurals of each of those pronouns and demonstratives.

'tân' acquires also an adverbial signification by the addition of the usual adverbial formatives; *e.g.*, 'tânây̆' (for 'tân-âgi'), Tam., *of myself*, *of yourself*, or *spontaneously*: and when appended to nouns of quality or relation its use corresponds to that of our adverbs *really*, *quite*, &c.; *e.g.*, 'meÿ tân,' Tam., *it is really true*, 'śari tân,' *quite right*.

One use to which the reflexive is put is peculiar to these languages, —viz., as an honorific substitute for the pronoun of the second person; and in this connexion either the singular, the plural, or the double plural may be used, according to the amount of respect intended to be shown. When used in this manner, it is not annexed to, or compounded with, the pronoun of the second person, but is used alone: and though, when it stands alone, it generally and naturally denotes the third person, yet when thus used honorifically for the second person, the verb with which it is connected receives the pronominal terminations not of the third person but of the second. This use of 'tân,' as an honorific pronoun of the second person, illustrates the possibility, if not the probability, of the origin of the Indo-European pronoun 'tu,' *thou*, from a demonstrative base.

A very interesting class of Tamil words, the nature of which has generally been overlooked, has originated from the honorific use of the reflexive pronoun. Its *inflexion*, or possessive, has been prefixed honorifically to most of the pure Drâvidian words which denote parents and other near relations, in a manner which somewhat resembles our modern periphrasis *Her Majesty*, *your worship*, &c. In general the plural 'tam' has been used in this connexion instead of the singular 'tan,' as a prefix of greater honour, but in some instances these compound words have become so corrupted that their constituent elements can scarcely be recognized. The Tamil 'tagappan,' *father*, is formed from 'tam-appan,' *their* (honorifically *his*) *father*, meaning, as it were, *his paternity*. 'tammei,' *mother*, is from 'tam-âÿi,' *her maternity*; and 'tâÿ,' *mother*, the more common word, is in like manner from 'ta-âÿi,' in which we find the crude 'ta' for 'tam.' 'tamayan,' *elder brother* (Tel., 'tammuḍu'), is from 'tam' and 'ayan' or 'eiyan,' *an instructor*, meaning *his tutorship*. 'tang-gei,' *younger sister*, is from 'tam,' and 'kei,' *a handmaid* (literally *a hand*), meaning *her handmaidenship*.* 'tambi' (Tel., 'tammu'), *younger brother*, and 'tandei' ('Tel., 'tandri'), *father*, evidently include the same honorific prefix 'tam' or 'tan;' but the nouns which form the basis of these words are so changed that they cannot now be recognized. 'tambirân,' a title of God, which is commonly applied to a particular class of Hindu abbots is formed from the same 'tam' and 'pirân' (probably from 'pra,' Sans., *before*, *first*), *Lord* or *God*, meaning *his lordship*, literally *his godship*: and this is perhaps the only word of this class the derivation of which has commonly been admitted by lexicographers.

Another remarkable use of the reflexive pronoun is the adoption of its possessive, or inflexional base, 'tan,' *of self* or *self's*, as the base of the abstract noun 'tan-mei' or 'tanam,' *quality* or *nature*, literally *selfness*; 'mei' is the regular formative of Tamil abstracts, like our English *ness*, or the Latin 'tas.' This word is identical in meaning with the Sanscrit 'tatvam,' *nature*, *property*, which is derived from

* Compare with this meaning of 'a younger sister,' the name of 'spinster' which is applied by ourselves to unmarried females; and also the derivation which is attributed to 'duhtri' ('duhitar'), Sans., *daughter*, viz., *a milk-maid* (or as Bopp regards it, *a suckling*), from 'duh,' *to milk*.

'tad' or 'tat,' *that*, and is possibly allied to it (though indirectly) in origin.

'tâ,' the base of the Drâvidian reflexive pronoun, has no connexion with, or resemblance to, any other pronoun of this family of languages; though it is unquestionably a pure Drâvidian root. If we look at its meaning and range of application it must, I think, have originated from some emphatic demonstrative base; and it will be found that there is no lack either in the Indo-European or in the Scythian family of demonstratives closely resembling 'tâ' or 'tâ-n.' We see examples of this resemblance in the Sanscrit 'ta-d,' *that* (from 'ta,' the demonstrative, and 'd,' the sign of the neuter singular); in 'tadâ,' *then, at that time;* and also (with the 't' weakened into 's') in 'sah,' *he.* The reflexive pronouns of this family, 'sva,' &c., are probably derived from the same base, though considerably altered. Compare also the Old Greek article, which is properly a demonstrative pronoun, 'τός,' 'τή,' 'τό;' and the corresponding German 'der,' 'die,' 'das.' We find the same or a similar demonstrative (with an annexed nasal, as in the Drâvidian 'tân') in the Doric, 'τῆν-ος,' *he, that,* which is the form from which the Æolian 'κῆν-ος,' and the later Greek 'ἐ-κεῖν-ος,' was derived (by a change similar to that by which the Hebrew pronominal suffix 'kâ' was derived from 'tâ'). The resemblance between 'τῆν' and 'tân' is certainly remarkable: and may not this Drâvidian reflexive pronoun, which is used honorifically as a pronoun of the second person, throw some light on that curious, indeclinable Greek word which is sometimes used as a form of polite address, viz., 'τᾶν' or ''ὦ τᾶν,' *Sir, My good friend,* &c., and which has been derived by some etymologists from 'τῆν-ος,' by others from an obsolete vocative of 'τύ' or 'τύνη?'

The same demonstrative, with a similar final 'n,' appears also in the Old Prussian 'tan's' (for 'tana-s'), *he;* and in the Scythian tongues, we find it, either nasalised or pure, in the Finnish remote demonstrative 'tuo,' and the proximate 'tama;' in the Lappish 'tat' *he,* 'tan,' *of him* (root 'ta'); and in the Ostiak remote demonstrative 'toma,' and proximate 'tema.'

The reflexive pronoun is used by the Seoni Gônd both as a reflexive and as a demonstrative. Thus, in the *Song of Sandsumjee,* in Dr. Manger's paper ('Journal of the Bengal Asiatic Society'), 'ten,' means *him* (not '*se,*' but '*illum*'); 'tunna,' *his;* and 'tâne,' *her* and *it.* The reflexive signification also appears in the same song in 'tunwa' (Tam. 'tan'), '*suus-a-um.*' This seems to prove that 'tâ' was originally a demonstrative.

The strongest argument, perhaps, for considering the Drâvidian 'tâ' or 'tân,' *self,* to be allied to the Scytho-Sanscrit demonstrative 'ta' is the circumstance that 'tan,' the inflexional base of 'tân,' is used in the formation of the word 'tanmei' or 'tanam,' *quality, selfness,* in precisely the same manner as the Sanscrit 'tad,' *that;* which forms the basis of the corresponding Sanscrit word 'tatvam,' *quality, thatness.* The Drâvidian word may have been, and probably was, framed in imitation of the Sanscrit (for so abstract a term is necessarily of late origin), but it cannot have been directly derived from the Sanscrit word. It seems very probable that both bases are remotely allied, and if they are so allied, their alliance carries us back to a very remote period: for whilst the Drâvidian reflexive pronoun retains the original demonstrative 't,' the corresponding reflexive in every one of the Indo-European tongues 'sva,' 'se,' &c.) had already allowed 't' to be weakened into 's,' before those tongues separated from the parent stem.

4. Plurals of the Personal and Reflexive Pronouns.

I class the plurals of these pronouns together because they are formed from the same pronominal bases as their singulars (which have already been investigated), and because they are all formed on one and the same plan, viz., either by the addition of a pluralising particle (generally 'm') to the pronominal base, or by the substitution of that particle for the singular formative. Exceptions exist, but they are few and trivial.

Comparison of dialects.—In the classical dialect of the Tamil, the plurals of the personal and reflexive pronouns ('nân,' *I,* 'nî,' *thou,* 'tân,' *self*) are 'nâm' or 'yâm,' *we;* 'nîr,' 'nîyir,' or 'nîvir' (instead of the more regular 'nîm'), *you;* and 'tâm,' *selves.* In the colloquial dialect a double plural has got into extensive use, which is formed by the addition to the classical plurals of 'gaḷ,' the sign of plurality which especially belongs to the class of *irrationals.* In consequence of the existence of these two sets of plurals, a difference in their use aud application has gradually established itself.

The classical or pure and simple plurals are now used in the colloquial dialect as honorific singulars; whilst the double plurals—'nânggaḷ' ('nâm-gaḷ'), *we;* 'nînggaḷ' ('nîm-gaḷ'), *you;* and 'tânggaḷ' (tâm-gaḷ'), *selves*—are used as the ordinary plurals. A double plural has crept into the Telugu also; *e.g.,* 'mîrulu' (for 'mîru'), *you,* and 'vârulu' (for 'vâru'), *they.* Another point of difference between 'nâm' and 'nânggaḷ,' the two Tamil plurals of the first personal pronoun, will be inquired into under a subsequent head. The formation of these secondary, double plurals of the Tamil and Telugu is in harmony with a usage which is observed in the Turkish. In that language 'ben,' *I*, is regularly pluralised into 'biz,' *we;* and 'sen,' *thou*, into 'siz,' *you;* but those plurals are sometimes pluralised over again by the addition of 'ler,' the ordinary suffix of plurality; *e.g.*, 'biz-ler,' *we*, 'siz-ler,' *you*.

In the verbal inflexions of the Tamil, the initial or radical consonant of each of the pronominal plurals (as of the corresponding singulars) disappears; and the pronoun is represented solely by the included vowel and the sign of plurality. The personal termination of the first person plural in the colloquial dialect is 'ôm;' in the classical dialect 'âm,' 'am,' 'êm,' 'em.' The termination of the second person plural is 'îr' or 'ir,' the representative of 'nîr.' The reflexive pronoun 'tâm,' *selves*, has no place in the verbal inflexions.

Of the three High Tamil or classical plurals which have been mentioned—'nâm,' 'nîr,' and 'tâm'—two form their plurals by substituting 'm' for the final 'n' of the singular, or by adding 'm' to the crude root. This I consider to be the regular method of pluralizing the personal pronouns; and the use of 'nîr,' *you*, instead of 'nîm,' is an abnormal exception. This appears on comparing it with 'nîng-gaḷ,' the corresponding plural in the colloquial dialect, which is formed from 'nîm'—the plural that is required by rule, and which is found in the ancient dialect of the Canarese. It also appears from the circumstance that 'nîr' is not the base of the oblique cases of the plural of this pronoun in any dialect of the Tamil. 'm' constitutes the sign of plurality instead of 'r' in the oblique cases of 'nîr,' precisely as in those of 'nâm,' *we*. 'nâm' is represented in the oblique cases in the classical dialect by 'nam' and 'em;' and by 'nam' and 'enggaḷ' ('em-gaḷ') in the colloquial dialect. In like manner, the oblique cases of the plural of the second personal pronoun are 'um' and 'num' in the higher dialect; and 'unggaḷ' ('um-gaḷ') in the colloquial. 'nin,' the abbreviation of 'nîn,' being used in the classics as the inflexion of the old singular, we should have expected to find the corresponding 'nim' (from 'nîm') in the plural: but both in the oblique cases and in the termination of the plural of the imperative, 'i' has given place to 'u,' and 'num' or 'um' has supplanted 'nim.' 'num,' the plural inflexion of the Tamil, is identical with the nominative plural of the Brahui, which is also 'num.'

In Telugu the second personal pronoun is pluralised in the nominative by 'r' instead of 'm,' *e.g.*, 'mîr-u,' *you;* and in Telugu, as in all the other Drâvidian dialects, 'r' invariably forms the plural of the personal terminations of the indicative mood of the verb. It will be seen, however, in the sequel that there are indications in Telugu that this use of 'r' is abnormal.

In Canarese the plurals of all the personal pronouns are formed in the ancient dialect with perfect and beautiful regularity; *e.g.*, 'ân,' *I*, 'âm,' *we;* 'nîn,' *thou*, 'nîm,' *you;* 'tân,' *self*, 'tâm,' *selves.* In the oblique cases the included vowel is shortened as usual; and the only other change which takes place is in the weakening (as in Tamil) of the radical 'a' of the nominative of the first person into 'e,' *e.g.*, 'emma,' *our*. In this particular, 'namma,' the form which has survived in the colloquial dialect is more regular, and evidently more ancient. The modern dialect substantially agrees with the ancient, the chief difference consisting in the softening, in the nominatives alone, of the final 'm' into 'vu;' *e.g.*, 'nâvu,' 'nîvu,' and 'tâvu,' instead of 'nâm,' 'nîm,' and 'tâm.'

In the personal terminations of the verb, the modern dialect uses 'êve,' 'evu,' and 'êvu,' as representatives of 'nâvu,' *we;* the 'e' of which forms corresponds to 'ên,' the termination of the Tamil singular. This final 'vu' of the modern Canarese is not euphonic, like the 'vu' of the Telugu singular, 'nî-vu,' *thou;* but is softened from, and is the representative of, an older 'm.' Though 'm' is the true sign of the plural of the second person, as of the other personal pronouns, 'r' is used instead in all the Canarese verbal terminations, as in those of all the other dialects. The ancient Canarese uses 'ir,' the modern 'iri' and 'îri.'

In Telugu the 'm' which constitutes the pronominal sign of plurality is not softened into 'vu' in the termination of the first person plural of the verb, as in Canarese. That termination is 'amu,' 'âmu,' 'emu,' 'êmu;' and in the preterite it takes the shape of 'imi,' through the influence of 'ti,' the preterite formative. The plural of the second person is represented by 'âru,' 'îri,' 'eru,' 'êru,' 'uru,' and 'ru;' of which 'r,' the pluralising suffix of 'mîru,' *you*, is the only essential element.

The Telugu differs from the Tamil-Canarese in occasionally using 'târ-u' instead of 'tâm-u,' as the nominative plural of the reflexive pronoun. This irregularity, however, like that of the pluralisation of the second personal pronoun by means of 'r' instead of 'm,' disappears in the oblique cases; the plural inflexion or possessive of this pronoun being 'tam-a,' in Telugu, as in the other dialects. 'tamar-u,' sometimes used instead of 'tâm-u,' is properly a possessive noun.

The Telugu plurals 'mêm-u,' *we*, and 'mîr-u' (or 'mîru-lu'), *you*, present some peculiarities which require to be separately inquired into.

In common with their singulars, the inflexions of these pronouns reject altogether the final consonant—the sign of number—and retain the long included vowel of the nominative unaltered. Thus, the inflexion or possessive of 'mêmu' is 'mâ,' and that of 'mîru' 'mî'—corresponding to the singular inflexions 'nâ' and 'nî.' The objective case, however, follows the rule of the Tamil and Canarese; *e.g.*, 'mamu' or 'mammu,' *us*, 'mimu' or 'mimmu,' *you*. It may, therefore, be concluded that the mode in which the inflexions 'mî' and 'mâ' are formed is irregular and of late origin; and that in Telugu, as in the other dialects, 'm' is to be regarded as the received and regular sign of the plural of the personal pronouns.

The chief peculiarity of these pronouns ('mêm-u' and 'mîr-u') in Telugu, is the change of the initial 'n' into 'm.' It has been seen that 'nâ' is the root of the primitive Drâvidian pronoun of the first person singular, and 'nî' that of the second; that the most essential portion of those pronouns is the initial consonant 'n;' and that the normal method of forming plurals from those singulars is by annexing to them a final 'm.' How then is it to be accounted for that the Telugu plurals have 'm' as their initial and radical, instead of 'n?'—'mêm-u' and 'mîr-u,' instead of 'nêm-u' and 'nîm-u' or 'nîr-u?'

I believe that this 'm' is not to be considered as the representative of an older pronominal root; but that it is merely the result of the euphonic attraction of the final 'm,' which constitutes the sign of plurality. I have been led to this conclusion by the following reasons:—

(i.) In the higher and more ancient dialect of the Telugu, 'memu,' *we*, is replaced by 'êmu;' precisely as 'ênu' is used in that dialect instead of 'nênu,' *I*. These older forms, 'ên-u' and 'êm-u,' are in perfect accordance with the Ancient Canarese 'ân' and 'âm,' and especially with the personal terminations of the Tamil verb, 'ên' and 'êm.' It is demonstrable that the Canarese 'ân' and 'âm' have been softened from 'yân' and 'yâm,' of which another form is the Malayâla 'ñjân' and 'ñjâm;' and I believe that these are derived by the ordinary change of 'n' into 'ñj' and 'y,' from the Tamil 'nân' and 'nâm.'

We thus arrive at the conclusion that the 'm' of the Telugu plural is abnormal, and that 'mêm-u' must have been formed from an older 'nêm-u;' and if, as I have supposed, the normal Drâvidian 'na' itself is allied to, and weakened from, a still older Scytho-Sanscrit 'ma,' the remembrance of this, or the surviving influence of the fact, would tend to facilitate a return of 'n' to 'm' in

Telugu; though I doubt not that the euphonic attraction of the 'm' which is used as a sign of plurality, is to be regarded as the immediate cause of that return.

(ii.) If the plural of the Telugu first person alone had 'm' for its basis, we might possibly suppose that 'm' to be radical and primitive, on account of 'm' being the basis of the corresponding Scytho-Sanscrit pronoun; but we find the same initial 'm' in the plural of the Telugu second person also. Now, as it cannot be doubted that 'nî,' the singular of that pronoun—agreeing as it does with the Behistun-Scythian and the Chinese, as well as with many of the Finnish forms—faithfully represents the primitive Drâvidian pronoun of the second person, it seems certain that 'mîm' (the supposititious nominative from which the objective 'mim-mu' has been derived) must have been altered from 'nîm.' We may, therefore, conclude that the same process took place in the pronoun of the first person also.

(iii.) The Telugu is more addicted to harmonic changes than any other Drâvidian dialect. It alters both vowels and consonants for harmonic reasons so frequently, that the change from 'nêm-u' to 'mêm-u,' and from 'nîm-u' to 'mîm-u,' would be thought by Telugu people a very natural and trivial one.

Possibly this change throws light on a termination of the imperative in Tamil which has not been accounted for.

The ordinary representative of the plural of the pronoun of the second person in Tamil imperatives is 'um,' a weakened form of 'num;' but in the poets we find also 'min,' *e.g.*, 'kêṇ-min' (theme 'kêḷ,' *to hear*,) *hear ye*, instead of the colloquial 'kêḷ-um.' Possibly this 'min' is an euphonic displacement of 'nim,' that very abbreviation of 'nîm' which we should expect to find used (instead of 'um') in the older dialect.

The Ku agrees with the Telugu, in the main, as to the mode in which it pluralizes the personal pronouns. Its nominatives are 'âm-u,' *we*, and 'îr-u,' *you*; but the inflexions of the same are 'mâ' and 'mî.' In the personal terminations of the verb the plural of the first person annexes 'âmu'; that of the second 'êru' or 'âru.'

The Malayâla plurals are nearly identical with those of the Tamil.

The only difference deserving of notice is that the included vowel is abbreviated in the nominative plural, as well as in the oblique cases; *e.g.*, 'ñjăngaḷ,' *we*, instead of 'nânggaḷ, and 'nĭngaḷ,' *you*, instead of 'nînggaḷ;' and that in the oblique cases the initial 'n' is not lost, and 'a' changed to 'i' in the first person and 'i' to 'u' in the second, as in Tamil, but the nominatives themselves are used unchanged as the bases of the oblique cases.

In Tulu the plural of the first person is 'namma,' instead of 'nâm,' the inflexion of which is 'nama,' as in High Tamil. The only representative of this plural in the verbal terminations is 'va.' There are two forms of the plural of the secoud person, as in Tamil; viz., 'îr,' corresponding to the Tamil 'nîr,' and the double plural 'nînggaḷ.' 'ar' represents this plural in the personal terminations of the verb.

The Tuda plural of the first person is 'ôm,' as in the personal termination of the verb in colloquial Tamil. The representative of this plural in the verbal inflexions is 'imi,' as in the Telugu preterite. The plural of the second person is 'nima.'

The Kôta plural of the first person is 'nâme,' which in the personal terminations of the verb becomes 'emme.' The nominative plural of the second person is 'nîye,' of which the inflexion is 'nima,' and the verbal ending 'irri.'

In Gônd the plural of the first person is 'amat,' of the second 'imat;' the final 't' of which forms is inorganic and abnormal. The inflexion, like that of the Telugu, is 'mâ' for the first person plural, and 'mî' for the second. The personal termination of the first person plural of the verb is 'âm' or 'ôm;' of the second, 'rit' or 'it.'

The Ûrâon and Râjmahal dialects form the plurals of their personal pronouns regularly by changing the final 'n' into 'm.' Compare the Ûrâon 'em,' *we*, with 'enan,' *I:* the Râjmahal 'nam,' 'om,' *we* with 'en,' *I*, and 'nim,' the base of the possessive 'nim-ki,' *your*, with the singular nominative 'nin,' *thou.*

In Brahui the plural of the first person is 'nan;' that of the second 'num,' which is identical with one of the Tamil plurals. In the verbal inflexions the final 'n' of 'nan,' *we*, represents the plural of the first person;' *e.g.*, 'aren,' *we are:* in the second person the final 'm' of 'num' disappears, and 'ri' is used instead, precisely as in the true Drâvidian dialects; *e.g.*, 'areri,' *you are.*

The result of the foregoing comparison is, that the first person forms its plural in all the Drâvidian idioms (with the solitary exception of the Brahui) by changing the final formative 'n' into 'm;' that the second person originally formed its plural in the same manner without exception, viz., by substituting 'm' for 'n,' though the verbal endings and the nominative of the isolated pronoun are now found to prefer 'r;' and that there is but one solitary and trivial exception (viz., that of an optional Telugu nominative) to the rule that the reflexive pronoun also forms its plural by discarding 'n' and annexing 'm.' Consequently we are now entitled to regard 'm' as the regular and ancient sign of plurality which is used by the Drâvidian personal pronouns.

'ar,' 'ir,' or 'r,' is the plural of all 'rationals' in the Drâvidian languages, with the exception of the three personal pronouns; and the existence of this exception constitutes 'r' a sign of the plural of the third person. How then has a termination which is peculiar to the third person found its way into the second? In this manner, I apprehend:—'nîr,' or more fully 'nîyir' (nî-(y)-ir,) means literally *thou + they;* and this compound would necessarily bring out the signification *you.* The Sanscrit 'yushmê' ('yu+smê'), *you,* is supposed to have a similar origin.

Extra-Drâvidian relationship.—We now proceed to inquire whether final 'm,' the distinctive Drâvidian plural of the personal pronouns, forms the plural of this class of words in any other family of languages.

'm' having a tendency to be weakened into 'n' (of which there are many examples in the terminations of Tamil nouns), and 'm' and 'n' being generally equivalent nasals, the use of a final 'n' as a sign of the plural of pronouns, may possibly be equivalent to that of 'm.' If so, we may adduce as examples of plurals allied to the Drâvidian the Brahui 'nan,' the Chaldee 'anân,' and the Ostiak 'men,' *we;* as also the Persian 'tan,' *you.*' A slight trace of the use of 'm' as a sign of the plural may be noticed in the Beluchi 'mimiken,' *we,* when compared with 'menik,' *I.* In the Ostiak, a Finnish dialect, the first person plural of the verb terminates in 'm,' whilst the plural of the corresponding pronoun terminates in 'n.' On comparing the Finnish proper 'olen,' *I am,* with 'olemme,' *we are,* we are struck with their resemblance to the Drâvidian rule. The resemblance, however, is illusory; for the 'm' of the Finnish 'me' is a sign of personality, not of plurality. 'me,' *we,* is the plural of 'ma,' the old Finnish *I;* of which 'na' (from which the 'n' of 'olen' arises) is, as I have shown, an euphonic modification. We can scarcely indeed expect to find in the pronouns of the Scythian languages any sign of plurality perfectly corresponding to that of the Drâvidian 'm;' for in those languages the personal pronouns are generally pluralized by a change of the final vowel, not by any change or addition of consonants: *e.g.,* Manchu 'bi,' *I,* 'be,' *we;* Magyar 'te,' *thou,* 'ti,' *you;* Ostiak and Finnish 'ma,' *I,* 'me' (or 'men'), *we.*

I have reserved till now the consideration of a series of close and remarkable analogies which run through the whole of the Indo-European family of languages, and which are found also in the North-Indian vernaculars. In those languages we find very frequent use of 'm' in the plurals of the personal pronouns, in which it either constitutes the final consonant, or occupies a place of evident importance;

and this 'm' in some instances appears to replace a final 'n' or '*n*' which is used by the corresponding singulars.

In the vernaculars of Northern India we find the following instances of the use of 'n' or '*n*' in the singular and 'm' in the plural. Hindi 'mai*n*,' *I*, 'ham,' *we;* 'tû,' 'tû*n*,' or 'tai*n*,' *thou*, 'tum,' *you:* Gujarâthi 'hu*n*,' *I*, 'hame,' *we;* 'tû*n*,' *thou*, 'tame,' *you:* Marâthi 'tû*n*,' *thou*, 'tumhi,' *you*. In Bengali and Uriya '*n*' disappears from the terminations of the singulars, but in the plural 'm' retains its place as in the other dialects: *e.g.*, Bengali 'toma' or 'tumi,' the inflexional base of the plural of the second person; and Uriya 'tumbha,' the base of 'tumbhamâni.' The same distinctive 'm' appears in the Pâli-Prâkrit 'tumhe,' *you*, 'amhe,' *we*. Compare also the New Persian 'shumâ,' *you*, and the final 'm' of 'hastêm,' *we are*.

Similar and very striking analogies meet us in Greek. Compare the singulars 'ἐγών' and 'τούν,' 'ἐγώνη,' and 'τούνη' with the plurals 'ἡμεῖς' and 'ὑμεῖς.' This resemblance too is strengthened when the vowels of the Greek plurals are compared with some of the corresponding Drâvidian ones: *e.g.*, compare 'ἡμ-εῖς' with the Telugu 'êm-u,' *we;*' and 'ὑμ-εῖς' with 'um,' which is the base of the oblique cases of the Tamil plural of the second person, and is used to represent that pronoun in the plural of the imperative.

It also deserves to be noticed, that in the Greek, Persian, Gaurian, &c., 'm' is not used indiscriminately by all nouns, or even by all pronouns, as a sign of plurality in general, but is invariably restricted to the pronouns of the first and second person—a usage which precisely accords with that of the Drâvidian languages.

A strong case for regarding the 'm' of the Indo-European idioms as allied to the plural 'm' of the Drâvidian family has doubtless now been established; and yet this resemblance, though so exact and consistent, will be found on investigation to be entirely illusory! On a more extended comparison it diminishes, and at last it disappears. Perhaps, indeed, no better illustration can be found than that which will now be adduced, of the danger of confiding in apparent resemblances, and of the value of comparison in philology.

The resemblance of the final 'n' of the North-Indian and of some Greek singulars to the final 'n' of the singulars of the Drâvidian pronouns, though probably accidental, is to be classed in a rather different category from that of the plural 'm.' The final '*n*' of the Hindi 'mai*n*,' 'tu*n*,' &c, is an euphonic and purely inorganic nasal, which adds nothing to the grammatical expression: this is also the character of the 'ν' of the Greek 'ἐγών' and 'τούν;' and the origin of those nasals is to be attributed to the euphonic influences from which the final 'n' of the Tartar 'men' and 'sen' proceeded; not, as I think, to the neuter termination of the Sanscrit pronouns 'ah-am' and 'tva-m.' On the other hand, the final 'n' of the Drâvidian pronouns is not a mere inorganic or euphonic addition, but is used distinctively as a sign of the singular, and in most of the dialects evinces greater persistency than the initial and radical 'n' itself.

Though, however, in actual use 'n' is a sign of the singular, it may possibly have proceeded originally from an euphonic origin; and this view is confirmed by the circumstance that in Canarese it is regarded as a formative, and accordingly is optionally dispensed with, and the crude, unformed root, without this addition, is occasionally used as the nominative singular. This 'n' may, therefore, after all, have some ulterior connexion with the final 'n' of the Græco-Gaurian, as well as the Scythian singulars.

This disturbing element being eliminated, we come now to the resemblance which is found to subsist between the Græco-Gaurian plural 'm' and the final 'm' of the Drâvidian plurals. On extending our comparison a few stages, so as to include those dialects which exhibit the original character of the Indo-European pronouns, no trace of a connexion between the one 'm' and the other, will be found to survive.

'ἡμεῖς' and 'ὑμεῖς' are not the oldest forms of the Greek plurals. For 'ἡμεῖς,' the Doric and Æolic dialects have 'ἄμες,' 'ἄμμες,' and 'ἄμμε:' for 'ὑμεῖς' they have 'ὔμες,' 'ὔμμες,' and 'ὔμμε:' of which forms, the oldest and most reliable appear to be 'ἄμμες,' or its uninflected type 'ἄμμε,' and 'ὔμμες' or 'ὔμμε.' When 'ἄμμε,' *we*, is now compared with the corresponding Prâkrit 'amhê,' with the Gujarâthi 'hame,' with the Zend (supposititious) 'ahme,' from which proceeds the possessive 'ahmâkem' (corresponding to the Prakrit 'amhâkam'), *our*; and finally with the Vedic-Sanscrit 'asmê,' *we*, it is evident that the last-mentioned form, 'asmê,' is the normal type from which all the rest are derived. The progression is very clear—'asmê,' 'ahmê,' 'amhê,' 'ἄμμε,' 'ἀμμέ-ες,' = 'ἡμεῖς,' 'hame,' 'ham.'

In like manner on comparing 'ὔμμες' or 'ὔμμε,' *you*, with the New Persian 'shumâ,' with the Zend 'yûshem' (in the oblique cases 'yusma'), and with the Vedic-Sanscrit 'yushmê' (for 'yusmê'), it is equally obvious that 'yusmê' is the root of the whole. 'yusmê,' *you*, the plural of 'tu,' *thou*, has probably been softened from 'tusmê,' = 'tu-smê' (as 'asmê' from 'masmê = 'ma-smê'): and this supposititious 'tusmê' (weakened into 'tuhmê,' like 'asmê' into 'ahmê') becomes a reality, when we turn to the Prakrit 'tumhê,' *you*,—from which comes directly the Gaurian 'tumbi,' 'tumbha,' 'tame,' 'tum,' &c.

It has now been ascertained that the Drâvidian final 'm' is to be compared, not with the apparently equivalent 'm' of 'ham' and 'tum,' but with the Vedic particle 'sme;' and the improbability of the existence of any connexion between these two is evidently very great. This improbability increases when the origin of 'sme' is investigated.

Bopp believes 'sma' to be a pronoun of the third person, and explains 'a-smê' (for 'ma-smê'), *we*, to signify *I+they*, and 'yu-smê' (for 'tu-smê'), *you*, to signify *thou+they*.

Moreover, though the 'm' which is derived from this 'smê' is found only in the plural in Sanscrit and Greek, yet in Zend, Pali, and Pracrit it is found also in the singular; *e.g.*, Pracrit 'mamammi = ('mama-sm'-i'), *in me*, 'tumammi' (= 'tuma-sm'-i'), *in thee*. Bopp supposes this use of 'sm'' in singular pronouns to be of late origin, and to have arisen from imitation of the plurals: but there is no proof whatever either that 'sm'' was originally a pronoun of the third person, or that the plural has a better right to it than the singular. Possibly it may have been a particle of specification, like the 'an' prefixed to the pronouns of the first and second persons in the Semitic languages. But whatever may have been its origin, it is now evident that it is entirely unconnected with the 'm' that forms the sign of plurality which is used by the Drâvidian personal pronouns.

Origin of this sign of plurality.—We have now to inquire whether the origin of this plural 'm' can be discovered in the Drâvidian languages themselves, seeing that no trace of it is discoverable in any other family. It appears to me to have been derived from 'um,' the conjunctive or copulative particle of the Tamil, and which appears to have been the primitive form of this particle in the other dialects also. On this supposition 'nâm,' *we*, and 'nîm,' *you*, resolve themselves into 'nâ-um,' '*egoque*,' and 'nî-um,' '*tuque*.' This view is corroborated by the extensive use which is avowedly made of this very 'um' in the formation of Tamil distributive and universal pronouns. Thus, 'evanum,' *every one*, 'engum,' *every where*, '*ubique*,' and 'epporudum,' *always, every time*, are unquestionably and avowedly derived from 'evan,' *who?* 'engu,' *where?* and 'epporudu,' *what time?* with the addition in each instance of the conjunctive particle 'um,' *and;* so that the compound pronoun *every one* is regularly expressed in Tamil by *who? and—; every where*, like 'ubique,' by *where? and—; always*, by *what time? and—*. In the same manner 'um' is annexed as an auxiliary to some affirmative universals for the purpose of widening their application; *e.g.*, 'ellâ-(v)-um,' Malayâlam, *all*, literally *all and—*, from 'ellâ,' *all*, and 'um,' *and*. This form is abbreviated in Tamil into 'ellâm;' which is regarded and treated by grammarians as a plural; and if the addition of 'um,' abbreviated to 'm,' undoubtedly constitutes pronominal distributives and universals, may not the sign of plurality which is employed by the personal pronouns be an abbreviation of the same 'um?' A parallel case appears in Ostiak, in which the sign of the dual number ('ga,' 'ka,' 'gai,' 'gan,' &c.) is derived by Castrén from 'ka' or 'ki,' *also*.

Twofold plural of the Drâvidian pronoun of the first person.—The ordinary plural of the Drâvidian first personal pronoun is constantly used, not only as a plural, but also as an honorific singular, precisely as the Royal and Editorial *we* is used in English; and the plural of every other Drâvidian pronoun may optionally be used as an honorific singular in the same manner. It is not, however, this twofold signification or use of the same pronoun to which I now refer; but the existence of two pronouns of the first person plural, which differ from one another in signification almost as much as the plural and the dual of other languages.

In all the Drâvidian dialects, with the exception of the Canarese and the higher dialect of the Tamil, there are two plurals of the pronoun of the first person, of which one denotes, not only the party of the speaker, but also the party addressed, and may be called *the plural inclusive;* the other excludes the party addressed, and denotes only the party of the speaker, and may be called *the plural exclusive.* Thus, if a person said *we are mortal*, he would naturally use the *we* which includes those who are spoken to, as well as the speaker and his party, or *the plural inclusive*: whilst he would use the *plural exclusive*, or that which excludes the party addressed, if he wanted to say, 'we' *are Hindus;* 'you' *are Europeans.*

There is a similar distinction between the two plurals of the first person which are used in the Marâthi and the Gujarâthi: *e.g.*, 'hame' in Gujarâthi, means *we—the party speaking;* whilst 'âpane' means *we—the party speaking, and you also who are addressed.* There is no connexion between the particular pronominal themes which are used for this purpose in Northern India and in the languages of the South; but the existence of so remarkable an idiom in the North-Indian family, as well as in the Southern, demonstrates the existence in the Northern family of an ancient under-current of Drâvidian, or at least of Scythian influences. The idiom in question is a distinctively Scythian one, and is one of those points which seem to connect the Drâvidian family with the Scythian group. There is no trace of this twofold plural in the Sanscrit, or in any of the languages of the Indo-European family, but it is found everywhere in Central Asia, in the languages which are spoken by the primitive, nomadic tribes. Thus the Manchu has 'mû,' *we—of the one party*, and 'be,' *we—the whole company*. The Mongolian has a similar idiom; and it is found also in the Polynesian languages, in many of the languages of America, and also in those of the Australian tribes.

All the Drâvidian languages do not use precisely the same plural pronouns as *inclusive* and *exclusive* plurals. The colloquial Tamil (with which the Malayâlam and Tulu agree) forms the plural exclusive from 'nâm,' the ordinary and regular plural, by the addition of 'gaḷ,' which is properly a neuter sign of plurality; by which addition 'nâm' becomes 'nânggaḷ' in Tamil; 'ñjangaḷ' or 'ñjangngaḷ' in Malayâlam; and 'engngal' in Tulu.

The Telugu, on the other hand, uses 'mêm-u' (answering not to the Tamil 'nânggaḷ,' but to 'nâm') as its plural exclusive; and as this is the simplest form of the pronoun, it seems better suited to this restricted use than the reduplicated form. The Telugu, though differing from the Tamil in this point agrees with the Tamil in using 'mêmu' as its honorific singular; and this use of the plural exclusive in Telugu as an honorific is more in accordance with philosophical propriety than the Tamilian use of the plural inclusive for this purpose: for when a superior addresses inferiors, it is evidently more natural for him to make use of a plural which excludes those whom he addresses, than one in which they would be included together with himself.

The Ku agrees with the Telugu, and uses 'âm-u' (identical in origin with the Tamil 'nâm') to express the restricted signification which the Tamil gives to 'nânggal.' Its plural inclusive is 'âju,' the oblique form of which is 'ammâ;' and the Telugu plural which corresponds to 'âju' (but which in meaning corresponds to 'nâm') is 'manam-u,' the base and inflexion of which is 'mana.' 'manam-u' is probably derived from 'mâ,' the inflexional base of 'mêmu;' with an euphonic addition, or possibly with a weakened reduplication.

II.—Demonstrative Pronouns.

The Drâvidian languages, like most, if not all, other primitive, uncompounded tongues, are destitute of pronouns (properly so called) of the third person, and use instead demonstratives signifying *this* or *that*, with the addition of suffixes of gender and number. In these languages 'he,' means literally *that man;* 'she,' *that woman;* and 'they,' *those persons or things.*

The words which signify *man* and *woman* have gradually lost the definiteness of their original signification, and shrunk into the position of masculine and feminine terminations. They are no longer substantives, but mere suffixes or signs of gender; and are so closely incorporated with the demonstrative bases that it requires some knowledge of the principles of the language to enable us to separate them. In comparison, therefore, with the Turkish and Ugrian languages, in which there is but one pronoun of the third person, the Drâvidian languages, which possess three, appear to considerable advantage. Nevertheless, the speech of the Drâvidians was originally no richer than the other Scythian idioms; and it has at length surpassed them only by the Aryanistic device of fusing *that-man, that-woman, that-thing,* into single, euphonious words.

The signification of *man* and *woman* still shines through in the masculine and feminine terminations; but no trace remains of the words by which *a thing* and *things* were originally expressed, and which are now represented only by 'd,' the sign of the neuter singular, and 'a,' that of the neuter plural.

Four demonstrative bases are recognised by one or another of the Drâvidian dialects, each of which is a pure vowel; viz., 'a,' the remote, 'i,' the proximate, and 'u,' the medial demonstrative; together with 'ê,' which is the suffix of emphasis in most of the dialects, but is a demonstrative in Ku. The first two, viz., 'a,' the remote, and 'i,' the proximate demonstrative, are the most widely and frequently used.

The medial 'u' is occasionally used by the Tamil poets, in Ancient Canarese, and in Tulu, to denote a person or object which is intermediate between the remote and the proximate; and it will be found that it has ulterior affinities of its own. 'ê,' the ordinary Drâvidian suffix of emphasis, is used as a demonstrative in Ku alone,—in addition however to 'a' and 'i;' *e.g.*, 'êvâru,' *they.* It appears also in the Ûrâon 'êdah,' *this,* the correlative of 'hûdah,' *that.* The use of 'ê' being chiefly emphatic, I refer the reader, for an account of it, to a subsequent head.

The ordinary remote and proximate demonstratives of the Drâvidian dialects are the simple, short vowels 'a' and 'i;' and it will be found that every other form which they assume is derived from this by some euphonic process.

1. *Demonstrative pronouns.*—The original character of the demon-

strative bases is best exhibited by the neuter singular; the formative suffix of which does not commence with a vowel, like 'an' and 'aḷ,' the masculine and feminine suffixes, but consists in a single consonant 'd,' with an euphonic vowel following it. The remote and proximate neuter singulars are in Tamil 'adu,' *that (thing)*, 'idu,' *this (thing)*; in Telugu 'adi,' 'idi;' in Canarese 'adu,' 'idu;' in Malayâlam 'ata,' 'ita;' in Gônd and Tuda 'ad,' 'id.'

'd' having already been shown to be the sign of the neuter singular which is used by pronominals and appellatives, and there being no hiatus between 'a' or 'i' and 'd,' and therefore no necessity for euphonic insertions, it is evident that the 'a' and 'i' of the neuter singulars cited above constitute the purest form of the demonstrative bases. In addition to 'adu' and 'idu,' the High Tamil sometimes uses 'adan' and 'idan.' These forms are probably derived from the annexation to 'ad' and 'id' of 'am,' which is dialectically and ordinarily convertible into 'an.' (*E.g.*, 'aʀ-an,' *virtue*, is identical with 'aʀ-am.') 'am' is a formative of neuter nouns; and I conceive that it was not added to 'ad-u' and 'id-u,' till it had ceased to be known and felt that 'd' was itself a sign of the neuter singular. 'dan,' the final portion of 'adan' and 'idan' is sometimes used in the high dialect, instead of 'du,' as the pronominal termination of the third person neuter singular of the participial noun, especially in the dative; *e.g.*, 'śeÿgiʀadan-ku' (euphonically 'śeÿgiʀadaʀ-ku'), instead of 'śeÿgiʀadu-kku,' *for* or *to the doing*.

The suffixes which are annexed to the demonstrative bases 'a' and 'i,' for the purpose of forming the masculine and feminine singulars and the epicene and neuter plurals, commence with a vowel. Those suffixes are in Tamil 'an,' for the masculine; 'aḷ,' for the feminine; 'ar,' for the epicene plural; and 'ei' or 'a,' for the neuter plural; and 'v' is the consonant which is most commonly used to prevent hiatus. The following, therefore, are the demonstrative pronouns of the Tamil, viz., 'avan,' '*ille*;' 'ivan,' '*hic*;' 'avaḷ,' '*illa*;' 'ivaḷ,' '*hæc*;' 'avar,' '*illi*;' 'ivar,' '*hi*;' 'avei,' '*illa*;' 'ivei,' '*hæc*.' I quote examples from the Tamil alone, because, though different formatives of number and gender are sometimes annexed in the other dialects, those differences do not affect the demonstrative bases. All the above suffixes of gender have already been investigated in the section on 'The Noun.' The mode in which they are annexed to the demonstrative bases is the only point which requires to be examined here.

The demonstrative bases being vocalic, and all the suffixes, with the exception of the neuter singular, commencing with a vowel, the euphonic consonant 'v' had to be used, to keep the concurrent vowels separate and pure.

'v,' though most frequently used to prevent 'hiatus,' is not the only consonant that is employed for this purpose. The Ku being but little attentive to euphony, it sometimes dispenses altogether with the euphonic 'v,' and leaves the contiguous vowels uncombined; *e.g.*, 'ââñju,' *he*, 'ââlu,' *she*. In Tulu 'y' is sometimes substituted for 'v,' *e.g.*, 'âye,' *he*: and even this 'y' disappears in the corresponding feminine, 'âḷ' (for 'avaḷ'), *she;* in which the two contiguous vowels are combined. Even the Tamil sometimes combines those vowels instead of euphonically separating them: *e.g.*, 'yâvar,' *who?* is commonly abbreviated into 'yâr;' and this is still further softened to 'âr,' in the colloquial dialect.

In the higher dialect of the Tamil, 'n' is often used euphonically instead of 'v,' especially in the personal terminations of the verbs. Thus, instead of 'irundân' (for 'irundavan'), *he was*, the poets sometimes say 'irundanan;' and for 'irundava,' *they* (neuter) *were*, the form which we should expect to find used, 'irundana' is universally used instead.

This euphonic 'v' has in some instances come to be regarded as an integral part of the demonstrative itself. In the nominative plural of the Gônd neuter demonstrative, the final and characteristic vowel 'a' has disappeared altogether, without leaving any representative; *e.g.*, 'av,' *those* (*things*), 'iv,' *these* (*things*). In the oblique cases 'a' is represented by 'e.' In Telugu, though the nominatives of the neuter plural demonstratives, 'avi' and 'ivi,' use 'v' merely as an euphonic, yet in the oblique cases, the bases of which are 'vâ' and 'vî,' the demonstrative vowels have got displaced; and 'v' stands at the beginning of the word, as if it were a demonstrative, and had a right *per se* to be represented. In the masculine singulars 'vâḍu,' '*ille*,' 'vîḍu,' '*hic*;' and in the epicene plurals 'vâru,' '*illi*,' 'vîru,' '*hi*,' 'v' euphonic has advanced a step further, and assumed the position of a demonstrative in the nominative, as well as in the inflexion. That this 'v,' however, is not a demonstrative, and that the use to which it is put in Telugu is abnormal, is shown by the fact that in 'dâ' and 'dî,' the inflexions of 'adi' and 'idi,' '*illud*' and '*hoc*,' the neuter singular demonstratives of the Telugu, 'd,' though certainly not a demonstrative, nor even euphonic, but simply a sign or suffix of neuter singularity, has been advanced to as prominent a position (by a similar euphonic displacement) as if it belonged to the root.

In Tulu 'avu,' which is properly the plural neuter, is used for the singular; whilst 'atu,' (corresponding to 'adu'), is used to signify *yes*. A similar use of a plural form for the singular appears in the Old Persian 'ava,' *it*, which appears to be derived from 'avâ,' *those*.

2. *Demonstrative adjectives.*—When the demonstrative bases 'a' and 'i' are simply prefixed to substantives, they convey the signification of the demonstrative adjectives *that* and *this*. When prefixed, they are indeclinable; but on thus prefixing them to substantives, either the initial consonant of the substantive is euphonically doubled, *e.g.*, 'annâḷ' ('a-(n)nâḷ'), Tam., *that day*; or if this euphonic doubling is not resorted to, the demonstrative vowels are lengthened. The Tamil invariably adopts the former plan: the latter is more common in the Malayâlam and Canarese. Where the substantive commences with a vowel, and 'v' is inserted as usual to prevent hiatus, the Tamil, by a dialectic rule of sound, doubles this 'v,' as if it were regarded as an initial consonant: *e.g.*, when 'ûr,' Tam., *a village*, receives this prefix, it becomes not 'avûr' ('a-(v)-ûr'), but 'avvûr.'

The origin of this doubling of the initial consonant of the word to which the demonstrative vowel is prefixed, is to be ascribed to the emphasis which is necessarily included in the signification of the demonstrative. Through this emphasis 'a' and 'i' assume the character, not of ordinary formatives, but of qualifying words; and the energy which they acquire influences the initial consonant of the following substantive, which is no longer an isolated word, but the second member of a compound.

In the same manner and from a similar cause, when Sanscrit words which commence with 'a' privative are borrowed by the Tamil, the consonant to which 'a' is prefixed is often doubled, at least in the colloquial dialect; *e.g.*, 'aññjânam' ('a-(ñj)-ñjânam,' *ignorance*.

The occasional lengthening of the demonstrative vowels, when used adjectivally, in Malayâlam, Canarese, and the other dialects (without the doubling of the succeeding consonant), is merely another method of effecting the same result. The emphasis which is imparted in this manner to the demonstrative, is equivalent to that which the doubled consonant gives; and hence when the demonstrative vowels are lengthened, from 'ă' and 'ĭ' to 'â' and 'î,' the succeeding consonant always remains single. The fact that the demonstrative vowels are short in the pronouns of the third person in each of the Drâvidian dialects without exception, shows that those vowels could not originally have been long, and that the use of long 'â' and 'î' as adjectival prefixes, instead of 'a' and 'i' is owing to emphasis. Some curious illustrations of the lengthening of a vowel through emphasis alone, are furnished by the common speech of the Tamil people; *e.g.*, 'adigam,' *much, large*—a word which is borrowed by the Tamil from the Sanscrit —when it is intended to signify *very much*, is colloquially pronounced 'adîgam.' Similar instances might be adduced from each of the colloquial dialects.

In addition to the use of the simple vowels 'a' and 'i,' and their equivalents 'â' and 'î,' as demonstrative prefixes, the Tamil makes much use also of a pair of derived demonstrative adjectives, viz., 'anda,' *that*, and 'inda,' *this; e.g.*, 'anda maram,' *that tree*, 'inda nilam,' *this piece of land*. These demonstrative adjectives are unknown to the other dialects of the family; and in the higher dialect of the Tamil itself they are unused. Their bases 'and',' 'ind',' are evidently identical with those of the Telugu adverbial nouns 'and-u,' 'ind-u,' *that* or *this (place or thing); e.g.*, 'indu-lô,' *in this*, 'andu-ku,' *to that*. I have no doubt that these Telugu words, 'andu' and 'indu,' are either derived by euphonization from the Tamil demonstrative pronouns 'adu' and 'idu,' or, which is more probable, from the addition to the demonstrative bases of the formative 'du,' nasalized to 'ndu;' in the same manner as in Tamil 'gu' and 'ḍu,' nasalized to 'ngu' and 'ṇḍu,' will be found to have been annexed to the same demonstrative bases, for the purpose of forming similar adverbial nouns. If to these adverbial nouns, 'and-u,' 'ind-u,' we now add 'a,' the formative of the relative participle, by annexing which so many adjectives are formed, we arrive at 'anda' and 'inda,' the Tamil demonstrative adjectives.

3. *Demonstrative nouns: their use as adverbs.* — The Drâvidian languages form nouns of place, time, and relation into demonstrative adverbs (which are adverbs in use only, but nouns in form) by prefixing to them the demonstrative bases.

The most frequently used words of this class are those which signify *then* and *now;* and they are formed by simply prefixing the demonstrative vowels—'a' (remote) and 'i' (proximate)—to any noun which signifies *time: e.g.*, from 'poṛudu,' *time*, the Tamil forms 'appoṛudu' ('a-(p)poṛudu'), *then, that time*, and 'ipporudu,' *now, this time;* from the corresponding noun 'puḍu,' the Telugu forms 'appuḍu,' and 'ippuḍu;' and from 'pôḷ' the Malayâlam forms 'appoḷ' and 'ippôḷ.' Each of these adverbs has the signification of a noun in the locative case; so that the expressions, *that time, this time*, signify, *in that time, in this time*, &c; but the case-signification, though understood, is not expressed. In the Drâvidian languages indeed, not nouns of time and place only, but all nouns may be used as adverbs, with or without the addition of the suffixes of cases; and all adverbs are either nouns or verbs.

A class of words which more nearly resemble our 'adverbs' than the compounds referred to above, are formed by annexing to the demonstrative bases certain formative suffixes: *e.g.*, compare the Tamil 'angu,' *there,* 'ingu,' *here;* 'andru,' *that day,* 'indru,' *to-day;*' the Telugu 'andu,' *in that place, there;* 'indu,' *in this place, here;* the Canarese 'andu,' *that day,* 'indu,' *to day;* 'alli,' *in that place, there,* 'illi,' *in this place, here;* also the High Tamil 'âṇḍu,' *there, then;* 'îṇḍu,' *here, now;* and the Tulu 'anchi,' *there,* 'inchi,' *here.* Similar adverbs are formed from the interrogative vowel 'e' by annexing the same formative terminations. In one of the examples given above, the ideas of place and time are evidently regarded as identical; and another, 'andu,' is an adverb of place in Telugu, and an adverb of time in Canarese. The Tamil 'andru,' *that day,* is evidently an euphonised form of the same word.

In the Tamil adverbs 'angu,' *there,* 'inga,' *here,* the formative which we find to be employed is 'gu'—one which is much used in the formation of ordinary nouns, and which in those nouns as well as in the adverbs before us, is often euphonized into 'ngu.' The primitive, unnasalised formative is seen in the corresponding Gônd adverbs 'iga,' *here,* 'haga,' or 'aga,' *there;* whilst in the Gônd 'inga,' *now,* we see that in that dialect also 'g' has occasionally been nasalised into 'ng.' We may compare also the Gônd adverbs 'hike,' *hither,* 'hoke,' *thither.*

The resemblance between the Gônd 'iga,' *here,* and the corresponding Sanscrit 'iha' is remarkable; yet it cannot be supposed that the Gônd word has been borrowed from the Sanscrit. The demonstrative base 'i' is the common property of the Indo-European and the Drâvidian families; but, though 'iga' seems to be as closely connected with 'iha,' as the Latin 'ego' is with the Sanscrit 'ah-am,' yet the Drâvidian formative 'gu,' 'ngu,' 'ku' (by suffixing which the demonstrative vowel becomes an adverbial noun) has no connection whatever with the merely euphonic 'h' of 'iha.'

The Canarese adverbs of place 'alli,' *there,* and 'illi,' *here,* are evidently derived from the High Tamil 'il,' *a house, a place,* which has been converted, by euphonic displacement, into 'li.' Notwithstanding this, 'il,' *a house,* is not contained in an isolated shape in Canarese.

The formative 'du,' euphonised to 'ndu,' which is found in 'andu,' and 'indu,' is one which is occasionally used in the formation of ordinary nouns, though not so frequently as 'gu.' (See the section on 'Roots.') It may have an apparent resemblance to the formative 'd' or 'th' of several Sanscrit adverbs, *e.g.*, 'athâ,' *so, thus;* 'tadâ,' *then, at that time;* but the connections and relationship of the Sanscrit formative are widely different from those of the Drâvidian one.

In the High Tamil adverbs, 'âṇḍu' and 'îṇḍu' ('â' and 'î,' for 'a' and 'i'), the cerebral 'ḍ' is suffixed as a formative instead of the dental; and it is nasalised accordingly by 'ṇ,' instead of 'n;' but I have no doubt that this 'ḍu' is from the same source, and is used for precisely the same purpose, as the dental suffix. In Telugu in a similar manner, 'aṭṭu,' *that*, an adjective and adverb, which is properly a demonstrative noun, exhibits the cerebral 'ṭ' instead of the more usual dental 'd' or 'nd.'

'âṇḍu,' in Tamil, means not only *then* and *there*, but also *a year*. This word has some apparent resemblance to words which signify *a year* in various other languages; *e.g.*, Ossete 'ans,' Latin 'an-nus,' Mongol 'on,' Manchu 'ania,' Tungusian 'anyan;' but the resemblance disappears on investigation, for the Tamil 'âṇḍu' (Tel. 'êṇḍu') is a modern corruption from 'yâṇḍu,' the word which is used for *year* in the poetry and in all ancient inscriptions; and 'yâṇḍu' is derived from the interrogative base 'yâ' and the formative 'ḍu,' nasalised to 'ṇḍu' (like 'iraḍu,' *two*, nasalised to 'iraṇḍu'), and means properly *when*, secondarily *a time*, and lastly *a year*.

Affiliation of the demonstrative bases: Extra-Drâvidian affinities.—There is only a partial and indistinct resemblance between the remote 'a,' proximate 'i,' and medial 'u,' which constitute the bases of the Drâvidian demonstratives, and the demonstratives which are used by the languages of Northern India.

In Bengali and Singhalese, 'ê' is used as a demonstrative; in Marathi 'hâ,' 'hî,' 'hen:' in the Hindustani we find 'vuh,' *that*, 'yih,' *this*; but in the oblique cases the resemblance increases; *e.g.*, 'is-kô,' *to this*. 'i' is used as the proximate demonstrative in the North-Indian languages more systematically than 'a' or any corresponding vowel is used as the remote; *e.g.*, Marathi 'ikaḍe,' *here*; Hindi 'idhar,' *hither*; Mar. 'itake,' *so much*.

A general resemblance to the Drâvidian demonstrative bases is apparent in several of the Himalayan languages; *e.g.*, Bodo 'imbe,' *this*, 'hobe,' *that*; Dhimal 'î,' 'û;' Ûrâon 'êdah,' 'hûdah.' The Rajmahal 'êh' and 'âh' are perfectly identical with the Drâvidian demonstratives, and form another evidence of the Drâvidian character of a portion of that idiom.

The connexion which appears to subsist between the Drâvidian medial demonstrative 'u' and the 'û' of the Ûrâon and Dhimal is deserving of notice. Perhaps the Drâvidian medial 'u' (Dhimal 'û,' Ûrâon 'hûdah') may be compared with the Old Hebrew masculine-feminine pronoun of the third person, 'hû;' and thus with the Old

Persian remote demonstrative 'hauva,' of which the first portion appears to be 'hu,' and the second 'ava,'—which 'ava' forms the base of the oblique cases. It may also be compared with the 'u' or 'o' which forms the remote demonstrative in some of the Scythian languages: *e.g.*, Finnish 'tuo,' *that*, 'tâma,' *this;* Ostiak 'toma,' *that*, 'tema,' *this.*' Compare also the Hind. 'vuh,' *that;* Bodo 'hobe.'

The Magyar demonstratives are more in accordance with the Drâvidian 'a' and 'i;' *e.g.*, 'az,' *that*, 'ez,' *this.* The demonstratives of the other languages of the Scythian family (*e.g.*, the Turkish 'bou,' *that*, 'ol,' *this*') are altogether destitute of resemblance.

When we turn to the languages of the Indo-European family, they appear in this particular to be closely allied to the Drâvidian. Throughout that family both 'a' and 'i' are used as demonstratives; though not to so large an extent, nor with so perfect and constant a discrimination between the remote and the proximate, as in the Drâvidian family. In Sanscrit 'a' is used instead of the more regular 'i' in most of the oblique cases of 'idam,' *this;* and the correlative of this word, 'adas,' means not only *that*, but also *this.* Nevertheless, 'a' is more generally a remote than a proximate, and 'i' more generally a proximate than a remote demonstrative. In derived adverbial words 'i' has always a proximate force; but 'ta,' the consonantal demonstrative, is more generally used than 'a.' The following are examples of each vowel:—'i-ha,' *here;* 'i-dânîm,' *now;* 'ta-dânîm,' *then:* also 'i-ti,' *so, this much*, 'a-tha,' *so, thus, in that manner.*

We may also compare the Old Persian 'avadâ,' *thither, in that direction;* and the corresponding proximate 'i-dâ,' *hither, in this direction.* The resemblance between these forms, notwithstanding the irregularity of their application, and the Drâvidian remote and proximate demonstrative bases, amounts to identity.

All irregularity disappears in the New Persian, which in this point accords as perfectly with the Drâvidian languages as if it were itself a Drâvidian idiom. Its demonstratives are 'ân,' *that*, 'în,' *this.* These demonstratives are adjectival prefixes, and naturally destitute of number; but when plural terminations are suffixed, they acquire a plural signification; *e.g.*, 'ânân,' *those (persons)*, 'înân,' *these (persons).* The same demonstratives are largely used in the modern Turkish, by which they have been borrowed from the Persian. 'ân' and 'în' are undoubtedly Âryan demonstratives. This is apparent when we compare 'ân' with the Zend 'aêm,' *that;* and that again with the

Sanscrit 'ayam;' but 'în' is still more clearly identical with the Zend 'îm,' *this.* The same 'îm' constitutes the accusative in Vedic Sanscrit (and is also identical with 'iyam,' the masculine-feminine singular of the Old Persian, and the feminine of the Sanscrit); but in Zend 'îm' is the nominative, not the accusative, and it is to this form that the New Persian is most closely allied.

The demonstrative base 'i' (without being restricted, however, to a proximate signification) appears in the Latin 'is' and 'id,' and in the Gothic 'is;' and the Drâvidian and New Persian distinction between the signification of 'a' and that of 'i,' has been re-developed in our English *that* and *this.*

Whilst the New Persian 'ân' and 'în' are closely connected with Sanscrit and Zend demonstratives, it does not follow that they are directly derived from either the one tongue or the other. On the contrary, the exactness with which the Persian discriminates between the remote and the proximate, leads me to conclude that it has retained more faithfully than either of those languages the primitive characteristics of the Pre-Sanscritic speech. If so, instead of supposing the Drâvidian dialects to have borrowed their demonstratives, which are still purer than the Persian, from the Sanscrit (which are irregular and greatly corrupted), it is more reasonable to suppose that the Drâvidian demonstrative vowels retain and exhibit the primeval bases from which the primary demonstratives of the Sanscrit and of all other Indo-European tongues have been derived.

Emphatic 'ê.'—It has been seen that in Ku 'ê' is used as a demonstrative; *e.g.,* 'êvâru' ('ê-(v)-âr'), *they;* and this may be compared with the demonstrative 'ê' of the Sanscrit 'êtat,' *this* (neuter), and the corresponding Zend 'aêtat.' In the other Drâvidian dialects, however, 'ê' is not used as a demonstrative, but is post-fixed to words for the purpose of rendering them emphatic. The manner in which 'ê' is annexed, and the different shades of emphasis which it communicates, are precisely the same in the various dialects, and will be sufficiently illustrated by the following examples from Tamil. When 'ê' is post-fixed to the subject of a proposition, it sets it forth as the sole depositary of the quality predicated; *e.g.,* 'kalvi-(y)-ê śelvam,' *learning (alone is) wealth;* when post-fixed to the predicate, it intensifies its signification; *e.g.,* 'kalvi śelvam-ê,' *learning is wealth (indeed):* when post-fixed to a verb or verbal, it is equivalent to the addition of the adverb *truly, certainly; e.g.,* 'alla-(v)-ê,' *(certainly) not.* In the colloquial dialect, it has often been annexed to the case-terminations of nouns without necessity, so that it has sometimes become in that connexion, a mere expletive; in consequence of which, in such instances, when emphasis is really required by a sign of case, the 'ê' has to be doubled; *e.g.*, 'ennâlêyê' ('ennâl-ê-(y)-ê'), *through me (alone)*.

The same sign of emphasis forms the most common vocative case-sign in the various Drâvidian dialects, the vocative being nothing more than an emphatic enunciation of the nominative. Compare with this the use of the nominative with the addition of the definite article as the vocative in Hebrew and in Attic Greek. The Persian '*é* of supplication' may also be compared with it.

Some resemblance to the use of 'ê' as a particle of emphasis may be discovered in the Hebrew '*he* paragogic' (pronounced 'eh' or 'ah,' according to the connexion), which is supposed to intensify the signification of the words to which it is annexed. The '*he* directive' of the same language is also, and not without reason, supposed to be a mark of emphasis; and its origin is possibly connected with that of the definite article. A still closer resemblance to the emphatic 'ê' of the Drâvidian languages is apparent in Chaldee, in which 'â' suffixed to nouns constitutes their 'emphatic state,' and is equivalent to the definite article of many other languages. The Persian '*é* of particularity,' the '*é* of ascription of greatness,' &c., in addition to the '*é* of supplication,' which has already been referred to, probably spring from a Chaldaic and Cuthite origin; though each of them bears a remarkable resemblance to the Drâvidian emphatic 'ê.'

Honorific demonstrative pronouns.—I have deferred till now the consideration of a peculiar class of honorific demonstratives, which are found only in Telugu and Canarese, and in which, I think, direct Âryan influences may be detected.

(1.) In all the Drâvidian dialects, the plural is used as an honorific singular when the highest degree of respect is meant to be expressed; but when a somewhat inferior degree of respect is intended, the pronouns which are used by the Telugu are 'âyana,' *he*, '*ille*,' and 'âme,' *she*, '*illa*;' with their corresponding proximates 'îyana,' '*hic*,' and 'îme,' '*hæc*.' These pronouns are destitute of plurals.

It can scarcely be doubted that an Âryan origin is to be attributed to these words; and this supposition would account for the circumstance that they are found in the Telugu only, and not in any other dialect of the family (except the Tulu 'âye,' *he*, is to be regarded as a connected form): it would also harmonise with their use as honorifics.

Compare 'âyana' with the Sanscrit masculine 'ayam,' '*ille*,' and 'îyana' with the Sanscrit feminine, and the Old Persian masculine-feminine 'iyam,' '*hic*,' '*hæc*.'

'âme,' '*illa*,' and 'îme,' '*hæc*,' the corresponding feminine pronouns of the Telugu, may be compared not only with the plurals of the Sanscrit pronoun of the third person ('ime,' mas., 'imâh,' fem., 'imâni,' neut.), but also with 'amum' and 'imam,' *him*, which are accusative singulars, and from which it is evident that the 'm' of the plural forms is not a sign of plurality, but is either a part of the pronominal base, or an euphonic addition. Bopp considers it to be the former, but Drâvidian analogies incline me to adopt the latter view; for it can scarcely be doubted that 'âme' and 'îme' are identical with 'âve' and 'îve,' another pair of Telugu pronouns (used when a little less respect is intended); and the 'v' of these forms seems to be the ordinary euphonic 'v' of the Drâvidian languages (which sometimes alternates with 'm'), and not part of the base.

(2.) When a little less respect is meant to be shown than is implied in the use of 'âyana' and 'îyana,' and of 'âme' and 'îme,' the Telugu makes use of 'atadu,' '*ille*,' 'âve,' '*illa*,' with their corresponding proximates 'itadu' and 'îve.' Here the Canarese substantially agrees with the Telugu; *e.g.*, 'âtanu,' '*ille*,' 'îtanu,' '*hic*'(Ancient Can. 'âtam,' 'îtam'). The final 'nu' of the Canarese is the formative of the masculine singular, corresponding to the Telugu 'du;' and the demonstratives 'a' and 'i' are often lengthened (as has already been shown) in Canarese. The Canarese feminines 'âke,' '*illa*,' 'îke,' '*hæc*,' do not appear so perfectly to accord with the Telugu 'âve,' 'îve;' the only real difference, however, is that the Telugu 'v' is purely euphonic, whilst the Canarese 'k' is a formative, the use of which constitutes 'âke' and 'îke' abstract pronominal nouns.

Both the above sets of Telugu pronouns are destitute of plurals, but both are pluralised in Canarese; *e.g.*, 'âtagalu,' 'îtagalu,' *those* and *these* (*men*); 'âkeyar,' 'îkeyar,' *those* and *these* (*women*).

I do not think that the Tuda 'adam,' *he*, *she*, *it*, is allied to any of the pronouns now referred to. I consider it to be a neuter singular which is synonymous with 'adu,' the neuter singular of the Tamil-Canarese, and which is used corruptly for the masculine and feminine, as well as for the neuter. The use of 'adam' as a neuter singular, instead of 'adu,' exactly corresponds to the use of 'adan' instead of 'adu' in High Tamil.

When the Telugu masculine of respect 'ata-du,' 'ita-du,' and the corresponding Canarese honorifics 'âta-nu,' 'îta-nu,' are scrutinised, it is evident that in addition to the vocalic demonstrative bases, 'a' and 'i,' which are found in Drâvidian demonstratives of every kind, the 'ta' which is subjoined to 'a' and 'i' possesses also somewhat of a demonstrative or pronominal signification. It cannot be regarded like 'v' as merely euphonic; and its restriction to masculines shows that it is not merely an abstract formative, like the 'k' of the feminine 'âke.' It can scarcely be doubted, I think, that the origin of this 'ta' is Âryan; for we find in all the Âryan languages much use made of a similar 'ta,' both as an independent demonstrative, and as an auxiliary to the vocalic demonstrative. 'ta-d,' Sans. *that*, is an instance of the former; whilst the secondary or auxiliary place which 'ta' or 'da' occupies in the Sanscrit 'êtad' ('ê-ta-d'), *this*, and 'adam,' 'adas,' ('a-da-m,' 'a-da-s'), *this*, or *that*, is in perfect agreement with the Telugu and Canarese 'â-ta-nu,' 'a-ta-ḍu.'

The final 'e' of 'âve,' 'îve,' 'âme,' 'îme,' 'âke,' 'îke,' is equivalent to the Tamil 'ei.' 'e' or 'ei' is an ordinary termination of abstracts in these languages, and a suitable one, according to Drâvidian notions, for feminine honorific pronouns.

III.—Interrogatives.

There are two classes of interrogatives in the Drâvidian languages, as in all others, viz., interrogative pronouns or adjectives such as, *who? which? what?* and syntactic interrogatives, such as, *is it? is there?*

Interrogative pronouns and adjectives resolve themselves in the Drâvidian tongues into interrogative prefixes, resembling the demonstrative prefixes already considered, by suffixing to which the formatives of number and gender we form interrogative pronouns. The interrogative particle itself, when simply prefixed to a substantive, constitutes the interrogative adjective *what?*

(1.) The first and simplest interrogative prefix is the vowel 'e.'

In all the Drâvidian dialects this prefix is used in the formation of pronominals, in precisely the same manner as the demonstrative bases 'a' and 'i.' It forms one of a set of three vocalic prefixes ('a,' 'i,' 'e'), which occupy one and the same position, obey one and the same law, and differ only in the particular signification which is expressed by each.

The unity of principle pervading these prefixes will be clearly apparent from the subjoined comparative view. The forms which are here exhibited are those of the Tamil alone; but in this particular all the dialects agree so perfectly with the Tamil, and with one another, that it is unnecessary to multiply examples.

	PROXIMATE DEMONSTRATIVE 'I.'	REMOTE DEMONSTRATIVE 'A.'	INTERROGATIVE 'E.'
Masculine sing...	ivan, *hic*	avan, *ille*	evan, *quis?*
Feminine do ..	ivaḷ, *hæc*	avaḷ, *illa*	evaḷ, *quæ?*
Neuter do ..	idu, *hoc*	adu, *illud*	edu, *quid?*
Epicene plural ..	ivar, *hi, hæ*	avar, *illi, illæ*	evar, *qui? quæ?*
Neuter do....	ivei, *hæc*	avei, *illa*	evei, *quæ?*

The interrogative vowel 'e' forms the basis also of various interrogative adverbs or adverbial nouns, in the same manner as the corresponding demonstrative adverbs or adverbial nouns are formed from 'a' and 'i:' *e.g.*, compare 'engu,' *where?* with 'angu,' *there,* and 'ingu,' *here;* 'endru,' *which day?* with 'andru,' *that day,* and 'indra,' *to-day.* A few adverbs of this kind are peculiar to the Canarese; *e.g.*, 'entha,' *of which kind?* 'ettalu,' *on which side?* 'elli,' *in which place? where?* The Tamil has also a regularly declined interrogative noun 'ennam,' *what?* which is derived from 'en' (commonly lengthened to 'ên'), *why?*

'e' is also prefixed adjectivally to substantives, in the same manner as 'a' and 'i;' and (as was observed in the case of those prefixes) it doubles the initial consonant of the substantive to which it is prefixed: *e.g.*, compare 'evvaṛi' (from 'vaṛi,' *a way*), *which way?* with 'avvaṛi,' *that way,* and 'ivvaṛi,' *this way.* In addition to this adjectival prefix, a regular interrogative adjective ('enda,' *what?* or *which?*) is formed by the Tamil, to correspond with the demonstrative adjectives, 'anda,' *that,* 'inda,' *this,* which are peculiar to that dialect. It is chiefly, however, in the colloquial dialect that these forms are used. The higher and more ancient dialect prefers the simple vowels 'a,' 'i,' 'e,' to express *that, this,* and *which?*

I need not call attention to the beautiful and philosophical regularity of this triple set of remote and proximate demonstratives and interrogatives. In no other language or family of languages in the world shall we find its equal or even its second. In addition to which, the circumstance that the demonstrative vowels are not only used in these languages with an invariable and exact discrimination of meaning which is not found in the Indo-European tongues (with the solitary exception of the New Persian), but are also associated with a corresponding interrogative vowel of which the Indo-European tongues are totally ignorant, tends to confirm the supposition which I have already expressed, that the Drâvidian family has retained some Pre-Sanscrit elements of immense antiquity; and, in particular, that its demonstratives, instead of being borrowed from the Sanscrit, represent those old Japhetic bases from which the primary demonstratives of the Sanscrit itself, as well as of various other members of the Indo-European family were derived.

The only peculiarity which requires notice in the use of this interrogative prefix, is the circumstance that it is occasionally lengthened to 'ê,' precisely as 'a' and 'i' are lengthened to 'â' and 'î.' In Tamil this euphonic lengthening is very rare. It is found only in the neuter-singular interrogative pronoun 'edu,' *what or which (thing)?* '*quid?*' which sometimes, especially in composition, becomes 'êdu;' and in the interrogative adverb 'en,' *why?* which is ordinarily lengthened to 'ên.' In Telugu this increase of quantity is more common. It appears not only in 'êmi' and 'êla,' *why?* but is ordinarily used as the interrogative prefix, where the Tamil invariably has short 'e.' Thus, whilst the Tamil has 'evvidam,' *what manner? how?* the Telugu says 'êvidham' instead. So also, whilst the Tamil occasionally only uses 'êdu,' '*quid?*' instead of the more classical 'edu,' the corresponding interrogative of the Telugu is invariably 'êdi,' and its plural 'êvi.' On the other hand, the Telugu masculine interrogative pronoun 'evvaḍu,' '*quis?*' preserves the same quantity as the Tamil 'evan;' and even when the prefix is used adjectivally, it is sometimes 'e' (not 'ê') as in Tamil, *e.g.*, 'eppuḍu' (not 'êpuḍu'), *what time? when?*

We have already seen that the base vowels of the Telugu demonstrative pronouns 'vâḍu,' '*ille*,' 'vîḍu,' '*hic*,' have shifted their position, the forms required by rule instead of 'vâḍu' and 'vîḍu' being 'avaḍu' and 'ivaḍu:' but as the interrogative pronoun is less used than the demonstrative, and therefore less liable to corruption, it has escaped this euphonic displacement of the base vowel; and in consequence we have not 'vêḍu,' '*quis?*' in accordance with 'vâḍu' and 'vîḍu,' as we might have expected, but 'evvaḍu' (for 'evaḍu'), in close accordance with the Tamil 'evan.'

In each of the Drâvidian languages, 'e' is commonly pronounced as 'ye,' and 'ê' as 'yê,' and in Telugu this 'y' is often written as well as heard; but as this is a characteristic of all words in each of the dialects which begin with this vowel, and not of the interrogatives alone, it is evident that it is merely a peculiarity of pronunciation, and that the 'y' in question is no part of the interrogative base

Compare with this Drâvidian interrogative the interrogative 'ê' of the Hebrew; *e.g.*, 'êpô, *where?* (compounded of 'ê' and 'pô,' *here*); and also 'êkâ,' *where?* or *how?*

Under the head of the Syntactic interrogative 'â,' a resemblance which subsists between this interrogative 'e' or 'ê' and the 'ê' of emphasis will be inquired into: and in that particular also it will be found that the Hebrew usage agrees with the Drâvidian.

(2.) The other interrogative of this class is 'yâ.'

'yâ' is not used at all in Telugu; but it is largely used in Canarese and somewhat more rarely in Tamil. In High Tamil 'yâ' is not only prefixed adjectivally to substantives (like 'a,' 'e,' and 'e'), *e.g.*, 'yâ-(k)kâlam,' *what time;* but it is even used by itself as a pronoun; *e.g.*, 'yâ-(ś)śeÿdây,' *what hast thou done?* It forms the basis of only one adverbial noun, viz., 'yâṇḍu,' Tam., *when? a year,* a correlative of 'âṇḍu,' *then,* and 'îṇḍu,' *now.* The only use to which 'yâ' is put in the colloquial dialect of the Tamil, is that of forming the basis of interrogative pronouns; a complete set of which, in Tamil as well as in Canarese, are formed from 'yâ;' *e.g.*, 'yâvan,' '*quis?*' 'yâvaḷ,' '*quæ?*' 'yâdu,' '*quid?*' 'yâvar,' '*qui?*' '*quæ?*' 'yâvei,' '*quæ?*' The Canarese interrogative pronouns accord with these, with a single unimportant exception. The neuters, singular and plural, of the Canarese are formed from 'yâva,' instead of 'yâ; *e.g.*, 'yâvadu,' '*quid?*' (for 'yâdu'), and 'yâvavu,' '*quæ?*' (for 'yâva'). This additional 'va' is evidently derived by imitation from the euphonic 'v' of 'yâvanu,' *he,* and its related forms; but it is out of place in connexion with the neuter, and is to be regarded as a corruption.

In Tamil a peculiar usage with respect to the application of the epicene plural 'yâvar,' '*qui?*' '*quæ?*' has obtained ground. It is largely used in the colloquial dialect with the signification of the singular, as well as that of the plural, though itself a plural only and without distinction of gender; and when thus used, 'yâvar' is abbreviated into 'yâr;' *e.g.*, 'avan yâr,' *who is he?* (literally *he who?*); 'avaḷ yâr,' *who is she?* 'yâr' has also been still further corrupted into 'âr,' especially in compounds.

The Gônd interrogatives 'bâ' and 'bô' appear to have been hardened from 'yâ.'

Extra-Drâvidian relationship.—There is no analogy between either 'e' or 'yâ' and any of the interrogative bases of the Indo-European family. Both in that family and in the Scythian group the ordinary base of the interrogative is the guttural 'k;' *e.g.*, Sanscrit, 'kim,' *what?* The same base appears in the Sanscrit interrogative initial syllables 'ka-,' 'ki-,' 'ku-,' which correspond to the Latin 'qu-,' the Gothic 'hva-,' and the English 'wh-.' We find the same base again in the Turkish 'kim' or 'kîm,' *who? what?* in the Magyar 'ki,' *who?* plural 'kik;' and in the Finnish 'kuka' (root 'ku').

In the absence of a real relative pronoun, the interrogative is used as a relative in many of the Scythian languages. The base of the Sanscrit relative pronoun 'ya' ('yas,' 'yâ,' 'yat'), bears a close apparent resemblance to the Drâvidian interrogative 'yâ.' The Sanscrit 'ya,' however, like the derived North-Indian 'jô,' and the Finnish 'yo' is exclusively used as a relative, whereas the Drâvidian 'yâ' is exclusively and distinctively an interrogative.

It has been conjectured that the Sanscrit 'ya,' though now a relative, was a demonstrative originally; and if (as we shall see that there is some reason for supposing) the Drâvidian interrogatives 'e' and 'a' were originally demonstratives, it may be supposed that 'yâ' was also a demonstrative, though of this no direct evidence whatever now remains. If 'yâ' were originally a demonstrative, the connexion which would then appear to exist between it and the Sanscrit relative would require to be removed a step further back; for it is not in Sanscrit that the relative 'ya' has the force of a demonstrative, but in other and more distant tongues, viz., in the Lithuanian 'yis,' *he;* and in the Slavonian 'yam,' and the Zend 'yim,' *him.*

Syntactic interrogatives, 'â' *and* 'ô.'—The interrogative prefixes 'e' and 'yâ,' are equivalent to the interrogative pronouns and adjectives, *who? which? what?* &c. Another interrogative is required for the purpose of putting such inquiries as are expressed in English by a change of construction; *e.g., is there? is it?* by transposition from *there is, it is.* This species of interrogation is effected in all the Drâvidian languages in one and the same manner, viz., by suffixing 'â' to the noun, verb, or sentence which forms the principal subject of interrogation; and in these languages it is by the suffix of 'â' alone, without any syntactic change, or change in the collocation of words, that an interrogative verb or sentence differs from an affirmative one: *e.g.,* compare the affirmative 'avan tandân,' Tam., *he gave,* with 'avan tandân-â?' *did he give?* and 'avan-âtandân?' *was it he that gave?* compare also 'adu ûr,' *that is a village,* with 'adu ûr-â?' *is that a village?* This interrogative is never prefixed to nouns or pronominals, or used adjectivally; but is invariably post-fixed, like an enunciated or audible *note of interrogation.*

'ô' is not unfrequently used like 'a' as a simple interrogative;

but its special and distinctive use is as a particle expressive of doubt. Thus, whilst 'avan-â' means *is it he?* 'avan-ô' means *can it be he?* or *I am doubtful whether it is he or not.* 'ô' is post-fixed to words in precisely the same manner as 'â,' and is probably only a weakened form of it, in which, by usage, the interrogation has become merged in the expression of doubt. It has acquired, however, as a suffix of doubt a position and force of its own, quite independent of 'â;' in consequence of which it is often annexed even to interrogative pronouns; *e.g.*, 'evan-ô,' Tam., *I wonder who he can be;* 'ennam-ô,' *what it may be I know not*—compound forms which are not double interrogatives, but which consist of a question 'evan,' *who?* or 'ennam,' *what?* and an answer 'ô,' *I am doubtful.—I know not.—There is room for further inquiry.*

'ko,' which seems to correspond in meaning to 'ô,' is used as a prefix of uncertainty by some Telugu pronominals: *e.g.*, compare 'anta,' *thus much,* 'inta,' *this much,* 'enta,' *how much?* with 'konta,' *some,* or, as if one should say, *I know not how much.*

This prefix is rare in Telugu, unknown in Tamil, and is possibly derived from the Sanscrit interrogative.

The use of 'â' as an interrogative suffix has not been derived from any language either of the Scythian or of the Indo-European family. It is altogether unknown to the Sanscrit; and the Cashmirian is the only Non-Drâvidian tongue in which it is found.

I am inclined to consider 'â,' the Drâvidian interrogative, as derived from, or at least as allied to, 'a' or 'â,' the remote demonstrative of the same family. The quantity of that demonstrative 'a' is long or short as euphonic considerations may determine; and though the interrogative 'â' is always long, yet in consequence of its being used as a post-fix, it is pronounced long by necessity of position, whatever it may have been originally. Hence the question of quantity may, in this inquiry, be left altogether out of account. The only real difference between them is the difference in location; 'a' demonstrative being invariably placed at the beginning of a word, 'a' interrogative at the end of it. If the interrogative 'a' were really connected with 'a,' the demonstrative, we should expect to find a similar connection subsisting between 'e' or 'ê,' the adjectival interrogative, and some demonstrative particle, with a similar interchange of places; accordingly this is found to be the case, for 'ê' is not only the ordinary sign of emphasis in all the Drâvidian tongues, but it is used in Ku as an adjectival demonstrative; and it is curious that in this instance also, there is a change of location, 'ê' emphatic being placed at the end of a word, 'e' interrogative at the beginning.

A similar change in the position of particles, to denote or correspond with some change in signification, is not unknown in other tongues. Thus in Danish, the article 'en' has a definite sense in one position and an indefinite in another; *e.g.*, 'en konge,' *a king*, 'kongen,' *the king*. But it is still more remarkable, and more corroborative of the supposition now advanced, that in Hebrew, one and the same particle, 'he' (for it is one and the same, and any difference that exists is merely euphonic), imparts emphasis to a word when post-fixed to it, and constitutes an interrogative when prefixed.

Distributive pronouns.—In all the Drâvidian tongues distributive pronouns are formed by simply annexing the conjunctive particle to the interrogative pronoun. Thus, from 'evan,' *who?* by the addition of 'um,' *and*, the conjunctive or copulative particle of the Tamil is formed, viz., 'evanum,' *everyone*, *whosoever* (literally *who?-and*); and from 'epporudu,' *when?* is formed in the same manner 'epporudum,' *always*, literally *when? and-*. In Canarese similar forms are found, though not so largely used as in Tamil; *e.g.*, 'yâvâgalû' ('yâ-âgal-û'), *always*; and in Telugu 'nu' (the copulative particle which answers to the Tamil 'um' and the Canarese 'û') is used in the same manner in the formation of distributives; *e.g.*, 'evvadunu' ('evvadu-nu'), *everyone*, 'eppudunnu' ('eppudu-(n)-nu'), *always*.

The Drâvidian languages have no pronouns properly so called besides those which have now been examined.

Instead of *relative pronouns*, they use verbal forms which are called by English grammarians *relative participles;* which see in the section on 'The Verb.' All other words which correspond either in meaning or in use to the pronouns of other languages will be found on examination to be nouns, regularly formed and declined.

SECTION VI.

THE VERB.

The object in view in this section is to investigate the nature, affections, and relations of the Drâvidian verb. I commence with some general preliminary remarks upon its structure.

(1.) A large proportion of Drâvidian roots are used indiscriminately, either as verbs or as nouns.

When case-signs are attached to a root, or when, without the addition of case-signs, it is used as the nominative of a verb, it is regarded as a noun: the same root becomes a verb without any internal change or formative addition, when the signs of tense (or time) and the pronouns or their terminal fragments are suffixed to it. Though, abstractedly speaking, every Drâvidian root is capable of this two-fold use, it depends upon circumstances whether any particular root is actually thus used; and it often happens, as in other languages, that of three given roots one shall be used solely or generally as a verbal theme, another solely or generally as the theme of a noun, and the third alone shall be used indiscriminately either as a noun or as a verb.

Herein also the *usus loquendi* of the various dialects is found to differ; and not unfrequently a root which is used solely as a verbal theme in one dialect, is used solely as a noun in another.

(2.) The inflexional theme of a Drâvidian verb or noun is not always identical with the crude root or ultimate base. In many instances formative or euphonic particles (such as 'vu,' 'ku,' 'gu' or 'ngu,' 'du' or 'ndu,' 'bu' or 'mbu') are annexed to the root,—not added on like isolated post-positions, but so annexed as to be incorporated with it. (See the section on 'Roots.') But the addition of one of those formative suffixes does not necessarily constitute the root to which it is suffixed a verb: it is still capable of being used as a noun, though it may be admitted that roots to which those suffixes have been annexed are more frequently used as verbs than as nouns.

(3.) The structure of the Drâvidian verb is strictly agglutinative. The particles which express the ideas of mood and tense, transition, intransition, causation, and negation, together with the pronominal fragments by which person, number, and gender are denoted, are annexed or agglutinated to the root in so regular a series and by so quiet a process, that generally no change whatever, or at most only a slight euphonic change, is effected either in the root or in any of the suffixed particles. [See this illustrated in the section on 'Roots.']

(4.) The second person singular of the imperative may perhaps be considered as an exception to the foregoing rule. The crude theme of the verb, or the shortest form which the root assumes, and which is capable of being used also as the theme of a noun, is used in the Drâvidian languages, as in most others, as the second person singular of the imperative; and the ideas of number and person and of the conveyance of a command, which are included in that part of speech, are not expressed by the addition of any particles, but are generally left to be inferred from the context alone. Thus, in the Tamil, sentences 'aḍi viṛundadu,' *the stroke fell;* 'ennei aḍi-ttân,' *he struck me;* and 'idei aḍi,' *strike thou this;* the theme, 'aḍi,' *strike*, or a *stroke*, is the same in each instance, and in the third illustration it is used without any addition, and in its crude state, as the second person singular of the imperative.

(5.) As the Drâvidian noun has but one declension, so the Drâvidian verb has only one conjugation and but very few irregular forms. Some European grammarians have arranged the Drâvidian verbs in classes, and have styled those classes *conjugations;* but the differences on which this classification is founded, are generally of a trivial and superficial character. The structure of the verb, its signs of tense, and the mode in which the pronouns are suffixed, remain invariably the same, with such changes only as euphony appears to have dictated. Consequently, though class-differences exist, they are not of sufficient importance to constitute different conjugations.

Such is the simplicity of the structure of the Drâvidian verb, that the only moods it has are the indicative, the infinitive, the imperative, and the negative, and that it has only three tenses, the past, the present, and the aorist or indefinite future. The ideas which are expressed in other families of languages by the subjunctive and optative moods, are expressed in the Drâvidian family by means of suffixed particles; and the imperfect, perfect, pluperfect, future-perfect, and other compound tenses, are expressed by means of auxiliary verbs.

In these respects the Drâvidian verb imitates, though it does not equal, the simplicity of the ancient Scythian verb. The modern Turkish has, it is true, an extraordinary number of moods—conditionals, potentials, reciprocals, inceptives, negatives, impossibles, &c., together with their passive, and also a large array of compound tenses; but this complexity of structure appears to be a refinement of a comparatively modern age, and is not in accordance with the genius of the Oriental Turkish, or Tartar properly so called. Remusat conjectures that intercourse with nations of the Indo-European race, some time after the Christian era, was the occasion of introducing into the Turkish language the use of auxiliary verbs and of compound tenses. 'From the extremity of Asia,' he says, 'the art of conjugating verbs is unknown.' The Oriental Turks first offer some traces of this; but the very sparing use which they make of it seems to attest the pre-existence of a more simple method.'

All the Drâvidian idioms conjugate their verbs, with the partial exception of the modern Malayâlam, which has retained the use of the signs of tense, but has rejected the pronominal terminations. Nevertheless, the system of conjugation on which the Drâvidian idioms proceed, is one of primitive and remarkable simplicity. The Gônd is the only Drâvidian dialect which has adopted a complicated system; and it has probably done so through the influence of its Kole or Himalayan neighbours.

(6.) The Drâvidian verb is more rarely compounded than the Indo-European one; and the compound of a verb with a preposition is especially rare. An inexhaustible variety of shades of meaning is secured in Sanscrit and Greek by the facility with which, in those languages, verbs are compounded with prepositions; and the beauty of many of those compounds is as remarkable as the facility with which they are made. In the Scythian tongues, properly so called, there is no trace of compounds of this kind; and though they are not unknown in the Drâvidian family, yet their use is not in harmony with the purer idiom; and when the component elements of such compounds are carefully scrutinised, it is found that the principle on which they are compounded differs widely from that of Indo-European compounds. The Drâvidian prepositions which are most frequently compounded with verbs are those which signify *over* and *under*, the use of which is illustrated by the common Tamil verbs 'mêʀ-koḷ,' *to overcome*, and 'kîṛ-(p)paḍi,' *to obey*. Drâvidian prepositions, however (or rather, post-positions), are properly nouns; *e.g.*, 'mêl,' *over*, literally means *over-ness, superiority;* and 'mêl-koḷ' (euphonically 'mêʀ-koḷ'), *to overcome*, literally signifies *to take the superiority*. These and similar verbal themes, therefore, though compounds, are not compounds of a preposition and a verb, but compounds of a noun and a verb; and the Greek verbs with which they are to be compared, are not those which commence with 'περί,' 'κατά,' 'ἀνά,' &c., but such compounds as 'πολιορκέω,' *to besiege a city*, literally *to city-besiege*; 'ναυπηγέω,' *to build a ship*, literally *to ship-build*. In such cases, whether in Greek or in Tamil, the first member of the compound (that is, the noun) does not modify the signification of the second (that is, the verb), but simply denotes the object to which the action of the verb applies. It is merely a crude noun, which is used objectively without any signs of case, and is intimately combined with a governing verb.

Drâvidian verbs acquire new shades of meaning, and an increase or diminution in the intensity of their signification, not by prefixing or combining prepositions, but by means of auxiliary gerunds, or verbal participles, and infinitives—parts of speech which in this family of languages have an adverbial force; *e.g.*, 'mundi (p)pônân,' Tam., *he went before*, literally *having-got-before he went*; 'śuRRi' ('śuttri) (p)pônân,' *he went round*, literally *rounding he went*; 'tâṛa (k)kudittân,' *he leaped down*, literally *so-as-to-get-down he leaped*.

Classification of Dravidian Verbs.

I. Transitives and Intransitives.

Drâvidian grammarians divide all verbs into two classes which are called in Tamil 'piRa vinei' and 'tan vinei,' *transitives* and *intransitives*, literally *outward action-words* and *self action-words*. These classes correspond rather to the 'parasmai-padam' and 'âtmanê-padam,' or *transitive and reflective voices*, of the Sanscrit, than to the active and passive voices of the other Indo-European languages.

The Drâvidian 'piRa vinei' and 'tan vinei,' or transitive and intransitive verbs, differ from the 'parasmai-padam' and 'âtmanê-padam' of the Sanscrit in this, that instead of each being conjugated differently, they are both conjugated in precisely the same mode. They differ, not in their mode of conjugation, but in the formative additions made to their themes. Moreover, all 'piRa vinei,' or transitive-verbs, are really, as well as formally, transitives, inasmuch as they necessarily govern the accusative, through the transition of their action to some object; whilst the 'tan vinei,' or intransitive verbs, are all necessarily, as well as formally, intransitives. The Drâvidian *transitives* and *intransitives* exactly resemble in force and use the *determinate* and *indeterminate* verbs of the Hungarian. The Hungarian *determinate* verbs, like the Drâvidian transitives, imply an object—an accusative expressed or implied, *e.g.*, 'szeretem,' *I love* (*some person or thing*); whilst the Hungarian *indeterminate* verbs, like the Drâvidian intransitives, neither express nor imply an object, *e.g.*, 'szeretek,' *I love, i.e., I am in love.*

In a large number of instances in each of the Drâvidian dialects, including entire classes of verbs, there is no difference between transitives and intransitives, either in formative additions to the theme, or in any structural peculiarity, the only difference is that which consists in the signification. Thus in Tamil, all verbs of the class which take 'i' or 'in' as the sign of the past participle are conjugated alike, whether they are transitives or intransitives; *e.g.*, from 'paṇṇ-u,' trans., *to make*, are formed the three tenses (first person singular) 'paṇṇu-giṟ-ĕu,' *I make*, 'paṇṇ-i-(n)-ên,' *I made*, and 'paṇṇu-v-en,' *I will make:* and in like manner from 'pês-u,' intrans., *to talk*, are formed, precisely in the same manner, the corresponding tenses 'pêsu-giṟ-ên,' *I talk*, 'pês-i-(n)-ên,' *I talked*, and 'pêsn-v-ên,' *I will talk.*

In a still larger number of cases, however, transitive verbs differ from intransitives, not only in signification and force, but also in grammatical form, notwithstanding that they are conjugated alike. The nature of the difference that exists and its rationale, are more clearly apparent in Tamil than in any other Drâvidian dialect; my illustrations will, therefore, chiefly be drawn from the Tamil.

There are three modes in which intransitive Tamil verbs are converted into transitives.

(1.) Intransitive themes become transitive, by the hardening and doubling of the consonant of the appended formative; *e.g.*, 'peru-gu,' *to abound*, by this process becomes 'peru-kku,' *to increase* (*actively*), *to cause to abound.* Transitives of this kind, which are formed from intransitives in actual use, are often called *causals*, and they are as well entitled to be called by that name as many *causal verbs* in the Indo-European tongues; but as there is a class of Drâvidian verbs which are distinctively causal (and which are formed by the annexing to the transitive theme of 'vi,' a causal particle; *e.g.*, 'paṇṇu-vi,' *to cause to make*, from 'paṇṇu,' *to make*), it will contribute to perspicuity to regard the whole of the verbs of which we are now treating, simply as transitives, and to reserve the name of *causal verbs* for the double transitives in 'vi.'

When transitives are formed from intransitives by doubling the consonant of the formative, it is in the theme or inflexional base itself that the change takes place: there is no change in any of the signs of tense, or in the mode in which those signs are added; and the hardened formative appears in the imperative, as well as in the other parts of the verb.

The nature of these formatives has already been investigated in the section on 'Roots;' and it has been shown that they are euphonic accretions, which, though permanently annexed to the base, are not to be confounded with it. I subjoin a few illustrations of this mode of forming transitives by the doubling and hardening of the consonant of the formative.

(i.) 'gu,' or its nasalised equivalent, 'ngu,' becomes 'kku;' *e.g.*, from 'pô-gu,' *to go* (in the imperative softened into 'pô'), comes 'pô-kku,' *to drive away;* from 'nî-ngu,' *to quit*, comes 'nî-kku,' *to put away.*

(ii.) 'śu' becomes 'śśu' (pronounced 'chu'); *e.g.*, from 'aḍei-su,' *to take refuge*, comes 'adei-chu,' *to inclose.*

(iii.) 'du,' euphonised into 'ndu,' becomes 'ttu;' *e.g.*, from 'tiru-ndu,' *to become correct*, comes 'tiru-ttu,' *to correct:* in like manner the cerebral 'ṇḍu' becomes 'ṭṭu;' *e.g.*, from 'tî-ṇḍu,' *to touch*, comes 'tî-ṭṭu,' *to whet.*

(iv.) 'bu,' euphonised into 'mbu,' becomes 'ppu;' *e.g.*, from 'nira-mbu,' *to be full*, comes 'nira-ppu,' *to fill.*

When intransitives are converted into transitives in this manner in Telugu, 'gu' or 'ngu' becomes, not 'kku' as in Tamil, but 'chu,' —a difference which is in accordance with dialectic rules of sound. Thus from 'tû-gu,' or 'tû-ngu,' *to hang, to sleep*, comes 'tû-chu,' or euphonically 'tû-*n*chu,' *to weigh, to cause to hang.*

The Telugu also occasionally changes the intransitive formative 'gu,' not into 'chu,' the equivalent of 'kku,' but into 'pu;' *e.g.*, from 'mêy,' *to graze*, comes 'mê-pu,' *to feed:* and as 'ppu' in Tamil is invariably hardened from 'bu' or 'mbu,' the corresponding Telugu 'pu' indicates that 'bu' originally alternated with 'gu;' for the hardening of 'gu' into 'pu' is not in accordance with Drâvidian laws of sound. This view is confirmed by the circumstances that in Telugu the use of 'pu' instead of 'chu' (and of 'mpu' instead of 'nchu') is in most instances optional, and that in the higher dialect of the Tamil the formative 'pp' sometimes supersedes 'kk;' *e.g.*, the infinitive of the verb *to walk*, may in that dialect be either 'naḍa-kka' or 'naḍa-ppa.' It is obvious, therefore, that all these formative terminations are mutual equivalents.

If the transitive or causal 'p' of such verbs as 'nira-ppu,' Tam., *to fill*, 'mê-pu,' Tel., *to feed*, were not known to be derived from the hardening of an intransitive formative, we might be inclined to affiliate it with the 'p,' which is characteristic of a certain class of causal verbs in Sanscrit; *e.g.*, 'jîvâ-p-ayâmi,' *I cause to live*, 'jñâ-p-ayâmi,' *I make to know.* It is evident, however, that the resemblance is merely accidental, for etymologically there is nothing of a causal nature in the Drâvidian formatives; it is not the formative itself, but the *hardening* of the formative which conveys the force of transition; and on the other hand, the real sign of the causal in Sanscrit is 'aya,' and the 'p' which precedes it is considered to be only an euphonic fulcrum.

It has already been shown (in the section on 'Roots') that the various verbal formatives now referred to are used also as formatives of nouns, and that when such nouns are used adjectivally the consonant of the formative is doubled and hardened precisely as in the transitives of verbs; *e.g.*, 'marattu,' *medicinal*, from 'marundu,' *medicine:* 'pâppu,' *serpentine*, from 'pâmbu,' *a snake*. When nouns are used to qualify other sounds, as well as in the use of transitive verbs, there is a transition in the meaning of the theme to some other object; and the idea of transition is expressed by the doubling and hardening of the consonant of the formative, or rather by the forcible and emphatic enunciation of the verb which that hardening of the formative necessitates.

(2.) The second class of intransitive verbs become transitives by doubling and hardening the initial consonant of the signs of tense.

Verbs of this class are generally destitute of formatives, properly so called; or, if they have any, they are such as are incapable of change. The sign of the present tense is in Tamil 'giR';' that of the preterite 'd,' ordinarily euphonised into 'nd;' and that of the future 'b' or 'v.' These are the signs of tense which are used by intransitive verbs of this class; and it will be shown hereafter that they are the normal tense-signs of the Drâvidian verb. When verbs of this class become transitives, 'giR'' is changed into 'kkiR;' 'd' or 'nd' into 'tt;' and 'b' or 'v' into 'pp.' Thus, the root 'śêr,' *to join*, is capable both of an intransitive sense, *e.g.*, *to join* (*a society*), and of a transitive sense, *e.g.*, *to join* (*things that were separate*). The tense-signs of the intransitive remain in their natural condition; *e.g.*, 'sêr-giR'-en,' *I join*, 'śêr-nd-ên,' *I joined*, 'śêr-v-ên,' *I will join*: but when the signification is active or transitive, *e.g.*, *to join* (*planks*), the corresponding parts of the verb are 'śêr-kkiR-ên,' *I join*, 'śêr-tt-ên,' *I joined*, 'śêr-pp-ên,' *I will join.*

The rationale of this doubling of the case-sign is evident. It is an emphasized, hardened enunciation of the intransitive or natural form of the verb; and the forcible enunciation thus produced is symbolical of the force of transition by which the meaning of the transitive theme overflows and passes on to the object indicated by the accusative.

In verbs of this class the imperative remains always unchanged; and it is the connexion alone that determines it to a transitive rather than an intransitive signification.

It should here be mentioned that a few intransitive verbs double the initial consonant of the tense-sign, and that a few transitive verbs leave the tense-sign in its original, unemphasized condition. Thus, 'iru,' *to sit, to be,* is necessarily an intransitive verb; nevertheless, in the present tense 'iru-kkiʀ-ên,' *I am,* and in the future 'iru-pp-ên,' *I shall be,* it has made use of the ordinary characteristics of the transitive: so also 'paḍu,' *to lie,* though an intransitive, doubles the initial consonant of all the tenses; *e.g.*, 'paḍu-kkiʀ-ên,' *I lie,* 'paḍu-tt-ên,' *I lay,* 'paḍu-pp-ên,' *I shall lie.* On the other hand, 'î,' *to give, to bestow,* though necessarily transitive, uses the simple, unhardened, unemphatic case-signs which are ordinarily characteristic of the intransitive; *e.g.*, 'î-giʀ-ên,' *I give,* 'î-nd-ên,' *I gave,* 'î-v-ên,' *I will give.* These instances are the result of dialectic rules of sound, and they are not in reality exceptions to the method described above of distinguishing transitive and intransitive verbs by means of the hardening or softening of the initial consonant of the case-signs.

(3.) A third mode of converting intransitives into transitives is by adding a particle of transition to the theme or root. This particle is 'du' in Canarese, and 'ttu' (in composition 'tu' or 'du') in Tamil; and may be regarded as a real transitive suffix, or sign of activity. We have an instance of the use of this particle in the Can. 'tâḷ-du,' *to lower,* from 'tâḷ-u,' *to be low,* and the corresponding Tam. 'tâṛ-ttu,' *to lower,* from 'tâṛ' or 'tâṛ-u,' *to be low.* When the intransitive Tamil theme ends in a vowel which is radical and cannot be elided, the transitive particle is invariably 'ttu,' *e.g.*, 'paḍu-ttu,' *to lay down,* from 'paḍu,' *to lie.* It might, therefore, be supposed that 'ttu' is the primitive shape of this particle; but on examining those instances in which it is compounded with the final consonant of the intransitive theme it appears to resolve itself, as in Canarese, into 'du.' It is always thus compounded when the final consonant of the theme is 'l' or 'ḷ,' 'ḍ'' or 'ʀ';' and in such cases the 'd' of 'du' is not merely placed in juxta-position with the consonant to which it is attached, but is assimilated to it, or both consonants are euphonically changed, according to the phonetic rules of the language. Thus 'l' and 'du' become 'ʀʀ-u' (pronounced 'ttr-u'), *e.g.*, from 'suṛal,' intrans., *to be whirled,* comes 'suṛaʀʀ-u' ('suṛattr-u'), trans., *to whirl.* 'ḷ' and 'du' become 'ṭṭu,' *e.g.*, from 'mîḷ,' *to return,* comes 'mîṭṭ-u,' *to cause to return, to redeem.* From these instances it is clear that 'du,' not 'ttu,' is to be regarded as the primitive form of this transitive suffix.

What is the origin of this transitive particle, or sign of activity, 'ttu' or 'du?' I believe it to be identical with the inflexion, or adjectival formative, 'attu' or 'ttu,' which was fully investigated in the section on 'The Noun,' and of which the Canarese form is 'ad',' the Tel. 'ṭi' or 'ti.' There is a transition of meaning when a noun is used adjectivally (*i.e.*, to qualify another noun), as well as when a verb is used transitively (*i.e.*, to govern an object expressed by some noun in the accusative); and in both cases the Drâvidian languages use (with respect to this class of verbs) one and the same means of expressing transition, viz., a particle which was originally a neuter demonstrative.

Nor is this the only case in which the Tamil transitive verb exhibits the characteristics of the noun used adjectivally, for it was shown also that the doubling and hardening of the consonant of the formative of the first class of transitive verbs is in exact accordance with the manner in which nouns terminating in those formatives double and harden the initial consonant when they are used to qualify other nouns. Another illustration of this principle follows.

(4.) The fourth (a distinctively Tamil) mode of converting intransitive verbs into transitives consists in doubling and hardening the final consonant, if 'ḍ' or 'ʀ.' This rule applies generally, though not invariably, to verbs which terminate in those consonants; and it applies to a final 'ṇḍ-u' (euphonised from 'ḍ-u'), as well as to 'ḍ-u' itself. The operation of this rule will appear on comparing 'vâḍ-u,' *to wither*, with 'vâṭṭ-u,' *to cause to wither;* 'ôḍ-u,' *to run*, with 'ôṭṭ-u,' *to drive;* 'tiṇḍ-u,' *to touch*, with 'tîṭṭ-u,' *to whet;* 'mâʀ-u,' *to become changed*, with 'mâʀʀ-u' (pronounced 'mâttr-u'), *to change.* The corresponding transitives in Telugu are formed in the more usual way by adding 'chu' to the intransitive theme, *e.g.*, 'mâʀu-chu,' *to cause to change*, 'vâḍu-chu,' *to cause to wither.*

Tamil nouns which end in 'ḍ-u,' 'ṇḍ-u,' or 'ʀ-u,' double and harden the final consonant when they are used adjectivally, or placed in an adjectival relation to a succeeding noun; *e.g.*, compare 'kâḍ-u,' *a jungle*, with 'kâṭṭ-u vaṛi,' *a jungle-path;* 'iraṇḍ-u,' *two*, with 'iraṭṭ-u nûl,' *double thread;* 'âʀ-u,' *a river*, with 'âʀʀu' (pronounced 'âttru') maṇal, *river sand.* Thus we are furnished by words of this class with another and remarkable illustration of the analogy which subsists in the Drâvidian languages between transitive verbs and nouns used adjectivally.

II. Causal Verbs.

There is a class of verbs in the Drâvidian languages which, though generally included under the head of *transitives*, claim to be regarded distinctively as *causals*. They have been classed with transitives both by native grammarians and by Europeans. Beschi alone places them in a class by themselves, and calls them 'êval vinei,' *verbs of command*, *i.e.*, verbs which imply that a thing is commanded by one person to be done by another.

Causals differ from transitives of the ordinary character, as well as from intransitives, both in signification and in form.

The signification of intransitive verbs is confined to the person or thing which constitutes the nominative, and does not pass outward or onward to any extrinsic object; *e.g.*, 'pô-giR-ên,' *I go*. The signification of transitive or active verbs, or, as they are called in Tamil, *outward action-words*, passes outwards to some object exterior to the nominative, and which is generally put in the accusative; *e.g.*, 'unnei anuppu-giR-ên,' *I send thee*: and as *to send* is *to cause to go*, verbs of this class, when formed from intransitives, are in some languages, appropriately enough, termed *causals*. Hitherto the Indo-European languages proceed 'pari passu' with the Drâvidian; but at this point they fail and fall behind: for if we take a verb which is transitive of necessity, like this one, *to send*, and endeavour to express the idea of *causing to send*, *i.e.*, *causing one person to send another*, we cannot by any modification of structure get any single Indo-European verb to express the full force of this idea: we must be content to make use of a phrase instead of a single verb; whereas in the Drâvidian languages, as in the Turkish and other languages of the Scythian stock, there is a form of the verb which will express the entire idea, viz., *the causal*: *e.g.*, 'anuppu-vi,' *to cause to send*, which is formed from 'anuppu,' *to send*, by the addition of the particle 'vi' to the theme.

Transitives are in a similar manner converted in Turkish into causals by suffixing a particle to the theme; *e.g.*, 'sev-dur,' *to cause to love*, from 'sev,' *to love*; and 'âtch-our,' *to cause to work*, from 'âtch,' *to work*.

There is a peculiarity in the signification and use of Drâvidian causal verbs which should here be noticed. Indo-European causals govern two accusatives, that of the person and that of the object; *e.g.* *I caused* him (acc.) *to build* the house (acc.): whereas Drâvidian causals govern the object alone, and either leave the person to be understood (*e.g.*, 'vîṭṭei (k)kaṭṭuvittên,' Tam., *I caused to build the house*, or as we should prefer to say, *I caused the house to be built*); or else the person is put in the instrumental; *e.g.*, *I caused to build the house* 'avanâlê' or 'avanei (k)koṇḍu,' *through him*, or *employing him*; that is, I *caused the house to be built by him*.

Though the Drâvidian languages are in possession of a true causal

—formed by the addition of a causal particle,—yet they sometimes resort to the less convenient Indo-European method of annexing an auxiliary verb which signifies *to make* or *to do*, such as 'śey̌' and 'paṇṇ-u' in Tamil, 'mâḍ-u,' in Can., and 'chêy-u,' in Tel. These auxiliaries, however, are chiefly used in connexion with Sans. derivatives, it being contrary to the Drâvidian idiom to combine indigenous particles with foreign themes. The auxiliary is annexed to the infinitive of the principal verb.

Tamil idiom and the analogy of the other dialects require that causals should be formed, not from neuter or intransitive verbs, but from transitives alone; but sometimes this rule is found to be neglected. Even in Tamil, 'vi,' the sign of the causal, is in some instances found to be annexed to intransitive verbs. This usage is not only at variance with theory, but it is unclassical and unidiomatical. In each of those cases a true transitive, derived from the intransitive in the ordinary manner, is in existence, and ought to be used instead. Thus, 'varu-vi,' Tam., *to cause to come*, is less proper, as well as less elegant, than 'varu-ttu;' and 'naḍa-ppi,' *to cause to walk, to guide*, than 'naḍa-ttu.'

The use of the causal, instead of the active, where both forms exist, is not so much opposed to the idiom of the other dialects, as to that of the Tamil. The use of one form rather than another is optional in Telugu and Canarese; and in some instances the active has disappeared, and the causal alone is used. Thus 'rappinchu,' or 'râvinchu,' *to cause to come*, the equivalent of the Tamil 'varu-vi,' is preferred by the Telugu to a form which would correspond to 'varu-ttu:' and instead of 'âkk-u,' Tam., *to cause to become, to make*, which is the active of 'âg-u,' and is formed by the process of doubling and hardening which has already been described, the Telugu uses the causal 'kâ-vinchu,' and the Canarese the corresponding causal 'âg-isu.'

The causal particle which is most commonly used in Tamil is 'vi;' *e.g.*, 'paṇṇu-vi,' *to cause to make*, from 'paṇṇu,' *to make;* and 'kaṭṭu-vi,' *to cause to build*, from 'kaṭṭu,' *to build*. Instead of 'vi' we sometimes find 'bi' or 'ppi,' according to the euphonic requirements of the preceding syllable. When the theme ends in a nasal, which it does but rarely, 'bi' is added to form the causal; *e.g.*, 'kâṇ-bi,' *to cause to see, to show*. [A more idiomatic word, however, is the proper transitive of 'kâṇ,' *see;* viz., 'kâṭṭ-u,' *i.e.*, 'kâṇ-ttu,' *to show*.] When the theme ends in a vowel which is of such a character that if a sonant follows it it will necessarily be hardened and doubled, 'vi' or 'bi' changes dialectically into 'ppi;' *e.g.*, from 'eḍu,' *to take up*, is formed the causal 'eḍu-ppi,' *to cause to take up*. 'vi' is undoubtedly the most common form of this particle in Tamil, and 'bi' is the rarest; yet 'bi' seems to be the original from which the others have been derived: for 'ppi' cannot have been derived from 'vi,' whereas 'bi,' after certain vowels, dialectically and necessarily becomes 'ppi;' 'vi' also will not harden into 'bi,' whereas 'bi' will readily and naturally soften into 'vi.' I conclude, therefore, that 'bi' may be regarded as the normal form of the causal particle.

In Telugu, causal verbs ordinarily end in 'inchu;' *e.g.*, 'chêў-inchu,' *to cause to do*, from 'chêў-u,' *to do;* 'mûў-inchu,' *to cause to shut*, from 'mûў-u,' *to shut;* and this 'inchu' might be supposed to be the Telugu shape of the causal particle: but it will be seen that in reality 'i' alone is to be regarded as the causal particle of the Telugu; and that 'i' is a softened, degraded form of 'vi,' the ordinary causal particle of the Tamil. The final 'nchu' of the Telugu causal is merely a nasalised formative, and is identical in origin with the Tamil formative 'kku.' This formative 'kku' is annexed to 'vi' in certain parts of the Tamil causal verb, viz., in the infinitive, and in the third person neuter of the aorist or future; and the identity of the Tam. 'kku' with the Tel. 'nchu' is apparent as soon as the Tamil infinitive is compared with that of the Telugu. *E.g.*, compare 'śeў-vikka,' Tam., *to cause to do*, with the Tel. 'chêў-incha,' and 'tiʀa-ppikka,' Tam., *to cause to open*, with the Tel. 'teʀa-pincha.' Here 'vikka' and 'ppikka' alternate with 'incha' and 'pincha;' and hence it appears that the 'nch' of the one dialect must as certainly be a formative as the 'kk' of the other is. Even in the Tamil of the southern Pândiya country, 'kk' systematically becomes 'ch.' Thus the correct Tamil 'maʀa-kka,' *to forget*, is 'maʀa-cha' in the southern patois, precisely as in Telugu. The chief difference between the Tamil and the Telugu, with respect to the use of this formative 'kk,' is that it is used by two parts of the Tamil verb alone, viz., the infinitive and the indefinite neuter, future, or aorist; whereas in Telugu it is added to, and compounded with, the theme itself, and is used accordingly by every part of the verb, even by the imperative. Ordinarily this formative 'chu' is used unchanged in Telugu; but when it follows 'i,' it is invariably euphonised or nasalised into 'nchu:' hence the causal verb of the Telugu terminates not in 'i-chu,' but in 'i-nchu,' pronounced 'intsu.' In like manner every verb the base of which ends in 'i,' terminates in 'inchu,' though it be not a causal; *e.g.*, 'jayi-nchu,' *to conquer*, from 'jayi,' a Sans. derivative.

We thus come back to the conclusion that 'i,' softened from 'vi,' is the regular causal particle of the Telugu. In a few instances the softening process by which 'vi' was changed into 'i' has been resisted; and in those instances 'vi' is the sign of the casual in Telugu, as in Tamil; *e.g.*, compare 'viḍa-vi-nchu' or 'viḍi-vi-nchu,' *to rescue, to cause to leave*, with the Tamil 'viḍu-vi.' The Tel. 'kâ-vi-nchu,' *to cause to become*, has retained this particle; whilst it has been lost by the corresponding Can. 'âg-i-su.' We occasionally find the causal formed by 'pi,' and even 'ppi' in Telugu as in Tamil; and though the use of these hardened forms is rare, yet their existence in Telugu serves still further to identify 'i' with the Tamil 'vi,' 'bi,' and 'ppi.' 'teʀa-pi-nchu,' Tel., *to cause to open*, is an example of the use of 'pi;' and 'teppinchu' ('te-ppi-nchu'), *to cause to bring*, from 'te-chu,' *to bring*, illustrates the use of 'ppi.' The Telugu verbs in 'chu,' 'nchu,' 'pu,' 'mpu,' &c., which are destitute of this causal particle under any form (*e.g.*, 'viḍu-chu' and 'viḍu-pu,' *to cause to quit, to rescue;* 'vanchu,' *to bend;* 'lêpu,' *to raise*) are to be regarded as transitives, not as causals. They are formed, not by annexing 'vi' or 'i,' but by the doubling and hardening of the final consonant of the formative (*e.g.*, compare 'lêpu,' *to raise*, with the corresponding Tamil 'eṛuppu,' the transitive of 'eṛumbu'); and the verbs from which they are so formed are not actives, but neuters. Instead, therefore, of saying that 'tîr-u,' *to end*, forms its causal either in 'tîr-chu' or 'tîr-pinchu,' it would be more accurate and more in accordance with Tamil analogies, to represent 'tîr-u' as the neuter, 'tîr-chu' as the transitive, and 'tîr-pi-nchu' as the causal. It is of the essence of the true causal that its theme is a transitive verb; *e.g.*, 'kaṭṭ-inchu,' *to cause to build*, from 'kaṭṭ-u,' *to build*.

In Canarese, causal verbs are formed by suffixing 'is-u,' or rather 'i-su,' to the transitive theme; *e.g.*, from 'mâḍ-u,' *to do*, is formed 'mâḍ-i-su,' *to cause to do*. This causal particle 'i-su' (in the ancient dialect 'i-chu') is annexed to the theme itself before the addition of the signs of tense, so that it is found in every part of the causal verb, like the corresponding Telugu particle 'i-nchu,' with which it is evidently identical. It has been shown that the Telugu 'i-nchu' must have been nasalised from 'i-chu' (the phonetic equivalent of the Tamil 'i-kku,' for 'vi-kku'); and now we find this very 'i-chu' in Canarese. The change in modern Canarese from 'i-chu' to 'i-śu' is easy and natural, 'ś' being phonetically equivalent to 'ch,' and 'chu' being pronounced like 'tsu' in Telugu.

An additional proof, if proof were wanting, of the identity of the Can. 'i-su' with the Tel. 'i-nchu,' is furnished by the class of derivative verbs, or verbs borrowed from the Sanscrit. Sans. derivative verbs are made to end in 'i' in the Drâvidian dialects (*e.g.*, 'jaẏ-i,' *conquer*); and those verbs invariably take in Telugu, as has been said, the formative termination 'nchu,' *e.g.*, 'jayi-nchu.' The same verbs invariably take 'i-su,' or 'y-isu,' in Canarese. Thus from the Sans. derivative theme, 'dhari,' *to assume*, the Telugu forms the verb 'dhari-nchu,' the Canarese equivalent of which is 'dhari-śu.'

These verbs are not causals; but the use which they make of the formative 'nchu' or 'su,' preceded by 'i,' illustrates the original identity of the Canarese causal particle 'i-su' with the Tel. 'i-nchu,' and of both with the Tamil 'vikku.' In Tamil, Sans. derivative verbs end in 'i' as in Canarese and Telugu, but the causal particle 'vi,' 'bi,' or 'ppi,' is never added, except it is desired to convert them into causals. Hence in Tamil no one is in any danger of confounding the true causal with the Sans. derivative. Generally the older and harsher sounds of the Canarese have been softened by the Tamil; and in particular, the Canarese 'k' has often been softened by the Tamil into 'ś' or 'ch:' but in the instance of the causative particle, exactly the reverse of this has happened; the Tamil 'bi' or 'vi' having been softened by the Canarese into 'i,' and the formative 'kk' into 'ś.'

The Canarese, like the Telugu, does not so carefully discriminate between transitive and causal verbs as the Tamil has been found to do. The true causal of the Tamil is restricted to transitive themes; but the Canarese, notwithstanding its possession of transitive particles, like those of the Tamil (*e.g.*, compare 'nera-hu,' to fill with 'neri,' *to be full*, and 'tiru-pu,' *to turn* (*actively*), with 'tiru-gu,' *to turn* (*of itself*), yet it often annexes the causal particle to intransitive themes; *e.g.*, 'ôḍ-i-su,' *to cause to run* (Tam. 'ôṭṭ-u'), from 'ôḍ-u,' *to run;* and 'naḍ-i-su,' *to cause to walk* (Tam. 'naḍa-ttu'), from 'naḍi,' *to walk*.

The oldest and purest form of the Indo-European causative particle is supposed to be the Sanscrit 'aya,' with 'p' prefixed after a root in 'â.' 'aya' becomes 'i' in Old Slavonic; and the resemblance between this and the Telugu 'i' is very close; nevertheless, the derivation of the latter from 'vi' or 'bi' and of the former from 'aya,' proves that the resemblance is purely accidental.

The Tulu forms its causal verbs in a different manner from the other Drâviḍian dialects, viz., by suffixing 'â' to the verbal theme, and then adding the signs of tense: *e.g.*, from 'marp-u,' *to make*, is formed 'marp-â-vu,' *to cause to make*. This greatly resembles the Hindustani causals; *e.g.*, 'chal-wâ-nâ,' *to cause to go*, from 'chal-nâ,' *to go;* and as the Hind. causative particle 'wâ' has probably been derived from the Sanscrit 'aya' or 'p-aya,' the Tulu 'â' may be supposed to proceed from the same or a similar source.

In Gônd 'ha' or 'h' is the causal particle, and is added to the present participle of transitive verbs, not to the theme.

III. The Passive Voice.

Each of the primitive Indo-European languages has a regular passive voice, regularly conjugated. The Sanscrit passive is formed by annexing the particle 'ya' (derived from 'yâ,' *to go*), to the verbal theme, and adding the personal terminations peculiar to the middle voice.

Most of the languages of the Scythian family also form their passives by means of annexed particles. To the verbal theme the Turkish suffixes in order to form the passive, 'il' or 'îl;' the Finnish 'et;' the Hungarian 'at,' 'et,' 'tet;' and to these particles the pronominal terminations are appended in the usual manner.

The Drâvidian verb is entirely destitute of a passive voice, properly so called, nor is there any reason to suppose that it ever had a passive. None of the Drâvidian dialects possesses any passive particle or suffix, or any means of expressing passivity by direct inflexional changes: the signification of the passive voice is, nevertheless, capable of being expressed in a variety of ways. We have now to inquire into the means which are adopted by the Drâvidian languages for conveying a passive signification; and it will be found that they correspond in a considerable degree to the means used for this purpose by the vernaculars of Northern India—which also are destitute of a regular passive voice.

In the particulars that follow all the Drâvidian dialects agree: what is said of one holds true of all.

(1.) The place of a passive voice is to a large extent supplied by the use of the neuter or intransitive form of the verb. This is in every dialect of the family the most idiomatic and characteristic mode of expressing the passive; and wherever it can be used, it is always preferred by classical writers. Thus, *it was broken*, is ordinarily expressed in Tamil by 'uḍeindadu,' the preterite (third person singular neuter) of 'uḍei,' intransitive, *to break or become broken;* and though this is a neuter, rather than a passive properly so called, and might literally be rendered *it has come into a broken condition*, yet it is evident that for all practical purposes nothing more than this is required to express the force of the passive. The passivity of the expression may be increased by prefixing the instrumental case of the agent, *e.g.*, 'ennâl uḍeindadu,' *it was broken by me*, or literally *it came into a broken condition through me.*

(2.) A very common mode of forming the passive is by means of the preterite verbal participle of any neuter or active verb, followed by the preterite (third person singular neuter) of the verbs *to become, to be, to go*, or (occasionally) *to end.* Thus, we may say either 'mugindadu,' *it is finished*, or 'mugind' âyittru,' literally *having finished it is become.* This form adds the idea of completion to that of passivity: not only is the thing done, but the doing of it is completed.

Transitive or active verbs which are destitute of intransitive forms, may in this manner acquire a passive signification.

Thus 'kaṭṭ-u,' *to bind or build*, is necessarily a transitive verb, and is without a corresponding intransitive; but in the phrase 'kôvil kaṭṭi âyittru,' *the temple is built*, literally *the temple having built has become*, a passive signification is acquired by the active voice, without the assistance of any passive-forming particle. 'pôyittru,' *it has gone*, may generally be used in such phrases instead of 'âyittru,' *it is become.*

Verbal nouns, especially the verbal in 'dal' or 'al,' are often used in Tamil instead of the preterite verbal participle, in the formation of this constructive passive; *e.g.*, instead of 'śeÿd' âyittru,' *it is done*, literally *having done it has become*, we may say 'śeÿdal âyittru,' which though it is used to express the same meaning, literally signifies *the doing has become, i.e., it has become a fact, the doing of it is completed.*

In these instances the use of the active as a passive (with the substantive verb) corresponds to the New Persian rule of using the same form of the verb as an active when it stands unsupported, and as a passive when followed by the substantive verb.

The Drâvidian constructive passives now referred to require the third person *neuter* of the auxiliary verb. The force of the passive voice will not be brought out by the use of the masculine or feminine, or by the epicene plural. If those persons of the verb were employed, the activity which is inherent in the idea of personality would necessitate an active signification; it would tie down the transitive theme to a transitive meaning; whereas the intransitive relation is naturally implied in the use of the neuter gender, and therefore the expression of the signification of the passive (viz., by the intransitive officiating for the passive) is facilitated by the use of the third person neuter.

A somewhat similar mode of forming the passive has been pointed out in the Hindustani and Bengali; *e.g.*, 'jânâ yâÿ,' Beng., *it is known*, literally *it goes to be known.* 'jânâ' is represented by some to be a verbal noun, by others to be a passive participle: but, whatever it be, there is some difference between this idiom and the Drâvidian one; for in the corresponding Tamil phrase 'terind' âyittru,' *it is known,* 'terind-u' is unquestionably the preterite verbal participle of an intransitive verb, and the phrase literally means *having known it is become.* 'terindu pôyittru,' literally *having known it is gone,* conveys the same signification. It is remarkable that a verb signifying *to go* should be used in the Drâvidian languages as a passive-making auxiliary, as well as in the languages of Northern India.

Occasionally Drâvidian active or transitive verbs themselves are used with a passive signification, without the addition of any intransitive auxiliary whatever. Relative participles and relative participial nouns are the parts of the verb which are most frequently used in this manner; *e.g.*, 'eṛudina suvaḍi uṇḍu; ach' aḍitta pustagam vêṇḍum,' Tam., *I have got a written book; I want a printed one.* In this phrase both 'eṛudina,' *written,* and 'ach'-aḍitta,' *printed,* are the preterite relative participles of *transitive* themes. The former means literally *that wrote;* yet it is used passively to signify *written,* and the latter means literally *that printed* or *struck off,* but is used passively as equivalent to *that is printed.*

The relative participial noun, especially the preterite neuter, is oftentimes used in the same manner; *e.g.*, in 'śonnadu pôdum,' Tam., *what was said is sufficient,* 'śonnadu,' literally means *that which said;* but the connexion and the usage of the language determine it to signify passively *that which was said;* and so distinctively in this case is the passive sense expressed by the connexion alone, that the use of the more formal modern passive 'śolla-(p)paṭṭadu,' would sound awkward and foreign. 'endra,' Tam., 'anêde,' Tel., *that is called,* literally *that spoke,* is another very common instance of the same rule. 'Iyêsu enbavar,' Tam., signifies literally, *Jesus—he who speaks;* but usage determines it to mean *he who is called Jesus.*

(3.) The verb 'uṇ,' *to eat,* is occasionally used in the Drâvidian languages as an auxiliary in the formation of passives. It is invaably appended to nouns (substantives or verbal nouns), and is never compounded with any part of the verb; *e.g.*, 'aḍi uṇḍân,' *he was beaten,* or *got a beating,* literally *he ate a beating;* 'paḍeipp' uṇḍén,' *I was created,* literally *I ate a creating.*

The same singular idiom prevails also in the North-Indian vernaculars. The particular verb signifying *to eat* which is used in those languages differs, indeed, from the Drâvidian 'uṇ;' but the idiom is identical, and the existence of so singular an idiom in both the northern and the southern family is deserving of notice. It is remarkable that the same peculiar contrivance for expressing the passive is found in the Chinese, in which also *to eat a beating*, means *to be beaten.*

(4.) The mode of forming the passive which is most largely used in each of the modern *colloquial* dialects of the Drâvidian family, is by means of the auxiliary verb 'paḍ-u,' *to suffer, to experience*, which is annexed to the infinitive of the verb signifying the action suffered; *e.g.*, 'kolla-(p)paṭṭân,' Tam., *he was killed*, literally, *he suffered a killing or a to kill.* It is also annexed to nouns denoting quality or condition; *e.g.*, 'veṭka-(p)pâṭṭân,' *he was ashamed,* literally *he suffered or experienced shame.* The ultimate base of a verb is sometimes used instead of the infinitive or verbal noun in construction with this auxiliary, in which case the base is regarded as a noun; *e.g.*, instead of 'aḍikka-(p)paṭṭân,' we may say 'aḍi paṭṭân,' *he was beaten,* or literally *he suffered a beating;* and where this form can be used, it is considered more idiomatic than the use of the infinitive.

It is evident that this compound of 'paḍ-u,' *to suffer*, with an infinitive or noun of quality, is rather a phrase than a passive voice.

It is rarely found in the classics; and idiomatic speakers prefer the other modes of forming the passive. 'paḍ-u' is often added, not only to active, but also to neuter or intransitive verbs; but as the intransitive expresses by itself as much of a passive signification as is ordinarily necessary, the addition of the passive auxiliary does not alter the signification; *e.g.*, there is no difference in Tamil between the intransitive 'teriyum,' *it appears*, or *will appear*, and 'teriya (p)paḍum;' or in Telugu between 'teliyunu' and 'teliya baḍunu,' the corresponding forms. In ordinary use 'paḍ-u' conveys the meaning of continuous action or being, rather than that of passivity; *e.g.*, 'irukka-(p)paṭṭa, Tam., is vulgarly used for 'irukkiRa,' *that is;* and I have heard a Tamilian say, 'nân nandrâÿ ŝâppiḍa-(p)paṭṭavan,' Tam., meaning thereby, not *I have been well eaten*, but *I have been accustomed to eat well.*

The Drâvidian languages, indeed, are destitute of passives properly so called; and, therefore, they resist every effort to bring 'paḍ-u' into general use. Such efforts are constantly being made by foreigners, who are accustomed to passives in their own tongues, and fancy that they cannot get on without them; but nothing sounds more barbarous to the Drâvidian ear than the unnecessary use of 'paḍu' as a passive auxiliary. It is only when combined with nouns that its use is thoroughly allowable.

In none of the Drâvidian dialects is there a middle voice, properly so called. The force of the middle or reflective voice is expressed constructively by the use of an auxiliary verb, viz , by 'koḷ,' Tam., *to take* (Tel. 'kon-u'); *e.g.*, 'paṇṇi-(k)koṇḍên,' *I made it for myself*, literally, *I made and took it*. This auxiliary sometimes conveys a reciprocal force rather than that of the middle voice; *e.g*, 'pêsi-(k) koṇḍârgaḷ,' Tam., *they talked together;* 'aḍittu-(k)koṇḍârgal,' *they beat one another*. The same usage appears in the other dialects also.

IV. The Negative Voice.

Properly speaking, the Drâvidian negative is rather a mood or voice than a conjugation. All verbal themes are naturally affirmative, and the negative signification is expressed by means of inflexional additions or changes. Nevertheless, it will conduce to perspicuity to inquire now into the negative mood or voice, before entering upon the consideration of the pronominal terminations and tenses.

The regular combination of a negative with a verbal theme is a peculiarity of the Scythian family of tongues. Negation is generally expressed in the Indo-European family by means of a separate particle used adverbially; and instances of combination like the Sanscrit 'nâsti,' *it is not*, the negative of 'asti,' *it is*, are very rare, and are found only in connexion with substantive or auxiliary verbs: whereas, in the Scythian languages, every verb has a negative voice or mood as well as an affirmative. The Scythian negative voice is generally formed by the insertion of a particle of negation between the theme and the pronominal suffixes; and this is as distinctive of the Drâvidian as of the Turkish and Finnish languages. Different particles are, it is true, used in the different languages to express negation; but the mode in which such particles are used is substantially the same in all.

In general, the Drâvidian negative verb has but one tense, which is an aorist, or is indeterminate in point of time; *e.g.*, 'pôgên,' Tam. ('pôvanu,' Tel., 'pôgenu,' Can.), *I go not*, means either *I did not, I do not*, or *I will not go*. The time is generally determined by the context. The only exception is in the Ku, in which there is a negative preterite, as well as a negative aorist. In most of the dialects there is only one mood of the negative in ordinary use, viz., the indicative. If an infinitive and imperative exist, it is only in classical compositions that they appear; and they are ordinarily formed by the help of the infinitive and imperative of the substantive verb, which are suffixed as auxiliaries to the negative verbal participle; *e.g.*, 'śeÿÿâd'-iru,' Tam., *do not thou*, literally *be thou doing not*.

In the Telugu alone, a negative infinitive, and a prohibitive or negative imperative, are in ordinary use even in the colloquial dialect.

In the Drâvidian negative voice, as in the affirmative, the verbal theme remains unchanged; and in both voices the pronominal terminations are precisely the same. The only point, therefore, which it is necessary to investigate here is *the means whereby the idea of negation is expressed.*

The Drâvidian negative is altogether destitute of signs of tense: it is destitute, not only of the signs of present, past, and future time, but even of the sign of the aorist; and in Tamil and Canarese the pronominal suffixes are annexed directly to the verbal theme. Thus, whilst the present, past, and future tenses (first person singular) of the affirmative voice of the Tamil verb 'vâṛ,' *to flourish,* are 'vâṛ-giṟ-ên,' 'vâṛ-nd-ên,' 'vâṛ-v-ên;' the corresponding negative is simply 'vâṛ-ên,' *I flourish not*—literally, as appears, *flourish-I,*—without the insertion of any sign of time between the theme and the pronoun.

What is the rationale of the Drâvidian negative?

The absence of signs of tense evidently contributes to the expression of the idea of negation: it may at least be said that it precludes the signification of the affirmative. In consequence of the absence of tense-signs the idea expressed by the verb is abstracted from the realities of the past, the present, and the future: it leaves the region of actual events, and passes into that of abstractions. Hence, this abstract form of the verb may be supposed to have become a negative mood, not by a positive, but by a negative process,—by the absence of affirmation, not by the aid of a negative particle. Is this to be accepted as the rationale?

If we examined only the Tamil and the Canarese, we might be satisfied with this explanation of the origin of the negative; for in the various persons of the negative voice in both languages there is no trace of the insertion of any negative particle; and though the vowel 'a' has acquired a predominant and permanent place in the verbal and relative participles, we should not feel ourselves warranted in considering that vowel as a particle of negation, without distinct, reliable evidence from some other source.

The only peculiarity in the personal forms of the Tamil negative is the invariable length of the initial vowel of the pronominal terminations. Thus, the initial 'a' of the neuter singular demonstrative being short, we should expect the Tamil of *it flourishes not* to be 'vâṛ-adu;' whereas it is 'vâṛ-âdu' or 'vâṛ-â.' This increase of quantity might arise from the incorporation and assimilation of some inserted vowel; but we might also naturally suppose it to be merely euphonic. The corresponding vowel is short in Telugu; but even in Telugu it is occasionally lengthened for the sake of emphasis; *e.g.,* 'palukâka' (instead of 'palukaka'), *without speaking.* In the Canarese negative we miss even this lengthening of the initial vowel of the pronominal terminations; *e.g.*, we find invariably 'bâḷ-adu,' instead of the Tamil 'vâṛ-âdu.' In the verbal and relative participles in both languages the vowel 'a' is inserted between the theme and the formative, and this 'a' is invariably short in Canarese and long in Tamil; *e.g.*, 'bâḷ-a-de,' Can., *not having lived*, or *without living;* Tam., 'vâr-âdu' or 'vâṛ-â-mal,' *without living.* The verbal noun in Tamil is 'vâr-â--mei,' *the not living.* The relative participle *that lived or lives not*, is in Can., 'bâḷ-a-da,' in Tam., 'vâr-â-da.' In these instances, if euphony alone had been considered, 'u,' the ordinary enunciative vowel, would have appeared where we find 'a:' it may, therefore, be concluded that 'a' (euphonically 'â' in Tamil) has intentionally been inserted, and that it contributes in some manner to grammatical expression.

It will be found that much light is thrown upon this subject by the Telugu. The pronominal terminations of the negative voice of the Telugu are identical with those of the present tense of the affirmative. In Tamil and Canarese the pronominal terminations of the verb commence with a vowel; but in Telugu verbs the pronoun is represented by the final syllable alone, and that syllable invariably commences with a consonant. Hence, if no particle of negation were used in the conjugation of the Telugu negative voice, the pronominal suffix would be appended directly to the verbal theme, and as every Telugu theme terminates in the enunciative 'u,' that 'u' would not be elided, but would invariably remain. What then is the fact?

On examining the Telugu negative, it is found that the vowel 'a' invariably intervenes between the theme and the pronominal suffix; and as the final enunciative 'u' of the theme has been elided to make way for this 'a,' it is evident that 'a' is not an euphonic insertion, but is a particle of negation. Compare 'chéy-a-nu,' Tel., *I do not*, with Tam., 'śey(y)-ên;' 'chêy-a-vu,' *thou dost not*, with Tam., 'śey(y)-ây;' 'chêy-a-mu,' *we do not*, with Tam., 'sey(y)-ôm;' 'chêy-a-ru,' *you do not*, with Tam., 'sey(y)-îr.' From this comparison it cannot be doubted that 'a' is regularly used in Telugu as a particle of negation. We find the same 'a' used in Telugu, as in Canarese and Tamil, in the negative verbal participle; *e.g*, 'chêy-a-ka,' *without doing;* in the relative participle, *e.g.*, 'chêy-a-ni,' *that does not;* and in the verbal noun, *e.g.*, 'chêy-a-mi,' *the not doing.* In each of these participials 'a' is used in the same manner by the Canarese, and 'â' by the Tamil: and that those vowels are not euphonics or conjunctives, but signs of negation, even in Tamil-Canarese, is now clearly proved by the evidence of the Telugu, in which a similar 'a' is used, not only by the participles, but by all the personal forms of the verb.

The Tel. verb *to go*, forms its ordinary negative, it is true, without any trace of this vowel of negation : *e.g.*, 'pônu,' *I go not*, 'pôvu,' *thou goest not*. This, however, is only an apparent irregularity, for it is certain that the correct forms are 'pôv-a-nu' and 'pôv-a-vu.'

The lengthening of the included 'a' of 'kânu,' *I become not*, is in accordance with the Telugu law of displacement, 'kânu' being instead of 'ak-a-nu' or 'ag-a-nu,' the equivalent of the Tamil 'âgên.'

We have thus arrived at the conclusion that 'a' is the sign of negation which is systematically used by the Drâvidian language in the formation of the negative voice of the verb. It has, it is true, disappeared from the conjugated forms of the Tamil and Canarese; but the analogy not only of the Telugu personal forms, but also of the Tamil and Canarese participles, proves that it must originally have been the common property of all the dialects. The negative 'a,' being succeeded in Tamil and Canarese by the initial vowel of the pronominal suffix, appears gradually to have got incorporated with it: and an evidence of this incorporation survives in the euphonic lengthening of the pronominal vowel in Tamil and Tulu.

It is desirable now to inquire into the participial and imperative formatives of the negative verb.

The negative verbal participle of the Tamil is formed by suffixing 'â-du' or 'a-mal;' *e.g.*, 'śey(y)-â-du' or 'śey(y)-â-mal,' *not doing*, or *without doing*. In the highest and lowest Tamil 'mei' is used as the formative of this participle instead of 'mal,' *e.g.*, 'vaṛuv-â-mei,' *without slipping*. 'mei' constitutes the ordinary termination of abstract nouns, and is added both to crude roots and to the relative participles of verbs; *e.g.*, 'tâṛ-mei,' *lowness, humility;* 'iru-kkindr-a-mei,' *a being* or *the being*. The formative termination of negative verbal nouns is identical with this abstract 'mei;' and 'mal,' the participial formative, is evidently equivalent to it, and probably the original form: for it is more likely that a final 'l' should have been softened away than added by use. The verbal noun of the Telugu negative verb ends in 'mi,' which is virtually the same as 'mei.' The other Tamil termination of negative verbal participles, 'du,' is an ordinary formative of neuter nouns of quality. The corresponding Canarese termination is 'de;' and in Tamil 'du,' with a subsequent emphatic 'ê,' is commonly used as a negative imperative or prohibitive; *e.g.*, 'śey(y)-â-d-ê,' *do not thou*,—a proof that the negative verbal participle in 'du' or 'de' is properly a verbal noun. The relative participle of the negative verb in each of the dialects, except the Telugu, is formed by suffixing 'a,' the sign of the relative, to the verbal participle in 'd-u,' eliding as usual the enunciative 'u;' *e.g.*, 'śey(y)-â-da,' Tam., 'gêy-a-da,'

Can., *that does or did not.* Many additional forms are constructed by the addition of the various tenses and participles of the substantive verb, and it is by the help of that verb that the negative imperative and negative infinitive in both Canarese and Tamil are ordinarily formed. The negative relative participle of the Telugu is formed by adding 'ni,' instead of the usual relative 'a,' to the negative particle; *e.g.*, 'chêy-a-ni,' *that does or did not.* This 'ni' is one of the Telugu inflexional increments, and is also used as a particle of conjunction, as will be seen under the head of the *relative participles.*

The negative verbal participle and negative imperative of the Telugu require to be separately investigated.

Mr. A. D. Campbell, in his Telugu Grammar, states that the negative verbal particle is formed by suffixing 'ka' to the infinitive of the affirmative voice; and that the prohibitive is formed in like manner by suffixing 'ku' or 'ka' to the infinitive, with the ordinary addition of 'mu' or 'mo.' In consequence of this representation, Dr. Stevenson has been led to consider 'ku' as a Telugu sign of negation, and to search for allied or equivalent particles in other Indian languages. The comparison of the negative verbs in the various Drâviḍian dialects which has just been made, proves that this representation is inaccurate, and that the 'a' to which the 'ka' and 'ku' aforesaid are suffixed is not the 'a' which forms the sign of the infinitive, but the negative particle 'a.' The suffixes of the forms in question, therefore, are not 'ku' or 'ka,' but 'a-ku' and 'a-ka,' or 'â-ka;' and thus 'chêy-a-ka,' *without doing*, or *not having done*, and 'chêy-a-ku' or 'chêy-a-ka,' *do not*, come into harmony with the other Telugu forms, viz., 'chêy-a-ni,' *that does not*, 'chêy-a-mi,' *the not doing;* and also with the negative participles and verbals of the other dialects.

The 'a' of the Telugu imperative and negative verbal participle being undoubtedly the sign of negation, it only remains to inquire into the origin of the 'ka' or 'ku' which is suffixed to it.

The participial suffix 'ka' is evidently used in Telugu for the same purposes as the Tamil suffixes 'du,' 'mal,' and 'mei,' and the Can., 'de.' Those suffixes, though used by verbal participles, are undoubtedly to be regarded as formatives of verbal nouns. I consider 'ka' also as proceeding from a similar origin; for in Telugu many verbal nouns are formed in this very manner by adding 'ka' to the root: *e.g.*, 'nammi-ka,' *confidence*, from 'nammu,' *to confide;* and 'kôri-ka,' *hope*, from 'kôru,' *to hope.* This 'ka' is 'kkei,' in Tamil (*e.g.*, 'nambi-kkei,' *confidence*), and 'ge' or 'ke,' in Canarese: it is a very common formative of verbal nouns, and is equivalent in use to the formatives of which 'd' or 't,' 'b' or 'p,' is the initial. When we compare Telugu derivative nouns ending in 'ka' (*e.g.*, 'teliyi-ka,' *semblance,* from 'teliyu,' *to appear*) with the negative verbal participles of the same language, which invariably end in 'ka' (*e.g.*, 'teḷiy-a-ka,' *not seeming*), it is evident that the particle 'ka' is not that by which the difference in meaning is expressed. The vowel 'a' which precedes 'ka' is evidently the seat of the difference. In those cases in which the derivative noun and the negative participle are absolutely identical in sound and appearance, the negative 'a' has been absorbed by the preceding long 'â' of the root. This is the cause of the similarity between 'râka,' *a coming,* and 'râka,' *not* or *without coming,* the latter of which is for 'râ-a-ka.'

In the dialect of the Kotas of the Nilgherry hills, 'p' is used as the formative suffix of the negative verbal participle instead of the Telugu 'k' and the Tamil-Canarese 'd;' *e.g.*, 'hôgâ-pe,' *without going,* corresponding to the Can. 'hôgade,' and the Tel. 'pôvaka.'

The Telugu prohibitive suffix 'ku,' or more commonly 'ka,' is, I believe, identical with 'ka,' the suffix of the verbal participle, just as the 'd' of 'dê,' the vulgar Tamil prohibitive, is identical with the 'd' of 'du,' the negative verbal participle in the same dialect.

Drâvidian imperatives are in general nothing but verbal nouns pronounced emphatically. Hence, the Tamil 'śey(y)-â-dê,' *do not thou,* is simply 'sey(y)-â-du,' *doing not,* with the addition of the emphatic 'ê:' and the Telugu 'chêy-a-ku,' or 'chêy-a-ka,' *do not thou,* is in like manner, I conceive, identical with the verbal participle 'chêy-a-ka,' *doing not,* or *without doing,* with an emphasis understood.

There is in classical Tamil a prohibitive particle which corresponds to this Telugu prohibitive, viz., 'aʀka;' *e.g.*, 'śey(y)-aʀka,' *do not.* The Tamil prohibitive is used in connexion with both numbers and every gender; and I believe that it is by usage only that the corresponding Telugu form is restricted to the second person singular; for when we compare the Tam. 'śey(y)-aʀka' and the Tel. 'chêy-aka,' we cannot doubt that they are identical. What is the origin of this Tamil prohibitive suffix 'aʀka?' it is derived from 'al' (pronounced 'aʀ' before 'k'), the particle of negation, and 'ka,' which is identical with 'ka' or 'ga,' a sign of the Tamil infinitive, optative, or polite imperative, apparent in such words as 'vâṛ-ga,' *may* (*he, thou, you, they,* &c.) *flourish.* All verbal nouns in Malayâlam end in 'ka' or 'ga,' and each of those verbals is used also as a polite imperative; *e.g.*, 'wari-ka' or 'wari-ga,' is either *a coming* or *mayest thou come,* according to the context: so that the infinitival, participial, or imperative formative appears to have been originally the formative of a verbal noun.

We should here notice the prohibitive particle of the Gônd, viz., 'mani' or 'minni.' This is not suffixed to the verb, but prefixed, like the Latin 'noli.' 'minni' closely resembles the Tamil suffix 'min,' in such words as 'śey(y)an-min,' *do not ye:* but the resemblance is purely accidental; for the prohibitive particle of 'śey(y)-an-min' is 'an' (euphonised from 'al'), and 'min' is not, as Beschi supposes, a prohibitive particle, but is a sign of the second person plural of the imperative, and as such is systematically used in the higher dialect by the imperative of the affirmative voice, as well as by the prohibitive; *e.g.*, 'poʀu-min,' *bear ye.* Possibly the Gônd prohibitive, 'mani,' is connected rather with the Hindustani 'mat' and the Sanscrit 'mâ,' and remotely with the Turkish particle of negation, 'me' or 'ma;' which is used like the Drâvidian 'a' in the formation of the negative voice of the verb. 'minni' also closely resembles 'inni,' the prohibitive particle of the Scythian tablets of Behistun.

Origin of 'a' the Drâvidian negative particle.—We have seen that 'a' is the Drâvidian sign of negation, and that it is inserted between the theme and the signs of personality and other suffixes to form the negative voice of the verb.

Is this 'a' connected with the 'alpha privative' of the Indo-European tongues? I think not, though this would be a more natural use of the 'alpha privative' than that of forming the temporal augment in Sanscrit and Greek, according to Bopp's theory. There is no trace of 'alpha privative' or any equivalent privative *prefix* in the Drâvidian languages; and its place is supplied by some post-fixed relative participle or verbal noun formed from 'il' or 'al;' *e.g.*, from 'nêr,' Tam., *straight* or *straightness*, is formed 'nêr-inmei' ('il-mei' euphonised), *crookedness, want of straightness.*

The negative 'a' of the Drâvidian negative verb is, I have no doubt, softened from 'al' or 'il,' the ordinary isolated particle of negation. This very sign of negation is sometimes used by the Tamil classics instead of 'a' in verbal combinations; *e.g.*, 'aʀig-il-îr, *you know not,* takes the place of the more common 'aʀi-(y)-îr:' compare also 'ninei-(y)-alâ,' *not considering;* 'śeÿg'-al-âdâr,' *they who will not do* or *they will not do.* In all these examples the 'al' is, I conceive, the negative particle 'al,' not the 'al' of the verbal noun. There cannot be any doubt whatever of the negative force of 'al' in the negative appellatives, which are formed from 'al-an' or 'il-an,' *he is not,* combined with verbal roots; *e.g.*, 'pêś-al-êm,' *we speak not,* 'uṇḍ-il-ei,' *thou eatest not* or *hast not eaten.* The Gônd regularly forms its negative voice by suffixing 'halle' or 'hille,' a barbarous euphonisation of the more correct 'al' or 'il;' and the dialect of the Kôtas makes a similar use of the particle 'illa,' This particle is also systematically used in forming the prohibitive, or negative imperative, of the High Tamil, in which connexion 'al' is ordinarily lengthened to 'âl' or 'êl;' *e.g.*, 'śel-êl,' *go not*, 'muni-(y)-êl,' *be not angry*. But it is also often retained unchanged; *e.g.*, 'sey(y)-aʀ-ka' ('aʀ' for 'al'), *do not*, and 'sey(y)-an-miṉ' ('an' for 'al'), *do not ye*. In modern vulgar Tamil 'illei' (for 'illa') is commonly subjoined to the infinitive of the affirmative verb to form an aoristic negative; *e.g.*, 'vara-(v)-illei,' (*I, thou, he*, &c.) *did not, do not, or will not come*. This form, though very common, is not classical, and has arisen from the tendency which compounds evince to break up in process of time into their component elements.

'al' or 'il' being the isolated particle of negation in the oldest Tamil dialect, and being still used in various verbal combinations, I conclude that 'a' the verbal sign of the negative, has been softened from 'al.' Several parallel examples of the softening away of a final 'l' can be adduced. 'dal,' the formative of many verbal nouns in Tamil, has become 'ta' in Canarese and Telugu; *e.g.*, 'śey-dal,' *doing*, Tam., is in Tel. 'chê-ta;' 'muʀi-dal,' Tam., *breaking*, is in Canarese 'muri-ta.' It will also be shown to be probable that 'a,' the suffix of the infinitive, has been weakened from another 'al;' and we have already seen that 'mei,' the Tamil suffix of the negative verbal noun appears to have been softened from 'mal,' the suffix of the negative verbal participle.

Whatever opinion we entertain respecting the derivation of 'a' from 'al,' the widely extended affinities of 'al,' 'âl,' or 'êl,' the prohibitive or negative imperative particle, are deserving of notice. The prohibitive particle of the Sântâl, a Kôl dialect, is 'âlâ;' the Finnish prohibitive also is 'âlâ;' the Ostiak 'ilâ;' and we find a similar prohibitive particle even in the Hebrew, viz., 'al;' Chaldee 'lâ.'

V. Appellative Verbs.

In some languages of the Scythian group, verbal terminations, or those pronominal fragments in which verbs terminate, are suffixed directly to nouns; which nouns become by that addition denominative or appellative verbs, and are regularly conjugated through every number and person; *e.g.*, from the noun 'paz,' *the Lord*, the Mordwin forms 'paz-ân,' *I am the Lord*; and from the possessive 'paz-an,' *Lord's*, it forms 'paz-an-ân,' *I am the Lord's*. Adjectives being merely nouns of quality in the Scythian languages, every rule which applies to nouns applies to adjectives also. In the New Persian, probably through the influence of the conterminous Scythian languages, there is a similar compound of a noun or an adjective, with the verbal terminations; *e.g.*, 'merd-em,' *I-am a man*, from 'merd,' *a man*, and 'em,' the contracted form of the substantive verb *I am*.

The agreement between the Drâvidian languages and those of the Scythian family with respect to the formation of appellative verbs of this character is complete. Any Drâvidian noun and any adjective may be converted into a verb in the more ancient dialects of each of the Drâvidian languages, and in some connexions even in the colloquial dialects, by simply suffixing to it the usual pronominal fragments: and not only may nouns in the nominative case be thus conjugated as verbs, but even the oblique case-basis, or old genitive, may in High Tamil, as in Mordwin, be adopted as a verbal theme.

Tamil grammarians call these verbs 'vinei-(k)kuʀippu,' literally *verbal signs;* and they have, not inappropriately, been styled *conjugated nouns* by an English writer on Tamil Grammar: but I think the best name is that which was given them by Beschi, viz., 'appellative verbs.'

Appellative verbs are conjugated through every number and person, but they are restricted to the present tense; or rather they are of no tense, for the idea of time is excluded from them.

Thus, from 'kôn,' Tam., *a king*, may be formed 'kôn-ên,' *I am a king;* 'kôn-ei,' *thou art a king;* 'kôn-êm,' *we are kings;* 'kôn-îr,' *ye are kings.* So also we may annex to the crude base the oblique or genitival formative 'in,' and then from the new constructive base 'kôn-in,' *of the king*, or *the king's*, we may not only form the appellative nouns, 'kôn-in-an,' *he who is the king's;* 'kôn-in-ar,' *they who are the king's* (each of which may be used also as an appellative verb, when it signifies *he is the king's*, or *they are the king's*); but we may also form the more distinctively verbal appellatives, 'kôn-in-ên,' *I am the king's*, 'kôn-in-êm,' *we are the king's*, &c. This use of the oblique or 'inflexion' as the basis of appellative verbs is a peculiarity of High Tamil; but the formation of appellative verbs from the nominative or crude base of nouns is common to the whole Drâvidian family. Thus, in Telugu (in which the vowel of the pronominal termination varies by rule in accordance with the preceding vowel), from 'sêvakuḍu,' *a servant*, or 'kavi,' *a poet*, we form the appellative verbs 'sêvakuṇḍa-nu,' *I am a servant;* 'kavi-ni,' *I am a poet:* 'sêvakuṇḍa-vu,' *thou art a servant;* 'kavi-vi,' *thou art a poet.* In the plural the Telugu has allowed the base of the noun (to which the pronominal terminations are affixed) to be pluralised, apparently from having forgotten that the plural sign of the pronominal termination was sufficient of itself; *e.g.*, it says 'sêvakula-mu,' *we are servants* (not 'sevakuṇda-mu'); whereas in Tamil the difference between 'aḍi-(y)-ên,' *I am (your) servant*, and 'aḍi-(y)-êm,' *we are (your) servants*, appears in the pronominal terminations alone; and the plan of denoting the plural which the Tamil has adopted is evidently more in accordance with the true theory of the appellative verb.

The Telugu appellative verb is destitute of a third person. It is obliged to be content with placing the isolated pronoun of the third person and the substantive noun in apposition, with a substantive verb understood; *e.g.*, 'vâḍu kavi,' *he (is) a poet*; 'adi ûru,' *that (is) a village*. The Tamil is in this particular more highly developed; for its appellative verbs are freely conjugated in the third person in each gender and number, by suffixing the final fragment of the pronoun; *e.g.*, from 'nal,' *goodness* or *good*, is formed 'nal(l)-an,' *he is good*; 'nal(l)-aḷ,' *she is good*; 'nal(l)-adu' or 'nan-dru' (for 'nal-du'), *it is good*; 'nal(l)-ar,' *they* (epicene) *are good*; 'nal(l)-ana' or 'nal(l)-a,' *they* (neut.) *are good*.

The neuter singular may appear to take a variety of forms; but on examination those various forms will be found to be identical; and the apparent differences which exist are owing either to the euphonic union of the final 'du' with some previous consonant, or to its euphonic reduplication.

The third person neuter, singular and plural (and occasionally the third person masculine and feminine also), of every species of Drâvidian verb, is often used not only as a verb, but also as a verbal or participial noun. Its primary use may have been that of a participial noun, and its use as a verb may be a secondary one: but at all events the two uses are found to be interchangeable; *e.g.*, 'irukkiʀadu,' means either *it is*, or *that which is*, or *the being*, according to the context.

It is especially with relation to appellatives that this twofold use of the forms of the third person must be borne in mind; for in the third person (singular and plural, masculine, feminine, and neuter) there is no difference whatever in spelling or pronunciation between appellative verbs and appellative nouns, and it is the context alone that determines which meaning is the correct one. Generally the appellative verb is more commonly used in the High dialect, and the noun in the colloquial dialect; but to this there are exceptions, and (*e.g.*) 'nalladu,' more frequently signifies in the colloquial dialect *it is well* than *that which is good*;—that is, it is used more frequently as an appellative verb than as an appellative noun.

It is certain, however, that the appellative verb, whatever person or gender it takes, is used more largely in the higher dialect of the

Tamil than in the lower; and its brevity and compression render it peculiarly adapted for metaphorical use.

Adjectives are formed into appellative verbs as well as nouns: but as the Drâvidian adjective is merely a noun of quality used adjectivally, the difference is more in terms than in reality: *e.g.*, 'oḷi-(y)-ei,' Tam., *thou art bright*, is literally *thou art brightness*; and 'iṅi-(y)-ei,' *thou art sweet*, is *thou art sweetness*. Appellative verbs are formed from adjectives, or nouns of quality, not only in the cultivated Drâvidian dialects, but even in the Ku, which is spoken by a barbarous race; *e.g.*, 'negg-ânu,' Ku, *I am good*, 'negg-âmu,' *we are good*.

When nouns of quality are used as the bases of appellative verbs or nouns they are generally adopted in their crude shape, as in the instances which have just been cited; but in many cases we find the particle 'iya' intervening between the crude base and the pronominal termination or sign of gender; *e.g.*, 'koḍ-iya-n' (as a verb), *he is cruel;* (as a noun) *one who is cruel*, or *a cruel man*; 'val-iya-n,' *a strong man* or *he is strong*, &c. This is the same particle which we have already seen to be used as an adjectival formative; *e.g.*, 'val-iya,' *strong*, 'per-iya,' *great*, 'siṟ-iya, *little*, &c., and I have stated that I conceive words like these to be relative participles. 'i' is identical with the 'i' of the past verbal participle, which is often used in Telugu as an adjectival formative without any addition; and the final 'a' is the sign of the relative, which is kept separate from 'i' by an euphonic 'y.' 'iya' is therefore the formative of the relative preterite participle, and 'val-i-(y)-a,' *strong*, means properly *that which was strong*. But though the form of the preterite tense is employed, the signification (as often happens, especially in the case of relative participles) is aoristic or without reference to time. This being the origin, as I conceive, of such forms as 'val-iya,' an appellative noun like 'val-iya-n,' *a strong man*, is in reality a participial noun, signifying *he who is strong*, and so of the other genders; and this explanation brings such forms into perfect harmony with other parts of the Drâvidian conjugational system, for participial nouns are regularly used in these languages as verbs.

In some instances, 'a,' the sign of the relative participle, is dispensed with, and the pronominal signs or signs of gender are elegantly suffixed to 'i,' the sign of the verbal participle, *e.g.*, 'peri-du,' Tam., *it is great*, or *that which is great*, instead of 'peri-(y)-a-du.'

On the other hand, in another class of instances, 'i' disappears, and 'a' alone remains. Words of this class, when deprived of their signs of gender, are commonly called adjectives, and undoubtedly it is as adjectives that they are used; but looking at their construction and force I would term them *relative participles of appellative verbs*.

In the words referred to, 'a,' the sign of the relative participle is directly annexed to crude substantive roots; *e.g.*, 'uḍei-(y)-a,' *belonging to*, more literally *which is the property of.* 'malei-(y)-a,' *hilly*, literally *which is a hill;* 'tî-y-a,' *evil*, literally *which is evil.* As 'uḍei-(y)-an,' considered as a noun, is certainly an appellative, signifying *he who owns, a proprietor*, and as the same word is used poetically as an appellative verb, when it signifies *he is the owner;* it seems evident that the proper light in which to regard 'uḍei-(y)-a' (and every similar word) is to consider it as the relative participle of an appellative verb used adjectivally.

Conjugational System.

Mode of annexing Pronominal Signs.—The persons of the Drâvidian verb, including the related ideas of gender and number, are formed by suffixing the personal or demonstrative pronouns or their fragmentary terminations, to the signs of tense.

The change which the pronouns undergo when they are appended to verbs as signs of personality have already been exhibited in the section on 'The Pronoun.' They consist chiefly in the softening away of the initial consonant; but in a few instances the final consonant has also been softened away, and nothing left but the included vowel. In Telugu, 'nî-vu,' the pronoun of the second person singular, has lost both its radical initial and its formative final; and in the personal terminations of the verb it is represented only by 'vu,' an euphonic addition.

In the Indo-European languages the personal signs of the verb are formed by suffixing pronominal fragments to the root; and those fragments are disguised in a still greater degree than in the Drâvidian languages, not only by frequency of use and rapidity of enunciation, but also by the love of fusing words and particles together, and forming them into euphonious compounds, which distinguishes that family of tongues. Sometimes one dialect alone furnishes the key to the explanation of the inflexional forms which are apparent in all. Thus, the origin of 'unt' or 'ant,' the sign of the third person plural in the various Indo-European languages (*e.g.*, 'fer-unt,' 'φέρ-οντι,' 'bhar-anti,' &c.) is found in the Welsh alone, in which 'hwynt' is a pronoun of the third person plural.

The various changes which the Drâvidian pronouns undergo on being used as the pronominal signs of verbs have already been stated in order. In Telugu, and partly also in Canarese, the pronominal terminations vary according to the tense; but this arises from the operation of the law of harmonic sequences (see the section on 'Sounds'), by which a vowel is affected by a preceding vowel, and changed so as to harmonise with it. What requires here to be investigated is simply the mode in which the pronominal signs are attached to the Drâvidian verb.

(1.) The pronominal signs of the Drâvidian verb, like those of the primitive Indo-European and Scythian languages, are suffixed, not prefixed. In the modern Indo-European vernaculars, most of the verbs have lost their old pronominal terminations, and the pronouns which are used as nominatives to verbs are usually isolated and placed first. Thus, instead of *love-I*, in accordance with the ancient 'am-o,' we have learnt to say *I love*,—an alteration of position which produces no change in meaning.

In the Semitic languages a change in the position of the pronoun from the termination of the verb to its commencement produces an important change in grammatical signification: the position of the pronouns or pronominal fragments determines the tense. When the pronominal fragments are prefixed, the tense of the verb is regarded as future or aoristic: it is regarded as past when they are suffixed. Prefixing the pronominal fragments denotes that the action of the verb has, as yet, only a subjective existence in the mind of the speaker or agent,— *i.e.*, it is future; suffixing them denotes that the action of the verb has already acquired an objective existence, apart from the will or wish of the speaker or agent, *i.e.*, it is past.

No peculiarity of this kind characterises the Drâvidian languages: the tenses are formed, not by means of the position of the pronouns, but by particles or signs of present, past, and future time suffixed to the theme; and the personal signs, as in the Turkish and Finnish families, are suffixed to the signs of tense. The only exception to this rule is that which forms the most characteristic feature of the Malayâlam—a language which appears to have been directly derived from the Tamil,—but which, in so far as its conjugational system is concerned, has relapsed into a condition nearly resembling that of the Mongolian, the Manchu, and other rude primitive tongues of High Asia. In ancient times, as may be gathered from Malayâla poetry, and especially from inscriptions preserved by the Syrian Christians and the Jews, the pronouns were suffixed to the Malayâla verb, precisely as they still are in Tamil. At present, the verb is entirely divested, at least in the colloquial dialect, of signs of personality; and with the pronouns. the signs of number and gender also have necessarily disappeared; so that the pronoun or nominative must in every instance be separately prefixed to the verb to complete the signification, and it is chiefly by means of this prefixed pronoun that a verb, properly so called, is distinguished from a verbal participle. Though the personal signs have been abandoned by the Malayâla verb, the signs of tense or time have been retained, and are annexed directly to the root as in the other dialects. Even in modern English some persons of the verb retain archaic fragments of the pronominal signs (*e.g.*, *lov*est, *lov*eth); but in the Malayâlam every trace of those signs has disappeared. Thus, whilst we would say in Tamil 'aḍittên,' *I beat;* 'aḍittây̆,' *thou didst beat;* 'aḍittân,' *he beat;* the Malayâlam uses in these and all similar cases the verbal participle 'aṭichu' (for 'aḍittu'), *having beaten*, with the prefixed pronouns *I*, *thou*, *he*, &c.: *e.g.*, 'ñjân aṭichu,' *I beat;* 'nî aṭichu,' *thou didst beat;* 'avan aṭichu,' *he beat.*

Though the pronominal signs have been lost by the Malayâla verb, they have been retained even by the Tuda; and notwithstanding the barbarity of the Gônds and Kus, their conjugational system is peculiarly elaborate and complete.

(2.) Another and distinctively Scythian peculiarity in the manner in which the personal signs are suffixed in the Drâvidian languages consists in their annexation, not directly to the root, as in the Indo-European family, but to the temporal participles. The first suffix to the root in the affirmative voice is that of the sign of tense, then follows the suffix of personality. Every pure Drâvidian affirmative verb is compounded of three elements, which are thus arranged and named by Tamil grammarians, viz., (i.) the 'pagudi' ('pracriti,' Sans.) or *root;* (ii.) the 'iḍei nilei,' or *medial particle, i.e.*, the sign of tense; and (iii.) the 'vigudi' ('vicriti,' Sans.), the *variation* or *differentia, i.e.*, the pronominal termination.

When the signs of tense are attached to the theme, some euphonic changes take place (not in the theme, but in the signs themselves), which serve, as has been shown, to distinguish transitive verbs from intransitives. Other euphonic changes also take place in accordance with Drâvidian laws of sound, which will be inquired into when those signs of tense are one by one examined. The changes which take place in the pronominal signs when they are annexed to the signs of tense have already been stated in the section on the 'Pronoun.'

In the Indo-European languages we meet with no instance of the annexation of the pronominal signs to the participles, *i.e.*, to the combination of the root with the signs of tense. We have no instance of the use of any form like 'amant-o,' instead of 'am-o,' to signify *I love.*

This, however, is the method which is invariably employed in the Drâvidian languages, and which constitutes an essential element in the family likeness by which they are pervaded. It is also distinctive of the Turkish. Thus, the Turkish 'ôlûrsen,' *thou art*, is formed from 'ôlûr,' *being*, the present participle of the verb 'ôl,' *to be*, with the addition of the pronoun 'sen,' *thou*. So also the Oriental Turkish 'bôlâmen,' *I am*, is formed from 'bôlâ,' *being* (theme 'bôl,' *to be*), and the pronominal suffix 'men,' *I*.

An important difference which is generally found to exist between the Drâvidian languages and the North Indian vernaculars should here be stated. In the languages of Northern India the present tense of a verb is ordinarily formed by annexing the substantive verb to its present participle, *e.g.*, 'karitechi,' Beng. ('karite-âchi'), *I am doing*, instead of *I do*.

In Telugu, probably through the influence of the North-Indian vernaculars, a similar usage prevails; but it is found in the present tense only, it may readily be dispensed with, and the simpler usage, which accords with that of all the other Drâvidian dialects, is undoubtedly the more ancient. In Tamil and Canarese this use of the substantive verb, as an auxiliary in the formation of the present tense, is unknown: it is used as an auxiliary only in the formation of the compound preterite and future tenses.

The Malayâlam occasionally uses the substantive verb in a similar manner to the Telugu, but with a somewhat different signification. In Telugu 'naḍuchutunnânu,' *I walk* (from 'naduchu-tu,' *walking*, and 'unnânu,' *I am*), has simply the meaning of the present tense, and is equivalent to the simpler form 'naḍuchutânu,' answering to the Tamil 'naḍakkiʀên,' and the Canarese 'naḍeyuttêne;' but in Malayâlam, whilst 'ñjân naṭakkunnu,' means *I walk*, 'ñjân naṭakkunnuṇṭa' has generally a progressive sense, *e.g.*, *I am walking* or *continuing to walk*.

(3.) It is a peculiarity of the Telugu that the third person of the preterite is sometimes left altogether destitute of the signs of time, person, number, and gender; and this peculiarity applies also to the third person of the aorist. Thus, whilst 'uṇḍitini,' *I was*, and 'uṇḍitivi,' *thou wast*, are supplied with the usual signs of tense and person, the third person of the same tense is simply 'uṇḍe-nu,' *he, she, or it was*, or *they were*, without distinction of number or gender, and without even the particle 'ti,' which constitutes the usual sign of the preterite. The aorist third person, with a similar absence of distinction, is 'uṇḍunu;' and in both cases the final 'nu' is merely a conjunctive suffix, like the corresponding Tamil 'um.' Sometimes even the aorist formative 'nu' is discarded, and the root alone is used as the third person singular. Thus (*he, she*, or *it*) *falls* or *will fall*, may either be 'paḍunu,' or simply 'paḍu.' The usage of poetical Tamil occasionally agrees with that of the Telugu with respect to the neuter gender, both singular and plural, especially in connexion with the negative voice of the verb : *e.g.*, 'śey(y)-â,' *it will not do*, is often used for 'sey(y)-âdu.'

A usage similar to that of the Telugu prevails in many languages which are widely different one from the other.

Thus, the New Persian uses for the third person singular of the preterite *the contracted infinitive*, as grammarians style it—an abstract verbal noun, which may be regarded as the theme of the verb. The Hebrew third person masculine of the preterite tense is also a verbal noun, without pronominal addition. We see a similar peculiarity in the third person of the *present* tense of the verb in some languages; *e.g.*, compare the three persons of the present tense of the Turkish substantive verb, 'ôlûrum,' *I am*; 'ôlûrsen,' *thou art*; 'ôlûr,' *he is*. Compare also the Armorican 'kanann,' *I sing*; 'kanez,' *thou singest*; 'kan,' *he sings*. Compare with these examples the Hungarian 'ismerek,' *I know*; 'ismersz,' *thou knowest*; 'and 'ismer,' *he knows*.

(4.) The Drâvidian verb, like that of many other languages, does not distinguish the genders of either the first person or the second, whether singular or plural; but in the third person it marks all existing distinctions of gender with peculiar explicitness and minuteness. Thus, without the use of isolated pronouns, and employing the inflections of the verb alone, we can say in Tamil 'varugiʀan,' *he comes*: 'varugiʀâl,' *she comes*; 'varugiʀadu,' *it comes*; 'varugiʀâr,' *they* (men and women) *come*, or honorifically *he comes*; 'varugiʀârgal,' *they* (men and women) *come*; 'varugindrana,' *they* (things) *come*.

FORMATION OF THE TENSES.—Most of the Drâvidian tenses are formed from participial forms of the verb; an inquiry into the participles is therefore a necessary preliminary to an inquiry into the tenses. Drâvidian verbs have two species of participles, one of which (called *relative participles*, because they include the signification of the relative pronoun), will be inquired into in a subsequent part of this section; the other, commonly called *verbal participles* or *gerunds*, and which are now to be considered, constitute the bases on which the tenses are formed. The *forms* which are assumed by the verbal participles will be inquired into in connexion with the signs of tense, from the consideration of which they cannot be severed. I content myself here with some general remarks on the signification and force of this class of words.

Verbal participles: their signification and force.—In ordinary Tamil and in Malayâlam, there is but one verbal participle, that of the past tense; in all the other dialects there is a verbal participle of the present tense as well as of the past. In this particular, therefore, the Tamil (with its daughter, the Malayâlam) may be considered as the poorest of the Drâvidian dialects. It partly makes compensation for the deficiency by the use in the classical idiom of a verbal participle of the future, which none of its sister dialects possesses. Even the classical idiom, however, is destitute of a present verbal participle. Properly speaking, the words which are called *verbal participles* are not *participles* at all, seeing that they do not *participate* in the nature of adjectives, as all the Indo-European participles do. They have somewhat of the signification of gerunds, inasmuch as in addition to the idea of time, they include more or less of the idea of cause. Nevertheless, as each of the Indo-European participles is commonly used also as a gerund, without losing the name of a participle, and as 'the gerund in *do*' (to which alone, amongst Latin gerunds, the Drâvidian participles have any resemblance) has a very restricted application, it appears advisable after all, to style these words participles instead of gerunds,—or more fully *verbal participles*, to distinguish them from what are called *relative participles.*

The following sentences will illustrate the force of the Drâvidian verbal participles.

(1.) *Present verbal participle.*—This verbal participle is unknown in Tamil and Malayâlam; but is commonly used both in Canarese and in Telugu. I quote the illustration which follows from the Canarese. '*Vikramârka, punishing the wicked and protecting the good, reigned over the kingdom.*' Here the English words *punishing* and *protecting*, are participles of the present tense, used gerundially; and the Drâvidian words which they represent, (in Canarese, 'sikshisuttâ' and 'rakshisuttâ) have precisely the same force. In this respect only there is a difference between them, viz., that the English participles are capable of being used also as adjectives, whereas the Drâvidian words, though called participles, cannot be used adjectivally, or in any other way than that here exemplified.

(2.) *Preterite verbal participle.*—'*Sâlivâhana, having killed 'Vikramârka, assumed supreme power.*' Though the English participle *having killed* which is here used, is a compound one (being formed from the present participle *having*, and the passive participle *killed*), its signification is that of a simple, uncompounded participle of the past tense, and the Drâvidian word which it represents ('kondru,' Tam, 'kondu,' Can.) is also a preterite active verbal participle. In this instance, neither the English participle nor the Drâvidian one is capable of being used as an adjective. In reality, they are both preterite gerunds or gerundials, though they retain the name of participles as a matter of convenience.

In those Drâvidian dialects in which there is a present, as well as a preterite, verbal participle (as in Canarese and Telugu), the present is used to express subordinate actions which are contemporaneous with that which is denoted by the principal and finite verb; whilst the preterite expresses subordinate actions which are antecedent in point of time to the principal action. In Tamil, the preterite participle is used to express all subordinate actions, whether simultaneous with the main action or antecedent to it; but though that participle is always a preterite in form, it possesses the force of a participle of the present tense, when the connexion requires it. In each of the dialects and in every connexion, the nominative of the final governing verb is the nominative of all the subordinate verbal participles.

The Drâvidian verbal participles may be compared with the Sanscrit 'indeterminate past participle' in 'tvâ;' *e.g.*, 'krutvâ,' *having done.* Like that participle they are indeclinable and indeterminate. One of the chief peculiarities, however, of these verbal participles is, that they have a continuative force, dispensing altogether with the use of conjunctions. In the Drâvidian languages, though nouns and pronouns are united by means of conjunctions, finite verbs are never so united. In every sentence there is but one finite verb, which is the last word in the sentence, and the seat of government; and all the verbs which express subordinate actions or circumstances, whether antecedent or contemporaneous, assume an indeterminate, continuative character, as verbal participles or gerundials, without the need of conjunctions or copulatives of any kind; so that the sense (and in Tamil the time also) waits in suspense for the authoritative decision of the final governing verb. Hence those participles might properly be called *continuative gerundials.* Tamilian grammarians class them, with infinitives and subjunctives, as 'vinei echam,' *verb-defects,* or *verbal complements,* *i.e.*, words which require a verb to complete the sense.

1. *The present tense.*—It may be stated generally that the present tense of the Drâvidian verb is formed by suffixing the pronominal signs to the present verbal participle, with such trivial changes only as euphony requires.

The exceptions to this general rule are as follows :—

(1.) In poetical Tamil the tenses are sometimes formed by suffixing the pronominal terminations to the relative participles, instead of the gerunds or verbal participles; *e.g.*, 'naḍanda(n)an' (equivalent to the colloquial 'naḍanda(v)an'), *he walked*, literally *a man who walked*. In such instances a verbal or participial noun is used with the force of a verb. This is not an uncommon usage in other languages also; and in colloquial Tamil the third person neuter of the verb, both singular and plural, is certainly a verbal noun in its origin, though used with the force of a verb; *e.g.*, 'naḍandadu,' *it walked*, literally means *a thing which walked*; and the plural 'naḍanda(n)a,' means literally *things which walked*. The peculiarity of the poetical dialect is the extension of this usage to each person of the verb; *e.g.*, 'naḍanda(n)en,' *I walked*, literally *I who walked*; 'naḍanda(n)am' or 'naḍanda(n)em,' *we walked*, literally *we who walked*.

This mode of forming the tenses has been developed from the Drâvidian custom of using participial and verbal nouns as the conjugational bases of verbs, and, so far, is in accordance with the genius of the language; but it has a constructive, artificial look, and it is an exception to the mode which prevails throughout all the other dialects of the family, whether colloquial or classical.

(2.) The Tamil has, properly speaking, no present verbal participle, but only a particle denoting present time, which is suffixed to the theme of the verb, and to which the pronominal signs are then suffixed for the purpose of forming the present tense. The combination, however, of the root and the particle of present time, forms virtually a present participle. I think it may, therefore, be assumed that the Tamil had a verbal participle of the present tense at a former period, which has now become obsolete, except in combination with the personal terminations, when it constitutes the present tense of the verb.

(3.) The sign of the present tense in the Ancient Canarese verb, is altogether unconnected with the formative of the present verbal participle. The present verbal participle of the ancient dialect is identical with that of the modern one, the temporal sign of which is 'tta' or 'utta,' whilst 'dap' or 'p' is the sign of the present tense of the verb in the ancient dialect; *e.g.*, 'bâḷdapen' ('bâḷ-dap-en'), *I live*.

(4.) The Telugu usage of employing the substantive verb in a modified form (viz., 'unnânu,' *I am*, 'unnâvu,' *thou art*, &c.) as an auxiliary in the formation of the present tense, can scarcely be called an exception to the general rule specified above; for this auxiliary is annexed to the present verbal participle, which is closely allied to that of the Canarese; and its use in this connexion is only a refinement of the grammarians, not a necessary element in the formation of the present tense.

These real or apparent exceptions being disposed of, it remains to inquire into the formation of the present verbal participles in the various dialects.

Formation of the Present.—In both the ancient and the modern dialect of the Canarese the verbal participle of the present tense is formed by suffixing to the verbal theme, 'uta,' 'ute,' 'utta,' 'utte,' or 'uttâ;' *e.g.*, 'bâḷ-uta,' *living;* 'ôd-ute,' *reading;* 'ond-utta,' *joining;* 'iḷi-(y)-utte,' *descending;* 'mâḍ-uttâ,' *doing.* Of these particles 'utta' is most commonly used. Probably this particle had but one 't' originally; and it seems also probable that the initial 'u' is euphonic, and derived from the final euphonic 'u' of the majority of the verbal themes. The primitive form of this particle would therefore appear to have been 'ta' or 'te.' The final vowel, 'a' or 'e,' is elided before the initial vowel of the pronominal signs, or rather perhaps, incorporated with it; *e.g.*, 'bâḷuttêne' ('bâḷ-utt'-êne'), *I live;* 'bâḷuttî' ('bâḷ'-utt'-î'), *thou livest.*

The present verbal participle of the Telugu is ordinarily formed by adding 'chu' (pronounced 'tsu') to the theme of the verb. Occasionally 'ka' is used to form the present participle instead of 'chu.' In the colloquial dialect 'tu' is used instead of 'chu;' and though it is possible that 'chu' may be the original, and 'tu' (from 'tsu') the corruption, yet it would be more in accordance with analogy to derive 'chu' from 'tu;' and this 'tu' so nearly resembles the Canarese 'ta' or 'te,' that we may safely conclude both forms to have been originally identical. Probably also 'du,' the particle which in most instances is inserted as a sign of tense between the verbal theme and the pronominal terminations of the Telugu aorist, springs from the same origin as 'tu.'

'chunnu' or 'tunnu,' the ordinary termination of the participle of the present tense in grammatical Telugu, is a compound form derived from 'chu' or 'tu,' the real and only sign of present time in this language, and 'unnu,' a participle of the substantive verb 'uṇḍu,' *to be,* used as an auxiliary.

I cannot offer any opinion respecting the origin of the use of 'tu,' 'ta,' or 'te,' as a sign of present time in Telugu-Canarese. We might propose to compare it with 'at' or 't,' the formative of the Sanscrit present participle, *e.g.*, 'jayat,' *conquering.* 'at,' however, is softened from 'ant' or 'nt,' the affinities of which lie in a widely different direction; besides which, this form is used only as a participle, not also as a gerund.

We might also compare the Telugu-Canarese formative with 'te' or 'ite,' the formative of the Bengali present participle, *e.g.*, 'karite,' *doing;* but this form is identical with that of the infinitive in the same language, and 'te' or 'ite' has been supposed, with reason, to be the dative or locative of a verbal noun. 'ka,' the secondary and less common formative of the Telugu present, may perhaps have been derived from 'gir' or 'kir,' the sign of the present tense in Tamil.

The Tulu sign of the participle of the present tense is 'v,' which is identical with the Tamil-Canarese sign of the future or aorist. The present participle is formed in Ku by suffixing 'i' or 'pi;' and in Gônd by suffixing 'i,' 'si' (properly signs of the preterite), or 'kun,' which is identical with the Malayâla 'kunnu.'

The sign of present time used by the Tamil and Malayâlam, differs considerably from that of the Telugu-Canarese.

The present tense in Tamil is formed by suffixing 'giʀ-u,' 'gindr-u,' or 'âuindr-u,' to the verbal theme, to one or other of which particles the pronominal signs are annexed. 'Ânindr-u' is a compound form, which is rarely used even by the poets, and is derived, I conceive, from 'â,' the ultimate base of 'â-gu,' *to be or become* (and which is not unfrequently used in this shape in the poets), and 'nindr-u,' *standing, abiding.* The other particles of present time, 'giʀ-u' and 'gindr-u,' are in common use, especially the former; *e.g.*, 'varu-giʀ-ân' or 'varu-gindr'-ân,' *he comes.* The only difference between them is that 'gindr-u' is considered more euphonious and elegant than 'giʀ-u,' and more suitable in consequence for poetry and elevated prose. I have no doubt that they are identical in origin, and that the one is merely an euphonised form of the other. In some connexions 'giʀ-u' and 'gindr-u' are changed by dialectic rules of euphony to 'kkiʀ-u' and 'kkindr-u,' viz., when they are attached to roots consisting of two short syllables (like 'paḍu', *to lie,* 'iru,' *to be,* 'naḍa,' *to walk*) the final vowel of which is regarded as a part of the root, and is incapable of being elided. It is a rule of the language that if in such cases the sonants 'g,' 'd,' 'b,' immediately follow, they shall be hardened, that is, converted into the corresponding surds 'k,' 't,' and 'p;' and in Tamil the only method of hardening sonants is by doubling them,—for it has already been shown that in this language the same consonant is a sonant when single and a surd when doubled. Hence we say in Tamil not 'iru-giʀ-ên,' *I am,* but 'iru-kkiʀ-ên.' A similar result follows in another and more numerous class of instances from a different cause. It has been shown in a former part of this section that transitive or active verbs are in many instances made to differ from intransitives by the hardening and doubling of the initial consonant of the sign of tense. In such cases 'giʀ-u' and 'gindr-u' become (not for the sake of euphony merely, but as a means of grammatical expression) 'kkiR-u' and 'kkindr-u.'

The Malayâlam uses the same sign of tense somewhat modified: the sign of present time in Malayâlam is 'unnu' or 'kkunnu,' suffixed to the verbal theme.

Where the Tamil would use 'gindru,' the Malayâlam has 'unnu;' and where the Tamil has 'kkindru,' there 'kkunnu' is used by the Malayâlam. The Malayâla particle is clearly a softened and euphonised form of the Tamil one. The Tamil compound sound 'ndr' is constantly converted into 'nn' in Malayâlam; *e.g.*, 'ondru,' Tam., *one*, is in Malayâlam 'onna,' and 'mûndru,' Tam., *three*, is in Malayâlam 'mûnna.' Even in vulgar colloquial Tamil the same or a similar tendency appears; 'ondru,' *one*, being commonly pronounced 'oṇṇu,' and 'mûndru,' *three*, 'mûṇu.' The Tam. 'gindru' and 'kkindru' would, therefore, naturally and dialectically be converted in Malayâlam to 'ginnu' and 'kkinnu.' The next point is the softening away of the 'g' of 'ginnu.' This has arisen from the circumstance that in Tamil 'g' is pronounced in the middle of a word so softly as to be little more than an indistinct, guttural breathing: in consequence of which it is used to represent the 'h' of the Sanscrit, and in the colloquial dialect it is often discarded altogether; *e.g.*, 'pôgiRên,' *I go*, is commonly pronounced 'pô-Rên;' and 'varugiRân,' *he comes*, 'vari-Rân' or 'vâ-Rân.' Hence 'ginnu' (from 'gindru') would naturally become in Malayâlam 'innu.' The only remaining difference is between the 'i' of 'innu' and the 'u' of 'unnu;' and this presents no difficulty, for even in Tamil 'i' is very often pronounced as 'u' by the vulgar, and the 'u' of the Malayâla 'unnu' is a middle sound between 'i' and 'u.'

The identity of the Malayâla sign of the present tense with that of the Tamil, cannot be doubted. Sometimes in Malayâla poetry the pronominal signs are suffixed to the signs of tense, as in Tamil; and in that connexion the identity of the signs of tense is clearly apparent; *e.g.*, compare 'aḍikkindrân' ('aḍi-kkindr-ân'), Tam., *he beats*, with the corresponding form in poetic Malayâlam, 'aṭikkunnân' ('aṭi-kkunn'-ân').

A priori it might have been supposed that the Malayâla 'unnu' or 'kkunnu' was related to 'chunnu' or 'tunnu,' the sign of the present participle in Telugu. The resemblance, however, is altogether illusory; for the Malayâla particle is derived from the Tamil 'gindru' or 'kkindru,' whilst the Telugu 'chunnu' is compounded of 'chu,' the real sign of present time, and 'unnu,' a participle of 'uṇḍu,' *to be;* which participle is in Malayâlam 'uṇṭa.'

I have said that I believe the Tamil 'giR-u' and 'gindr-u' are identical in origin, and that the one is merely an euphonised form of the other. I have no doubt that 'gindr-u' is the secondary form, and that it has been derived from 'giR-u.' There are many instances of words ending in 'RU' converted euphonically into 'ndru,' of which one will suffice as an example, viz., 'mûru,' Can., *three*, which has been converted into 'mûndru,' Tam., but *per contra* there is no instance extant of 'ndr' being simplified into 'r' or 'R;' and the fondness for nasal sounds which is inherent in the Drâvidian languages, forbids the supposition of any such change ever having taken place. If this view of the case is correct, it detracts somewhat from the claim of the Malayâlam to high antiquity, for it proves that it was subsequent to the change of 'kkiR-u' to 'kkindr-u,' *i.e.*, subsequent to the commencement of the phonetic refinement of the Tamil language, that the Malayâlam acquired a separate existence and a distinct place of its own amongst the Drâvidian dialects.

The origin and ulterior relationship of 'giR,' as a sign of present time, is as completely enveloped in mystery as that of the corresponding Telugu-Canarese 'chu,' 'tu,' 'ta,' 'te.'

I notice (but it is scarcely deserving of notice) the slight resemblance in sound between 'gindr-u' and 'ant,' 'ent,' 'and,' 'ende,' &c., the formative of the Indo-European present participle, of which sometimes the nasal is discarded, as in the Sanscrit 'jayat,' *conquering*, and sometimes the dental, as in the English *singing* and the Scotch *singin*.

No greater importance is to be attributed to the slight resemblance of 'giR' to 'our' or 'ur,' the formative of the present participle in Turkish; for I have no doubt that this 'ur' is derived from 'dur,' *est*, the impersonal substantive verb.

2. *The preterite tense.*—The mode in which a language forms its preterite, constitutes one of the most distinctive features in its grammatical character, and one which materially contributes to the determination of the question of its relationship.

In the Semitic languages past time, or the objective reality of past events, is denoted by placing the verbal theme first, and suffixing to it the sign of the personal agent. In the primitive Indo-European languages the preterite appears to have been most commonly formed by means of the reduplication of the root or verbal theme; but this reduplication has in many instances been so softened and euphonised, that it has dwindled into the mere use of a different vowel in the preterite from that which forms part of the root. The Indo-

European preterite was also frequently formed by means of a prefixed temporal augment; a prefix which Bopp considers to be identical with 'alpha privative,' but which is supposed, with greater probability, by Meyer, to be identical with 'a,' a relic of the auxiliary verb *to have*, which is still prefixed to verbs in the Celtic languages as a temporal augment, *i.e.*, as a sign of past time.

In a large proportion of the verbs in the Germanic tongues, in the Modern Persian, in the Turkish and Finnish families of languages, in the vernacular languages of Northern India, and, with a few exceptions, in the Drâvidian languages, the preterite is formed by suffixing to the verbal theme a particle, generally a single consonant only, which is significant of past time.

The Drâvidian preterite tense is ordinarily formed, like the present, by annexing the pronominal signs to the preterite verbal participle. It is in that participle that the idea of past time resides: by it alone that idea is expressed: the changes that are made when the pronominal signs are added, will be shown to be euphonic merely, not structural; and in the Malayâlam (in which the pronominal signs are not annexed), that part of speech which corresponds to the Tamil preterite verbal participle, expresses by itself the past tense of the verb. Consequently an inquiry into the Drâvidian preterite tense, resolves itself into an inquiry into the formation of the preterite verbal participle.

The preterite verbal participle is used in Tamil with a wider range of signification than in any other dialect, though its proper and inherent meaning is that of the preterite alone. The Tamil being destitute of a present verbal participle, uses the preterite verbal participle instead; in consequence of which, in a Tamil sentence, the question of time is in abeyance till it is determined by the tense of the final governing verb. This statement applies to the verbal participle alone, not also to the preterite tense of the finite verb; which is restricted in Tamil to the expression of past time, precisely as in the other dialects.

We have now to inquire particularly into the Drâvidian methods of forming the preterite. They divide themselves into two—(i.) by reduplication of the final consonant; and (ii.) by suffixing a sign of past time.

(1.) The formation of the Preterite by Reduplication of the Final Consonant.—This mode of forming the preterite is adopted by a very small number of verbs in each of the Drâvidian dialects; but its existence cannot be doubted, and it is a mode which is as interesting as it is remarkable. In the Indo-European languages, when the preterite is formed by means of reduplication, it is the root which is doubled, or at least the first syllable of the root; but in the Drâvidian dialects the reduplication is that of the final consonant alone. The verbal themes which form their preterites in this manner are those which end in 'ḍ-u,' 'g-u,' or 'ʀ-u,' preceded by a single short vowel, *e.g.*, in Tamil, 'paḍ-u,' *to suffer;* 'pug-u,' *to enter;* and 'peʀ-u,' *to obtain,* the preterites of which are 'paṭṭ-ên, *I suffered;* 'pukk-ên,' *I entered;* and 'pettr-ên,' *I obtained.* In each of the above examples the final consonants—'ḍ,' 'g,' and 'ʀ'—are doubled, and being thus doubled, are converted by rule into the corresponding surds 'ṭṭ,' 'kk,' and 'ʀʀ' (pronounced 'ttr'). Whilst the above and similar verbs form their preterites in this manner in the classical dialect of the Tamil, in the modern colloquial dialect some of those very verbs have adopted the more ordinary method of denoting past time by means of a suffixed particle or consonant. Thus 'pukk-ên,' *I entered,* has been superseded in the modern dialect by 'pugu-nd-ên,' and 'nakk-ên,' *I laughed,* by 'nagei-tt-ên.' The Canarese forms the preterites of this class of verbs in exact agreement with the Old Tamil; *e.g.*, 'nakk-anu,' *he laughed,* from 'nag-u,' *to laugh:* and the Telugu, though less systematic in this point, exhibits the operation of the same rule, especially in the relative participles of the preterite.

This Drâvidian reduplication differs materially in form from that of the Indo-European languages; but it appears to proceed from a similar principle, and it constitutes, so far as it goes, an interesting point of resemblance between the two families.

(2.) The formation of the Preterite by Suffixing some Particle or sign of Past Time.—This, with the exception of the very few verbs included in the previous class, is the method of forming the preterite which is invariably adopted by the Drâvidian languages, and which may be regarded as their characteristic mode. For the purpose of thoroughly investigating this important subject, it will be desirable to inquire into the practice of each dialect *seriatim.*

i. *The Canarese preterite.* — The most characteristic Canarese preterite is formed by annexing 'd' (euphonically 'd-u') to the verbal theme. This addition constitutes the preterite verbal participle; *e.g.*, 'iḷi-d-u,' *having descended,* 'nuḍi-d-u,' *having spoken:* to which the pronominal terminations are suffixed to form the preterite tense; *e.g.*, 'iḷi-d-enu,' *I descended,* 'nuḍi-d-i,' *thou saidst.* All verbal themes (both in the ancient and in the modern dialect, and whether transitive or intransitive) which end in 'i' or 'e,' form their preterites in this manner, together with many themes ending in 'u.'

All the apparent irregularities that exist are merely modifications of the 'd' in question. Thus, sometimes 't' is substituted for 'd;' *e.g.*, 'aritanu,' *he knew*, instead of 'aridanu' (corresponding to the Tamil 'aʀindân'): sometimes the 'd' of the preterite combines with the final consonant of the root, and converts it into 'dd' or 'tt;' *e.g.*, 'iddanu,' *he was*, instead of 'irudanu' (Tam, 'irundân'); 'eddu,' *having risen*, instead of 'eḷudu' (Tam. 'eṛundu'); 'uttu,' *having ploughed*, instead of 'uḷudu' (Tam. 'uṛudu'); 'nintu,' *having stood*, instead of 'niludu' (Tam. 'nindru').

Another Canarese preterite is formed by suffixing 'i' to the crude verbal theme; *e.g.*, 'mâḍ-i,' *having done*, from 'mâḍ-u,' *to do*. Between this 'i' and the pronominal terminations, 'd' is inserted in the formation of the preterite tense; *e.g.*, 'mâḍ-i-(d)-enu,' *I did;* 'bâḷ-i-(d)-anu,' *he lived*. This mode of forming the preterite characterises most verbs ending in 'u' in the modern dialect. The final 'u' of such verbs is merely euphonic, not radical, and is elided on 'i' being annexed; and the 'd' which is inserted between 'i' and the pronominal signs, though possibly identical in origin with the 'd' which constitutes a sign of the preterite, is merely euphonic, in so far as the use to which it is now put is concerned.

In a considerable number of instances the formation of the preterite in 'i' appears to be a modern corruption. Intransitive verbal themes ending in 'u' form their preterite in 'd' in the ancient dialect; and it is in the modern dialect alone that 'i' forms their preterite: *e.g.*, instead of 'bâḷ-i' (modern), *having lived*, the ancient dialect has 'bâḷ-d-u;' and as the ancient dialect is undoubtedly more authoritative than the modern, 'd' or 'd-u' may be considered as the legitimate form of the preterite of this class of verbs. This conclusion is confirmed by the analogy of the Tamil, in which the corresponding verbal theme forms its preterite verbal participle by suffixing 'nd'—an euphonised form of 'd;' *e.g.*, 'vâṛ-nd-u,' *having flourished*, which is the equivalent, not of the modern Can. 'bâḷ-i,' but of the ancient 'bâḷ-d-u.'

How is this diversity in the formation of the preterite to be accounted for? Can 'i' have been derived in any manner from 'd?' An argument in favour of this supposition may be deduced from the circumstance that the ancient 'bâḷ-d-en,' *I lived*, which is in perfect dialectic agreement with the Tamil 'vâṛ-nd-ên,' has in the modern dialect become 'bâḷ-i-d-enu.' Even in the ancient dialect itself, though this 'i' is generally unknown, it makes its appearance in the preterite relative participle; which is 'bâḷ-i-d-a,' *that lived*, not 'bâḷ-d-a,' though the corresponding Tamil is 'vâṛ-nd-a.' If we may judge, therefore, from these instances, 'i' seems to have come into existence as a vocalic bond of connexion between the root and the sign of the preterite.

In a similar manner, the future, both in Canarese and in Tamil, often makes use of 'u' as a bond of union between the verbal root and 'v,' the sign of tense; *e.g.*, 'bâḷ-u-v-enu,' modern Can., and 'vâṟ-u-v-ên,' colloquial Tam., *I shall live*, instead of the ancient and more correct 'bâḷ-v-en,' Can., and 'vâṟ-v-ên,' Tam. In this case the 'u' is certainly euphonic; though it has not come to be used as 'i' has, to express grammatical relation, or in lieu of the sign of tense which it is employed to euphonize.

If we had to account for the insertion of 'i' before 'd' in such instances only as have been mentioned, we might be content with the supposition of its euphonic origin; but the use of 'i' as a sign of the preterite, has a much wider range. All *transitive* verbs ending in 'u,' both in the ancient dialect of the Canarese and in the modern, form their preterite verbal participles by suffixing 'i;' and there is nothing to show that those verbs ever formed their preterites in any other manner. A very large number of verbs of this class form their preterites in Tamil also by suffixing 'i;' and in Telugu the preterite is formed by suffixing 'i' to the root, not of one class of verbs only, but of all, with the exception of the small class of reduplicative verbs.

This statement applies, it is true, to the preterite verbal participle of the Telugu, not to the preterite tense of the verb, which generally suffixes or inserts, as a tense-sign, some additional consonant or particle: but in Malayâlam the preterite verbal participle constitutes by itself the preterite tense, without the addition of any pronominal signs; and in that dialect 'i' is the only sign of past time which is used by a large number of verbs. Thus 'pâḍ-i,' which means *having sung*, in the other dialects, signifies in Malayâlam (*he, she, or it*) *sang:* 'i' is, therefore, in that dialect a distinctive sign of the preterite in the class of verbs referred to; and it is to be remembered that the addition of the pronominal terminations, though the means of expressing personality, effects no change in the means whereby *time* is expressed.

The extent and prevalence, therefore, of the use of 'i' as a sign of the preterite, may seem to forbid our supposing it to have been in all cases derived from an euphonization of 'd;' and as 'd,' on the other hand, cannot have been derived from 'i,' it might appear probable that 'd' and 'i' are distinct and independent signs of past time.

I have no doubt that of these two signs of past time 'd' is to be considered as the older and more characteristic.

We have seen that in many instances in which the modern Canarese has 'i,' the ancient dialect and the Tamil have 'd.' Not in those instances only, but universally, the Telugu uses 'i' as the sign of the preterite; but the greater antiquity of the grammatical forms of the Tamil and the Old Canarese, precludes the supposition that their most characteristic sign of past time has been corrupted from that of the Telugu. In addition to which, it will be shown that in the Telugu itself there are traces of the existence of an old sign of the preterite agreeing with that of the Tamil and the Ancient Canarese. It would, therefore, appear that two modes of forming the preterite being in existence, an older in 'd' and a more recent in 'i,' the modern form has in many instances, particularly in Telugu, superseded the more ancient: and the prevalence of 'i' in Telugu and Gônd, would seem to prove that this form, whether an indigenous corruption or derived from foreign influences, entered the South-Indian family of languages from the Telugu quarter.

In the Indo-European family of languages we find similar interchanges amongst the signs of past time; and though in some instances one form or mode may have been derived from another, yet this cannot have been the case uniformly; *e.g.*, the *weak* Germanic conjugations cannot have been corrupted from the *strong*, or *vice versâ;* though it seems certain that the *strong* method of forming the preterite was more ancient than the *weak*, and though it is also certain that the former mode has in very many instances been superseded by the latter.

It remains to inquire into the origin of the 'd' which is inserted in Canarese between 'i' and the pronominal terminations, and also between 'i' and the sign of the relative participle. It appears to be used (whatever be its origin) merely for the purpose of preventing *hiatus* between concurrent vowels; *e.g.*, 'mâḍi-(d)-enu,' *I did*, 'mâḍ-i-(d)-a,' *that did*. *Hiatus* is generally prevented in the Drâviḍian languages by the insertion of a nasal, or of one of the semi-vowels, 'y' and 'v;' and it seems extraordinary that 'd' should be used for this purpose. It is true that in some of the inflexions of Canarese nouns, *e.g.*, 'mara-d-a,' *of a tree*, 'd' might seem to be used euphonically; but it has been shown in the section on 'The Noun,' that that 'd' is the remnant of a neuter demonstrative, and is used as an inflexional increment: it is not, therefore, a precedent for the use of 'd' for the prevention of *hiatus* merely. Possibly the use of this 'd' by the Canarese verb may thus be accounted for:—a consonant for preventing hiatus between the sign of the preterite and the subsequent signs of personality and relation being required, the Canarese preferred using for this purpose an old sign of the preterite which still survived. Thus, 'd' was not a new invention, but an old and partially obsolete particle used for a new purpose, and placed in a position in which it would not have appeared, but for the use to which it had already been put.

ii. *The Tamil preterite.*—The preterite is ordinarily formed in Tamil, as in Canarese, in two ways; viz., by suffixing either 'd' or 'i' to the verbal theme. In the former case, 'd' itself is more rarely used than some euphonization of it or related consonant; but such secondary forms invariably resolve themselves into 'd.' Thus, when a theme with 'l' as its final letter is followed by 'd' as the sign of the preterite, the compound becomes 'ndr;' *e.g.*, the preterite verbal participle of 'pôl,' *like*, is not 'pôl-d-u' but 'pôn-dr-u.' Sometimes, however, when 'd' follows 'l,' the compound becomes 'RR,' pronounced 'ttr;' *e.g.*, from 'kal,' *to learn*, comes not 'kal-d-u,' but 'kaRR-u' ('kattr-u'), *having learned.* 'ḷ' followed by 'd' becomes 'ṇḍ;' *e.g.*, from 'mâḷ,' *to die*, comes 'mâṇḍ-u,' *having died.* Sometimes, however, when 'd' follows 'ḷ,' the compound becomes 'ṭṭ;' *e.g.*, from 'kêḷ,' *to hear*, comes 'kêṭṭ-u,' *having heard.* These and similar combinations are merely instances of euphonization, in accordance with the fixed phonetic rules of the language; and in each case it is in reality 'd' alone which constitutes the sign of past time.

In some verbs the primitive 'd' still remains unchanged and pure; *e.g.*, 'uṛu-d-u,' *having ploughed*, from 'uṛu,' *to plough;* or with a conversion of the dental 'd' into the cerebral 'ḍ;' *e.g.*, 'kaṇ-ḍ-u,' *having seen*, from 'kâṇ,' *to see.*

The euphonization of 'd' which occurs most frequently, and is most characteristic of the Tamil, is its conversion into 'nd.' This conversion takes place without phonetic necessity, and solely through that fondness for nasalisation which is so deeply inherent in the Tamil and Telugu, and by means of which the formatives 'gu,' 'du,' and 'bu' have so generally been changed to 'ngu,' 'ndu,' and 'mbu.' In the majority of cases in Tamil in which 'd' (preceded by a vowel or semi vowel) once formed the sign of the preterite, it has been nasalised into 'nd;' whilst the Canarese wherever it has preserved the primitive 'd,' has preserved it unnasalised and pure. Thus whilst the Tamil preterite of 'iru,' *to be*, is 'iru-nd-ên,' *I was*, the corresponding Canarese is 'iddenu' (for 'iru-d-enu'); and whilst the preterite of the Tamil verb 'vâṛ,' *to flourish*, is 'vâṛ-nd-ân,' *he flourished*, the equivalent in Ancient Canarese is 'bâḷ-d-am.' The higher dialect of the Tamil retains some traces of the primitive, un-nasalised purity of this sign of the preterite; *e.g.*, 'viṛu-nd-u,' *having fallen*, from 'viṛu,' *to fall*, is occasionally written by the poets 'vîṛ-d-u.' ('vîr' is phonetically equivalent to 'viṛu.') It is curious to notice the progress of nasalisation which is apparent in this verb on comparing the Canarese 'biddu' (for 'biḷ-du'), the High Tamil 'vîṛdu,' the modern Tamil 'viṛundu,' and the Malayâlam 'vînu.'

Another change which 'd' undergoes in Tamil consists in its being hardened and doubled in certain cases, so as to become 'tt.'

This happens to 'nd' as well as to 'd,' a clear proof of the development of the former from the latter; and when the 'd' of 'nd' is doubled, the nasal entirely disappears. Just as the doubled form of 'ng' is 'kk,' and that of 'mb' 'pp;' so the doubled form of 'nd' is 'tt.' In some instances, this change is merely euphonic; *e.g.*, 'paḍu,' *to lie*, an intransitive verb, takes for its preterite, not 'paḍu-d-ên' or 'paḍu-nd-ên,' but 'paḍu-tt-ên,' *I lay*. Such cases, however, are rare, and in general the use of 'tt' as a sign of the preterite instead of 'd' or 'nd' is a means of distinguishing transitives or active verbs from intransitive: *e.g.*, the 'tt' of 'tâṛ-tt-ên,' *I lowered*, is formed by the doubling and hardening of the 'nd' (the equivalent of 'd') of the corresponding intransitive 'tâṛ-nd-ên,' *I got low*. See the further explanation of this subject under the head of 'The Classification of Verbs.'

The second mode of forming the preterite in Tamil, as in Canarese, is by suffixing 'i' to the verbal theme. The themes which form their preterite in this manner are those which terminate in 'u' euphonic, and of which the radical portion consists either in one long syllable or in two syllables, whether short or long. In this connexion, as in prosody, a vowel which is long by position is equivalent to one which is naturally long. The following are examples of the classes of verbs which take 'i' for their preterite:—(long syllable) 'pâḍu,' *to sing;* (long by position) 'paṇṇ-u,' *to make;* (two short syllables) 'eṛud-u,' *to write;* (one syllable short, and one long by position) 'tirupp-u,' *to turn.*

All verbs of which the final consonant is a liquid semi-vowel ('l,' 'ḷ,' 'r,' 'ṛ,' not 'v' or 'ʀ'), whatever number of syllables they may contain, form their preterite by means of 'd' or some of its modifications: such verbs are therefore exceptions to the above rule.

Even in the class of Tamil verbs which take 'i' as their preterite suffix, there are traces of the prevalence of 'd' at a more ancient period. Thus, whilst *thou didst go* is in the ordinary dialect 'pô-(n)-ây' (properly ' pôg-i-(n)-âÿ,' from ' pô,' or ' pô-gu,' *to go*), in the poets ' pô-d-i' is sometimes used instead: so instead of ' â-(n)-âÿ' (for ' âg-i-(n)-âÿ,' from ' â-gu,' *to become*), *thou becamest*, the poets sometimes use ' â-d-i.' In these instances the Canarese also, even in the colloquial dialect, says ' pôdi' and ' âdi.'

Even ' nd' is sometimes ' d' only in Tamil poetry; *e.g.*, ' varu-d-i,' *thou camest*, is found instead of the more modern ' va-nd-âÿ' (for ' varu-nd-âÿ'); and it is evident that this form, ' varu-d-i,' exactly corresponds to the forms quoted above, ' pô-d-i' and ' â-d-i.'

Notwithstanding, therefore, the prevalence of ' i' as a sign of the preterite in Tamil, as in Canarese (though in a less degree than in Canarese), there seems to be some reason for regarding it as an innovation, or at least as a less ancient, less characteristic, and less widely used sign than ' d.' ' n' is inserted in Tamil (as ' d' in Canarese) between the ' i' which constitutes the sign of the preterite of certain classes of verbs and the pronominal terminations, and also between the sign of the preterite and the sign of the relative participle; *e.g.*, from ' pâḍ-i,' *having sung* (the preterite verbal participle of ' pâḍ-u,' *to sing*), is formed ' pâḍ-i-(n)-ân,' *I sang*; ' pâḍ-i-(n)-âÿ,' *thou didst sing*; ' pâḍ-i-(n)-ân,' *he sang:* so also ' pâḍ-i-(n)-â,' the relative participle *that sang.* Whatever be the origin of this ' n,' it cannot be doubted that its *use* in Tamil is at present wholly euphonic; and this statement applies also to the use of the same ' n' in the preterite relative participle of the Telugu. It in no respect contributes to the expression of grammatical relation; and when used by the relative participle in Tamil, it may optionally and elegantly be changed into ' y,' which is one of the semi-vowels that are systematically used for the prevention of *hiatus;* *e.g.*, instead of ' pâḍi(n)a,' *that sang*, we may write with perfect propriety ' pâḍi(y)a.' We see a parallel use of ' n' in the Turkish verb, in the frequent insertion of an euphonic ' n' between the theme and the infinitival particle, and also between the theme and the sign of the passive. The most weighty argument in confirmation of the euphonic origin of the Tamilian ' n' in question, is derived from the use of ' n' as an euphonic fulcrum, or means of preventing *hiatus* in the Drâvidian languages generally, and even in connexion with another part of the Tamil verb. Thus, in the classical plural neuter of the present tense, ' varugindrana' (' varu-gindr-ana'), *they (things) come*, the ' n' of the pronominal termination ' ana' is undoubtedly equivalent to the ' v' of the isolated plural neuter ' avei' (for ' ava'); and is used merely for the euphonic prevention of *hiatus* between the first ' a,' or the demonstrative vowel, and the final ' a,' or the sign of the neuter plural. (' a(n)a' or ' a(v)a' is equivalent to ' a-a.')

If the Tamil and the Telugu alone were concerned, we should perhaps be justified in considering the purely euphonic origin of the 'n' in question to be a settled point; but a difficulty arises on comparing those languages with the Canarese. Wherever the Tamil and Telugu use 'n' in the formation of the preterite tense and the preterite relative participle, there the Canarese uses 'd:' *e.g.*, 'mâḍi-(d)-enu,' *I did*, not 'mâḍi-(n)-enu;' and 'mâḍi-(d)-a,' *that did*, not 'mâḍi-(n)-a.' Now, though this 'd' of the Canarese is certainly euphonic in its present use, it has been shown that there is reason for suspecting it to be derived from 'd,' the old sign of the preterite; and if this supposition be correct, it would follow that the Tamilian 'n,' which corresponds so perfectly to the Canarese 'd,' is derived from the same source as 'd,' and euphonically altered from it. The 'n' of the Tamil preterite, therefore, as well as the 'd' of the Canarese, may testify to the primitive universality of the use of 'd' as a sign of past time. Whether 'd' (= 'n') was originally a sign of the preterite or not, the conversion of 'd' into 'n' in this connexion, viz., in the preterite tense, and especially in the preterite relative participle, is analogous to the change of 'ta' or 'da' to 'na' in the past participle of the Indo-European tongues; especially in the German, from which the final 'n' of our own past participles (such as 'fallen') has been derived.

iii. *The Malayâla preterite.*—The Malayâla preterite is substantially the same as the Tamil: the only real difference consists in the disuse in Malayâlam of the pronominal terminations. The sign of past time is invariably the same in each language; with only such modifications of sound as are dialectic and regular. That which constitutes the preterite verbal participle in Tamil, is in Malayâlam the preterite tense of the verb; *e.g.*, 'naḍandu,' in Tamil signifies *having walked;* the corresponding Malayâla word 'naṭannu,' means (*he, she, it or they*) *walked.*

The only thing which it is necessary to notice here, is the difference which exists in Malayâlam between the past tense of the verb and the past verbal participle or gerund, and the agreement of the latter in appearance with the past relative participle. By analogy 'naṭanna,' *having walked,* which is the past participle, should have been used as the past tense of the verb, whereas 'naṭannu' is the form used instead: 'naṭanna' is also the relative participle *that walked.*

How are we to account for these things?

I conceive that 'naṭannu,' the finite verb, is an abnormal form: it should have been 'naṭanna,' and thus identical with the past verbal participle. But after the pronominal terminations were laid aside, it appears to have been felt that something was necessary to distinguish the past participle, which is a continuative, from the past tense of the verb, which is a final; and from this feeling the merely enunciative half sound of the 'a' of 'naṭanna' was emphasized, and thus gradually transformed into 'u,' which, though merely an enunciative in Tamil, has a more distinctive position in Malayâlam. Whilst this change was going on, the enunciative 'a' of the past participle remained unchanged, inasmuch as it was a continuative word, and not a seat of emphasis.

The explanation of the resemblance between 'naṭanna,' *having walked*, the past verbal participle in Malayâlam and 'naṭanna,' *that walked*, the past relative participle, is very easy. A reference to the Tamil shows that the resemblance is only apparent. 'naṭanna,' the past verbal participle, corresponds to the Tamil 'naḍand-u,' the final 'u' of which is merely enunciative and euphonic, and is invariably elided when followed by another vowel; and in like manner the final 'a' of the Malayâla past participle is merely enunciative. It is that euphonic, constantly elided 'a' which dialectically answers to the Tamil 'u.' (*e.g.*, compare 'ad-u,' Tam., *it*, with the Malayâla 'at-a;' 'âʀ-u,' Tam., *a river*, with 'âʀ-a,' Mala.; 'ondr-u,' Tam., *one*, with 'onn-a,' Mala.) Hence arises the rule that this final 'a' is not to be dwelt upon in pronunciation, but enunciated with rapidity. Whereas the final 'a' of 'naṭanna,' *that walked*, is identical with 'a,' the sign of the relative participle in all the Drâvidian languages, and which was in its origin, as I conceive, a sign of the genitive. This latter 'a' contributes largely to grammatical expression, and cannot be elided without destroying the sense, whilst the former 'a' is inorganic and merely euphonic.

iv. *The Telugu preterite.*—In Telugu all preterite verbal participles, without exception, are formed by adding 'i' to the theme. Even those verbs which form their preterites by suffixing 'd' or some modification of it in Tamil, Canarese, and Malayâlam, form their preterites in Telugu by suffixing 'i;' *e.g.*, 'koṇ-ḍu,' Tam. and Can., *having bought*, is in Telugu 'kon-i' and 'kaṇ-ḍu,' Tam. and Can., *having seen*, is 'kan-i.'

Notwithstanding the universality of this rule, there are traces even in Telugu of the use of a particle corresponding to the 'd' of the other dialects as a sign of past time. Though the preterite verbal participle never takes any suffix but that of 'i,' some parts of the preterite tense of the verb in the higher idiom of the language, viz., the first and second persons both singular and plural, insert the particle 'ti' between the 'i' of the verbal participle and the pronominal terminations. It cannot be doubted, I think, that this 'ti,' which is found nowhere but in the preterite, is allied to the 'd' which is inserted in the same place in the Canarese preterite. Thus, whilst both in Canarese and in Telugu the preterite verbal participle of 'âḍ-u,' *to play*, is 'âḍ-i,' *having played;* in both dialects 'ti' or 'd' is suffixed to 'i' before adding the personal terminations; *e.g.*, compare Can. 'âḍ-i-d-enu,' *I played*, Tel. 'âḍ-i-ti-ni.' It has already been shown to be probable that the 'd' thus inserted by the Canarese, though now used to so large an extent euphonically, was originally a sign of the preterite, identical with the 'd' which is still used for that purpose by many verbs. This view derives confirmation from the Telugu, in which the corresponding 'ti' does not appear to be used euphonically at all, and certainly is not used for the prevention of *hiatus;* for there is no *hiatus* and no necessity for an euphonic insertion between the aforesaid 'âḍi' and 'ni,' the pronominal fragment, or in the second person between 'âḍi' and 'vi.' Moreover, there is no instance of such a particle as 'ti' being used merely for euphony in any of the Drâvidian dialects. It therefore follows that we must regard 'ti' as a sign of past time—subordinate indeed to 'i,' and unused in the third person of the preterite, but immediately allied to 'd,' the past tense-sign of the Tamil and Canarese, and testifying to the existence of a time when 'd,' or its equivalent 'ti,' was the ordinary sign of the preterite in Telugu, as in the other dialects. In some Telugu verbs, 'ti' is combined in such a manner with the final consonant of the theme, as to prove beyond doubt its identity in origin and force with the Tamil 'd:' *e.g.*, 'chês-ti-ni,' Tel., *I did* (for 'chêsi-ti-ni'), is evidently equivalent to the Tam. 'śeÿ-d-ên;' and 'koṇ-ṭi-ni,' *I bought* (for 'koni-ti-ni'), is equivalent to 'koṇ-ḍ-ên.' So also when 'ê,' the Telugu conditional particle, answering to the Tamil 'âl,' is suffixed to the preterite tense of a verb for the purpose of giving to it the meaning of the subjunctive, it appears evident that the ancient sign of the preterite of the Telugu must have been, not 'i,' but 'ti' or 'it;' *e.g.*, compare the Telugu 'chêst-ê,' *if (I, thou, he, &c.) did or do* (abbreviated from 'chês-it-ê'), with the Tamil 'śeÿd-âl.'

We have seen that the Tamil inserts 'n' between the preterite verbal participle and the pronominal terminations in many instances in which 'd' is used for this purpose in Canarese. The colloquial dialect of the Telugu makes much use of 'nâ' or 'na' in the same connexion; *e.g.*, 'âḍ-i-(nâ)-nu,' *I played*, (answering to the Tamil 'âḍ-i-(n)-ên'), instead of the more ancient and elegant 'âḍ-i-ti-ni.' The Tamil 'n' used in this connexion separates two vowels, and might therefore be considered as purely euphonic; but the Telugu 'nâ' or 'na' comes between a vowel and a consonant, and must, therefore, have a more important use than that of preventing *hiatus.* 'ti' and 'nâ' alternate in the formation of the Telugu preterite tense, 'ti' being preferred in the more classical dialect, 'nâ' in the more vulgar: and this seems to confirm the supposition that the 'n' of 'nâ,' like the Tamil 'n,' is derived from the old preterite 'd.' We can hardly fail to regard these particles as identical, when we examine an instance in which they are used as equivalents in all three dialects; *e.g.*, compare 'ay-i-(nâ)-nu,' Tel., *I became;* 'â-(n)-ên,' Tam. for ('âg-i-(n)-ên'); and 'â-(d)-enu,' Can. (for 'âg-i-(d)-enu').

On the whole, therefore, it may be concluded that the Telugu agrees with the other dialects in exhibiting distinct and deep-seated traces of the ancient use of 'd' or 't' as a sign of the preterite, notwithstanding the universal prevalence in Telugu at present of the use of 'i,' as the sign of the preterite verbal participle.

I may here take occasion to guard against an illusory resemblance to which my attention was once called, viz., the resemblance which subsists between the Telugu preterite verbal participle 'veichi,' *having placed*, and the corresponding Tamil participle 'veittu,' which is vulgarly pronounced 'veichi.' The 'tt' of the Tamil 'vei-tt-u,' being simply the hardened and doubled form of 'd,' is the ordinary sign of the preterite; and if there were any real alliance between 'tt-u,' through its provincial pronunciation, and the Telugu 'ch-i,' we should undoubtedly have here an instance of the use of 'tt,' *i.e.*, of 'd,' in modern Telugu as well as in Tamil, as a sign of the preterite verbal participle, and consequently of past time. The resemblance, however, is altogether illusory. The 'ch' of the Telugu 'veichi' corresponds, not to the 'tt' of the Tamil 'veittu,' but to the 'kk' which constitutes the formative of so many verbs and nouns in Tamil. 'kk' makes its appearance in the infinitive of this very verb, viz., 'vei-kk-a,' *to place*, the Telugu of which is 'vei-ch-a.' 'kk' is vulgarly pronounced 'ch' in the southern part of the Tamil country; and the same pronunciation universally obtains in Telugu. The imperative or theme of this verb in Telugu is not 'vei,' as in Tamil, but 'veich-u' (with the addition to 'vei' of the formative 'ch-u,' which is equivalent to the Tamil 'kk-u'); and from this 'veich-u,' the preterite verbal participle 'veich-i,' is regularly formed, in this, as in all other cases, by the addition of 'i.' If the corresponding Tamil verb formed its preterite in the same manner, its verbal participle would be 'vei-kk-i,' not 'vei-tt-u.' A case in point in illustration of this, is the Tam. 'tû-kk-u,' *to lift, to weigh* (Tel. 'tû-ch-u'), the preterite verbal participle of which is 'tû-kk-i' (Tel. 'tû-ch-i').

v. *Preterites of minor dialects.*—In Tulu, 't' constitutes the characteristic mark of the preterite tense, and 'ti,' the preterite insertion of the Telugu verb is the sign of the Tulu preterite verbal participle.

In Gônd 'si' or 'ji,' apparently softened from 'ti,' forms the verbal participle of the preterite; but the perfect tense is formed by suffixing 'tt,' *e.g.*, 'kei-tt-ân,' *I have called;* 'kei-si,' *having called.* In Seoni Gônd also the preterite or conjunctive participle suffixes 'si;' *e.g.*, 'wunk-si,' *having spoken:* but the past participle is formed by suffixing 'tûr;' *e.g.*, 'wunk-tûr,' *spoken;* and the past tense simply suffixes 't;' *e.g.*, 'wunk-t-an,' *I spoke,* 'wunk-t-i,' *thou didst speak.* An imperfect or progressive tense is formed in both those dialects by inserting 'und' or 'nd,' the substantive verb, between the root and the pronominal terminations.

These instances tend to confirm the supposition that 'd,' or some modification of it, is the oldest and most characteristic sign of the Drâvidian preterite, and that the use of 'i' is of secondary origin.

Origin of the Drâvidian signs of past time.

(1.) The most probable conjecture that I can offer respecting the origin of 'i,' is one which confirms the supposition of its secondary character. I conceive it to have been originally a vowel of conjunction, employed for the purpose of euphonically connecting the verbal theme, and the true sign of past time, 'd' or 'd-u.'

Where the theme terminated in a hard consonant, euphony would require some such vocalic bond of connexion; *e.g.*, the Old Canarese, 'bâḷ-d-en, *I lived,* is undoubtedly somewhat harsh to an ear that is attuned to Drâvidian phonetics; and it was natural that it should be softened, as it has been in modern Canarese, into 'bâḷ-i-d-enu.' We see a precisely similar euphonic insertion of 'i' in the Latin 'dom-i-tus' (instead of 'dom-tus'), *tamed,* and the Sanscrit 'pîḍ-i-tah' (instead of 'pîḍ-tah'), *pressed.* Subsequently we may suppose the true preterite 'd' to have gradually dropped off; whilst 'i' remained, as being the easier sound, with the adventitious signification of the preterite. There are many instances in all languages of euphonic additions coming to be used instead of the parts of speech to which they were attached; *e.g.*, in the Telugu verb 'vu' is used to represent the second person singular of the pronoun instead of 'nî,' *thou*, though 'vu' was originally only an euphonic addition to 'nî,' by which it was converted into 'nîvu.'

It deserves notice that wherever 'i' is used in Canarese or in Tamil, instead of 'd,' as a sign of the preterite, the use of 'd' would in that instance be harsh and uncouth; and that on comparing the Tamil verbs which form their preterite in 'i' with those that suffix 'd,' no reason but euphony can be alleged why the one suffix should be employed rather than the other: consequently euphonic causes must have contributed to the development of 'i.'

This supposition of the origin of 'i' from the vocalic conjunction of 'd' with the verbal theme, would also account for the circumstance that wherever 'i' is followed by a vowel (whether the initial vowel of the pronominal terminations, or the 'a' which constitutes the sign of the relative participle), it picks up again the 'd' which it had gradually lost, and uses it as an euphonic bond of conjunction, either in its original shape of 'd,' as in Canarese, or in its nasalised shape of 'n,' as in Tamil and Telugu. The manner in which 'ti' is separated from the theme in some Telugu preterites, *e.g.*, 'kon-i-ti-ni' ('koṇ-ṭi-ni'), *I bought*, confirms this supposition of the euphonic origin of 'i.'

(2.) 'd,' the older and more characteristic sign of the Drâvidian preterite, has many interesting affinities with corresponding signs of past time in various Indo-European and Scythian languages.

I have no doubt that it has an ulterior, though remote, connexion with 't' or 'ta' (alternating with 'na'), the ordinary suffix of the Indo-European passive particle; *e.g.*, 'jñâ-ta-h,' Sans., *known;* Greek 'γνω-τό-ς;' Latin '(g)nô-tu-s;' 'bhug-na-s,' Sans., *bent;* Gothic 'bug-a-n(a)-s.' In Gothic this suffix is 'd' or 't;' in New Persian invariably 'd.'

In Sanscrit the participle which is formed from 'ta' is in general distinctively passive; but a few traces exist of a preterite signification, only however in connexion with neuter verbs; *e.g.*, 'ga-ta-s,' *one who went;* 'bhû-ta-s,' *one who has been.* A preterite signification predominates also in the active participles formed by suffixing 'tavat' (derived from the passive 'ta'); *e.g.*, 'kru-tavat,' *was making;* and in the indeterminate past participle, or gerund, which is formed by suffixing 'tvâ;' *e.g.*, 'kru-tvâ,' *having made* or *through making.*

Though there is probably an ultimate connexion between the preterite 'd' of the Drâvidian languages and the passive (and secondary preterite) 't' of the Sanscrit, the use of this suffix is too essential a characteristic of the Drâvidian languages, and too rare and exceptional in Sanscrit, to admit of the supposition that the former borrowed it from the latter.

The 'l' which constitutes the sign of the preterite in Bengali, has been supposed by Professors Max Müller and Bopp to be derived from the past participial 't' of the Sanscrit; *e.g.*, 'karilâm,' *I did*, is derived by them from 'karita,' Sans., *done*, followed by the personal termination 'âm.' This supposition is confirmed by the conformity of 'karilâm' to the New Persian 'kardem,' *I did*, and by the use in Marathi of a similar preterite in 'l,' which is supposed to be derived in like manner from the Sans. passive participial 't;' *e.g.*, 'mî kelo-*m*,' *I did*, 'mîn gêlô-*n*,' *I went*. The interchance of 'ḍ' and 'ḷ' is of frequent occurrence; and possibly the Sanscrit 't' may have become 'd' before it was corrupted into 'l.' There is no proof of this, however, and the 'l' which is used as the equivalent of 't' or 'd' in the formation of the Slavonian preterite, 'byl' (Pers. 'bûd,' Sans. 'bhûta-s'), *he was*, shows that 't' may have passed into 'l' immediately, without the middle point of the cerebral 'ḍ.'

Whether the preterite 'l' of the Bengali and Marathi is derived directly from the Sanscrit passive participial 't,' or whether it has descended from the Old Scythian vernacular of Northern India, it is interesting to notice the fact of the conformity in this important particular, between the Drâvidian languages and those of the Gauda family. We should notice, however, this important difference between the two, that whilst the Gauda preterite 'l,' in so far as it is derived from the Sanscrit, appears to be only a secondary constructive preterite, the Drâvidian 'd' exhibits no trace whatever, either of connexion with any passive participle or of a constructive origin.

In the New Persian, 'd' invariably forms the sign of the preterite; *e.g.*, 'bû-d-em,' *I was*; 'bur-d-em,' *I bore*. The participle which constitutes the verbal theme in Persian, and which has a formative that is passive in Sanscrit, has an active as well as a passive preterite signification; *e.g.*, 'burdeh,' means either *borne* or *having borne*, according to the context. The preterite tense has in Persian been developed out of a passive participle; and this appears to have happened through the influence of the past time which is inherent in the perfect passive.

In the Germanic tongues, 't' or 'd' not only forms the perfect passive participle, as in Sanscrit, Latin, and Zend; but is used also to form a regular preterite tense. The Sanscrit 't' of 'gata-s,' *who went*, forms the preterite of neuters only; but the Gothic 't' appears systematically in the preterites of a numerous class of active verbs; and is found not only in the participle, but in the regular preterite tense; *e.g.*, 'bauh-ta,' *I bought;* 'thah-ta,' *I thought;* and 'vaurh-ta,' *I made.*

It is not my object to endeavour to trace the *origin* of the suffix in question. Whether the 't' of the passive participle is identical, as I conceive, with that of the indicative preterite, or whether it springs from a different origin,—whether 't' or 'd,' the sign of the preterite, is derived from 'dhâ,' *to set, to make,* from 'thun,' *to do,* or from the demonstrative 'ta,'—I am not about to inquire. My belief is, that the real origin of this suffix cannot now be ascertained; it has simply been my object to point out in various languages of the Indo-European family, and in the western branches more than in the Sanscrit, the existence of a mode of forming the preterite (viz., by suffixing 'd' or 't' to the root) which closely resembles that which forms a characteristic of the Drâvidian languages.

The formation of the preterite by suffixing 'd,' is not confined to the Indo-European family, but prevails also in the Turkish and Ugrian tougues.

'd' is the sign of past time which is used by the Turkish; *e.g.*, compare 'sewer-im,' *I love,* with 'sewer-d-im,' *I loved;* and this 'd' is inserted, as in Tamil and Canarese, between the root and the pronominal signs. Compare the present 'îm,' *I am,* with the preterite 'i-d-um,' *I was.* Notice also 'ôl-d-um,' *I was,* and the equivalent form in Oriental Turkish, 'hôl-d-îm.'

In Finnish, the preterite is regularly formed by suffixing 't.' The preterite participle from which the perfect tense is formed terminates in 'ut,' 'yt,' 'et,' &c.; *e.g.*, 'oll-ut,' *having been,* from the theme 'ol,' *to be.*

The Hungarian forms its preterite in a similar manner; *e.g.*, the preterite participle of 'le-nni,' *to become,* is 'le-tt,' *having become;* and from this is regularly formed the perfect 'le-tt-em,' *I have become.*

It especially deserves notice, that these Turkish, Finnish, and Hungarian signs of the preterite are totally unconnected with the passive participle. They are distinctive signs of past time, and of that alone; and as such they are suffixed to all indicatives, whether active or neuter, and are appended, in addition to the sign of passivity, to passive forms, only when those passives are also preterites. In this particular, therefore, the analogy between the Drâvidian preterite and the Turko-Ugrian is closer and more distinctive than the Indo-European analogies which have been pointed out: it may be said indeed to amount to identity.

3. *The future tense.*—The present and preterite tenses of the Drâ-

vidian verb are formed from present and preterite participles, by suffixing the pronominal terminations. The future is without a verbal participle or gerund, except in High Tamil, in which there is a rarely used verbal participle of the future, ending in 'vân;' nevertheless, the future tense is formed virtually in the same manner as the other tenses, by suffixing a sign of future time to the verbal theme, and adding to that sign the pronominal terminations.

In the Drâvidian languages there are two future formations. One, which is more distinctly a future than the other, is found in Canarese and Telugu alone; the other, which is contained in all the dialects, inclusive of the Canarese and Telugu, is an indeterminate, aoristic future, and is called by Telugu grammarians 'the aorist.'

It should here be observed also, that the use of the present for the future is exceedingly common in all the Drâvidian dialects.

(1.) *The more distinctive future.*—In modern Canarese this constitutes the second form of the future, in consequence of being less used than the other. It is formed by inserting 'iy,' or 'î,' or 'd,' between the theme and the pronominal signs, and lengthening the vowel which immediately follows this future particle, viz., the initial vowel of the pronoun; *e.g.*, 'mâḍ-iy-ênu,' *I will do;* or, 'nuḍi-d-ênu,' *I will say.*

In Telugu also, this future assumes a two-fold form, from the optional use of two inserted particles, corresponding to the 'iy,' or 'î,' and 'd' of the Canarese. One form inserts 'ê' between the theme and the pronominal terminations; *e.g.*, 'chês-ê-nu,' *I will do;* which 'ê' is optionally changed to 'î,' in the third person neuter plural; *e.g.*, 'chês-î-ni,' *they (neut.) will do.* The other form of the future, which is still more rarely used, inserts 'eda;' *e.g.*, 'chês-eda-nu,' *I will do;* except in the third person singular, and the third person neuter plural, in which 'eḍi' is used instead of 'eda;' *e.g.*, 'chês-eḍi-ni,' *they (neut.) will do.*

(2.) *The aoristic future, or aorist.*—Of this future also there are several forms.

In Tamil, the most commonly used form of the future is that which inserts 'v,' 'b,' or 'pp,' between the theme and the pronominal signs; *e.g.*, 'śey̆-v-ên,' *I will do;* 'kâṇ-b-ên,' *I will see;* 'naḍa-pp-ên,' *I will walk.* 'b' appears to be the original form of this particle; for on this supposition we can easily account both for 'v' and 'pp.'

In certain cases the initial consonant of the temporal particle, or the particle itself, if composed of a single consonant, would require to be doubled, *e.g.*, after the vowels 'a' and 'i,' and when the doubling of the tense sign is the method adopted for converting an intransitive verb into a transitive. In those cases we find 'pp' used as the sign of the future instead of 'v;' *e.g.*, 'vaḷar-pp-ên,' *I will rear*, is the future transitive of 'vaḷar-v-ên,' *I will grow*. And we may hence conclude that 'b,' not 'v,' was originally the sign of the future of the intransitive, for 'b' when doubled becomes 'pp' by rule; and whilst it is certain that 'b' will readily change into 'v,' no instance of the change of 'v' into 'b' in Tamil can be adduced. Notwithstanding this, 'b' is now used only after a final nasal; *e.g.*, 'tin-b-ên,' *I will eat;* 'en-b-ên,' *I will say.*

In consequence of 'b' invariably becoming 'pp' after the vowel 'i,' 'pp' is the sign of the future of all Tamil causals; *e.g.*, 'kaṭṭu-vi-pp-ên,' *I will build.*

In classical Tamil there is a future verbal participle or gerund, in 'vân,' which when hardened becomes 'ppân;' *e.g.*, 'śeÿ-vân,' *being about to do;* 'paḍi-ppân,' *being about to learn.* The principal element in this is the future tense-sign 'v;' and this participle in 'vân' or 'ppân,' constitutes the sign of the infinitive in Malayâlam; *e.g.*, 'iri-ppân,' *to be*, 'urukku-vân,' *to dissolve.*

The Tamil future formed from 'v' or 'b,' is destitute of a relative participle, and uses instead the aorist future in 'um.' Generally also, that aorist is used instead of the more distinctive future in the third person singular neuter. Thus, whilst *he will be* is 'iru-pp-ân,' *it will be* is ordinarily 'iru(kk)-um,' not 'iru-pp-adu;' and forms like 'iru-pp-adu' are in general used only as participial nouns. In this respect the Tamil is less regular than the Canarese, in which the ordinary third person neuter singular of the future tense is 'iru-v-adu.'

The future is sometimes formed by the Tamil poets by adding 'g' (or 'kk') to the root, instead of 'b' (or 'pp'); *e.g.*, 'śeÿgên' (for 'śeÿvên'), *I will do;* 'aḍeikkên' (for 'aḍeippên'), *I will obtain.* I am inclined to think these forms identical in origin, for 'g' often changes into 'v.'

Another future formation of the Tamil may be called the defective aoristic future, inasmuch as its reference to future time is still less distinct and determinate than the future in 'v,' and as it is restricted to two forms, the third person singular neuter, and the relative participle. This defective future is formed by suffixing 'um' to the formed theme; 'eṛud-um,' *it will write.* The future in 'um' is not considered by Tamil grammarians as distinct from, and independent of, the future in 'v;' but is strangely enough considered as a part of it.

Its claim, however, to be regarded as a distinct future formation is confirmed by the Malayâlam, in which it is the only future in ordinary use; *e.g.*, 'ñjân eṛut-um,' *I will write*, 'nî eṛut-um,' *thou wilt write;* the other form corresponding to the Tamil future in 'v,' being used in the poetry alone. In the Tamil of prose and conversation the future in 'um' is used in connexion with the neuter of the third person singular alone; but in the poetry it occasionally takes a wider range of application, and is sometimes construed even with the masculine-feminine plural, as in Malayâlam.

The future in 'um,' when used in Tamil as a relative participle, does not differ from the form of the same future which is used as the third person singular neuter. The forms are identical; *e.g.*, 'pôg-um,' *it will go*, 'pôg-um,' *which will go;* they may therefore be regarded as one.

'um' is added, not to the crude root of the verb, or that form which is used as the imperative, but to the formed theme, or that verbal noun which forms the basis of the infinitive, and the equivalent of which constitutes in Telugu the inflexional basis of every part of the verb.

The base to which the future 'um' is suffixed, may safely be assumed to be a verbal noun, even in Tamil, though it rarely appears in a separate shape.

The following instances will show the relation subsisting between the Tamil infinitive and the aoristic, impersonal future, in virtue of the formation of both on the basis of the formed verbal theme, or assumed verbal noun, in question:—compare 'pôg-a,' *to go*, 'pôg-um,' *it will go;* inflexional theme 'pô-gu:' 'pôkk-a,' *to cause to go, to get rid of*, 'pôkk-um,' *it will get rid of;* inflexional theme 'pô-kku:' 'irukk-a,' *to be*, 'irukk-um,' *it will be;* inflexional theme 'iru-kku.' In those cases in which intransitive verbs are converted into transitives by doubling the initial consonant of the tense-sign (*e.g.*, 'vaḷar-giṟ-ên,' *I grow*, hardened into 'vaḷar-kkiṟ-ên,' *I rear*), the infinitive and the aoristic future of the transitive verb are formed upon the basis of a theme which terminates in the formative 'kk-u' (the equivalent of which is 'ch-u' in Telugu), whilst the unformed theme, or ultimate root, is the basis of the corresponding forms of the intransitive; *e.g.*, compare 'vaḷar-a,' *to grow*, 'vaḷar-um,' *it will grow*, theme 'vaḷar,' with 'vaḷar-kk-a,' *to rear*, 'vaḷar-kk-um,' *it will rear;* theme 'vaḷar-kku.'

It is evident from a comparison of these illustrations that the above 'g' or 'k' is no part of the sign of future time; it belongs to the formative, not to the future; the infinitive as well as the aoristic future is built upon it; and the Telugu formative which corresponds to it has a place in every part of the verb.

The future in 'um' is altogether impersonal, no pronominal terminations are ever added to it, and in consequence it is well adapted to be used as a relative participle, the relative participles being used alike by all persons, numbers, and genders.

The particle 'um' which constitutes the sign of future time, is identical in form, and is also, I believe, identical in origin and force, with 'um,' the conjunctive or copulative particle of the Tamil. It is also identical with 'nu,' the impersonal suffix of the third person singular and plural of each gender of the Telugu aorist, a tense which perfectly corresponds with the one now under consideration. 'nu' is a conjunctive particle in Telugu also; and it is probable that this particle has been chosen, both in Tamil and in Telugu, to be the characteristic sign of the aorist, because of its suitableness to express the idea of continuity. This tense, it is true, frequently denotes the future; but it is much more frequently used to express continuous action, or what is habitually done. Thus, 'mâḍ-u pul tin(n)-um,' Tam., is to be translated, not *the ox will eat grass*, but *the ox eats* (*i.e. habitually eats*) *grass*, or *grass is the ox's food.*

When the relative participle of this aoristic future, coupled to a noun signifying time, is followed by a finite preterite verb, the future in Tamil takes the sense of the imperfect; *e.g.*, 'nân var-um poṛudu, pôrei (k)kaṇḍên,' *when I was coming* (literally *when I shall come*), *I saw the battle.* In respect of this capacity of the aoristic future for becoming a historical preterite, it resembles the future tense of the Semitic languages.

The High Tamil (and also the Telugu) often uses the formed theme or verbal noun referred to, without the addition of 'um,' as an aorist; *e.g.*, 'parapp-u,' instead of 'parapp-um,' *it will spread*, or *which will spread.* This form is rarely used except by the poets, and is even more distinctively an aorist than the aorist future in 'um.' The final 'u' does not belong to the particle 'um,' but is the ordinary euphonic, enunciative 'u,' and accordingly is often elided.

The Canarese, with which the Tulu agrees, forms its ordinary future by inserting 'v' between the theme and the pronominal terminations, in accordance with the first Tamil future, viz., that in 'v.' Like it, this Canarese future has often an indeterminate, aoristic sense; but it is more regular than the Tamil, inasmuch as it never changes 'v' into 'b' or 'pp,' in the modern dialect, but uses 'v' as the invariable sign of future time. It is not obliged also, like the Tamil, to borrow its third person singular neuter from another formation, but forms it, like the other persons, by means of 'v;' *e.g.*, 'iru-v-adu,' *it will be;* and it has also a relative participle of its own; *e.g.*, 'bâḷu-v-a,' *that will live;* compare 'âgipa,' Ancient Canarese, *that will become,* (answering to the modern 'âg-iruva').

The Telugu tense which corresponds to the Tamil and Canarese aoristic futures is still more distinctively an aorist than they, though with an inclination in general to the idea of futurity. By English grammarians this tense is commonly called, not 'the future,' but 'the aorist.' It is formed by inserting 'du' between the theme and the pronominal terminations; with the exception of the third person singular and plural, in which 'nu' alone, the equivalent of the Tamil 'um,' is added to the theme. Compare the Tam. 'âg-um,' *it will become, it will be,* with the Telugu aorist 'avu-nu,' (*he, she, it, they, &c.*) *will become.* Probably the Tel. aoristic formative 'du' is allied to 'tu,' the particle of present time.

The Gônd makes use of 'k' as the sign of the future, in connexion with the first and second persons of the verb; *e.g.,* 'wunkî-k-a,' *I will speak.* Compare the 'g' or 'kk' which is sometimes used as the sign of the future by the High Tamil.

Affinities of the sign of the future.—The most characteristic and most extensively used sign of the future in the Drâvidian tongues, is evidently the 'v' or 'b' of the Tamil, Canarese, and Tulu. It is remarkable that in Bengali also, the sign of future time is 'v,' pronounced 'b;' and this Bengali 'b' has been connected by Max Müller with the 'b' or 'bo' which forms the most characteristic sign of the Latin future, and which is considered to be a relic of an old substantive verb. The 'd' of the Drâvidian preterite has been proved to have so wide a range of affinities both in Europe and Asia, that it cannot be considered improbable that the Drâvidian futuric 'b' also possesses some ulterior Indo-European affinities.

As in the case of the sign of the preterite, it will be found that the closest analogies are those of the Ugrian languages. In Finnish, 'wa' or 'va' is the sign of the future participle which is used as an auxiliary in the formation of the future tense; *e.g.,* 'ole-wa,' *about to be:* and the sign of the future infinitive is 'wan;' *e.g.,* 'ole-wan,' *to be, to be about to be;* with which we may compare the Tamil future gerund, and Malayâla infinitive in 'vân.' In the Hungarian, the future participle is formed by suffixing 'vö;' *e.g.,* 'lê-vö' (Finnish 'ole-wa'), *being* or *about to be.*

4. *Compound tenses.*—It is unnecessary to enter into an investigation of the Drâvidian compound tenses, inasmuch as in all the dialects they are formed in the simplest possible manner, by suffixing the various tenses of the substantive verb to the verbal participles of active

verbs. Thus, *doing I was* will represent the imperfect (also *doing I came*); *doing-keeping* (*i.e.*, *keeping a doing*) *I was*, a more continuative imperfect; *having done I am*, the perfect; *having done I was*, the pluperfect; *having done I shall be*, the future perfect.

A vast number of auxiliary verbs are used in all the Drâvidian dialects, in conjunction with infinitives and verbal participles, for the purpose of expressing compound ideas; but as the use of those auxiliaries pertains rather to the idiom or syntax of the language than to the grammatical structure, and is sufficiently explained in the ordinary grammars, it would be out of place to inquire into them here.

Relative participles.—It is a remarkable peculiarity of the Drâvidian languages, that they have no relative pronouns whatever, and that the place of the relative pronoun is supplied by a part of the verb which is called 'the relative participle,' a participle which is invariably followed by a noun, and preceded by the words or phrases that depend upon the relative.

The vernaculars of Northern India have relative pronouns derived from the Sanscrit relatives 'yah,' 'yâ,' 'yad,' *who, which;* but of those pronouns they make little use, probably through an under-current of Drâvidian, or at least of Pre-Sanscrit influences. In those languages a sentence which contains a relative is ordinarily divided into two members; and the demonstrative pronoun which forms the nominative of the second member of the sentence, is used instead of a relative. Thus instead of saying, *the man who came yesterday has come again to-day*, they would prefer to say, *a man came yesterday*, he *is come again to-day*. The Drâvidian languages sometimes make use of a similar idiom, but only in the hurry of conversation. They are not obliged to have recourse to any such arrangement, the signification of the relative, together with that of the definite article, being contained in, and distinctly expressed by, the relative participle of the verb. Thus they would say in Tamil, 'vanda-âḷ,' *the person who came*, literally *the-who-came person*. In like manner instead of 'vanda,' the preterite, they might use the present relative participle; *e.g.*, 'varugiṟa âḷ,' *the-who-is coming person*, or the future 'varum âḷ,' *the-who-will-come person*.

The name given to the relative participle by Tamil grammarians, is 'peÿr echam,' *noun-defect*, or *noun-complement*, *i.e.*, a word which requires the complement of a noun to complete its signification. This name is given to it because it participates so largely in the nature of an adjective, that it is invariably followed by a noun, to which it stands in the relation of a relative, and which it connects with the antecedent clauses.

Like other Drâvidian adjectives, it undergoes no alteration on account of the number or gender of the related noun; but inasmuch as it is a verb as well as an adjective (*i.e.*, a participle *participating* in the nature of both parts of speech), it is capable of governing a preceding noun, equally with any other part of the verb to which it belongs; *e.g.*, 'nûlei eṛudina pulavan,' Tam., *the poet who wrote the book*, literally *the-who-the-book-wrote poet;* 'kâṭṭil tirigiʀa yânei,' Tam., *the elephant that wanders in the jungle*, literally *the-that-in-the-jungle-wanders elephant.*

The relative suffix most largely used in the Drâvidian languages is 'a,' which is appended to the verbal participle or gerund, to convert it into a relative participle. Thus, in Tamil, the (assumed) present verbal participle of 'uṛu,' *to plough*, is 'uṛu-giʀ,' *ploughing;* from which, by suffixing 'a,' is formed the present relative participle 'uṛugiʀ-a,' *that ploughs.* The preterite verbal participle of the same verb is 'uṛu-d-u,' *having ploughed*, (of which the final 'u' is merely enunciative,) from which, by the addition of the same 'a,' is formed the preterite relative participle 'uṛu-d-a,' *that ploughed.*

When the preterite verbal participle ends, not in 'd-u,' but in 'i,' 'n' (alternating with 'y'), is euphonically inserted between the concurrent vowels 'i' and 'a;' *e.g.*, from 'eṛud-i,' *having written*, is formed 'eṛud-i-(n)-a,' or 'eṛud-i-(y)-a,' *that wrote.* In all these particulars, the Malayâlam perfectly agrees with the Tamil. The future relative participle of the Tamil is not formed from 'a,' but terminates in 'um,' being identical with the aoristic future third person singular neuter.

The Canarese has in this point the advantage not only of the Tamil, but of all the other dialects; inasmuch as it forms its future relative participle also by suffixing 'a;' *e.g.*, 'mâḍu-v-a,' *which will do.* On the other hand, the relative participle of the present tense in Canarese is defective, being formed by means of the relative participle of the future, used as an auxiliary: *e.g.*, 'bâḷ-utt-iruva,' *which lives*, literally *which will be living.* The preterite relative participle is formed, like that of the Tamil, by suffixing 'a;' the only difference is, that between the final 'i' of the verbal participle and the relative 'a,' 'd' is inserted euphonically instead of 'n;' *e.g.*, 'mâḍ-i-(d)-a,' *which did*, from 'mâḍ-i,' *having done.*

The Telugu agrees with the Tamil in forming its present and preterite relative participles by suffixing 'a,' and in inserting 'n' between the 'i' in which the preterite verbal participle of that dialect invariably ends, and the relative 'a;' *e.g.*, from 'avu-tunnu,' *becoming*, is formed 'avu-tunn-a,' *that becomes;* and from 'ay-i,' *having become,* is formed 'ay-i-(n)-a,' *that became.*

The suffix of the relative participle of the negative voice of the verb is 'a' in Tamil, Malayâlam, and Canarese, in Telugu it is 'ni.'

It is now evident that 'a' may be regarded as the characteristic relative suffix of the Drâvidian languages. The only exceptions are 'ni,' the negative relative suffix of the Telugu; the suffix of the aoristic future relative in several of the dialects, viz., 'ni' in Ku, 'um' in Tamil, and 'eḍu,' 'eḍi,' 'ê' or 'êṭi' in Telugu; and 'ti' the sign of the preterite relative participle in Tulu and Ku.

Not only are the greater number of relative participles formed by suffixing 'a,' but, as was observed in the section on 'The Noun,' most Drâvidian adjectives also receive the same suffix. Ultimate nouns of quality or relation are capable of being used as adjectives, without any change or addition; *e.g.*, 'siR-u,' *small,* 'per-u,' *great;* but more commonly these nouns are converted into quasi relative participles, and rendered thereby more convenient for use as adjectives; *e.g.*, 'siR-i-(y)-a,' *small,* 'per-i-(y)-a,' *great.* The preterite relative participles of regular verbs are also frequently used as adjectives; *e.g.*, 'uyar-nd-a,' *high,* literally *that was high;* 'tâṟ-nd-a,' *low,* literally *that was low.* Tamil adjectives like 'per-i-(y)-a,' agree so exactly with preterite relative participles like 'paṇṇ-i-(y)-a' (for 'paṇṇ-i-(n)-a'), *which made,* that they may safely be regarded as preterite relative participles in form, though unconnected with the preterite or any other tense in signification.

Another class of Tamil adjectives receive the suffix of the future or aorist relative participle, *i.e.*, 'um,' which is suffixed like 'i-(y)-a' to the crude noun of quality; *e.g.*, 'per-um,' *great,* 'pas-um,' *green.* There is no difference in meaning between these two classes of adjectival formatives, the use of the one rather than the other being determined solely by euphony or usage; but on the whole 'um' is considered more elegant than 'i-(y)-a.'

Origin of the relative suffixes.—The Tamil aorist or future suffix 'um,' has already been shown to be identical with the conjunctive or copulative particle. I regard all the other relative suffixes as originally signs of the *inflexion,* or possessive case signs, expressing the signification of *endowed with, possessed of, having, which has,* &c.

In the older Scythian languages, a relative participle is used, as in the Drâvidian languages, instead of a relative pronoun; and the existence of a family likeness in so remarkable a particular is a proof of the existence of a family relationship between the Scythian group and the Drâvidian. The particle which is suffixed in the Scythian languages for the purpose of forming a relative participle out of a verbal participle, is identical with the sign of the possessive case. In Manchu this particle is 'ngge' or 'ninge' (corresponding to the Turkish 'niug'); in Mongolian 'don' or 'ton:' and the addition of this possessive case-sign converts the verbal participle (*i.e.*, the theme with the tense-sign attached) into a verbal adjective or relative participle, precisely as in Tamil or Canarese. Thus in Manchu, from 'aracha,' *written*, which is the verbal participle of 'ara,' *to write*, is formed the relative participle 'aracha-ngge,' *which wrote*, literally *the-written-having*.

The language of the Scythian tablets of Behistun has also a relative suffix, 'pi,' answering to the Mongolian 'ki,' which is appended, as in the Drâvidian languages, to the theme in the formation of relative participles.

Looking at the analogy of the Scythian languages, and at the genius of the Drâvidian languages themselves, I have no doubt that 'a,' which forms the most common Drâvidian relative suffix, is identical with 'a,' the oldest and most characteristic sign of the possessive case. The other particles also which are used as suffixes of the relative will be found to have a similar nature.

Though the sign of the relative participle in Ku differs from that which prevails in the other dialects, yet 'ni,' the sign of the aorist relative participle, is identical with the sign of the *inflexion* or possessive case, which is also 'ni.' 'ni,' the sign of the negative relative participle in Telugu, appears to bear the same relation to 'ni,' a sign of the Telugu inflexion. 'ti,' the sign of the preterite relative participle, both in Tulu and in Ku, is the most commonly used sign of the inflexion in Telugu; and the various suffixes of the Telugu aorist relative participle are apparently adjectival formatives, corresponding in origin to 'ti,' the sign of the neuter inflexion in the same language.

Though the use of a relative participle, instead of a relative pronoun, is characteristic of the Scythian tongues; yet both the Turkish and the Finnish languages possess a relative pronoun as well. The use of such a pronoun is foreign to the grammatical structure of those languages, and has evidently been borrowed from the usage of languages of the Indo-European stock. It is certain that the Turkish has been much influenced by the Persian; and the Oriental Turkish, though it has borrowed from the Persian a relative pronoun, rarely uses it, and ordinarily substitutes for it a suffixed particle of its own, in a genuine Scythian manner.

Formation of Moods.

The investigation of the structure of the Drâvidian verb may now be considered as completed; for in each dialect of the family the verb has, properly speaking, only one mood, the indicative; and the forms which correspond to the conditional, the imperative, and the infinitive moods of other languages, are verbal nouns or compounds, rather than moods. Nevertheless it is desirable, at this point, to inquire into the manner in which those moods are formed.

(1.) *The conditional or subjunctive.*—In most of the Indo-European languages, and even in the Turkish and Finnish, the subjunctive is a regularly conjugated mood, distinct from the indicative, with pronominal terminations of its own. In the Drâvidian languages the subjunctive is formed by simply postfixing to different parts of the verb, either a particle corresponding in meaning to '*si*' or *if*, or the conditional forms of the substantive verb, which includes the same particle, and which signifies *if it be.* Different particles are used for this purpose in the different dialects, and they are not in each dialect suffixed to the same part of the verb; but the principle on which they are suffixed, and the use to which they are put, are the same in all.

In Canarese the conditional particle is 're,' which is derived probably from 'ir-u,' the theme of the verb *to be:* it is appended to the relative participle of the preterite, and that participle being inpersonal, the condition applies, without change of form, to all persons, numbers, genders, and times; *e.g.*, 'mâḍida,' *that did,* on receiving this suffix becomes 'mâḍida-re,' *if (I, thou, he, she, they,* &c.) *do, did, or shall do.* Person, number, and gender are expressed by the prefixed pronoun, and time by the subsequent finite verb. The use of the relative participle—a form which always requires a noun to complete its signification—shows that 're' is regarded as a noun, and that a closer rendering of the construction would be *in the event of (my, your,* &c.) *doing,* more literally *in the event that (I, you,* &c.) *have done (so and so).*

The most essential and ancient form of the Telugu conditional consists in annexing 'in' or 'ina' to the ultimate conjugational base; *e.g.*, 'chûch-in,' *if (I, thou, he,* &c.) *should see.* This 'in' is evidently identical with the 'in' which is used for the same purpose and in the same manner in Tamil; and as the Tamil 'in' is a sign of the ablative or locative, signifying *in the event,* so must the Telugu 'in' or 'ni' be identical in origin with the 'na' or 'ni' which the Telugu uses as a locative. In Telugu the various conditional particles which are in ordinary use are parts of the substantive verb, more or less regular in form, each of which is used to signify *if it be.* The particle which is commonly used for this purpose in the higher dialect is 'ê-ni,' the conditional form of the verb 'avu,' *to be or become,* a form which corresponds to the High Tamil 'ây̆-in,' and means, as will be seen, *in being, i.e., in the event of being.* This particle or auxiliary, 'ê-ni,' is appended not to the verbal or relative participle, but to the personal terminations of the verb. It may be appended to any tense, as to any person; but whatever tense it is attached to, the time of that tense is rendered aoristic, and is determined, as in Canarese, by the context, especially by the tense of the succeeding verb. The manner in which 'êni' is post-fixed in Telugu exactly corresponds to the use that is made of 'âgil' or 'ânâl' in Tamil, and of 'ây̆in' in High Tamil; *e.g.,* 'chêsitin'-êni,' *if I did or do* (literally *if it be (that) I did*), and 'chêsitim'-êni,' *if we did or do,* are equivalent to the Tamil 'śey̆dên-ây̆in,' *if I did,* and 'śey̆dôm-ây̆in,' *if we did.*

In the colloquial dialect of the Telugu the conditional particle commonly used is simply 'ê,' which is suffixed, not to any tense at pleasure like 'ê-ni,' but only to the preterite; and is not appended, as 'ê-ni' is, to the personal termination, but to the root of the preterite, or as I conceive it to be, the old preterite verbal participle; *e.g.,* 'chêsit-ê,' or rather 'chêst-ê,' *if (I, thou, he, &c.) did or do.* I consider this 'ê' to be either the particle of emphasis, or rather perhaps an abbreviation of 'ê-ni,' the 'ê' of which alone represents the substantive verb. 'ê' is equivalent to 'avu' or 'ay̆i,' and 'ni,' as will be seen, is a locative case-sign, equivalent to the Tamil 'iṉ.'

Another mode of expressing the conditional mood in the colloquial dialect of the Telugu agrees with the Canarese in this, that the particles are suffixed to the relative participle. The particles thus suffixed are 'aṭṭ-ayitê' and 'aṭṭ-âyenâ;' the first part of both which compounds, 'aṭṭ-u,' is a particle of relation meaning *so as, as if.* 'ayitê' ('ayit-ê') is the ordinary conditional of 'avu,' *to be,* being an emphasised form of 'ayi-ti,' the impersonal preterite, or old preterite verbal participle of 'avu.' 'âyenâ,' is emphasised from 'âyenu,' properly 'ayenu,' *it was,* the third person of the preterite tense of 'avu.'

In Tamil, the most ancient and characteristic mode of forming the conditional mood is by suffixing the locative case signs 'il' or 'in,' to the formed verbal theme, *i.e.*, that assumed verbal noun which forms the basis of the infinitive and the aoristic defective future. Thus, from the formed theme 'pôg-u,' *going*, is formed the infinitive 'pôg-a,' *to go*, and 'pôg-um,' *it will go:* and from the same base by the addition of the locative, 'il' or 'in,' is formed the conditional 'pôg-il' or 'pôg-in,' *if (I, thou, &c.) go.* From 'var-u,' *coming*, is formed 'var-a,' infinitive, *to come;* 'var-um,' *it will come;* and also 'var-il' or 'var-in,' *if (I, &c.) come.* In like manner, from 'âg-u,' *being*, is formed the infinitive 'âg-a,' *to become or be;* 'âg-um,' *it will be;* and also 'âg-il,' *if (I, &c.) be.* 'âg-in' (the equivalent of 'âg-il'), has been softened into 'ây̆-in;' and this is identical in origin and meaning with the Telugu 'ê-ni' ('for 'avu-ni') referred to above, and is subjoined to the personal terminations of verbs in the same manner as 'ê-ni.' This conditional 'il' or 'in' is undoubtedly identical with 'il' or 'in,' the Tamil sign of the ablative of motion, which is properly a sign of the locative, signifying *in, at*, or *on;* and of this 'in,' the Telugu equivalent, in accordance with dialectic laws, is 'ni,' which is also occasionally used as a locative.

This being the case, the signification of 'âg-il' or 'ây̆-in,' is evidently *in being, i.e., in the event of being;* and this is equivalent to the phrase *if it be.* Hence 'âg-il,' 'ây̆-in,' and 'ê-ni,' are well suited to be used as conditional auxiliaries, and appended to the various personal terminations of verbs.

The second mode of forming the conditional in Tamil, consists in the use of the above-mentioned conditional forms of the substantive verb, viz., 'âg-il' and 'ây-in' (and also a commoner form, 'ân-âl') as auxiliaries to other verbs; and when thus used, they are post-fixed, like the corresponding Telugu 'êni,' to any person of any tense: *e.g.*, 'śey̆dên-âgil,' *if it be that I did*, or *if I did*, literally *in the (event of its) being (that) I did;* 'śey̆vên-âgil,' *if I shall do*, literally *in the (event of its) being (that) I shall do.*

This mode of forming the Tamil conditional, though not confined to the classics, is but rarely used in the colloquial dialect: it is chiefly used in elegant prose compositions.

A third form of expressing the sense of a conditional mood in Tamil is by appending the particle or noun 'kâl' to the past relative participle; *e.g.*, 'śey̆da-(k)kâl,' *if (I, &c.) do or did;* 'uvari olitta-(k)kâl,' *if the sea should roar.* The conditional form which is most commonly used by the vulgar, is a corruption of this, viz., 'śey̆dâkkâ,' or even 'śey̆dâkki;' and the Ku conditional also is formed by appending 'kka.' 'kâl' being appended to a relative participle, it is evidently to be considered as a noun; and it may either be the crude Sanscrit derivative 'kâl' (for 'kâl-am'), *time*, used adverbially to signify *when*, a use to which it is sometimes put in Tamil; or, less probably, the pure old Drâvidian word 'kâl,' *a channel, a means*. The literal meaning, therefore, of 'śeÿda-(k)kâl' will be, *when (I) do or did*, a form which will readily take from the context a conditional force; *e.g.*, in the following Tamil stanza,—*When you have done* ('seÿda-(k)kâl') *a good action to any one, say not, 'when will that good action be returned?'*—it is evident that *when you have done* is equivalent to *if you have done*. The signification of *when* is still more clearly brought out by the use of 'kâl' in connexion with the future relative participle; *e.g.*, 'śeÿ(ÿ)ung-kâl,' *if (he, they, &c.) should do*, literally *when (they) shall do*, or *in the time when (they) shall do*. This mode of expressing the conditional mood is exceedingly common in the Tamil poets.

The fourth Tamil mode of forming the conditional is by suffixing 'âl' to the abbreviated preterite relative participle, *e.g.*, 'śeÿd-âl,' *if (I, &c.) do*. If we looked only at examples like 'śeÿd-âl,' we might naturally suppose 'âl' to be suffixed to the preterite *verbal* participle ('śeÿd-u'), the final 'u' of which is regularly elided before a vowel; and this form of the conditional would then perfectly agree with the second Telugu mode, *e.g.*, 'chêst-ê.' If we look, however, at the class of verbs which form their preterite in 'i,' and their preterite relative participle in 'n-a,' we shall find that 'âl' is added to the relative, not to the verbal participle, and that the two vowels ('a' and 'â') are incorporated into one; *e.g.*, the conditional of 'âg-u,' *to be*, is not 'âg-i-âl,' but 'ân-âl,' evidently from 'ân-a' ('âg-i-(n)-a'), *that was*, and 'âl.' Besides, the verbal participle must be followed by a verb or some verbal form; but 'âl' is a noun, and therefore the participle to which it is suffixed must be a relative participle, not a verbal one. In colloquial Tamil, 'âl' is suffixed to impersonal forms of the verb alone; but in the higher dialect 'âl,' or its equivalent 'êl,' may be suffixed to any person of any tense; *e.g.*, 'śeÿdanei-(y)-êl,' *if thou hast done*; 'śeÿguvên-êl,' *if I shall do*. It is also suffixed to the relative participle, as I conceive 'âl' is in the ordinary dialect; *e.g.*, 'śeÿgindra-(v)-âl,' 'śeÿda-(v)-âl,' *if (I, thou, &c.) should do*. This 'śeÿda-(v)-âl' of the High Tamil illustrates the origin of the more common colloquial form 'śeÿd-âl.'

This conditional particle 'âl' has been corrupted, I conceive, from 'kâl,' the particle already mentioned, and is not, I think, to be confounded with 'âl,' the sign of the instrumental case in Tamil. 'âl' is rarely used as a sign of the conditional in the higher dialect, in which 'kâl' is generally preferred.

One form of the conditional mood is expressed by *if* (*e.g.*, *if I do*); another is expressed by *though*, or *although* (*e.g.*, *though I do*, or *though I have done*). This second form of the conditional is generally expressed in the Drâvidian languages by suffixing the conjunctive particle to one of the conditional particles already referred to. Thus, in Tamil, 'śeÿd-âl' signifies *if* (*I*, &c.) *do;* whilst 'śeÿd-âl-um' signifies *though* (*I*, &c.) *do*. 'um,' the conjunctive or copulative particle, having the sense of *even*, as well as that of *and*, the literal meaning of this phrase is *even if* (*I*) *do*. The same particle 'um' is suffixed to the preterite verbal participle to bring out a preterite signification; *e.g.*, 'śeÿd'-um,' *though* (*I*, &c.) *did*, literally *even having done*.

In the superior dialect of the Telugu the conjunctive particle 'yu' (answering to the Tamil 'um') is appended to the conditional particle, when the reference is to the present time, and to the preterite relative participle (in that case 'nu' is substituted for 'yu') when past time is referred to.

The Canarese adds 'rû' and 'âgyu' to the relative participle, when the conditional sense is that of *although*. 'rû' is 're,' with the copulative 'û' annexed; and 'âgyu' is 'âgi,' *having been*, with the addition of the same 'û,' like the Tam. 'ânâl-um.'

2. *The imperative.*—In the Drâvidian languages the second person singular of the imperative is generally identical with the root or theme of the verb. This is so frequently the case, that it may be regarded as a characteristic rule of the language.

In a few instances in Tamil there is a slight difference between the imperative and the verbal theme; but those instances scarcely constitute even an apparent exception to the general rule, for the difference is caused not by the addition of any particle to the root, for the purpose of forming the imperative, but merely by the softening away of the formative suffix or the final consonant of the theme, for the sake of euphony; *e.g.*, 'var-u,' *to come*, takes for its imperative 'vâ,' Tel., 'râ;' the plural (or honorific singular) of which is in High Tamil 'vammin,' in Telugu 'rammu.'

It has been seen that there is a class of Tamil verbs which form their transitives by doubling the initial consonant of the sign of tense. Such verbs also, however, use the simple unformed theme as their imperative, and, in so far as that mood is concerned, make no distinction, except in their connexion and force, between transitives and intransitives. Thus, 'keḍ-u,' is either *spoil* or *be spoiled*, according to the connexion, whilst every other part of the verb takes a form suited to its signification; *e.g.*, the infinitive of the intransitive is 'keḍ-a,' that of the transitive 'keḍukk-a.' The Telugu, on the other hand, generally makes a distinction between the imperative of the transitive and that of the intransitive; *e.g.*, whilst the intransitive *be spoiled*, is 'cheḍu,' the transitive is not also 'cheḍu,' but 'cheʀuchu' (for 'cheḍuchu'), a form which would be 'keḍukku' in Tamil.

A large number of Telugu verbs use as their verbal theme, not the ultimate root, but a species of verbal noun ending in 'chu,' 'pu,' or 'mpu.' This accounts for the presence of 'chu,' which is in itself a formative, in the imperative 'cheʀuchu,' and not only in the imperative, but through all the moods and tenses of the Telugu verb. The Tamil uses the equivalent verbal noun (ending in 'kku') as the base of its transitive infinitive, and of the third person singular neuter of the future or aorist of its transitive; *e.g.*, 'keḍukk-a,' *to spoil*, and 'keḍukk-um,' *it will spoil;* but in every other part of the verb it uses the root alone (including only the inseparable formative, if there be one) as its inflexional theme. Hence it is easier to ascertain the primitive, true root of a verb in Tamil than in Telugu.

The ascertained use of a species of verbal noun as the imperative and inflexional basis of certain classes of Telugu verbs, leads to the conclusion that every Drâvidian imperative, whatever form it may take, is to be considered as a verbal noun. The crude root is the imperative in Tamil; and yet that even the Tamil imperative is a verbal noun appears from this, that the pronoun which the second person plural of that imperative employs, is not the nominative, or any portion of the nominative, of the Tamil pronoun of the second person, but the oblique case or genitive, viz., that form of the pronoun which is used in construction with nouns; *e.g.*, 'keḍ-um,' *spoil ye*, or *be ye spoiled*, is formed by suffixing to the verbal theme, not 'nîr,' *you*, but 'um,' *your*,—a proof that the imperative in Tamil has the grammatical significance of a verbal noun, and that it is the context and the energy of its enunciation that constitute it an imperative.

The particle 'mu' or 'mî,' is often added to the inflexional base of the verb, or verbal theme, to form the imperative in Telugu. The same practice obtains in the Ku; and even in Tamil 'mô' is sometimes suffixed to the singular of the imperative and 'min' to the plural, —only, however, in the classical dialect. In Telugu, nevertheless, as in Tamil, the verbal theme is more commonly used as the imperative without the addition of any such particle; and it seems probable that 'mu' or 'mî,' the only remaining relic of some lost root, is added as an intensitive or precative, like the Tamil 'ên;' *e.g.*, 'vârum-ên,' *Oh do come.* 'aṇḍi,' which is added to the root in Telugu, to form the second person plural of the imperative, is the vocative of an obsolete noun, *Sirs* (sometimes used honorifically to mean *Sir*); it is probably identical with 'andar,' an honorific plural suffix of the Canarese (*e.g.*, 'av-andar-u,' *they*); and the other signs of the same part of the verb in Telugu ('ḍi,' 'uḍi,' and 'uḍu' or 'ḍu'), are evidently abbreviations of 'aṇḍi.'

'min' (also 'minîr'), the particle occasionally used to form the plural of the imperative in classical Tamil, is perhaps only a metamorphosed pronoun, and equivalent to 'nim,' the oblique case of the old 'nîm,' *you;* and probably 'in,' the suffix of the imperative plural in Malayâlam, has been softened from 'min.'

3. *The infinitive.*—It has been customary in Drâvidian grammars, especially in the Telugu, to call various verbal nouns infinitives; as '*the infinitive in* 'uṭa,'' '*the infinitive in* 'aḍam-u,'' and '*the infinitive in* 'êdi.'' This use of terms is not sufficiently discriminative; for though each of those forms may be used with the force of a *quasi* infinitive in certain connexions, yet the two first are properly verbal nouns, and the third is a participial noun: each is capable of being regularly declined, and each possesses a plural. The Tel. 'paḍu-ṭa,' is identical with the Tamil 'paḍu-dal,' *suffering;* whilst the infinitive proper, *to suffer,* is in both languages 'paḍ-a.' I have no doubt that the true infinitive was originally a verbal noun also, and this origin of the Drâvidian infinitive will, I think, be proved in the sequel; but the *usus loquendi* of grammatical nomenclature requires that the term *infinitive* should be restricted to those verbal nouns which have ceased to be declined, which are destitute of a plural, and which are capable of being used absolutely.

Both in Tamil and in Telugu an infinitive in 'u' is occasionally used: it is identical with the root in Telugu and with the conjugational theme in Tamil; and therefore seems to be rather a verbal noun used absolutely than a formed infinitive.

The Malayâla infinitive 'vân' or 'ppân,' is properly a future gerund, and is used as such in High Tamil.

The true Drâvidian infinitive is generally formed by suffixing 'a' to the verbal theme. This is invariably the mode in which the infinitive is formed in Telugu; *e.g.*, 'chêŷ-a,' *to do.* Ordinarily in Tamil and Canarese the infinitive is formed in the same manner; but a verbal noun is also much used in Canarese as an infinitive, with the dative case-sign understood or expressed; *e.g.*, instead of 'mâḍ-a,' *to do,* they prefer saying 'mâḍ-al-ke' (in the modern dialect 'mâḍ-ali-kke'), *for doing,* or (without the case-sign) 'mâḍ-al' or 'mâḍ-alu,' *doing* or *to do.* Similar constructive infinitives are occasionally used in classical Tamil also, instead of the true infinitive in 'a;' *e.g.,* 'śol-laʀku' ('śollal-ku'), *for saying,* and 'śollal,' *saying,* with the sign of the dative understood, instead of 'śoll-a,' *to say.* There is also another infinitive, or honorific imperative in 'ga,' which is occasionally used in classical Tamil; *e.g.,* 'aʀi-ga,' *to know,* or *mayest (thou) know,* a form which will be inquired into presently. Notwithstanding these apparent exceptions, 'a' is to be considered as the regular Drâvidian sign of the infinitive.

Professor Max Müller, noticing that the majority of Tamil infinitives terminate in 'ka,' supposes this 'ka' to be identical in origin with 'ku,' the dative-accusative case-sign of the Hindi, and concludes that the Drâvidian infinitive is the accusative of a verbal noun. It is true that the Sanscrit infinitive and Latin supine in 'tum' is correctly regarded as an accusative, and that our English infinitive *to do,* is the dative of a verbal noun; it is also true that the Drâvidian infinitive is a verbal noun in origin, and never altogether loses that character; nevertheless, the supposition that the final 'ka' of most Tamil infinitives is in any manner connected with 'ku,' the sign of the Drâvidian dative and of the Hindi dative-accusative, is erroneous. A comparison of various classes of verbs and of the various dialects shows that the 'ka' in question proceeds from a totally different origin.

The Tamil infinitive terminates in 'ga' ('g-a') only in those cases in which the verbal theme ends in a formative 'gu' (g-u'); and in many instances in which 'g' appears in the infinitive (as in the verbal theme) in the ordinary dialect, 'v' replaces it in the poets: *e.g.* 'nôga,' *to be pained,* is not so much used by the classics as 'nôva.' 'ppa' is also used in the higher dialect instead of 'kka;' *e.g.,* 'naḍappa,' *to walk,* for 'naḍakka.' These interchanges of the formative consonant, which is the termination of the verbal theme, and to which the infinitival 'a' is added, are in perfect agreement with the Telugu; and from both it is apparent that 'a' alone is the sign of the infinitive. Tamil verbs ending in the formative 'g-u' are intransitives; and when they are converted into transitives, the formative is doubled for the purpose of denoting the increased intensity of signification. In such cases the formative 'g-u' is converted into 'kk-u;' and accordingly the infinitive of all such verbs ends in 'kk-a.'

Thus, the verb 'pô,' *to go,* takes 'gu' for its intransitive formative, and hence its verbal theme is 'pô-gu;' from which is formed the aorist 'pôg-um,' *it will go,* the verbal noun 'pôg-al,' *going,* and the infinitive 'pôg-a, *to go.* The corresponding transitive verb is 'pô-kku,' *to drive away* ('gu' being converted into 'kku'); and from this is formed in like manner 'pôkk-um,' *it will drive away,* and also the infinitive 'pôkk-a,' *to drive away.* In some instances the intransitive shape of the verb has no formative; and when it is converted into a transitive, the initial consonant of the tense-sign is hardened and doubled: *i.e.,* 'giR' becomes 'kkiR, 'd' or 'nd' becomes 'tt,' and 'v' or 'b' becomes 'pp.' In such instances the verbal theme on which the infinitive is constructed takes the doubled formative, 'kk-u:' *e.g.,* compare 'vaḷar-a,' *to grow,* with 'vaḷar-kk-a,' *to rear.* This formative, 'kk' however, appears not only in the infinitive but also in the aorist 'vaḷar-kk-um,' *it will rear.*' A very large number of Tamil verbs, including many transitives, have no formative termination whatever; and the infinitive of such verbs is formed by simply suffixing 'a' to the root; *e.g.,* 'vâṛ-a,' *to flourish,* and 'kâṇ-a,' *to see.* In the event of the root of a verb of this class ending in 'i' or 'ei,' 'y' is inserted between the root and the sign of the infinitive; *e.g.,* 'aRi-(y)-a,' *to know;* 'aḍei-(y)-a,' *to obtain.* This 'y,' however, is clearly euphonic. When an intransitive root is converted into a transitive by annexing 'tt-u' to the root, *e.g.,* 'tâṛ-tt-u,' *to lower,* the infinitive simply elides the euphonic 'u' and suffixes 'a;' *e.g.,* 'tâṛ-tt-a.'

From a comparison of these instances, it appears indubitably certain that 'a' alone is the normal suffix of the Tamil infinitive, and that the 'g' or 'kk' which so often appears, belongs to the formative of the verbal theme, not to any supposititious case-sign.

What then is the origin of the infinitival suffix 'ga,' which is occasionally used in classical Tamil; *e.g.,* 'aRi-ga,' *to know,* instead of the ordinary 'aRi-(y)-a,' and 'śeÿ-ga,' *to do,* instead of 'śeÿ(ÿ)-a?' This form is chiefly used as an optative, or as conveying a wish or polite command; *e.g.,* 'nî aRi-ga,' *mayest thou know!* It does not follow, however, from this, that it would be correct to regard it as a form of the imperative originally; for the ordinary infinitive in 'a' is often used by the poets in the same manner, and not unfrequently even by the peasants.

I am persuaded that the 'g' of 'ga' is simply the usual formative 'g' or 'g-u' of verbal nouns, and that its use is primarily euphonic. The same formative 'g' is found to be used in connexion with other parts also of the very verbs which are given as examples of this rule. Thus, not only is 'aRi-ga,' *to know,* used instead of 'aRi-(y)-a,' but 'aRi-g-il-ir,' *you know not,* instead of 'aRi-(y)-il-îr,' or 'aRi-(y)-îr; and just as 'śeÿ-ga,' *to do,* is used instead of 'śeÿ(ÿ)-a,' so we find 'śeÿ-gu-v-ên,' *I will do,* instead of 'śeÿ-v-ên.' The 'g' which makes its appearance in these instances, is in its origin the formative 'g-u,' as appears by the second example; but it is used rather for euphony than any other cause. It is also to be noticed, that the formative 'gu' may be appended to any verbal root whatever, as a fulcrum to the inflexional forms, provided only that the euphony is improved by it, or that the prosody requires it. This view of the origin of the 'ga' in question, is conformed by the evidence of the Malayâlam, for in that dialect 'ga' is the formative of verbal nouns, answering to the Tamil 'gei;' *e.g.*, 'wariga,' *a coming;* and yet the very same form is used as a polite imperative; *e.g.*, 'nî wariga' (Tam. 'varuga'), *mayest thou come!* Here we see not only a verbal noun used as an imperative, but we see the infinitive of one dialect treated as a verbal noun in another. The Tamil verbal noun which directly answers to the Malayâla 'wariga,' *a coming*, is 'varugei;' and 'varuga' in Tamil has ceased to be used as a verbal noun, and been restricted to the use of an infinitive and imperative; but it is evident from the identity of both with the Malayâla 'wariga,' that both are verbal nouns in origin. The Malayâla 'wariga' is regularly declined; *e.g*, 'wariga-(y)-âl,' *through the coming.* We thus come back to the conclusion, that 'a,' not 'ga,' is the true infinitival suffix of the Tamil.

On examining the Telugu we shall find that the only sign of the infinitive which is recognised by that language is 'a.' The various formatives which, as we have seen, are inserted between the Tamil verbal root and the suffixes of the infinitive, form in Telugu part of the verbal theme itself, and are found not only in one or two connexions, but in every mood and tense of the verb, including the imperative. In Telugu, therefore, the only difference between the imperative and the infinitive is, that the latter elides the enunciative 'u' of the former, and substitutes for it its own distinctive suffix 'a.' Thus, whilst the imperative of the verb *to open*, is in Tamil 'tiʀa,' and the infinitive 'tiʀa-kk-a;' the formative 'kk' which appears in the Tamil infinitive, and which might be supposed to form part of the infinitival suffix, appears in Telugu (in its dialectically softened form of 'ch'), not only in the infinitive, but also in the imperative and throughout the verb; *e.g.*, 'teʀa-ch-a,' infinitive, *to open;* 'teʀa-ch-u,' imperative, *open thou.* At the same time, the Telugu sign of the dative case 'ku' or 'ki' is never softened into 'ch' in any connexion; consequently, there is no possibility of connecting the Telugu sign of the infinitive with that of the dative. Moreover, the formative 'ch' is often replaced, especially in the imperative and infinitive, by 'p;' *e.g.*, 'naḍu-p-a,' infinitive, *to walk*, instead of 'naḍu-ch-a,' corresponding to the Tamil 'naḍa-kk-a,' of which the imperative and theme is 'naḍa.' Hence, it cannot be doubted, that the Tamil 'g' and 'kk,' and the corresponding Telugu 'ch' and 'p,' alternating (after 'i') with 'nch' and 'mp,' are merely formatives, without any special connexion with the suffix of the infinitive, which is 'a' alone.

In most instances in Canarese the formatives referred to above are discarded altogether, and the 'a' which constitutes the sign of the infinitive is suffixed to the crude verbal root. Thus, whilst the verb 'ir-u,' *to be*, takes 'iru-kk-a' for its infinitive in Tamil, the simpler Canarese infinitive is 'ir-a.'

Origin of the infinitival suffix 'a.'—I conceive that 'al' was originally the sign of the infinitive in all the Drâvidian dialects, and that 'a' is a weakened form of 'al.' Several analogies may be adduced which render the softening of 'al' into 'a,' not only possible, but probable. It has been shown that 'a,' the verbal sign of negation, is probably derived from 'al,' the ordinary negative particle. The following analogy is more decisive. Much use is made in Tamil of a verbal or participial noun ending in 'dal;' *e.g.*, 'alei-dal,' *a wandering*, from 'alei,' *to wander;* 'muʀi-dal,' *a breaking*, from 'muʀi,' *to break*. In Canarese the final 'l' of those and similar verbal nouns has systematically disappeared; *e.g.*, 'ale-ta,' *a wandering*, 'muri-ta,' *a breaking*.

The Telugu also has softened away the final 'l' of the same class of words; *e.g.*, compare the Tamil 'mêÿ-(t)tal,' *pasturage*, with the corresponding Telugu 'mê-ta;' 'chê-ta,' Tel., *an act*, with 'śeÿ-dal,' Tam.; and 'naḍa-ta,' Tel., *walk, conduct*, with 'naḍa-(t)tal,' Tam. Even in Tamil also, 'naḍa-(t)tei' alternates with 'naḍa-(t)tal.'

It has already been stated that the verbal noun in 'al,' with or without the dative case-sign, is used instead of the infinitive in 'a' in both dialects of the Canarese and in classical Tamil. In Gônd also, the sign of the infinitive is 'alle,' amplified from 'al;' *e.g.*, 'aiâlle,' *to be*, which is evidently identical with the Tamil verbal noun, 'âgal,' *being*—a form occasionally used in the higher dialect as an infinitive. Now, as the Drâvidian infinitive undoubtedly partakes of the character of a participial or verbal noun, and is considered by native grammarians as a verbal participle or gerund of the present or aorist tense; as it is certain that it is intimately associated with a verbal noun in 'al,' one of the most characteristic in the language, and which denotes not the abstract idea of the verb, but the act; and as 'al' in other connexions has been softened into 'a,' we seem to be justified in coming to the conclusion that 'a,' the infinitival suffix, has been weakened from 'al,' and, consequently, that 'âg-a,' *to be*, is identical with 'âg-al,' *being*.

A parallel instance of the softening away of the final consonant of the infinitive appears in the Indo-European tongues. The sign of the infinitive is in Persian and Gothic 'an,' but in Frisian 'a;' *e.g.*, 'mak-a,' *to make*.

The present infinitive of the Finnish is apparently identical with the Drâvidian, being also in 'a;' *e.g.*, 'oll-a,' *to be;* but it appears probable that this 'a' was originally preceded by a nasal, for the corresponding Esthonian infinitive is 'olle-ma,' and the sign of the infinitive in Hungarian is 'ni.'

On the supposition that the Drâvidian infinitive terminated originally in 'l,' there is a remarkable, but probably accidental, resemblance to it in the Armenian, in which 'l' is the infinitival suffix; *e.g.*, 'ber-e-l,' *to carry* (compare Tam. 'poR-al,' *bearing* or *to bear*); 'ta-l,' *to give* (compare Tam. 'ta(r)-al,' *giving* or *to give*).

Use of the infinitive.—If we look at the force and use of the Drâvidian infinitive, we shall discover conclusive reasons for regarding it as a verbal or participial noun. It is not only used as in other languages to denote a purpose or end, *e.g.*, 'var-a (ś)śollu,' *tell (him) to come*, but also in the following connexions. (i.) The majority of Drâvidian adverbs are infinitives of neuter verbs; *e.g.*, *he knocked down*, would be in Telugu 'paḍa goṭṭenu,' in Tamil 'viṛa (t)taḷḷinân;' in which phrases *down* means *to fall*, *i.e.*, *so as to fall*. Through the same idiom 'âg-a,' the infinitive of the verb *to become* (in Tel. 'kâ,' or 'gâ'), is ordinarily added to nouns of quality to convert them into adverbs; *e.g.*, 'nandr'-âga,' Tam. *well*, from 'nandr-u,' *good*, and 'âg-a,' *to become*. (ii.) The infinitive is elegantly used with an imperative signification (in accordance with the Hebrew idiom), or rather as an optative, seeing that it conveys a wish rather than a command; *e.g.*, 'nî vâṛ-a' (more frequently 'vâṛ-ga'), *mayest thou flourish!* The infinitive of the verb *to be*, also regularly forms an optative, or polite imperative, by being annexed to the future tense of any verb; *e.g.*, 'śeÿvâÿ-âga,' *mayest thou do*, from 'śeÿvâÿ,' *thou wilt do*, and 'âga,' *to become*, literally, *may it be (that) thou wilt do*. (iii.) It is used as a kind of ablative absolute; *e.g.*, 'poṛudu viḍind' irukk-a, ên tûngugiRaÿ,' Tam., *the sun having arisen, why sleepest thou?* In this instance, 'viḍind' irukk-a,' (literally *to be—having arisen*,) is in the perfect tense, but 'irukk-a' is not a preterite infinitive, but is the ordinary present or aorist infinitive of the verb 'ir-u,' *to be*. The infinitive used in this manner is styled a verbal noun in Malayâlam, and is capable of being regularly declined, which proves that it is a noun. The Malayâlam prefers to use as an infinitive 'vân,' which is properly a gerund of the future; but some of the uses to which it puts its verbal noun in 'ga,' 'ka,' or 'kka,' show that that verbal is identical with the Tamil infinitive; *e.g.*, 'ellâwarum kêḷkka,' Mal., (Tam. 'ellârum kêṭka,') *in the audience of all* is literally *so as that all should hear*, or, *whilst all were hearing*. (iv.) A series of infinitives is often elegantly used, somewhat as in Latin, to express minor actions that take place contemporaneously with the principal action; *e.g.*, they would say in Tamil 'mugil eṛumba' (*whilst the clouds were rising*), 'vânam iruḷ-a' (*whilst the sky was gathering blackness*), 'maṛei poṛindu peÿ(ÿ)-a' (*whilst the rain was falling abundantly*), 'ûrâr tiru-viṛâ naḍattinârgaḷ' (*the villagers celebrated their sacred festival*). (v.) The reduplication of any infinitive expresses exactly the force of the Latin gerund in 'do;' *e.g.*, 'pôg-a pôg-a, balan koḷḷum,' '*vires acquirit eundo;*' more closely, *as it goes—as it goes* (literally *to go—to go*) *it gathers strength*.

These illustrations prove that the Drâvidian infinitive has the force of a gerund or verbal participle, or of a verbal noun, as well as that of the infinitive properly so called. The examples adduced are all from the Tamil, but parallel examples could easily be adduced from each of the other dialects.

Formation of Verbal Nouns.

Drâvidian verbal nouns divide themselves into two classes, viz.—participial nouns, which are formed from the relative participle, and verbal nouns of each tense and retaining the time of the tense to which they belong, which are always formed directly from the theme, and are determinate in point of time.

1. *Participial nouns.*—The greater number of nouns of this class are formed by suffixing the demonstrative pronouns, or their terminations, to the present and preterite relative participles; *e.g.*, from 'śeÿgiʀa,' *that does* (the present relative participle of 'śeÿ,' *to do*), is formed 'śeÿgiʀa-(v)-an,' *he that does;* 'seÿgiʀa-(v)-aḷ,' *she that does*, &c. In like manner from the past relative participle 'śeÿda,' *that did*, is formed 'śeÿda-(v)-an,' *he that did;* 'seÿda-(v)-al,' *she that did*, &c.; and by simply adding the appropriate terminations, participial nouns of any number or gender (but always of the third person only) may be made at pleasure. A similar series of future participial nouns exists, or may be constructed if required; *e.g.*, 'ôduvân,' *he who will read, or is accustomed to read*. The Tamil future in 'v' or 'b' is destitute of a relative participle; but its existence is implied in that of future participial

nouns, like 'pôva-du,' *that which will go,* and 'kâṇba-(v)-an,' *he who will see,* and must have ended like the future relative participle of the Canarese, in 'va,' 'ba,' or 'ppa.' The Tamil aoristic future in 'um,' though a relative participle as well as a future tense, forms no participial nouns, probably in consequence of 'um' being in reality a conjunctive particle, not a true suffix of relation. Negative participial nouns of each number and gender are formed exactly like the affirmative participial nouns, by suffixing the various demonstrative terminations to the negative, instead of the affirmative, relative participle.

These participial nouns are declined like other nouns; nevertheless, being parts of the verbs, they have the same power of governing nouns as the verbs to which they belong; *e.g.*, 'vîṭṭei (k) kaṭṭinavan-ukku,' *to him who built the house.*

In these respects all the Drâvidian dialects are so perfectly agreed that it is needless to multiply quotations.

There is a peculiarity about the words which are used as neuter participial nouns in Tamil which requires to be noticed. Each of them is used in three different significations, viz.—as the third person neuter of the verb, as a neuter relative-participial noun, and as a verbal-participial noun. Thus, 'śeÿgiʀadu' in the first connexion means *it does*; in the second, *that which does;* in the third, *the doing* or *to do.* I have termed it in the third connexion 'a verbal-participial noun,' to distinguish it from the ordinary verbal nouns, which are formed from the theme, not from participles, and from which the idea of time is excluded. It is a verbal noun in use, though participial in origin. I am persuaded that of these three senses the original and most correct one is the last, viz., that of the verbal-participial noun; for the relative-participial noun ought by analogy to be 'seÿgiʀa-(v)-adu,' not 'śeÿgiʀ-adu;' and whilst it is certain that a participial or verbal noun might easily be used as the third person neuter of the verb, in accordance with the analogy of many other languages, it is difficult to see how the third person neuter of the verb could come to be used so regularly as it is as a verbal-participial noun. This species of participial noun, though neuter or without personality, includes the idea of time: it has three forms, in accordance with the present, the past, and the future tenses of the verb; *e.g.*, 'śeÿgiʀadu,' *the doing;* 'śeÿdadu,' *the having done;* and 'śeÿvadu,' *the being about to do.* Each of these forms may be pluralised, as far as usage permits, when it is used as the third person neuter of the verb, or as a relative-participial noun; but when used abstractly as a verbal-participial noun it is not pluralised. The participial noun formed from the future is one of the most commonly used forms of the verbal noun in Canarese, *e.g.*, 'iḷiyu-v-adu,' or 'iḷivu-du,' *the act of descending,* from 'iḷi,' *to descend.*

Words of this kind have sometimes been called infinitives; and it is true that they may generally be rendered in the infinitive on translating them into English, *e.g.*, 'appaḍi seÿgiʀadu sari (y) alla,' Tam., *it is not right to do so.* But this is simply because the English infinitive itself is sometimes used as a verbal noun, and *to do* is equivalent to the participial noun, *the doing.* The phrase might be more closely rendered, *the doing thus (is) not right.* Verbal nouns of this class become more allied to infinitives when they are put in the dative; *e.g.*, 'seygiʀadu-kku,' *for the doing, i.e., to do.* As the pronoun 'adu' becomes optionally 'adan,' so the participial noun 'śeÿgiʀadu' may become 'seÿgiʀadan.' This change, however, is exceedingly rare except in the dative; and in that connexion 'śeÿgiʀadan-ku,' euphonically 'śeÿgiʀadaʀ-ku,' is more common in written compositions than 'śeÿgiʀadu-kku.'

The Tamil alone possesses an abstract relative-participial noun, expressing in the form of a declinable participle, the abstract idea denoted by the verb. It is formed by appending 'mei,' the suffix of abstracts, to the present or preterite relative participle of any verb: *e.g.*, from 'irukkindr-a,' *that is* (the present relative participle of 'iru,' *to be*), by the addition of 'mei' Tamilians form 'irukkindra-mei,' *being.* The use of this form is confined to classical compositions; but the abstract derivative *nouns* which are formed by annexing 'mei' to the crude verbal theme (*e.g.*, 'poʀu-mei,' *patience,* from 'poʀu,' *to bear*) are much used even in the colloquial dialect. The relative-participial noun in 'mei,' whilst it is declined like a noun, has the governing power of a verb; but the corresponding verbal derivative in 'mei' has the force of a substantive only.

The Tamil suffix 'mei' is 'me' in Canarese, 'mi' in Telugu. In several of the Scythian tongues we find a suffix used which bears a considerable resemblance to this. The suffix of the participial noun in Finnish is 'ma' or 'mâ:' in Esthonian 'ma' is the suffix of the infinitive: supines are formed in Finnish by suffixing 'man:' the Turkish infinitival suffix is 'mak' or 'mek.' Possibly we may also compare with this Drâvidian 'me' or 'mei,' the old Greek infinitive in 'μεν,' and such nouns as 'ποίη-μα,' 'δεσ-μό-ς,' and 'σχισ-μή,' each of which exhibits an old participial suffix.

2. *Verbal nouns.*—Drâvidian verbal nouns are indeterminate with respect to time, being formed, not from participles, but from the verbal root or the formed theme; but they express the act, not the abstract

idea, of the verb to which they belong, and hence are called by Tamil grammarians 'toṛil peÿr,' *nouns of operation.*

Verbal nouns are carefully to be distinguished from verbal dérivatives, or substantives derived from verbs. The latter, though derived from verbs, are used merely as nouns; whereas the verbal noun, properly so called (like the participial noun), is construed as a verb. In several Drâvidian grammars written by Europeans this distinction has not been attended to; and Tamil words like 'naḍei' or 'naḍappu, *walk,* have been classed with verbal nouns like 'naḍakkei,' 'naḍakkudal,' and 'naḍakkal,' *walking.* Though, however, each of these words may be translated *walking,* the first two are simply substantives; and adjectives, not adverbs, must be used to qualify them; whereas 'naḍakkudal,' the corresponding *noun of operation,* is a true verbal noun, and is qualified by adverbs, precisely as the verb itself, 'naḍa,' *to walk,* would be. Thus, we can say 'nîdi(y)âÿ naḍakkudal,' *acting or walking justly;* but we could not use the adverb 'nîdi(y)âÿ' to qualify either 'naḍappu' or 'naḍei.' It would be necessary to qualify those words by the adjectival form 'nîdi(y)âna,' there being nearly the same difference between 'naḍappu' and 'naḍakkudal' that there is in English between *behaviour* and *behaving.*

A verbal noun in 'gei' or 'kkei' is often used in Tamil, *e.g.,* 'irukkei,' *the being,* 'śeÿgei,' *the doing;* but though this is used as a verbal noun, *e.g.,* 'appaḍi irukkei-(y)-âl,' *seeing that it is so,* more literally *through its being so,* yet the forms which are most commonly used as verbals, and which have the best claim to that character, are those which terminate in 'al:' *e.g.,* 'śeÿ(ÿ)-al,' or 'śeÿ-dal,' *doing;* 'naḍakk-al' or 'naḍakkudal,' *walking.* Whether the suffix appended be 'al' or 'dal,' it is generally suffixed, not to the crude root, but to the formed verbal theme, *i.e.,* to that which forms the basis of the infinitive and of the defective future or aorist: *e.g.,* the verbal noun that is formed from 'ir-u,' *to be,* is not 'ir-al,' but 'iru-kk-al,' *being;* and from 'naḍ-a,' *to walk,* is formed not 'na-ḍ-al,' but 'naḍa-kk-al.' Notwithstanding this, 'al' or 'dal' is sometimes added directly to the ultimate base: *e.g.,* not only have we 'pôg-al' or 'pôgu-dal,' *going,* but also 'pô-dal;' and not only 'âg-al' or 'âgu-dal,' *becoming,* but also 'â-dal.' Probably, however, in these instances the right explanation is, that the formative 'g' of 'pô-gu' and 'â-gu' has been softened by use. The 'd' of 'dal' is clearly a formative of the same character and force as the 'g' of 'gei' or 'kkei;' and this is proved by the circumstance that the 'd' is doubled and converted into 'tt' when the verb becomes a transitive instead of an intransitive, or when euphonic considerations require: *e.g.,* comp. 'kuṟei-dal,' intransitive, *a being curtailed,* with 'kuᴚei-ttal,' transitive, *a curtailing.* It is evident that this 'd' is unconnected with the 'd' which constitutes the sign of the preterite tense of many verbs; for the verbal noun in 'dal' is as indeterminate with respect to time as that in 'al' or that in 'kkei;' and the corresponding Telugu forms are 'ṭa' and 'ḍam-u;' *e.g.,* 'chêyu-ṭa' or 'chêsu-ṭa,' or more commonly 'chêya-ḍam-u,' *doing.*

The distinction which has been shown to exist between verbal nouns, properly so called, and verbal derivatives, furnishes, I conceive, some confirmation of the hypothesis that the infinitive in 'a' has been softened from 'al,' the Tamil suffix of verbal nouns.

3. *Verbal derivatives.*—It is not my intention to enter fully into the investigation of the formatives of *verbal derivatives,* or substantives derived from verbs, most of those formatives being merely euphonic, and their number in the various dialects being very great. It may be desirable, however, to direct the reader's attention to a few of the more characteristic and interesting modes in which the Drâvidian languages form nouns of this class.

(1.) The first class of derivative nouns (if indeed it is correct to consider them as *derivatives*) consists of those that are identical with verbal themes; *e.g.,* compare 'kaṭṭ-u,' *a tie,* and 'kaṭṭ-u,' *to tie.*

(2.) Some verbal themes become nouns by the doubling and hardening of the final consonant; *e.g.,* 'eṛutt-u,' *a letter,* from 'eṛud-u,' *to write;* 'pâṭṭ-u,' *a song,* from 'pâḍ-u,' *to sing.* This is especially a Tamil method of forming derivative nouns, for some of the corresponding Telugu nouns are formed differently; and where they do resemble the Tamil, the resemblance consists only in the hardening, and not also in the doubling of the final consonant; *e.g.,* 'pâṭa,' Tel., *a song,* from 'pâḍ-u,' *to sing.* The Telugu differs also from the Tamil in changing the final or enunciative 'u' of the verbal root into 'a.' Compare 'âṭ-a,' *play* (Tam. 'âṭṭ-u'), from 'âḍ-u,' *to play.* The Tamil mode of doubling, as well as hardening, the final consonant, seems most in accordance with Drâvidian analogy; for it is when a sonant is doubled that it is naturally converted into a surd, and when it is not doubled, it should be pronounced as a sonant.

It is remarkable how many purposes are served by the doubling of Drâvidian final consonants. (i.) It places substantives in an adjectival relation to succeeding substantives; (ii.) it converts intransitive verbs into transitives; (iii.) it forms a sign of the preterite tense; and (iv.) it forms derivative nouns from verbal themes.

(3.) A remarkable mode of forming derivatives is that of lengthening the included vowel of monosyllabic verbal roots: *e.g.,* in Tamil, from 'paḍ-u,' *to suffer*, comes 'pâḍ-u,' *suffering;* from 'min,' *to glitter*, comes 'mîn,' *a star*. Nor is this method found only in the classics: it appears in words of the most familiar class; *e.g.*, 'nâkk-u,' *the tongue*, from 'nakk-u,' *to lick*. The Tamil simply lengthens the root vowel in forming derivatives of this class, and leaves the final consonant unchanged; but the Telugu and Canarese harden the final consonant, in addition to lengthening the root vowel; *e.g.*, from 'paḍ-u,' *to suffer*, they form not 'pâḍ-u,' but 'pâṭ-u,' *suffering*. See the section on 'Roots.'

(4.) Abstract nouns are formed from verbal themes by suffixing 'mei;' *e.g.*, 'tâṟ-mei,' *humility*, from 'târ,' *to be low*. The same suffix forms abstracts also from nouns of quality or relation and pronominals; *e.g.*, 'peru-mei,' *greatness*, from 'per-u,' *great*, and 'tan-mei,' *nature, quality*, from 'tan,' *itself*, literally *self-ness*. This suffix is in Telugû 'mi;' *e.g.*, 'kali-mi,' *wealth*, from 'kalu-gu,' *to accrue*.

(5.) Many nouns are formed from verbs in Tamil by suffixing 'am,' and at the same time doubling and hardening the final consonant of the verbal theme. 'ng' being the equivalent of 'g,' 'nd' of 'd,' 'ṇḍ' of 'ḍ,' and 'mb' of 'b,' 'ng' on being doubled becomes 'kk,' 'nd' becomes 'tt; 'ṇḍ' becomes 'ṭṭ,' and 'mb' becomes 'pp;' *e.g.*, from 'tûng-u,' *to sleep*, is formed 'tûkk-am,' *sleep;* from 'tirund-u,' *to become correct*, comes 'tirutt-am,' *a correction;* from 'tôṇḍ-u,' *to dig*, comes 'tôṭṭ-am,' *a garden;* and from 'virumb-u,' *to desire*, comes 'virupp-am,' *a desire*.

In most instances the Telugu (and the Canarese always) rejects the final 'm' of nouns of this class; *e.g.*, 'tûng-a,' Tel., *sleep*, instead of the Tamil 'tûkk-am.' Though the final consonant, if 'g,' 'd,' 'b' (or their equivalents), is always doubled before this 'am' in Tamil and Malayâlam, verbal themes which end in other consonants often become nouns by simply annexing 'am;' *e.g.*, 'uÿar-am,' *height*, from 'uÿar,' *to be high;* 'âṟ-am,' *depth*, from 'âr,' *to be deep*.

Possibly this 'am' is derived from the Old Canarese sign of the objective case. 'am' being in that dialect a sign of objectivity, it might naturally be used as a formative of abstract neuter nouns; and it is certain that this would be in accordance with analogy, for this is evidently the reason why the nominative singular of so many Indo-European neuter nouns is formed by suffixing 'am' or 'um,' which is properly the sign of the accusative.

(6.) A vast number of verbal derivatives in all the Drâvidian dialects, are formed by suffixing to the verbal themes those favourite and multifariously used formatives, 'g,' 'd,' 'b,' under various modifications, and with various vowel terminations.

i. The 'g' formative becomes in Tamil 'gei,' *e.g.*, śeÿ-gei,' *an action*, from 'śeÿ,' *to do;* it is nasalised to 'ngei,' *e.g.*, 'kâ-(ng)gei,' *heat*, from 'kâÿ,' *to burn;* or is doubled and hardened into 'kkei,' *e.g.*, 'paḍu-kkei,' *a bed*, from 'paḍ-u,' *to lie*. The corresponding Canarese formatives are 'ke' or 'ge,' with not unfrequently the prefix of an euphonic 'i.' The Telugu nouns which take this formative terminate in 'ka' or 'ki;' *e.g.*, 'êli-ka,' *government*, from 'êl-u,' *to govern*, and 'uni-ki,' *residence*, from 'uṇḍu,' *to be, to dwell.*

ii. The 'd' formative is in Tamil 'di;' *e.g.*, 'keḍu-di,' *ruin*, from 'keḍ-u,' *to spoil:* being doubled and hardened it becomes 'tti;' *e.g.*, 'uṇar-tti,' *sensibility*, from 'uṇar,' *to feel, to be sensible.* This 'tt' is generally softened into 'chi;' *e.g.*, 'pugaṛ-chi' (instead of 'pugaṛ-tti'), *praise*, from 'pugaṛ,' *to praise.* This formative is 't' instead of 'd' in Canarese and Telugu. It appears in Canarese under the forms of 'ta' and 'te;' *e.g.*, 'hogaḷ-te,' *praise*, from 'hogaḷ' (Tam. 'pugaṛ'), *to praise;* 'kâÿ-ta,' *producing fruit*, from 'kâÿ,' *to fruit.* In Telugu we find 'ta' or 'ṭa' and 'ti;' *e.g.*, 'alaśa-ṭa,' *fatigue*, from 'alay-u' ('alaś-u') *to be tired;* 'tiṇ-ṭa,' *eating*, from 'tin,' *to eat;* 'mû-ta,' *a lid*, from 'mû-yu,' *to shut;* and 'naḍi-ti,' *conduct*, from 'naḍu-chu,' *to walk.*'

iii. The 'b' formative is in Tamil generally softened into 'v,' *i.e.*, 'vi' or 'vu;' *e.g.*, 'kêḷ-vi, *hearing*, from 'kêḷ,' *to hear*, and 'maṟei-vu,' *concealment*, from 'maṟei,' *to conceal.* In some instances, however, 'b' is euphonised into 'mb' ('mbu'); *e.g.*, 'vê-mbu,' *the Margosa tree*, from 'vê-ÿ,' *to be umbrageous;* 'pâ-mbu,' *a snake*, from 'pâ-ÿ,' *to spring.* 'b' cannot retain its proper sound before a vowel, and when single either becomes 'v' or 'mb;' and that the 'vu' which is so common a formative in each Drâvidian dialect was softened from 'bu,' appears from the circumstance that when it is doubled it becomes 'ppu;' *e.g.*, 'naḍa-ppu,' *a walking;* 'iru-ppu,' *a being;* 'mû-ppu,' *old age.* In Telugu this formative is 'vu,' 'vi,' or 'pu;' *e.g.*, 'châ-vu,' *death*, from 'cha-chchu,' *to die* (corresponding Tam. and Can. 'śâ-vu,' from 'śâ'); 'digu-vu,' *the bottom*, from 'dig-u,' *to descend;* 'teli-vi,' *understanding*, from 'teli-yu,' *to know;* 'chêru-pu,' *nearness*, from 'chêr-u,' *to draw near;* 'êḍu-pu,' *a weeping*, from 'êḍu-chu,' *to cry* (corresponding Tam. 'aṛa-ppu,' from 'aṛa'). The Canarese uses in this connexion 'vu' alone; *e.g.*, 'ira-vu,' *a being*, corresponding to the Tamil 'iru-ppu.'

4. *Nouns of agency or operation.*—The participial nouns of the Drâvidian languages are largely used as nouns of agency; but such nouns are also formed in each of the Drâvidian dialects in a more

direct and primitive manner by suffixing 'i' to the verbal root; *e.g.*, 'uṇ(ṇ)-i' (Tam. and Can.), *an eater*, from 'uṇ,' *to eat;* 'kol(l)-i' (Tam. and Can.), *a killer*, from 'kol,' *to kill.* The Drâvidian languages in borrowing feminine derivative nouns from the Sanscrit, change the final 'î' of the Sanscrit feminine into short 'i;' *e.g.*, 'sunda-rî,' Sans., *a fair woman*, becomes 'sundari.' But this final 'i' of feminine derivatives, which is directly borrowed from the Sanscrit, is not to be confounded with the more distinctively Drâvidian 'i,' by suffixing which nouns of agency or operation are formed, without reference to gender, whether masculine, feminine, or neuter. It is also to be distinguished from the 'i' which in Sanscrit is sometimes used as a suffix of nouns of agency, generally masculines, *e.g.*, 'kav-i-s,' *a poet*, literally *a speaker*, in borrowing which from the Sanscrit, the Drâvidian languages invariably reject the sign of the nominative, and use the crude theme (*e.g.*, 'kavi') instead.

Possibly 'i,' the Drâvidian suffix of nouns of agency, may have sprung from the same origin as the 'i' by which similar nouns are sometimes formed in Sanscrit; but it is certain that it has not been directly borrowed from the Sanscrit, and it does not appear even to have been introduced into the Drâvidian languages in imitation of it. Its independence of a direct Sanscrit origin will sufficiently appear from the following statement of the manner in which it is used.

(1.) Drâvidian nouns of agency which are formed by suffixing 'i,' are destitute of gender: their gender depends entirely upon the context; *e.g.*, 'panei-(y)-êR-i,' Tam., *a Palmyra climber* (from 'panei,' *a Palmyra*, and 'êR-u,' *to climb*), may be considered as masculine, because men only are climbers of the palmyra; 'maṇ-veṭṭ-i,' Tam., *a native spade, a hoe* (from 'maṇ,' *the ground*, and 'veṭṭ-u,' *to dig or cut*), is in like manner neuter by the necessity of the case: but both these nouns, and all similar nouns, when regarded from a grammatical point of view, are destitute of gender in themselves, and may be applied at discretion to objects of any gender.

(2.) Nouns of agency may be formed in this manner from primitive, underived nouns, as well as from verbal roots; *e.g.*, 'nâR-kâl-i,' Tam., *a chair*, literally *that which has four feet*, from 'nâḷ-u,' *four*, and 'kâl,' *a foot.*

(3.) When nouns of agency are formed from verbs, the suffix is often added, not to the crude root, but to the conjugational theme, or that form of the root which appears in the infinitive and in the defective aorist; *e.g.*, 'uṇg-i,' Tam. (as well as 'uṇ(ṇ)-i'), *an eater.*

(4.) My chief reason for regarding this suffix as a true and ancient Drâvidian form, and as independent of the Sanscrit, whatever may have been its ulterior relation to it, consists in the very extensive use which is made of nouns of agency formed by means of this suffix, not only in the Tamil classics, but also in the language of the peasantry. It appears in the names of plants and animals, in the names of many of the objects of nature, in old compounds, in proverbs, in nicknames, in the very highest and in the very lowest connexions, and to a much larger extent in all these varieties of use, than in Sanscrit. The following Tamil examples cannot be supposed to have been derived from Sanscrit precedents:—'kaḷ(ḷ)-i,' *cactus*, from 'kaḷ,' *toddy, sweet sap;* 'veḷ(ḷ)-i,' *silver*, from 'veḷ,' *to be white;* 'pul-i,' *the cheetah*, or *leopard*, from 'pul,' *small;* 'uvar-i,' *the sea*, from 'uvar,' *saltness;* 'âṛ-i,' *the sea*, from 'âṛ-u,' *to be deep.* Compare also the following compounds, 'vaṛi-kâṭṭ-i,' *a guide*, literally *a way-shower;* 'vânam-pâḍ-i,' *the lark* literally *the heaven-singer;* 'toṭṭâl-vâḍ-i,' *the sensitive plant*, literally *if (one) touch, the witherer*, or as we should prefer to say, *touch-me-and-I-wither.*

Adverbs.—It is unnecessary in a work of this kind to enter into the investigation of the Drâvidian adverbs, for, properly speaking, the Drâvidian languages have no adverbs at all: every word that is used as an adverb in the Drâvidian languages is either a verbal theme, or the infinitive or gerund of a verb; and illustrations of the manner in which those words acquire an adverbial force will be found in the ordinary grammars of each of the Drâvidian dialects.

SECTION VII.

GLOSSARIAL AFFINITIES.

THE comparison of the vocables of languages was often conducted in so loose and unscientific a manner, without definite principles, without regard to dialectic changes, and to the neglect of the comparison of grammatical forms and structure, that this branch of philology has fallen into indiscriminate and not undeserved disgrace. I admit that a comparative vocabulary, however carefully prepared, is of much less philological value than a comparative grammar. Isolated nouns and verbs are very apt to get corrupted in the lapse of time, and to adopt one phase of meaning after another, till the original meaning is overlaid or forgotten; whilst declensional and conjugational forms—the bones and sinews of a language—retain for ages both their shape and their signification with marvellous persistency. Nevertheless, I regard the comparison of vocables, when carefully and cautiously conducted, as an important *help* to the determination of lingual affinities; and it will be found, I think, that the following vocabularies bear independent testimony, in their own degree, to the very same result at which we arrived by grammatical comparison, viz., that whilst the Drâvidian idioms exhibit traces of an ancient, deep-seated connexion with Pre-Sanscrit—the assumed archaic mother-tongue of the Indo-European family—their relationship to the languages of the Scythian group, especially to the Ugrian tongues, is closer, more distinctive, and more essential than any other.

I.

Indo-European Affinities.

Section I.

Sanscrit Affinities.

Before entering upon the comparison of Drâvidian with Sanscrit vocables, it is desirable to disentangle the subject from extraneous matter by a preliminary examination of words which appear to have been borrowed by the Sanscrit from the Drâvidian languages.

I have long felt persuaded that some words of pure Drâvidian origin have found their way into Sanscrit vocabularies; and I have no doubt that a still larger number of words have been introduced into Sanscrit from the North-Indian vernaculars. I have also already stated my opinion (in the section on 'Sounds') that it was from the Drâvidian languages that the Sanscrit borrowed its 'cerebral' consonants.

There is probably almost as large a proportion of Drâvidian words in Sanscrit, as of British words in English: but this fact has generally remained unnoticed or unknown; and wherever any word was found to be the common property of the Sanscrit and any of the Drâvidian tongues, it was at once assumed to be a Sanscrit derivative. Doubtless, the number of Sanscrit derivatives, properly so called, which have been introduced into the Drâvidian languages is very great; but those words are always recognised and admitted to be derivatives by Tamil and Telugu lexicographers, and carefully distinguished from *national* or native Drâvidian words. In a few cases, as might be expected, but in a few cases only, some doubt exists whether a particular word was borrowed by the Sanscrit from the Tamil, or by the Tamil from the Sanscrit. Sanscrit lexicographers and grammarians were not so discriminative as their Drâvidian brethren; and if any writer had happened to make use of a local or provincial word, that is, a word belonging to the Drâvidian vernacular of the district in which he resided (and it was natural that such words should occasionally be used, for variety of metre or some other cause, especially after Sanscrit had ceased to be a spoken tongue), every such word, provided only it were found written in Sanscrit characters, was forthwith set down in the vocabularies as Sanscrit. Some words of Greek or Roman origin, such as 'denarius,' '*ὥρα, λεπτὸν*' (in the sense of *a minute of a degree*), and even the Greek names of the signs of the Zodiac, have found their way into Sanscrit. If so, it may be concluded that a much more considerable number of words belonging to the old Drâvidian vernaculars must have obtained a footing in the Sanscrit vocabularies.

The grounds or conditions on which I conclude any word contained in the Sanscrit lexicons to be of Drâvidian origin, are as follows:—

(i.) When the word is an isolated one in Sanscrit, without a root and without derivatives, but is surrounded in the Drâvidian languages with collateral, related, or derivative words; (ii.) when the Sanscrit possesses other words expressing the same idea, whilst the Drâvidian tongues have the one in question alone; (iii.) when the word is not found in any of the Indo-European tongues allied to the Sanscrit, but is found in some of the Scythian idioms, or at least in every Drâvidian dialect however rude; (iv.) when the derivation which the Sanscrit lexicographers have attributed to the word is evidently a fanciful one, whilst Drâvidian lexicographers deduce it from some native Drâvidian verbal theme of the same or a similar signification, from which a variety of words are found to be derived; (v.) when the signification of the word in the Drâvidian languages is evidently radical and physiological, whilst the Sanscrit signification is metaphorical, or only collateral; (vi.) when native Tamil and Telugu scholars, notwithstanding their high estimation of the Sanscrit, as the language of the gods, and the mother of all literature, classify the word in question as a pure Drâvidian one;—when any of these reasons are found to exist, and more especially when several or all of them coincide, I conceive we may safely conclude the word in question to be a Drâvidian not a Sanscrit derivative. I here subjoin a selection of such words.

Words borrowed by the Sanscrit from the Drâvidian tongues.

akkâ, *a mother.* For the exclusive Scythian relationship of this word, and proof of its derivation by the Sanscrit from the Scytho-Indian vernaculars, see the list of 'Scythian Affinities.'

attâ, *a mother, an elder sister, a mother's elder sister.*—See 'Scythian Affinities.'

aṭavi, *a jungle, a forest.* The root of this word is represented in Sanscrit dictionaries to be 'aṭa,' *to go,* because a forest is a place where birds, &c., *go;* which is evidently a fanciful derivation. All the Drâvidian languages contain a primary root 'aḍ,' the radical signification of which is *nearness, closeness;* and this monosyllabic root is modified and expanded so as to signify every variety of *closeness*. Amongst other derived words we have in Tamil 'aḍar,' *to be crowded, to grow thick together* (like the trees of a forest); and I have no doubt that it was from this verbal root, not from any native Sanscrit one, that 'aṭavi' (in Tamil and Telugu 'aḍavi,') was derived. Even the formative 'vi' is one which is distinctively Drâvidian; *e.g.*, 'kêḷvi,' Tam., *hearing*, from 'kêḷ,' *to hear*.

aṇi, âṇi, } *the pin of the axle of a cart;* derived, it is said, from 'aṇ-a,' *to sound*. On comparing this word with the Tamil 'âṇi,' *a nail, a pin or peg of any kind*, it is evident that they are not different words, but one and the same; and the only question is *which is the original?* The Tamil word is connected with a family of roots, each of which has a real affinity in signification to that of *a nail*, considered as *a fastening; e.g.*, 'aṇ-ei,' *to embrace, to tie;* 'aṇ-i,' *to put on;* 'aṇ-avu,' *to cleave to;* 'aṇ-u,' *to touch*. The derivation of the Sanscrit word from this Drâvidian root is, therefore, beyond comparison more natural than that which Sanscrit lexicographers have devised.

ambâ, ammâ, } *mother*, vocative 'ammă.' This word is found also in some of the Western Indo-European dialects; *e.g.*, Old High German and Oscan 'amma;' Icelandic 'amma' (*grandmother*); German 'amme' (*nurse*).

Notwithstanding this, I am inclined to believe that it was from the Drâvidian languages that this word found its way into the Sanscrit.—See proofs of its Ṡcytho-Indian character in the 'Scythian Affinities.'

arê, *interjection of calling to an inferior:* no derivation given. Compare with this the Telugu 'arê,' and the Tamil 'aḍê' or 'aḍâ;' which are used in exactly the same manner as the Sanscrit interjection. The dialectic interchange of 'd' and 'r,' has so often been illustrated, that 'arê' may safely be considered as equivalent to 'aḍê.' The supposition of their identity is strengthened by comparing the Sanscrit reduplication 'arêrê,' with the corresponding Tamil reduplication 'aḍaḍâ.'

Whilst the Sanscrit interjection is underived and perfectly isolated, the equivalent Tamil interjection claims to be derived from a Tamil root; viz., from 'aḍi,' *a slave*, the primary signification of which word is *the lowest part of anything; e.g., the sole of the foot*. The corresponding interjection addressed to women in Tamil is 'aḍi,' and this becomes 'aḍê' by the addition of 'ê' *emphatic*, which is the ordinary sign of the vocative case. So closely is the meaning of *a slave* still connected with these interjections in Tamil, that I have heard persons when thus addressed turn round angrily and say, *did you buy me, that you call me* 'aḍi?'

âli, *a woman's female friend.* Probably from 'âlu,' *a wife, a woman*, in poetical and vulgar Telugu, and also in Gônd.

kaṭu, *sharp, vehement, pungent:* assumed Sans. derivation 'kaṭ-a,' *to go.* The corresponding Drâvidian word is in Tamil 'kaḍ-u.' In Telugu 'kaṭu' is represented as Sanscrit, and 'kaḍ-u,' with the very same meaning, as native Telugu. The most important derivative of this root in Sanscrit is 'kaṭuk-ah,' masculine, or 'kaṭuk-î,' feminine, *mustard.* The word 'kaṭu' is deeply rooted in Sanscrit, and is *à priori* unlikely to have been borrowed from the Drâvidian tongues; and yet it cannot be doubted, I think, that its origin is Drâvidian.

Not only are the direct derivatives of this word much more numerous in Tamil than in Sanscrit, but collateral themes and meanings are also very abundant, whereas in Sanscrit no correlative root exists. 'kaḍ-u,' Tam., *to be sharp*, is one of a cluster of roots which are united together by a family resemblance. Some of those are 'kaḍ-u-gu,' *to make haste;* 'kaḍ-i,' *to cut, to reprove;* 'kaḍ-i' (with another formative), *to bite;* 'kaRi,' identical with 'kaḍi,' *curry;* 'kaḍu-kaḍu' (a mimetic word), *to appear angry.* Moreover, the Sanscrit 'kaṭuk-(ah or î),' *mustard*, appears to have been derived from the Tam. 'kaḍugu,' *mustard;* for nouns formed from verbal themes in this manner, by suffixing the formative 'ku,' pronounced 'gu,' are exceedingly abundant in Tamil.

kalâ, *any practical art, mechanical or fine:* assumed derivation 'kala,' *to sound.* The Tamil makes use of the same word ('kalei' for 'kala'), but includes in the signification every science, as well as every art. We cannot, I think, doubt the derivation of 'kalei' or 'kalâ,' from the primitive Tamil root 'kal,' *to learn*, (another derivative of which is 'kalvi,' *learning.*)

The other meanings of the Sanscrit word 'kalâ,' are so entirely unconnected with this, that it is evident that two different words spelled in the same manner (one of them Drâvidian), have erroneously been supposed to be one and the same.

kâvêr-i, *saffron,* also *the river Cavery* (from its muddy colour): assumed root 'kava,' *to colour.* Greek name of the same river, χάβηρις.

Possibly this word may be of true Sanscrit origin. I may suggest, however, the possibility of the origin of the name of the river Kâvêri, from the Drâvidian 'kâvi,' *red ochre,* and 'êʀ-u,' Tel., *a river,* or 'êr-i,' Tam., *a sheet of water.*

kûcha-h, *a female breast, especially that of a young unmarried woman:* derivation 'ku,' *to sound.* There is a much more natural derivation in the Tamil word 'kûcha-m,' *bashfulness,* a verbal noun from 'kûś-u,' *to be shy, to be ticklish.*

kûj-a, *to utter a cry, as a bird.* Probably this word is mimetic; we may compare it, however, with corresponding Drâvidian words, which also appear to be mimetic; viz., Tam. 'kû-vu;' Tel. 'kû-su;' Can. 'kû-gu;' each of which is derived from a Drâvidian root, 'kû,' *an inarticulate cry.* Compare also our English '*coo.*'

kuṭi, *a house;* related words 'kuṭiram,' also 'kuṭêrah,' *a cottage, a hut,* and 'kuṭumba,' *a family:* assumed derivation 'kuṭa,' *crooked.* There cannot be any doubt of the derivation of 'kuṭa-m,' *a water pot,* from 'kuṭa,' *crooked;* but the other words are probably of Drâvidian origin. In Tamil 'kuḍi' means *a house, a habitation,* also *an inhabitant, a farmer;* related Tamil words are 'kuḍil' and 'kuḍiśei,' *a hut;* a provincial form of the latter of which is 'kuchu.' In Telugu and Canarese 'guḍi' means *a temple,* and 'guḍishi' or 'guḍise,' *a hut.* In Hindustani 'guṭi' means *a house.* By all native grammarians, these words are considered to be of pure Drâvidian origin; and the existence of the same root in all the Finnish tongues favours the supposition that it was not borrowed by the Drâvidian languages from the Sanscrit, but by the Sanscrit from those languages. Compare the Finnish 'kota,' Tscheremiss 'kuda,' Mordwin 'kudo,' Ostiak 'chot,'—each signifying *a house.* Was the Saxon 'cot' also derived from this same Scythian or Finnish source?

kuṇi, kûṇi, } *having a crooked or withered arm.* Compare this with 'kûn,' Tam., *crook-back;* and especially with 'kun-i,' Tam. *to stoop,* an undoubted Drâvidian root, from which it is probable that both the Tam. 'kûn,' and the Sanscrit 'kuṇi' or 'kûṇi' have been derived.

kûla, *a pond or pool:* assumed derivation 'kûl-a,' *to cover.* Compare the Tamil 'kuḷ-am' and the Tel. 'kol-anu,' *a tank, a pool.*

We can scarcely doubt that the Sanscrit word is identical with the Drâvidian one; and if so, it must have been derived from it, for the Tam. 'kuḷ-am,' *a tank,* is unquestionably a verbal noun from 'kuḷ-i,' *to bathe,* a pure Drâvidian root.

kôṭṭa, kôṭa, } *a fort, a stronghold:* assumed derivation 'kuṭa,' *to be crooked,* or 'kuṭṭa,' *to cut.* The Drâvidian dialects make use of the same or a similar word for *a fort,* viz., 'kôṭa' in Tel., 'kôṭe' in Can., and 'kôṭṭei' in Tam.

The Tamil having another and very ancient word for *a stronghold,* viz., 'araṇ,' which is certainly a Drâvidian root, it may be concluded that 'kôṭṭei' has been borrowed from the Sanscrit. But where did the Sanscrit itself obtain this word? Probably from a Tamil root after all; for the Sanscrit derivations of 'kôṭa' are very fanciful, whilst we could not desire a better or more natural derivation than the Tamil 'kôḍ-u,' *a line, a line of circumvallation,* which is sometimes used to denote also *a walled village, a fortification.* 'kôḍ-u,' when used adjectivally, becomes 'kôṭṭ-u.'

khaṭvâ, *a couch, a cot:* assumed derivation 'khaṭṭ-a,' *to screen.* Compare the Tam. 'kaṭṭ-il,' *a cot,* from 'kaṭṭ-u,' *to tie or bind, to build.* The word 'katt-u' is thoroughly and essentially Drâvidian, and one which abounds with derivatives and related words.

sava-m, *a corpse.*

sâva-m, adj., *relating to a dead body.*

These words are said to be derived from 'sava,' *to go;* but this derivation is much less probable than the Drâvidian verbal root 'śâ,' Tam. and Can., *to die.* The vowel of 'śâ' is short in the Telugu 'cha' (for 'śa'), in the corresponding verbal theme 'chachu;' and both in Tamil and Canarese it is short in the preterite tense. 'śâ' is undoubtedly a pure Drâvidian root; and it re-appears in the Samoïede 'chawe,' *dead.* Probably also the Sanscrit 'shei' ('sâyati'), *to waste away,* and 'shô,' *to be destroyed,* have some ulterior connexion with it.

sâya, *the evening:* assumed derivation 'sho,' *to destroy, to put an end to.* The Tamil 'śây,' *to lean, to incline,* a pure Drâvidian word, seems to be a much more natural derivation, *the evening* being the period when the sun *inclines* to the west.

nânâ, *several, various, multiform.* Bopp derives 'nânâ' from certain assumed obsolete demonstratives signifying *this and that.*

It is more likely to have been derived from the Tamil 'nâl-u' or 'nân-gu,' *four,* this numeral being constantly used in the Drâvidian languages to signify *several, various,* or *an indefinite number of moderate extent.* By a corresponding usage the numeral *ten* is taken to represent any large indefinite number. Thus a Tamilian will say, *I was told so and so by four persons,—i.e., by several persons;* or, *we must do as ten people do,—i.e., as the world does.* The numeral adjective 'nâlâ' (from 'nâl-u,' *four*) is regularly used in Tamil to signify *various,* though literally meaning *four-fold;* and the euphonic change of 'l' into 'n' in the High Tamil 'nân-gu,' *four,* shows how 'nânâ' may have originated from 'nâlâ.' The Tamil Dictionary gives us, amongst other instances of the use of 'nâlâ,' one which is identical with the instance of the use of 'nânâ' given in the Sanscrit Dictionary, viz., 'nâlâ vidam,' *in various ways,* literally *in a four-fold way;* which we may compare with the corresponding Sans. 'nânâ vidha,' *in various ways.*

With respect to the Drâvidian origin of this word, the testimony of the Tamil stands alone; for in the Canarese and Telugu Dictionaries 'nânâ' is regarded as Sanscrit.

nîra-m, *water:* assumed derivation 'nî,' *to obtain.* This derivation shows that the word was not familiar to the Sanscrit lexicographers. 'nîram' is rarely used, in comparison with 'ap' (connected with 'aqua'), and 'uda' (connected with 'unda' and 'ὕδωρ'). 'jala,' another Sanscrit word for *water,* is supposed to have been borrowed from the northern vernaculars; whilst I have little or no doubt that to 'nîra' a Drâvidian origin should be ascribed. The corresponding Dravidian word is 'nîr' or 'nîr-u;' and this is the only word properly signifying *water* which the Drâvidian dialects possess. The Telugu ordinarily uses 'nîḷḷu' for 'nîru,' *i.e.,* the plural ('nîrulu,' corrupted to 'nîḷḷu') for the singular; but 'nîru,' the singular, is also occasionally used.

'nîr' is in Gônd softened to 'îr,' and in Brahui it has become 'dîr.' The Malayâlam alone commonly uses for *water* another word, viz., 'veḷḷam,' which properly means *a flood.* This word is used in Tamil to denote *the water with which rice-fields are flooded;* and it has probably thence come to signify *water* in Malayâlam. Even in that dialect, however, 'nîr' is also used. In Tamil the adjective 'taṇ,' *cool*, is so frequently prefixed to 'nîr,' that in the colloquial dialect the compound 'taṇṇîr,' *water*, literally *cold water*, has superseded the original and simple noun.

Whilst I have no doubt that 'nîr' is a true Drâvidian word, it may have descended to the Drâvidian family from some Japhetic source older than the Sanscrit; and hence, it may have some ulterior connection with the Greek 'νηρός' and 'ναρός,' *wet*, (and through them with the modern Greek 'νήρο,' *water*), though these words are supposed (and perhaps correctly) to be derived from 'νάω,' *to flow*.

paṭṭa-m
paṭṭana-m
pattana-m, } *a city, town, or village:* assumed derivation 'paṭa,' *to surround.* The Tamil has borrowed the word 'paṭṭanam' from the Sanscrit; and yet, as in the case of 'kôta,' *a fort*, it will be found, I think, that the Sanscrit word itself was derived originally from the old Drâvidian vernaculars. Professor Wilson conjectures that, 'paṭṭam' is probably identical with the 'pettah,' of Southern India; but the word from which I conceive it to have been derived is 'paṭṭi,' Tam. *a fold for cattle, a pound, a small village*,—a word which constitutes the final portion, or termination, of the names of so many towns and villages in the south; *e.g.*, 'Kôvil-paṭṭi,' *Temple-town.* In Canarese the same word is 'haṭṭi; *e.g.*, *Dim-hutty.* The Old Sanscrit seems to have adopted this word 'paṭṭi,' in addition to its own 'pura' (which is a true Indo-European word), and formed from it first 'paṭṭa-m,' and then 'paṭṭana-m.'

The word 'pettah,' *a suburb* (Tam. 'pêṭṭei'), which is referred to by Wilson, belongs to a different root from 'paṭṭi,' and cannot have been the origin of the Sans. 'paṭṭam.' 'pêṭṭei' is derived from 'pêḍu,' Tam. *a suffix to the names of villages;* which, again, is identical with 'pâḍu' and 'pâḍi,' *a place*, each of which is suffixed to names of villages like 'pêḍu.'

panno, Prakrit, *gold.* This word is supposed by Ellis to be derived from the Sans. 'suvarṇa.' I think it much more probable that it was adopted into the Prakrit from the Tam. 'pon,' or the Tel. 'ponn-u,' *gold.*

palli, *a city, a town, a village.* This is without doubt identical with the Drâvidian word 'paḷḷi,' which is added to various names of places in the South; *e.g.*, *Trichinopoly*, properly 'Trisirâpaḷḷi.'

The Drâvidian origin of this word is sufficiently proved by the circumstance that it is chiefly, if not exclusively, used to denote places which are within the limits of the Drâvidian tongues.

bhaj-a, *to share.*

bhâga, *a portion.* I am doubtful whether to regard these words as derived from the Tamil 'pag-u,' *to divide, to share*, or to suppose both the Sanscrit and the Tamil to be derived from a common and earlier source. Probably the former supposition is in this case the more correct. At all events the Tamil 'pag-u' is a pure, underived Drâvidian root. The noun formed from it, signifying *a share*, is 'pang-u' ('ng' for 'g,' as is often the case); and a collateral root is 'pag-ir,' meaning also *to share.* The Sanscrit word 'pangu' means *lame*, and is altogether unconnected with the Tamil one.

mîna-m, *a fish;* assumed derivation 'mî' ('mînâti'), *to hurt.*

The Drâvidian word for *fish* is 'mîn,' a word which is found in every dialect of the family, and is the only word signifying *fish* which these languages possess. 'mîn' is found even in the small list of decidedly Drâvidian words contained in the Râjmahal dialect. The Gônd has 'mînd.' It seems much more probable that the Sanscrit-speaking people borrowed this word from the Indian aborigines, and then incorporated it in their vocabulary with other words signifying the same object, than that the Drâvidian inhabitants of the Malabar and Coromandel sea-boards were indebted for the word which denoted so important an article of their food and commerce, to a race of inland people coming from the North-West.

Moreover the derivation of 'mîn,' which is supplied by the Drâvidian languages, is as beautiful as the Sanscrit derivation is uncouth.

The root of 'mîn,' *a fish*, is 'min,' Tam., *to glitter, to be phosphorescent.* Hence *the glow-worm* is 'min-mini' by reduplication; and 'mîn,' a verbal noun which is formed from 'min' by the lengthening of the included vowel (like 'pêʀu,' Tam., *a birth*, from 'peʀu,' *to bear*, and 'kôḷ,' *reception*, from 'koḷ,' *to receive*), signifies in poetical Tamil *a star*, as well as *a fish; e.g.*, 'vân-mîn,' *a star* (literally *a sky-sparkler*); and 'aʀu-mîn,' *the Pleiades*, literally *the six stars.* Who that has seen the phosphorescence flashing from every movement of the fish in tropical seas or lagoons at night, can doubt the appropriateness of denoting the fish that dart and sparkle through the waters, as well as the stars that sparkle in the midnight sky, by one and the same word, viz., a word signifying *that which glows or sparkles?*

valacsha-m, *white;* assumed derivation 'vala,' *to go.* Much more probable is the derivation of this word from the Drâvidian 'veḷ,' *white.* Compare also the related Drâvidian words 'veḷi,' *space, the open air;* 'veḷḷi,' *silver;* 'veḷicham,' *light.* The Hungarian 'vilaga,' *light,* appears to be an allied word. Has the Slavonian 'veli,' *white,* been borrowed from a Scythian source? or is it one of those ultimate analogies which bind both families together?

val-a, *to surround.*

valaya-m, *a circlet, a bracelet.* The Drâvidian languages have borrowed the Sanscrit *noun,* with or without modification; but the verb from which the noun has been formed was itself, I doubt not, borrowed by the Sanscrit from the Drâvidian languages. The corresponding Drâvidian root is 'vaḷ-ei,' *to bend, to crook,* metaphorically *to surround.* This word has a larger store of secondary meanings and wider ramifications than the Sanscrit verb. It is also used as a noun, without any formative addition, when it signifies *a hole, a sinuosity; e.g.,* 'eli-vaḷei,' Tam., *a rat-hole.* Whilst the Tamil makes occasional use of the Sanscrit 'valayam,' *a bracelet, an armlet;* it also uses 'vaḷeiyal,' a verbal noun formed from 'vaḷei,' its own verbal root, to signify the same thing. Taking these various circumstances into consideration, I conclude that the Drâvidian verb has certainly not been borrowed from the Sanscrit, and that the Sanscrit verb has probably been derived from the Drâvidian.

In the foregoing list of Drâvidian words which have found a place in the vocabularies of the Sanscrit, I have not included the names of various places and tribes in Southern India which are mentioned in the Sanscrit historical poems, and which have in consequence found a place in the dictionaries. In general the vernacular origin of those words is admitted by Sanscrit lexicographers. In one case, however, a Sanscrit origin has erroneously been attributed to a Drâvidian word of this class. 'Malaya,' *a mountain or mountainous range in Southern India,* is represented as being derived from 'mala,' Sans., *to hold or contain (sandal-wood).* The real origin is unquestionably the Drâvidian 'mal-a' or 'mal-ei,' *a hill or mountain*, and also *a hilly or mountainous country*; and the range of mountains referred to under the name of 'Malaya' is doubtless that of the Southern Ghauts or the 'Malayâla' country, which was called 'Male' by the Arabian geographers.

I now proceed to point out the existence of some real Sanscrit affinities in the vocabularies of the Drâvidian languages. The words which are contained in the following list are true, underived Drâvidian roots, yet they are so closely allied to certain Sanscrit words, that they must be concluded to be the common property of both families of tongues.

Possibly one or two words may have been borrowed at an early period by the one language from the other; but in most cases, if not in every case, there is a preponderance of evidence in favour of the mutually independent origin of both the Sanscrit word and the Drâvidian one, from a source which appears to have been common to both. The various words appear to be too deeply-seated in each family of languages, to have too many ramifications, and (whilst they retain a family likeness) to differ too widely, either in sound or in signification, to allow of the supposition of a direct derivation of the one from the other. Moreover, notwithstanding the general resemblance of the Drâvidian words contained in the following list to the Sanscrit ones with which they are compared, and notwithstanding the prejudice of native grammarians in favour of everything Sanscrit, these words are invariably regarded by native scholars as independent of the Sanscrit, and as underived, 'national' Drâvidian words. Consequently, if a connexion can be traced, as I think it can, between these words and the corresponding Sanscrit ones, it must be the connexion of a common origin. I place in another and subsequent list those Drâvidian words which are more directly allied to the Greek or Latin, the Persian, or some other Extra-Indian member of the Indo-European family, than to the Sanscrit. In this list I place those Drâvidan words which appear to be allied to the Sanscrit alone, or more directly to the Sanscrit than to any other Indo-European language; and it is remarkable how few such words there are, compared with those of the other class. A comparison of the two following lists will, I think, lead to the conclusion that the Indo-European elements which are contained in the Drâvidian languages were introduced into those languages before the Sanscrit separated from its sisters, or at least before the Sanscrit, as a separate tongue, came in contact with the Drâvidian family.

The Drâvidian words which follow are quoted from the Tamil, if it is not expressly mentioned that it is otherwise. Where it is certain that the final vowel or syllable of a Drâvidian word is no part of the root, but is a separable formative accretion, or a particle which has been added merely for euphony, or for the purpose of facilitating enunciation, I have separated such vowel or syllable from the genuine portion of the word by a hyphen.

aḍi, *to strike, to beat, to kill.*
ud-ei, *to kick, to stamp.* Compare 'ut-a,' Sans., *to strike, to knock down.*

aḍ-ei, *to get in, to obtain, to possess.* Compare 'aḍ-a,' Vedic Sans., *to occupy or possess.*

an-u, Tel., en, Tam., } *to speak, to say.* Compare 'aṇ-a,' Sans., *to sound.*

ûr-u, *to creep;* in the higher dialect of the Tamil, *to ride (as in a palanquin).* Compare Sans. 'ur-a,' *to go.*

kaḍ-a, *to pass, to pass by or over.* Compare 'kaṭ-a,' Sans. *to go.*

kaṛudei, *an ass;* Tel. 'gaḍide;' Can. 'katte.' Compare Sans. 'khara,' *an ass.* The Sanscrit word is borrowed and used by the Tamil poets; but it is never confounded with 'kaṛudei,' which is considered to be a purely Drâvidian word. Nevertheless, 'kaṛudei' is evidently allied to 'khara' in origin, and also to the Persian 'char,' and the Kurdish 'kerr.' Compare especially the Laghmani 'karatik,' *a female ass.*

kinna, Can. *small;* Tuda 'kin;' Tel. 'chinna;' Tam. 'śinna.' Compare 'kaṇa,' Sans. *small, a minute particle;* also 'kaṇiga,' *the smallest, the youngest.* There is no doubt of the Tamil 'śinna' having been softened from 'kinna;' but I have some doubt whether the 'n' has not been corrupted from 'ṉ,' for the ultimate root to which 'śinna' is referred by Tamil scholars is 'śiṟ-u.'

kudirei, *a horse;* Can. 'gudure.' Compare Sans. 'ghôḍa,' *a horse,* 'ghôṛati,' *to go as a horse.* The Drâvidian languages have borrowed 'ghôḍa' from the Sans. (in Tamil 'gôṛam,' 'gôḍagam'); but 'kudirei' is regarded as an underived, indigenous Drâvidian word. It is evident, however, that the two words are ultimately related.

kir̤-u, *to cut, to scratch, to rend.*
kir̤-i, *to tear.* Compare 'khur-a,' Sans. *to cut, to scratch.*

keḍ-u, *to spoil or destroy*, or (intransitively) *to be spoiled or destroyed:* verbal noun 'kêḍ-u,' *ruin;* relative participle 'keṭṭa' ('ṭṭ' for 'ḍḍ'), *bad.*

Compare the Sanscrit 'khid-a,' *to suffer pain or misery*, and its verbal noun 'khêda,' *sorrow, distress.* Compare also 'khiṭ-a,' *to terrify*, and its derivative 'khêṭa,' *bad, low.*

If these words are allied to the Drâvidian one, as they appear to be, it must be in virtue of a common origin; for there is not a more distinctively Drâvidian word in existence than 'keḍ-u.'

śiʀ-ei, *to shave:* base 'siʀ'.' Compare Sans. 'kshur-a,' *to scrape*, and 'kshaura,' *shaving.* Compare also the corresponding Greek verbs 'ξυρ-άω,' 'ξυρ-έω,' *to shave;* our English *shear*, from the Germ. 'scheer;' and even the Greek 'κείρ-ω,' *to share.*

śil-ir, *to tremble, to have the hair standing on end.* Compare 'chêl-a,' Sans. *to shake, to tremble.*—See also subsequent list under 'kuḷir,' *cold.*

śe, *to be red.* This root forms the basis of many Tamil adjectives and nouns (*e.g.*, 'śen,' *red*); but is not used anywhere in its primitive unformed shape. Compare 'sôṇa,' Sans. *to be red.*

taḍ-i, *a stick, a club;* verbal theme 'taḍi,' *to be thick or heavy.* Compare 'taḍ-a,' also 'taḍ-i,' Sans. *to strike, to beat.*

tûv-u, *to sprinkle gently (as dust).*
tû-ʀu, *to drizzle, to scatter, to spread abroad (as a report).*

The transitive of 'tu-ʀu' is 'tû-ʀʀu' (pronounced 'tûttru'), *to winnow;* and a derivative from 'tûvu' is 'tûsi,' *dust.* The ultimate root of all these words evidently is 'tû.' Compare 'dhû,' Sans. *to shake, to agitate;* a derivative from which is 'dhûli,' *dust.* Compare also 'tûsta-m,' *dust* (assumed derivation 'tûs-a,' *to sound*), with which our own word '*dust*,' is evidently identical.

From the Sanscrit 'dhûli,' the Tamil has borrowed 'tûḷi' and also 'tûḷ,' *dust:* 'tûs-i,' on the other hand, is a pure Drâvidian word, allied to the Turkish 'tus' or 'tusan,' *powder*, and possibly to the Mongolian 'toghoz; and there cannot be any doubt of the Tamil verbs 'tûv-u' and 'tûʀ-u' being underived Drâvidian themes. 'dhû' or 'tû' appears, therefore, to be the common property of both families of languages; whilst it is in the Drâvidian family that the original meaning of this root appears to have been most faithfully preserved.

nad̤-a, *to walk.* Compare the Sanscrit theme 'nat̤-a,' *to dance, to act, to shake;* derivatives from which are 'nat̤a-m,' *dancing,* 'nát̤a-ka-m,' *a drama, a play.* It seems improbable that the Sanscrit word has been borrowed from the Drâvidian tongues; and yet it is certain that the Drâvidian word has not been borrowed from the Sanscrit, for the Telugu and Canarese make a broad distinction between the Sans. derivative 'nat̤inchu' or 'nat̤isu,' *to dance,* and their own theme 'nad̤uchu' or 'nad̤i,' *to walk;* and whilst the Sanscrit has many words signifying *walking,* the Drâvidian languages have 'nad̤',' *alone.* Probably, therefore, both words have been derived from a common source.

pâd̤-u, Tam. Tel., and Can. *to sing.* Compare Sans. 'pat̤h-a,' *to read, to recite.* The Sans. 'pat̤h-a' is, I have no doubt, the theme from which the corresponding Tel. 'pat̤h-i,' and the Tamil 'pad̤-i,' *to read,* have been borrowed; and the Tamil 'pâd̤a-m,' *a lesson,* is clearly derived from the Sans. 'pât̤ha,' *reading.* 'pâd̤-u,' *to sing,* however, and 'pât̤t̤-u,' *a song,* (Tel. 'pât̤a,' Can. 'pât̤-u,' Gônd 'pât̤â,') are certainly not derivatives from the Sanscrit; but I suspect them to be ultimately related to 'pat̤h-a' and 'pât̤ha,' as descended from some ancient source common to both. The ideas expressed are nearly related; for the *reading* of all Hindus (and of all Orientals) is a sort of intoned 'cantilena;' and even the Sanscrit derivative 'pad̤i,' *to read,* often receives in colloquial Tamil the meaning *to sing.*

pâl, Tam. and Can. *a portion, a part, a class.* Compare Sans. 'phal-a,' *to divide;* also Lat. 'par-s,' *a portion.*—See especially the Semitic affinities of this word.

piʀa, *other; e.g.,* 'piʀa-n,' *another man;* 'hera' (for 'pera'), Can. Compare 'para,' Sans. in the sense of *different,* a sense which it often bears. It is with this preposition, and not with 'pra,' *before, forward,* that I think the Tamil 'piʀa,' *other,* should be compared.

The use of the Tam. 'piʀa,' and that of the Sans. 'para' (in the signification adduced above) are identical; and we might naturally suppose the Tamil word to have been derived from the Sanscrit. The Tamil, however, whilst it admits that 'para' was borrowed from the Sanscrit, regards 'piʀa' as an indigenous theme. The 'R' of 'piRa,' is unknown to the Sanscrit, and is considered to be a distinctive mark of Drâvidian words. Moreover, the Tamil ascribes to 'piRa' the meaning of *other* alone, whilst the Sanscrit 'para' has a much wider range of signification.

It is remarkable that the Tamil has another root, 'piR-a-gu,' *after*, (ultimate base 'piR,') which is considered to be perfectly independent of, and unconnected with, 'piRa,' *other;* and yet that this very meaning, *after*, is one of the many significations which are attributed to 'para' in Sanscrit.

It may be concluded, I think, that 'para' and 'piRa,' are radically allied; and yet the supposition that the one is derived from the other, is quite inadmissible. Each is too deeply seated in its own family of tongues to allow of this supposition, and we are therefore driven to conclude, that both have been derived from a common source.

pâl, *milk*. The Drâvidian languages do not contain the verbal theme from which this word is derived. We may compare it with the Sanscrit 'pâyasa,' *milk*, and also with 'pâya,' *water*, Zend 'péo,' Affghan 'poï;' all of which words are derived from 'pâ,' Sans. *to drink*, a root which runs through almost all the Indo-European languages.

Possibly the Drâvidian 'pâl,' *milk*, may be a verbal noun formed from this very theme; for a large number of verbal nouns are formed in Tamil by simply adding 'al' or 'l' to the root. Notwithstanding this, the purely Drâvidian character and connexions of this word 'pâl,' preclude the supposition of its *direct* derivation from the Sanscrit 'pâ.'

pêś-u, *to speak*. Compare 'bhâsh-a,' Sans. *to speak*.

pû, *a flower*, or *to blossom*, Tam., Tel., and Can. Compare 'phull-a,' Sans. *to blossom*, and 'pushpa,' *a flower*.

Indo-European Affinities.

Section II.

EXTRA-SANSCRITIC OR WEST INDO-EUROPEAN AFFINITIES, VIZ.:

Drâvidian words which appear to be specially allied to words that are contained in the languages of the Western or non-Sanscritic branches of the Indo-European family.

Some of the words which are contained in the following list have Sanscrit as well as Classical or West-Âryan analogies; but they have been placed in this, rather than in the preceding, list, because the West-Âryan affinities are clearer, more direct, and more certain than the Sanscrit ones. The greater number, however, of the words that follow, though indubitably connected with the Western tongues, and especially with the Greek and Latin, exhibit no analogy whatever to any words contained in the Sanscrit.

If the existence of this class of analogies can be clearly established, it must be concluded either that the Drâvidians were at an early period near neighbours of the West-Âryan tribes, subsequently to the separation of those tribes from the Sanscrit-speaking people, or that both races were descended from a common source.

The majority of the Drâvidian words which exhibit West-Âryan analogies, do not belong to that primary, rudimental class to which the words that the Drâvidian languages have in common with the Scythian are to be referred. Nevertheless, they are so numerous, many of them are so remarkable, and, when all are viewed together, the analogy which they bring to light is so distinct, that an ultimate relation of *some* kind between the Drâvidian and the Indo-European families, may be regarded as conclusively established.

As before, the Drâvidian words are to be regarded as Tamil, except it is stated that they are taken from some other dialect.

aś-ei, *to shake.* Compare '*σεί-ω*,' *to shake, to move to and fro.*

arn-vi, *a waterfall;* from 'ar-u,' *to ebb, to trickle down.* Compare 'riv-us,' Latin, *a brook*, English '*river*;' also the verbal theme of those words, '*ῥέ-ω*' or '*ῥύ-ω*' (as in '*ῥύη*'), *to flow.*

al-ei, *to wander, to be unsteady:* 'alei,' as a noun, means *a wave.* Compare '*ἀλά-ομαι*,' *to wander;* Germ. 'welle,' Armen. 'alik,' *a wave.*

av-â, *desire;* also 'âv-al,' a verbal noun, derived from an obsolete root 'âv-u,' *to desire.* Compare Sans. 'av-a,' of which one of the rarer meanings is *to desire.* The affinity between 'avâ' and the Latin 'ave-o,' *to desire,* is still more complete, inasmuch as this is the only meaning of the word in Latin, as in Tamil.—See also 'Semitic Affinities.'

avv-a, Tel., *a grandmother.* In Tuda 'avva,' means *a mother;* in Canarese 'avva' or 'avve' means either *a mother* or *grandmother,* or, generally, *an old woman.* The ordinary Tamil form of this word is 'auv-ei,' an honorific term for *a matron, an elderly lady,* but 'avv-ei' is also used. Compare the Latin 'av-us,' *a grandfather;* 'avi-a,' *a grandmother.* The root of the Latin word appears to have been applicable to any elderly relation; *e.g.,* 'av-unculus,' *a maternal uncle.*

âvi,' *a spirit,* literally *vapour, breath;* then *life,* and also *a spirit:* verbal theme 'âvi,' *to yawn, to breathe.* Compare the Gothic 'ahma,' *spirit;* the Sanscrit 'âtma,' *self,* or *soul;* the Greek 'ἄνεμος,' *wind;* the Latin 'anima,' and the Tamil 'ânma,' *soul* or *spirit.* Compare also the High Tamil 'ân-dal,' *the breath.* The resemblance of the Tam. 'âvi' to the Greek 'ἄω,' *to blow,* is especially remarkable.

iṛ-u, *to draw, to pull.* Compare 'ἐρύ-ω,' *to draw.* Compare also 'eḷe,' the Canarese equivalent of 'iṛu,' with 'ἕλκ-ω,' *to drag,* a word which is probably related to 'ἐρύ-ω,' through that alliance of 'r' to 'l' which is apparent in all languages.

iru-mbu, *iron;* from 'iru' or 'ir,' the ultimate root, and 'mbu,' a formative, euphonised from 'bu' or 'vu:' Tel. 'inumu.' Compare the Saxon 'iren,' Danish 'iern,' Armenian 'ergad.' The 'r' of these words has been hardened from 's,' as appears from comparing them with the German 'eisen' and the Sanscrit 'ayas.' None of these words, however, though possibly they may have some ulterior connexion with the Tamil, seems to be so nearly related to 'iru' as the Motor (a Samoïede dialect), 'ur.'

în-u, *to bring forth young,* said of cattle only. Compare Engl. '*to yean,*' Sax. 'eanian.'

uyar,' *high;* when used as a verb, *to raise.* Compare 'ἀείρ-ω' *to raise up;* also 'ἀερ' in 'ἀερ-θείς' (Aor. pass. past), and in the adverb 'ἀέρ-δην,' *lifted up.* Compare also 'ἀήρ,' *the air;* Armenian 'wor,' *high;* Ossete 'arw,' *heaven.*

ur-i, Can., *to burn;* Tam., 'er-i.' Compare 'ur-o,' Lat., *to burn;* Armenian 'ôr,' *fire;* Affghan 'or,' 'wur.' There are also very remarkable Semitic analogies; *e.g.*, Hebrew 'ûr,' *fire*, and 'ôr,' *light*.

uṛ-u, *to plough.* Compare Lat. 'ar-o;' Greek 'ἀρό-ω;' Lithuanian 'aru.' 'uṛu-dal,' *tillage*, may also be compared with the equivalent Greek 'ἀρο-τὸς.'

uḷ-ei, *mire.* Compare 'ἕλ-ος,' *a marsh*.

ûḷ-ei, *a howling.* Lat. 'ululo,' *to howl;* Greek 'ὀλολύζω;' English 'howl.'

eÿ, *to shoot (an arrow), to cast (a dart).* Compare 'ἰὸς,' *an arrow;* 'ἵω,' *to shoot, to cast;* 'ἕω,' *to send.*

eṛ-u, *to rise, to get up.* Compare Lat. 'ori-or,' *to rise, to get up.* 'eṛu jñâyiʀu,' Tam., *the rising sun*, may be compared with the Latin 'ori-ens sol.'

eḷl-â, *all.* The Canarese 'ellar,' *all they*, corresponding to the Tamil 'eḷlôr' (for 'ellâr'), together with the Tamil 'eḷlîr,' *all ye* (from 'ell,' *all*, and 'îr,' for 'nîr,' *you*), prove that the ultimate Drâvidian root of this word is 'el.' A vowel has been euphonically added to 'el' (at first a short vowel, afterwards lengthened), in consequence of which addition the consonant is doubled by dialectic rules.

Compare Ossete 'al,' 'ali,' 'all;' Saxon 'eal;' Danish 'al;' English 'all.' Probably the Greek 'ὅλ-ος' and the Hebrew 'kol' are allied rather to our own 'whole,' Lat. 'salv-us,' Sans. 'sarva,' than to the Drâvidian and Germanic 'el,' *all.*

ôr-am, *border, brim, margin, coast.* Compare Lat. 'ora,' *border, margin.* 'ôr-am' has no connexion with any Drâvidian word signifying *mouth;* and possibly the derivation of the Lat 'ora,' from 'os,' 'oris,' may be open to question. The corresponding word in Gujarathi, Marathi, and Hindi, is 'kôr.'

kaḍ-i, *to cut, to rend, to reprove.* 'katti,' *a knife.* Compare Sans. 'krit-a,' *to cut*, but especially the English 'cut;' Norman 'cotu,' Welsh 'cateia;' Latin 'caed-o.' Compare also the Persian and Ossete 'kard,' *a knife*, and the Sanscrit 'karttari,' which words, however, are more nearly related to 'krut-a,' Sans., than to the English 'cut.'

kaṇ, *the eye;* 'kâṇ' (in the preterite 'kaṇ'), *to see*, also *to mark, to consider, to think.* In the latter sense it becomes euphonically 'kaṇṇu' in Tamil, but the base remains unchanged. In Telugu, the ordinary 'n,' the nasal of the dental row, is used instead of 'ṇ,' the cerebral nasal.

Compare the Welsh 'ceniaw,' *to see;* English 'ken,' *view, power or reach of vision.* In Webster's English Dictionary 'kanna' is said to be *an eye* in Sanscrit; whereas it is exclusively a Drâvidian word. This mistake may be compared with that of Klaproth in representing 'kuruta,' *blind,* as a Sanscrit word, instead of referring it to the Drâvidian languages, to which alone it belongs. Possibly the Drâvidian 'kaṇ,' *to see, to consider,* may have some ulterior connexion with the Gothic 'kunn-an,' *to know;* Greek 'γνῶ-ναι;' Sans. 'jñâ;' Latin 'gna' ('gnarus'), Old High German 'chann.'

The different shades of meaning which are attributed in Greek to 'γνῶ-ναι' and 'εἰδέ-ναι,' seem to corroborate this supposition; for the latter is represented as meaning *to know by reflection, to know absolutely,* whereas the former means *to perceive, to mark,* and may therefore have an ulterior connexion with the Drâvidian root.

karaḍi, *a bear;* from 'karaḍu,' *rough, knotty, uneven,* the ultimate base of which must be 'kara' or 'kar.'

The Tuda word for *a bear* is 'kar.' Compare the Persian 'chars,' Kurd 'harj,' and even the Latin 'urs-us.' Compare also the Samoïede 'korgo,' and the Tungusian 'kuti.'

kaṛug-u, *an eagle.* Compare Persian 'kergish,' Ossete 'kartziga.'

kaḷ-a, Can., *to steal;* Tam., 'kaḷavu,' *a theft;* Malayâlam, 'kaḷḷ.am,' *a lie.* Compare Latin 'clep-o,' *to steal;* Greek 'κλαπ-είς.'—See also 'Scythian Affinities.'

gav-i, Can., *a cave, a cell;* Tam., 'keb-i,' *a cave.* The equivalent Sanscrit words are 'guhâ,' *a cavern,* from 'guh-a,' *to conceal,* and 'gaha,' *a cave, a forest,* from 'gah-a,' *to be impervious.* 'guhâ' has become in Tamil 'kugei;' but the Tamil 'kebi' and the Can. 'gavi,' are altogether independent words.

Compare with them the Latin 'cave-a,' *a cavity, a den,* from 'cav-us,' *hollow;* theme 'cav-o,' *to hollow out:* and with this compare the Tel. 'kapp-u,' *to cover over,* the origin of the Tamil 'kapp-al,' *a ship,* and also, probably, of 'keb-i,' and 'gav-i,' *a cave.*—See also 'Scythian Affinities.'

kâÿ, *to be hot, to burn*. The Telugu 'kâgu,' Can. 'kây-u,' *to burn*, and the Can. 'kâge,' *heat*, compared with the Tamil 'kânggei,' show that the ultimate root is 'kâ,' to which 'y' or 'gu' is added dialectically as a formative. The only Sanscrit word which seems to be at all related to this Drâvidian one, is 'kâm-a,' *to desire;* and we should not, perhaps, have suspected it to be related, were it not for its connexion with the Hebrew 'ḥâm-ad,' *to desire*, and the derivation of that word from 'ḥâm-am' (base '.âm'), *to be warm*.

Compare with the Drâvidian 'kâ' or 'kâÿ,' the Greek 'καί-ω' (Attic 'κά-ω'), *to burn, to be hot*. The words seem absolutely identical. Liddell and Scott represent 'κάω' to be connected with the Sanscrit 'such-a,' *to dry*. How much more nearly connected with the Drâvidian 'kâÿ!' Besides, the Drâvidian languages have another word which seems to have a real relation to 'sush-a,' viz., 'suḍ-u,' *to burn*.

ki, Gônd, *to do;* Ku 'gi;' Kôta 'ke;' Can. 'gêy-u;' Tel. 'chêÿ; Tam. 'śeÿ.' The harder form is always to be regarded as the primitive one, and hence 'chêy' and 'śeÿ' are to be referred to the Can. 'gêy,' and that to an ultimate 'ke,' allied to the Gônd 'ki.'

Compare the Old Persian 'ki,' *to do;* a root which is probably related to the Sans. 'kri,' but more nearly still to the Drâvidian words now quoted. The Pracrit form of 'kar' (for 'kri') is 'ka;' *e.g.*, 'ka-da,' *made*, instead of 'kar-da:' and the corresponding Marathi is 'ke;' *e.g.*, 'ke-lâ,' *made*. The Kotra has 'kek,' *to do*.

kiṇḍ-u, *to stir, to search, to turn up the ground*. Compare 'κεντ-έω,' *to prick, to goad, to spur on*.

kiṛa, *old* (not by use, but with respect to length of life). Compare Sans. 'jaras,' *age*, but especially the Greek words signifying *age, aged*, viz., 'γῆρα-ς,' 'γήραι-ός,' 'γεραι-ός,' 'γέρ-ων.'—See also the Scythian affinities of this word.

kiṛa-mei (base 'kiṛa'), *a week*, literally *property, possession*, each portion of a week being astrologically regarded as the *property* or *inheritance* of some planet. Compare Ossete 'kuri,' 'kôre,' *a week;* Georgian 'kuire.' Possibly these words are derived from the Greek 'κυρι-ακή,' *Sunday, the Lord's day;* but whence is the Greek word derived? from 'κύρι-ος,' *a Lord, a possessor*, the base of which seems to be allied to the Tamil 'kiṛa,' *possession*.

kiḷ-ei, *a young branch.* Compare Ossete 'kalius;' Servian 'galusa;' Greek 'κλάδος,' *a young shoot, a branch.* The theme of the Greek word is 'κλά-ω,' *to lop, to break;* and the Tamil 'kiḷ-ei,' considered as a verbal theme, means not only *to sprout,* but also *to pluck off.* 'kiḷḷ-u,' *to pinch, to pluck,* is a collateral theme.

kupp-ei, *sweepings, refuse, dung, a dung-heap.* Compare 'κόπρος,' *dung, dirt, a farm-yard.*

kuʀ-u, *short, brief:* derivative verb 'kuʀu-gu,' *to diminish:* collateral root 'kuʀ-ei,' *a defect, to be or make defective.* Compare Persian 'chord,' *short,* German 'kurz;' Latin 'curt-us,' *short, small, defective.* On comparing the Latin word 'curt-us,' with such words as 'sert-us,' *connected,* from 'ser-o,' it may be concluded that 'curt-us,' is derived from an obsolete verbal theme 'cur-o,' which would be identical with the Tamil 'kuʀ-u.'

kuru-ḍu, *blindness, blind;* ultimate base 'kuru' (like 'kiṛa,' the ultimate base of 'kiṛaḍu,' *old*). Compare Persian 'kûr;' Kurd 'kor;' Ossete 'kurm,' *blind.*

kuri, Can., *a sheep;* Tuda 'gurri.' Compare Irish 'kaora;' Georg. 'chhuri.'

kuḷ-ir, *cold,* Tam. and Can.: ultimate base, by analogy, 'kuḷ;' Telugu and Canarese 'chali,' *cold:* collateral root, 'śilir,' Tam., *to tremble.* 'kûdal' and 'kûdir,' *cold,* are doubtless derivative or allied words. Compare German 'kühl;' Saxon 'cyl,' 'col,' 'cele;' Russian 'cholod;' English 'cool,' 'cold;' Latin 'gelu;' English 'chill.'—See also 'Scythian Affinities.'

kêḷ, *to hear,* Tam. and Can. Compare Latin 'aus-*cul*-to,' *to hear, to listen;* also the Greek 'κλύ-ω,' *to hear;* Welsh 'clyw,' *hearing;* Irish 'cluas,' *the ear;* Lithuanian 'klau,' *to hear;* Latin 'clu-o,' *to be called.*—See also the Scythian affinities, which are still closer than these.

kol, *to kill.* Compare Russian 'kolyu,' *to stab;* and especially the English 'kill' and 'quell.'—See also 'Scythian Affinities.'

śâkk-u, *a sack.* Compare Greek 'σάκκ-ος' or 'σάκ-ος,' *a sack.*—See also 'Semitic' and Scythian Affinities.

Greek lexicographers derive this word from a Greek etymon; but we can suppose it to have sprung from a Greek base only on the supposition (which is an inadmissible one) that the Greeks were the great carrying traders of antiquity. The Tamil word 'sâkk-u,' denotes *a loose bag of coarse cloth*, but not also as in Hebrew and Greek, *the coarse cloth itself of which the bag or sack is made.* Those languages, therefore, would appear to come nearer than the Tamil to the original source of the word.

śâtt-u, *to close a door, to shut;* Saxon 'scytt-an,' *to shut in;* Dutch 'schutt-en,' *to stop;* English 'to shut.'

śâḍ-i (pronounced 'jâḍi'), *a jar.* Compare Spanish 'jarra;' English 'jar.'

śâl, *a bucket.* Compare 'σηλ-ία,' *any flat board or tray with a raised rim.*—See also 'Semitic Affinities.'

śivar-u, Can., *a splinter.* Compare English 'a shiver.'

śîʀ-u (pronounced 'süʀ-u'), *to hiss.* Compare 'συρ-ίζω,' *to pipe*, also *to hiss;* Latin 'su-*surr*-us,' *a whispering*, or *whistling.* Our English word '*hiss*' is evidently mimetic; but 'śîʀu' and its allied roots bear no trace of an imitative origin.

śuḍ-u, Tam. and Can., *to heat, to burn, to fire:* related root 'śuḍ-ar,' *to shine.* Compare. Persian 'sus-an;' Kurd 'sodj-an;' Ossete 'suds-in,' *to burn.* Compare also Sans. 'sush-a,' and Latin 'sicc-o,' *to dry.* Probably Sans. 'kuḍ-a,' *to heat, to burn*, contains the same base.

śepp-u, *to speak.* Compare 'ἔπ-ω' (for 'Ϝέπ-ω'), *to speak.*

śel,' *to go, to proceed.* This is unquestionably a pure Drâvidian root, and abounds in derivatives; *e.g.*, 'śel,' *the white ant;* 'śel-avu,' *expenditure;* 'śel-vam,' *prosperity.* It forms its preterite also in a manner which is peculiar to pure Drâvidian verbs.

It is obviously allied to the Sans. 'shal-a,' *to go or move*, 'shêl-a,' *to move, to tremble;* 'chal-a' and 'char-a,' *to go, to shake, to totter;* and also to the Hindustani derivative, 'chal,' *to go.* Close as these analogies are, 'śel' appears to bear an equally close resemblance to 'cel,' the obsolete Latin root, signifying *to go*, from which are formed 'celer,' and also 'excell-o' and 'præ-cell-o.' The same root is in Greek 'κελ;' *e.g.*, 'κέλ-ης,' *a runner*, and 'κέλλω,' *to urge on.*

tag-u, *fit, proper, worthy.* Compare 'δίκ-αιος,' *right, proper, just.*

tayir, *curds.* Compare 'τυρ-ός,' *cheese.*

tin, *to eat;* 'tindi,' *food.* Compare 'τένδ-ω,' *to gnaw, to eat daintily;* 'τένθης,' *a gourmand.*

tiʀ-a (pronounced nearly like 'toʀa'), *to open;* 'tiʀ-a-vu,' *an opening, a way, a means.* Compare Greek 'θύρα,' *a door;* German 'thur;' Old High German 'tor;' Gothic 'daur; Sanscrit 'dvâra.' These words are commonly derived from the Sanscrit theme 'dvru,' *to cover;* but as they all mean not the door-*leaf,* but the door-*way,* and metaphorically *a way,* or *means,* this derivation is far inferior to that of the Drâvidian 'tiʀa' or 'toʀa' (Can. 'teʀa'), *to open.*

tîṇḍ-u, *to touch, to kindle.* Compare Gothic 'tandya,' *I kindle.* Possibly there may be a remote connexion also with the Sans. 'dah,' *to burn,* the intensitive of which is 'dandah.' On the other hand, the 'ṇ' of the Tam. 'tîṇḍ-u' is probably euphonic, for it disappears in the Can. 'tîḍ-u.'

teḷ, *clear.* Compare 'δῆλ-ος,' *clear, manifest.*

tol-ei (base 'toḷ'), *distance,* adverbially *distant.* As a verb, 'tol-ei' signifies *to end, or come to an end.* Compare 'τῆλ-ε,' *far off,* which Buttmann derives from 'τέλ-ος,' *an end.*

tripp-u, Tel., *to turn;* also, by corruption, 'tippu;' Can. 'tiru-pu;' Tamil 'tiru-ppu.' These are causal or active verbs, and the corresponding neuter or intransitive verb signifying *to turn,* is in Tel. 'tiru-gu,' in Tamil 'tiru-mbu.' The Canarese has 'tiru-hu,' 'tiru-vu,' and 'tiru gu.' There are also a few related themes; *e.g.,* 'tiru-gu,' Tam., *to twist* or *turn;* from which is derived 'tirugal,' *a mill.* From a comparison of all these words, it is manifest that their common base is 'tiru,' to which various formative additions have been made, for the purpose of expressing modifications of meaning. 'tiru' itself, also, has evidently arisen through the phonetic necessities of the language, from 'tru' or 'tri,' which is to be regarded as the ultimate base. Compare Greek 'τρέπ-ω,' *to turn;* which bears a remarkable likeness to the Tel. 'tripp-u,' and the initial portion of which (with that of our English 'turn'), seems closely allied to the Drâvidian base, 'tru' or 'tri.' Probably the Sanscrit 'tarku,' *a spindle,* is not a collateral word, but one which has been directly borrowed by the Sanscrit from the Drâvidian tongues.

naś-u, *to crush, to squash.* Compare 'νάσσ-ω,' *to squeeze close, to stamp down.*

nar-a, Can., *a tendon, a sinew, catgut;* sometimes, but improperly, *a vein* or *artery:* adjectivally *wiry, stringy.* Tel. 'naramu;' Tam. 'narambu;' Rajmahal 'nâru.' 'nara' or 'nar' appears to be the ultimate base; with which compare the Latin 'nerv-us' and the Greek 'νεῦρ-ον,' *a tendon, a ligament.*

nin-ci, *to think, to remember;* Can., 'nen-i.' This word is undoubtedly a Tamil primitive, and is probably connected with 'neñjju,' Tam., *the soul,* literally *the upper part of the chest, the diaphragm.* [With respect to this double signification of the word 'neñjj-u,' compare the twofold meaning of 'φρήν,' in Greek, viz., *the diaphragm or chest* (supposed to be the seat of the mental faculties), and also *the mental faculties* themselves.]

If there is any analogy between the Drâvidian 'nin' or 'nen,' and the Sanscrit 'man,' *to think,* it comes to light only by comparing it with the corresponding Greek word 'νό-εω,' by reduplication 'νενό-ημαι.' 'μνά-ομαί,' *to think on, to remember,* and 'μέν-ος,' *wish,* are in perfect accordance with the Sanscrit 'mana,' and are probably more ancient than 'νό-εω;' of which the initial 'ν' has possibly been changed from 'μ.' The Drâvidian 'nen' or 'nin' has in like manner, I conceive, been changed from an older 'men' or 'min,' allied to 'man-a' and 'μέν-ος.'

nînd-u (also 'nîñj-u'), *to swim;* 'nîch-u' and 'nîtt-al,' *swimming.* Tel. 'îd-u,' Can. 'îch-u,' *to swim;* Tel. derivative noun, 'îta,' *swimming.* A comparison of these words shows that the final 'ndu' of the Tamil verb has been euphonised from 'du.' I have no doubt that the base of this verb is simply 'nîd' or 'nî;' of which 'mî,' Can., *to bathe,* is probably a collateral form.

Compare 'nî' with the Latin 'no' ('navi'), *to swim;* Greek 'νέ-ω,' also 'νή-χω;' Sanscrit 'nau;' Greek 'ναῦ-ς,' *a boat.* Compare also 'nîd-u' (the supposititious original of both 'nînd-u' and 'îd-u') with the Latin secondary verb 'nat-o.' Bopp derives these Indo-European words from 'snâ,' Sans., *to bathe;* but their root is not, I conceive, in Sanscrit. It is only in the Classical and in the Drâvidian tongues that it is found.

neÿ, *to weave.* Probably 'nûl,' *a thread,* and also *to spin,* is a word of collateral origin. As 'pâl,' *milk,* may have been derived rom 'pâ,' *to drink,* and 'tûḷ,' *dust,* from 'tû,' *to scatter,* so 'nûl,' *a thread,* may be supposed to be derived from an obsolete 'nû,' *to spin:* and this root would naturally be concluded to be a correlative of 'neÿ,' *to weave.*

Compare 'νέ-ω,' *to spin,* 'νῆ-μα,' *a thread;* and more especially the Latin 'neo,' which not only means *to spin, to entwine,* but also, secondarily, *to weave; e.g.,* 'tunicam quam molli neverat auro.' Virg.

A collateral root, and one which bears, perhaps, a still closer analogy to the Drâvidian 'neÿ,' *to weave,* is that which we find in the German 'näh-en,' *to sew;* Latin 'nec-to,' *to knit, to join;* and Sanscrit 'nah-a,' *to bind, to tie.*

paḍ-u, *to suffer, to receive or feel an impression;* a word which is used as an auxiliary in all the Drâvidian languages in the formation of passive verbs: derivative noun, 'pâṭ-u,' Tel. and Can., *a suffering.*

Compare Latin 'pat-ior,' and Greek 'παθ-εῖν,' each of which has precisely the same meaning as the Drâvidian verb.

paḍ-u, Tel. *to fall.* This verb is identical in Telugu with the preceding one; but the meaning, *to fall,* which it bears in Telugu, in addition to that of *to suffer,* suggests a different set of affinities. Even in Tamil it means *to hit,* or *to light,* as well as *to suffer, or receive an impression.* Compare Slavonian 'pad,' *to fall;* Sanscrit 'pat,' *to fall, to fly;* Zend 'pat,' *to fly;* Latin 'pet' in 'im-pet-o,' *to fall upon;* Greek 'πέτ-ομαι,' *to fly,* and also 'πίπτ-ω,' *to fall.*

paṇ, *to make, to work, to produce:* colloquial form 'paṇṇu;' Tel. 'pannu.' This word is evidently allied to the Sanscrit 'paṇ-a, *to do business, to negotiate;* the noun corresponding to which, 'paṇa,' means *business,* hence *property.* This noun, 'paṇa,' has been borrowed by the Drâvidian languages; but the only signification which it bears is *money.* Whilst 'paṇa-m,' *money,* is always admitted by Drâvidian grammarians to be a Sanscrit derivative, they regard 'paṇ(ṇ)-u,' *to make, to work,* as a primitive Drâvidian word; and this view is confirmed by the circumstance that it stands at the head of a large family of derivatives and collaterals; some of which are 'paṇṇ-ei,' *tillage, a rice-field;* 'paṇ-i,' *service, humility;* 'paṇikku,' *a design, a clever performance;* 'paṇi,' Malayâlam, *difficulty, toil;*

'pani,' Tel., *work*. It is especially worthy of notice that 'paṇ-i,' as a verbal root, signifying *to be subservient, to obey, to worship*, has become in its turn the parent of a host of derivative words.

I have no doubt that 'paṇ,' *to make, to work*, has an ulterior connexion with the Sanscrit 'paṇ-a,' *to negotiate;* but it appears to have a still closer connexion with the Greek 'πον-έω,' *to toil, to work hard*, 'πόν-ος,' *work, a task*, and 'πέν-ομαι,' *to work, to toil*. Compare also the Babylonian 'ban-as,' *to do, to make*.

pamp-u, Tel., *to send:* a softened form of the same word is 'ampu,' from which is derived the Tamil 'anuppu,' *to send*, and 'ambu,' *an arrow;* also the Tel. 'ampa,' *an arrow*, and 'ampakam,' *dismission*. It is obvious from a comparison of these words, that the Telugu has best preserved the original form. Telugu grammarians suppose 'pampu,' *to send*, to be a causal from 'pô,' *to go;* and it is certain that some causals are formed in Telugu by adding 'mp' to the root. This supposition, however, would lead us to expect 'pômpu' instead of 'pampu;' and it is inconsistent with the existence of a causal formed from 'pampu' itself, viz., 'pamp-i-inchu,' *to cause to send*, corresponding to the Tamil 'anuppu-vi.' I therefore, think that 'pamp-u,' *to send*, should be regarded as a primitive word.

Compare the verb 'pamp-u' with Greek 'πεμπ-ω,' *to send*, and the noun 'pamp-u,' *a dismission*, with 'πομπ-ή.'

paḷ-e, Can., *old, long in use, of ancient date;* Tamil 'paṛa.' Compare 'παλαι-ός,' *old, ancient, antiquated;* 'πάλαι,' *in olden time*.

paṛ-u, *to fruit, to become ripe;* 'paṛa-m,' *a ripe fruit;* Can. 'paḷa' ('ṛ' changed into 'ḷ'); Tel. 'paṇḍu' ('ṛ' changed dialectically into 'ḍ' and then nasalised). Compare Persian 'ber,' *fruit;* Armenian 'perk;' Latin 'fru-or,' 'fru-x.' Compare also the Sanscrit 'phala,' *fruit;* a word which has been borrowed by the Tamil in the sense of *effect* or *profit*, but which is never confounded by it with its own 'paṛa-m.' I suspect this root to be identical in origin with the preceding one. In Tamil *to be old* or *long in use*, is 'paṛa;' *to be ripe*, 'paṛu;' and both the words themselves and the ideas they express seem to be allied.—See also, however, the Semitic analogies of this word.

pal, *many, various;* 'pal-ar,' *many people;* 'pal-a,' *many things.* The ordinary adjectival form of this word, which is used without discrimination of number or gender, is 'pala;' but 'pal' is more classical. There is also a verb formed from the same base, 'pal-gu,' *to become many, to be multiplied, to increase.*

If there is any connexion between this word and the Sanscrit 'puru' (for 'paru') *much,* it is a very distant one; whereas 'pal' appears to be closely allied to the Greek 'πολύς,' 'πολύ,' *many, much,* and the Latin 'plus.' Compare 'palar,' *many persons,* with 'οἱ πολλοί,' *the many, the majority.* The Sanscrit 'puru' is derived from 'prî,' *to fill* ('pi-par-mi'); but the Tamil 'pal' is an ultimate root.

paḷḷ-i, *a town, a village, a school, a mosque;* in Travancore *a church,* and generally *a place of concourse.* Compare 'πόλις,' *a city,* from 'πολέω,' *to haunt, to frequent.*

'palli' is found in Sanscrit dictionaries; but I consider it to be a purely Drâvidian word.

piy̆kk-u, *to rend in pieces, to card, to comb cotton, to pick.* Compare 'πέκ-ω,' *to comb;* English 'to pick.'

pir-i, *to divide;* also 'pôṛ,' *to cleave.* Compare Sanscrit 'phal-a,' *to divide;* but especially the Latin 'par-s,' *a portion;* also 'portio,' from the supposititious root 'por-o' or 'par-o,' *to apportion, to divide.* The Greek 'πόρ-ω,' in the sense of *im*-par-*ting,* is doubtless an allied word. The closest and most remarkable analogies, however, are those which we find in the Semitic vocabulary,—which see.

piḷḷ-ei, Tam., *a child;* Tel. 'pilla;' Can. 'piḷḷe;' Latin 'puell-us,' 'puell-a,' *a boy, a girl.* If the Latin word is derived from 'puer-ulus,' it is probably unconnected with 'pill-ei.' Perhaps a more reliable affinity is that of 'fil-ius,' 'fil-ia,' *a son, a daughter,* supposed to mean literally *a suckling.*—See also the 'Scythian Vocabulary.'

pugaṛ, *to praise.* Compare Old Prussian 'pagir-u,' *I praise,* and the corresponding noun 'pagir-sna,' *praise.*

puʀ-am, *a side,* especially *the outside, the exterior; e.g.,* 'appuʀam,' *that side;* 'ippuʀam,' *this side:* adjectivally 'puʀ-attu,' *external:* adverbially 'puʀambâga' (puʀam-b'-âga'), *externally:* as a verbal theme 'puʀappaḍu' ('puʀa-(p)-paḍu'), *to set out:* Can. 'pora-ge,' *outside:* 'pora-ḍu,' *to set forth.* There is, doubtless an ulterior connexion between 'puRa-m,' *the outside, externally,* and 'piRa,' *other;* yet they are not to be regarded as one and the same word; and 'puRam' has affinities of its own, as well as meanings of its own. Compare Greek 'παρά,' *beside,* in which one of the meanings of the Drâvidian word appears, whilst the meaning of *side* is not conveyed by the correlative Sanscrit 'para.' Compare especially the Latin 'foris,' *abroad;* 'forum,' *a public place;* 'fori,' *the decks of a ship,* with the Canarese 'pora,' *outside.* This seems a more natural derivation of 'foris' than the Greek 'θύρα,' *a door,* a word which I have connected with the Drâvidian 'tiRa,' *to open.* In the Drâvidian languages 'f' is unknown, and 'p' is always used instead.

pûś-ei, *a cat,* especially in the South-Tamil idiom. In the Cashgar dialect of the Affghan, 'pusha' signifies *a cat.* Compare Irish 'pus,' *a cat;* English 'puss.'

pill-i, Tel., *a cat.* 'pul-i,' signifies *a tiger,* or more commonly *a cheetah,* or *hunting leopard,* in all the Drâvidian dialects, and *a cat* also in Canarese. Compare Persian 'pelang,' *a tiger;* but especially the Latin 'feles' or 'felles,' *a cat,* a word which is also used to denote various animals of a similar character.

per-u, *great,* also 'per-ia:' another form of the same adjective in Tamil, and probably a more ancient one, is 'par-u.' Possibly 'pal-a,' *many,* is a related root, seeing that there appears to be the same relation between 'per-u' or 'par-u,' *great,* and 'pal-a,' *many,* that there is between 'siR-u,' *small,* and 'sil-a,' *few.* 'per-u,' *great,* is also used as a verbal theme, and in that connexion it signifies *to increase.*

Compare Sanscrit 'puru,' *much,* 'varh' and 'vih,' *to grow;* but especially the Zend 'berez' and 'barez,' *great.*

peR-u, *to bear, to bring forth, to obtain, to get or beget:* verbal noun 'pêR-u,' *a bringing forth* or *birth, a thing obtained* or *a benefit.* 'piR-a,' *to be born, to proceed from,* is doubtless a related word; and there is probably a relationship between these words (especially the latter) and 'piRa,' *other, foreign;* 'puRa-m,' *the exterior,* and even 'poR-u,' *to bear* or *sustain.* Compare the Latin 'par-io,' 'pe-per-i,' *to bring forth, to acquire.* Possibly the ultimate base of all these words is the Indo-European preposition, 'pra,' signifying *progressive motion, expansion, excess,* &c.; and the Zend form of this preposition, 'fra,' indicates the propriety of classing the Latin 'fru-x' with the other derivatives. See also the Semitic Vocabulary.

pêÿ, *a demon.* Compare the English 'fay,' *an elf;* French 'fée.'

peiy-an, *a boy, a servant;* also 'pay-an,' 'pay-al,' and 'peiy-al:' Mala. 'pei-tal;' Can. 'hei-da.' The termination 'al' is that of the neuter verbal noun; and consequently 'payal' might be applied to a youth of either sex, though restricted in Tamil to the masculine. The Malayâlam has 'âṇ pei-tal,' *a boy,* 'peṇ pei-ṭal,' *a girl.*

Compare Greek 'παῖς,' 'παιδ-ὸς,' *a boy* or *girl, a servant;* Laconian 'πόιρ;' Latin 'puer;' Persian 'bach,' *a boy,* 'puser,' *a son;* Swedish 'poike;' English 'boy.'—See Scythian Affinities.

poʀ-u, *to sustain, to bear, to suffer patiently:* 'poʀ-u-ppu,' *responsibility;* 'poʀ-u-mei,' *patience.* Compare Gothic 'bair-an,' *to bear;* Greek 'φέρ-ω;' Latin 'fer-o.' The Tamil distinguishes between this word and 'piʀ-a,' *to be born,* though both are probably from the same base. The Latin in like manner distinguishes between 'par-io' and 'fer-o,' whilst the Gothic tongues make no difference between 'bear,' *to sustain,* and 'bear,' *to bring forth.* They constitute one word, from which is formed the past participle *to be born* or *borne,* and also the noun *birth.*

poṛ-u-du, *time:* theme 'poṛ.' Compare Sanscrit 'vâr-a,' *time;* Persian 'bâr,' the theme of 'bâri,' *once;* Latin 'ber,' the suffix of time, which appears in the names of the months from Septem-*ber* to Decem-*ber.*

povv-u, *to rise, to be puffed up, like bread:* a real Tamil word, though a local, vulgar one. Compare English 'to puff,' and Dutch 'boff-en,' also 'pof,' *a blast which swells the cheeks.*

pô, *to go;* also 'pô-gu' (with the usual formative addition of 'gu'). The second person singular of the imperative of 'pôgu' is 'pô.' Laghmani (an Affghan dialect), 'pâk,' *to go;* Greek 'βά-ω,' *to go;* Latin 'va-do,' *to march;* Hebrew 'bô,' *to come,* occasionally *to go.*

pôḍ-u,' *to put.* Compare Dutch 'poot-en,' *to set or plant;* Danish 'pod-er,' *to graft;* English 'to put.'

biḷ-u, Can., *to fall;* Tam. 'viṛ-u.' Compare English 'to fall;' German 'fallen.'

mag-an, *a son, a male;* Tulu 'mag-e.' Compare Gothic 'mag-us,' *a boy, a son,* from the verbal theme 'mag,' originally *to grow,* then *to be able;* Gaelic 'mak,' *a son;* Tibetan 'maga,' *son-in-law.* Compare also Latin 'mas,' *a male.*

may-ir, *hair.* Compare Persian 'mui;' Armenian 'mas,' *hair.*

maR-a, *to forget.* Compare Lithuanian 'mirsz,' *to forget.*

mâ, *a male,* particularly the male of the lion, elephant, horse, and swine; *e.g.*, 'ari-mâ,' *a male lion.* Compare Latin 'mas,' *a male.*

mâṛg-u, *to die, to be bewildered, to mingle:* related theme 'mâṛ-u,' *to be confused, to be lazy.*

Compare Latin 'marc-eo,' *to wither, to be faint, to be languid or lazy,* and also the Greek 'μαραίνω,' which in the passive voice signifies *to waste away,* or *die.* Possibly all these words have a remote connexion with 'mri,' Sanscrit, *to die.*

It is evident, however, that there is a closer and more special connexion between the Latin and Greek secondary themes here adduced and the Tamil.

mig-u, *much, great:* as a verbal theme, *to be much.* 'miñj-u,' *to abound* (from 'mij,' nasalised), is probably a collateral root. Related words, Tel., 'migal-u,' *remainder, that which is too much;* 'migula' and 'migala,' adverb and adjective, *much, exceedingly,* also 'mikkili,' the same. Can. 'mig-u,' *to exceed,* also 'migil-u,' both as a verb and as a noun; ancient dialect of Canarese 'migal,' *much;* 'mogga,' and also 'mokkaḷa,' *a mass, a heap, an assemblage.*

The Sanscrit 'mahâ,' *great,* from 'mah,' *to grow,* is frequently used in the Drâvidian dialects, but it is always considered to be a Sanscrit derivative, not the original base from which the Drâvidian words have been derived. This view is confirmed by the circumstance that the Drâvidian languages have no word signifying *much,* except 'mig-u,' and its correlatives. The Drâvidian words quoted above, bear a much closer resemblance to the corresponding words in the Classical and Germanic tongues than to the Sanscrit. Thus, the Latin 'mag-nus,' 'mag-is;' the Persian 'mih' or 'meah;' the Greek 'μέγα' or 'μεγάλος;' the Old High German 'mihhil;' Norse 'mikil;' Danish 'megen;' English 'migh-t;' Scottish 'mickle,' are more closely connected with the Tam.

'migu,' the Can. 'migal' and 'mokkala' and the Tel. 'migala' and 'mikkili,' than with the Sans. 'mah-ât.' The final 'l' of the Drâvidian words seems to be 'a particle of specialisation.' —See the section on 'Roots.'

mûṛg-u, *to plunge, to sink.* 'amiṛ' appears to be a softened form of the same word; and probably the 'g' of 'mûrgu' is only a formative. Compare Latin 'merg-o,' *to plunge, to immerse.* The preterite being 'mersi,' not 'merxi,' possibly the 'g' of 'mergo' is a formative addition like the 'g' of the Tam. 'mûṛ-g-u.'

mugil, Tam. and Ancient Can., *a cloud.* Compare Sanscrit 'mêgha,' *a cloud,* from 'mih' ('mêhati'), *to sprinkle.* The word 'mêgha,' has been borrowed from the Sanscrit by the Drâvidian languages, and is now more commonly used than 'mugil.' The latter, however, is found in the classics, is much used by the peasantry, and is undoubtedly a pure Drâvidian word. Doubtless 'mêgha' and 'mugil' are ultimately allied; but there is a direct and special connexion between the Drâvidian word and the Greek '*ὀ-μίχλ-η*,' *a cloud,* the Lithuanian 'migla,' the Slavonian 'mgla,' and the Gothic 'milh-ma;' in each of which the 'l' of 'mugil' retains its place.

muyal, *to labour, to endeavour.* Compare Latin 'mol-ior,' *to endeavour, to strive;* Greek '*μῶλ-ος*,' *the toil of war;* English 'to moil,' *to labour or strive.*

muRumuRu, *to grumble, to murmur.* A very similar word, 'moRumoRu,' *to murmur,* would naturally be regarded as identical with 'muRumuRu;' but a different origin is ascribed to each. 'moRumoRu' is said to be simply and solely a mimetic word, one of a large class of imitative, reduplicated exclamations; *e.g.,* 'he said 'moRu-moRu;'' *i.e., he spoke angrily:* 'his head said 'kiRu-kiRu;'' *i.e., it went round.* 'muRumuRu,' on the other hand, is not purely imitative, but seems to be regularly formed by reduplication from 'muRu,' the base of 'muRukku,' *to twist, to chafe;* and the signification of *grumbling,* and *being discontented,* has arisen from that of *chafing.*

Whatever be the derivation of the Tamil word, it may be compared with the Latin 'murmuro,' *to mutter.* The Latin word is evidently an imitative one, the reduplication of the syllable 'mur' being used to signify the continuance of a low muttering sound. 'mur' has doubtless some connexion with the base of 'musso,' 'mussito,' *to mutter or grumble.* Compare also the Greek expression *to say* 'μῦ μῦ,' *to mutter, to grumble.*

The Old Prussian 'murra,' *to murmur,* is evidently related. —See also the 'Scythian Vocabulary.'

The Tamil word means not only *to utter a muttering sound,* but also *to express discontent, to be angry;* and in this it goes beyond the meaning of the corresponding Latin 'murmuro.' *Muttering,* is in Tamil expressed by 'muṇa-muṇa,' a somewhat similar, yet independent, imitative word.

mûkk-u,' *the nose:* theme 'mûg-u,' Can., *to smell;* related Tamil verbs 'mugar' and 'môkk-u,' *to smell.*

Compare Greek 'μυκτήρ,' *the nose.* The Greek word is said to be derived from 'μύζω,' *to moan, to mutter, to suck in,* or from 'μύξα,' *the discharge from the nose* (Latin 'mucus'). It is worth consideration, however, whether the Drâvidian derivation is not, after all, a more probable one.

mett-a, Tel., *a bed, a cotton bed, a cushion;* Tamil 'mett-ei;' Canarese 'mott-e.' The word seems to be a derivative from 'mel,' Tam., *soft, fine.*

Compare Latin 'matta,' *a mat, a mattrass;* Slavonian 'mat;' Saxon 'meatta:' also the Hebrew 'mittâh,' *a bed, a cushion.*

The Tamil seems to give the best and most natural derivation of these words.

mel, *fine, thin, soft, tender;* mell-a,' *softly, gently.*

Compare Latin 'moll-is,' *soft, tender, pliant;* Greek 'μαλακός,' *soft, gentle, tender.* The derivation of the Latin 'mollis, from 'movilis,' is inconsistent with the connexion which certainly subsists between 'mollis' and 'μαλακός;' and the resemblance of both to the Drâvidian 'mel' is remarkable. Compare Sanscrit 'mridu,' *soft,* which is in Tamil 'med-u.'

râÿ, Tel., *a stone.* Bearing in mind the mutual interchange of 'r' and 'l,' we may perhaps compare this word with the Greek 'λᾶ-ας' or 'λαί-α,' *a stone.*

val-i, *strength;* 'val-i-ya,' *strong;* 'van-mei' ('val-mei'), *strength.* The Drâvidian languages have borrowed, and frequently use, the Sanscrit 'bala' (in Tamil 'balan,' 'balam,' and even 'valam'); and it might at first be supposed that this is the origin of 'vali,' &c. I am persuaded, however, that the words cited above have not been derived from the Sanscrit, but have been the property of the Drâvidian languages from the beginning. The Drâvidian 'val' has given birth to a large family, not only of adjectives and nouns, but also of derivative verbs, which have no connexion whatever with anything Sanscrit; *e.g.*, 'vali,' *a spasm;* 'vali,' *to row*, &c.; and if this word is not to be regarded as Drâvidian, this family of languages must be supposed to be destitute of a word to express so necessary and rudimental an idea as *strong*. 'val,' also, more closely resembles the Latin 'val-eo,' *to be strong*, and 'val-idus,' than the Sanscrit 'bala-m.'

vaḷ, *fertility, abundance;* 'vaḷ-ar,' and many related verbs, *to rear, to cause to grow.* Compare Latin 'al-o,' *to nourish*. Connexion doubtful.

viṇḍ-u, *the wind.* Compare Latin 'vent-us;' English 'wind.' The Tamil word is said to be derived from 'viṇ,' *the sky:* its resemblance to 'vent-us' is, therefore, probably accidental.

viʀei, *to shiver from cold, to grow stiff from cold.* 'vʀi' was probably the primitive form of this theme.

Compare Greek '*φρισσ-ω*,' *to tremble, to shiver;* '*ῥιγ-έω*,' *to shiver or shudder with cold;* '*ῥῖγ-ος*,' *frost, cold, a shivering from cold;* also Latin 'frig-eo,' *to be cold;* 'frig-us,' *cold;* 'rig-eo,' 'rig-or,' *to be stiff, as from cold;* English 'to freeze.'

vîṇ, *useless, vain.* Compare Latin 'van-us,' *empty, unreal, frivolous, vain.*

vêṇḍ-u, *to wish, to want.* Compare English 'want' from Saxon 'wanian,' *to fail.* If the 'ṇ' of the Tamil word is euphonic, as it appears to be from comparison with 'beḍ-u,' the corresponding Canarese word, this resemblance is merely accidental.

vêʀ-u, *different, other.* Compare Latin 'var-us,' the secondary meaning of which is *different, dissimilar;* also 'var-ius,' *diversified, various, different from something else.*

vrây̆, Tel., *to write;* Tam. 'eṛud-u.' If these words were originally identical, as it is probable they were, the Telugu 'vray̆' must have lost a final 'd.' Compare English 'to write.'—See also 'Scythian Affinities.'

II.

Semitic Affinities,

OR,

Drâvidian words which appear to be allied to the Hebrew and its sister tongues.

The number of such words in the Drâvidian languages is not great; and it might be supposed that in attempting to prove the existence of this class of affinities, in addition to affinities of the Indo-European and Scythian classes, I prove nothing by attempting to prove too much. I submit, however, the following list of words to the scrutiny and judgment of those who may entertain this supposition; and they will find in it, if I mistake not, clear evidence of the existence of a few highly interesting points of resemblance between the Drâvidian vocabulary and that of the Hebrew.

In some of the instances which will be adduced, the Semitic vocables are allied to the Indo-European as well as to the Drâvidian languages; but it will be found that the Drâvidian analogies are closer and more direct than the Indo-European, and it is for that reason that the words are inserted in this list rather than in the preceding one. In some instances, again, the only analogies to the Semitic vocables are such as are Drâvidian.

If the existence of Semitic affinities in the Drâvidian languages is established, those affinities cannot be explained by supposing them to have been introduced by the Jews who have settled on some parts of the Malabar coast; for the Jews, whether 'black' or 'white,' have carefully preserved their traditional policy of isolation: they are but a small handful of people at most; they have never penetrated far into the interior, even on the Malabar coast, whilst on the Coromandel coast, where the Tamil is spoken, they are entirely unknown; and the Drâvidian languages were fully formed, and the Tamil and Telugu were, it is probable, committed to writing long before the Jews made their appearance in India. Whatever words, therefore, appear to be the common property of the Hebrew and the Drâvidian languages, must be regarded either as indicating an ancient, pre-historic intermixture or association of the Drâvidians with the Semitic race, or as constituting traces of the original oneness of the speech of the Noachidæ.

app-â, *father!* vocative of 'app-an.' This word is found unaltered in all the Drâvidian dialects. The Mech also, a Bhutân dialect, has 'appa' for *father;* the Bhotiya 'aba;' the Singhalese 'appâ.' Analogies will also be found in the Scythian vocabulary.

In all the languages of the Indo-European and Semitic families, the ultimate base of the words which denote *father*, is 'p' or 'b,' and that of the words which denote *mother* is 'm.' The difference between those two families consists in this, that the Indo-European words *commence* with the consonants 'p' or 'm;' *e.g.*, 'pater,' 'mater;' whilst in the Semitic languages, those consonants are preceded by a vowel; *e.g.*, Hebrew 'âb,' *father*, 'êm,' *mother*. In this particular the Drâvidian languages follow the Semitic rule; *e.g.*, Tam., 'app-an,' *father*, 'amm-âḷ,' *mother*. The resemblance between 'appan' (vocative 'appâ'), and the Chaldee 'abbâ,' *father* (Syriac 'âbô') is very remarkable. It is so close, that in the Tamil translation of Gal. iv, 6, ''abba,' *father*,' there is no difference whatever, either in spelling or in sound between the Aramaic word 'abbâ' (which by a phonetic law becomes 'appâ' in Tamil), and its natural and proper Tamil rendering 'appâ;' in consequence of which it has been found necessary to use the Sanscrit derivative 'pitâ-(v)-ê,' instead of the Tamil 'appâ,' as the translation of the second word.

amm-â, *mother!* vocative of 'amm-ei' or 'amm-âḷ,' *mother*.

Compare Hebrew 'êm' or 'imm,' *mother;* Syriac 'âmô.' See also the Scythian and Indo-European affinities of this word, which are still closer than the Semitic.

âʀ-u, *a river;* Tel. 'êʀ-u;' Malayâlam 'âʀ-a:' correlative root 'êri,' Tamil, *a natural reservoir of water*. Compare Hebrew 'ôr' or 'yeôr,' *a river;* Coptic 'jaro.'—See also 'Scythian Analogies.'

al, *not*. In Tamil, 'al' negatives the attributes of a thing; 'il,' its existence: 'êl' (and sometimes 'al'), is prohibitive. The vowel is transposed in Telugu, and 'lê' (the base of 'lêdu'), used instead of 'il.' Compare the negative and prohibitive particles of the Hebrew, 'al' and 'lô;' also the corresponding Arabic and Chaldaic 'lâ.' 'lô' in Hebrew negatives the properties of a thing, like 'al' in Tamil, and another particle ('ain') is used to negative the existence of it. This idiom is one which remarkably accords with that of the Drâvidian languages.

Compare also the Chaldee 'lêth,' *it is not*, a compound of 'lâ,' the negative particle, and 'îth,' the substantive verb *it is* (a compound resembling the Sanscrit 'nâsti'), with the corresponding Telugu 'lêdu,' *it is not*, which is compounded of 'lê,' the negative particle, and 'du,' the formative of the third person neuter of the aorist.—See also 'Scythian Affinities.'

av-â, *desire:* a related word is 'âval,' also *desire*, which is a verbal noun derived from the assumed root 'âv-u,' *to desire* (Marathi 'âvaḍ,' *love*). Compare Hebrew 'avvah,' *desire*, a verbal noun derived from 'âvâh,' *to desire.*

The ultimate base of the Hebrew 'âv' or 'av' is identical not only with the Tamil 'âv' or 'av,' but with the Latin 'av-eo,' *to desire*, and the Sanscrit 'av-a,' of which *to desire* is one of the rarer meanings. Compare also Hebrew 'âbâh,' *to will.*

ir-u, *to be;* Brahui 'ar.' Compare Babylonian 'ar,' *to be;* also Coptic 'er' or 'el,' and the Egyptian auxiliary 'ar.'

The Drâvidian word appears to mean primarily *to sit*, secondarily *to be*, *i.e.*, to be 'simpliciter,' without doing anything.

iʀ-a, the ultimate base of 'iʀa-ngu,' neuter, *to descend*, and its transitive 'iʀa-kku,' *to cause to descend.* Compare Hebrew 'yârad' (biliteral base 'yar'), *to descend.*

ur-i, Can., *to burn;* Tamil 'er-i.' Compare Hebrew 'ûr,' *fire*, 'ôr,' *light.*—See also 'Indo-European Affinities.'

ûr, *a city, a town, a village.* Compare Hebrew ''âr' or ''îr,' *a city;* Babylonian 'er.'

eʀ-i, *to cast, to shoot.* Compare Hebrew 'yârâh' (biliteral base 'yar'), *to cast, to shoot.*

erum-ei, *a buffalo;* Gônd 'armi,' *a she buffalo;* Telugu 'yenumu;' Canarese 'emmeyu.' These synonyms (in which 'm' is used as a radical) seem to prove that the final 'mei' of the Tamil word 'erumei,' has no connexion with 'mei,' the formative termination of Tamil abstract nouns, but represents an essential part of the root. Compare Hebrew 'rêm,' *a buffalo* or *wild ox.*

kûr, *a sharp point.* Compare Hebrew 'kûr,' *to pierce, to bore.*

śâkk-u, *a loose bag of coarse cloth, a sack;* Malayâlam 'châkk-a.' Compare Hebrew 'sak,' *a sack.*—See also the Greek affinities of this word.

We find the same word in many languages; *e.g.*, Celtic 'sac;' Finnish 'sakki;' Magyar 'saak.' The use of this word in Genesis xlii., is unquestionably more ancient than its use in Greek, or in any other Indo-European tongue. The Babylonians having been the great carrying traders of the earliest period of human history, it would seem probable that the word 'sak' was originally theirs, and if so, Semitic. It is remarkable that though this word is in Tamil, it is not in Canarese or Telugu; nor is it in Sanscrit. Possibly it is a relic of the commerce which the old Phenicians and Hebrews carried on with the Malabar coast. They brought with them to Palestine the Old Tamil and Malayâlam name of the peacock, 'tôk-a' ('thûka' in the Book of Chronicles); and they left behind them in India their word for *sack*.

śâl, *a bucket.* Compare Hebrew 'sâl,' *a basket;* Greek '*σηλ-ία*,' *a tray.*

śâÿ, *to lean, to incline.* Compare Hebrew 'shâ'an' (biliteral base, 'sha'' or 'sha'), *to lean.*

śina-m, *anger:* verbal theme 'śina-kku,' *to be angry.* Compare Hebrew 'sânê;' Chaldee 'senê,' *to hate;* Hebrew 'sinah,' *hatred.* The corresponding Canarese word being 'kini,' *to be offended,* 'sina-m' is probably softened from 'kina-m.' The analogy is therefore somewhat doubtful.

śiʀ-u, *to hiss.* Compare Hebrew 'shârak' (biliteral base 'shar'), *to hiss;* Greek '*συρίζω*,' *to pipe, to hiss.*

śum-ei, *a burden:* verbal theme 'suma-kku,' *to bear, to carry.* Compare Hebrew 'sâmak' (biliteral base 'sam'), *to support, to uphold, to weigh heavily on.*

śuv-ar, *a wall.* Compare Hebrew 'shûr,' *a wall.*

śevv-ei, *equal, level, correct:* base 'śev' or 'śe.' A nasalised, adjectival form of the same root is 'sen;' *e.g.*, 'śen-Tamiṛ,' *correct Tamil, the classical dialect of the Tamil language.* From 'se,' 'sev,' or 'sen,' is formed 'semm-ei' ('sen-mei'), an abstract of the same meaning as 'sevvei.' Compare Hebrew 'shâvâh;' Chaldee 'shevâ' (biliteral base 'shav' or 'shev'), *to be equal, to be level.* If the Sanscrit 'sama,' *even,* is at all connected with the Tamil 'sev' or 'sen,' the connexion is very remote; whereas the Tamil and the Hebrew word seem to be almost identical.

nâṭṭ-u, *to fix, to set up, to establish:* ulterior verbal theme 'naḍ-u,' *to plant.* Compare Hebrew 'nâtâ'' (biliteral base 'nat'), *to plant, to set up, to establish.*

nîṭṭ-u, *to lengthen, to stretch out;* formed by causative reduplication of the final consonant from 'nîḍ-u' (also 'nîḷ'), *long.* Compare Hebrew 'nâtâh' (biliteral base 'nat'), *to stretch out.*

nôkk-u, *to look direct at, to address.* Compare Hebrew 'nôkaḥ' (base 'nok'), *straight forward, over against.*

paṛ-u, *to become ripe, to fruit;* 'paṛa-m,' *a ripe fruit.* Compare Hebrew 'pârâh,' *to be fruitful, to bear fruit;* 'pâraḥ,' *to blossom, to break forth:* biliteral base of both 'par.' Especially compare 'perî,' *fruit.* Compare also Armenian 'perk,' and Persian 'ber,' *fruit.* Doubt is thrown upon the affinity of these words with the Drâvidian 'paṛ-u,' by the apparent connexion of that word with 'paṛ-a,' Tam., *to become old, to be accustomed.*

pâl, *a part, a portion, a class;* Canarese 'pâl-u:' collateral Tamil roots 'pir-i,' *to divide;* 'piḷ-a,' also 'pôṛ,' *to cleave.* The regularity of the dialectic interchange of 'r' and 'l' confirms the supposition that 'pâl' and 'pir-i' are related roots. Compare Hebrew 'pâlâh,' 'pâlâ,' 'pâlaḥ,' 'pâlag,' 'pâlal;' and also (by the interchange of 'r' and 'l'), 'pârash,' 'pâras,' and Chaldee 'perâs,' *to separate, to divide, to distinguish,* &c. All these words, like the Tamil 'pâl' and 'pir-i' (and also 'pagir,' *to divide*), include the idea of *separation into parts.*—See also the Indo-European analogies of these roots; *e.g.*, Sanscrit 'phal-a,' *to divide;* Latin 'par-s,' and 'por-tio,' *a portion.* It is evident, however, that the Semitic analogies are the closest.

peR-u, *to obtain, to bear or bring forth, to get or beget:* verbal noun 'pêR-u,' *a bringing forth or birth, a thing obtained, a benefit:* collateral root 'piR-a,' *to be born;* Gônd 'pirra,' *to spring forth;* also 'piRa,' Tam., *other, different.* Compare Hebrew 'pârâh,' *to be fruitful;* 'perî,' *fruit;* 'pâraḥ,' *to blossom, to break forth.* Whether the connexion between 'paṛ-am,' Tam., and 'perî,' Heb., *fruit,* be real or only apparent, I have no doubt of the existence of an intimate relation between 'peR-u,' *to bear,* 'piR-a,' *to be born,* and the Semitic words which are here adduced, as well as the Latin 'par-io,' 'pe-per-i.'

bâ, Can., *to come;* Gônd 'wai;' Tamil 'vâ' or 'var;' Telugu 'râ;' Tuda 'wô.' Compare Hebrew 'bô,' *to come, to come in;* Babylonian 'ba,' *to come*

mâÿ, *to die, to put to death.* Compare Hebrew 'mûth,' *to die.* Compare also 'muwo,' *dead,* in the Lar, a Sindhian dialect.

mâR-u, *to change;* Can. *to sell.* Compare Hebrew 'mûr,' *to change or exchange,* of which the 'niphal' is 'nâmar,' as if from a base in 'mârar' or 'mâr.' The corresponding Syriac 'môr,' means *to buy.*

miśukka-n, *a poor, worthless fellow;* 'misukk-ei,' *a worthless article.* Compare Hebrew 'miskên,' *poor, unfortunate.*

The Hebrew word is commonly supposed to be derived from 'sâkan;' but Gesenius considers the 'm' of 'miskên' to be a radical letter, not a servile. This word has found its way (probably by means of the Saracens) into several European languages; *e.g.*, French 'mesquin.' The Tamil does not contain the root of this word; and it may therefore be supposed to have borrowed it an early period from some Semitic dialect, after the manner of 'sâkk-u,' *a sack.*

At all events, the coincidence between 'miskên' and 'misukkan,' is one which deserves to be noticed.

meṭt-a, Tel. (Tam. 'mettei;' Can. 'motte'), *a bed, a cotton bed, a cushion.* The Drâvidian word appears to be derived from 'mel,' *soft.* Compare, however, the Hebrew 'mittâh,' *a bed, a cushion, a litter,* from 'nâtâh,' *to stretch out.*

III.

Scythian Affinities,

OR,

Drâvidian words which exhibit a near relationship to words contained in some of the languages of the Scythian group, particularly to the Finnish dialects.

The majority of the affinities that follow are clearer, more direct, and of a more essential character than the Indo-European or Semitic affinities which have been pointed out in the preceding lists. Many of the words which will be adduced as examples are words of a *primary* character, and of almost vital necessity—words which carry authority and convey intuitive conviction, in comparisons of this kind. Some of the Drâvidian words in the following list have Sanscrit or Indo-European affinities, as well as Scythian; a very few also have Semitic affinities; but I have preferred placing them in this list, because the Scythian affinities are not only the most numerous, but the closest that appear to exist. Such words, though they are but few, are of peculiar interest, as tending to prove the primitive oneness of the Scythian and Indo-European groups of tongues.

For the important Scythian affinities which are apparent in the Drâvidian pronouns and numerals, see the sections devoted to those parts of speech.

akk-a, Can. and Tel., *elder sister;* Tamil 'akk-âḷ;' Marathi 'akâ.' In Sanscrit, 'akkâ,' signifies *a mother;* and an improbable Sanscrit derivation has been attributed to it. I believe this word to be one of those which the Sanscrit has borrowed from the indigenous Drâvidian tongues; and the proof of this supposition is furnished by its extensive use in the Scythian group. The Sanscrit signification of this word, *a mother,* differs, it is true, from the Drâvidian, *an elder sister;* but a comparison of its significations in various languages, proves that it was originally used to denote *any elderly female relation,* and that the meaning of the ultimate base was probably that of *old.*

The following are Scythian instances of the use of this root with the meaning of *elder sister,* precisely as in the Drâvidian languages:—Tungusian 'oki' or 'akin;' Mongolian 'achan;' Tibetan 'achche;' a dialect of the Turkish 'ege;' Mordwin 'aky;' other Ugrian idioms 'iggen.'

The Lappish 'akke,' signifies both *wife* and *grandmother.* The Mongol 'aka,' Tungusian 'aki,' and the Uigur 'acha,' signify *an elder brother:* whilst the signification of *old man* is conveyed by the Ostiak 'iki,' the Finnish 'ukko,' and the Hungarian 'agg.' Even in the Ku, a Drâvidian dialect, 'akke,' means *grandfather.* The ultimate base of all these words is probably 'ak,' *old.* On the other hand 'akka,' in Osmanli Turkish, means *a ўounger sister;* and the same meaning appears in several related idioms. It may, therefore, be considered possible that 'akka' meant originally *sister;* and then *elder sister,* or *younger sister,* by secondary or restricted usage.

It is proper here to notice the remarkable circumstance that the Drâvidian languages, like those of the Scythian group in general, are destitute of any common term for *brother, sister, uncle, aunt,* &c., and use instead a set of terms which combine the idea of relationship with that of age; *e.g., elder brother, younger brother, elder sister, younger sister,* and so on.

The derivation of 'akka,' from a root signifying *old,* would appear to be the more probable one.

att-an, *father.*

âtt-âḷ, *mother.* We find in the Sanscrit lexicons 'attâ,' *a mother, an elder sister, a mother's elder sister;* also 'atti,' in theatrical language, *an elder sister.* I regard this word also as probably of Drâvidian origin; and it will be found that in one or another of the related meanings of *father* or *mother,* it has a wide range of usage throughout the Scythian tongues. The difference in quantity between the Tamil 'âtt-âḷ' or 'âtt-ei,' and the Sanscrit 'attâ,' does not appear to be of much consequence; and the change of 'tt' in some Drâvidian dialects into 'ch' or 'tch,' is in perfect accordance with generally prevalent laws of sound. Hence the Malayâla 'achchh-an' (pronounced 'atchhan'), and the Canarese 'ajj-a,' are identical with the Tamil 'att-an;' and probably the Hindi and Marathi 'âjâ,' *a grandfather,* is a related word, if not identical. The related words, 'ătt-ei,' Tamil; 'att-e,' Canarese; 'att-a,' Telugu, have also the meanings of *mother-in-law, sister-in-law, paternal aunt;* and the coresponding Singhalese 'att-â,' means *a maternal grandmother;* meanings which are not found in Sanscrit.

For the Scythian analogies of these words, compare Finnish 'aïti,' *mother,* together with the following words for *father,* viz., Turkish 'ata;' Hungarian 'atya;' Finnish 'âtta;' Tcheremiss 'âtyâ;' Mordwin 'atai;' Ostiak 'ata.' Compare also Lappish 'aija,' *grandfather,* and also 'attje.' It is remarkable that 'atta' is also a Gothic theme; *e.g.,* 'attan,' *father,* 'aithein,' *mother.*

ann-ei, *mother:* honorifically *elder sister.* 'ann-ei' and 'amm-ei' are probably correlative forms of the same base, 'm' being sometimes softened into 'n.'

Compare however Finnish 'anya,' *mother;* Mordwin 'anai;' Ostiak 'ane;' and also 'anna' and 'ana' in two dialects of the Turkish. The Hindi 'annî,' *a nurse,* is probably the same word.

app-an, *father*. Compare the following words for *father-in-law*, viz., Ostiak 'ûp,' 'ôp;' Finnish 'appi;' Hungarian 'ip,' 'ipa,' 'apos.'—See also 'Semitic Analogies.'

amm-âḷ, amm-ei, amm-an, } *mother:* the word is also used honorifically in addressing matrons. The following are correlative words, 'amm-âÿ,' *maternal grandmother, aunt by the mother's side*, and 'amm-ân,' *mother's brother*. Compare Samoïede 'amma,' *mother;* Jeneseï 'amma' or 'am;' 'Estrian 'emma;' Finnish 'emâ.' Compare also Ostiak 'in-a,' *woman, wife;* Hungarian 'eme.'—See also Semitic analogies. The Sanscrit 'ambâ' or 'ammâ,' *mother*, properly a name or title of Durgâ, is doubtless derived from the Drâvidian word. The bloody rites of Durgâ, or Kâli, were probably borrowed from the demonolatrous aborigines by the Brahmans; and 'amma,' *mother*, the name by which she was known and worshipped—her only Drâvidian name—would naturally be borrowed at the same time.

From the same source is derived the Scindian 'amâ' and the Malay 'ama,' *mother*.

It is remarkable that in one or two Drâvidian dialects the words which denote *father* and *mother*, have mutually changed places. In Tulu, 'amm-e,' is *father;* 'appe,' *mother;* and in Tuda the former is 'en,' the latter 'aph.' Compare the Mongolian 'ama,' *father*.

In Tibetan and its sister dialects, 'pa' or 'po' denotes *a man;* 'ma' or 'mo,' *a woman:* and these words are post-fixed to nouns as signs of gender; *e.g.*, 'Bot-pa,' *a Tibetan man*, 'Bot-ma,' *a Tibetan woman*.

ar-u, âr-u, } *precious, dear, scarce*. Compare Hungarian 'aru,' 'âr,' *price;* Finnish and Lappish 'arwo.'

al, êl, } *the prohibitive particle*, 'noli;' *e.g.*, 'koḍêl' (from 'koḍ-u,' *give*), *give not:* Sântâl prohibitive 'âlâ.' Compare Lappish 'ali' or 'ele;' Ostiak 'ilâ,' and Finnish 'âlâ.'—See also 'Semitic Analogies.'

avva, Tel., *a grandmother;* Tuda 'avva,' *a mother;* Tamil 'avv-a,' *a matron, an elderly woman*. Compare Mordwin 'ava,' *mother*. —See also 'Indo-European Analogies.'

al-ei, *a wave;* Can. 'ale:' as a verbal theme 'alei,' means *to wander*, *to be unsteady.* Compare Finnish 'allok,' *a wave;* Armenian 'alik.'

âʀ-u, *a river;* Telugu 'êʀ-u.' Compare Lesghian 'or;' Avar 'nor;' Yakutan (Siberian Turkish), 'oryas;' Lappish 'wiro;' Ostiak 'jeara.' Compare also Armenian 'aru;' Coptic 'jaro;' and Hebrew 'ôr,' 'yeôr.'

âm, *it is, yes.* Compare Vogoul 'am,' *yes.*

iru-mbu, *iron.* Compare Motor (a Samoïede dialect), 'ur,' *iron.*—See also 'Indo-European Analogies.'

îd-u, Tel., *to swim;* Tamil 'nîñj-u.' Compare Ostiak 'ûdem;' Finnish 'uin,' *to swim.*

uyarka, *high:* infinitive (used adverbially) of 'uyar,' *to be high;* Râjmahal idiom, 'arka,' *high.* Compare Samoïede 'arka,' *high.*

uḷ, *to be in, to be:* as a noun, *a being, an entity:* as a post position *in, within;* Ancient Canarese 'ôl.' As a verb 'uḷ' is very irregular; and the 'ḷ,' though radical, has generally been euphonised into 'ṇ.' The primitive form and force of the root are apparent in the Tamil appellative verb 'uḷḷadu' ('uḷ(ḷ)-adu'), *it is, there is;* the Canarese 'uḷḷavu' ('uḷ(ḷ)-a-vu'), *there are;* and such nouns as 'kaḍavuḷ' ('kaḍa-(v)-uḷ'), Tamil, *God,* literally *the surpassing or transcendent Being.* 'uḷḷadu' has in Tamil been euphonised into 'uṇḍu' (like 'koḷ-du,' *having taken,* into 'koṇḍu'); and this euphonised appellative forms the inflexional base of the Telugu verb *to be.* Compare with 'uḷ,' *to be,* the Ugrian substantive verb 'ol,' *to be; e.g.,* Tcheremiss 'olam,' *I am;* Syrianian 'voli,' *I was;* Finnish 'olen,' *I am.* Compare also the Turkish 'ôl,' *to be.*

The primitive meaning of the Drâvidian 'uḷ,' seems to be *within,* in which sense it is still used as a post position in Tamil.

eṛud-u, *to write.* Compare Hungarian 'ir,' *to write;* Manchu 'ara;' Finnish 'kir.'

elu-mbu, *bone.* Compare Finnish 'lua;' Samoïede 'luy,' *bone.*

okk-a, Malayâlam, *all.* Compare Mordwin 'wok,' *all.*

katt-i, *a knife.* Compare Tungusian 'koto,' *a knife.*—See also 'Indo-European Affinities.'

kaḍ-i, kaR-i, } *to bite.* Compare Lappish 'kask,' *to bite.*—See also 'Indo-European Affinities.'

kaṭṭ-u, *to bind, to tie.* Compare the following words, each of which has the same signification:—Hungarian 'kot;' Ostiak 'katt-em' (*to fasten, to catch*); Syrjanian 'kuta;' Finnish 'keitt;' Lappish 'karet.'

kaṇṇîr, *tears.* Compare Finnish 'kônyv.' The Tamil word ('kaṇ-nîr') literally signifies *eye water;* so that it is doubtful whether this resemblance is not accidental.

kapp-al, *a ship, a vessel,* originally a verbal noun from 'kapp-u,' Tel., *to cover over:* derivative Telugu noun 'kapp-u,' *a covering.* The verb is not found in Canarese or Tamil, but the Canarese noun 'kapp-u,' *a subterraneous room, a pit-fall for catching elephants* (covered over with branches of trees and grass), and the Tamil noun 'kappal,' *a ship,* properly *a decked vessel,* in contradistinction to 'paḍugu,' *an open vessel,* are evidently identical in origin with the Telugu verb and noun.

The Malay word for *ship* is 'kapâl;' but this has probably been borrowed directly from the Tamil, and forms one of a small class of Malay words which have sprung from a Drâvidian origin, and which were introduced into the Eastern Archipelago, either by means of the Klings (Kalingas) who settled there in primitive times, or by means of the Arab traders, whose first settlements in the East were on the Malabar coast, where the Malayâlam, the oldest daughter of the Tamil, is spoken. The following Scythian words for *ship* appear to be really analogous to the Tamil, and have certainly not been borrowed from it:—Vogoul 'kap' or 'kaba;' Samoïede 'kebe;' Jenesei 'kep;' Yerkesian 'kaf;' Ostiak 'chap.'—See also the analogies adduced under the word 'kebi,' *a cave.*

kar-u, *black;* euphonised from 'kâr;' Gujarathi 'karo.' Compare Turkish 'kara;' Calmuck 'chara;' Mongolian 'chara,' 'kara;' Manchu 'kara;' Japanese 'kuroi.' These Scythian affinities are too distinct to admit of the smallest doubt. There is possibly an ulterior, but doubtful, connexion between this Scytho-Drâvidian root and the Sanscrit 'kâla,' *black,* or Tamil 'kâḷ-am,' from which there is a derivative, 'kâṛa-g-am,' that throws light on the relation of 'kâla' to 'kar-u.' Possibly also 'kri,' the radical portion of 'krishna,' Sanscrit, *black*, may be related to the same Scythian theme.

kara-ḍi, *a bear;* probably from 'kara-ḍu,' *rough.* Compare Samoïede 'korgo;' Tungusian 'kuti,' 'kuuti.'—See also 'Indo-European Affinities.'

kaṛug-u, *an eagle.* Compare Ostiak 'kuruk,' *an eagle.*—See also 'Indo-European Affinities.'

kaṛutt-u, *the throat;* also 'kur-al,' *the wind-pipe.* Compare Vogoul 'kuryd,' *the throat;* Finnish 'kurko,' 'kero,' 'kerri; Kurd 'g'eru;' Lappish 'karas,' 'kirs;' Slavonian 'gorlo.'

kal, *a stone.* Compare Lappish 'kalle,' also 'kedke' or 'kerke;' Lesghian 'gul;' Kamtschadale 'kual,' 'kualla.' Probably these words have an ulterior connexion with the Finnish 'kiwi;' Hungarian 'kô;' Ostiak 'key,' 'kaück.' Compare also (through the interchange of 'l' and 'r') the Tamil 'kâṛ,' *gravel, a pebble;* with the Greek 'χερ-άς,' *gravel,* and 'χερ-μάς,' *a stone;* and the Armenian 'k'ar,' 'kuar,' *a stone.* The Drâvidian root cannot be traced farther than 'kal,' *a stone;* but the corresponding Lappish 'kalle,' appears to be derived from, or connected with, 'kalw-at,' *to become hard.* Compare also 'karra,' Lappish, *hard, rough.*

kaḷḷ-am, Malayâlam, *a lie;* Tamil 'kaḷa-vu,' *a theft.* Compare Lappish 'keles,' *a lie.*

kâʀʀ-u (pronounced 'kâttr-u'), *wind.* Compare Kangazian (a Turkish dialect) 'kat,' *wind;* Sojoten (a Samoïede dialect) 'kat;' other Samoïede dialects 'chat,' 'kada' (also *a storm,* 'charru'); Georg. 'kari;' Jurazen 'chada.'

kâÿ, *to heat, or be hot, to burn, to boil.* Compare Finnish 'keite,' 'keitta,' *to boil, to cook;* Hungarian 'keszil.' Compare especially the Indo-European Affinities of this word.

kâl, *foot;* Tuda 'kôl;' Tulu 'kâr.' Compare Mongol 'kôl;' Ostiak 'kur;' Tungusian 'chalgan,' 'halgan;' Permian 'kok;' Ossete 'kach,' 'koch;' Vogoul 'lal;' Korean 'pal;' Canton-Chinese 'koh.'

kiṛ-a, *old, aged.* Compare Oriental Turkish 'chari;' other Turkish idioms, 'kar,' 'kart;' Wotiak 'keres;' Lesghian 'heran.'—See also the Indo-European analogies of this word.

kîḷ, Can., *below;* Tamil 'kîṟ.' Compare Wolgian 'kilgi,' 'kelga,' *deep.* From the Tamil 'kîr' is derived 'kiṟ-angu,' *a bulbous root;* with which we may perhaps compare the Slavonian 'koren;' Jenseï 'koryl,' *a root.*

kudir-ei, *a horse;* Canarese 'gudur-e.' The Sanscrit 'ghôḍa,' *a horse,* has doubtless an ulterior connexion with the Drâvidian word; but I cannot suppose the Drâvidian word to have been directly borrowed from the Sanscrit one, for the Tamil occasionally borrows and uses 'ghôḍa' (in Tamil 'ghôṛam,' also 'gôḍagam;' Telugu 'gurram-u'), in addition to its own 'kudir-ei.' Both words seem to be derived from a common origin. The Scythian analogies are Jeneseï 'kut' and Lesghian 'kota.' Compare also Malay 'kuda.'

kuḍ-i, *a habitation;* 'kuḍ-il,' 'kuḍis-ei,' *a hut, a cottage.* In Telugu and Canarese 'guḍ-i,' means *a temple.* A similar word, 'kuṭa' or 'kuṭi,' is also contained in Sanscrit; but it appears to be one of those words which the Sanscrit has borrowed from the Drâvidian tongues. It has a place in each of the dialects of the Finnish family; *e.g.,* Mordwin 'kudo,' *a house;* Tscheremiss 'kuda;' Finnish 'kota;' Ostiak 'chot;' Lappish 'kata.' I suspect the Saxon 'cot' had a Finnish origin.

kuḷ-ir, *cold, to become cold:* ultimate base 'kuḷ;' related words 'kûd-al' and 'kûd-ir,' *cold;* also Telugu and Canarese 'chali,' *cold.* 'śil-ir,' Tamil, *to tremble,* seems to be a collateral root.

With 'kuḷ-ir,' compare Lappish 'kal-ot,' *to freeze;* Finnish 'cyl-ma;' and with 'chali' (Telugu and Canarese), compare Permian 'cheli,' *cold.*—See also 'Indo-European Affinities.'

kei, *hand;* Canarese 'kye,' 'keiyyi;' Telugu 'chêyi.' A comparison of these words seems to show that 'kêÿ,' was the primitive form of this root. Possibly there is a remote ulterior connexion between the Sanscrit 'kara,' *the hand,* and the Drâvidian word: possibly, also, as 'kara' is supposed to be derived from 'kri,' *to do* (or 'hri,' *to take*), so 'kêÿ,' *the hand,* may be derived from, or connected with, the Drâvidian 'ki,' 'gi,' 'gê,' 'cheÿ' or 'śeÿ,' *to do.* There appears also to be a special resemblance between the Tamil 'kei' and the Greek 'χείρ;' yet when the Greek genitive 'χερ-ός' is compared with the Old Latin 'hir' and the Sanscrit 'kara,' it is obvious that it is with the latter that 'χείρ' is to be connected, rather than with the Tamil 'kei. The analogies of the Drâvidian

2 I 2

word seem to be exclusively Scythian. Compare Hungarian 'kêz' (pronounced 'keis'); Finnish 'kchêsi' (root 'kâ;' *e.g.*, genitive 'kâ-an'); Estnian 'kâsi;' Ostiak 'ket;' Lappish 'kât;' Permian 'ki;' Lasian 'ke; Mingrelian 'che;' Quasi-Qumuq (a Turkish dialect), 'kûya.' Compare also Persian 'kef.' The Hungarian has both 'kar' and 'kêz;' but the former is used to signify *arm*, the latter *hand*, a distinction which seems to prove that those roots, though perhaps ultimately related, have long been independent of one another.

keb-i, *a cave;* Canarese 'gav-i;' also 'kapp-u,' Canarese, *a subterraneous room, a pit-fall.* Compare Mongol and Manchu 'kobi,' *a cavity, a cave;* Ostiak 'kaba,' 'kebi,' 'kavi,' *a chamber.*

Compare also 'kapp-al,' Tamil, *a ship*, from 'kapp-u,' Telugu, *to cover over.*—See 'Indo-European Affinities.'

kev-i,' Can., *the ear;* Telugu (euphonically softened) 'chevi;' Tuda 'kavi;' Brahui 'khaff:' related words 'kâd-u,' *the ear*, and 'kêḷ,' *to hear*. Compare the following Scythian words signifying *the ear:*—Samoïede dialects 'ko,' 'ku,' 'kus;' Korean 'kui;' Ossete 'k'us;' Kurd 'g'oh;' Turkish dialects 'kulak.'

kêl-u, Ancient Telugu, *the hand.* Compare Kuralian 'kell' and Georgian 'cheli,' *the hand.*

kêḷ, *to hear;* 'kêḷ-vi,' *hearing.* Compare Finnish 'kuul-en,' *to hear;* Syrjanian 'kyla;' Tcheremiss 'kol-am;' Hungarian 'halla;' Lappish 'kull-et' ('kullem,' *hearing*); Ostiak 'kûdl-em.' Notice the change of the final 'l' of the other Finnish dialects into 'dl' in Ostiak, a single cerebral consonant, precisely similar in sound to the final 'ḷ' of the corresponding Tamil 'kêḷ.'—See also the Indo-European affinities of this word.

kol, *to kill.* Compare Finnish 'kuol,' *to die;* Tcher. 'kol-em;' Syrj. 'kula;' Hung. 'hal.' See also 'Indo-European Analogies.'

kôn, *a king, a ruler;* in honorific usage *a shepherd*, or *man of the shepherd caste.* Another form of the same word is 'kô,' *a king, a god.* It is hard to determine whether 'kô' or 'kôn' is to be regarded as the primitive form of this word. Compare the Turkish and Mongolian 'khân,' also 'khagân,' *a ruler;* Ostiak 'khon;' Scythian of the Behistun tablets, 'kô,' *a king.*

kôṛ-i, *the domestic fowl;* Gônd 'kôrh;' Seoni Gônd 'kôr,' *a hen* ('gogori,' *a cock*). This word is the common term which is used in the Drâvidian languages for both the cock and the hen. If it is required to express the gender 'sâval,' *a cock*, or 'peṭṭei,' *a hen*, is prefixed adjectivally to the common term 'kôṛi.'

The Sanscrit 'kukkuṭa,' *a cock*, from 'kuk-a,' *to scratch* does not seem to have any affinity with the Drâvidian 'kôṛ-i.' The Scythian analogies, on the other hand, are close and direct. Compare Vogoul 'kore;' Ostiak 'korek,' 'kurek;' Permian 'korech,' 'kuryg,' 'kuraga.' Probably the North-Asian tongues borrowed this word directly from the Drâvidian; for the domestic fowl had its origin in India, where the wild variety still exists; and when it was introduced into Upper Asia, the name by which it was known in India would naturally be introduced along with the fowl itself. That name being, not Sanscrit, but Drâvidian, it would appear that the domestic fowl must have been introduced from India into Central and Northern Asia, prior to the irruption of the Âryan race, and the consequent cessation of intercourse between the Drâvidians and the other members of the Scythian family.

The Drâvidian word has found its way into two languages of the western branch of the Indo-European family, viz., the Persian and the Russian. Compare Persian 'khor-os,' *a cock*; 'kour-ek,' *a poulet*; and the Russ 'kûr,' *a cock*; 'kûr-itsa,' *a fowl*; diminutive 'kûr-otchka,' *a chicken*.

śâral, *rain driven by the wind:* in the usage of the Southern Tamilians, *the rain brought by the south-west monsoon*. Compare Samoïede 'sarre;' Permian 'ser;' Wotiak 'sor,' *rain*.

śâ, or śâg-u, *to die;* Telugu 'chachu' (base 'cha'). Compare Samoïede 'chawe' and 'chabbi,' *dead*.

cheḍ-u, Telugu *bad*. Compare Ostiak 'jat,' *bad*.

chêṟ-u, *mud*. Compare 'chedo,' 'zerta,' 'choti,' and 'chat',—Lesghian words for *clay*.

tal-a, Telugu, *the head;* Tamil 'tal-ei.' Compare Mongol 'tologoi;' Calmuck 'tolgo;' Buriat 'tulgai;' Samutan (a Tungusian dialect) 'döll,' 'dollokin;' other Tungusian dialects 'düll,' 'del,' 'deli.'

tî, *fire*. The more commonly used Tamil word for *fire* is 'neruppu;'

Telugu 'nippu:' but 'tî' is the more classical word; and it is much used by all classes of people in the southern districts of the Tamil country. It is used also in Tulu.

The Scythian affinities of this word 'tî,' are peculiarly distinct; *e.g.*, Samoïede 'tu,' 'tui,' 'ti,' 'ty;' Mantchu 'tua;' Hungarian 'tüz;' Ostiak 'tût;' Tungus 'togo;' Lesghian 'tze,' 'zi,' 'zie;' Finnish 'tuli;' Lappish 'tall.' Compare also Gaelic 'teine;' and Welsh 'taan;' Persian 'tigh;' Sanscrit 'têjas.'

tûs-i, *dust, powder.* Compare Turkish 'tus,' 'toosan;' Mongol 'toghoz,' *dust.*

tôl, *skin.* Compare Vogoul 'toul,' 'towl,' *skin.*

nakk-u, *to lick:* derivative noun 'nâkku' or 'nâ,' *the tongue.* Compare Ostiak 'nal,' *to lick,* and 'nâl,' *the tongue:* Samoïede 'nawa,' *the tongue.*

nag-ei, *to laugh, laughter.* Compare Ostiak 'nâg-am,' *to laugh;* 'nâch,' *laughter.*

nâÿ, *a dog;* Tuda 'noi.' Compare Mongol 'nogai,' *a dog;* Calmuck 'nokoi,' 'nochoi.'

nu, Telugu copulative particle *and.* Compare Ostiak 'no,' *and.*

nett-i, *the forehead;* Telugu 'nud-ur.' Compare Lesghian 'nata,' 'nodo,' 'nete-bek,' *the forehead.*

neÿ, *ghee, clarified butter, oil.* Compare Avar (Turkish family of idioms), 'na,' 'nah,' 'nach,' *butter.*

nôḍ-u, Canarese *to see, to look.* Compare Mongol 'nüdu,' *the eye.*

ñjâyiʀ-u, *the sun.* Compare Hungarian 'nar,' *the sun;* 'nyâr' ('ñjâr'), *summer;* 'nap,' *a day:* also Mongol 'nar-an,' *the sun;* Ostiak 'naï;' Affghan 'nmar.'

pas-u, *green;* 'pul,' *grass.* Hungarian 'pusit,' *grass;* Vogoul 'piza;' Ostiak 'pady.'

pay-an, peiy-an, pay-al, peiy-al, } *a boy, a servant.* Malayâlam 'peidal;' Canarese 'heida,' *a boy* or *girl.* The words terminating in 'an' are masculines; those in 'al' and 'dal' are verbal nouns. 'dal' is as common a formative of verbal nouns even in Tamil as 'al,' and the two forms are mutually convertible. Both 'payal' and 'peidal' are necessarily abstracts, and are therefore capable of denoting either sex. 'payan,' Tamil, is restricted to signify *a boy*.

The theme or base of these words is evidently 'pay' or 'peiy,' which are equivalent sounds, and of which the 'y' seems to have been converted from, or is convertible into 'ś,' if we may judge from 'paśan-gaḷ,' which is often used as the colloquial plural, instead of 'payan-gaḷ.'

Compare the following Ugrian words for *son:* Vogoul 'py,' 'pu;' Mordwin and Syrj. 'pi;' Wotiak 'pyes;' Finnish 'poika;' Hungarian 'fiu;' Estrian 'poeg;' Ostiak 'pach,' 'poch,' 'pagul,' 'pagam,' 'pyram;' Lappish 'patja.' The Swedish 'poike' is evidently derived from the Finnish 'poika;' and the Greek 'παῖ-ς' and the Latin 'pu-er' are evidently related roots. See 'Indo-European Affinities.'

The Drâvidian languages appear to contain the ultimate theme of all these words, viz., 'pei,' Tam., *to be green* or *fresh*, a word which has been softened from 'pas-u' ('pay-u,' convertible into 'pei'), *green*, by a common Drâvidian law. The derivation of 'pay-an,' *a boy*, from this root would account for its conversion in vulgar usage (in the plural) into 'pas-an,' and it would also explain why 'al' and 'dal,' which are formatives of verbal nouns, are often used as terminations.

paṛ-a, *old (by reason of use)*; Canarese 'paḷa-ya;' 'paṛas-u,' Tamil. *old, what is old*. Compare Mordwin 'peres;' Syrj. 'pörys;' and Ostiak 'pirich,' *old*.

pal, *tooth*. Compare Lappish 'pane,' 'padne;' Wolgian 'padne,' 'paï,' 'pin;' Ostiak 'pank,' 'penk,' 'pek;' Tcher. 'py.'

pâl, *a part, a division*. Compare the following Ugrian words signifying *a half*:—Samoïede 'peâleâ;' Tcher. 'pêle;' Lappish 'beâle;' Ostiak 'pêlek;' Hungarian 'fél.' See also 'Semitic Affinities.'

piḍ-ú, *to catch*. Compare Finnish 'pidan,' *to catch*.

piʀ-agu (base 'piʀ' or 'pin'), *behind, after*. Compare Ostiak 'pir,' 'pira,' *behind, hindermost;* Finnish 'pera.'

piḷḷ-ei, *a child*. Compare Yarkand Tartar 'billa,' *a child;* Hindi 'pillâ,' *a cub, a pup*. See also 'Indo-European Affinities.'

pug-ei, *smoke.* Compare the following words signifying *vapour* in the Turkish dialects, 'bug,' 'buch,' 'bugu.' Compare also the English 'fog.'

peṇ, *a female;* Canarese 'heṇn-u.' Compare Lappish 'hene,' *a female.*

pokkul-i, Telugu *the navel.* Compare Ostiak 'puklam,' *the navel.*

bayir, Canarese *the belly;* Tamiḷ 'vayiʀ-u;' Gônd 'pir.' Compare Kangazian (a Turkish dialect), 'bar,' *the belly;* Armenian 'por;' Albanian 'bark;' Ostiak 'perga;' Mordwin 'pak.'

bâḷ, Canarese *to exist;* Tamil 'vâṛ,' *to flourish, to live prosperously.* Compare Oriental Turkish 'bôl,' *to exist.*

man-a, Canarese *a house:* classical Tamil 'man-ei.' Compare Samoïede 'men,' *a house;* Vogoul 'unneh.'

mar-am, *a tree, wood;* Canarese 'mar-a;' Telugu 'mân-u' (for 'mrân-u'). Compare Lappish 'muor,' 'muorra,' *a tree, wood;* Quasi-Qumuk Turkish 'murm,' 'murch;' Mongol 'modo;' Tomsk. 'madji;' Finnish 'mezza;' Lettish 'mes.'

maʀ-i, *a foal, the young of the horse, the ass,* &c. Compare Mongol 'mori,' *a horse;* Manchu 'morin;' Breton 'mor;' German 'mähre.'

mal-a, Canarese *a hill, a mountain;* Tamil 'mal-ei.' This Drâvidian root has found its way into the Sanscrit lexicons as the base of 'Malaya,' the Sanscrit name of the Southern and Western Ghauts—'Malayâlam,' or as the Arabian geographers called it, *Male.* It has probably given their name also to the Mal-dives, the 'dives' (Sanscrit 'dwîpa'), or *islands,* pertaining to Male or Malayâlam.'

Compare Albanian 'malli,' *a hill;* Vogoul 'molima;' Permian 'mylk;' Wolgian (by a change of 'l' into 'r'), 'mar;' Samoïede 'mari;' Avar 'mehr;' Finnish 'mâgi.'

muʀumuʀu, *to mutter, to grumble.* Compare Finnish 'muraj,' and Hungarian 'morog,' *to murmur.* See also 'Indo-European Affinities.'

menj, Gônd, *an egg:* plural 'mensk.' Compare Hungarian 'mony,' *an egg:* Finnish 'muna;' Samoïede 'muna.' Canarese 'moṭṭe' is more remote.

vân, *heaven.* Compare Mordwin 'mânel,' *heaven;* Tungus. 'ñyan;' dialect of the Kookies and Bungoos in the Chittagong hills, 'van.'

vâÿ, *the month.* Compare Samoïede 'aiw-a,' *month;* Lappish 'saiwe;' Hungarian 'ayak.'

viṛ-i, *to watch.* Compare Finnish 'wir-ot,' *to watch;* Hungarian 'vir-ad.'

velich-am, *light.* Compare Hungarian 'vilaga,' *light.*

APPENDIX.

I.

Are the Pariars of Southern India Dravidians?

It is commonly supposed by Anglo-Indians, that certain tribes and castes inhabiting Southern India, especially the Pariars and similar low-caste tribes, belong to a different race from the mass of the inhabitants. The higher castes are styled 'Hindus,' or else 'Tamilians,' 'Malayâlis,' &c., according to their language and nation; but those names are withheld from some of the ruder and more primitive tribes, and from the Pariars and other agricultural slaves. As this supposition, and the use of words to which it has given rise, are frequently met with both in conversation and in books, it seems desirable to enquire whether, and to what extent, this opinion may be regarded as correct.

The term 'Hindu' as used by some, is one which pertains to religious nomenclature. When they speak of certain classes as 'Hindus,' they mean that they are followers of the Brahmanical religion, or the religion of the Purânas; and according to this use of words (which is open to serious objection, inasmuch as it is the use, not of a theological, but of a geographical term, to denote one out of several religions which prevail within the region to which the term applies), the tribes and classes whose religion differs from that of the Brahmans are not 'Hindus.' In this sense it is true, that the Tudas and the Gônds are not Hindus, and that the majority of the predatory, wandering tribes, and of the lower castes are not Hindus, or at least are not 'orthodox Hindus;' though, geographically, it is certain, that they have as much right to the name of Hindus as the Brahmans themselves.

Some, again, use the term 'Hindu' as synonymous with 'Âryan.' They call the Brahmans and the higher castes of Northern India

'Hindus,' but withhold the name from the aboriginal races. This seems a still more improper use of words, inasmuch as it denationalizes not only the low-caste inhabitants of the northern provinces, but also the whole of the Drâvidian inhabitants of the Dekhan and the Peninsula; notwithstanding the proofs that exist that they crossed the Sind, Hind, or Ind-us, and occupied the 'Sapta Sindhu,' or 'country of the seven rivers,'—the Vêdic name of India—before the arrival of the Âryans, and that they have, therefore, a better claim to be called 'Hind-us' than the Âryans themselves. To deprive the Drâvidians and other aboriginal races of the name of 'Hindu,' is as unjust as it would be to deprive all persons of Anglo-Saxon descent of the name of 'Englishman,' and to restrict that name to the descendants of Norman families.

There are some, again, who with the error now mentioned, conjoin an additional one. They suppose the higher castes of the Tamil, Telugu, and other Drâvidian peoples, to be identical in origin with the Âryan races of Northern India, and the lower castes alone to have a Non-Âryan origin. Hence they call the high-caste Drâvidians 'Hindus,' and withhold that name from the Pariars, &c., not on geographical, but on ethnological grounds. I apprehend, however, that the Non-Âryan origin both of the higher and of the lower castes of Drâvidians, has been proved when the Non-Âryan structure of the Drâvidian languages has been established; and, therefore, this use of words may be passed by without further remark, as arising simply from misapprehension.

The Pariars (called in Telugu Mâlars) are not the only caste or class of people in the Drâvidian parts of India, who are commonly regarded as outcasts, nor are they the lowest or most degraded of those classes; but partly because they are the most numerous servile tribe (their numbers amounting on an average to at least a tenth of the entire population), and partly because they are more frequently brought into contact with Europeans than any similar class, in consequence of the majority of the domestic servants of Europeans throughout the Madras Presidency being Pariars, they have come to be regarded by some persons as *the* low-caste race of Southern India. Hence, besides the above-mentioned errors in the application of the name 'Hindu,' there are various popular errors afloat respecting the origin of the Pariars and their position in the caste scale, which require to be noticed before entering on the question now to be discussed, 'are the Pariars Drâvidians?'

Europeans were generally led to suppose, on their arrival in India several generations ago, that the Pariars were either the illegitimate offspring of adulterous intercourse, or were persons who had been excluded from caste for their crimes. This notion was invented and propagated by the Brahmans and the higher castes, and originated, in part, in their wish to justify their exclusive, unsocial behaviour towards the Pariars, on principles which they supposed that Europeans would approve. In part, also, it originated in an error arising from the uncritical habit of the Hindu mind; viz., the error of transferring to Southern India and to the Drâvidian tribes, the fictions which were devised in Northern India to account for the origin of the new castes or, so called, 'mixed classes,' of the North. Those northern castes or classes came into being through the operation of two causes; first, from the sub-division of the original castes of Vaisyas and servile or Sûdra Âryans, in accordance with the progressive sub-division of labour; and secondly, from the introduction of one tribe after another within the pale of Âryan civilization, as the religion and civil polity of the Sanscrit-speaking race spread throughout the country, and the aborigines were transformed from Mlêchchas into Sûdras. In Manu and the Shastras, no mention is made of either of these causes; but the new or mixed castes are attributed exclusively to fictitious mixtures of the older castes. The more respectable of the new castes are attributed to the legal intermarriage of persons belonging to different castes of recognized respectability. Another and inferior set of castes are attributed to the adulterous intercourse of persons of equal respectability, but of different caste, or of high-caste men with low-caste women; whilst the lowest castes of all are represented to have sprung from the adulterous intercourse of high-caste women with low-caste men, and are said also to constitute the receptacle of persons who had been socially excommunicated for offences against their caste.

Whatever amount of truth may be contained in this representation of the origin of the castes of Northern India (and I think it most probably a fiction throughout), it may confidently be affirmed that the Drâvidian castes had no such origin. The only 'mixed caste' known in Southern India, is that which consists of the children of the dancing girls attached to the temples. Of this class the female children are brought up in the profession of their mothers, the males as temple florists and musicians. In all ordinary cases, when children are born in adultery, if there is no great disparity in rank or caste between the parents, the rule is that the caste of the child of adulterous intercourse is that of the less honourable of the two castes to which its parents belong. Where considerable disparity exists, and where the dereliction of rank is on the woman's side—as for example, where a high-caste woman, or even a woman belonging to the middling castes, has formed an intimacy with a Pariar man (and in the course of a residence amongst the Hindu people for seventeen years, I have heard of several such cases), neither the caste of the father nor any other caste has any chance of being recruited or polluted by the addition of the woman's illegitimate offspring. The child never sees the light; the mother either procures an abortion or commits suicide.

To suppose, therefore, as Europeans have sometimes been led to suppose, that the entire caste of Pariars (including its subdivisions, and the 'left hand' castes corresponding to it) has come into existence in the surreptitious manner described above, or that it is composed of persons who have been excluded from caste for their crimes, is a baseless dream, which is too preposterous for serious refutation. Though it is probable that it was from the statements of natives that the Anglo-Indian community originally derived this notion, yet I never met with any natives, learned or unlearned, by whom the notion appeared to be entertained; and the Pariars themselves, who regard their lowly caste with feelings of pride and affection, which are very different from what might be expected of them, would resent this representation of their origin, if they had ever heard of it, with indignation.

Anglo-Indians who are not acquainted with the vernacular languages, often designate Pariars as 'outcasts,' as persons who are 'without caste,' or as persons who have 'no caste to lose.' It is true that the Pariar servants of Europeans will sometimes vaunt that they belong to 'master's caste;' and many masters know to their cost that their Pariar servants practise no scrupulous, superstitious distinctions respecting meats and drinks. Notwithstanding this, to suppose that the Pariars have literally 'no caste,' is undoubtedly a mistake. The Pariars constitute a well defined, distinct, ancient caste, independent of every other; and the Pariar caste has subdivisions of its own, its own peculiar usages, its own traditions, and its own jealousy of the encroachments of the castes which are above it and below it. The Pariars, though, perhaps, the most numerous caste in the country, belong to the lowest division of castes, and are not fabled to have sprung from even the least noble part of Brahma; nevertheless, they are not the lowest of the castes which are comprised in this lowest division. I am acquainted with ten castes in various parts of the Tamil country, which are certainly lower than the Pariars in the social scale; and in this enumeration I do not include the Paḷḷars, a caste between whom and the Pariars there is an unsettled dispute respecting precedence. The treatment which the Pariars receive from the castes above them, is doubtless unjust and indefensible; but it is not generally known by those Europeans who sympathize in the wrongs of the Pariars, that, whenever they have an opportunity, the Pariars deal out the very same treatment to the members of castes which are inferior to their own, *e.g.*, the caste of shoemakers, and the low-caste washermen; that they are, equally with the higher castes, filled with that compound of pride of birth, exclusiveness, and jealousy which is called 'caste feeling;' and that there is no contest for precedence amongst the higher castes of longer standing, or of a more eager character, than that which is carried on between the Pariars and the Paḷḷars. In the insane dispute about pre-eminence, which is always being carried on in Southern India, between the 'right hand' and the 'left hand' castes, the Pariars range themselves on the right hand, the Paḷḷars on the left; and it is chiefly by these two castes that the fighting part of the controversy is transacted.

Now that Europeans are better acquainted with Indian affairs, the theory of the illegitimate origin of the Pariars is more rarely found to be entertained; and, as the study of the native languages extends, the supposition that they are 'outcasts,' or that they have 'no caste,' will soon disappear likewise.

The question which is really before us having been cleared of popular errors and extraneous matter, we now come to the consideration of that question itself. 'Are the Pariars Drâvidians?' Are the forest tribes, the lower castes, and the so-called 'out casts,' that speak the Drâvidian languages, especially the Tamil Pariars and Telugu Mâlars (who may be taken as the representatives of the class), of the same origin and of the same race as the Drâvidians of the higher castes? Whilst both classes have a right to be called 'Hindus,' are the higher castes alone Drâvidians, Tamilians, Malayâlis, &c.? and are the Pariars and people of similar castes to be regarded as belonging to a different race?

On the whole I think it more probable that the Pariars are Drâvidians; nevertheless, the supposition that they belong to a different race, that they are descended from the true aborigines of the country—a race older than the Drâvidians themselves—and that they were reduced by the first Drâvidians to servitude, is not destitute of plausibility.

It may be conceived that as the Âryans were preceded by the Drâvidians, so the Drâvidians were preceded by an older, ruder race, of whom the Dôms and other 'Chandâlas,' of Northern India, and the Pariars and other low tribes of the Peninsula, are the surviving representatives. If this primitive race existed prior to the arrival of the Drâvidians, it would naturally happen that some of them would take refuge from the intruders in mountain fastnesses and pestilential jungles —like the Râjîs or Dôms of the Himalayas, the Weddas of Ceylon, and the Mala-(y)-arasers of the Southern Ghauts; whilst others, probably the majority of the race, would be reduced to perpetual servitude, like the Pariars, Puliars, and Pallars.

The history of the subjection of the Pre-Âryan Sûdras of Northern India, would thus form the counterpart and supplement of the history of the subjection of a much older race. Though, however, all this may be conceived to be possible, and though there may not be any *à priori* improbability in it, it is more to the purpose to state such circumstances and considerations as appear to be adducible in its support.

(1.) The Pariars, the Pallars, the Puliars, and several other low caste tribes, are slaves to the higher castes, and appear always to have been in an enslaved condition; and it is more natural to suppose that they were reduced to a servile condition by conquest, than to suppose that entire tribes were enslaved by the operation of ordinary social causes. If then, the castes referred to were a subjugated people, they must have settled in the country at any earlier period than their conquerors, and probably belonged to a different race.

(2.) The low-caste inhabitants of Southern India (whether they be slaves like the Pariars; vagrants like the Korawas, or basket makers; or freemen and proprietors of land, like the Shânârs, or palmyra cultivators), are distinguished from the entire circle of the higher castes by clear, unmistakable marks of social helotry. The title of 'Sûdra,' which has been assumed by the higher castes, or which was conferred upon them by the Brahmans, is withheld from the low-caste tribes; they are not allowed to enter within the precincts of the temples of the *Dii majorum gentium;* and wherever old Hindu usages survive unchecked, as in the native protected states of Travancore and Cochin, the women belonging to those castes are prohibited from wearing their 'cloth' over their shoulders, and obliged to leave the entire bust uncovered, in token of servitude.

It may be argued, that broadly marked class distinctions like the above-mentioned, which separate the people of at least twenty different castes or tribes from the rest of the population, are incompatible with the supposition of an original identity of race.

(3.) There are various traditions current amongst the Pariars to the effect, that the position which their caste occupied in native society at some former period was very different from what it is now, and much more honourable. Wilks observes that there is a tradition that the Canarese Pariars were once an independent people, with kings of their own. The Tamil Pariars sometimes boast that at an ancient period, theirs was the most distinguished caste in the country. They say that they were reduced to their present position, as a punishment for the haughty behaviour of their ancestors to some ancient king; on which occasion the Vellâlars, or caste of cultivators, who are now called 'Tamirar,' or Tamilians, *par excellence*, were raised to the place which had previously been occupied by themselves. There is a similar but more distinct tradition that the Korawas, or gipsy basket makers, were once 'kings' of the hill country in the extreme south.

(4.) In various parts of the country Pariars enjoy peculiar privileges, especially at religious festivals. Thus, at the annual festival of 'Êgâttâl,' *the only mother*—a form of Cali, and the tutelary goddess of the 'Blacktown' of Madras,—when a 'tâli,' or bridal necklace (answering to our wedding ring), was tied round the neck of the idol in the name of the entire community, a Pariar was chosen to represent the people as the goddess's bridegroom. Similar privileges are claimed by Pariars in other parts of the country, especially at the worship of divinities of the inferior class, such as the village 'ammas,' or *mothers*, and the guardians of boundaries; and these peculiar rights which are conceded to them by the higher castes, may be supposed to amount to an acknowledgment of their Pre-Drâvidian existence, or at least to an acknowledgment of their ancient importance; like the privileges claimed at the coronation of Rajput princes by the Bhills, a northern race of aborigines.

It has always been the policy of Hindu rulers, to confer a few empty privileges upon injured races as a cheap compensation for injuries; and it has generally been found, where an inquiry has been made, that such privileges possess a historical signification.

(5.) The strongest argument which can be adduced in support of the Pre-Drâvidian origin of the Pariars and other low-castes, consists in the circumstance that the national name of 'Tamilians,' 'Malayâlis,' 'Kannadis,' &c., is withheld from them by the *usus loquendi* of the Drâvidian languages, and conferred exclusively upon the higher castes. When a person is called a 'Tamiran,' or 'Tamilian,' it is meant that he is neither a Brahman, nor a member of any of the inferior castes, but a Drâvidian Sûdra. The name is understood to denote, not the language which is spoken by the person referred to, but the nation to which he belongs; and as the lower castes are never denoted by this national name, it would seem to be implied, that they do not belong to the nation, though they speak its language, but belong, like the Tamil-speaking Brahmans and Mahommedans, to a different race.

I may here mention an argument which is occasionally urged in support of the same view of the case, which is founded upon a mistake. It has been said that the name Pariar, or Pariah, is synonymous with that of the 'Paharias,' a race of mountaineers near Calcutta; and hence it is argued that the Pariahs may be considered, like the Paharias, as a race of Un-Âryan, Un-Drâvidian aborigines. It is a mistake, however, to suppose that there is any connection whatever between those two names. The word 'Pariar,' properly 'Paʀeiyar,' is the Tamil plural of 'paʀeiyan' ('paʀei-(y)-an'), which denotes not *a mountaineer*, but *a drummer*, a word which is regularly derived from 'paʀei,' *a drum*, especially *the great drum used at funerals.* The name 'Pariar' is, in fact, the name of a hereditary occupation, the Pariars being the class of people who are generally employed at festivals, and especially at funerals, as drummers. It is true that their numbers are now so great, that many of them are never so employed, and that the only employment of the great majority is that of agricultural slaves; but whenever and wherever the din of the 'paʀei' happens to be heard, we may be assured that a 'Paʀeiyan' is the person who is engaged in beating it. As the whole caste, though the most numerous in the circle of the low-castes, is denominated by this name, it appears probable that originally *drumming* was their only employment. If so, they must have been much less numerous at a former period than they are now. The origin of the epithet 'Mâlar,' which is applied to the Telugu Pariars, is unknown.

Though the circumstances and arguments that have now been alleged in favour of the Un-Drâvidian origin of the lower castes, possess a considerable degree of strength, I proceed to show that they are not perfectly conclusive, and that they are to some extent counter-balanced by considerations which are adducible on the other side.

(1.) The argument which is drawn from the servile condition of the Pariars fails to establish the conclusion; because it is certain that there are many slaves in various parts of the world who do not differ from their masters in race, though they do in status. The Russian serfs are Slavonians, and the Magyar serfs Magyars, equally with their masters. Illustrations of the inconclusiveness of the argument may be drawn also from Drâvidian life.

The Shâṇârs, the highest section of the lowest division of castes, are generally proprietors of the land which they cultivate, and many of them are almost on a level with the Drâvidian Sûdras. The more wealthy of the Shâṇârs have slaves in their employment, some of whom, called 'Kaḷḷa Shânârs,' belong to a subdivision of the Shâṇâr caste. These servile Shâṇârs appear to have been slaves from a very early period; and yet they are admitted even by their masters to belong to the same race as themselves. There are also servile subdivisions of some of the higher or unquestionably Drâvidian castes. Thus, a portion of the Maravas of the southern provinces, are slaves to the Poligars, or Marava chieftains; and even of the 'Vellâlas,' or Tamilian cultivators, there are not a few families who are slaves to the temples.

Various circumstances might contribute to the reduction of the Pariars, &c., to servitude, irrespective of difference or identity of race. In the wars of barbarous nations, it often happens that both conquerors and conquered belong to the same race, and even to the same tribe. In a civilized age, the conquerors may be content with governing and taxing the conquered; but in a ruder age, and especially in a tropical climate, where labour is distasteful, the vanquished are ordinarily reduced to the condition of slaves. In such cases we shall meet with a phenomenon exactly parallel to that of the Pariars, viz., a servile tribe speaking the language and exhibiting the physiological peculiarities of their masters, and yet separated from them by an impassable barrier. Other causes, however, in addition to that of war, may have been in operation, such as poverty, or a state of society resembling the feudal system, or even a trade in slaves like that which in Africa sets not only nation against nation, but village against village. At all events, taking into account the probability that these and similar social evils may have existed, it does not seem more difficult to account for the enslaved condition of the Pariars, without supposing them to have been a different race from their masters, than it is to account for the serfdom of the Russian peasantry, or the existence of slavery amongst nearly all the primitive Indo-European races, without the help of any such supposition.

It is worthy of notice also, that whilst the Pariars, Pallars, and Puliars are slaves, a much larger number of the castes that are included in the lower division—including some of the very lowest—are composed of freemen.

(2.) The traditions that have been mentioned respecting the honourable position formerly occupied by the Pariars, do not establish the point in hand. Supposing them to rest upon a historical foundation, they prove, not an original difference of race, but only the ancient freedom of the Pariars, and the respectability of their social rank, before their reduction to slavery.

(3.) The circumstance that the entire circle of the lower castes, including the Pariars, are separated from the higher by badges of social distinction, and denied the national name, is one which must be admitted to possess great weight. Though the argument which may be deduced from this circumstance is a very strong one, it does not appear, however, to be absolutely conclusive, for it is in accordance with the genius of Hindu legislation, to punish poverty by civil and social disabilities; and high-caste pride might naturally take the shape of an exclusive appropriation even of the national name.

We find a parallel use of words in the Sanscrit Shâstras, in which nations that are admitted to be of Kshatriya origin (*e.g.*, the Yavanas and Chînas), are termed Mlêchchas, not in consequence of difference of race, but solely in consequence of their 'disuse of Brahmanical rites.' There is a still closer parallel in the law of Manu, that Brahmans who took up their abode in the Drâvida country—in Manu's time an uncleared forest—should be regarded as Mlêchchas.

(4.) There is nothing in the physiology of the Pariars, in their features, or in the colour of their skin, which warrants us to suppose that they belong to a different race from their high-caste neighbours. The comparative blackness of their complexion has led some persons to suppose them to be descended from an imaginary race of Negro aborigines; but this hypothesis is unnecessary, as well as gratuitous. The swarthiness of the complexion not only of the Pariars, but also of the Puliars of the Malayâla country—a still blacker caste,—is adequately accounted for by their continual employment for many ages in the open air, exposed to the full force of the vertical sun. If the Fellahs, or labourers, and Bedouins, or wandering shepherds, of Egypt, are admitted to be Arabs of pure blood, notwithstanding the deep brown of their complexion, it is unnecessary to suppose the Pariars, who labour in a hotter sun than that of Egypt, to be of a different race from the rest of the Drâvidians, in order to account for their complexions being a shade darker.

Such of the Pariars as have had the good fortune to be placed in more favourable circumstances, are found to be as fair as the high-castes. When Pariars have risen to a position of competence and comfort, and Sûdras have become impoverished, and been obliged to work hard in the sun all day, their mutual difference of complexion is reversed, as well as their social position; and in the second, or at least in the third generation the Sûdra becomes dark, the Pariar fair.

I admit that the features of the Pariars differ from those of the high-caste 'cultivators,' as the features of every caste in India differ from those of every other caste; yet there is no difference between the 'cultivator' and the Pariar in the shape of their heads. Not only from their peculiarities of feature and dress, but even from the shape of their heads, we are generally able to distinguish Tamilians or Telugus from the Turco-Tartar Mahommedans of India. But looking at the shape of their heads alone, and leaving complexion and features out of account, it is impossible to distinguish a Tamilian, or high-caste Drâvidian, from a Pariar or any other member of the low-castes. Difference in feature is of little or no account in this inquiry, for it is notorious that castes which proceed from the same origin differ from one another both in features and in mental characteristics, as widely as if they inhabited different and distant countries.

The robber castes of Kallars and Maravars, differ as much from the higher castes in their features as the Pariars, and in habit of mind they differ still more. Nevertheless, they claim to be considered as Sûdras. The caste title of the Maravars, 'Dêva,' is the same as that of the old kings of the Pândiya and Chôla dynasties. Chieftains of their race still possess the principalities of Shevagunga and Râmnâd, which are called 'the two Maravas;' and the latter, the prince of Râmnâd, has claimed from an ancient period to be considered as Sêtupati, or hereditary 'guardian of Rama's bridge.'

The other predatory tribe, the Kallars, have a king of their own, the Tondiman Rajah, or Rajah of Poodoocottah; they claim a relationship to the ancient kings of the Chôla country; and they are regarded by the Tamilian Veḷḷâḷars, or 'cultivators,' as next in rank to themselves.

It is possible, and even probable, that these robber castes settled in the Tamil country subsequently to the settlement of the mass of the population; but it does not follow that they belonged to an Un-Drâvidian race. For the course which I have supposed the Kallars and Maravas to have followed, is precisely that which was followed on the decline of the power of the Pândiyas, by various Telugu and Canarese castes that are unquestionably Drâvidians.

(5.) The essential unity of all the Drâvidian dialects argues the unity of the race, inclusive of the lower castes.

The mixed origin of the Hindus of the Gaura provinces may be conjectured, not only from historical notices, but from an examination of the component elements of the northern vernaculars. In those vernaculars we can trace the existence of two lingual currents, the Sanscrit and the Scythian, the one running counter to the other; but in no dialect of the Drâvidian languages are such traces discoverable of any extraneous idiom which appears to have differed in character from that of the mass of the language.

All the grammatical forms of primary importance in all the Drâvidian dialects cohere together and form one harmonious system. If the Pariars and the other servile castes are supposed to be a different race from the Drâvidians, and the only surviving descendants of the true aborigines, it will be necessary to regard the isolated mountain tribes, the Tudas, Gônds, &c., as remnants of the same aboriginal race; and if this theory were correct, the languages of those long isolated tribes, should be found to differ essentially from the Telugu and the Tamil. On the contrary, no essential difference in grammatical structure, or in the more important names of things, has been discovered in them; but the Gônd and the Ku, the Tuda and the Kôta dialects, belong demonstrably to the same family as the more cultivated Drâvidian tongues.

It is also worthy of notice, that though the Pariars and the other servile classes in the plains live in hamlets by themselves, removed to a considerable distance from the villages in which their high-caste masters reside, there is no trace amongst them of any difference in idiom, of peculiar words, or of peculiar forms of speech. The only difference which is apparent, consists in their mispronunciation of Sanscrit derivatives, arising from their general want of education; and in many instances, even this difference is not found to exist.

On the whole, therefore, the supposition that the lower castes in the Drâvidian provinces belong to a different race from the higher, appears to me to be untenable. It seems safer to hold, that all the indigenous tribes who were found by the Âryans in Southern India, belonged to one and the same race. It is probable enough that the Drâvidians were broken up into hostile tribes before the Âryan immigration, and that the distinctions, not only of richer and poorer, but also of master and slave, had already come into existence amongst them. Those distinctions may have formed the foundation of the caste system, which their Brahmanical civilizers introduced, and which was moulded by degrees into an exact counterpart of the caste system of Northern India.

II.

Are the Nilgherry Tudas Dravidians?

The Tudas, or aboriginal inhabitants of the Nilgherry Hills, are commonly supposed to belong to a different race from the Drâvidians of the plains. The reasons that have been adduced in support of this supposition appear to me inconclusive. Unfortunately, so much exaggeration and error are included in those reasons arising from the sentimental interest with which everything connected with the Tudas has been invested by tourists, that there is not much satisfaction in dealing with the question.

(1.) The difference of the religion of the Tudas from what is called Hinduism, or the Brahmanical religion, is alleged to prove that they belong to a different race to their low country neighbours.

It is quite true that the Tuda religion differs greatly from the Brahmanical; but it will be shown in another portion of this Appendix that the original religion of the majority of the Drâvidians of the plains differed from Brahmanism as widely, and that the religion of the Gônds and Kus, who are as certainly Drâvidians as the Tamil people themselves, is very different from the religion of the Brahmans, and not unlike that of the Tudas.

(2.) The manners and customs of the Tudas are said to be altogether *sui generis*, and such as to indicate an origin different from that of the people of the plains.

Many of the customs of this tribe are certainly remarkable, but it is a mistake to regard them as peculiar to the Tudas, and *sui generis*. Polyandria is practised by the Tudas, but it is practised also by the Coorgs, whose Drâvidianism cannot be questioned; and female infanticide is not confined to the Tudas, but is unfortunately too well known in various parts of India.

The Tudas are not the only Indian people who live a wandering, pastoral life; who subsist entirely upon milk and grain; who dwell in huts formed of twisted bamboos; who wear no covering upon their heads; who let their hair grow to its full length; or who never wash their clothes or bodies from their birth to their death.

Each of those customs is practised by various other Indian tribes, though not all of them, perhaps, by any tribe but the Tudas: and though the Tudas may observe some customs of minor importance which are quite peculiar to themselves—(*e.g.*, the Tuda men do not, like other long-haired Drâvidians, tie their long hair in a knot like women, but allow it to cluster round the head in natural curls. The bamboo huts, also, in which they dwell are built on the plan of a perfect equilateral arch),—yet the observance of a few peculiar customs by a caste which is so isolated as the Tudas, cannot be regarded as a proof of difference of race; for every caste in India, whether Âryan or Drâvidian, whether high or low, has some custom or another which is entirely peculiar to itself,—generally some peculiarity in dress, in the ornaments worn by the women, or in the manner in which their houses are built.

(3.) The Tudas are said to be a fine manly race, with European features, Roman noses, hazel eyes, and great physical strength; and hence it is concluded that they differ from the Tamilians and other Drâvidians in origin, as well as in appearance.

It is certain that the Tudas are an athletic, hardy, fine-looking race, as might be expected from their simple mode of life and the bracing mountain air which they breathe; but it is also certain that many of the statements that are commonly made, both in conversation and in books, respecting their physical characteristics are mere romance. As regards size and strength of body they will not bear a comparison with the natives of the north-western provinces, or even with the Telugu palanquin bearers. The supporters of the Celtic or Indo-European origin of the Tudas are wont to rest the chief weight of their theory in the Roman noses of their protégés; but aquiline noses are not unfrequently met with amongst the people of the plains, though they have not had the good fortune to attract so much of the notice of tourists: and after all, the nose which is most commonly seen on the Tuda face is not an aquiline nose, but simply a large nose. Even if it were universally aquiline, it would reveal nothing respecting the origin of the Tudas; for physiology makes little account of noses, but much of heads, and the shape of the heads of the Tudas does not differ materially from that of the low country Drâvidians. Even their features do not differ from those of the people of the plains to a greater degree than their isolated situation for many ages would lead us to expect. It is true that the Tudas have hazel eyes and naturally curling hair; and this alone would give them a different appearance from the black-eyed, straight-haired people of the plains. The colour of their eyes may be, and probably is, the result of their long residence in the temperate climate of the hills; but this circumstance, when considered as an argument for difference of race, is neutralized by the dark colour of their hair, approaching to black, and especially by the darkness of the colour of their skin. It has not been noticed by writers on the Nilgherries, but it is nevertheless a fact, that, notwithstanding the long residence of the Tudas on a cold, cloudy, mountain region, the colour of their skin is considerably darker than that of the more modern hill race, the Badagars, a race of people who immigrated from the Canarese country not many centuries ago, and is many shades darker than that of the majority of the natives of the Malabar coast.

The darkness of the complexion of the Tudas appears to prove that they came originally from the eastern or sun-burnt side of the range of Ghauts; and that long before they took up their abode on the hills they had formed a constituent portion of the low country population. It should be observed also, that this inference exactly accords with the results that were deduced from the examination of the Tuda language which is contained in the Introduction. It was there shown that the language of the Tudas was essentially Drâvidian, and that it is, on the whole, more nearly allied to the Tamil, the language which is spoken in the plains on the eastern side, than to any other dialect.

After weighing the various considerations that have now been adduced, we may, I think, safely adopt the conclusion that the Tudas belong to the same race and stock as the mass of the Drâvidians, though long separated from the rest of the race, and isolated from its civilization. It may, at least, be confidently asserted that the evidence of the Drâvidian origin of the Tudas greatly preponderates over that of every other supposition.

III.

Dravidian Physical Type.

My object in making a few remarks on the physical type of the Drâvidian race is merely that of guarding the reader against certain commonly received errors. Lingual comparison is, I believe, the only guide to a knowledge of the pre-historic relationship of the Drâvidian family on which any reliance can safely be placed; and though I admit that, in some instances, physiology has contributed much to the discovery of the affiliation of races, it seems to me, in so far as the study has hitherto been pursued, that it is at fault in this instance.

I must here premise that my remarks relate exclusively to the Drâvidian race properly so called, not to the aboriginal or Nishâda races of India generally. Many of the physical characteristics which Mr. Hodgson attributes to the 'Tamulians,' may undoubtedly be observed in the Bhutân and Sub-Himalayan tribes, and in a smaller degree in the Sântâls and other Koles; but the inexpediency of using, as a general appellation so definite a term as 'Tamulian,' appears from the error into which some recent writers have fallen of attributing the same or similar physical characteristics to the Drâvidians or Tamulians of Southern India, who differ as much from the Himalayan tribes as do the Brahmans themselves.

Mr. Hodgson thus distinguishes the 'Arians' from the 'Tamulians:'

'A practised eye will distinguish at a glance between the Arian and Tamulian style of features and form—a practised pen will readily make the distinction felt—but to perceive and to make others perceive, by pen or pencil, the physical traits that separate each group or people of Arian or of Tamulian extraction from each other group, would be a task indeed! In the Arian form their is height, symmetry, lightness and flexibility: in the Arian face an oval contour with ample forehead and moderate jaws and mouth; a round chin, perpendicular with the forehead, a regular set of distinct and fine features; a well raised and unexpanded nose, with elliptic nares; a well-sized and freely opened eye, running directly across the face; no want of eyebrows, eye-lash, or beard; and lastly a clear brunet complexion; often not darker than that of the most southern Europeans.

In the Tamulian form, on the contrary, there is less height, less symmetry, more dumpiness and flesh : in the Tamulian face, a somewhat lozenge contour caused by the large cheek bones, less perpendicularity in the features to the front, occasioned not so much by defect of forehead or chin, as by excess of jaws and mouth ; a larger proportion of face to head, and less roundness in the latter; a broader, flatter face, with features less symmetrical, but perhaps more expression, at least of individuality; a shorter, wider nose, often clubbed at the end and furnished with round nostrils ; eyes less, and less fully opened, and less evenly crossing the face by their line of aperture ; ears larger, lips thicker ; beard deficient ; colour brunet, as in the last, but darker on the whole, and, as in it, various. Such is the general description of the Indian Arians and Turanians.'

Mr. Hodgson states also in several places that a Mongolian stamp is impressed on all the aborigines of India. 'Look steadfastly,' he says, 'on any man of an aboriginal race, and say if a Mongol origin is not palbably inscribed on his face.'

Probably there was little if any reference to the Tamulians, properly so called, in this striking and accurate description of the Brahmans of Northern India and of the forest tribes of the Himalayas and the Vindhyas; but through the vague use of the appellation 'Tamulian,' it is evident that Prof. Max Muller has been led to suppose the same description applicable to the Drâvidians proper, or aboriginal inhabitants of the south. Founding his theory on this description, which he quotes and eulogizes (in his *Turanian Researches*, included in *Bunsen's Outlines of Universal History*),—he says: 'From the most ancient times to the period of the Puranas, we meet everywhere with indications, more or less distinct, of two races brought into contact in the Indian peninsula :' and again, 'The traveller in India to the present day, though he would look in vain for the distinctive features of a Brahman (?), a Kshattriya, or a Vaisya, feels the conviction irresistibly growing upon him, as he passes along the streets of cities, or the roads of villages, *whether north or south of the Vindhyas*, that everywhere he is brought in contact with at least two races of man, distinct in mind as well as in body.' It is evident also from a quotation from a paper of Dr. Stevenson's, which he subjoins, that by those 'two races of man' he understood 'the higher and lower orders of natives'—'the Brahmans and other castes allied to them, and the lower or non-Âryan castes of the Hindu population.' We thus arrive at the conclusion that Mr. Hodgson's description of the physical peculiarities which he calls 'Tamulian,'—that is, as he understands the term Turanian or Mongolian—has come to be accepted as a faithful pourtraiture of the Un-Brahmanical Hindus generally, including the Un-Brahmanical classes south of the Vindhyas, *i.e.*, the entire mass of the Drâvidian people. The Professor quotes also those notices from the Puranas in which the type of the Nishada features is given.—He is 'a being,' they say, 'of the complexion of a charred stake, with flattened features, and of dwarfish stature.' 'The inhabitants of the Vindhya mountains are called his descendants. According to the Matsyapurâṇa, they were as black as collyrium. According to the Bhâgarata-purâna, they had short arms and legs, were black as a crow, with projecting chin, broad and flat nose, red eyes and tawny hair. The Padma-purâna adds a wide mouth, large ears, and a protuberant belly, and particularises their descendants as Kirâṭas, Bhillas, Bahanakas, Bhramaras, and Pulindas.' In the next chapter the Professor states that he 'accepts for his starting point this general distinction between Âryas and Nishâdas, which, whether suggested by physical features or proved by the evidence of grammar, may be considered as an undisputed fact;' and he then proceeds to inquire 'whether they can be subdivided into distinct groups.'

Finally he distinguishes, yet on lingual evidence alone, between 'two classes of Nishâdas, the Tamulic, in the narrower sense of the word, and the Bhotîya or Sub-Himalayan.'

Another recent writer, Dr. Logan, treating of the Drâvidians exclusively, thinks that there is a strong Melanesian or Indo-African element in the Tamil physiology; and accounts for it by the supposition that a negro race overspread India and Ultra India, not only before the arrival of the Âryans, but even before the arrival of the Scythians. He sees an evidence of this in the colour of the Drâvidians, and in the exceeding variety of physical type and features which he observes amongst them. Yet even in his opinion, and in this point at least I think he is quite correct, the Tamilians are 'intellectually more Europeanised than any other Tartaro-Iranian race.'

The tide evidently runs so strongly against my Drâvidian friends, that it seems almost fool-hardy to attempt to resist it; and yet I am persuaded that it has arisen in the main from misapprehension. I am persuaded that the physical type of the Drâvidians is not Mongolian, is not tinged with negro peculiarities, is not essentially different from that type which is called Caucasian or Indo-Germanic; and that whilst the distinct, indubitable evidence of their language requires that the Drâvidians should be affiliated with the Scythian race, physiological considerations throw, in this instance, so little light upon the subject that they would admit of our affiliating them, if it seemed necessary, with the Indo-Europeans.

Leaving out of account, for the present, the question of colour, it does not appear to me that there is any essential difference between the heads or features of the Drâvidians and those of the Brahmans.

There is, it is true, a great variety of feature, as well as of colour, apparent amongst the Drâvidians; but though the varieties of feature, or rather of physiognomy, which one observes are numerous, they are generally so minute and unimportant that in the absence of any class-difference in the shape of the head, they are consistent with the supposition of oneness of blood, and may safely be referred to local, social, and individual causes of difference. The long continued operation of the caste-law of the Hindus appears to me to be quite sufficient to account for the differences of feature, colour, and expression that are observed to exist.

Like oil and water in the same vessel, or ingredients which may be mixed mechanically, but will not combine chymically, the various castes into which the Drâvidians were arranged by their Brahman preceptors have lived side by side for ages, probably in some instances for twenty-five centuries, without commingling. For ages there has been no intermarriage, no social intercourse, no common bond of sympathy. Rank has become hereditary, as well as caste; and not only rank, but even intellect, temperament, character, and physical characteristics. In consequence of the separation of caste from caste for so many ages through the prohibition of intermarriage, unmistakeable points of difference both in features and in mental temperament have been developed.

It would be surprising indeed if under such circumstances 'varieties of man' did not make their appearance, and if ethnologists, looking at the question from a distance, did not sometimes doubt whether they could all be referred to a single race of pure blood. 'Some,' says Dr. Logan, speaking of the Tamilians in particular, 'are exceedingly Iranian, more are Semitico-Iranian, some are Semitic, others Australian, some remind us of Egyptians, while others again have Malayo-Polynesian, and even Simang and Papuan features.'

In no country in the world are features and complexion so variable as in India; but caste, as it exists in India, and especially as it affects the condition of the lower classes, is unknown in every other country in the world.

Separate for ever from the society of their fellow countrymen a class of agricultural labourers or slaves: prohibit all intermarriage with families in more easy circumstances: require them to live by themselves in wretched wigwams, removed to a considerable distance from the village which is inhabited by the respectable householders: compel them to work hard the whole year round in the open air in an inter-tropical climate—in a country where the sun comes twice in the year right over head: let all possibility of their rising to a higher condition of life, or obtaining a more sedentary, shady employment be for ever precluded: prohibit education: pay them no wages: feed them scantily and clothe them still more scantily: encourage drunkenness and the eating of carrion: prohibit the women from dressing themselves with ordinary regard for decency:—treat them, in short, for twenty centuries as the Brahmans and high-caste Drâvidians have treated the Pariars and other low-castes, and it will be quite unnecessary to have recourse to Dr. Logan's theory of their intermixture with a primitive race of Africans or Negritoes in order to account for the coarseness of their features, their dwarfishness, or the blackness of their skin. Notwithstanding all this, though the Pariars, as a class, are darker than any other class in the Carnatic, we find amongst them as great a variety of colour as amongst other classes of Hindus; and occasionally we may notice complexions that are as clear as those of the higher castes, together with considerable regularity of features.

The question, however, which is before us now is, not 'are the Pariars of the same race as the high-caste Drâvidians?' but 'to what race do the Drâvidians themselves belong?'—'Do those who are admitted to be Drâvidians of pure blood resemble most the Âryans or the Mongolians?' this is the question really at issue.

In comparing the physical type of the Drâvidians with that of Mongolians and Âryans, it is unfair to restrict the comparison to the lower classes of Drâvidians; for the South-Indian Sûdras, or high caste Drâvidians, claim to be regarded as the purest representatives of their race. Their institutions and manners have been Âryanised; but it is pure Drâvidian blood which flows in their veins. There *may* possibly be some doubt whether the lower castes were not intermixed with an anterior race: but the higher castes call themselves Tamilians, Telugus, Malayâlis, &c. *par excellence*; and their special right to those national appellations is always admitted, in terms at least, by the lower castes themselves.

When we compare the physical type of cultivated, high caste Drâvidians with that of the Brahmans, no essential difference whatever, and very little difference of any kind, can be observed.

In many instances the features of the high-caste Drâvidian women are more delicately formed and more regular than those of Brahman women themselves, whilst their complexions are at least equally fair;

and if any difference appears, it consists not in Mongolian breadth of face, but in greater elongation and narrowness. The Drâvidian type of head will even bear to be directly compared with the European. Compare, for instance, the heads of the Tamil or Telugu Munshis, translators, and Pandits in any Zillah court with that of the presiding English judge; and it is evident that the Drâvidian heads differ from the English only in being smaller and narrower,—with a preponderance in the former of the signs of subtilty and suppleness, in the latter of straightforward moral and mental energy.

It is especially deserving of consideration, that the Nilgherry Tudas, who of all Drâvidian tribes have been most thoroughly guarded by their secluded position from Bhramanical influences, instead of being more Mongol-like or Negro-like than the Âryanised Drâvidians, are so distinctively Caucasian in the opinion of many persons, that they have been regarded as Celts, Romans, Jews, &c., and the chief difficulty that exists is that of inducing people to be content with the statement, that the Tudas are proved by their language to be identical in origin with the Drâvidians of the plains.

Amongst the lower class of the Drâvidians, I have occasionally observed a type of head which is somewhat inclined to be what is called Mongolian, that is, it exhibits unusual breadth across the cheek bones, a pyramidal forehead, a somewhat oblique position of the eyes, and a pyramidal nose with a broad base.

On the other hand, Mongolian smoothness of skin, scantiness of hair, flatness of face, and the peculiar monotonous olive hue of the Mongolian complexion are never met with; and it should be observed that the other elements of the Mongolian type which one does occasionally notice, though it is chiefly, if not solely, amongst the lower classes that they are seen, yet they do not constitute the class-type of any caste whatever; nor are they ordinarily or frequently met with, but are exceptional instances, which scarcely at all affect the general rule; and I have no doubt that similar exceptional instances could easily be pointed out amongst the lower classes of our own race.

The physical type of a race should be determined by the shape of the head and the more permanent peculiarities of feature alone, irrespective of the complexion or colour of the skin; for every one who has lived in India must have learned to regard colour as a most deceptive evidence of relationship and race. It is true that the Brahmans as a class are much fairer than the Pariars as a class; but the conviction is forced upon the mind of every observer, by the hundreds of instances which he meets with in daily life, that the colour of the features of the Hindus is purely a result of the external circumstances in which they are placed, with respect to climate, occupation, and mode of life. They are dark-complexioned in proportion as they are exposed to the sun in out-door labour, and fair in proportion as they live a sedentary life; and consequently colour, if an evidence of anything specific, is an evidence only of the social status of the individual and his family. It is vain, therefore, to expect from considerations of colour and complexion any real help towards determining the race to which the Drâvidians belong.

The influence of climate alone, in darkening or blanching the colour of the skin is greater than is commonly supposed; and India furnishes innumerable instances of this influence. One of the best of Indian instances of the influence of climate in modifying colour with which I am acquainted, is furnished by the extreme fairness of the complexion of the greater proportion of the natives of the Malabar coast, compared with the very dark hue of a like proportion of the natives of the coast of Coromandel, who belong to the same or similar castes, and who follow similar occupations. The natives of the Coromandel coast are exposed for ten months in the year to a very high degree of dry heat, in a level country, bare of wood.* The natives of the Malabar coast are exposed to a similar degree of heat for not more than two months out of the twelve, and a similar degree of drought is on that coast unknown: their sky is almost always laden with moisture; the quantity of rain that falls is always double, generally treble, the quantity that falls on the eastern coast in the same latitude. The country is everywhere well wooded, and the houses of the people are generally nestled in deep, cool groves; and, in consequence, in the same degree of latitude, and with a difference in longitude of only a degree or half a degree, the skin of the people on the western side of the Ghauts (or central mountain range of Southern India) is as much fairer than that of the people on the eastern side, as the complexion of the Brahmans of any province is fairer than that of the labouring classes in the same province. Notwithstanding this difference in complexion, there is no difference in race, for the Malayâlis are demonstrably descended from an early colony of Tamilians; and an equally remarkable difference in complexion is apparent amongst the members of those Tamil castes, of whom a portion have settled in Malayâlam.

* In my own neighbourhood in Tinnevelly, I never knew the thermometer fall lower at any period of the year, day or night, than 76°. For about eight months in the year it averaged 84°, and for about two months rose above 90°. The maximum, which it rarely reached in the shade, was 96°.

The average fall of rain in the same neighbourhood, during the six years in which I registered it, was only 25 inches!

Towards the southern extremity of the Peninsula, the breadth of the central mountain range is greatly diminished, and there is easy access from the Tamil country into Travancore by the Aramboly pass. By this pass, and by similar breaks and gaps still farther south, the Tamilians of the old Pândiya kingdom forced their way into Malayâlam, and possessed themselves of the province of South Travancore. The government of this province has again reverted to the Travancorians, in whose hands it has been for several centuries; but the bulk of the population continue to be Tamilians, as far as the vicinity of Trivandrum, the Travancore capital. Up to that limit the majority of the people on the Travancore side of the mountain barrier belong to the same castes as in the East India Company's district of Tinnevelly, on the eastern side; they speak the same language, and follow the same occupations; they occasionally intermarry, and their features are perfectly similar; yet, notwithstanding all this, they differ so materially with respect to colour, that a stranger would naturally suppose them to belong to different races. A remarkable instance of difference of colour under these circumstances is furnished by the Shânârs, or palmyra cultivators, who are found in considerable numbers on each side of the Ghauts, up to the very foot of the mountains. In the vicinity of Neyâttangkarei, a Travancore village, the Shânârs on the western side of the mountain range, are separated from their fellow caste-men on the eastern side, by a space of only about fifteen miles as the crow flies; and the only difference in their circumstances, is the difference in the climate, which is caused by the precipitation of the moisture of the south-western monsoon on the western side of the Ghauts, and its interception from the eastern side. In consequence of this difference in the climate alone, the Shânârs who reside on the eastern side of the Ghauts, are amongst the blackest of the Tamilians, while on the Travancore side, the same class of people, engaged in the same occupations, are as fair as the Brahmans of the Carnatic, and in some instances even fairer. This fact, which is patent to the observation of every one in the neighbourhood, is perhaps the most remarkable proof in existence, of the immense influence of climate in modifying the colour of the skin.

Another and better known evidence, is furnished by the circumstance that many of the descendants of the Portuguese who settled in India several centuries ago, are now blacker than the Hindus themselves. The class of people referred to are a mixed race, descended from European fathers and native mothers, yet instead of being the fairer for their admixture with European blood, many of them are of a darker colour than the natives from whom, on the maternal side, they are descended. Even amongst the Brahmans, though a perfectly pure, unmixed race, differences of colour are frequently observed. It is supposed to be unlucky to meet 'a black Brahman,' or 'a fair Pariar,' the first thing in the morning. The Brahmans of Northern India are generally fairer than those of the south, with the exception of the Nambûris, or high-caste Brahmans of the Malabar coast, who appear to be the fairest of their race.

Professor Max Müller (in his valuable paper on the Bengali in the Reports of the British Association), thinks he finds in the Gônds, and other Un-Âryanised Drâvidians, evidences of the existence of a race 'closely resembling the Negro;' and says that, 'the existence of the same dark race in the South of India, is authenticated by Strabo.' On the contrary, Strabo's statement, when not merely alluded to, but translated, will be found to corroborate the view which I have taken. He says, 'the Southern Indians resemble the Æthiopians *in colour:* but *in features* and *in hair*, they resemble the rest of the Indians (for on account of the moisture of the climate the hair does not become woolly); but the Northern Indians resemble the Egyptians.'

This statement of Strabo throws light on a passage in Herodotus, in which a black race, apparently Hindus, are said to have been brigaded with the fairer Indians in the army of Xerxes. He says, 'Æthiopians from the eastward—from the sun-rising—from Asia—marched with Indians, but differed not from other Æthiopians except in their language and their hair; for the Libyan Æthiopians have the woolliest hair of all men, but those people are straight-haired.' Herodotus supplies us with a fact, Strabo with the right explanation of that fact. Herodotus is silent with respect to the *features* of the Eastern Æthiopians; Strabo asserts that their features resembled those of the rest of the Indians.

Though there is little or nothing of a distinctively Mongolian character in the features and heads of the Drâvidians, considered generally; and though consequently physiology does not furnish any reliable evidence in support of their Mongolian or Scythian origin, it is unsafe to draw any conclusion from this circumstance. The danger of arguing from negative evidence respecting matters which are so fleeting and changeable as features and complexion, is illustrated by the change which has passed over the features of the Mahommedans of India. The Mahommedans of India are partly descended from the Affghan, and partly from the Mogol invaders; but the great majority are descendants of the Tartar-Turkish soldiers and camp-followers, who accompanied both the Affghans and the Mogols. Probably most of the Affghan invaders of India were Seljukian Turks; the Mogols were, as their name imports, Mongolians; and the hordes that followed the fortunes of both classes of invaders, were a mixed race—a 'colluvies gentium'—comprising various tribes and races of Mongolian and Tartar-Turkish origin, called by the Hindus Turushkas, in Tamil Turukkar, or more commonly Tulukkar, *i.e.*, Turks.

The proportion of Persians and other races of Indo-European origin, who accompanied the Affghans and Mongols in their expeditions, was exceedingly small; and though the Mahommedans have occasionally made proselytes amongst the Hindus, by force or the prospect of secular advantages, and have occasionally robbed Hindus of their wives and daughters, the disturbing influence of these accessions to their ranks has been so small, that it may be left altogether out of account. Hence, the Mahommedans of India may be regarded as a Tartar-Mongolian people; and we might naturally expect to observe in them those physiological peculiarities of the High Asian races which must have characterised the majority of their ancestors on their first arrival in India, and which are still apparent in all their distinctiveness, not only in the Mongolians, but in the Siberian Turks. Notwithstanding this, we generally search in vain amongst the Indian Mahommedans for signs of their Tartar origin. With the exception of a somewhat greater breadth of face and head, and a more olive complexion, they do not now differ from the Hindus, properly so called, in any essential point. They exhibit, it is true, special peculiarities of physiognomy and expression; but every Hindu tribe or caste has, in like manner, a peculiar physiognomy of its own, by which it differs from every other tribe. A change appears to have passed over the physiology of the Mahommedans of India similar to that which the Magyars and the Osmanli Turks have experienced since they settled in Europe, and which has transformed them from Tartars into Europeans. As, therefore, there cannot be any doubt of the original Mongolianism of the majority of Indian Mahommedans, or of the absence from them now of almost every thing that is Mongolian, so, though little or nothing that is distinctively Mongolian is now apparent in the features or physiology of the mass of the Drâvidians, they may, notwithstanding this, be descended from as purely a Scythian or Mongolian ancestry as the Mahommedans are known to be; or at least, we may conclude that there is nothing in the physiological view of the question which is opposed to the argument derived from lingual comparison.

Perhaps, however, on the whole, the safest conclusion is, that the mass of the Drâvidians, though as truly Scythians as the Mongolians themselves, were, even at the time of their entrance into India, free from those peculiarities of feature that are called Mongolian. We cannot safely conclude that the Mongolian type of features was from the beginning the inheritance of the whole of the Scythian tribes. It appears more probable that that type was developed in the course of time in the steppes of High Asia; and it is certain that the tribes amongst whom it has acquired a peculiar degree of permanence, are the Tibetans and the Mongolian nomades, who still inhabit the original seats of their race.

It is remarkable that the only Indian tribes which are now distinctly characterized by Mongolian peculiarities, are those which entered India by the north-east, and which are probably of Tibetan origin. The Garos and other forest tribes on the Bhutân frontier, as described by Mr. Hodgson, seem to be decidedly Mongolian; and the Koles and Santâls are probably descended from the same or a similar stock. The existence at an early period in the vicinity of Orissa, of barbarous tribes differing in appearance from the rest of the Hindus, and exhibiting a Mongolian or foreign type, is attested by the following passage in the *Periplus Maris Erythraei.* After referring to the region watered by the Godavery and Kistna, the author says: 'After this, keeping the sea on the right hand and sailing northwards, we come upon certain barbarous tribes, as the '*κιῤῥάδαι*' (Sans. 'Kirâṭas'), *a race of people with* flattened noses (evidently Mongolians), also the horse-faces and the long-faces, all of whom are said to be cannibals. Then sailing eastwards, and having a certain sea on the right, we come to the Ganges.'

The distinct statement of Strabo which has already been quoted, joined to the negative evidence of this passage, proves that at the Christian era, the civilized, cultivated Drâvidians (the Pândiyas, Calingas, Ândhras, &c.), did not materially differ in physiognomy or personal appearance from the northern Hindus; and that certain barbarous inhabitants of the jungles, who are barbarians still, were the only tribes that appeared to be distinctively Mongolian. The Gondali of Ptolemy, probably the Gônds, who are classed among 'the Bitti,' and distinguished from 'the Phyllitae' (probably the Bhills), are not said to have differed in appearance from the more cultivated Drâvidians.

Some writers, I think erroneously, speak of the 'jet blackness' of the Gônds; and the Rajmahal people are said to be black. Notwithstanding this, according to the account of that accurate observer, Dr. Buchanan Hamilton, the features of the Males or Rajmahal hill people, do not essentially differ from the Âryan type. 'Their lips are full, but not at all like those of the Negro. Their faces are oval, not shaped like a lozenge as those of the Chinese are. Their eyes, instead of being hid in fat and placed obliquely like those of the Chinese, are exactly like those of Europeans.'

We have seen that some of the Vindhya Nishâdas are described in the Purâṇas to be 'as black as crows;' but without debating the accuracy of the amiable portrait of those primitive tribes, which the Purâṇas have drawn, and which waits to be tested by Mr. Hodgson's pencil, it will suffice for the present to remind the reader that those very Purâṇa writers entertained so different an impression respecting the true Drâvidians of the south, that they fell into the opposite error of Âryanising them, and supposed the Calingas, Pândiyas, Kêraḷas, and other Drâvidians to be descended from colonies of Âryans from Oude.

IV.

Ancient Religion of the Dravidians.

Religious usages are sometimes found to throw light on the origin or relationship of races. Similarity in the religious ideas and practises of any two primitive tribes strengthens the evidence of their relationship derived from similarity of language. Let us see whether any light can be thrown on the question of the relationship of the Drâvidians by an inquiry into their religious usages. A priori, this inquiry seems likely to lead to some definite result, inasmuch as the religions of the ancient Indo-European nations and the old Scythian religions of Upper Asia present many essential points of difference.

In the earliest times we find amongst the nations of the Indo-European family the universal prevalence of certain tenets and usages, which each of those nations appears to have inherited from the common progenitors of the race. The *doctrine* which was most characteristic of the whole family was that of the Metempsychosis; their *objects of worship* were either the elements of nature personified, or a Pantheon of heroes and heroines; and the most characteristic of their *religious usages* was the maintenance of a distinct order of priests, generally hereditary, who were venerated as the depositaries of all ancient traditions and spiritual power.

In whatever race these religious peculiarities appear to have prevailed, we shall probably find on inquiry that there are weighty reasons for attributing to that race an Indo-European origin or relationship: and in like manner a family likeness (exceedingly dissimilar from the particulars now mentioned) will be found to characterize the religious practises of the nations of the Scythian group.

In endeavouring to ascertain the characteristics of the primitive Drâvidian religion, we are met by a serious but not insurmountable difficulty. The Brahmans, by whom the Âryan civilization was grafted on the ruder Drâvidian stock, laboured assiduously to extirpate the old Drâvidian religion, and to establish their own in its room; and they are generally supposed to have succeeded in accomplishing this object.

Notwithstanding their success however, it is still possible in some degree to discriminate between the doctrines and practices which were introduced by the Brahmans and the older religion of the Drâvidian people. If, for instance, any usages are found to prevail extensively in Southern India, and especially amongst the ruder and less Âryanised tribes. which are derived neither from the Vêdas nor from the Purânas, neither from Buddhism nor from Jainism, such usages may be concluded to be relics of the religious system of the Drâvidian aborigines. Many such usages do actually exist. Several religious systems widely differing from the Brahmanical are discoverable amongst the Drâvidian nations, and are especially prevalent amongst the rude inhabitants of the jungles. Hence, we are not quite destitute of the means of comparing the characteristics of the ancient Drâvidian religion, prior to the introduction of Brahmanism (or what is commonly called Hinduism), with the religious usages that prevailed amongst the Scythian races.

The system which prevails in the forests and mountain-fastnesses throughout the Drâvidian territories, and also in the extreme south of the Peninsula amongst the low caste tribes, and which appears to have been still more widely prevalent at an early period, is a system of demonolatry, or the worship of evil spirits by means of bloody sacrifices and frantic dances. This system was introduced within the historical period from the Tamil country into Ceylon, where it is now mixed up with Buddhism. On comparing this Drâvidian system of demonolatry and sorcery with 'Shamanism'*—the superstition which prevails amongst the Ugrian races of Siberia and the hill-tribes on the South-Western frontier of China, which is still mixed up with the Buddhism of the Mongols, and which was the old religion of the whole Tartar race before Buddhism and Mohammedanism were disseminated amongst them—we cannot avoid the conclusion that those two superstitions, though practised by races so widely separated, are not only similar but identical.

I shall here point out the principal features of resemblance between the Shamanism of High Asia and the demonolatry of the Drâvidians,† as still practised in many districts in Southern India.

* This word *Shamanism* is formed from *Shaman*, the name of the magician-priest of the North Asian demonolaters. 'Shaman,' though a name appropriated by demonolaters, is of Buddhist origin, and was adopted from the Mongolians. It is identical with 'Samaṇa,' the Tamil name for a Buddhist, and is derived from the Sanscrit word 'Srâmana.' The use of this word *Shaman* in Siberia, must be of comparatively modern origin; but the system of religion into which it has been adopted and incorporated is one of the oldest superstitions in the world.

† I beg to refer the reader for a full account of the peculiarities of the Drâvidian demonolatry, to a small work of mine called *The Shânârs of Tinnevelly*, published by the Society for the Propagation of the Gospel. I think I have proved in that work that the demonolatry of the Shanars (the palmyra cultivators

(1.) The Shamanites are destitute of a regular priesthood. Ordinarily the father of the family is the priest and magician; but the office may be undertaken by any one who pleases, and at any time laid aside.

Precisely similar is the practice existing amongst the Shânârs and other rude tribes of Southern India. Ordinarily it is the head of the family, or the head-man of the hamlet or community, who performs the priestly office; but any worshipper, male or female, who feels so disposed, may volunteer to officiate, and becomes for the time being the representative and interpreter of the dæmon.

(2.) The Shamanites acknowledge the existence of a supreme God: but they do not offer him any worship. The same acknowledgment of God's existence and the same neglect of his worship characterize the religion of the Drâvidian demonolaters.

(3.) Neither amongst the Shamanites nor amongst the primitive, un-brahmanized demonolaters of India is there any trace of belief in the metempsychosis.

(4.) The objects of Shamanite worship are not gods or heroes, but demons, which are supposed to be cruel, revengeful, and capricious, and are worshipped by bloody sacrifices and wild dances. The officiating magician or priest excites himself to frenzy, and then pretends, or supposes himself, to be possessed by the demon to which worship is being offered; and after the rites are over he communicates, to those who consult him, the information he has received.

The demonolatry practised in India by the more primitive Drâvidian tribes is not only similar to this, but the same. Every word used in the foregoing description of the Shamanite worship would apply equally well to the Drâvidian demonolatry; and in depicting the ceremonies of the one race we depict those of the other also.

of Southern India) did not originate with the Brahmans, or in any local development of the religion of the Brahmans; but that on the contrary, the element of demonology which is contained in the later Puranic system, was borrowed from this old Drâvidian superstition.

It is admitted to be a fact that the Buddhists of Ceylon borrowed their demonolatry from the Drâvidians of the Old Pândiya Kingdom: if so, it cannot be unreasonable to suppose that it was from the same or a similar source that the Brahmans borrowed the demoniacal element which is contained in the later Puranas. I apprehend that we have a mythical record of the adoption of the aboriginal demonolatry into the later Brahmanical system, and of the object in view in this alliance, in the Puranic story of the sacrifice of Daksha. According to that story, Siva (*i.e.*, Vedantic Brahmanism) found himself unable to subdue the old elementary divinities, and to secure to himself the exclusive homage at which he aimed, till he called in the aid of the demons (the demonolatry of the aborigines), and put himself at their head in the person of his ('pro-re-nata') son, Vîra-Bhadra; a demi-god, whose wife, emanation, or representative, Bhadra-Câli, is regarded by the Shânârs as their patroness and *mother*.

Compare the following accounts of the demonolatrous rites of the Shamanites of Siberia and those of the demonolaters of India.

The description of the Shamanite worship is formed from a series of arranged quotations from Prichard's account of the descriptions which various Russian travellers and ecclesiastics have given of the superstitions of the Ostiaks, the Samoïedes, the Siberian Turks, and other Pagans inhabitants of Northern Asia. The account of the Drâvidian superstitions is taken from my paper on 'the Tinnevelly Shanars,' a paper which was written before I was aware of the identity of the demonolatry of Siberia with that of Tinnevelly.

Shamanite Demonolatrous Rites.—'When the Shaman, or magician, performs his superstitious rites he puts on a garment trimmed with bits of iron, rattles, and bells: he cries horribly, beats a sort of drum, agitates himself, and shakes the metallic appendages of his robe; and at the same time the bystanders increase the din by striking with their fists upon iron kettles. When the Shaman, by his horrible contortions and yells, by cutting himself with knives, whirling and swooning, has succeeded in assuming the appearance of something preternatural and portentous, the assembled multitude are impressed with the belief that the demon they are worshipping has taken possession of the priest, and regard him accordingly with wonder and dread. When he is quite exhausted with his exertions, and can no longer hold out, he makes a sign that the spirit has left him, and then imparts to the people the intimations he has received.'

Shânâr Demonolatrous Rites.—'When it is determined to offer a sacrifice to a devil, a person is specially appointed to act the part of priest; for devil-worship is not, like the worship of the deities, appropriated to a particular order of men, but may be performed by any one who chooses. The officiating priest is styled a 'devil-dancer.' Usually the 'head man,' or one of the principal men of the village officiates; but sometimes the duty is voluntarily undertaken by some devotee, male or female, who wishes to gain notoriety, or in whom the sight of the preparations has awakened a sudden zeal.

'The officiating priest is dressed up for the occasion in the vestments and ornaments which are appropriated to the particular devil that is worshipped. The object in view in donning the demon's insignia is to strike terror into the imagination of the beholders; but the party-coloured dress and grotesque ornaments, the cap and trident and jingling bells, of the performer, bear so close a resemblance to the usual adjuncts of a pantomime that an European would find it difficult to look grave.

'The musical instruments, or rather the instruments of noise, which are chiefly used in the devil-dance are the tom-tom, or ordinary Indian drum, and the horn; with occasionally the addition of a clarionet when the parties can afford it. But the favourite instrument, because the noisiest, is that which is called 'the bow.' A series of bells of various sizes is fastened to the frame of a gigantic bow; the strings are tightened so as to emit a musical note when struck; and the bow rests on a large empty brazen pot. The instrument is played on by a plectrum, and several musicians join in the performance. 'One strikes the strings of the bow with the plectrum, another produces the bass by striking the brazen pot with his hand, and a third beats time and improves the harmony by a pair of cymbals.

'When the preparations are completed, and the devil-dance is about to commence, the music is at first comparatively slow, and the dancer seems impassive and sullen; and either he stands still or moves about in gloomy silence. Gradually, as the music becomes quicker and louder, his excitement begins to rise. Sometimes to help him to work himself up into a frenzy he uses medicated draughts; cuts and lacerates his flesh till the blood flows; lashes himself with a huge whip; presses a burning torch to his breast; drinks the blood which flows from his own wounds; or drinks the blood of the sacrifice, putting the throat of the decapitated goat to his mouth. Then, as if he had acquired new life, he begins to brandish his staff of bells, and dance with a quick, but wild, unsteady step. Suddenly the *afflatus* descends. There is no mistaking that glare, or those frantic leaps. He snorts, he stares, he gyrates. The demon has now taken bodily possession of him; and though he retains the power of utterance and of motion, both are under the demon's control, and his separate consciousness is in abeyance. The bystanders signalize the event by raising a long shout attended with a peculiar vibratory noise.

'The devil-dancer is now worshipped as a present deity; and every bystander consults him respecting his disease, his wants, the welfare of his absent relations, and the offerings which are to be made for the accomplishment of his wishes.

'As the devil dancer acts to admiration the part of a maniac, it requires some experience to enable a person to interpret his dubious or unmeaning replies, his muttered voices and uncouth gestures; but the wishes of the parties who consult him help them greatly to interpret his meaning.'

It seems to me unnecessary to say anything more in proof of the substantial identity of the demonolatry of the Drâvidians of India with the Shamanism of Northern Asia. It may be alleged that similarity in mental characteristics and social circumstances alone might give rise to this similarity in religious ideas and practises, but it seems far more probable that both the superstitions which have now been described have sprung from a common origin: and I may add that the conformity which has been traced between the old religion of the Drâvidians and that which was once the religion of all the Scythian nations corroborates the supposition of the Scythian relationship of the Drâvidian race.

Whilst the demonolatrous rites which I have now described appear to have constituted the prevailing superstition of the ancient Drâvidians, we meet also with traces of the existence of systems that correspond in part to those which prevailed amongst the Indo-European races.

The religion of the Kunds or Kus, though it contains a demonolatrous element, may be described as in the main a worship of gods of rivers and mountains, of gods of the earth and the sky, and of the gods of elements and *genii loci*. It is in part an elementary worship, which may be allied in principle to that of the Âryans, but which differs widely from it in spirit and form, and appears to be quite independent of it in origin. This remark especially applies to that section of the Kus which practises human sacrifices, and delights in cruelty and gloom. A worship of gods of rivers and mountains similar to that of the Kus is found amongst the Koles, and also amongst the Sub-Himalayan and Bhutân tribes described by Mr. Hodgson; and it seems not improbable that it was from those tribes that the Ku religion was derived.

Amongst the Drâvidians of the plains no trace of the worship of the elements has ever been discovered. Indeed there is reason to believe that the old Vêdic or elementary worship of the Brahmans had already merged into the mythological and mystical system of the Purâuas, before the Brahmans effected a settlement in the South.

So far as appears, every Drâvidian usage which is not of Brahmanical origin is either identical with Shamanism or allied to it.

The religion of the Tudas of the Nilgherry hills exhibits some peculiarities which are analogous to the earliest Brahmanical religion, or the religion of the Vêdas, together with some which are regarded as Scytho-Druidical.

The peculiar veneration with which the Tudas worship the manes of ancestors; their sacrifices to secure the peace of the dead; their worship of *genii loci* by means of offerings of milk and clarified butter; their freedom from the worship of idols; the religious veneration with which they appear to regard a sacred bell, which is hung up in their temples, or dairies; their abstinence from flesh, and living entirely on grain and milk; their exclusion of women from all share in the rites of worship, and even from the precincts of their temples; their practice of polyandria and female infanticide;—these and analogous peculiarities of the religious system and social life of the Tudas accord to a certain extent with usages which prevailed in the earliest ages amongst most of the tribes of the Indo-European race.

There is no trace amongst the Tudas of hero-worship or of Âryan mythology, of the doctrine of the transmigration of souls, or of the existence of a priestly caste,—all of which are distinctive portions of the Indo-European system. Nevertheless the peculiarities of the religion of the Tudas which have been mentioned above may be suspected to have had an Âryan origin, or at least to have been shaped and tinged by Âryan influences. Our ignorance of the history of the Tudas (an ignorance which has not been dispelled by the speculations of Captain Congreve), and of the circumstances which compelled them to take refuge in the Nilgherry hills, renders it exceedingly difficult, if not impossible, to determine whether their religion sprang from the same Scythian origin as the Drâvidian demonolatry, or whether it is to be placed to the account of their early association with some Indo-European race. We must look to further and more accurate research for the solution of this problem.

The religion of the Tudas has sometimes been regarded as 'Druidical,' 'Celto-Druidical,' or 'identical with the religion of the ancient Celts;' but, with the exception of the performance of some of their rites in the deep gloom of sacred groves, a practice which was not peculiar to the Celts alone, but which prevailed amongst various ancient nations, it does not appear that there is anything distinctively or certainly Druidical in the existing system of the Tudas.

The supposition of the Druidical character of the Tuda religion has arisen from the error of attributing to the Tudas various remains and usages which were peculiar to an earlier and probably extinct race.

Those remains consist of cairns or burrows, cromlechs, kistvaens, and circles of upright, loose stones, which are nearly identical in form with those that are found in Europe in the ancient seats of the Celts: and whatever mystery may hang over the origin of those remains and over the race of which they are the only surviving relics, there seems no reason for hesitating to style them, in a general sense, Druidical.

In the cairns or barrows referred to, vases, cinerary urns, and other vessels of glazed pottery are often found, which sometimes contain human bones, more or less charred, and mixed with ashes, sometimes a little animal charcoal alone. Most of these vessels have a peculiar glaze of a rich red colour, with a zig-zag ornamentation : some have a black glaze. Brass and iron implements of agriculture and of war have often been discovered in them : in several instances a bell has been found, as in some of the Celtic barrows in England; and occasionally gold ornaments have come to light. Though these remains seem to be undoubtedly Druidical, they can hardly lay claim to an antiqnity equal to that of many Druidical remains found in Europe.

The rich glaze of the pottery; the elegance of the shape of some of the vessels (compared with the rude cinerary urns discovered in the British barrows); the presence of implements of iron; the representations of processions with musical instruments and led horses, which are rudely sculptured on the sides of some of the cromlechs; the presence of gold ornaments;—all these circumstances denote a superior civilization to that of the primitive Celts, and therefore a later origin of the relics. If it be true, as it is confidently asserted (though I have been unable to ascertain the truth of the statement), that a Roman aureus was discovered in one of the barrows, the race by which those Druidical rites were practised must have survived for several centuries after the Christian era.

At first it was supposed that cairns and other Druidical remains were discoverable only on the Nilgherry hills; and hence it was natural that these remains should at first be attributed to the Tudas, the aborigines of the Nilgherries, and who are as peculiar in their customs as in their language. On further research it was found that the people to whom those remains belonged had practised agriculture and made use of horses; whereas the Tudas were ignorant of agriculture, appeared to have always lived a pastoral, wandering life, and were ignorant even of the existence of the horse. It was subsequently discovered that the Tudas neither claimed the cairns and cromlechs as belonging to themselves or their ancestors, nor regarded them with reverence; that their rites of sepulture are altogether different from those of the ancient people who used those cairns; and that they ascribed them to a people still more ancient than themselves, by whom they assert that the plateau of the Nilgherries was inhabited prior to their arrival. Sometimes they designated the cairns as burial places of the 'Curbs,' *i.e.*, of the Curubas or Curumbars, a race of nomade shepherds who once overspread a considerable part of the Tamil country (probably the 'nomadic Sôras' of Ptolemy), and of whom a few scattered relics still inhabit the slopes of the Nilgherries. It appeared, however, on making inquiry of the Curubas, that they neither practised Druidical rites themselves, nor supposed the barrows to be the work of their ancestors; so that the problem still remained unsolved. It was at length ascertained that similar cairns or barrows, containing a great variety of similar remains, but of a more advanced order and in a better condition, existed in immense numbers on the Âna-mala hills,—a range of hills on the south side of the great Coimbatoor gap, which form the commencement and the northern face of the Southern Ghauts; and further investigation proved their existence, not only in mountain ranges, but in almost every part of the Dekhan and Peninsular India, from Nagpore to Madura, and also in various districts in the presidency of Bombay.

Similar remains are found also in Circassia and Russia; and circles of stones surrounding ancient graves are found both on the Southern Arabian coast and in the Somali country in Africa.

This discovery has had the effect of disconnecting the cairns, and other Druidical remains of the Nilgherries from the Tudas, almost as completely as from any other Drâvidian race or tribe that now exists; and the question of the origin of the relics which have been discovered in such numbers not only in the Nilgherries, but in many other parts of India, and in the plains as well as on the mountains, and also the ulterior question of the relationship and history of the people of whom these relics are the only monuments that remain, have now become problems of a more general and of a deeply interesting character. Captain Meadows Taylor has discovered and examined a large number of these remains at Rajan Koloor, in Sorapoor, and also at Siwarji, near Ferozabad, on the Bhima; and has devoted much attention to the comparison of them with similar remains found in England. He calls them 'Scytho-Celtic,' or 'Scytho-Druidical.'

It is probably correct to regard them as Druidical; but they are not on this account necessarily Celtic, for the practice of rites of a Druidical character and the use of cairns and barrows were not confined to the Celts, but appear to have prevailed also amongst the Finns, the Euraskians, and the other Scythians by whom Europe was inhabited prior to the arrival of the Celtic race; and traces of the same system of religion and sepulture have been discovered in various parts of Northern and Central Asia. The other term, 'Scytho-Druidical,' seems an unobjectionable one.

It is a remarkable circumstance that no class of Hindus know anything of the race to which these Druidical remains belonged, and that neither in Sanscrit literature nor in that of the Drâvidian languages is there any tradition on the subject. The Tamil people generally call the cairns by the name of 'pâṇḍu-kuṛis.' 'kuṛi' means a *pit* or *grave*, and 'pâṇḍu'* denotes *anything connected with the* Pâṇḍus,' or Pâṇḍava brothers, to whom, all over India, ancient mysterious structures are generally attributed. To call anything 'a work of the Pândus' is equivalent to terming it 'Cyclopean' in Greece, 'a work of the Picts' in Scotland, or 'a work of Nimrod' in Asiatic Turkey; and it means only that the structure to which the name is applied was erected in some remote age, by a people of whom nothing is now known. When the Tamil people are asked 'by whom were these pâṇḍu-kuṛis built and used?' they sometimes reply, 'by the people who lived here long ago;' but they are unable to tell whether those people were their own ancestors or a foreign race, and also when and why those 'kuṛis' ceased to be used. The answer which is sometimes given is that the people who built the cairns were 'a race of dwarfs who lived long ago, and who were only a span or a cubit high, but were possessed of the strength of giants.'

The supposition that the builders of the cairns had settled in India earlier than the Drâvidians, and were expelled by the Drâvidians from the plains and forced to take refuge in the hills and jungles, where they gradually died out, would accord with some of the circumstances now mentioned; but it is inconsistent with the proofs which we meet with of the civilization of the race, and in particular with their acquaintance with the art of glazing pottery, an art which is unknown to the modern Hindoos themselves. If we should suppose, on the other hand, that they were a race of nomadic 'Scytho-Druidical' shepherds, who wandered into India, *after* it was peopled and settled (perhaps about the Christian era), and then wandered out again, the circumstance that the Druidical remains are found most plentifully in remote mountainous regions renders this supposition an improbable one. The improbability of the supposition would, however, be diminished, if we were to suppose that this shepherd people, instead of retracing their steps and wandering out of India, formed alliances with the Drâvidians, and gradually merged in the mass of the Drâvidian race.

Whether the people to whom these Scytho-Druidical remains belonged were or were not Drâvidians (a point which cannot be settled till we know something more of them), it cannot be regarded as pro-

* This word 'Pâṇḍu' is not to be confounded (as Captain Congreve has confounded it) with 'Pâṇḍi' or 'Pâṇḍiya,' the name of the ancient dynasty of Madura. Possibly both words may be derived from the same etymon; but historically they are unconnected and independent. It may be added also that some Tamil scholars derive 'Pâṇḍi,' the title of the Madura dynasty, not from the Sanskrit 'Pâṇḍu,' but from 'Paṇḍu,' a Tamil word, signifying *ancient*, from the ultimate root 'paṛ-a,' *old*.

bable that their religious usages and rights of sepulture had their origin in India.

The resemblance of the barrows and their contents (with the cromlechs, &c.) to the Druidical remains which are discovered in the ancient seats of the Celtic race in Europe, is too exact and remarkable to be accounted for on any other supposition than that of their derivation from the same origin. Hence the people by whom Druidical rites were introduced into India must have brought them with them from Central Asia; and this favours the conclusion that they must have entered India at a very early period—a period perhaps as early as the introduction of Druidical rites into Europe. On this supposition it is necessary to suppose that they kept themselves separate from the various races that entered India subsequently, and that they imitated the civilization of the newer immigrants without abandoning their own peculiarities.

It remains, however, as great a mystery as ever that those people have everywhere disappeared, and that not even a tradition of their existence survives.

On a review of the various particulars which have been mentioned above respecting the religious usages of the Un-Âryanised Drâvidians, including the Kus and the Tudas, and also the unknown race that practised Druidical rites, it seems unquestionable that the majority of the ancient Drâvidian inhabitants of India were demonolaters or Shamanites, like the majority of the ancient Scythian tribes of Upper Asia, whilst it also seems probable that there existed amongst some Drâvidian tribes a strong under-current of Indo-European, and possibly of Druidical tendencies.'

This result exactly accords with the supposition which has already been deduced from lingual comparison respecting the relationship or affiliation of the Drâvidian race, viz., that in basis and origin it is distinctively Scythian, with a small but very ancient admixture of an Indo-European element.

PRINTED BY HARRISON AND SONS, ST. MARTIN'S LANE.